Praise for *Extreme Money*

"A true insider's devastating analysis of the financial alchemy of the last 30 years and its destructive consequences. With his intimate first-hand knowledge, Das takes a knife to global finance and financiers to reveal the inner workings without fear or favor."

—Nouriel Roubini, Professor of Economics at NYU Stern School of Business and Chairman of Roubini Global Economics

"Das describes the causes of the financial crisis with the insight and understanding of a financial wizard, the candor and objectivity of an impartial observer, and a wry sense of humor that reveals the folly in it all."

—Brooksley Born, Former Chairperson of the U.S. Commodity Futures Trading Commission (CFTC)

"This is the best book yet to come out of the financial crisis. Das is a graceful, witty writer, with an unusually broad range of reference. He is also a long-time master of the arcana of the netherworlds of finance and nicely balances historical sweep with illuminating detail. *Extreme Money* is lively, scathing, and wise. "

—Charles Morris, Author of *The Two Trillion Dollar Meltdown: Easy Money, High Rollers, and the Great Credit Crash*

"Like Hunter S. Thompson's *Fear and Loathing in Las Vegas*, *Extreme Money* launches you into a fascinating and disturbing alternative view of reality. But now greed predominates, the distorted world of finance is completely global, and the people making crazy decisions can ruin us all. This is an informative, entertaining, and deeply scary account of Hades's new realm. Read it while you can. "

—Simon Johnson, Ronald A. Kurtz Professor of Entrepreneurship at MIT Sloan School of Management and Author of *13 Bankers: The Wall Street Takeover and the Next Financial Meltdown*

"You know when Lewis Caroll, Max Weber, Alan Greenspan, and Sigmund Freud all appear on the same early page that you are about to read an intellectual tour de force. Das is an authoritative and colorful critic of modern markets, and here he weaves financial history and popular culture into an entertaining and blistering social critique of how so many people have come to chase endless financial reflections of the real economy. *Extreme Money* speaks truth to power. "

—Frank Partnoy, George E. Barrett Professor of Law and Finance at the University of San Diego and Author of *F.I.A.S.C.O*, *Infectious Greed*, and *The Match King*

"*Extreme Money* is a highly entertaining, richly detailed account of how fools and charlatans, masquerading as investment professionals, pillage the world economy. Das is modern finance's Candide: a cool, precise, globetrotting observer of decades of delusion and rapacity. The serial revelations of his picaresque tour will amuse, enlighten, and enrage both lay people and market insiders."

—Yves Smith, Founder of www.nakedcapitalism.com and Author of *ECONned: How Unenlightened Self Interest Undermined Democracy and Corrupted Capitalism*

"Most books written about the global financial crisis have been written by those who only became wise after the event. Das is not one of them. Long before the collapse of Lehman Brothers, he warned about the flaws in modern finance. *Extreme Money* is his account of what went wrong. Read it! "

—Edward Chancellor, Member of GMO's Asset Allocation Team and Author of *Devil Take the Hindmost: A History of Financial Speculation*

"A rich analysis told with color and verve."

—Philip Augar, Author of *Reckless: The Rise and Fall of the City*

Praise for *Traders, Guns & Money*

"…a distinctly timely book…tries to reach out to the mathematically challenged to explain how the world of derivatives "really" works…explaining not only the high-minded theory behind the business and its various products but the sometimes sordid reality of the industry, illustrated by lively anecdotes…very up to date, covering some of the new areas of finance, such as credit derivatives…also gives an excellent sense of the all-important cultural aspect of the business, detailing the complexities of trading-floor politics, the dangerously skewed incentive systems, the obsession with money and the cultural chasm that separates derivative traders from many of their clients—and from many other parts of the bank."

—Gillian Tett, Financial Times, London

"…an acerbic expose…Funny, readable and peppered with one-liners from Groucho Marx, "Traders, Guns & Money" offers an ideal primer for anyone tempted to take a walk on the derivative side."

—James Pressley, Bloomberg

"Long before the 2008-09 credit crisis and collapse, one of the strongest warnings about the dangers of derivatives came from Satyajit Das…. it reads more like a crime novel than a financial book."

—Barry Ritholtz

"...a scalpel of a book that pulls back the skin on the derivatives and risk management industry to expose the blood, guts and circulatory system underneath."

—Nina Mehta, Financial Engineering News

"*Traders, Guns & Money* is one the most entertaining investment books I've read in a long time…this is possibly the best insider account of a career in investments since Michael Lewis's book *Liar's Poker*."

—www. dna.bloggingstocks.com

"…this revealing insider's account …the book is peppered with cautionary tales …Das wittily exposes the mechanisms behind the arcane language…."

—Carol Kennedy, UK Corporate Director

"…given the dramatic impact of derivatives, this book is a must-read."

—NYSSA News

"…contains more than investor advice, with plenty of tales of gluttonous excess and trading floor antics…."

—Cameron Dueck, South China Morning Post

"The murky and complex world of finances and derivatives is scrupulously and frantically told in this brilliant narrative…a collection and recollection of exquisite financial tales well worth your time."

—Convergence

"…an amusing, down-to-earth look behind the scenes of the derivatives market …There were several times I laughed out loud…."

—www.runningofthebools.typepad.com

Extreme Money

Extreme Money

Masters of the Universe and the Cult of Risk

Satyajit Das

Vice President, Publisher: Tim Moore
Associate Publisher and Director of Marketing: Amy Neidlinger
Executive Editor: Jim Boyd
Editorial Assistant: Pamela Boland
Development Editor: Russ Hall
Senior Marketing Manager: Julie Phifer
Assistant Marketing Manager: Megan Graue
Cover Designer: Chuti Prasertsith
Managing Editor: Kristy Hart
Project Editor: Jovana San Nicolas-Shirley
Proofreader: San Dee Phillips
Indexer: Larry Sweazy
Senior Compositor: Gloria Schurick
Manufacturing Buyer: Dan Uhrig

FT Press offers excellent discounts on this book when ordered in quantity for bulk purchases or special sales. For more information, please contact U.S. Corporate and Government Sales, 1-800-382-3419, corpsales@pearsontechgroup.com. For sales outside the U.S., please contact International Sales at international@pearson.com.

Printed in the United States of America

First Printing August 2011

ISBN-10: 0-13-279007-6
ISBN-13: 978-0-13-279007-9

Pearson Education LTD.
Pearson Education Australia PTY, Limited.
Pearson Education Singapore, Pte. Ltd.
Pearson Education North Asia, Ltd.
Pearson Education Canada, Ltd.
Pearson Educatión de Mexico, S.A. de C.V.
Pearson Education—Japan
Pearson Education Malaysia, Pte. Ltd.

Library of Congress Cataloging-in-Publication Data

Das, Satyajit.

Extreme money : masters of the universe and the cult of risk / Satyajit Das.

p. cm.

ISBN 978-0-13-279007-9 (hbk. : alk. paper)

1. Money. 2. Finance. I. Title.

HG221.D257 2012

332—dc22

For Jade Novakovic

without whom there is nothing

"It is hard to change Gods."
Fyodor Dostoevsky, *The Possessed*

Contents

Part II: Fundamentalism

Part III: Alchemy

About the Author

Satyajit Das is an international specialist in the area of financial derivatives, risk management, and capital markets, with a global reputation.

Das presciently anticipated many aspects of the Global Financial Crisis in his 2006 book *Traders, Guns & Money: Knowns and Unknowns in the Dazzling World of Derivatives*. In a speech that year—"The Coming Credit Crash"—he argued that: "an informed analysis of the structured credit markets shows that risk is not better spread but more leveraged and (arguably) more concentrated amongst hedge funds and a small group of dealers. This does not improve the overall stability and security of the financial system but exposes it to increased risk of a 'crash' during a credit downturn." He has continued to be a respected commentator on subsequent developments in the crisis.

He was featured in Charles Ferguson's 2010 Oscar-winning documentary *Inside Job* and a 2009 BBC TV documentary *Tricks with Risk*. He has appeared on TV and radio—ABC and SBS (Australia); BBC (UK); Bloomberg (USA); CNBC (UK and Asia); SABC, Summit TV and e-TV (South Africa); Canadian Broadcasting and Business New Network (Canada); and NZ Radio. He is a frequent interviewee and widely quoted in the financial press in the United States, Canada, UK/ Europe, South Africa, Australia, New Zealand, and Asia.

Between 1988 and 1994, Das was the Treasurer of the TNT Group, an international transport and logistics company with responsibility for the Global Treasury function. Between 1977 and 1987, he worked in banking with the Commonwealth Bank of Australia, Citicorp Investment Bank, and Merrill Lynch.

Since 1994, Das has acted as a consultant to financial institutions and corporations in Europe, North America, Asia, and Australia. He provides advice on trading, pricing/valuation, and risk management of derivative transactions/financial products. He also presents advanced seminars on financial derivatives/ risk management and capital markets for derivatives and finance professionals throughout the world. Between 2000 and 2007, he was a consultant to and Director of Rand Merchant Bank, a division of First Rand Group of South Africa.

He is the author of *Traders, Guns & Money: Knowns and Unknowns in the Dazzling World of Derivatives—Revised Edition* (2006 and 2010), an insider's account of derivatives trading and the financial products business filled with black humor and satire. The book has been described by the Financial Times, London as "fascinating reading...explaining not only the high-minded theory behind the business and its various products but the sometimes sordid reality of the industry." James Pressley at Bloomberg included the revised edition of the book in his list of 50 top business titles published since January 1, 2009.

Das is also the author of a number of key reference works on derivatives and risk management including *Swaps/ Financial Derivatives Library—Third Edition* (2005) (a four-volume, 4,200-page reference work for practitioners on derivatives) and *Credit Derivatives, CDOs and Structured Credit Products—Third Edition* (2005).

He has published widely on financial issues in professional journals and newspapers.

His blogs can be found on a number of online financial sites, including www.nakedcapitalism.com, www.roubini.com, www.minyanville.com, www.eurointelligence.com and www.prudentbear.com.

Das is also the author (with Jade Novakovic) of *In Search of the Pangolin: The Accidental Eco-Tourist* (2006, New Holland), a travel narrative on eco-tourism.

Prologue

Hubris

Hubris—in Classical Greek tragedy, insolent defiance caused by excessive pride toward the Gods.

Subprime Dialects

"Vhat does a poor American defaulting in Looneyville, West Virginia, have to do with me?" Behind his high-tech, titanium composite glasses with an unlikely red-and-white polka dot design, Doktor Flick's anxious tone betrays uncharacteristic insecurity. Looneyville, I learned, was a real town. In 2007, U.S. citizens were falling behind in payments on their mortgages in record numbers in Gravity Iowa; Mars, Pennsylvania; Paris, Texas; Venus Texas; Earth, Texas; and Saturn, Texas.

Since 2000, housing prices in the United States had increased dramatically, driven by a combination of low interest rates, a strong and growing economy, and an innate desire for home ownership. U.S. President George Walker Bush, a former investment banker, set out his administration's agenda for "an ownership society in America" clearly on December 16, 2003: "We want more people owning their own home. It is in our national interest that more people own their own home. After all, if you own your own home, you have a vital stake in the future of our country."[1]

Unknown to most, the housing boom was driven primarily by strong growth in the availability of money. Banks and mortgage brokers fell over themselves to lend to new homebuyers. *Innovative* mortgage products enabled people traditionally denied loans to borrow. George Bush was full of praise for the bankers and their new *affordability* products.

During the Puyo hearings into the 1907 stock market crash, J.P. Morgan stated the required qualities of a borrower: "A man I do not trust could not get money from me on all the bonds in Christendom."[2] In the early 2000s, bankers no longer looked deeply into the soul and character of potential borrowers. You filled in a form, usually online. You stated your financial position. The value of a house was assessed using computer models based on comparable properties. Like drive-by shootings, there were *drive-by valuations*, where the valuer literally drove past the property. If the property value was insufficient to justify the loan, then the valuer added the required margin for *curb value*.

By 2006, loans were available to anybody. The borrowers came to be known as NINJAs (no income, no jobs, or assets). In 2006, U.S. house prices began to fall. Borrowers stopped making payments on these mortgages.

"What is this subprime business?" The American Dialect Society voted *subprime* the word of 2007. The term described the suspiciously cheap mortgages that were sold to hapless individuals. It was synonymous with deceitful, cynical sales practices of banks, and mortgage brokers that ended with thousands of people losing their homes.

Exploding ARM was the colloquial description of an adjustable-rate mortgage. The interest rate goes up so fast that borrowers, who could afford the original monthly payments, cannot afford the increased payment (sometimes 40–80 percent higher). *Jingle mail* refers to mail received by banks from borrowers who cannot afford mortgage repayments and so abandon their homes and mail the keys to the lender. *Liars' loans* (known as *no-doc loans*, *low-docs*, and *stated-income loans*) describe loans where potential home buyers do not have to provide any proof of their financial position but state their income and assets. The loans practically beg borrowers to lie about their income. 2007 introduced the *Implode-O-Meter*—a website tracking falling house prices, defaults on mortgages, and ultimately the housing finance débâcle.

Doktor Flick (the title is honorific) was head of international banking for a medium-sized German Landesbank, owned by the state (Lander). Limited growth at home had encouraged aggressive overseas expansion. Now, a bunch of Americans irresponsibly refusing to make their mortgage payments threatened Doktor Flick's empire.

"Finished, it must be nearly finished." Inadvertently, the German has spoken, almost exactly, the opening words of Samuel Beckett's somber and hopeless existential drama Endgame. It was finished, but not quite in the way that Doktor Flick had imagined. Within a few months, the melange of his banks' special purpose vehicles (SPVs) would collapse, with losses of billions of dollars. In a world of global money flows, what happened in America no longer stayed in America.

Best in Show

"Bad?" Mailer breaks the long silence looking at me contemplatively over his Martini. "Very. Very bad." I respond. "Long?" Mailer's turn. "Years. Many years." It is autumn 2007. I am in London to brief Mailer's bank on conditions in credit markets. Mailer ruminates on my gloomy prognostications, drains his drink, and tries to order another. The bartender has trouble understanding Mailer's Bostonian rolled vowels and laryngeal consonants.

When I first met Mailer, he introduced himself as: "Mailer Stevenson. Managing director. Fixed income. Graduate School of Business, Chicago." Mailer then worked at a white-shoe Wall Street firm. Used to describe pedigreed investment banks, "white shoe" is a reference to "white bucks," a laced suede or buckskin shoe once popular among upper-class, Ivy League-trained bankers. Losing out in the internecine wars that break out periodically in investment banks, Mailer moved to London to lead the trading operations of Euro Swiss Bank (ESB), a major European bank. He had recently returned to his old Wall Street employer, heading global bond trading. Forty something, a former star college athlete somewhat gone to middle-aged fat, intellectually agile, liberal in attitude, Mailer is the epitome of the new financial superclass that rules the world.

A small group of men causing a commotion interrupts our reveries. The young men are wearing T-shirts under their jackets—a style made famous in the long-running TV series *Miami Vice* by the actor Don Johnson. A roll of pound notes mollifies the bouncer, concerned about the establishment's dress code. Designer T-shirts, it seems, are not T-shirts in the strictest sense.

Mailer and I know two of the men—Joachim Margin and Ralph Smitz, hedge fund managers who run JR Capital. Everybody assumes that J R are the initials of the first names of the founders. In fact, they stand for *Jolly Roger*. The fund's logo is a stylized skull and crossbones once flown to identify a ship's crew as pirates. Like the original, the logo's background is blood red, and the skull and bones are black.

The next day, JR will be crowned Hedge Fund of the Year and Hedge Fund Manager of the Year at the all-star gala Global Finance Forum. Mailer's bank is also getting an award—Fixed Income House of the Year. Mailer bought that prize of course.

The idea behind industry awards is that clients and peers vote on who is the best. A dealer voted best "something in something somewhere" uses it prominently to solicit clients. Polling is supposedly anonymous and independent. Like democracy, the process is obscure. Mailer "heard" that his bank would be crowned Fixed Income House of the Year. If this were correct, he explained to the magazine arranging the awards, then he would buy a platinum sponsorship of the award event (cost $100,000) and take a full-page ad (cost $40,000). By a strange coincidence, Mailer's bank did indeed win the award.

The black T-shirts are emblazoned with a bold pattern in small diamonds: 10/40. 10 is the $10 billion of money JR now manages; 40 is the 40 percent return that JR earned for its investors last year. The two principals took home a cool $250 million each for their efforts. Margin and Smitz once worked for Mailer at ESB. "Punks!"—Mailer's insults are from a different era.

The Physical Impossibility of Death in the Mind of Someone Living

JR has commissioned a famous architect to design the hedge fund's new offices. "They are going to put sharks in tanks." The piscine predators turn out to be installations, *objets d'art*.

Damien Hirst—the best known of a group of artists dubbed young British Artists (YBAs)—is the artist of choice for conspicuously consuming hedge fund managers. *The Physical Impossibility of Death in the Mind of Someone Living*, Hirst's most iconic work, is a 14-foot (4.3-meter) tiger shark immersed in formaldehyde in a vitrine, weighing more than 2 tons.

The shark was caught by a fisherman in Australia who was paid £6,000—£4,000 to catch it and £2,000 to pack it in ice and ship it to London. Charles Saatchi (the advertising guru) bought the work for £50,000. Over time, the shark decomposed. Its skin became heavily wrinkled and turned a pale green. One of its fins fell off. The formaldehyde solution in the tank turned murky. The threatening effect of a tiger shark swimming toward the viewer was lost. Curators tried adding bleach to the formaldehyde. This only increased the rate of decay of the cadaver. In the end, the curators removed the skin, which was then stretched over a weighted fiberglass mold.

In December 2004, Saatchi sold the work to Steve Cohen, founder and principal of the über hedge fund SAC Capital Advisers, which manages $20 billion. Cohen paid $12 million for *The Physical Impossibility of Death in the Mind of Someone Living*, although there are allegations that it was *only* $8 million.

At one time, Saatchi had explored giving away his collection to a new British museum. Ken Livingstone, later London's mayor, argued that an aquarium built for the same cost would attract more tourism. Author Rita Hatton pointed out that *The Physical Impossibility of Death in the Mind of Someone Living* was both an aquarium and a tourist attraction.[3] JR was rumored to have commissioned Hirst to create an installation for its new offices, using white pointer sharks, a feared large predator.

Retreat

The bad blood between Mailer and JR dates to Mailer's time as the head of fixed income at ESB. Each year, the bank held its Global Strategy Session (GSS) at Versailles. Sceptics referred to it secretly as the **G**od **S**un King **S**peaketh. Eduard Keller, the young, urbane, and snappily dressed chief executive of ESB, was the Sun King.

Keller, a former management consultant, knew little about banking. He spoke of *competitive gaps* (ESB lagged other banks) that Mailer had been hired to *bridge*. There were *voids*, a reference to businesses that ESB were not in. ESB needed to *harness*, *seed*, and *harvest*. Occasionally, it also needed to *cull*. In le Roi Soleil's reign, people met in their *teams*, *formations*, *waves*, *wavelets*, or *currents*. Ideas had to be *socialized* in endless meetings and committees. ESB had grown astonishingly in size and profitability during Keller's period as CEO. No one actually knew why or whether it was the result of his leadership. Nobody cared.

The philosopher Alasdair MacIntyre noted: "One key reason why the presidents of large corporations do not, as some radical critics believe, control the US is that they do not even succeed in controlling their own corporations."[4] Tolstoy had written about the Battle of Borodino in a similar vein: "It was not Napoleon who directed the course of the battle, for none of his orders was carried out and during the battle he did not know what was going on." Keller's reign at ESB was Napoleonic.

At the 2005 GSS, "The state of the world" session turns out to be a journalist with a best-selling book on globalization. His speech is spiced with "When I had dinner/lunch/tea/tamarind juice with such and such." According to him, "global think" will usher in a new age of endless prosperity and wealth for all denizens of the blue planet, driven by free market economics, democracy, and global trade.

"The state of markets" turns out to be a Nobel-Prize laureate economist who reports "sound prospects," "dampened risk," and "subdued volatility." The BRIC (Brazil, Russia, India, and China) economies will power the world with endless demand for commodities and "stuff," interest rates will remain low and stock markets will always go up.

"The state of mind" is Swami Muktinanda, who strides on to the stage in saffron robes finished off with elegant Gucci loafers. He urges the audience to harness the spiritual energy of the cosmos, trying to get everyone to levitate.

Swiss Inquisitions

After lunch, Mailer and I wait in an anteroom to begin serious discussions about the proposal to set up a hedge fund.

Historically, banks took deposits from savers and lent them to companies and individuals to buy things—property, plant, machinery, houses, cars, and so on. Investment banks provided advice to companies and arranged share issues and bond issues to finance their business. In the late twentieth century, the universal bank or financial supermarket emerged. As the nomenclature implies, these banks did *everything*. In the past, banks acted as middlemen standing between borrowers or lenders taking minimal risk. To increase profits, banks now took risks with their shareholders' and depositors' money. The Sun King was turning ESB into a universal banking powerhouse.

A strategy report prepared by consultants concluded: "ESB's risk profile was conservative relative to its peers providing opportunities to enhance shareholder returns by significantly increasing its trading activities." They should "increase risk." To bridge "the gap," ESB should invest in hedge funds, freewheeling shops that traded anything that moved.

Margin and Smitz propose starting a hedge fund. Initially ESB will invest $500 million and lend the fund up to $6 billion secured over its investments. After the fund has a successful track record, the bank's own wealthy customers and institutional clients will be allowed to invest in the fund. Margin and Smitz's company, the manager of the fund, will be paid 2/20: 2 percent of the assets under management and 20 percent of any investment earnings. In return, ESB will receive a 20 percent share of Margin and Smitz's fund management company.

Idea of an Investment

At the meeting Margin and Smitz are joined by Stone (the chief financial officer), Benoit (the chief operating officer), and Woori (the chief risk officer). Amid the chiefs, I am the only Indian.

Margin and Smitz take the audience through the obligatory PowerPoint presentation. "I have done some analysis...." Mailer is prone to the use of the personal singular pronoun *I* where the personal plural pronoun *we* would be more appropriate. In reality, I, not Mailer, had analysed the proposed investment strategy, the script by which a trader or fund manager attempts to make money.

Nonprofessionals are astonished as to how banal all investment strategies are when stripped of the marketing gloss that is used to sell them. A *long-short* strategy is where the investor buys something they expect to go up and short sells something that they expect to go down. It is called *market neutral* or *relative value*. Long-short is differentiated from *long only* where the investor can buy things that presumably they think will go up.

Short selling involves selling something that you don't own but hope to buy back at a lower price when the price goes down. You can sell tickets to a sought-after concert by the latest hot band for $200 for delivery in 1 week. You don't own the tickets but you think that ticket prices will fall before you have to deliver them. If they do, then you buy the ticket for say $160 before the week is out and deliver to the person who bought it for $200, making $40.

The *carry trade* entails borrowing in a currency that has low interest rates. The Japanese yen is a perennial favorite as interest rates there have been close to an anorexic 0.00 percent for many years. You take the money and invest it in something earning more than the interest rate you pay and pocket the difference.

You can lose—that's risk. The thing that you thought would go up comes down, and the thing you thought would come down goes up. Yen interest rates go up, and the yen goes up in value against whatever currency you invested in.

Your instincts and history say that on average the investment strategy works. Details are worked out and tested. You work out which share you think will go up or down. It could be based on tedious fundamental analysis—you pore over financial statements that are out-of-date or fraudulent, and you talk to management who lie to you if they talk to you at all. Alternatively, you use *technical* or quantitative filters to identify stocks. You *buy the dip*—purchases of stocks that have fallen by a certain amount. Your quant, an analyst with several quantitative degrees who is grossly over-qualified for the task at hand, tests the strategy, using historical data.

The process fleshes out the details of the investment idea. In the long-short, it will tell you what you should buy and what you should sell. In the carry trade, it will tell you which currency to borrow in and which currency to invest in. Do you buy and sell stock in the same industry, geography, or currency? In the carry trade, how do you define high and low rates and what kind of investments and borrowing do you do and for how long? The process gives you an idea of the risks. How often will the strategy work? What kind of profits does it produce? How often will it lose money and how much?

Margin and Smitz's answers to my probing are vague, reminiscent of the investment strategy in a prospectus during the South Sea bubble: "A company for carrying on an undertaking of great advantage, but nobody to know what it is."

Ambush

"I have analyzed a number of your past trades in detail." Margin and Smitz look at me, surprised. Dr Woori, the Korean nuclear physicist in charge of risk, has supplied me details of Margin and Smitz's trading, unaware of the reasons for my interest. "Now let's take the gold trade...."

In the gold trade, they purchased shares in MG, a small Canadian gold-mining company, and short sold gold against the position. MG's share price was *undervalued*, not reflecting the value of the gold in the ground that could be mined and sold. The investment strategy benefits from the fact that MG shares are not properly valued based on the gold content. It looks good, at least in Excel spreadsheets.

The short gold position protected any investor from a sudden unexpected fall in the gold price. If the gold price fell, then the shares would also fall, as MG's gold reserves would be worth less. The fall in prices would create profits on the short gold position, as you could buy gold at the lower price, deliver it to the buyer at the agreed higher price and lock in a profit. The loss on the shares would be offset by the gain on the short gold position. The position is hedged, free of risk, at least in theory.

"My analysis shows that the positions were highly risky." Mailer is all smiles at my unrelenting assault—he likes *offense.* The investment strategy is based on the relationship between MG shares and the gold price. What if MG had already locked in the price of the gold by agreeing the price for future sales with buyers? What if MG gold reserves were not as large as supposed? What if MG could not raise the funds to expand the mines? What if ESB could not borrow the gold for the short sales? I pile on the "what if's." Dr. Woori pointed out the very same risks to ESB management in a memo from which I copied liberally.

"Academic bullshit," Margin interrupts. "Gold's there. Independent reserve assessments. No forward gold sales! Management. You're a complete moron." When agitated, Margin speaks in a strange, rapid, barely intelligible staccato.

I keep going. "Even if you are right, how does ESB exit the position? What would happen if MG's share price never aligned to the gold price? What would you do? Buy the company and mine the gold and deliver into the short gold position? You need government approval to buy the mine. Your regulator doesn't allow you to own 100 percent of any company." I move to my killer point. "In any case, the trade lost money—a lot of money."

"In detail we drown." The Sun King has trouble with the order of nouns and verbs in English. "We are drowning in detail," Dr. Woori corrects emphatically in his perfect diction and Oxford-educated English. "Return needs risk," Keller continues. "The returns are insufficient to compensate for the risk." I moan. Like Cassandra I know that no one will ever believe my predictions. Keller's mind is made up. ESB must increase risk taking to enhance "shareholder return" to close the "gap." All I can see are gaps in the strategy. The meeting is over.

Early next morning, waiting for a taxi to the airport at an hour unsuited to the working habits of French taxi drivers, I run into the Sun King. He gets up habitually at 4.30 a.m., starting the day with cardiovascular exercises and a Pilates session. He follows a rigid diet that begins with a breakfast of raw fruit. In earlier times, bankers were better fed and watered. Exercise was considered eccentric. I wonder whether Keller knows that at the 1943 Allied Casablanca Conference, Harry Hopkins, one of Franklin D. Roosevelt's advisers, found Winston Churchill in bed, clad only in a pink bathrobe, drinking a bottle of red wine for breakfast.

"Good for the brain is exercise," Keller states. "Your contribution yesterday. Very interesting. I have asked Dr. Woori to look at your ideas on risk." With that he is gone.

On the way to the airport in a rattling Peugeot taxi driven by a disgruntled North African from the *banlieues*, we drive past the Versailles palace, resplendent in the morning light. A few years later, Ken Griffin, the founder of the mega hedge fund Citadel, will rent Versailles to stage his wedding.

Mega Presentations

Four thousand participants cram into the 2007 Global Finance Conference, staged that year in London. The opening address is from the British Chancellor of the Exchequer. The Chancellor's intellectual signature is a naïve belief in the primacy of finance, banking, and money in general. He has made London money friendly and is lionized by *the City* for it.

Modern economies have long ceased to make anything. The major activity is money: investing it, borrowing it, trading it, making it, and spending it. Money generates derivative industries like property speculation, luxury car dealerships, personal trainers, and company-paid-for lifestyle coaches, butlers, and valets—all essentials of a modern life of conspicuous consumption in the modern service economy.

The Chancellor's allusion to London's superiority over New York as a center of money elicits a negative reaction from the large contingent of American financiers. Mailer bristles with indignation: "If you're good enough to make it in New York, you can make it anywhere."

Government mandarins and academics vouchsafe the contribution of finance to society at large. Bankers talk of innovation and the *golden age of finance*, the money to be made, and the money they are making. Regulators speak of *market responsive* regulations. One bank chief executive notes: "The regulators are finally under control!" There is the dull repetitious quality of minimalist music.

The lunchtime guest speaker—a rock star noted for his charity work—enters to a blast of his hit song from 30 years ago. The audience, which was in nappies when he enjoyed his popularity, looks confused, not recognizing the tune. Unconstrained by anything as restrictive as a lectern or notes, the speaker celebrates his own "humanitarian achievements," and concludes:

"I tell you this—the paradigm for the future century must be a new order or else there will be new global disorder."

Fording Streams

The focus of days two and three of the Global Finance Conference is learning and development—"learning talent." My understanding that talent was innate and skill was acquired is obviously incorrect.

Whereas once a basic business degree or (for those with higher aspirations) an MBA (Master of Business Administration) was sufficient, these days the qualification of choice is the M.Fin. (Master of Finance), M.App.Fin. (Master of Applied Finance), M.Sc. (Fin.) (Master of Science in Finance), CFA (Certified Financial Analyst), CQF (Certificate in Quantitative Finance), and so on. Perhaps there should be a new qualification—MMM (Master of Making Money).

The alphabet soup feeds an industry, providing the training that is necessary to keep up to date or risk losing the qualification. Multiple streams cater for the varied audience—fascists, anarchists, neo-cons, Fabian socialists, Marxist-Leninists, Friedmanites, Keynesians, Roundheads, Cavaliers, and militant vegans.

There are sessions at the conference on structured finance, structured products, structured trade finance, structured commodities—in fact, anything with *structured* in front of it. There are multiple streams on commodities. There are entire floodplains devoted to private equity, hedge funds, and emerging markets (especially the BRIC economies of Brazil, Russia, India, China). A technical session is titled "Combining gamma diffusion methods and eigenvectors within and without Black-Scholes-Merton frameworks for modelling mean reverting energy prices in an emerging market context—a non-technical overview."

Liquidity and Leverage

Mailer invites me to his bank's post-conference soirée at Tate Modern on the south side of the Thames river across from St Paul's Cathedral. The five-story-high, 3,400 square meters of the massive turbine hall that once housed the electricity generators of the former Bankside Power Station have been converted into an entertainment space.

There is a champagne bar, a vintage whisky tasting area, and a Tiffany space displaying expensive jewelry celebrating the occasion. The theme is the roaring twenties—jazz, cocktail waitresses dressed as flappers, and art deco décor, including a scale model of the Chrysler Building minus Fay Wray and King Kong. Guests mingle and network while enjoying multiple champagne salutes. Music from Leverage, an amateur, banker-led jazz band, entertains the guests. A French competitor's party features a rock band called La Liquidité.

Tate staff offers private guided tours of artworks dating back to 1900. A highlight of the collection is a massive Joseph Beuys tableau—a collection of sleds, each with its blanket, flashlight, and edible fat, extending out of the back of a Volkswagen bus. Nearby there is a massive suspended felt-covered piano. The obsessive images and totems seem a strange accompaniment for the age of capital.

I leave early to party hop. My Indian heritage has gotten me an invitation to the Indian Bankers' Association party themed "India Shining," a shameless sales pitch for investment in India. A minister extols the virtues of India, citing statistics on growth, resource availability, and opportunities. There is no mention of the fact that the vast majority of the Indian population has no access to sanitation, clean water, education, or healthcare. There is no mention of the aging colonial era infrastructure where inadequate electricity supply results in daily *load shedding* or *brownouts* interrupting power supplies for several hours most days.

An American banker finds India fascinating and full of opportunity. "A billion people, a billion consumers, wow!" He is fascinated that I, an Indian, do not speak Indian but Bengali, one of the hundreds of languages spoken in India. "Wouldn't it be easier if everybody just spoke, you know, Indian?" Dan Quayle, a former U.S. vice-president, once apologized to Latin Americans that he could not speak Latin.

Along the Thames outside the Tate, there is a collection of ice sculptures of men and women sponsored by a broker drawing attention to a new initiative in carbon permit and emission trading—expected to be the next mega profitable field. In the gentrified old streets of London, I notice indigent people wrapping themselves in cardboard and newspaper against the chill of the early spring evening. Near the all-night supermarkets, automatic teller machines (ATMs) and London Underground train stations, the cry of the homeless—"Any spare change, please?"—echoes.

Democracy of Greed

A year earlier, in 2006, I attended the Money Show in America, a massive annual showcase of investments and financial management for ordinary individuals. If the Global Finance Conference is champagne and caviar, then the Money Show is beer and pizza.

In the massive hall, nubile young male and female hucksters shamelessly tempt passers-bys into booths selling investments, financial newsletters, and personal financial advice. The Money Show targets the new democracy of greed—combining the frenzy of an auction and the deep faith of an evangelical gathering. There is, as economist John Kenneth Galbraith observed, a deep "conviction that ordinary people were meant to be rich."[5]

Money managers and hucksters try to separate visitors from their hard-earned savings; in the words of American comedian Woody Allen, "Giving you investment advice until you don't have anything left."[6]

Before the 1929 stock market crash, many systems for predicting the stock market gained currency. One system saw price falls in months containing the letter "r." Another system made stock picks on the basis of comic book dialogue. Evangeline Adams, the famous fortune teller, predicted stock market movements using the movements of the planets. Mark Twain, in his novel *Pudd'nhead Wilson*, probably offered the soundest investment advice: "October: this is one of the peculiarly dangerous months to speculate in stocks. The others are July, January, September, April, November, May, March, June, December, August, and February."

Contrarian investor Victor Niederhoffer chronicled his trading secrets in his best-selling 1997 book *Education of a Speculator* before blowing up his fund with large losses shortly afterward. Ironically, Niederhoffer once observed that it is inconceivable that anybody would divulge a truly effective get-rich scheme for the price of a book.

Pick and Pay

At the Money Show, a bank is publicizing its new home loan product—the *pick and pay* mortgage loan. The borrowers *pick* the amount of the loan, the term of the loan, and what they want to *pay* each month. The repayments selected stay at the agreed level for 2 years after which the bank resets the payments. The product brings expensive dream homes within the reach of everybody.

Repayments do not cover the interest cost of the loan. On any reasonable assumption, repayments will more than double after the first 2 years. The account executive corrects me: "Re-fi! You haven't factored in the re-fi!" At the end of 2 years you *re-fi*, taking out a new loan to repay the old loan. Slick charts and interactive graphics show prices of American houses increasing at 10, 20, or 40 percent each year. Increasing house prices enable increased borrowing to pay off previous borrowing in a spiral of wealth creation. The small print of the loan in the product disclosure statement (PDS) sets out large, punitive early payment penalties and re-fi costs. On a $400,000 mortgage, the account executive stands to make 3 percent or more—$12,000.

There is also *equity access*, where people who own their house free of a mortgage takes on a new loan to access the price appreciation, spending the money on whatever they want. *Reverse mortgage* is where people in retirement borrows against their residence to cover retirement expenses. And there is a *legacy mortgage*, in which the borrowers take out a loan for 99 years and bequeath the mortgage to their progeny to repay.

Black Sea Real Estate

The speaker at the real estate seminar is a 30-something man in a shiny silk suit and a headset. He is big on rhetorical questions:

> Do you know what is the hottest real estate market in the world today? It's the Black Sea coast in Bulgaria. Do you know why? It's the cheapest waterfront in the world today. Just $40,000 gets you prime beachfront property. What would you get for that amount in Florida, Mexico, Spain? Think about it. Prices have doubled in the last six months. Do you know what gains I expect over the next two years? 500 percent. That's right! You will get back five times what you invest. Can you imagine that? Only smart people can imagine that. Are you smart? Do you dare to be rich?

The speaker pauses and looks carefully at his audience. "Or are you a loser? Do you want to stay a loser?"

I grapple with magnificent Black Sea beachfront bungalows overlooking rocky, pebble-strewn beaches, a heavily polluted sea and a smoke-belching Chernobyl vintage nuclear power plant. The speaker's other favored investment destination is the Persian Gulf emirate of Dubai, where prices have appreciated 150 percent over the last 2 years. Soaring oil prices and demand from other property players diversifying their investment portfolios *guarantee* massive gains.

World RE Investment Portfolios, Inc., the speaker's company, is selling seminars not real estate. At the conclusion of the speech, assistants fan out, buttonholing attendees to sign them up for further seminars to gain in-depth knowledge about the path to riches by the Black Sea, in Dubai, and further afield. The cost is $25,000 for a series. If you want a personal one-on-one with the "Divine One," then the cost is $50,000 for a 2-hour audience.

"Best investment I ever made," a fellow attendee tells me. "I'm signing up for a personal coaching session. Just to 'fine tune' what I've been doing." What he has "been doing" turns out to be a portfolio of 200 homes in various countries assembled over the last 7 years. He purchased a property next to his house for his aged parents, but they became seriously ill and died before they could move in. The property appreciated in value. He sold it and was left with a profit on his first *trade*. He reinvested the gain in another property. He now buys property, and as soon as the property rises in value, he increases the mortgage amount to take out his initial investment and starts the whole thing all over again. "Banks are pretty relaxed now about lending these days. They lend you the full amount, no questions asked. You really don't need to have any money to start. Not like in the old days."

He is worth $20 million on paper. "Not bad for a garage mechanic." It is all tied up in the properties. "I don't want to sell. There's so much upside." If he needs spending money, then he borrows it. He has around $180 million in debt. The consistent message is "Debt is in; debt is good."

Life on the Margin

In the ST trading seminar, participants are divided into small groups. I share my computer terminal with a couple—Mary, a lively middle-aged woman and her husband, Greg.

She is a homemaker but was a secretary in a brokerage firm. She found juggling a family (two young children) and a job difficult. Mary believes that she can fit stock trading into her schedule and make more money than she would from a job. "One of my neighbors has been doing it for ages and she makes $5,000 a week. It can't be that hard, can it?"

Greg, a machinist, has worked for the same machine tool maker for more than 20 years. A private equity firm recently bought the company with a lot of borrowed money. "There have been changes," Greg mumbles. He has doubts about trading but sees the need for more money. "The mortgage, two cars, school fees, college fees, healthcare, holidays," he ticks them off. They saw a financial adviser who calculated what they needed to retire. It is well in excess of what their pensions and other retirement savings could ever amount to. "That's when I said we gotta do something! Didn't I, Greg?" Mary interjects.

The seminar introduces us to trading in *contracts for differences (CFDs)*, *futures* and *options*, *derivatives*—Warren Buffett's infamous "weapons of mass destruction." You can bet on fluctuations in prices of any financial asset—share prices, currencies, interest rates, commodity prices, and so on. You put up a mere 2 percent: With $20,000 you can take positions in $1,000,000 worth of shares. If the share price goes up, say 10 percent, then you make $100,000 with your $20,000 investment—a return of five times or 500 percent. That's leverage.

Normally, if a stock is trading at $100, you outlay $100—the full price. For a $10 increase in the price of the stock (10 percent increase) you make a profit of $10 equivalent to a return of 10 percent (gain of $10 divided by investment of $100). Using leverage you can buy the stock using $10 of your own money and borrowing $90 of other people's money. For the same $10 increase in the value of the stock, you still make $10, but your return is now 100 percent (gain of $10 divided by investment of $10). Leverage enhances returns in percentage terms. It can also enhance the return in dollars. If you had $100, then normally you could only buy one share. But with leverage, you can now buy 10 shares (investment [$100] plus borrowing [$900] to buy 10 shares at $100 for a total outlay of $1,000), enabling you to increase the amount of any gains in dollars.

But leverage works for both increases and decreases in the value of what is purchased. As the borrowing must be repaid in full with interest, leverage increases the risk. For a $10 decrease in the value of the stock, you lose $10, but where leveraged, the fall wipes out your entire investment of $10 (a return of *negative* 100 percent).

Archimedes said: "Give me a lever long enough and a fulcrum on which to place it, and I shall move the world." In the modern world, money games are based on a similar principle: "Give me enough debt and I shall make you all the money in the world."

Racing Days

The only way to trade successfully, we are told, is to buy ST's computer programs ($995). Then there are training DVDs ($495), manuals ($195), trading newsletters ($350 per year) and trading paraphernalia such as trade blotters for keeping tabs on your trades. You open an account with an affiliated broking firm (2 percent commissions on trades) by signing up and investing $20,000. If you sign up immediately, then you get a free copy of the firm's founding father's cheap self-published work *Trade Your Way to Wealth and Independence*. "You get $199 of value right there."

All I see is the Marx Brothers' *Day at the Races*, in which Chico is a con artist selling racing tip books containing horse racing tips. Chico offers the gullible Dr. Hugo Hackenbush, played by Groucho Marx, a $1 racing tip book. Groucho buys the tip book, which predicts that Z-V-B-X-R-P-L will win the next race. Unable to decipher the text, Groucho consults Chico, who offers a code book to decode the letters. The code book is free but there is a $1 printing charge. Chico also offers an alternative—a *free* master code book, without a printing charge, but with a $2 delivery charge. Groucho is outraged at the delivery charge, as he is standing right next to the con artist. Chico agrees to make the delivery charge $1 for such a short distance. In the end, Groucho spends $6 on the master code book and a set of four Breeder's Guides to decipher the master code book. By the time he has assembled his library of literary material on horses, the race Groucho wanted to bet on is over.

As I leave the seminar, Mary and Greg are signing up for ST's trading system. I think of the famous speculator Jesse Livermore, immortalized in Edwin Lefèvre's *Reminiscences of a Stock Operator*:

> The sucker play is always the same: To make easy money. That is why speculation never changes. The appeal is the same: Greed, vanity, and laziness. The merchant who would not dream of buying and selling stockings or percales on the advice of fools goes to Wall Street and cheerfully risks his money on the say so of men whose interest is not his interest, or tipsters who have not grown

> rich at the game they want him to play. He thinks his margin will take the place of brains, vision, knowledge, experience, and of intelligent self-surgery. Whether the stock market goes his way or against him, his hope is always fighting his judgment—his hope of gaining more that keeps him from taking his profits when he should: his hope of losing less that keeps him from taking a relatively small loss. It is a human failing![7]

Livermore, "the man with the evil eye," was a famous speculator making and losing several fortunes. By 1940 Livermore, once wealthy and owner of a yellow Rolls Royce, a yacht, and a huge sapphire ring, was reduced to poverty. His suicide note read: "My life was a failure."

Dr. Doom

"Only Roubini and Faber agree with you," says Mailer, passing judgment on my analysis of the global financial situation. "Between them they have predicted 12 of the last 3 recessions."

Roubini—Dr. Nouriel Roubini—is *Dr. Doom*. Born in Turkey of Iranian parents, the professor of economics, who runs a private consulting business, has been pessimistic about the finances of the world for as long as most can remember. Faber—Dr. Marc Faber—shares the Dr. Doom title. An investment analyst and entrepreneur, originally from Switzerland, Faber resides in Thailand from where he publishes the *Gloom Boom Doom* newsletter. His website features Kaspar Meglinger's macabre paintings, *The Dance of Death*. They are *perma-bears,* believing that the world is in the grip of a giant bubble, supported by abundant and cheap debt provided by accommodating central bankers.

"The VC [vice-chairman] thought you were seriously depressed. Needed antidepressants. Therapy," Mailer continues. "Your analysis was interesting. We need a 'correction'. Definitely. But it's not serious."

The *analysis* shows a dizzying spiral of debt. Borrowings by the U.S. government, corporations and individuals have reached around 350 percent (three and a half times) of what America produced in a year: gross domestic production (GDP). Consumer borrowing is at a record level. Every man, woman, and child in the United States (a supposedly rich country) has borrowed around $4,000 each from their Chinese counterparts (who are supposedly less well off). Complex, incomprehensible, untested financial products have accumulated unnoticed, outside regulatory purview. Banks are lending money to companies and people who will never ever be able to pay them back. Speculation and games shuffling money are rampant.

But there is no market for bad news. In 2007, I was approached to speak at a conference of fund managers. After selecting someone else, the organizer shared her reasoning. "We are nervous about the gloomy picture you might paint and any messages that wouldn't provide some sense of salvation. As our clients pay to attend our conference; we don't want them to feel that they are paying to be made depressed."

It is difficult to be rational in money matters. Investors and bankers are reluctant to forgo gains that keep piling up in defiance of the perma-bears' perennial doomsday predictions. Only the strongest person or self-sacrificing saint can leave easy money on the table, quarter after quarter, year after year. Irrespective of how much knowledge of financial history you have or how careful you are in your analysis, it is difficult to avoid being caught up in the madness of crowds.

"We are making record profits," Mailer says, as he ticks off new initiatives—hedge funds, private equity vehicles, new derivatives, new structured investment vehicles; expanding and opening offices in India, China, Russia, Brazil, and Dubai. "Heard of Madoff?" he asks. "We may be doing something with him."

Once, Mailer had been skeptical of the things that he now embraced with enthusiasm. All successful financiers have selective amnesia, remembering what fits their current worldview. Walter Bagehot, the famed economic historian and founder of *The Economist*, noted that people are most credulous when they are making money. In 1925, the author F. Scott Fitzgerald summed it up in *The Great Gatsby*: "Gatsby believed in the green light, the orgiastic future that year by year recedes before us. It eluded us then, but that's no matter—tomorrow we will run faster, stretch out our arms farther."[8]

Extreme Money

Alain de Botton wrote that he found "few seconds in life are more releasing than those in which a plane ascends to the sky."[9] It was conducive to "internal conversations."[10] On the flight home, I try to order my thoughts.

The master narrative of the world is now economic and financial as much as social, cultural, or political. Identities are defined and reinvented around money. Individual economic futures increasingly depend on financial success. Businesses and governments define their performance by financial measures.

Ordinary people borrow money to buy houses, cars, and things. They save for their children's education, vacations, or retirement. Financiers invest the savings in markets to make more money. They buy shares, property, and other investments. The money is invested in private equity funds that borrow heavily to buy companies, cut staff, and costs, strip them of assets and then resell them at vast profits to other investors. Hedge funds try to make money by placing complex bets on minuscule price movements or on an event taking or not taking place.

Financiers cut and dice risk into tiny slices according to investor requirements using super computers relying on arcane mathematics that only French bankers understand. Mortgages and toll roads or airports are transformed into securities sold to fund managers and pension funds that provide retirement income for individuals. Financiers colonize new frontiers converting natives to their new religion.

On the plane, I watch a program on *extreme sports*—adventure activities featuring danger, high levels of exertion, or spectacular stunts. *BASE jumping* (**b**uilding, **a**ntenna, **s**pan and **e**arth) involves parachuting off physical structures. Bored skateboarders practice *street luge* going fast downhill in cities. *Buildering* is free climbing up skyscrapers without any safety nets. The *Verbier extreme* requires snowboarders to find daring ways to descend a mountain. *Extreme ironing* involves a skydiver ironing mid-skydive, up a mountain or under water.

Extreme sports are not competitive in the traditional sense. People push the limits of physical ability and fear creating a *rush* as the brain releases dopamine, endorphins, and serotonin to create a temporary feeling of inexplicable euphoria. Money, too, is increasingly an extreme sport. As Gordon Gecko, played by Michael Douglas, tells his son-in-law in Oliver Stone's *Wall Street Money Never Sleeps*, the 2010 reprise of the original, it isn't about the money; it's about the game!

We live and work in the world of *extreme money*—spectacular, dangerous games with money that create new artificial highs in growth, prosperity, sophistication, and wealth. Once used to value and exchange ordinary goods, money has become the main way to make money. To make a billion dollars, it is no longer necessary to actually make anything. The rule of extreme money is that everybody borrows, everybody saves, everybody is supposed to get wealthier. But only skilled insiders get richer, running and rigging the game.

Money and the games played are intangible, unreal, and increasingly virtual. Electronic displays flashing red or green price signals are the distilled essence of the financial world. Traders do not experience the underlying reality directly but only in terms of gains or losses—money made or lost that can be lost or made back in the next few seconds.

The author Tom Wolfe once summed up the world of money by citing the Austrian economist Joseph Schumpeter: "Stocks and bonds are what he called evaporated property. People completely lose touch of the underlying assets. It's all paper—these esoteric devices. So it has become evaporated property squared. I call it evaporated property cubed."[11] Extreme money is eviscerated reality—the monetary shadow of real things.

The Greek word *Hubris* means arrogant, excessive pride that often results in fatal retribution. In Greek tragedy, it describes the actions of mortals that challenge the gods or the laws. It results in the mortals' inevitable downfall. At the Global Finance Conference, at the Money Show, in my conversations with Mailer, I felt the overweening self-confidence and overreaching ambition that comes before fall. Hubris is followed by *Nemesis*. In Greek mythology, she is the god of retribution and downfall.

Mankind mistook money, a lubricant of society and the economy, for an end in itself. It created a cult and worshipped the wrong deity, building ever more elaborate edifices and liturgies dedicated to its worship. It was a one-way street. It is now too late to turn back.

Extreme Money tells that story. It is essentially the story of the modern world.

Part I

Faith

Faith—confidence of belief based not on proof but trust in a person, thing, or teaching.

In the later half of the twentieth century, a *money culture* dominated. Money changed from a mechanism of exchange into something important in its own right. It ceased to be a claim on real things, becoming instead a way to create wealth, increase economic activity, and promote growth.

Money came to dominate individual lives, through saving for retirement and debt to finance consumption. Companies relied on money games to boost profit. Newly deregulated banks took advantage of the new opportunities to move into central roles in modern economies. Cities and countries became *financialized*.

Financialization was reinforced by the media, which increasingly provided 24/7 coverage of money matters.

1

Mirror of the Times

There's old money; then there's new money. Old money is the stuff of storied Mayflower descendants in the Hamptons or hyphenated names and titles in London's South Kensington. New money is the arriviste stuff brandished by Russian oligarchs who buy *Chealski* football club, and hedge fund managers with a taste for modern art works called *The Physical Impossibility of Death in the Mind of Someone Living*.

There's hard money, there's fiat money, and there's debt. Gold, greenbacks, dollars, pounds, euros, loonies (Canadian dollars), aussies (Australian dollars), kiwis (New Zealand dollars), Chinese renminbi, Indian rupees, Russian roubles, Brazilian reals, South African rands, Kuwati dinars, Saudi riyals, and the Zambian kwatcha. In the film *Other People's Money*, Lawrence Garfield, aka Larry the Liquidator, played by Danny de Vito, tells his lawyer that everyone calls it "money" because everybody loves "money."

In truth, money exists only in the mind. It is a matter of trust. With trust, comes the possibility of betrayal. The late Michael Jackson understood money's essence, urging people to lie, spy, kill, or die for it.[1]

Some Kinda Money

There are different sorts of money. Most of the participants at the Portfolio Management Workshop run by a prestigious business school were in their late 20s or early 30s, already managing other people's money. One man did not fit the typical attendee profile. Almost 80 years old—tall, straight-backed, and gaunt—he was there to learn to manage his own money better. He told an interesting story about gold.

He was a boy when the great earthquake struck San Francisco at 5:12 a.m. on Wednesday, April 18, 1906, one of the worst natural disasters in U.S. history. The man and his family survived the earthquake and subsequent fire, managing to get out of the destroyed city by boat. His father paid the boatman, who would not accept money, in gold, secreted away for emergencies. Gold, the *sweat of the god* as the Incas called it, is *hard* money. It is the only money when chaos ensues.

In the 1970s many Indians emigrated in search of a better life. Indian foreign exchange controls prevented legal conversion of worthless Indian rupees into real money—American dollars or British pound sterling. Emigrants resorted to *Hawala* or *Hundi*—an informal money transfer system.

You needed an introduction to a money broker. You paid him your rupees. In return you received a small chit of paper on which were scrawled a few words in Urdu, a language spoken mainly in Pakistan and India. This chit had to be presented to another money broker outside India to receive the agreed amount of dollars. There was no guarantee that you would receive the promised dollars. It was a pure leap of faith. Hawala is paper money, based entirely on trust and honor.

In July 2008, a bank in Zimbabwe cashed a check for $1,072,418,003,000,000 (one quadrillion, seventy-two trillion, four hundred eighteen billion, three million Zimbabwe dollars). In the 28 years since independence, Zimbabwe, the former colony of Rhodesia, progressed from one of Africa's richest states into an economic basket case. The government's answer to economic collapse was to print money until the Zimbabwe dollar became worthless. This is *mad* money—paper money made valueless through inflation and its extreme mutation *hyper*inflation.

Inflation in Zimbabwe was 516 quintillion percent (516 followed by 18 zeros). Prices doubled every 1.3 days. The record for hyperinflation is Hungary where in 1946 monthly inflation reached 12,950,000,000,000,000 percent—prices doubled every 15.6 hours. In 1923, Weimar Germany experienced inflation of 29,525 percent a month, with prices doubling every 3.7 days. People burned Marks for heat in the cold Northern German winter. It was cheaper than firewood. The butter standard was a more reliable form of value than the Mark. The German government took over newspaper presses to print money, such was the demand for bank notes. The abiding image of the Weimar Republic remains of ordinary Germans in search of food pushing wheelbarrows filled with wads of worthless money.

To avoid calculators from being overwhelmed, Gideon Gono, the governor of Zimbabwe's central bank who despised *bookish economics*, lopped 10 zeros off the currency in August 2008. It did not restore the value of the Zimbabwe dollar but made it easier to carry money.

You receive a letter, a fax, or an email. The letter is from the wife of a deposed African or Asian leader, a terminally ill wealthy person, a business being audited by the government, a disgruntled worker, or corrupt government official who has embezzled funds. He or she is in possession of a large amount of money—in the millions—but cannot access the money. You will receive 40 percent if you can help retrieve the money or deal with it according to the *owner's* instructions. You just need to send a little money.

It's a scam. Any money you send is lost. This is *bad* money. Scammers are known as Yahoo millionaires. "Ego" or "pepper" is money. To be fooled in a scam is to "fall mugu." "Dolla chop" refers to the receipt of money from a victim.

Money is pure trust and faith. Money itself can have value—gold. It can have no intrinsic value—paper. Money can be easily debased. It can corrupt and, in turn, be corrupted.

Trading Places

In trade, two parties willingly exchange goods and services. The economist Adam Smith observed that people have an intrinsic "propensity to truck, barter, and exchange one thing for another."[2] Trade originally involved *barter*, the direct exchange of goods and services. If you have two items to trade, then you agree a rate of exchange—for example, five of this is worth one of that. If you have 100 items, then traders would have to remember 4,950 exchange ratios. For the 10,000 different items that a supermarket may stock, you need to remember 49,995,000 exchange ratios.

In the eighteenth century the French opera singer, Mademoiselle Zelie, performed in French Polynesia during her world tour, receiving one-third of the box office—3 pigs, 23 turkeys, 44 chickens, 5,000 coconuts, and considerable amounts of fruit. Unable to consume the payment, Mademoiselle Zelie's fee equivalent to 4,000 francs—a considerable sum at the time—was wasted.[3] When naturalist A.R. Wallace was exploring the Malay Archipelago, he planned to obtain food through barter. But he found that the indigenous people did not want the commodities he brought. Wallace nearly starved as his and the Malays' needs rarely coincided.[4]

The problems of barter are overcome where traders negotiate through a medium of exchange—*money*. Money allows separation of buying and selling in the process of exchange. Any traveler in the Malay Archipelago today carrying cash or an American Express or Visa card is unlikely to suffer the indignities and privations of Wallace.

Barter still exists. During the Cold War era, communist economies bartered for essential goods. The UK exchanged Russian grain for Rolls Royce jet engines that were used to power Soviet MiG fighters in the Korean conflict. "Returned with interest," Glynn Davies, a monetary historian, grimly noted. In 2010, North Korea's cash-strapped totalitarian regime, through its Bureau 39, offered several tons of ginseng, a curly white root claimed to improve memory, stamina, and libido, to settle $10 million in accumulated debt owed to the Czech Republic.[5]

The Invention of Money

Money is universally accepted as payment, a claim on other things—food, drink, clothing, operatic arias, travel, knowledge, or sex. It is a medium of exchange, a measure of the market value of real goods and services, a standard unit of value, and a store of wealth that can be saved and retrieved in the safe knowledge that it will be exchangeable into real things when retrieved.

Commodity money is anything that is simultaneously money but is a desired tradable commodity in its own right—money that is good enough to eat. Humans have experimented with dried fish, almonds, corn, coconuts, tea, and rice.[6]

The ancient Aztec cultures used cacao. The large green-yellow pods of the cacao tree produce a white pulp that, when dried, roasted, and ground, becomes chocolate. Some European pirates seized a ship full of cacao beans—a true El Dorado worth more than galleons filled with gold doubloons. Unaware of the value of the cargo and mistaking it for rabbit dung, the pirates dumped the cacao into the ocean.[7]

Commodities have intrinsic value and their supply cannot be changed easily. But restrictions on the availability of a commodity can artificially limit the amount of money, in turn limiting the volume of activity and trade. If water were used as a form of commodity money, then hoarding it to preserve wealth would reduce the amount available. People might die of thirst, but they would die rich. Commodities are also difficult to store, so inhibiting the capacity to amass and store wealth.

In economic chaos, war or collapse, commodity money reappears. In post-Saddam Iraq, mobile phone credit became a popular quasi-currency, rivaling banks and the Hawala system. Prostitutes asked for payment by way of mobile phone airtime credits, leading to the nickname *scratch-card concubines*. Even kidnappers asked for ransoms to be paid in the form of high-value phone cards.

Over time, more permanent forms of money have developed—massive stone tablets, animal skins and fur, whale teeth, and shells, especially the cowrie shell (the ovoid shell of a mollusk commonly found in the Indian and

Pacific Ocean). Ultimately commodity money focused on precious metals, gold and (to a lesser extent) silver, until superseded by paper.

Fiat or *paper money* is the promise by the government or state to pay you whatever it says on the paper—usually in the form of more paper. It relies on acceptance—the trust of everyone to exchange often dog-eared and toxic notes into real things. Where gold relies on a deep-rooted mythology, paper money relies on a system of trust and faith as well as the sanctity and integrity of the underlying legal system.

Credit money—the last form of money—is a future claim against someone that can be exchanged for real goods and services. The person lending money trusts the borrower to repay the money lent at the agreed time in the future.

British economist John Maynard Keynes once gave his friend Duncan Grant, the artist, money as a birthday gift. Grant was enraged: "The thing is good as a means and absolutely unimportant in itself." Keynes thought of money as "a mere intermediary without significance in itself which flows from one to another is received and dispensed and disappears when its work is done."[8]

Barbarous Relic

Gold—chemical symbol *Au* and atomic number 79—is a dense, malleable, and highly ductile lustrous metal that does not rust in air or water, making it useful in dentistry and electronics. Gold has qualities desirable in money—it is rare, durable, divisible, fungible (each unit is exactly identical and equivalent to other units of gold), easy to identify, and easily transported and possesses a high value-to-weight ratio. The *gold standard* was the basis of money for substantially all of human economic history.

Gold bullion is stored in ultra secure vaults, such as Fort Knox and the Bank of England. The gold is in 400 troy ounce bars—each bar weighs about 28 pounds (11 kilograms). At a price of $1,200/ounce, each bar is worth around $480,000. The bars have an assay mark recording the quantity and quality of the gold and the mint at which it was produced.

The bullion is stored in sealed lockers. At an appointed time, burly men dressed in drab gray uniforms move bars of gold from one numbered locker to another, settling purchases and sales. This movement of gold bullion over a short distance once signaled major changes in the fortunes and wealth of countries and kings.

In all human history, only about 161,000 tons of gold have been extracted, equivalent to about two Olympic standard swimming pools. Gold's monetary role confers extraordinary riches on those who control it and was once the key to wealth and economic dominance.

In the 1890s, the issue of gold became central to the U.S. presidential campaign of William Jennings Bryan. Southern farmers in the United States borrowed from north-eastern bankers to finance their farms, equipment, and crops. The debt had to be repaid in gold. As gold prices rose and the price of farm produce fell, the farmers' earnings fell, and their debt repayments grew, fueling resentment. The farmers wanted more money in circulation and advocated silver as well as gold currency—known as *bimetallism*.

At the 1896 Democratic Convention, Bryan spoke passionately: "You shall not press down upon the brow of labor this crown of thorns. You shall not crucify mankind upon a cross of gold."[9] Bryan was defeated in the 1896 and 1900 election by William McKinley and the United States adopted the gold standard in 1900.

The bimetallism debate spawned Frank Baum's satire on the currency debate, the *Wizard of Oz* (actually the *Wizard of Ounce*—of gold). Dorothy, the Kansas farm girl, represented rural America. The Scarecrow, Tinman, and cowardly Lion represented farmers, factory workers, and Bryan respectively. Dorothy and her companions' journey down the golden road is the 1894 Coxey march of unemployed men (named after its leader Jacob Coxey) to secure another public issue of $500 million of paper money and to obtain employment. Baum's plot has Dorothy and her companions exposing the fraud of evil wizards and witches, representing bankers and politicians, and establishing a new monetary order based on gold and silver. Dorothy returns to Kansas City courtesy of her magic silver slippers. In the film, Dorothy's slippers are red rather than silver, a concession to Hollywood cinematography.[10]

In Ian Fleming's 1959 novel *Goldfinger*, James Bond, Agent 007, is sent to investigate Auric Goldfinger, the mysterious Swiss financier who is smuggling gold. Goldfinger's plot is to boost the value of his gold through an audacious attack on the Fort Knox gold depositary. Goldfinger plans to contaminate the gold by exploding a nuclear device—a *dirty bomb*. Goldfinger's own stock of uncontaminated gold would increase in value astronomically. Bond discerns the plot through dazzling mental arithmetic—Fort Knox's $15 billion dollars of gold equated to more than 400 million ounces, which would weigh over 12,000 tons, making it difficult to carry off.

Thirst for gold fueled war and conquest. The Spanish, who followed Columbus, took approximately half a century to strip the major treasures of gold and silver accumulated by the indigenous people of South and Central America. In the process, the Spanish enslaved and virtually wiped out the native population until they literally ran out of things to loot. Today, armed groups fight for control of gold mines in the Democratic Republic of Congo to purchase weapons and finance wars. As the more easily accessible rich deposits of gold have been exhausted, mining gold in more remote, inhospitable, and fragile environments leads to irreversible damage.

Gold's mythological power has fueled the imagination of mankind for much of its history. Financial historian Peter Bernstein wrote: "Gold has...this kind of magic. But it's never been clear if we have gold—or gold has us."[11]

In India, gold is the ultimate store of wealth that can be pawned or used as security to raise money quickly. A child's baptism or eating of its first solid food, usually rice, requires offerings of gold. Marriage traditions require a dowry of treasure—heavy necklaces, ornate bangles, dangling earrings, jewel-encrusted rings, delicate headpieces, and saris woven with gold thread. For Indian women, gold may be the only real property they own—their only *nest egg*.

Although few believe in its once assumed magical properties, the attachment to gold has persisted into the twenty-first century. In *Goldfinger*, Colonel Smithers explained the monetary role of gold: "Gold and currencies backed by gold are the foundation of international credit.... We can only tell what the true strength of the pound is...by knowing the amount of [gold] we have behind our currency."[12] As the global financial crisis consumed the world in 2007 and 2008, individuals purchased 150 tons of gold in the form of coins. Investors poured money into special funds that bought up 1,000 tons of gold. Gold prices increased from around $800 per troy ounce in December 2007 to more than $1,400 per ounce by early 2011.

Harry "Rabbit" Angstrom, the central character in John Updike's 1970s novels about American suburban life, spent $11,000 on the purchase of 30 gold krugerrands (a South African minted gold coin). Rabbit explained the purchase to his wife: "The beauty of gold is, it loves bad news."[13] John Maynard Keynes famously described gold as "a barbarous relic."

The Real Thing

Adam Smith captured the essence of paper (or fiat) money—the promise that it can be exchanged into real goods and services:

> When the people of any particular country has such confidence in the fortune, probity, and prudence of a particular banker, as to believe he is always ready to pay upon demand such of his promissory notes as are likely to be at any time presented to him; those notes come to have the same currency as gold and silver money, from the confidence that such money can at any time be had for them.[14]

Paper money is now the dominant currency, and the dollar is the dominant form of paper money. The word derives from a large silver coin worth three German Marks—*taler*. American economist John Kenneth Galbraith observed that: "If the history of commercial banking belongs to the Italians and of central banking to the British, that of paper money issued by a government belongs indubitably to the American."[15]

The U.S. dollar is sometimes referred to as the greenback, a reference to the green-inked backs of one of the first currencies authorized by the Legal Tender Act of 1862 during the U.S. Civil War. Greenbacks were not convertible into anything but constituted legal tender, that is, a creditor could not legally refuse to accept them as payment for any debt.

The current dollar, introduced in 1914, is three-quarters cotton and one-quarter linen. Approximately half the bills are one dollar denominations. The average life span of a bill varies—a $1 note lasts a mere 18 months whereas a $100 bill can last several years. Each bill is designed to be folded 4,000 times before it tears. Four hundred and ninety $1 bills weigh 1 pound (454 grams). One million dollars in $1 bills would weigh more than one ton. One trillion dollars in $1 bills would weigh one million tons.

Less than 8 percent of all dollars are in the form of paper money or coins. The vast majority of dollars exists in the form of entries in the accounts of borrowers or lenders. Paper money is an abstraction or, as most of it does not exist physically, the abstraction of an abstraction. Its sole reason for existence is as a medium of exchange. There are no limits to the amount of money that can be created.

Paper money can be easily damaged or destroyed. There is *counterfeit money*—a fake imitation of real money passed off as the real article. The real problems with paper money are subtler. As Baron Rothschild once boasted: "Give me control over a nation's currency and I care not who makes its laws."

In 1716 John Law, a self-taught banker, inveterate gambler, and convicted murderer, established the Compagnie d'Occident (the Mississippi Company) to exploit the wealth of Louisiana, then a French colony. In his pamphlet *Money and Trade Considered with a Proposal for Supplying the Nation with Money*, Law advocated using paper money to create wealth.

Law's Banque General printed money by lending large sums to investors to purchase shares of the Mississippi Company, so driving the price higher. The vast quantities of paper money were supposedly guaranteed by reserves of gold coin. Law, now the duc d'Arkansas, actually issued paper money equal to over twice the gold available in the country. He was using the two companies to create vast fictitious profits for both. The pyramid scheme, where investors in the Mississippi Company received *profits* from subsequent investors, eventually collapsed. Today, governments have a monopoly in printing money.

Fear of reduction in the value of paper money meant that it was backed by gold for much of its history. The strange thing is that gold has almost no value as a commodity and is not itself a great store of value.

In 2009, gold bugs excitedly speculated about gold prices reaching $2,300. Even at that price gold would merely match its January 1980 value, after adjusting for inflation. The holder had earned nothing on the investment over almost 30 years! The gold price in 2010 adjusted for inflation was the same as the price in 1265. Dylan Grice of Société Générale summed up the case for gold as a store of value:

> A fifteenth-century gold bug who'd stored all his wealth in bullion, bequeathed it to his children and required them to do the same would be more than a little miffed when gazing down from his celestial place of rest to see the real wealth of his lineage decline by nearly 90 percent over the next 500 years.[16]

The Hotel New Hampshire

The Hotel New Hampshire, written by John Irving, the author of *The World According to GARP*, is populated with unlikely characters—Egg, Win, Iowa, Bitty Tuck, a Viennese Jew named Freud, and Sorrow, a dog repeatedly restored through taxidermy. In July 1944, a similarly dysfunctional group of politicians, economists, and bankers gathered in Bretton Woods, New Hampshire, at the Mount Washington Hotel, to establish the post-Second World War international monetary and financial order. The pivotal figures were John Maynard Keynes, representing the UK, and Harry Dexter White, representing the United States.

Selected as one of *Time*'s 100 most influential figures of the twentieth century, John Maynard Keynes was the author of *General Theory of Employment, Interest, and Money* and one of the fathers of modern macroeconomics. A product of the English elite and a member of the Bloomsbury group, Keynes was equally at home among academics, politicians, businessmen, bankers, philosophers, and artists. An incorrigible pamphleteer and prolific author, he influenced public policy in a manner that has rarely been surpassed. Keynes was also a successful investor. Managing the endowment fund of King's College, Cambridge, he outperformed the stock market over two decades, increasing the value of the portfolio by around ten times. A study concluded that: "On the basis of modern portfolio evaluation measures…Keynes was an outstanding portfolio manager 'beating the market' by a large margin."[17]

Harry Dexter White, a descendant of Jewish Lithuanian Catholic immigrants, was an economist and a senior U.S. Treasury department official. White may have also been a Soviet spy, who passed confidential information about the negotiations to the Russians.

Bretton Woods took place against the background of a still raging brutal war, the rise of fascism, and the economic experience of the Great Depression. The focus was on establishing free trade based on convertibility of currencies with stable exchange rates. In the past, this problem was solved through the gold standard where the standard unit of currency was a fixed weight of gold. Under the gold standard, the government or central bank guaranteed to redeem notes upon demand in gold.

The gold standard was not feasible for the post-war economy. There was insufficient gold to meet the demands of growing international trade and investment. The communist Soviet Union, emerging as a rival to the United States in the post-war order, also controlled a sizeable proportion of known gold reserves. Keynes' bold solution was a world reserve currency (the *bancor*) administered by a global central bank. White rejected the proposal: "We have been perfectly adamant on that point. We have taken the position of absolutely no."

The United States was the undisputed preeminent economic and military great power as well as the world's richest nation and the biggest creditor. The British and the French, devastated by two world wars, needed American money to rebuild their economies. White's view prevailed.

Bretton Woods established a system of fixed exchange rates where countries would establish parity of their national currencies in terms of gold (the *peg*). All countries would peg their currencies to the U.S. dollar as the principal *reserve currency* and, after convertibility was restored, would buy and sell U.S. dollars to keep market exchange rates within plus or minus 1 percent of parity (the *band*).

The U.S. dollar was to have a fixed relationship to gold ($35 an ounce). The U.S. government would convert dollars into gold at that price. The dollar was *as good as gold*. It was more attractive because dollars—unlike gold—earned interest. The U.S. dollar reigned supreme as the world's currency, taking over the role that gold had played in the international financial system.

Barbarism—gold—had triumphed. George Bernard Shaw would have been pleased: "You have to choose between trusting the natural stability of gold and the...honesty and intelligence of the members of the government...I advise you...to vote for gold."[18] The gold standard would remain in place until 1971.

Collapse

The Bretton Woods system was ultimately undermined by the decline in U.S. power. In 1944, the United States produced half of the world's manufactured goods and held more than half its reserves ($26 billion in gold reserves out of an estimated total of $40 billion globally). Over time, the burden of the Cold War and being at the center of the global financial system weighed heavily on the United States.

In the 1960s, President Lyndon Johnson's administration ran large budget deficits to pay for the Vietnam War and its Great Society programs. This created inflation and increased dollar outflows to pay for the expenditures. The dollar became overvalued relative to the German Deutsche Mark and the Japanese yen. Faced with the choice of devaluing the dollar or imposing protectionist measures, President Johnson argued: "The world supply of gold is insufficient to make the present system workable—particularly as the use of the dollar as a reserve currency is essential to create the required international liquidity to sustain world trade and growth."[19] It was the *Triffin dilemma*, identified by Belgian-American economist Robert Triffin in the 1960s. As the dollar was the global reserve and trade currency, the United States had to run large trade deficits to meet the world's demand for foreign exchange.

By the early 1970s, the ratio of gold available to dollars deteriorated from 55 percent to 22 percent. Holders of the dollar lost faith in the ability of the United States to back currency with gold. On August 15, 1971, President Richard Nixon unilaterally closed the gold window, making the dollar inconvertible to gold directly. The *Nixon Shock* was announced in an address on national television on a Sunday evening. The President risked antagonizing fans of the popular TV program *Bonanza* to make the announcement before markets opened.

Frantic efforts to develop a new system of international monetary management followed. The Smithsonian Agreement devalued the dollar to $38/ounce, with 2.25 percent trading bands. By 1972, gold was trading at $70.30/ounce. Other countries began abandoning the link between their currency and the dollar. In February 1973, the world moved to the era of floating currencies with no link to dollars or gold. It was the final transformation of money. The last link to something tangible was severed. The greenback was no longer as good as gold. It could not be exchanged into anything except identical notes—itself.

Max Weber, the father of social science, defined the state as the agency that successfully monopolizes the legitimate use of force. Now the state, through its monopoly over the printing presses, controlled money and the economy. Money would be henceforth a matter of pure trust. American dollars still bear the words: "In God We Trust." But God was not directly responsible for control of money; it was governments and central banks.

In Lewis Carroll's *Alice in Wonderland*, Humpty Dumpty observes: "When I use a word it means just what I choose it to mean—neither more nor less." Alice responds: "The question is whether you can make words mean so many different things." Unhesitatingly, Humpty Dumpty cuts through to the heart of the issue: "The question is which is to be master—that's all."[20] Governments could create money, making them undisputed masters. Keynes recognized the risk: "By a continuing process of inflation, government can confiscate, secretly and unobserved, an important part of the wealth of their citizens."[21]

Some found the prospect of governments controlling money disturbing. In his study of the human unconscious, Sigmund Freud noticed a striking association between money and excrement: "I read one day that the gold which the devil gave his victims regularly turned into excrement."[22] Many feared that governments would turn their money into human waste.

Former U.S. Federal Reserve Chairman Alan Greenspan once flirted with this problem:

> Under the gold standard, a free banking system stands as the protector of an economy's stability and balanced growth.... The abandonment of the gold standard made it possible for the welfare statists to use the banking system as a means to an unlimited expansion of credit.... In the absence of the gold standard, there is no way to protect savings from confiscation through inflation.[23]

Money Machines

The word *bank* has its origins in the word for the *table* or *bench* on which bankers did their transactions. Originally, the table or bench may have been an altar. The Templars, a military order of religious knights dedicated to the task of liberating the Holy Lands from the Infidels, can lay claim to being the first truly global financial supermarket.

Modern banking practice began in Italy in the Renaissance. Great banking families in Venice, Florence, Genoa, and Pisa profited from financing growing trade. To avoid religious prohibitions on usury, the banks dealt in *bills of exchange*—documents, traditionally arising from trade, that order the payment of a known sum of money to a designated person at a specified time and place. Banks bought and sold these documents, effectively lending (buying a bill of exchange with money) and borrowing (selling a bill and receiving money). Bills of exchange overcame the need to transport gold. They were faster and more secure. The bills circulated as an early form of pure money.

Banks allowed idle gold or money to circulate freely. It would be deposited with a bank or used to buy a bill (a debt collectable at a future date with interest). The original holders of $100 still had their money, but the bank and whoever it lent to also had the $100. The money that was lent would come back to the bank or another bank as a deposit. The money could then be re-lent and recirculated in a continuing, endless process.

This process—*reserve* or *fractional banking*—is the quintessential element of modern finance. Banks keep only a fraction of their deposits in reserve to meet the needs of withdrawals by depositors and lend out the rest. The practice expands the supply of money, allowing merchants, businesses, and investors to increase the scale and scope of their activities. The only limit is the requirement for banks to keep a minimum fraction of their deposits as reserves.

The banking system that evolved in the Renaissance survives remarkably unchanged to this day. It is the basis of money machines—a financial perpetual motion device. John Kenneth Galbraith summed it up:

> The study of money, above all other fields in economics, is one in which complexity is used to disguise truth or to evade truth, not to reveal it. The process by which banks create money is so simple that the mind is repelled.[24]

Not everybody supported these developments. In 1802, Thomas Jefferson in a letter to Albert Gallatin, secretary of the Treasury, warned:

> If the American people ever allow private banks to control the issue of their money, first by inflation and then by deflation, the banks and corporations that will grow up around them will deprive the people of their property until their children will wake up homeless on the continent their fathers conquered.[25]

Debt Clock

Paper money represents a claim on itself. Debt or credit money is a future claim against a person or entity that can be used today for the purchase of goods. Credit is a world of sweet nothings, mere promises. The word *credit* is from the Latin *credere*, to trust. Keynes recognized this aspect of debt: "The importance of money flows from it being a link between the present and the future."[26]

Debt enables borrowers to consume in excess of their earnings or available resources. Credit also provides the essential mechanism for making money from money. The lenders charge for the money borrowed, enabling them to become *rentiers*—people who live from income derived from interest, rent, or gains from trading. The German poet Heinrich Heine understood the significance: "Men can choose whatever place of residence they like; they can live anywhere, without working, from the interest on their bonds, their portable property, and so they gather together and constitute the true power."[27] To Karl Marx, the author of *Das Kapital* and father of communism, this was another "ism"—*parasitism*.

Debt introduces new risks. The person on whom your claim is may be unable to pay. If the interest rate on the borrowing is too low, then the lender will lose, as the money received back will be insufficient to compensate for the effects of the rising prices (inflation). But the ultimate risk of debt is subtler still.

Charles Ponzi, an Italian immigrant, created an eponymous fraudulent scheme that paid very high returns to investors—not from actual profits, but from their own money or money paid by subsequent investors. Originally, Ponzi had the idea of arbitraging international reply coupons (IRCs). Postal reply coupons can be sent from one country to a correspondent in a foreign country to be used to pay the postage of a reply. IRCs were priced at the cost of postage in the country of purchase but were eligible for exchange into stamps to cover the cost of postage in the country where redeemed. After the First World War, the fall in the value of the lira decreased the cost of postage in Italy in U.S. dollar terms. This allowed an IRC bought cheaply in Italy to be exchanged for U.S. stamps of a higher value. Ponzi's company—the Securities Exchange Company—raised money to exploit this difference in prices by offering a 50 percent return on investment in 45 days. About 40,000 people invested $15 million in the scheme.

On July 26, 1920, the *Boston Post* and Clarence Barron, a financial analyst who published the *Barron's* financial paper, revealed that there were only about 27,000 coupons actually circulating, whereas the investments made with the Securities Exchange Company required 160,000,000 postal reply coupons. The U.S. Post Office confirmed that postal reply coupons were not being bought in any great quantity at home or abroad. Ponzi had diverted the investors' money to support payments to earlier investors and to support his extravagant personal lifestyle. Ponzi was indicted for fraud and ultimately deported. He reportedly said, "I went looking for trouble, and I found it."

Debt can be a monetized Ponzi or *pyramid* scheme. To be self-sustaining, the modern monetary system—printing money, reserve banking, and debt—requires a Darwinian scheme in which the only ones who survive are those who can induce others into even greater debt.

Borrowers have to pay interest and ultimately repay the amount borrowed. But the interest and the amount borrowed may not be paid back, therefore requiring more borrowing that continues until the borrower collapses under the weight of debt. The only way out is for borrowers to induce new borrowers into larger amounts of debt to allow them to pay off their own debts. The system works, like any Ponzi scheme, as long as everyone believes the debt can be paid back and the market value of assets bought with that debt keeps rising. The economy inexorably gravitates toward debt-fueled consumerism, inflation, and increasing debt. This leads to a constant cycle of credit booms and bust.

In the second half of the twentieth century, credit money gradually became the primary form of money, leading to an explosion of debt.

In 1947 the directors of the *Bulletin of Atomic Scientists* at the University of Chicago created the *doomsday clock*. The *minutes to midnight* represent the time remaining to catastrophic destruction (midnight) of the human race from global nuclear war. In 1989 Seymour Darst, a New York real estate developer, created the financial equivalent. He installed the *national debt clock*—a billboard-size digital display on Sixth Avenue (Avenue of the Americas) in Manhattan, New York, that constantly updates to show the current U.S. public debt and each American family's share of it.

When this clock was originally erected, the U.S. national debt was under $3 trillion. The clock was switched off from 2000 to 2002 when the national debt briefly fell. Subsequently, as the debt started to rise, the clock was restarted. By 2009, the debt exceeded $10 trillion, requiring Douglas Darst, Seymour's son, to arrange for a new clock with extra capacity.

In the 1950s, Herman Kahn, a strategist at the RAND Corporation, and Ian Harold Brown, a risk analyst, proposed a *doomsday machine*. It consisted of a computer linked to a stockpile of hydrogen bombs, programmed to detonate them and bathe the planet in nuclear fallout at the signal of an impending nuclear attack from another nation. In Stanley Kubrick's film *Dr Strangelove or: How I Learned to Stop Worrying and Love the Bomb*, there is speculation about whether the Russians possess this technology.

Currently, the doomsday clock reads around 5 minutes to midnight. In 2008, as the global financial crisis gripped the world, the financial equivalent of the doomsday machine—an unstable system of money and unsustainable levels of debt—reached midnight and imploded.

Money Is Nothing

At each step of the transition from commodity to paper to credit, money became more unreal, and detached from the real goods and services that money can be exchanged for. Money transformed itself from a mechanism for trade into an object in its own right. Modern technology—digital money—further stripped money of corporeality. Money exists as pure information, with no intrinsic value. It is nothing and everything. Making money, lending it, borrowing money, and making money from money is central to human existence and activity. As the Roman poet Horace noted eons ago: "Make money, money by fair means if you can, if not, by any means money."

Modern money is inherently worthless, but everybody accepts it as real. Paul Seabright, a professor of economics, identified two traits that underpin systems of trust including money: the capacity to weigh up the costs and benefits of trusting others and the instinct to return favors in kind or seek revenge when trust is betrayed. When it is working well, the system enables strangers to deal with each other safely. When the fragile trust fails, people withdraw their money from banks, and they seek the refuge of cash. Ironically, in times of crisis, people seek paper money that has no intrinsic worth, illustrating the power of the monetary illusion.[28]

The trust that underlies money sometimes works in reverse—*alternative* paper money. Irving Fisher, a prominent American economist of the early twentieth century, suggested an alternative currency—*stamp scrip*—which would be periodically taxed with a stamp, forcing holders to spend rather than hoard it. The idea was based on the *Wära*, an alternative currency used in Schwanenkirchen, a Bavarian coal-mining village, in 1931.

Today, Bavaria has the *Chiemgauer*, introduced in 2003, which can be used alongside the euro in more than 600 shops and firms. In England, in

Lewes, Sussex, the *Lewes pound* circulates alongside the pound sterling. (One Lewes pound can be exchanged for one pound sterling.) The notes feature Thomas Paine, the eighteenth-century activist reformer, not the Queen. In the United States there are at least 12 local currency schemes. The largest is the *Berkshares* program in the rural region of southern Massachusetts.

These alternative currencies encourage local business and emphasize community values. They are a gesture of defiance against the control of governments, banks, and global money. At their heart is a quaint but powerful notion of ordinary people supporting each other in a complex and often alien world.

The Mirrored Room

The genius of money made possible the modern economy and the money culture. Georg Simmel, a German sociologist and contemporary of Freud, argued that money imitated the world around it: "There is no more striking symbol…of the world than that of money."[29]

Money is the ultimate Faustian bargain—a pact with the devil in return for earthly power, wealth, or knowledge. In the second part of *Faust*, Johann Wolfgang von Goethe has Faust and Mephistopheles visit the Emperor who lacks the money to pay his retinue of soldiers and servants as well as his lenders. Mephistopheles comes to the aid of the Emperor, obtaining his permission to print paper money. Faust has the Emperor sign a note that anticipates modern money: "To whom it may concern, be by these presents known, this note is legal tender for one thousand crowns and is secured by the immense wealth safely stored underground in our Imperial States." The Emperor is incredulous: "And people value this the same as honest gold?"[30] Mephistopheles arranges for thousands of notes to be printed and uses this to pay off the Emperor's creditors.

Money, ultimately, is the truest mirror for the times and human beings. The benign surface reflects back the image of the world that money can make possible. Money, like a mirror, is nothing but takes on the reality of things it can be converted into. Money reveals something of the original that is not otherwise evident. As William Shakespeare wrote: "And since you know you cannot see yourself, so well as by reflection, I, your glass, will modestly discover to yourself, that of yourself which you yet know not of."[31]

In 1966, the artist Lucas Samaras, in his construction *Mirrored Room*, created the ultimate metaphor for modern money. The work consists of a small room containing one door, a table, and a chair. All surfaces of the room—walls, floor, ceiling, the table, and the chair—are covered with mirrors. Entering the room, the viewer sees their image reflected, fragment by fragment, expanding in number and detail but dwindling in size until it is no longer identifiable. The work is a statement of isolated, narcissistic splendor. Samaras described the feeling as "suspension." The striking feature of the *Mirrored Room* is the feeling of infinity and abstraction.[32]

If money is a mirror of the times, then *Mirrored Room* is the ultimate symbol for extreme money. Money now is endless, capable of infinite multiplication and completely unreal. The world is involved in creating, manipulating, and chasing reflections of real things. Finance is the interplay of the real and its endless reflections. In the end, money would change the real world—*financialize it*.

2

Money Changes Everything

The *Financial Times* advertises the new Zeitgeist: "We live in financial times." Earlier, Heinrich Heine, the German poet, also identified the change: "Money is the God of our time."[1] In the later half of the twentieth century, individuals became true believers.

Human history is a sequence of 'ations' —civiliz*ation*, industrializ*ation*, urbaniz*ation*, globaliz*ation*; interspersed with actual or threatened annihil*ation* (war, genocide, or the mutually assured destruction [MAD] pact of the Cold War). The most recent "ation" is financializ*ation*—the conversion of everything into monetary form (known as another "ation" —monetiz*ation*). Increasing wealth, increasing consumption, increased borrowing, and the need to save for retirement has financialized individual lives. It has provided scope for other "ations"—manipul*ation* and, its sibling, exploit*ation*.

Mrs. Watanabe Goes to Wall Street

Nothing illustrates the financialization of everyday life better than Japan. Foreigners—*gaijin* (loosely, "round eyes")—find Japan strange, especially its toilets. Japanese toilets are fitted with blow dryers, seat heating, massage options, water jets, automatic lid opening and closing, automatic flushing, deodorizing, heating, and air conditioning. Some feature music to relax the user's sphincter (*Frühlingslied* Op. 62 No. 6 by Felix

Mendelssohn). Female toilets feature an *otohime*—a black, square, motion sensor—that when activated produces the sound of flushing water to avoid others overhearing the noise of your bodily functions.

Japanese finance is equally strange. It is famed for its stockbrokers, who go door-to-door seeking to entice individuals to invest in stocks and other financial products, and its female speculators—collectively *Mrs. Watanabe*, a common surname.

Japan has the world's largest pool of savings—estimated at more than ¥1,500,000 billion (more than $15,000 billion), built up through legendary frugality and thrift during Japan's rise to prosperity after the Second World War.

Yuki Wada, a 35-year-old homemaker and blogger, is a *setsuyaku no tatsujin* (master penny-pincher). She recycles bath water to do her laundry and clean the toilets, keeps energy costs down by cutting power to most of her home when she goes out and selects appliances based on electricity usage. Wada polishes her shoes using saved tangerine peels and washes her floors with sour milk. A staple of talk shows, she even shares her tips on saving money with government officials.

Japanese savings are kept in bank accounts or literally under the bed—known as *tansu* savings, after the traditional wooden cupboards in which Japanese store possessions. Japanese women invest these savings.

Japan survived the stock market crash of 1987, but its *bubble* economy collapsed at the end of 1989. A boom based on excessive debt and overvalued shares and property ended, leading to the *ushinawareta junen*—the lost decade. Losses on bad loans triggered bank failures, requiring massive government intervention. Interest rates fell to near zero, and the economy ceased to grow. Today, the Japanese stock market is around 75 percent below its 1989 level. The Japanese economy remains moribund.

Forced to hunt for higher returns, older retired Japanese dependent on investment earnings moved their retirement savings (*toranoko*—Tiger's cub) from bank accounts, paying a derisory 0.01 percent per annum, into riskier investments. Attracted by the high returns offered, 5 percent per annum, money went into investment funds—Asian Infrastructure *nantoka nantoka* Fund, Emerging Market High Yield *nantoka nantoka* Fund, and so on. (*Nantoka* means "something or other" or "what-you-ma-call-it"). The bulk of investments went into foreign-currency-denominated bonds and deposits.

FX Beauties Club

Young, usually 30-something, computer-literate Japanese women, known as the *clickety-clicks*, traded, online. Borrowing (up to) $98 of every $100, they traded the euro, U.S. dollar, Australian dollar, New Zealand dollar, pound sterling, and exotic currencies such as the South African rand and Turkish lira.

A celebrity cult of housewife traders—*pin-up Mrs. Watanabes*—grew. There is Fumie Wakabayashi, a 31-year-old author of the book *I Like Stocks* and creator of a Nintendo DS investment game. There is Yukiko Ikebe, the *kimono trader*, who made profits of an estimated ¥400 million ($4 million) on commodity futures and currency over 3 years, becoming a regular on the investment lecture circuit and writing the book *The Secret of FX*. Another famous housewife-trader is Mayumi Torii, a 41-year-old single parent, who quickly earned $150,000 from margin trading in currencies. She wrote a book on her investing strategies and founded a support group for home traders, the *FX Beauties Club*. (FX is short for foreign exchange.)

Some housewife traders trade compulsively, staying up to trade during European and North American hours. They ride the volatility, trying to get in and out quickly to make money. Fumie Wakabayashi admitted that in her youth she occasionally did *drunk trading* after too many cocktails.

Such speculative trading benefited from high interest rates in foreign currencies and gains from falls in the value of the yen against overseas currencies. At the peak, Mrs. Watanabe accounted for around 30 percent of the foreign exchange market in Tokyo. Mrs. Watanabe's buying and selling at banks and brokerages became a guide to changes in the value of the yen. In the 1964 pound sterling crisis, the British politician Harold Wilson described financial speculators as the "gnomes of Zurich." Mrs. Watanabes now wielded similar influence in currency markets.

Professional traders, hedge funds, and banks followed Mrs. Watanabe's actions and mimicked them via the *yen carry trade*—investors borrowed in yen at low interest rates, converted it into foreign currencies and invested the money at higher rates. Investors enjoyed the *carry*—the difference between the income (high interest rates in the foreign currency) and the cost of borrowing (low interest rates in yen).

Investors played these games with borrowed money. Larry the Liquidator in the film *Other People's Money* confesses that he loves one thing more than money: *other people's money*.

Mrs. Watanabe ignored the risk of loss of her investment as long as the high income kept rolling in. As long as the yen did not increase in value against the currency of the investment, the strategy worked. During the early 2000s, the strategy was profitable, as the yen steadily weakened, falling to 20-year lows. In 2007, the yen began to rise and returns on investments around the world fell. Mrs. Watanabe, together with more sophisticated hedge funds, was forced to dump assets bought with borrowed money, losing billions.

In Japan, there are strict cultural taboos against money that is not earned by honest effort— "with sweat from the brow." But even Japan had embraced financialization. The rest of the world followed. As Cole Porter sang in the 1930s, now almost anything went.

Plutonomy

For most people, money was the link between work and the essential victuals of life. It also provided financial independence and protection against uncertainty. For a small group, wealth provided social acceptance, power, and influence. It became a means for self-expression, a statement of status and selfhood. As F. Scott Fitzgerald observed: "Let me tell you about the very rich. They are different from you and me. They have more money."[2]

In his 1899 book *The Theory of the Leisure Class*, Thorstein Veblen, a Norwegian-born American economist, created the term *conspicuous consumption*, meaning the waste of money or resources by people to establish higher status. *Conspicuous leisure* was the waste of time by people to achieve the same thing. By the late twentieth century, it was unnecessary even to spend money on useless things and wasteful pursuits. Control of large sums of money—a large bank balance, real estate or stock holdings, and investments in exclusive hedge funds—were proof of membership of the leisure classes.

Ajay Kapur, a CitiGroup investment analyst, coined the term *plutonomy* to describe the global split between the rich and the rest. Wealth was highly concentrated in the United States, Canada, and UK. Europe, excluding Italy, and Japan were more egalitarian. In emerging economies, a small group also controlled most of the wealth. The top 1 percent of households in the United States accounted for about 20 percent of overall U.S. income, about the same share of income as the bottom 60 percent of households. The top 1 percent of households accounted for more than 30 percent of net worth, greater than the entire bottom 90 percent of households put together. Writer Robert Frank observed that the wealthy inhabited a different country—*Richistan*.[3]

Gains from recent economic growth flowed disproportionately to the wealthy, who benefited from market-friendly governments, favorable tax regimes, protection of property rights, globalization, and technological change, and financial innovation and deregulation. The top 10 percent of earners received the majority of the benefits of the *productivity miracle* of 1996–2005.[4]

Wealthy plutocrats both powered and benefited from economic growth. The *Forbes* 400 richest people in 2006 controlled $1,250 billion, up $92 billion from 1982. To make it on to the list in 2006 you had to have a billion, compared to $75 million in 1982. This money was invested, making more money to fund consumption or simply to attest to wealth. For the wealthy, financialization of life was trading and speculation; using money was a means to an end and an end in itself. This even changed the source of wealth, with almost a quarter of the 2006 rich owing their fortunes to the finance sector compared with less than one-tenth in 1982.

Trickling Down, Trading Up

Most of the population generally got richer, not über or even mega rich, but comfortable. Middle-class incomes increased broadly throughout the world.

In 1914, Henry Ford doubled workers' pay from $2.34 to $5 per day and introduced a new, reduced working week. Ford argued that paying people more would enable workers to afford the cars that they were producing. The U.S. auto industry pioneered the basic wage in 1948. Harley Shaiken, a labor economist at the University of California at Berkeley, observed: "The most important model that rolled off the Detroit assembly lines in the 20th century was the middle class for blue-collar workers."[5]

In *trickle-down economics*, benefits flow down from the top to the bottom. During the Great Depression, Will Rogers, the humorist, defined it as: "Money was all appropriated for the top in hopes that it would trickle down to the needy." In the 1970s, the process went into reverse. The auto industry and heavy industries in the United States and developed countries declined. Technological change deskilled some jobs, driving declines in the earnings of low and middle-income workers. Increasing international trade and globalization meant that jobs were outsourced to developing countries, where labor costs were lower. This brought new wealth to emerging nations but depressed wages and living standards in developed countries. Immigration, both legal and illegal, affected incomes, especially in lower-skilled jobs. The changing labor market and erosion of safety nets meant that individuals and families, other than the plutocrats, lived a precarious existence.

Some borrowed to finance consumption or resorted to financial speculation to offset declining income and safeguard their future, increasingly with borrowed money. Home equity—the difference between the current value of the family home and the amount owed on it—provided the initial financial stake. George Bernard Shaw knew this connection between speculation and wealth: "Gambling promises the poor what property performs for the rich, something for nothing."

Fumie Wakabayashi, the Japanese housewife trader, started trading hoping to earn more than the ¥900 ($9) per hour wage of a waitress or a receptionist. She wanted to be a nurse but could not afford tuition fees after her father's business went broke. Yukiko Ikebe started trading to supplement her earnings from teaching flower arranging and later, when she married and had children, to earn extra money for children's toys and clothes.

Mayumi Torii began trading to become economically independent after her first marriage ended in divorce and she had to support herself and her son.

Kapur was interested in how plutonomy affects consumption, which accounts for 65 percent of the world economy. Concentration of wealth means that national spending, profits, and economic growth are disproportionately dependent on the fortunes of the rich. As the rich buy luxury goods and services, Kapur recommended the less wealthy buy shares in Tiffany's and Louis Vuitton, even if they could not afford the company's products.

I Shop, Therefore I Must Be!

Economic policies emphasized consumerism, linking material possessions and consumption with happiness. In *The Limits to Power*, Andrew Bacevich identified the nouveau-Jeffersonian trinity—"Whoever dies with the most toys wins," "Shop till you drop" and "If it feels good, do it."

In his 1958 book *The Affluent Society*, John Kenneth Galbraith argued that society had become obsessed by the production and consumption of ever increasing levels of goods, most of which were not essential. As Ronnie Shakes, the comedian, wryly observed: "I spend money with reckless abandon. Last month I blew five thousand dollars at a reincarnation seminar. I got to thinking, what the hell, you only live once."

Consumers purchased an increasing range and volume of products—"the desire to get superior goods takes on a life of its own."[6] Increased borrowing financed the increased production and consumption of goods.

Advertising fostered demand. In humorist Will Rogers' words, advertising was "the art of convincing people to spend money they don't have for something they don't need."

In his three best-selling books *The Hidden Persuaders* (1957), *The Status Seekers* (1959), and *The Waste Makers* (1960), Vance Packard, an American journalist, highlighted the use of psychological techniques to manipulate consumers. Status and fear of loss of status was used to sell goods. Planned obsolescence increased demand for products, long before they required replacement.

> A toothbrush does little but clean teeth. Alcohol is important mostly for making people more or less drunk. An automobile can take one reliably to a destination and back.... There being so little to be said, much must be invented. Social distinction must be associated with a house...sexual fulfillment with a particular...automobile, social acceptance with...a mouthwash [and so on]. We live surrounded by a systematic appeal to a dream world which all mature, scientific reality would reject. We, quite literally, advertise our commitment to immaturity, mendacity and profound gullibility. It is the hallmark of our culture.[7]

Consumerism increased sales, encouraging businesses to invest. Economic growth required expanded production and higher earnings. Alan Greenspan noted: "Human psychology being what it is, the initial euphoria of a higher standard of living soon wears off.... The new level is quickly perceived as 'normal.' Any gain in human contentment is transitory."[8] For sociologist Zygmunt Bauman consumption was an "appeal to forever-elusive happiness." Bauman's phrase *liquid-modernity* described a process in which individuals desperately reinvented themselves through consumption.

Consumerism exploited deep-seated human anxieties and changes in society. In July 1989, addressing the students of Dartmouth College, the Russian American writer Joseph Brodsky described modern lives:

> You will be bored with your work, your spouses, your lovers, the view from your window, the furniture or wallpaper in your rooms, your thoughts, yourselves...you'll try to devise ways of escape. Apart from...self-gratifying gadgets...you may take up changing jobs, residence, company, country, climate, you may take up promiscuity, alcohol, travel, cooking lessons, drugs, psychoanalysis...you may lump them together...for a while that may work. Until the day...when you wake up...with a heap of bills from your travel agent and your shrink, yet with the same stale feeling toward the light of day pouring through your window.[9]

For Americans, the attacks of September 11, 2001 added to the sense of insecurity. After the attacks, President George W. Bush urged Americans to go shopping as the best way to help them and the country recover. In 2008, after a terrorist attack at the Taj Mahal Hotel in Mumbai, India, Suketu Mehta, author of *Maximum City,* echoed George Bush: "The best answer to the terrorists is to dream bigger, make even more money, and visit Mumbai more than ever."[10]

Spend It Like Beckham!

Consumers emulated the tastes, preferences, and lifestyles of people higher in the social hierarchy. The rich needed to "keep up with the Gateses." The British were "keeping up with the Beckhams." Wealth gives rise to different concepts of equality. Asked whether the privatization of state assets that was the basis of his fabulous wealth had been fair, one Russian billionaire responded: "Of course not! One of the other oligarchs got a bigger oil company than I did."

Key positional goods essential to success included a trophy wife or husband, a large expensive house in an up-market suburb, and an expensive foreign luxury car. (Some SUVs were OK!) Expensive clothes, preferably from a bespoke tailor on Savile Row, topped off by a Burberry coat and a gold Rolex watch, were essential. Golf, membership of exclusive country clubs,

people's savings were insufficient to meet their needs when they could no longer work. The process of saving and investment for retirement further financialized lives.

Otto Eduard Leopold von Bismarck, Count of Bismarck-Schönhausen, Duke of Lauenburg, Prince of Bismarck (the Iron Chancellor) introduced provisions for old age, sickness, accident, and disability pensions in the 1880s. In 1942, a committee chaired by Sir William Beveridge, a British economist, released a report—*Social Insurance and Allied Services* (known as the *Beveridge Report*)—that formed the basis of the post-Second World War British Labour government's welfare agenda—the National Health Service, child allowances, and unemployment benefits. State-supported pensions and benefits became an integral part of post-war economies.

Beveridge attacked want, proposing a revolution to create "a better world than the old world."[17] Beveridge sought to guarantee security of a minimum income. Bismarck's motivation was preventing revolution:

> I will consider it a great advantage when we have 700,000 small pensioners drawing their annuities from the State, especially if they belong to those classes who otherwise do not have much to lose by an upheaval and erroneously believe they can actually gain much by it.[18]

Universal if modest government-sponsored welfare arrangements became part of most liberal democracies. In time, employer-supported occupational pension and medical schemes emerged for most workers.

Retirement savings could be PAYG (pay-as-you-go) systems in which welfare was funded through taxes or future income. In funded systems, contributions by the worker, employer, or government were invested to meet future payments. There were defined benefit (DB) schemes where the benefit was fixed, a percentage of final salary, irrespective of contributions. There were also defined contribution (DC) schemes where the contribution was specified, but the benefit received depended upon the contributions and returns earned.

PAYG systems offering DBs worked well while the labor force was growing and the number of pension recipients was small. Over time, payments increased, reflecting increased life expectancy driven by better living standards and improvements in medical science and healthcare. At the same time, the aging population and declining birth rates meant that inflows into the funds declined.

At General Motors (GM), pioneers of employee benefits, legacy responsibilities grew because its workforce began to shrink as the bulge of workers hired in the middle of the century retired and began drawing pensions. Productivity improvements and cost pressures meant that the company was making more vehicles than in the early 1960s but with about one-third of the employees. In 1962, GM had 464,000 U.S. employees and was paying benefits to 40,000 retirees—a dependency ratio of one pensioner to 11.6 employees. By the early 2000s, it had 141,000 workers and paid benefits to 453,000 retirees—a dependency ratio of 3.2 to 1.

In 1889, the Iron Chancellor set the retirement age at 70 years, when average life expectancy was around 45. In 1908, Lloyd George set the British retirement age at 70 years, when few survived past 50. In 1935, America set the official pensionable age at 65 years for the social security system, when the average lifespan of Americans was around 68 years. The schemes were never meant to cover workers for ever-lengthening lives after retirement, in a society with less and less workers and taxpayers to support the retired. The entire system began to unravel.

Tax Avoidance

Limiting the universal system to a social safety net for the needy, governments instituted schemes designed to wean people off the public teat into personal retirement plans. Companies closed DB plans to new employees or converted them into DC schemes.

In the 1970s, citing pressures in the social security system and low saving rates, the U.S. government introduced individual retirement accounts (IRAs) with tax incentives. IRAs did not catch on, and the government introduced further concessions. Under Clause 401(k), workers were allowed to contribute cash bonuses to their IRAs on the basis that they could delay the tax on them.

In 1980 Ted Benna, while restructuring an employee pension fund, wondered whether regular income could be sheltered in the same way under the vaguely worded clause. The Internal Revenue Service agreed with Benna, triggering an explosion of retirement plans that allowed employees to contribute a part of their before-tax earnings to retirement savings. Similar retirement arrangements were introduced around the world, transforming individual finances and promoting populist capitalism.

Corporate pension schemes and individual retirement portfolios created vast pools of money that had to be invested. U.S. 401(k) accounts alone now hold close to $3 trillion, with annual inflows of hundreds of billions. Globally, close to $30 trillion is held by pension funds. The simple idea of providing for retirement expanded into a vast industry of consultants, actuaries, financial planners, and investment managers. In the feeding frenzy, after deduction of all fees and expenses, there was less and less left for the golden years.

Risk shifted from governments and companies back to the individual. If the funds underperformed, then retirements were not golden but silver or copper. If the employer went bankrupt, then the employee might not receive their entitlement where the plan did not have enough money.

Enron's employee pension plan invested over half its money in Enron stocks. When Enron filed for bankruptcy, employees suffered a double loss, losing not only their jobs but also their retirement savings. Grief counselors were called in to help employees come to terms with their bereavement.

Even if the entire plan works, under the DC schemes now common, there is no guarantee that the contributions and investment earnings will be sufficient.

For example, assume that you currently make $50,000 per year ($962 a week). Assume that your income rises by the rate of inflation (3 percent per annum), you have a working life of 40 years and you save 10 percent of your income ($5,000) each year. If you earn 6 percent per annum consistently over time, you will have around $1.2 million at retirement. If prices have gone up at 3 percent per annum, then what costs $1 today will cost $3.25 40 years in the future. The $1.2 million is only worth around $370,000 in today's money (around seven times your annual earnings).

You can draw an income equivalent to $25,000 (half your current income) adjusted for inflation for 20 years after you retire. You can't afford to live longer or better. You will have to focus on the *have-tos* rather than the *could-haves*, *should-haves*, or *would-haves*. If your investment earnings are 1 percent lower (5 percent per annum) then you can draw only the equivalent of $18,000 (36 percent of your current income). If you save 1 percent less each year, then you have only $22,000 each year (44 percent of your current income) to live on. There is no margin for error.

Japanese Curse

Japan is doubly cursed. The Japanese live a long time, and since 1989—when the bubble economy collapsed—interest rates, stock, or property investment returns have been microscopic.

Frugal Japanese saved a large portion of their income to try to provide adequately for their retirement. Retirees ran down savings or joined Mrs. Watanabe in speculating on foreign currencies and exotic financial products offering higher returns.

There was a boom in *pokkuri dera,* especially in the ancient capitals of Kyoto and Nara, shrines where older Japanese go to pray for a quick and painless death. Financial worries were a factor in one-fifth of suicides. Jumping in front of trains proved a common means for ending one's life—but Japan Railway charged families for the cost of the inconvenience and cleaning up after a suicide.

Inability to get welfare and inadequate pensions led to the rise of neo-geriatric crime. One 70-something invalid using an umbrella as a makeshift walking stick robbed a Nagoya convenience store of ¥50,000

($500) at knifepoint. Increasing numbers of elderly Japanese resorted to crime in the hope of being incarcerated, receiving free accommodation, free food, and the company of people their own age. The increase in pensioner prisoners required special wards fitted with metal walkers and support rails appropriate for senior citizens.

Legendary Japanese longevity had another, darker side. While trying to track down a citizen to present him with an award for living well past 100 years, Japanese authorities discovered the man had been dead for decades. His relatives had stored the body in their apartment, hiding news of his death, to continue receiving his pension, which was essential to support the surviving family members.

In the aftermath of the global financial crisis, falls in the value of retirement saving and low returns on investments revealed a Japanese future for the retirees of the world. A policy of low interest rates robbed retirees reliant on earnings on their savings perversely when the economy cried out for spending. Banks benefited from the massive subsidy, borrowing for almost nothing earning significant margins from lending out the funds or simply buying government bonds. A deliberate policy of creating inflation was designed to transfer wealth from savers to over-indebted borrowers.

Bank of England deputy governor Charles Bean advised:

> Savers shouldn't necessarily expect to be able to live just off their income in times when interest rates are low. It may make sense for them to eat into their capital.... Very often older households have actually benefited from the fact that they've seen capital gains on their houses.[19]

Retirees should simply sell their homes, which held most of their accumulated savings, and live in a public park consuming their savings.

The God of Our Time

Thomas Friedman, the globe-trotting journalist and confidant of anyone important, embraced the age of capital:

> Your parents probably had very little idea of where or how their pension funds were invested. Now...workers are offered a menu of funds, with different returns and risks, and they move their money around like chips on a roulette table.[20]

The bit about the roulette was correct.

Money even invaded the most intimate human acts. Two people are depicted having sex in Roy Andersson's film *You the Living*. A thin man is portrayed mounted by an overweight woman, wearing a Bismarck military helmet. During the entire sexual act, the man talks about his investments. He invested his savings and extra earnings from playing the tuba at funerals in mutual funds recommended by his bank. He has lost 34 percent of his investment. His pension is going to be lower than he expected. Throughout the entire scene, the woman astride him moans in carnal ecstasy.

Around 2002, a developing country defaulted on its debt. Following protracted negotiations, agreement was reached that the *bad* debt would be replaced with a smaller amount of new *good* debt, with all investors losing around half their original investment. The country's finance minister, accompanied by a vast retinue of assistants and bankers, embarked on a road show to sell the deal.

In Tokyo, the meeting attracted a vast throng of aged Japanese retirees, who had invested their savings in the defaulted securities, on the recommendations of financial advisers to earn interest rates higher than those available in Japan. At the end of the minister's presentation, a frail, ancient Japanese woman stood up and spoke. In a quiet steady voice, she explained the hardships that the loss had caused. She wanted to know "whether there was any chance she would see any of her money before her life ended."

3

Business of Business

In 1922 U.S. President Calvin Coolidge famously observed: "The business of America is business." The economist Thorstein Veblen saw a clear difference between industry, *producing things*, and business, *making money from producing things*. In the age of capital, business rapidly financialized.

Originally, business people invested in factories and businesses that produced and sold things. Now, in the twentieth century, business people sought to make money in ways not necessarily directly linked to the making of things. Speculators can make money from trading oil even if they do not actually produce, refine, or consume oil. They can make money irrespective of whether the oil business is good or bad, the price high or low. Business profited from disturbing the balance of the system, especially from uncertainty and volatility.

Financialization required money, specifically securities. Shares and bonds could be traded and manipulated more easily than the factories, railroads, and businesses that they were claims over. In 1908, *McClure's Magazine* understood that the old *physical frontier* of American history had been replaced by a new *financial frontier*. It was essential to make issuing, purchasing, and trading securities as safe as "producing farm land." The *speculation economy* had begun.[1]

Limited Consciences

The corporation allowed businesses to raise money from large numbers of people, combining their capital and economic power. Corporate securities limited the investor's liability to the amount of their investment, allowing the participation of ordinary individuals as their wealth increased.

Limited liability allowed investors to escape personal financial responsibility for a company's debts, encouraging speculation with other people's money. In Gilbert and Sullivan's satiric opera *Utopia Limited* Mr. Goldbury, a company promoter, sings:[2]

> Though a Rothschild you may be, in your own capacity,
> As a Company you've come to utter sorrow,
> But the liquidators say, "Never mind—you needn't pay,"
> So you start another Company Tomorrow!

In the late seventeenth century in London's financial district—the lanes around Lombard Street and Cornhill—stockbrokers, known as *jobbers*, sold shares in frequently dubious companies to investors. In 1696, concerned about the exploitation of credulous investors, England's Commissioners of Trade wrote that shares were being sold "to ignorant men, drawn in by the reputation, falsely raised and artfully spread, concerning the state of [the company]."[3]

Formed in 1710 to carry on trade with Spain's colonies in South America, the South Sea Company promised investors great profits. The stock increased by more than 900 percent. But in 1720, the stock price collapsed as shareholders tried to sell their shares, realizing that the company was worthless. The English Parliament enacted the 1720 Bubble Act, outlawing the creation of all joint stock companies not authorized by royal charter. In 1825, the need to raise capital to finance industry led to the Act's repeal.

A Brilliant Daring Speculation

Originally, companies were floated to raise funds for speculative projects—railways, canals, new inventions, and mining ventures (usually the latest "gold rush"). During the Internet bubble in the 1990s, companies desperately sought to stick virtual claim pegs into the new frontier of cyberspace.

Oscar Wilde, in *The Ideal Husband*, captured the sense of feverish speculation:[4]

> *Sir Robert Chiltern* This Argentine scheme is a commonplace Stock Exchange swindle.
>
> *Mrs. Cheveley* A speculation, Sir Robert. A brilliant daring speculation.

Sir Robert Chiltern Believe me, Mrs. Cheveley, it is a swindle. Let us call things by their proper names. It makes things simpler.

In the late nineteenth century, speculation took the form of overcapitalization, *watered stock*. The term originally referred to the practice of bloating a cow with water to increase its weight before sale. American stock promoters inflated claims about a company's assets and profitability and sold stocks and bonds in excess of the true value. The promoters contributed property to the new corporation (for example, worth $5,000) in return for stock at an inflated par value (for example, $10,000), enabling the value of the assets to be written up. The overvalued stock was sold to investors.

Financialization of business reached its zenith with *shareholder value*. In 1981, in a speech at New York's Hotel Pierre, Jack Welch, chief executive officer (CEO) of General Electric (GE), stated the company's objective as returning maximum value to stockholders.[5] Companies should only make investments and take on businesses providing returns above the firm's cost of capital.

Incorporation increases the separation between owners and managers of the business. In their 1932 book, *The Modern Corporation and Private Property*, Adolf Berle and Gardiner Means argued that companies were akin to feudal kingdoms run by "princes of industry" in their own, not the shareholder's, interests. Investors seeking to control the activities of managers embraced shareholder value.

This fitted the *great expectation machine*[6]—the needs of the pension funds, insurance companies, and professional investment managers who pooled and managed the savings and pension contributions of individuals. Investors want a simple mechanism to evaluate the companies they invest in. Disliking uncertainty, they prefer the financial world to be a predictable and highly ordered place. Shareholder value quickly became the preferred narrative and language of communication between companies, their managers, and investors. As remuneration became linked to performance via bonuses and grants of shares or stock options, managers embraced shareholder value.

With little control over the business, shareholders invested initially only for dividends paid by the company. Speculative shares were companies with uncertain ability to pay dividends, such as the Lucky Chance Oil Company of West Virginia.

Investors eventually became preoccupied with appreciation in stock prices. Companies became fixated on enhancing shareholder wealth by boosting the stock price. In investor presentations, Bernie Ebbers, CEO and later convicted criminal, would put up a chart of WorldCom's rising share price and ask his audience: "Any questions?" In March 2009, Welch would change his mind, calling shareholder value "the dumbest idea in the world."[7]

Dirty Tricks

Higher shareholder value requires increasing earnings, reducing the amount of capital used by the business, or decreasing the cost of that capital. You can improve the *real* business. Business improvements are risky and very slow, akin to watching grass grow. *Financial* changes are easier, more predictable and, most important, quicker. *Financial engineering* replaced *real engineering*. Rather than making things, trained engineers joined banks to provide turbo-charged financial structures for companies.

Until its spectacular implosion, Enron epitomized the new economy. Under Kenneth "Kenny Boy" Lay and Jeffrey Skilling, the merged Omaha-based InterNorth and Houston Natural Gas evolved from a natural gas producer and pipeline company into a trading company. Enteron, the original selected name of the merged firm, meant "intestine" in Greek and was hastily changed. Enron had "no meaning other than what we make it mean."[8]

Enron's center of gravity was its main trading floor in Houston, not its pipelines or natural gas operations.

There was the *old economy* business—generating and distributing energy. Then there was the *new economy* business—trading energy and ultimately everything. Enron shifted from the low return and regulated business of managing physical assets to the higher return unregulated business of trading. The *asset lite* strategy was the brainchild of Skilling, a Harvard MBA and an ex-McKinsey management consultant. The hallmark of Enron was the creative use of intellectual capital and money rather than physical assets.

Instead of managing the firm's risk, the company's financial operations increasingly augmented revenues by profits from trading in financial instruments. Companies now traded foreign exchange, bonds, commodities, equities, and derivatives.

For example, in the 1980s the yen appreciated, creating havoc among Japanese exporters, who were reliant on the cheap yen for competitiveness. Exporters changed strategy, moving production facilities offshore. Unfortunately, you cannot move a car plant to Mobile, Alabama, overnight. Japanese companies used *zaitech* or *zaiteku* (financial engineering) to cover up the weak profitability of their businesses.

In 2007, Porsche, the German sports car manufacturer, increased pretax earnings by around €3.7 billion to €5.8 billion, up 276 percent from €2.1 billion the previous year. The boost came from a profit of €3.6 billion from trading derivatives on shares (related to Porsche's holding in another German carmaker, Volkswagen). During the same period, core earnings from Porsche's car business fell around 30 percent.

Financialization of industry quickly spawned jokes: "How many workers does it take for Toyota to make a motor car?" Answer: "Four. One to design it, one to build it, and two to trade the long bond."[9]

In 1994, Metallgesellschaft, a German commodity producer, lost $660 million in oil trading. Proctor & Gamble lost $157 million in interest rate trading, revealing what the *gamble* in the company's name was about. In 1996 Sumitomo, a Japanese trading house, reported $2.6 billion in losses after discovering that Yasuo Hamanaka, a trader known as *Mr. Five Percent* because of his clout in copper markets, had manipulated the price.

In 2004, China Aviation Oil (Singapore) Corporation, a foreign subsidiary of a Chinese government-owned company, lost $550 million on speculative oil-futures trades. In 2005, Liu Qibing, a copper trader who executed trades on behalf of China's State Reserve Bureau, mysteriously went missing after making wrong bets on copper futures contracts that potentially cost hundreds of millions of dollars.[10] In 2008, companies in China, Korea, Taiwan, Hong Kong, India, and Latin America lost heavily as a result of speculative currency transactions.

In January 2011, providing definitive confirmation that trading by companies was a piscine affair, the Japanese carmaker Honda announced losses of ¥15 billion ($180 million) from trading in shrimp and shellfish. The company apologized deeply via its website "for causing great worry and trouble."

Financialization also took simpler, more conventional forms. Automobile companies offered financing to buyers, insurance, and other financial services, which were more profitable than the cars themselves. The financial businesses could also borrow larger sums and operate with higher leverage.

GM set the standard with General Motors Acceptance Corporation. Starting life financing GM dealers and new car buyers, it evolved into a bank. As the earnings from financial operations grew, GM increasingly resembled a bank that owned an unprofitable car company on the side. By the time the venerable symbol of American capitalism filed for bankruptcy in 2009, the burden of its liabilities to its retired employees meant that the company was "not even a car company. It's a health care provider with an auto manufacturer on the side."[11]

Companies exploited accounting rules to increase earnings or remain asset lite. Traditionally, earnings are recognized when cash is or is about to be received, progressively over the life of a contract. *Mark-to-market* accounting allowed revenues over the entire contract life to be recognized *immediately*. An electricity producer could book the entire future revenue that might be received over the useful life of the plant when the plant went into operation.

Skilling's decision to join the company had been conditional on Enron being able to adopt mark-to-market accounting, "a lay-my-body-across-the-tracks-issue."[12] Mark-to-market accounting accelerated growth, with future profits being brought to account at the start of the contract, creating an urgency to increase deal flow to maintain earnings growth.

Complex accounting provisions—special purpose entity rules (SPE)—allowed companies to shift assets *off balance sheet*, avoiding the need to record investments and associated borrowings as the firm's assets and liabilities. This reduced the amount of reported assets used to generate earnings, boosting *return on capital*—the key to shareholder value.

Companies aggressively reduced their cost of capital by substituting cheaper debt for expensive equity. Alan Greenspan, chairman of the Federal Reserve, supported the rush to debt: "Rising leverage appears to be the result of massive improvements in technology and infrastructure...experience...has made me reluctant to underestimate the ability of most households and companies to manage their financial affairs."[13]

Companies used cash flow from operations or new borrowings to repurchase their own shares to boost their stock price. Alan Greenspan put the practice down to a slowdown in innovation and excess capital.[14] Stock buybacks left the company with more debt and a weaker financial position.[15]

In 1987 Standard Oil of Ohio (Sohio), once part of the grand dame of oil companies but now owned by Britain's BP, advertised in leading financial magazines—"Standard Oil not standard thinking."[16] An arty graphic depicted a drop of oil in which a reflection of an oil well was visible. The text mentioned "a new very active management strategy," a subtext for financialization. "Assets not strategic to Standard Oil have been divested" spoke of redeploying the firm's capital by divesting underperforming investments. "We have also become fast creative traders" declared the trend to trading in financial instruments for profit. The text ended: "in a world of oil sheikhs and oil shocks, the more liquid we are the more solid." The advertisement spoke of a financial strategy. The *oil company* had become the *oil bank*.[17]

Marriages and Separations

Corporations restructured constantly, acquiring and disposing of assets and companies, making comparison of performance over time impossible. Merger activity was the *market for corporate control*. Like Ronin, lord-less mercenary Samurai, groups of corporate managers competed for control of assets, providing the necessary discipline on errant businesses.

The weapon of choice was the *hostile takeover*, the brainchild of Siegmund "Siggy" Warburg, founder of S.G. Warburg, the UK investment bank that is now part of UBS, the Swiss bank. Traditionally, mergers were friendly affairs agreed between the parties. Breaking with convention, in 1958, Reynolds/Tube, advised by Warburg, sought to acquire British Aluminium (BA) without the agreement of the target's board. Lord Portal, chairman of BA, haughtily rejected the offer as it would be giving away "a powerful empire for the price of a small kingdom." Instead, BA sought a friendly alliance with Alcoa to prevent the hostile takeover. But Warburg, an outsider to the moribund English financial establishment, masterminded a stunning tactical triumph in which Reynolds/Tube gained majority control of BA, despite fierce opposition.[18]

The hostile takeover of BA by Reynolds "was a very expensive one for the client. In fact, Warburg gave Reynolds poor advice. British Aluminium was not worth it at that price."[19] The advice may have been poor but Warburg did not do poorly out of the transaction. Acquisitions became common as a new generation of more aggressive businessmen assumed power.

In January 2000, Time Warner and AOL agreed to merge.[20] Time Warner was a sprawling conglomerate with publishing, film, television, entertainment, and media interests. AOL, originally America Online, was a young Internet company synonymous with the catchy "You've got mail" campaign. Time Warner had $26 billion in revenues, $6 billion in cash flows, a large amount of debt, and was valued at $83.5 billion prior to the merger. AOL had revenues of $5.2 billion and had made $879 million over the previous year, one of the few Internet companies to make money. AOL was valued by the stock market at $163 billion. AOL bought Time Warner for $165 billion.

At the press conference announcing the merger, overturning their respective traditional corporate cultures, Gerald Levin, Time Warner's chairman, appeared in an open-necked shirt and khakis, while Steve Case, AOL chairman, was clad uncharacteristically in a suit and tie. Case would be the chairman of the combined entity. The stock's new ticker symbol would be AOL. Time Warner shareholders got 45 percent of the new AOL Time Warner, despite being the more senior partner.

Levin endorsed Internet stocks: "The new media stock valuations are real." Media observers argued that it marked the end of old media, "go digital or die." The blogosphere was triumphant—a 14-year old Internet startup was taking over the world's largest media conglomerate.

AOL's value was its grossly overvalued stock. Riding the Internet boom to perfection, building up the stock price to stratospheric levels, AOL's shares were a currency to purchase real income and cash-producing assets. Stock prices no longer represented any real underlying business or earnings. It was monopoly money, convertible into something real if others believed in its value.

In 2002, as the Internet bubble collapsed, AOL Time Warner took the largest writedown in corporate history, recording a loss of $54 billion. Old media managers reasserted control, forcing out Case and Levin.

Rio Tinto was *old economy*, formed in 1873 when British investors purchased the eponymous copper, silver, and gold mine in Huelva, dating back thousands of years to Iberians, Tartessians, Phoenicians, Greeks, Romans, Visigoths, and Moors. By the twenty-first century, Rio Tinto was one of the world's largest diversified mining and resources group operating globally.

Rio Tinto's chief executive Tom Albanese persuaded the University of Alaska at Fairbanks to create a new degree course combining geology and economics. Albanese's reign at Rio Tinto was more about deal-making than extracting minerals.

In May 2007, just a few months into Albanese's tenure, Rio outbid Alcoa, an American aluminum firm, to purchase Alcan, a Canadian rival, for $38 billion. A price that looked high became ridiculous with the onset of the global financial crisis. The purchase was funded by $40 billion in debt. The acquisition had assumed rising commodity prices, driven by the emergence of China and India, would underpin Rio's earnings.

Shortly afterward Rio Tinto was subject to a hostile takeover bid from rival BHP Billiton. The bid valued Rio at $190 billion. Rio and Albanese rejected the bid. In late 2008, China experienced a sharp economic slowdown, sending metal prices plunging. $9 billion of debts falling due in 2009 and $10 billion in 2010 compounded Rio's problems. As Rio's stock market value fell, BHP dropped its bid, citing the target's large borrowings.

Undeterred, Albanese and Rio sought salvation in another transaction with Chinalco, a largely state-owned Chinese aluminum firm. The Chinese firm would pay $12.3 billion for up to 50 percent of nine Rio mines and also purchase $7.2 billion in convertible bonds that would give it the right to raise its stake in Rio from 9 to 18 percent. This deal also fell over, forcing Rio to enter into a joint venture with BHP on some of its iron ore mines. In 2010, that deal too duly collapsed.

The beneficiary of serial deal making was banks and investment banks. They earned huge fees from advising firms, lending money to finance transactions, designing and distributing complex corporate securities to investors, and entering into derivative transactions with the company.

The House That Jack Built

No firm captured the financialization of business better than GE, the firm built by John Francis "Jack" Welch, its chief executive between 1981 and 2001.[21] Historically, GE was founded on industrial innovation and engineering excellence—the light bulb, the first U.S. jet engine. Under Welch, the company financialized, building up GE Credit (now known as GE Capital) into a major part of its business.

During Welch's tenure, GE evolved from a company with 425,000 employees and $25 billion in revenue to a company with 310,000 employees and $125 billion in revenue. The ruthless downsizing earned Welch the nickname "Neutron Jack," a reference to a nuclear device that killed people but left property untouched. As GE's stock performed well, investors, shareholders, and investment bankers loved it.

Assuming charge of GE, Welch had to overcome the opprobrium of the *c* word—*conglomerate*. GE had a bewildering range of businesses—consumer products, turbines, jet engines, medical technology, media, and a finance business.

Combinations of unrelated businesses had been fashionable in the go-go 1960s. The "nifty fifty"—stocks like Ling-Temco-Vought (LTV), ITT Corporation, Litton Industries, Textron, Teledyne, and Gulf and Western Industries were the darlings of investors. Low interest rates and an equity market that rose and fell with metronomic regularity allowed the conglomerates to buy companies at temporarily deflated values, anticipating the leveraged acquisitions of the 1980s and 2000s. Investors saw conglomerates as an unstoppable new power and pushed up stock prices, allowing them to borrow more to buy more companies.

In the 1970s, higher inflation and rising interest rates caused the profits of the conglomerates to fall sharply. Poor businesses bought on the promise of being rejuvenated on to a higher growth track remained underperforming. Promised synergies remained promises. Investors eventually sold off conglomerate shares savagely.

With conglomerates out of fashion, the new preference was for *pure plays*—firms with clear-focused businesses. Welch was forced to fight the *conglomerate discount*, the company's share price traded well below the values of the individual businesses. GE's mission was recast to be number one or two by market share in every one of its businesses. As with all management strategy, the number one or number two rule was not always adhered to. Simply, by changing the definition of market, it was possible to meet the test. But investors and shareholders liked the focus on *market leadership*. Sales of noncore assets, savage cost cutting, and reduction in employee numbers pleased investors even more.

Welch came up with a succession of other *big ideas*, introducing management controls and planning tools that focused on allocating capital to businesses, suspiciously similar to those of Alfred Chandler from the 1960s. To improve product quality and reduce costs, Welch introduced *six sigma*, based on statistical tools for process and production control, originally developed by Allied Signal, Motorola, and the Japanese. Welch was not beyond naked opportunism, creating www.DestroyYourBusiness.com during the Internet boom, promoting digital technology to improve productivity.

GE managers, trained at the firm's Crotonville facilities (dubbed *cretinville* by sceptics), celebrated its *integrated diversity*, as well as its *silo-less*, *boundary-less*, and *learning organization*. Jack's gospel of GE *values*, supplying *organizational style* and acting as *professional change agents* spread. Welch now wanted his gravestone to say "People Jack."

Capital Ideas

The initiatives accentuated the positive features of GE's diverse conglomerate structure. GE's undisclosed business model was driven by opacity, complex relationships between its industrial and financial business, a reliance on continual mergers and acquisitions and earnings smoothing.

GE ran its old low-growth industrial business for earnings and cash flow, simultaneously diverting funds to aggressively grow its financial services business. GE Capital lent to customers to secure orders for power plants, wind turbines, and aircraft engines. Financial services were integral to selling GE products to customers, counteracting the slower growth and lower profitability of mature industrial businesses.

Consistent profits from its portfolio of industrial businesses maintained the parent's pristine AAA credit ratings (signifying the highest quality of borrower), keeping borrowing costs low. GE grew its financial businesses to the limit of its credit rating, borrowing far more than any comparable industrial company to enhance its return on equity, earnings, and share price. By the early 2000s, GE was leveraged around ten times: $10 of borrowings, much of it short term, for every $1 of share capital. GE Capital was contributing in excess of 40 percent of GE's earnings.

GE was also a merger and acquisition machine selling its low-margin industrial operations and buying profit and growth through purchases of financial businesses. Each year, it completed hundreds of deals involving billions of dollars. GE's policy was to aim for 80 percent of growth from existing businesses and 20 percent from acquisitions. In reality, half of its growth came from acquisitions.

Despite protestations that the firm managed businesses not earnings, GE's continuous restructuring of its portfolio and its growing financial services operations provided opportunities to realize gains and losses to smooth earnings to meet market expectations. GE used its insurance units' reserves, corporate pension fund, and commercial property arm to adjust earnings. During periods of strong equity market gains, GE boosted its profits by suspending contributions to its pension plan. GE sold buildings in the final weeks of a quarter to help meet its earning projections. GE was increasingly a product of financial engineering.

The size and complex structure of GE made it difficult to understand and analyze—should GE be classified as an industrial or a financial firm? GE studiously maintained a constructive ambiguity, increasing the lack of transparency and making detailed like-for-like comparisons difficult.

The nature of the firm made the relatively few investment analysts who covered the company reliant on management, especially Welch, who was GE's best share salesman. In analyst briefings, Welch typically replied to questions identifying each analyst by their first name. As *The Economist* noted: "[GE treats] analysts, journalists and other outsiders as if they either belong to the family and are believers, or do not."[22] Investors, reassured by a word from Jack and the company's capability to meet or marginally beat carefully cultivated earnings expectations, bought GE shares unquestioningly. Other businesses copied the GE formula.

WWJD—Watch What Jack Did!

Welch understood and exploited the growing power of the business media. He was a master of the *management narrative*—the artful stories and self-conscious recipes used to manage analysts' and investors' image of a company. Welch understood the value of a pithy sound grab to convey a big idea: "Every idea you present must be something you could get across easily at a cocktail party with strangers."[23] He cunningly avoided sophistication and "sounding smarter than anyone else."[24]

An entire literature provided uncritical and hagiographic portraits of GE and its CEO—*29 Leadership Secrets from Jack Welch*, *Business the Jack Welch Way*, *the Welch Way: 24 Lessons from the World's Greatest CEO*, and so on. Despite disagreement on the number of secrets or lessons, the books cited evidence in support of preconceived positions—"GE is a great company" and "Jack Welch is God."

Part of the narrative was Welch's humble beginnings and modest rewards as a CEO in an era of unparalleled excess. Unfortunately the mythology unravelled in the course of his divorce from Jane Beasley, Welch's second wife, whom he married in 1989. The couple had a prenuptial agreement but Jane hired William Zabel, a New York divorce lawyer well known for obtaining substantial divorce settlements for clients.

Welch leaked information that Jane had had an affair with a handsome Italian chauffeur and bodyguard. In Welch's view, Jane was a second wife who married a successful CEO. During their 13-year marriage, she enjoyed a lavish lifestyle. She had not made any contribution to Welch's career. Ironically, in his memoir *Jack: Straight from the Gut*, Welch reported that Jane was a perfect partner accompanying him on his corporate trips. Jane gave up her business career devoting herself to her husband, even taking up golf to play with Welch's business associates. Welch even noted that Jane introduced him to the Internet.

Annoyed at an ongoing dispute over her monthly living expenses and the negotiations, Jane lodged an affidavit outlining Welch's assets, liabilities, expenses, and income and other details of Welch's lifestyle, exposing details of the retirement package agreed by GE. In 2000, his last full year at GE before retirement, Welch received compensation, including bonus and salary, totaling $16.7 million. He remained a consultant to the company on $86,535 annually for his first 30 days of work, with a payment of $17,307 for every additional day. GE was paying for Jack Welch's living expenses in retirement, including cars, aircraft, apartments, mobile phones, flowers, security systems, and vitamins.

"People Jack" was entitled to floor-level seats to New York Knicks games, courtside seats at the U.S. Open, VIP seating at Wimbledon, a box at the Metropolitan Opera, a box at Red Sox games, and a box at Yankee games. GE paid four country club fees; limousine services; security services, satellite TV, communications, and computer equipment at his four homes; and security and all the costs associated with his New York apartment, from wine and food to laundry, toiletries, and newspapers. GE also covered dining bills at the Jean Georges restaurant in the Manhattan apartment building where he lived.

The resulting outcry forced Welch to give up the perks he believed he was entitled to after 40 years of service to GE. Jane Welch received an amount believed to be around $180 million in the divorce settlement. But Welch remains high on the list of most admired management leaders.

Welch's successor at GE, Jeffrey Immelt, inherited a company at the end of its growth strategy reliant on GE Capital. Immelt tried to reorganize the company, increasing transparency. He expanded into alternative energy, which raised the eyebrows of Welch, a climate change nonbeliever. But Immelt also relied on large acquisitions to transform GE. In 2004, GE was among the largest purchasers of investment banking services, paying fees of more than $450 million to financial advisers. Immelt was truly a chip off the Welch block. When the global financial crisis exposed the weaknesses of its business model, GE's stock price and performance went into meltdown, or as one journalist christened it *Immeltdown*.

Business Dealings

Finance gradually replaced industry, with trading and speculation becoming major activities. In his classic nineteenth-century work *Lombard Street*, Walter Bagehot cautioned that: "Common sense teaches that booksellers should not speculate in hops, or bankers in turpentine; that railways should not be promoted by maiden ladies, or canals by beneficed clergymen."[25] The advice was seen as quaint and irrelevant in the modern age.

Facing pressure from investors for quick tangible results, corporate managers and boards resorted to financialization. Peter Drucker, the management scholar, identified the reason:

> Dealmaking beats working, dealmaking is exciting and fun, and working is grubby. Running anything is primarily an enormous amount of grubby detail work.... Dealmaking is romantic, sexy. That's why you have deals that make no sense.[26]

The death of the owner manager and the rise of the MBA-trained professional managers meant that those running companies lacked *domain knowledge*—the specific knowledge and skills to run a company operationally. Maryann Keller, writing about General Motors, noted the change: "the best way to achieve success at GM is to be a good finance man…juggling numbers in order to present the picture people want to see."[27] You only managed the things that you could measure. Eventually the business of business became money. Like individuals, they became habitués of *The Mirrored Room*.

In *Other People's Money*, Andrew "Jorgy" Jorgenson (played by Gregory Peck) faces off against "Larry the Liquidator"— the private equity investor who is seeking to take over his family company. Jorgy tells the assembled shareholders that at least the old robber barons built something tangible—a coalmine, a railroad, even banks. The new entrepreneurs of post-industrial America use other people's money to buy up businesses, create nothing and leave behind nothing, except the paper that cannot cover the pain of the people whose lives are wrecked.

Money came to drive individual lives and businesses. Heinrich Heine, the German poet, saw the reality of this future: "this is based on the most unreliable of elements, on money…which is more fluid than water and less steady than air."[28]

4

Money for Sale

Nature abhors a vacuum. Taking advantage of the financialization of business and everyday life, banks moved to fill the gap.

In the film *Ferris Bueller's Day Off*, an economics teacher, played by Ben Stein, launches into an improvised soliloquy, asking his apathetic students whether anyone has seen the "Laffer Curve." He asks if anyone knows what Vice-President Bush Senior called this in 1980. No one knows. "Something-d-o-o economics. 'Voodoo' economics."

The 1930s Hollywood film *White Zombie* incorrectly associated voodoo, African beliefs syncretized with Christianity, with exotic superstitions and occult practices. Unscrupulous practitioners made a fortune out of fake potions, powders, fetishes, and talismans to ward off evil. In the 1980s, U.S. President Ronald Reagan embraced *voodoo economics*. At about the same time, banks created *voodoo banking*.

It's a Wonderful Bank!

Every Christmas, Frank Capra's film *It's A Wonderful Life* is repeated. For some, it probably isn't Christmas until they have seen it again. James Stewart plays every banker George Bailey, who owns and runs the town's bank. *It's a Wonderful Life* portrays a world where the bank acts as an intermediary between savers and borrowers, and bankers are respected members of the community.

Until recently, banks were simple. Regulators set the rates that the bank could pay its depositors, the rates it could charge borrowers, and the amount it could lend. There was little trading. Exotics remained exotic. The world worked to the *3-6-3* rule—borrow at 3 percent, lend at 6 percent, hit the golf course at 3.00 p.m.

Following the 1929 stock market crash and the collapse of the banking system, the Glass-Steagall Act of 1933 (named after Democratic Senator Carter Glass of Lynchburg, Virginia, and Democratic Congressman Henry B. Steagall of Alabama) separated *commercial* banking (taking deposits and lending money) and *investment* banking (advising, arranging, underwriting, and trading securities). Regulation sought to prevent conflicts of interest where the same institution was lending (granting credit) and investing (using credit). It recognized that institutions accepting deposits wielded financial power through control of other people's money. Proponents of regulation argued that this power should be limited, to ensure soundness and competition for loans or investments.

In the United States, government insurance of deposits meant that the taxpayer could be required to pay out if an insured bank suffered trading losses. Trading in securities exposed firms to losses that could threaten depositors. Some argued that banks conditioned to limit risk were not equipped to undertake more speculative activities.

In the 1980s, the controls over banks and banking were gradually loosened. President Reagan and UK Prime Minister Margaret Thatcher favored less government involvement in the economy. In parts of the world like France, deregulation of the financial system was accompanied by privatization of government-owned banks.

Proponents of deregulation argued that distinctions between loans, deposits, and securities were increasingly difficult in practice. In 1977, Merrill Lynch, a securities firm with a large brokerage network known as *the thundering herd*, launched the cash management account (CMA)—a mutual fund investing in short-term securities offering investors daily access to money, checking facilities, and the convenience of having their pay deposited directly. It was, in reality, a checking or operating account that paid attractive rates of interest. At the time, banks were not allowed to pay interest on checking accounts, placing them at a competitive disadvantage.

Banks argued that perceived conflicts of interest could be managed by enforcing separation of activities—*firewalls* or *Chinese walls*. The ability to expand into broader financial services would reduce risk through diversification of activity. Proponents pointed to Europe, where *universal* banks undertook both banking and securities businesses.

In 1999, the *coup de grâce* was administered by Phil Gramm (Republican of Texas) and Jim Leach (Republican of Iowa), who introduced legislation repealing the Glass-Steagall Act. The repeal paved the way for *financial supermarkets*—one-stop money shops taking deposits, making loans, providing advice, underwriting and trading securities, managing investments, and providing insurance. Byron Dorgan, one of only eight senators who voted against the abolition, presciently observed that "this bill will in my judgement raise the likelihood of future massive taxpayer bailouts."[1]

Giant financial supermarkets destroyed old banking traditions. Walter Bagehot, the nineteenth-century British economist, saw banking as the preserve of titled families: "The banker's calling is hereditary; the credit of the bank descends from father to son; this inherited wealth brings inherited refinement."[2] The chairman of Hambros Bank, a leading London merchant bank, was more specific: "Our job is to breed wisely."[3] Inherited refinement gave way to a more industrial form of banking. In David Gaffney's novel *Never Never*, a bank manager describes the new regime:

> "You're not selling enough," [the regional manager] says. "You should be moving more product. Loans, insurance, second mortgages, personal pensions. I say ... that's not what banking is about in this area. It's about helping people. They haven't got the money to be buying things."[4]

Banking became a commercial activity driven by shareholder returns. With increasing competition, banks resorted to *voodoo* to meet investor expectations.

Pass the Parcel

Banks took short-term deposits, using the money to make longer-term loans. The major risk was that the borrower did not pay you back. It was a simple, unexciting business. The bank's capability to grow depended on its own shareholders' capital and its capability to garner deposits. The shareholders received predictable, modest returns. Figure 4.1 sets out the traditional banking model.

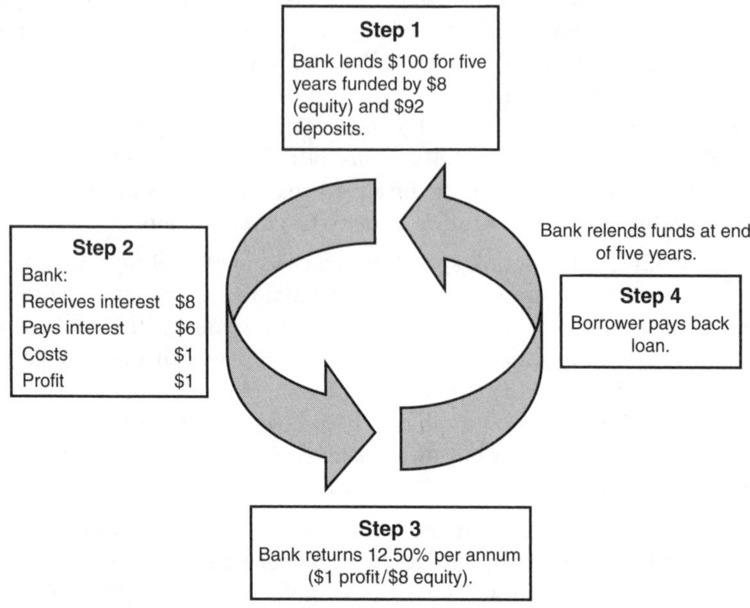

1. The bank raises $92 in deposits from clients, combining it with $8 of its own shareholders' capital.
2. This money ($100) is lent to a client, say for 5 years.
3. The bank receives $8 in interest. It pays $6 in interest to its depositors. The bank has operating costs of $1. The profits before tax of $1 ($8 minus $6 minus $1) translate into a return for bank shareholders of 12.50 percent per annum ($1 in profits, divided by $8 of shareholders' capital).
4. When the loan is paid back, the whole process repeats.

Figure 4.1 Traditional banking model

In the new *originate-to-distribute model*, banks underwrote the loan, warehousing it on the balance sheet for a short time using its own money, before parceling the loans into securities to be sold to investors, in a process known as *securitization*. Figure 4.2 sets out the originate-to-distribute banking model.

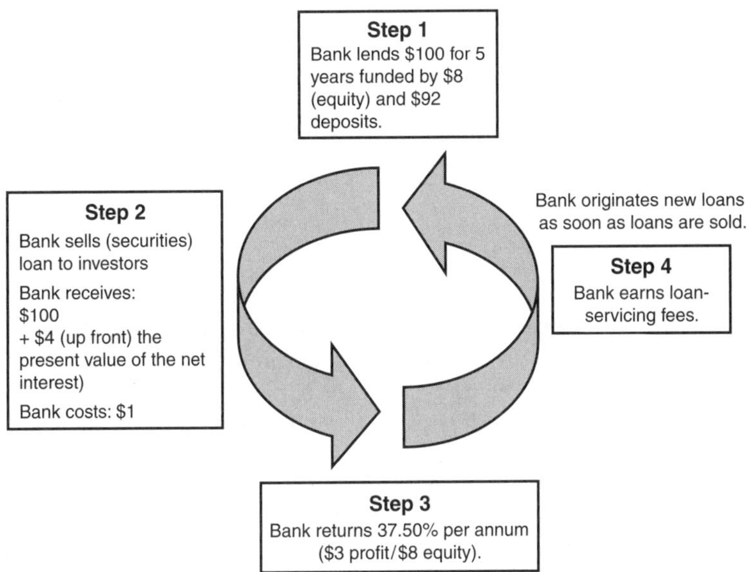

1. The bank still raises $92 in deposits from clients, combining it with $8 of its own shareholders' funds to lend $100 to a client for 5 years.
2. Instead of holding the loan for its entire life (5 years), the bank holds the loans until it has a sufficient number and amount to package them up and sell them to investors, such as pension funds, insurance companies, and investment managers.
3. When the loan is sold, the bank receives the amount loaned ($100) plus the current or present value of the net interest (the difference between what the borrower pays and what the investor purchasing the repackaged loans receives). This amount is $4. After operating costs of $1, the bank has profits before tax of $3 ($4 minus $1), translating into shareholder returns of 37.50 percent per annum ($3 in profits divided by $8 of shareholders' capital).
4. The bank continues to administer the loan during its life, receiving loan servicing fees. After the loans have been sold, the bank's capital and funding are freed up, and it can repeat the process again.

Figure 4.2 Originate-to-distribute model

In the originate-to-distribute model, banks tied up capital for a short time (until the loans were sold off). The same capital could be reused as the process is repeated. Interest earnings over the life of the loan are discounted back and recognized immediately. Banks increase the *velocity of capital*, effectively sweating the same capital harder to increase returns. If a bank turned over its entire loan book twice a year, its returns would be 75 percent per annum!

Other financial products, primarily derivative contracts, essentially forms of price insurance, were used in the same way. The CEO of one bank noted that they had become "a moving company and not a storage company."

Loan Frenzy

By increasing throughput, making more loans and selling them off to eager investors, banks created a money machine. Banks traditionally earn the net interest rate margin (the difference between what the borrower pays and what it must pay to depositors) over the life of the loan—*annuity income*. When loan assets are sold off, the earnings from the loan are recognized *up-front*. Over the remaining life of the loan, the bank earns modest fees for administering it. Each year, banks now needed to make more and more loans to meet the expectation machine's demand for higher earnings.

Access to cheap deposits to fund loans traditionally gave commercial banks an advantage over investment banks and nonbank lenders. The originate-to-distribute model allowed investment banks, mortgage brokers, and independent credit card providers to make loans and sell them off. They could now obtain cheap funding from investors. The competition led to lower profit margins, forcing everyone to increase loan volumes to meet investor demand for higher returns. Everybody had to run harder just to stay where they were.

The race was to find borrowers. Banks outsourced the origination of the loans to brokers, incentivized by large upfront fees. Everybody first lent to the soundest borrowers. Then, less creditworthy borrowers (previously denied access to credit) entered the market. Then came even more risky loans—subprime mortgages for NINJA borrowers and loans to private equity funds and hedge funds.

Traditional lending practices relied on character. After his bank avoided losses on property loans in the early 1970s, Lord Poole of Lazards set out his successful lending criteria: "I only lent money to people who had been at Eton [an elite English school with a distinguished alumni]."[5] Who qualified for loans, on what terms and at what rate, now relied on *credit scores*—a numerical expression of the risk based on statistical analysis of financial information. The models relied on purely historical factors that sometimes did not reflect changes in the world. Information fed into the models was not checked.

Loans relied on the value of collateral securing the debt. Borrowers put up a portion of the price of the asset, agreeing to cover any fall in value with additional cash. Little attention was paid to the accuracy and stability of the value of the collateral. The ability to repay the loan diminished in importance. As the value of the collateral was expected to increase, it was assumed that you would refinance your loan to pay back the previous borrowing.

Bankers argued that loans to low-quality borrowers were not risky, as the banks did not plan to hold on to them. Banks were only at risk in the period before the loans were sold. All this underpinned an unprecedented growth in lending.

Plastic Fantastic Money

The average American has around five credit cards. In 2005, there were 6.1 billion credit card offers to Americans.

In 1992, Emily Grant received a letter from American Express: "We don't invite most people to apply for the American Express Card. We are inviting you." Emily Grant happened to be the daughter of James Grant, founder of *Grant's Interest Rate Observer*. In a caustic piece,[6] Grant pointed out that his daughter was 11 years old, received an allowance of $2.50 each week and could probably pay the $55 annual fee but that would leave little remaining funds in her savings account. Shortly afterward, Grant's 10-year-old son Philip received his own offer to apply for the even more prestigious *gold* Amex card: "Charges are approved based on your ability to pay, as demonstrated by your spending and payment patterns, and by your personal resources." Grant wrote that Philip's resources were an allowance of $1.50 each week, and his savings were negligible, following heavy investments in raffle tickets for a school fair.

The modern credit card grew out of merchant credit schemes to purchase fuel or items from department stores. Ralph Schneider and Frank McNamara created Diners Club, which pioneered the concept of customers paying different merchants using the same card, eliminating the need for multiple cards. In 1958, American Express commenced operations, ultimately creating a worldwide credit card network. Visa evolved out of the BankAmericard created in 1958 by Bank of America. Other banks created MasterCard, which eventually incorporated Citibank's proprietary Everything Card. Copying the concept, Barclays Bank launched Barclaycard in the UK in 1966.

In the mid-1980s, John Reed, then head of consumer banking at Citibank, expanded the acceptance and use of credit cards with an audacious campaign. Citi mailed credit cards with a small limit to householders based on their postal codes, filtering out undesirable neighborhoods. The scheme helped the rapid adoption of credit cards, but Citibank at first experienced high bad debts because many card holders could not or did not pay the bank back for things they bought. Over time, the business became very profitable for the bank.

The idea of the credit card—a simple revolving loan for individuals—has remained constant. Financial institutions issue credit cards to approved customers, allowing them to use it to make purchases up to a specified limit at businesses that accept the card. When a purchase is completed, the card issuer pays the business. Each month, the cardholder may repay the entire amount owed by a specified date. Alternatively, the cardholder must make a minimum payment, usually a defined minimum proportion of the bill. If the cardholder does not pay the bill in full (known as *revolvers*), the card issuer charges a high rate of interest on the unpaid balance.

Card issuers make money from the cardholder—annual fees and interest on balances owed. Card issuers also make money from businesses that accept the card—a merchant discount of 1–5 percent of each purchase and a flat per-transaction charge.

In the 1990s, credit cards based on the value of the card holder's home emerged. Rising home prices and repayments of their mortgages meant that many homeowners were rich *on paper*—the value of the house was greater than the amount owed on their mortgage. A credit card secured against this value allowed individuals to unlock their *home equity*.

Credit card marketing is slick—"Life Flows Better with Visa"; "Live richly, Citibank"; "Priceless! For everything else there's MasterCard." Cards are linked to the good life and the consumption that goes with it. Each dollar spent may generate bonus points toward a prize or air miles. Cards related to an entity like a university, return a percentage of the spending on the card to the affinity group. In developing countries, a credit card is frequently a sought after symbol of Western modernity, signifying sophistication and progress. Consumers agreed with Marshall McLuhan, the Canadian media theorist: "Money is a poor man's credit card." Nobody wanted to be *poor*.

Credit cards are now even *objets d'art*. Specialists in numismatics (the study of money) and exonumia (the study of money-like objects) collect old paper merchant cards, metal tokens once used as merchant credit cards and early credit cards made of celluloid plastic, fiber, and paper.

In October 2008, MasterCard launched its diamond credit card, inlaid with a 0.02-carat gem and laced with gold. The card featured an image of a peacock for female cardholders and a winged horse for men. It targeted new super-rich billionaires created by the oil and minerals boom of recent years in commodity-rich Kazakhstan. Kazkommertsbank, the second largest bank in Kazakhstan, planned to issue 1,000 cards, at a rate of about 30 a month, to VIP customers. Each card had an annual fee of $1,000 and a credit limit of $50,000, more than twice the limit on MasterCard platinum cards.

The instant gratification provided by readily accessible money replaced restraint and deferred consumption. In the new economy, there were three kinds of people: the haves, the have-nots, and the have-not-paid-for-what-they-haves.[7]

Casino Banking

Banks also began to trade financial instruments, taking the advice of *Fear of Flying* author Erica Jong: "If you don't risk anything then you risk even more."

Initially, banks traded currencies and government bonds. Volatility of currencies increased following the collapse of the Bretton Woods agreement and the demise of the gold standard. Volatility of interest rates increased, following removal of controls on interest rates and a rise in inflation as a result of the oil shocks of 1974 and 1979. Derivatives—different forms of price insurance on currencies, interest rates, and equities—began trading in the 1970s.

As volatility forced businesses and investors to hedge their financial risks, banks moved into the *protection racket*. Initially, they acted primarily as an intermediary, matching transactions between clients. Over time, banks began to take positions without having a matching counterparty. Competition meant margins kept getting lower. Competitors shamelessly copied new products, reducing profits. Banks maintained earnings through higher volumes, innovation, and increased risk taking.

Increasing volumes meant finding new customers to trade with. Hedge funds, that traded frequently and aggressively, became important clients. Banks created prime brokerage units to settle and clear trades, lend to, and raise capital for hedge funds. With growing wealth and sophistication, investors moved out of bank deposits into equity, bonds, or mutual funds. Banks created or purchased wealth management businesses (fund managers and private banks) to meet the demand for investment products. Wealth management clients became major purchasers of securities or financial products created by the banks. Major banks expanded geographically, especially into emerging markets, where similar products could be created and sold to new clients.

In trading, banks rely on their counterparts to perform contractual obligations, sometimes over many years. Needing to overcome the risk of dealing with less creditworthy clients, banks created a system known as collateral—clients lodged an initial deposit (an agreed percentage of the contract value), agreeing to top up this amount as necessary to minimize risk. Banks now could trade with anybody and did.

Complexity grew rapidly, with banks creating exotic products, usually derivatives, to trade with clients. Increased computing power and quants, highly trained staff with mathematical or quantitative skills, accelerated this process. Banks managed the risks and calculated their earnings using complex models.

If one bank offered an option with a somersault, then a second offered the same with a somersault and pike, while a third marketed one with a triple somersault and pike ending in a double tuck. In a surreal sequence, banks created instruments using models that few understood, which they traded with clients who did not understand what the product was and had no way of pricing or valuing it. The level of knowledge of clients was often inversely proportional to the complexity of the product.

Banks increasingly speculated on price changes to supplement shrinking margins from client transactions. Traders used information gained from trading with clients to make money. Banks all wanted to become *flow monsters*—institutions that traded with everybody, capturing a large share of total trading volume.

Banks now invested their own money in transactions, becoming principals in deals. Where they lent money to an investor to purchase a business, the banks co-invested alongside the client. Clients liked banks investing in transactions they financed or advised upon to ensure better alignment of their interests. Advisory work in mergers and acquisition and corporate finance became conditional on extension of credit at skimpy margins. Banks *seeded* or invested in hedge funds to gain preferential access to business. Investing their own funds allowed banks to make ends meet. But traders were now betting the house's money.

Classically trained bankers quoted Herodotus: "Great deeds are usually wrought at great risk." Traders stayed with Lillian Carter, mother of President Jimmy Carter: "I don't think about risk much. I just do what I want to do. If you gotta go, you gotta go." It was a long way from George Bailey's wonderful world. Banks should all have heeded Mark Twain's acid wit: "There are two times in a man's life when he should not speculate: when he can't afford it, and when he can."

Confidence Tricks

Originally created to help facilitate German war reparations after the First World War, the Bank of International Settlement (BIS) established the basic framework under which banks operated, from its HQ in Basel, Switzerland. The first set of global bank regulations, known as *Basel 1*, emerged in the early 1980s.

Banking involves risks. Borrowers may not pay back loans—*credit risk* or *default risk*. Banks may lose money trading if prices move against them—*market risk*. Depositors may want their money back—*liquidity risk*. Liquidity risk arises because banks take deposits typically for short periods (less than 12 months) to make loans for longer terms (up to 30 years)—known as *maturity transformation*. Basel 1 required banks to maintain capital, a buffer or reserves (shareholders' money), against loss. They were required to hold cash or securities that could be readily sold to raise funds to meet the needs of depositors wanting to take out their money.

The eighteenth-century English playwright Susannah Centlivre observed that: "Tis my opinion every man cheats in his own way, and he is only honest who is not discovered." *Regulatory arbitrage*—the process of exploiting gaps in bank regulations—evolved into a business model.

Banks reduced the amount of expensive capital, transferring loans, investments, and trading into a network of unregulated off-balance-sheet vehicles, which did not need to hold as much capital as the bank itself. Frequently, the real risk remained with the banks. Banks reduced *real* capital—common shares—by substituting creative hybrid capital instruments that were cheaper. High income was used to attract fund managers and "mom and pop" (ordinary) investors, while disguising the (less obvious) risks. Banks used these new forms of capital to finance repurchase of their shares to boost returns. CitiGroup repurchased $12.8 billion of its shares in 2005 and an additional $7 billion in 2006, just before its share price plunged as the bank suffered huge losses.

Banks decreased their equity and cash reserves, assuming they could always buy these resources from the market at a price in case of need—this came to be known as *purchased* capital and *purchased* liquidity. Banks had reduced the amount of capital and spare cash at the same time as they were increasing loan volumes, taking on more risk and increasing leverage. The bank's return on capital, the measure investors looked at, increased as the denominator (capital) fell and simultaneously the numerator (return) rose. Like David Hockney, the English artist, bankers knew that: "The moment you cheat for the sake of beauty you are an artist."

The financial system became more fragile and dangerous as banks became larger. As Baltasar Gracian, the Spanish philosopher and writer, noted in the seventeenth century: "One deceit needs many others, and so the whole house is built in the air and must soon come to the ground."

The Citi of Money

On April 6, 1998 Citicorp and Travelers merged to create CitiGroup in a $83 billion deal that was another "deal of the century." Sandy Weill, chief executive of Travelers, and John Reed, chief executive of Citicorp, announced the merger at New York's Waldorf Astoria Hotel. The men wore matching ties dotted with red umbrellas—the original logo of Traveler.

The merger combined Travelers' insurance, brokerage, and securities businesses and Citicorp's international banking operations. It was to be the ultimate *universal bank* or *financial supermarket*, with hundreds of millions of customers in more than a hundred countries.

The Travelers/Citicorp juggernaut would use its huge balance sheet to make large loans to companies and leverage this to sell the clients a variety of other advisory services or financial products. The institution's unparalleled reach would offer a one-stop-shop for individuals—payments, credit cards, mortgages, savings, and investment products. But as the baseball player Yogi Berra noted: "In theory there is no difference between theory and practice but in practice there is."

Synergies and cross-selling benefits failed to emerge. Competition limited CitiGroup's gains. Other commercial banks built or bought investment banks to compete. *i-Banks*, the new buzzword for investment banks, shamelessly derivative of Apple's 'i' products—particularly Morgan Stanley, Goldman Sachs, and Merrill Lynch (collectively dubbed MGM)—changed their business models to match the universal banks.

At an internal conference in the early 1990s, John Thornton, a Goldman Sachs managing director, outlined a business model. Eschewing the traditional PowerPoint presentation, Thornton used a felt pen to draw dots on a white board. "These are the important people in the world." Thornton then drew overlapping circles around the dots. "Inside these circles are the people they know, the deals they do, the ideas they are thinking about. Pretty much everything that happens in the world, happens in these circles." Pointing to where most of the circles overlapped, Thornton summed up investment banking: "This is where I want to be. That is our strategy."[8]

Thornton's vision was old school—advise clients and underwrite debt and equity issues. Instead, investment banks now transformed themselves into commercial banks. They began lending to clients, in part to protect their advisory franchises from the likes of Citi that were keen to use their lending power to muscle in. Investment banks raised capital to compete with their commercial and universal banking peers. Even mighty "Gold Man Sex," as foreign clients called the firm, abandoned its hallowed partnership structure to raise the capital needed to support a burgeoning balance sheet and support trading operations.

Citi was born with a golden foot in its mouth. In the 1980s, ill-fated forays into lending to Latin America led to multibillion dollar losses. Citi Chairman Wriston had earlier inaccurately believed: "Countries don't go bust." In the early 1990s, Citi nearly collapsed because of poor real estate lending. In the aftermath of the bust of the Internet bubble, Citi's star telecommunications analyst Jack Grubman was accused of spruiking WorldCom stock in return for investment banking business. Grubman described his role in the following terms: "What used to be a conflict is now a synergy."[9]

In 2004, Citi was criticized and then fined for disrupting European markets in the *Dr. Evil trade*, rapidly selling €11-billion-worth of bonds via an electronic platform, driving down the price, and then buying it back at cheaper prices. In 2007, Citi was fined by the National Association of Security Dealers for violations relating to mutual fund sales practices. In June 2009, Japanese authorities prosecuted Citi for breaches of regulations, following on earlier problems in 2004. The most global thing about Citi was its unending list of problems with regulators in different jurisdictions.

In the end, Citi too came to rely on voodoo banking to boost its lackluster performance. It rapidly increased its lending and risk taking heeding humorist Will Rogers' advice: "You've got to go out on a limb sometimes because that's where the fruit is." In the global financial crisis, CitiGroup would suffer near-fatal losses, necessitating majority government ownership.

Sign of the Times

As John Manyard Keynes observed: "A sound banker, alas, is not one who foresees danger and avoids it, but one who, when he is ruined, is ruined in a conventional way along with his fellows, so that no one can really blame him."[10] Celebrated commercial and investment banks from the United States, UK, Germany, Switzerland, and France followed similar strategies.

Profits were driven by rapid and large growth in lending, trading revenues, and increased risk taking. High returns were underwritten by an extremely favorable economic environment, not, as bankers argued, *innovation*. As John Kenneth Galbraith, in *A Short History of Financial Euphoria*, identified:

> Financial operations do not lend themselves to innovation. What is recurrently so described and celebrated is, without exception, a small variation on an established design.... The world of finance hails the invention of the wheel over and over again, often in a slightly more unstable version.[11]

The Economist summarized the era:

> Over the past 35 years it has seemed as if everyone in finance has wanted to be someone else. Hedge funds and private equity wanted to be as cool as a dot.com. Goldman Sachs wanted to be as smart as a hedge fund. The other investment banks wanted to be as profitable as Goldman Sachs. America's retail banks wanted to be as cutting-edge as investment banks. And European banks wanted to be as aggressive as American banks.[12]

They would all end up wishing they could be back precisely where they started.

Elite athletes sometimes use drugs to boost performance. Voodoo banking enabled banks to enhance short-term performance while risking longer-term damage. The problem was they put everybody, not just themselves, in harm's way. In 2008, discovering the casino banking practices of financial institutions, regulators reacted like Captain Renault (played by Claude Rains) in *Casablanca*. They confessed that they were truly shocked to find that gambling was going on in regulated banks.

5

Yellow Brick Road

Money transformed cities and entire countries. Financial centers replaced industrial and trading districts in importance. New York, London, Frankfurt, Tokyo, Hong Kong, and Singapore emerged as major financial centers. Because trading is electronic, location did not matter. The convergence of financiers to particular locations reflected English economist Alfred Marshall's 1890 observation: "The mysteries of the trade become no mystery, but are, as it were, in the air."[1]

The players did not make things or trade goods. Instead, they traded trillions of dollars, euros, yen, bonds, shares, commodities, and derivatives. Much of the activity did not generate true value or represent direct additions to the goods and services produced in the economy. It increased debt and the circulation of money, as well as trading and speculation.

In 2009 Paul Volcker, a former chairman of the Federal Reserve, questioned the role of finance: "I wish someone would give me one shred of neutral evidence that financial innovation has led to economic growth—one shred of evidence.... [U.S. financial services increased its share of value-added from 2 percent to 6.5 percent] Is that a reflection of your financial innovation, or just a reflection of what you're paid?"[2] The only financial innovation over the past 20 years that impressed Volcker was the automated teller machine.

In the financial centers, high rewards enjoyed by people associated with finance trickled down. Entire cities and districts became gentrified, with bustling streets, chi-chi restaurants, trendy bars, and luxury label retailers. The financial centers were at the epicenter of this new self-confident, Starbucks society.

Monumental Money

In New York, a 70-story tower at 40 Wall Street, originally the home of Bank of Manhattan Trust that became Chase Manhattan Bank, was briefly the world's tallest office building. It was quickly eclipsed by the Chrysler Building, an art deco masterpiece celebrating the dominance of America's industrial economy. The iconic Seagram and General Motors Building paid homage to America's industrial power.

Marking the shift from industry to finance, new hallmark buildings were increasingly built for financial institutions. In 1977, the 59-floor, 915-foot (279-meter) CitiGroup Center, featuring a 45°-angled top and a unique stilt-style base, opened as the group's headquarters. The location in mid-town Manhattan was immortalized by *The Ramones*, the punk rock band, in *53rd and 3rd*, a song that refers to this famous meeting place for male prostitution.

In London, Swiss Reinsurance created its infamous "Gherkin." Near Madrid, Banco Santander, a major Spanish bank, built a vast campus. The Frankfurt skyline was dominated by the Deutsche Bank building whose twin towers were dubbed "debit" and "credit."

The CitiGroup Center was initially structurally unsound, being too weak to withstand 70-mph (113 km/h) winds. The problem was corrected. Later the building was reinforced against possible terrorist attack. CitiGroup itself was not reinforced against financial turmoil.

The Battle of the "Pond"

In London, the *City* or the *Square Mile* is synonymous with the UK's financial services industry. But the City is not in the City any more. Hedge funds congregate in Mayfair around Curzon Street, St James's Square, or Berkeley Square. A few miles away the Docklands financial industry is centered around Canary Wharf.

Canary Wharf is located on the site of the West India Docks on the Isle of Dogs, once one of the busiest ports in the world. In the 1980s, Michael von Clemm, former chairman of Credit Suisse First Boston, promoted the idea of converting the run-down, unused docks into a new business district. Today, major banks, along with legal, accounting, and media firms that support the financial services industry, occupy its glass towers. Canary Wharf symbolizes the changed economic geography of the UK and London's growth as a financial center.

New York's *FiDi* (Financial District) is similarly diffuse. For American journalist H.L. Mencken, Wall Street was "a thoroughfare that begins in a graveyard and ends in a river." Many Wall Street firms and hedge funds now congregate in Mid-Town. Others are based in Stamford, Connecticut, an hour from New York's Grand Central Station.

Wall Street is an idea—the power of money. The contrast between Wall Street and the Main Street symbolizes the clash between the interests of money and business and the interests of ordinary individuals. Steve Fraser subtitled his book on Wall Street *America's Dream Palace*, acknowledging its deep financial, political, ethical, and cultural significance.

New York focuses on the large domestic American market, its large companies, and investors. It raises money from American investors for foreign companies or helps foreign investors make American investments. New York has huge volumes in share trading; the New York Stock Exchange is the world's biggest market for trading stocks. America controls around 40 percent of the global investment management business, insurance companies, pension funds, mutual funds, and hedge funds. America has some of the world's largest commodities and derivative exchanges.

London is an entrepôt center—a trading post where goods were imported and exported, usually without paying duties. The City's origins are in its overseas trading network developed over centuries. London acts as a center matching borrowers and investors, most of whom are located outside the UK. London's *métier* is innovation and flexibility, especially in structured finance, complex derivatives, cross-border financing, and hybrid products combining insurance and banking.

London profits from its proximity to and capability to take advantage of legal, tax, and regulatory differentials in Europe and other places. The London Stock Exchange proclaims itself to be the most international capital market, with hundreds of international companies listed on its main market. London dominates European share trading, as well as global currency and derivatives trading.

London's role is all the more remarkable given that the UK's industrial power waned almost a century ago. Two world wars and the loss of empire inflicted physical, human, and economic damage.

Michael Lewis, describing Salomon Brothers' London office in the 1980s, identified a cultural problem:

> Our Englishmen...tended to be the refined products of the right schools...work was not an obsession or even...a concern.... [They] had a reputation...of sleeping late, taking long liquid lunches, and stumbling through their afternoons. One New York trader referred to them as Monty Python's Flying Investment Bankers.[3]

The feeling was mutual. One English merchant banker described Goldman Sachs as: "nothing more than high-priced interlopers who produce a massive stream of impractical ideas that have no relevance." The banker gave the Americans credit only "for making a lot of noise."[4]

Cool Britannia

Under Margaret Thatcher, things changed. Exchange controls were abandoned in 1979. Freer capital movements allowed London to recapture its position as an international market. In 1989 the government implemented the *Big Bang*, reforms ending the City's archaic practices. Financial regulations were overhauled, becoming more market friendly. In 2001 a single regulator—the Financial Services Authority (FSA)—was created to oversee financial markets.

London's resurgence was helped by Wall Street's stumbles. John F. Kennedy's interest equalization tax (closing access to the U.S. market for foreign borrowers) prompted the creation of the London based euro dollar market—attributed to Siegmund Warburg. Tighter regulations and accounting rules, such as the Sarbane-Oxley (SOX) laws passed in the aftermath of the Internet stock scandals, discouraged foreign companies from listing on American stock exchanges or raising money there.

London had two priceless advantages—location in the right time zone between the growing markets of Asia and the United States, and the primacy of English law in international finance.

The success of London as a financial center mirrors the prestigious annual Wimbledon Tennis Championships. The tournament is held in England, staffed by Englishmen (eastern Europeans and South Asians actually), contested and won generally by foreigners but generates wealth and cultural standing for the UK. The last English man and woman to have won a major title are Fred Perry in 1936 and Virginia Wade in 1977. London is a leading center for international finance where almost all the major players were American, European, Japanese, or Asian. A governor of the Bank of England suggested that this was precisely how things ought to be.[5]

London and the financial services sector became the engine for UK's growth and prosperity, supplanting the commercial and trading activity of the British Empire. Gordon Brown, the chancellor of the Exchequer under Tony Blair and then prime minister, harbored secret dreams of a Scandinavian-style social welfare state with low taxes funded by the growth of the City. In 2007, he told bankers: "What you have achieved for...financial services we...now aspire to achieve for the whole of the British economy." Alistair Darling, Gordon Brown's successor as chancellor, was no less loquacious describing financial services as "absolutely critical" to the economy. Ed

Balls, when economic secretary to the Treasury, perhaps harking back to his days as a journalist, was triumphal: "I have absolutely no hesitation when I say to you that London is—now, today—the world's greatest global financial center."[6] The mainly foreign bankers applauded.

Superlatives celebrated the new age:

> Italian derivative traders, American corporate financiers, Lebanese arbitrageurs, Dutch brokers, Moroccan rocket scientists, German bond salesman, Swiss equity market makers, Japanese swappers and even the stray Essex forex boy. There is no other financial center in the world with a talent pool to match that of the City.[7]

In the sixteenth century, Tome Pires, a Portuguese apothecary in *Suma Oriental*, an account of his travels, wrote similarly about the magical city of Malacca, then one of the most important trading ports in the world. Pires records no less than 84 languages being spoken in Malacca, more than equal to modern financial centers like London and New York.[8]

Barbarian Invasions

Minor financial centers also developed, usually concentrating in specific areas. Chicago became a dominant force in commodity and derivatives trading. Bets on currencies, shares, and bonds could be placed next to bets on corn, wheat, live hogs, and pork bellies. Geneva and Zurich emphasized discrete private banking and wealth management, augmented by favorable secrecy, tax, and regulatory regimes.

Asia and the Middle East built hubs from scratch. In the bubble economy of the 1980s, foreign banks flocked to Tokyo, dazzled by the large domestic market and the world's largest pool of savings. When the bubble burst in 1989 and the Japanese economy entered a prolonged recession, Tokyo slipped off the international radar.

Hong Kong and Singapore pursued ambitious programs built around their proximity to growing Asian markets, especially China and India. Shanghai and Mumbai increasingly aspired to this role. *Shang Kong*, a combination of Shanghai and Hong Kong, was mooted as a joint financial center providing a gateway to China.

Dubai drew on the Middle East's vast oil wealth, *petro-dollars*, to create the Dubai International Financial Centre (DIFC), offering freedom from tax, unrestricted foreign ownership, free movement of money and things unavailable in the region—alcohol and female companionship.

The DIFC, a 110-acre (45-hectare) city within a city, is dominated by the high-rise, architectural signature of money, especially the distinctive

15-story Gate building housing the executive offices of the DIFC Authority, regulators, and leading international financial institutions. The DIFC was not vaguely Arabic. Most of the businesses and workers were foreign, attracted by fairy tales of mythical wealth and tax-free salaries. The Emirates in United Arab Emirates seemed to stand for **E**nglish-**m**anaged **I**ndian-**r**un **A**rabs **t**aking **e**xcessive **s**alaries.

As the financial crisis hit, a belief that the emerging markets would be immune from the malaise led banks to seek refuge in new centers. Unemployed and underemployed bankers were told: "It's either Shanghai, Dubai, Mumbai or good-bye!"[9] In 2010, as Dubai experienced its own financial crisis, the DIFC's rents, once the second-most expensive after London, fell by two-thirds in a desperate effort to make the district more attractive.

Unlikely Centers

Ireland, historically a poor, agrarian economy, reinvented itself. In the 1970s, Ireland entered the European Union (EU) (then known as the European Economic Community). Influx of EU money, a well-educated population, low taxes, limited regulations, and business-friendly governments transformed Ireland into the *Celtic tiger*. In the late 1980s, Ireland established a financial center in Dublin—creatively named the International Financial Centre. Continental banks, especially from Germany, set up units in Dublin, raising money that was then channeled into various investments. Money flowed in and out, and profits were transferred back to the parent. The proximity to London helped.

Indigenous Irish banks grew rapidly, and a seemingly endless supply of easy money drove the Irish economy. Between 1997 and 2001, growth averaged around 9 percent per annum, faster than other comparable European countries. Output per person rose from $17,200 in 1995 to $33,000 in the early 2000s, 20 percent above the EU average.

The new prosperity centered on property, fueled by cheap and abundant debt. House prices spiraled ever higher, feeding a construction boom. Derelict parts of Dublin were converted into cultural facilities, eating and drinking places catering to the new financial classes.

If Ireland is an island off an island off the coast of Europe, then Iceland is an island off an island off an island off Europe. Iceland, too, reinvented itself through financial services. In 2003, the three largest banks in Iceland had assets equal to the country's modest annual domestic production. In the years that followed, the banks' assets grew to $140 billion, over eight times Iceland's domestic production. The banks raised money overseas and lent it to buy stocks and real estate.

Between 2003 and 2007 the Icelandic stock market increased by around 900 percent, while Reykjavik house prices tripled. Icelanders' wealth grew by around three times. Icelandic entrepreneurs fanned out across the globe, buying companies and making investments. The Icelandic banking system drove this unprecedented growth.

Financial centers, and the mobile, cosmopolitan financiers who worked in them, dominated the economies of developed nations. Federico García Lorca, the Spanish poet, once captured the essence of the cities of money:

> Rivers of gold flow there from all over the Earth, and death comes with it. There, as nowhere else, you feel a total absence of the spirit: herds of men who cannot count past three, herds more who cannot get past six, scorn for pure science and demoniacal respect for the present. And the terrible thing is that the crowd that fills the street believes that the world will always be the same and that it is their duty to keep that huge machine running, day and night, forever.[10]

History shows that financial centers are ephemeral. Pingyao, in the province of Shanxi, was China's banking capital in the nineteenth century under the Qing dynasty. At the height of the city's history, many banks operated in Pingyao, financing trade in silk, tea, and wool. Today, the Rishengchang, meaning "sunrise over prosperity," reputedly the first bank in China, is a museum. On display are the remains of opium dens and mahjong rooms where prostitutes, hired by the banks, were once used to win business from potential customers.

El-Dollardo Economics

Money also shaped the developing world in complex ways. Historically, many emerging countries were colonial properties of developed countries. *El-Dorado economics* emphasized conquest and plunder, especially of gold and silver that could be coined into money. All natural resources were exploited, including people, who could be enslaved or used as cheap labor. Colonialism was driven by its profits, expanding the power of the developed nations and spreading their religious and political philosophy.

Colonizers argued they brought civilization to indigenous populations. The reality was death, subjugation, displacement, or destruction of cultures and civilization, sometimes ancient. Commenting on the devastation wrought on the New World by transmission of Western diseases, one observer noted: "Europe had much to give and little to receive in the way of human infections."[11]

Following decolonization after the Second World War, former colonial powers established zones of influence using emerging nations as cheap sources of resources or labor or markets for Western goods. Over time, some countries with high rates of savings became sources of capital for developed countries. *El-Dollardo economics* now ruled a world of globalized trade and capital flows.

The Unbalanced Bicycle

China exemplified this new global monetary order. Under Deng Xiaoping, leader of the Communist Party from 1978, China undertook *Gaige Kaifang* (reforms and openness)—changing domestic, social, political, and economic policy. The centerpiece was economic reforms that combined socialism with elements of the market economy. In embracing markets, Deng famously observed: "It doesn't matter if a cat is black or white, so long as it catches mice."

Robert Hart, nineteenth-century British trade commissioner for China, once wrote: "[The] Chinese have the best food in the world, rice; the best drink, tea; and the best clothing; cotton, silk, fur. Possessing these staples and their innumerable native adjuncts, they do not need to buy a penny's worth elsewhere."[12] China now engaged with the global economy, reversing the traditional policy of economic self-reliance.

Modeled on the post-war recovery of Japan, China used trade to accelerate the growth and modernization of its economy. Special economic zones (SEZ), for example in Shenzen, located strategically close to Hong Kong, were established to encourage investment and industry, taking advantage of China's large, cheap labor force. Benefiting from rising costs in neighboring Asian countries, China attracted significant foreign investment, technology, management, and trading skills, from countries keen to outsource manufacturing to lower cost locations.

Parts of China became the world's factory of choice. Imported resources and parts were assembled or processed and then shipped out again. A buoyant global economy ensured a growing market for China's exports.

Deng represented a change in philosophy: "Poverty is not socialism. To be rich is glorious." The strategy proved startlingly effective, bringing about profound change. By 2011, Colonel Sanders and KFC were better recognized than Chairman Mao in China.

The strategy was decidedly trickle-down economics, as Deng himself acknowledged: "Let some people get rich first." Later, Deng would grouse: "Young leading cadres have risen up by helicopter. They should really rise step by step."

Foreign Treasure

China exported more than it imported, creating large foreign reserves that by 2011 totaled over $2.7 trillion. The Asian crisis of 1997–8 encouraged China to build even larger surpluses as protection against the destabilizing volatility of short-term foreign capital flows that almost destroyed many Asian countries. A history of political instability and the absence of extensive social welfare systems forced the Chinese to save a large portion of their income. The reserves and savings became a giant lending scheme, allowing China to finance and boost global trade, accelerating its own growth.

The build-up of foreign reserves in central banks of emerging markets and developing countries was really a liquidity creation scheme reliant on the U.S. dollar's position in trade and as a reserve currency in the post-Bretton-Woods era.[13]

Dollars received from exports and foreign investment have to be exchanged into Chinese renminbi. To maintain the competitiveness of exporters, China invested the foreign currency overseas to mitigate upward pressure on the renminbi. As reserves grew, China invested 60–70 percent of its reserves in dollar-denominated investments, primarily U.S. Treasury bonds and other high-quality securities. Only the large, liquid dollar money markets could accommodate China's large investment requirements. The historically unimpeachable credit quality of the United States was attractive. The recycled dollars flowed back to the United States, helping finance America's large trade and budget deficits.

Thomas Mun, a director of the East India Company, argued that the purpose of trade was to export more than you imported. Countries should amass *foreign treasure*, using it to acquire foreign colonies to control essential natural resources. The strategy required reducing domestic consumption and imports while increasing export of goods manufactured with imported foreign raw materials. China had followed Mun's seventeenth-century mercantilist policies.[14]

Global trade and investment (much of it export related) now drove China's economy. In 2007, Chinese Premier Wen Jiabao warned that Chinese growth was becoming increasingly "unstable, unbalanced, uncoordinated and ultimately unsustainable." China was not alone, as other countries such as Germany, Japan, South Korea, and Taiwan used similar strategies to boost growth.

Chinese funds helped keep American interest rates low, encouraging increasing levels of borrowing, especially among consumers. The increased debt fueled further consumption, housing, and stock market bubbles, enabling consumers to decrease savings as the paper value of investments rose. The consumption fed increased imports from China, creating further outflows of dollars via the growing trade deficit. The overvalued dollar and an undervalued renminbi exacerbated U.S. demand for imported goods.

Low U.S. interest rates also drove American pension funds and investors to seek out more risky investments. This fed the market for junk bonds, securitized debt, private equity, and hedge funds, which promised the higher returns needed to finance retirement income.

According to Andy Warhol, such behavior was innate: "Buying is...American.... In Europe and the Orient people like to trade—buy and sell, sell and buy—they're basically merchants...[Americans] really like...to buy—people, money, countries."[15] In 2006, the economic historian Niall Ferguson and economist Moritz Schularick termed this symbiotic relationship *Chimerica*. The neologism combined the two countries but also referred to the legendary *chimera*—a grotesque monster of the imagination.[16]

Fool's Gold

An economic order where some nations save and others borrow this money to fund consumption, buying goods from the savers, is inherently unstable. China had effectively lent Americans the money to purchase its goods and now faced the prospects that the loans would never be repaid.

Deterioration in the U.S. economy and additional borrowing placed increasing pressure on the U.S. government's debt rating, reducing the value of Treasury bonds and the currency. The inscription on dollar bills—"In God we trust"—probably needed to read "I hope my redeemer liveth."[17] Premier Wen Jiabao expressed China's concern: "If anything goes wrong in the U.S. financial sector, we are anxious about the safety and security of Chinese capital."[18]

China's trillions in foreign currency reserves, a large proportion denominated in dollars, could not be sold without massive losses because of their sheer size, far larger than the normal trading volumes. China was learning Keynes' famous observation: "If I owe you a pound, I have a problem; but if I owe you a million, the problem is yours."

China tried to reduce the purchase of dollars, switching into real assets like commodities. But China was forced to purchase more dollars and U.S. Treasury bonds to preserve the value of *existing* holdings. Forty years ago, John Connally, then the U.S. Treasury secretary, accurately identified China's problem: "It may be our currency, but it's your problem."[19]

In investing its reserves and savings heavily in dollars, China had stepped on a bounding mine, which does not explode when you step on it but when you *step off*. The Chinese used to refer to dollars affectionately as *mei jin*, literally "American gold." China's dollar investments were not the real thing—merely iron pyrite, *fool's gold*.

Liquidity Vortex

Money was now central to everything. Global money flows were built on traditional domestic banks, which pushed leverage to extreme levels. Off-balance-sheet structures added to the supply of money. The foreign exchange treasure maintained by China and other nations were another part of the global credit process. The export of savings, such as Japanese savings via the yen carry trade, was a further part.

This money pulsed through the world, pumping up the price of assets to create the illusion of wealth, transforming individual lives, businesses, cities, and entire countries. Through prices, financial markets provided a real-time poll on government policies and corporate decisions. But as Charles Mackay observed in 1841: "Money…has often been a cause of the delusion of the multitudes. Sober nations have all at once become desperate gamblers, and risked almost their existence upon the turn of a piece of paper."[20] John Maynard Keynes, too, warned about speculation:

> Speculators may do no harm as bubbles on a steady stream of enterprise. But the position is serious when enterprise becomes the bubble on a whirlpool of speculation. When the capital development of a country becomes a by-product of the activities of a casino, the job is likely to be ill done.[21]

As the financial crisis hit, it became clear that the power of money to transform economies, business, and lives had been greatly over-estimated. The amount of money available was also far less than thought. It had just been the same money that had flowed around ever faster. When asked what happened to his fortune, the soccer star George Best responded: "I spent 90 percent of my money on women, drink and fast cars. The rest I wasted!" Slowly, the world awoke to the realization that it had wasted a staggering amount of wealth that did not exist in the first place.

6

Money Honey

The scholar Marshall McLuhan elliptically noted that "the medium is the message." The medium is newspapers, books, television, and increasingly the Internet. The message now was *money*. Banker Walter Wriston anticipated it: "Information about money has become almost as important as money itself."[1]

Once, newspapers gave more space to sport than financial news. When asked about the reason, Richard Harwood, the assistant managing editor of the *Washington Post*, replied: "I guess it is because we think sport is more interesting to readers than business and economics. I know it is to me."[2] In the 1980s, business and financial news went mainstream, reflecting the increasing importance of money matters. The world rapidly became an endless discussion of money, directed at people who either did not have much of it or had a lot.

Printing It

In 1888, Horatio Bottomley launched the *Financial Times (FT)*, originally known as the *London Financial Guide*, a four-page journal targeting the financiers in the City. In 1889, Dow Jones created *The Wall Street Journal (WSJ)*, the *Journal*, for the financial community in the north east of America. The FT sought to be the friend of "the honest financier and the respectable broker." The WSJ sought to provide readers with facts on the market.

Today, newspapers provide a mix of company news, market news, and political developments as they might affect the market. Most take American broadcaster Ted Koppel's advice seriously: "People shouldn't expect the mass media to do investigative stories. That job belongs to the 'fringe' media."

If someone is directly quoted in a story, then they are generally seeking to lift their profile. A "source close to the company" is the time-honored method of leaking a story that would cost you your job. "Market sources" refers to simple gossip. Politician Donald Rumsfeld summed it up: "Anyone who knows anything isn't talking and anyone with any sense isn't talking. Therefore, the people that are talking to the media, by definition, are people who don't know anything and people who don't have a hell of a lot of sense."[3]

Specialized magazines cater to the fetishes of their target audience. There are even newsletters that report on the average recommendations of other investment newsletters: "the path of least resistance continues to be up."

Personal finance writers provide sound tips for financial success. If you give up a $4 Starbuck's latte each day for 40 years, you will save $1,460 each year, $58,400 over 40 years. If you can invest the savings in the market at the end of every year and earn 20 percent each year on your investment, what will you have at the end of 40 years? $10,722,032. If you invest your $121.67 savings from foregone lattes at the end of each month, you will have $20,365,160 in your latte retirement fund. As Albert Einstein supposedly noted "compound interest is the eighth wonder of the world."

Column Inches

Columnists, *name* journalists or authorities known for being famous rather than for their output, express opinions on the topic *du jour*. Opinion pieces provide opportunities for banks to get their views in front of the masses. Only the fact that the piece is attributed to the analyst (for personal recognition) and the company (for marketing value) is important. It helps to come up with the *big idea*.

In 2001, Jim O'Neill, an analyst with Goldman Sachs, came up with the BRIC (Brazil, Russia, India, and China) economies. CRIB was rejected as infantile. It was marketing genius. The now ubiquitous acronym pithily captured the increasing power of emerging countries in the global economy. As investors and companies flooded into the BRIC economies, Goldmans, the *thought leaders*, earned large fees from providing advice, raising money, and investing it. In India in 2007, when a fund management company was listed on the Mumbai Stock Exchange, its share price went up sharply because one of the management team had worked with O'Neill on the BRIC research.

In 2010, O'Neill introduced a new acronym for favored *frontier* markets—CIVETS (Colombia, Indonesia, Vietnam, Egypt, Turkey, and South Africa). A cat-like omnivore, whose musky anal gland secretions are the basic ingredient for perfumes, replaced the solidity of building materials. Eager for column inches, a competitor coined the term MIST (Mexico, Indonesia, South Korea, and Turkey).

In early 2011, as North Africa and the Middle East, including Egypt, was rent apart by political uprisings, an anonymous blogger joked that emerging market investors were hunting in the "MIST" for "CIVETS" with only a "BRIC."

Sure-fire moneymaking ideas are highly sought after. Comedians John Bird and John Fortune (the Long Johns) captured the quality of financial advice in a YouTube comedy sketch. One John tells the other that State Street Global Markets has issued research stating that "market participants did not know whether to buy the rumor, sell the news, do the opposite, do both, or do neither, depending on which way the wind is blowing." Then, a few days later, ABN-AMRO analysts provided clients with even more telling advice: "we are back to 'happy days' again."[4]

In early 2010, a controversy developed in Australia over financial institutions paying news networks to allow their analysts to appear on news bulletins. Was this advertising? The media regulator ruled that the financial news did not constitute a *factual program* and therefore it did not have to investigate the matter.[5]

Zdener Urbanek, the dissident Czech novelist, observed that assumptions about what was written are dangerous:

> In dictatorships.... We believe nothing of what we read in the newspapers and nothing of what we watch on television, because we know it's propaganda and lies. Unlike you in the West. We've learned to look behind the propaganda and to read between the lines and, unlike you, we know that the real truth is always subversive.[6]

Thomas Jefferson, the third president of the United States, agreed: "The man who reads nothing at all is better educated than the man who reads nothing but newspapers."

Video Money

Financial TV in the United States was once the permanently tanned, urbane Louis Rukeyser and *Wall Street Week*. Rukeyser, a journalist, became an award-winning presenter, helping educate ordinary people about economics and business. Rukeyser was calm, measured, plainspoken, and thoughtful. Discussing a hairpiece manufacturer, he quipped: "If your money seems to be hair today and gone tomorrow, we'll try to make it grow back by giving the bald facts on how to get your investments toupee."[7]

The arrival of cable and satellite news channels, CNBC (formerly the Consumer News and Business Channel) and Bloomberg, specializing in coverage of business and financial markets, changed financial TV globally. The networks broadcast throughout the day, providing reports on business, updates on financial markets, stock market indices and commodities prices, interviews with chief executives and business leaders, and commentary. The growing interest in stocks and money matters culminated in the *day trader* phenomenon.

Most day traders were small-time investors risking their own money—American Mrs. Watanabes trading part time. Between 1997 and 2000, during the euphoric dot.com bubble, day traders traded stocks like Intel or Microsoft as well as ephemeral companies like pets.com or boo.com. Day traders made large numbers of trades during a single day as they bought and sold online in a frenzy to take advantage of news and opportunities. Some day traders worked out of *trading alleys* housing *stations* (a desk and computer with high-speed connection to the electronic broker). In the corner, a large plasma screen TV was permanently tuned to CNBC or Bloomberg.

From 1997 to 2000, as the NASDAQ rose from 1,200 to 5,000, investors with next to no experience made substantial profits buying and selling technology stocks. Professional traders made larger profits, exploiting the arbitrage opportunities created by day traders. In March 2000, the dot.com bubble burst, temporarily ending the day trading bubble.

Studs, Starlets

When Rukeyser's show ended after 32 years, new stars emerged in the United States—"Mad" Jim Cramer, Money Honey, the Street Sweetie, and Suze Orman. If Rukeyser was sedate charm and genteel bonhomie, then the new financial news presenters were studs and starlets of *financial pornography*.

The new era was defined by Jim Cramer, host of CNBC's *Mad Money*, making loud animal noises, doing his Ozzy Osbourne routine and abusing guests as he doled out stock tips. Appearing on TV in a diaper to illustrate the relationship between Kimberly-Clark, a consumer products company, and the price of oil, Cramer explained:

> I was going through all the different ingredients in a diaper, and it's all the ethyls, you know, the polypropylene, polyethylene, polyvinyl.... So, right before the camera starts, I pull the diaper on...and I do the whole piece straight, and I know that I've got people's attention because I'm wearing the diaper.[8]

Maria Bartiromo allegedly tried to get trademark protection of her nickname—"Money Honey." Like many TV financial anchors, she frequently *is* the news. In 2007, she was featured in a story involving Todd Thompson, a senior CitiGroup executive, and the bank's corporate jet. Thompson left the bank shortly afterward. The incident fueled jokes harking back to an earlier era when a senior banker married a stewardess on the corporate jet: "Before landing, please return the flight attendant to the upright position."

Erin Burnett is the "Street Sweetie." On the *Morning Joe* program on MSNBC, commenting on a clip showing President Bush with two other world leaders, Burnet referred to the president as the "monkey in the middle." Given her own show, *Street Signs*, Street Sweetie was keen to interview important people the world cared about—CEOs, presidents, and Angelina Jolie.

The biggest star in the firmament is the polymath Susan "Suze" Orman—award-winning TV host, financial adviser, best-selling author, and $80,000-per-speech motivational speaker. She hosts *The Suze Orman Show*, a weekend financial advice show on CNBC, and *Suze Orman's Financial Freedom* on QVC.

Her hallmark "Can I afford it?" segment has callers asking Orman's permission to borrow money or purchase a must-have item. Orman's response, untypical of the age, is generally virulently *anti-debt*, drawing on her own life experiences. Callers with high levels of debt are advised not to borrow more, in her characteristic Joan Rivers' hectoring style peppered with well-practiced slogans from her books: "People first, then money, then things"; "Truth creates money. Lies destroy it."

Suze Orman is a charismatic melange of pop psychologist, trusted counselor, and tele-evangelist. Orman's common sense channels Benjamin Franklin's *Poor Richard's Almanac* and *The Way to Wealth*: "a penny saved is a penny earned." Her anticonsumerism and antimaterialism message sells.

Cramer's diaper stunt and Orman's "Can I afford it?" segment are both deeply symbolic of the new *anyone-can-become-rich* age of money that financial TV portrays.

Financial Porn

Financial TV is pornography—sleazy, intrusive, seeking to titillate, and shock. During a crisis, these programs can be compulsive. Once, pornographic scripts had a passing interest in improbable plot and implausible dialogue. In the Coen brothers' film *The Big Lebowski,* Jackie Treehorn bemoans falling standards in adult entertainment. Competition from cheap amateur pornographic films means that professionals can no longer afford the extra investment in story, production value, and feeling. Financial TV never bothered with plot, dialogue, or production values, focusing only on the action.

The 24/7 Joycean stream-of-consciousness financial noise machine calls for successive, rolling segments—pre-market, market, post-market, recapping today's market and, finally, looking forward to tomorrow's market. The formula requires an anchor or two. The only part of Louis Rukeyser's legacy that survives is the fashion sense. Rukeyser was voted the best-dressed man in finance and America's most sartorially elegant TV host. *Playboy* magazine described him as a "rakish raconteur." Today's TV hosts are well dressed, impeccably groomed, and perfectly coiffed.

Rudimentary sets create the illusion of overlooking a frenetic exchange or a city panorama, made possible by computer imagery. The occasional outside shot on the steps of a stock exchange or outside some monumental bank headquarters interrupts the visual monotony.

The fare is constant financial news and interviews with in-house (paid) and outside (unpaid) *experts*. A ticker-stream of breaking stories and market information scrolls along the peripheries of the screen. Graphs and various visuals assault the senses. The soundtrack is a series of video game noises, typically when the screen changes. The amphetamine-charged pace features interviewers and guests repeatedly interrupting and constantly talking over each other. Presenters take the title of CNBC's signature show—*Squawk Box*—literally.

The editorial approach requires drama:

> Human beings have an innate desire to be told and to tell dramatic stories.... I am at a loss to name a single operatic work that treats coronary artery disease as its subject but I can name several where murder, incest, and assassination play a key part in the story.[9]

This is money, Jerry Springer or Howard Stern *shock-jock* style.

Speedy Money

Through the day, a succession of guests is interviewed on the topic of the moment—news, just released statistics, government policy announcements, or the latest *good* or *bad* news. TV follows its print rival: "If it bleeds, it leads!" The aim is to shed light on the impact of the news *on the market*. But as Donald Rumsfeld astutely observed: "The problem is that people think that news is something that is announced before it happens, as opposed to something that is reported when it does happen."[10]

Each interview is about 5 to 10 minutes—only divine beings get longer. Presenters are unlikely "to use a word that might send a reader to the dictionary" (to use William Faulkner's observation about Ernest Hemingway).

Sensible interviewees offer equivocal opinions to preserve plausible deniability. Rumsfeld once masterfully set out the mechanisms of evasion: "I'm working my way over to figuring out how I won't answer."[11] The alternative is former U.S. Vice-President Dan Quayle's formula: "I believe we are on an irreversible trend toward more freedom and democracy—but that could change."

There are experts who do not know: "I was born not knowing and have had only a little time to change that here and there."[12] There are those who have theories: "If the facts don't fit the theory, change the facts."[13] There are the fanatics: "one who can't change his mind and won't change the subject."[14] Then there are politicians, like Sarah Palin, a former governor of Alaska and vice-presidential candidate: "Well, let's see. There's—of course—in the great history of America rulings, there have been rulings."[15]

In 1891 W.J. Stillman, writing in the *Atlantic Monthly*, commented about the effects of an earlier technological innovation—the telegraph—on journalistic standards:

> [It has] transformed journalism from what it once was, the periodical expression of the thought of the time, the opportune record of the questions and answers of contemporary life, into an agency for collecting, condensing and assimilating the trivialities of the entire human existence.... The frantic haste with which we bolt everything we take, seconded by the eager wish of the journalist not to be a day behind his competitor, abolishes deliberation from judgment and sound digestion from our mental constitutions. We have no time to go below surfaces.[16]

During the global financial crisis, CNBC's *Power Lunch* hosted a segment—"Turning the corner"—with Dr. Doom, Nouriel Roubini, together with the former derivative trader, financial philosopher, and best-selling author known variously as Nassim Taleb, Nicholas Nassim Taleb, NNT, or simply the *Black Swan* (his best-known work).

Bill Griffeth, the interviewer, and his co-host Michelle Caruso-Cabrera, started off upbeat: "What would it take to make you bearish on this economy right now?" Dr. Doom summarized the position: "It's ugly!" Dr. Doom's prophecy that the current recession was likely to be three times as long and three times as deep as previous recent recessions did not please Griffeth: "But that's not the end of the world, is it?" The Black Swan was gloomy: "We have the same people in charge, those who did not see the crisis coming." The hosts tried in vain to look for positive statements.

On live TV, the more dubious a proposition or unreliable a fact, the greater the authority and confidence with which it is stated. Constant repetition diminishes skepticism. Rumors, suppositions, and half-baked statistics become believable and ultimately accepted facts.

Analysis of Jim Cramer's *Mad Money* share buy-and-sell recommendations show that the recommendations affect share prices of the companies mentioned but that the effects are short-lived. His stock recommendations are neither extraordinarily good nor unusually bad, whatever their entertainment value.[17]

Stock traders have cited the *Rukeyser Effect*—mention on *Wall Street Week* could cause a spike in the company's stock price. There was little relationship between the mention and the stock's performance,[18] a claim that Rukeyser strongly disputed. One commentator provided an ingenious defense: "It is mathematically impossible for the thirty million viewers of this show to beat the market, since they are the market."[19]

The global financial crisis painfully exposed many Wall Street media savvy stars that failed to anticipate the sharp turn in financial fortunes. Bennett W. Goodspeed, best known for *The Tao Jones Averages*, a treatise on *whole-brained* investing, used the phrase *articulate incompetents* to describe money-losing fund managers and financiers who frequently appeared in the media.

Bill Gross, a founder of the investment management firm Pimco (Pacific Investment Management Company), cleverly used the opportunities afforded by financial TV. Articulate, witty, and attractive, Gross became a regular on Louis Rukeyser's *Wall Street Week*. Gross acknowledged the benefits of his ubiquitous media presence: "It doesn't do you any good to be good if nobody knows about you."[20]

Simon Johnson, a former chief economist for the International Monetary Fund and a professor at the Sloan School of Management at MIT, observed: "I think we pay undue deference to people who are very rich and have been successful in the financial sector in this country. We think they are the gurus who think they have unique expertise, and if Bill Gross tells us there will be a panic, it must be true."[21]

Jon Stewart, host of *The Daily Show*, joined in endorsing financial TV: "If I had only followed CNBC's advice, I'd have a million dollars today, provided that I'd started with $100 million."

Literary Money

The literate read money books—investment books, trading books, memoirs, biographies of the rich, sure-fire strategies from financial gurus, history of money books, financial disaster books, or multi-volume technical books full of stochastic calculus and the recipe for chocolate financial muffins. Books like *Why the Real Estate Boom Will Not Bust*, *Profit from Property*, *Secrets of Wealth* or *Why the Bust is Really a Boom* reflect the words of *Daily Show*'s Jon Stewart: "You cannot, in today's world, judge a book by its contents."

Books on money are examples of a well-defined genre—the self-improvement book, once feared and avoided. In one Monty Python skit on such endeavors, a man opens his door to find a self-confessed burglar, only allowing him into the house after repeated assurances that he really is a burglar and not an encyclopedia salesman.

Books on money hide a dirty secret—everybody wants a do-it-yourself plan to get rich, quickly and easily. Investment results tell a different story. Groucho Marx remarked at the time of the 1929 stock market crash (writing in *Groucho and Me*): "Some of the people I know lost millions. I was luckier. All I lost was two hundred and forty thousand dollars.... I would have lost more but that was all the money I had."

In 1999, James Glassman and Kevin Hassett published a book—*36,000: The New Strategy for Profiting from the Coming Rise in the Stock Market*. Glassman, an investment columnist for the *Washington Post*, and Hassett, a former senior economist with the Federal Reserve, inverted normal investment logic by arguing that over the long term shares were no riskier than bonds and that the traditional risk premium (higher return) demanded by investors could be eliminated. The Dow Jones Industrial Average, trading at the time around 11,000, was forecast to more than triple.

In a 1929 article "Everybody ought to be rich" in the *Ladies' Home Journal*, John Raskob, a director of General Motors, wrote in a similar vein. An investment in shares of just $15 a month would, with dividends reinvested, increase in value to about $80,000 after 20 years. But Raskob, the man who wanted his readers to invest in stock for long-term wealth, was selling his shares even before his article appeared, avoiding the 1929 crash.

In support of their argument, Glassman and Hassett pointed to the fact that 6 years earlier in January 1993 the Dow had been around 3,300. A reviewer in the *Publishers Weekly* noted the only thing missing was an exhortation to buy stocks for the Gipper—one George Gipp, an American college football player, immortalized by Knute Rockne's famous "Win just one for the Gipper" speech later used as a political slogan by Ronald Reagan. For many authors (David Elias, *Dow 40,000: Strategies for Profiting from the Greatest Bull Market in History*; Charles W. Kadlec, *Dow 100,000*), it was an act of faith that the stock market would go up. Louis Rukeyser once drew investors' attention to the risk of falling as well as rising markets: "Trees don't grow to the sky."[22]

Glassman and Hassett's book was not without fans. One reviewer on Amazon.com was very grateful: "This book was one of the reasons I got completely out of the stock market in late '99 early 2000. When I read this pustulous piece of putrescent puffery I just knew I had to get out. THANK YOU KEVIN AND JAMES!!!!!" Another Amazon reviewer was concerned about the possibility of an inadvertent error: "What a strange place to find a typo misprint! But overall, surely this book is too pessimistic. Times may be hard, but it doesn't seem likely that the Dow will really fall as low as 3,600. If it does, that will surely be the time to buy!"

Like Irving Fisher, the eminent but unfortunate Yale economist who in 1929 suggested publicly that stock prices had reached "a permanent and high plateau" shortly before the great stock market crash, Glassman and Hassett got the timing wrong. The dot.com bubble burst shortly after the book was published. Undeterred by Glassman and Hassett's experience, in the early 2000s Robert Zuccaro published *Dow, 30,000 by 2008—Why It's Different This Time.* The author graciously admitted that some of his conclusions clashed with conventional opinions.

At the time of writing, the market is trading at around 13,000 and has never touched the 36,000 level or even 30,000. Glassman and Hassett argued that they never suggested that the Dow would be at 36,000 soon. They should have taken E.M. Forster's counsel: "No author is entitled to whine. He was not obliged to be an author."

The only way to get rich from a *get-rich* book may be to follow Brother Ty's seventh law—write a really successful get-rich book. Brother Ty is a fictional character in Christopher Buckely and John Tierney's book *My Broker: A Monk Tycoon Reveals the 7 1/2 Laws of Spiritual Growth*. Brother Ty struggles to poke fun at the real genre. Get-rich investment and trading-secrets books are already inadvertently funny because of their fatuous seriousness and absence of irony or self-deprecation.

Bernard Baruch, the famous financier and investor, once offered the following guide to investment success:

> If you are ready and able to give up everything else, to study the whole history and background of the market and all the principal companies whose stocks are on the board as carefully as a medical student studies anatomy, to glue your nose at the tape at the opening of every day of the year and never take it off till night; if you can do all that and in addition you have the cool nerves of a great gambler, the sixth sense of a kind of clairvoyant, and the courage of a lion, you have a chance.[23]

Money for All

From modest origins as a mechanism of exchange and store of value, money has evolved into something much more. Infinitely malleable, it is the reflection of the world, but also a shaper of worlds.

Individual lives and business activities are increasingly molded by money. Banks and financiers have become dominant forces in the world. The interplay of the real world and its endless monetary reflection now drives economies and cities. News about money is everywhere and deeply embedded in popular culture. It is a fragile construction that echoes Marshall McLuhan: "All media exist to invest our lives with artificial perceptions and arbitrary values."

In 1999, with the American economy in the grip of a speculative mania, *Wired*, the magazine that exemplified the dot.com era, envisioned *ultra prosperity*. By 2020, average household income in the United States would triple to $150,000, and families would be served by their very own household chefs.[24] The Dow would be at least 50,000, probably on its way to 100,000. The arithmetic behind the forecasts was vague.

In the summer of 1999, James Glassman, enjoying the attention that *Dow 36,000* was receiving, faced off against Barton Biggs, Morgan Stanley's skeptical equity strategist, in a debate on the *new economy*. Glassman argued that the Internet was the most important invention of the twentieth century. He was mirroring the views of Kevin Kelly, executive editor of *Wired*:

> How many times in the history of mankind have we wired up the planet to create a single marketplace? How often have entire new channels of commerce been created by digital technology? When has money itself been transformed into thousands of instruments of investment?[25]

Biggs argued that the entire reasoning was fatuous but lost the debate 180 votes to 2 on a show of hands. Even his wife voted against him.[26]

Faith in money was now everything. Finance fundamentalism ruled.

Part II

Fundamentalism

Fundamentalism—movement that stresses the superiority, infallibility, and authority of its beliefs in matters of faith, morals, history, and prophecy.

The "financial revolution" elevated economic theory to the status of an all-powerful religion.

The central belief was the ability to create continuous growth and improved living standards, without destructive "boom-bust" economic cycles. Policy makers and economists would achieve these outcomes by adjusting the economic flight controls. Camouflaged as a "science" in dense jargon and mathematics, the system was actually political ideology focused on the role of markets and governments in economies. The ideas of influential economists, like John Maynard Keynes and Milton Friedman, were subsumed into political agendas to shape the money economy.

7

Los Cee-Ca-Go Boys

For a quarter of a century, the Berlin Wall symbolized the difference between the free markets of the West and the socialist economies of the East. On June 12, 1987, speaking at the Brandenburg Gate to commemorate the 750th anniversary of Berlin, U.S. President Ronald Reagan issued a challenge to Mikhail Gorbachev, the general secretary of the Communist Party of the Soviet Union: "Tear down this wall!" On November 9, 1989, the Berlin Wall came down.

At the fall of the Wall, when asked "Who won?", Western political scientists cited the triumph of capitalism over socialism. The economists' response was "Chicago." The University of Chicago radically changed how the world thought about economics, politics, and business, with a system based on: "belief in the efficacy of the free market as a means for organizing resources…skepticism about government intervention into economic affairs and…emphasis on the quantity theory of money as a key factor in producing inflation."[1]

In the early part of the twentieth century, work in theoretical physics was centered around the Cavendish Laboratory (Cambridge, England), Göttingen (Germany), and the Institute of Theoretical Physics (Copenhagen, Denmark). Under Niels Bohr, the Nobel-prize-winning Danish physicist, and his German protégé Werner Heisenberg, the "Copenhagen Interpretation" became dominant. Generations of physicists once asked: "What is

Copenhagen's view of this?" Generations of economists now asked: "What is Chicago's view of this?" As remote from real life as quantum physics, the Chicago School was highly influential for more than 50 years.

Dismal Science

Thomas Carlyle, the Victorian historian, christened economics the "dismal science." American satirist P.J. O'Rourke described economics as "an entire scientific discipline of not knowing what you're talking about."[2]

Economics focuses on how production and financial systems work or should work. *Macroeconomics* focuses on growth, employment, production, inflation, and monetary and government budgetary (fiscal) policy. *Microeconomics* tries to analyze the behavior of firms or individuals, and how things like prices are determined and markets work.

In his 1776 work *The Wealth of Nations*, Adam Smith argued for a self-regulating market system in which narrow self-interest could order economic activity:

> It is not from the benevolence of the butcher, the brewer, or the baker that we expect our dinner, but from their regard to their own interest. We address ourselves, not to their humanity but to their self-love, and never talk to them of our own necessities but of their advantages.[3]

Capitalism created wealth and progress, but at high social cost. Economic theory was preoccupied with the business cycle—especially painful and disruptive *boom-bust* cycles.

The 1929 stock market crash brought to an end the long boom of the jazz age. During this period, led by the United States, the world's dominant economy, there were sharp increases in economic activity and the prices of stocks, commodities, and other assets. The crash was the largest fall in share prices ever recorded, with the U.S. market collapsing by around 90 percent and taking 25 years to recover its pre-crash highs. In the recession that followed, U.S. prices fell by one-third and unemployment reached 25 percent of the workforce. Global trade collapsed. The recession turned into the Great Depression, from which the world would not emerge until after the Second World War.

President Herbert Hoover sought to keep budgets balanced, preserve a sound currency, and avoid interfering in the adjustment process. The U.S. government refused to bail out banks. The Federal Reserve tightened the supply of money to maintain the value of the dollar. Economic orthodoxy dictated that the fall in values and elimination of bad loans or unsound investments would lead to recovery. It was *tough love*.

As the depression threatened to overwhelm societies, John Maynard Keynes argued for government spending to stimulate demand by supporting income and spending power. He broadened the remit of governments to manage the economy: "[the answer] is not to be found in abolishing booms and thus keeping us permanently in a semi-slump; but in abolishing slumps and thus keeping us permanently in a quasi-boom."[4]

Frederick Hayek, a prominent member of the Austrian School, opposed any interference in markets. Downturns were essential to allow capitalism and markets to purge and renew themselves. If Keynes' views were shaped by the Great Depression, then Hayek's quest for idealistic renewal was influenced by the epic collapse of the Austro-Hungarian Empire in the First World War.

Keynes' *General Theory of Employment, Interest and Money*, Hayek believed, was primarily motivated by the political and economic problems of the period. Keynesian economics would not solve the problems but would create inflation. Keynes was equally critical of Hayek's work, commenting that one article started "with a mistake" and then moved on to "bedlam." Another article constituted "a farrago of nonsense." Although he got on well with the Austrian personally, and thought Hayek's 1944 *The Road to Serfdom* was "a grand book," Keynes was unpersuaded, concluding: "what rubbish his theory is."[5]

Joseph Schumpeter's worldview was shaped by his role as Austria's minister of finance, paying off debts incurred in the collapse of central European financial institutions. Intending to be the world's greatest economist, lover, and horseman, the colorful, thrice-married Austrian acknowledged only having to work at his horsemanship. Capitalism's strength, Schumpeter argued, was *creative destruction*, where economic incentives encouraged entrepreneurs to develop new ideas to take advantage of profit opportunities, sweeping away old defunct businesses and processes. The destruction was the inevitable and unavoidable cost of a vibrant system that renewed itself periodically.

Schumpeter saw the Great Depression as part of the adjustment that would wipe out unsustainable debts and poor investments, allowing economic renewal. Keynesian economics was legitimizing interference in the natural process.

For many politicians and economists, the severity of the Great Depression, the inability of markets to restore full employment and the rising human cost highlighted the failure of the *invisible hand*. Keynes gained credence and, for the next four decades, dominated economic thinking and policy. The ability of governments and central banks to fine-tune the economy through a judicious mix of budgetary and monetary policy as well as regulation became accepted faith.

In the 1960s, the University of Chicago's Milton Friedman challenged Keynes as the foremost public figure in economics of the twentieth century. The Chicago Interpretation updated and reinstated classical economic theory with a dash of pure laissez-faire economics. Proof that markets were self-adjusting was couched in elegant, impenetrable statistical analysis. Like quantum physics, economics now relied on mathematics to describe reality.

The physicist Paul Dirac observed that: "In physics, we try to tell people in such a way that they understand something that nobody knew before. In the case of poetry, it's the exact opposite."[6] Economics, as practiced at Chicago, with its mix of dogma, political fundamentalism, and mathematics, was neither poetry nor physics.

Theories—rational expectations, real business cycle theory, portfolio theory, efficient market hypothesis, capital structure theory, capital asset pricing models, option pricing, agency theory—rolled off the academic production line. Many economists received recognition in the form of the Nobel prize in Economics (technically the "Severige Riksbank [Swedish Central Bank] Prize in Economic Sciences in Memory of Alfred Nobel" founded in 1968). Some historians assert that every recent economics Nobel prize winner was either from the University of Chicago, was at Chicago at the time of doing their prize-winning work, had at some time visited the city or had simply inhaled the campus air—especially bottled and sent to them.

In January 1971, Richard Nixon recanted opposition to budget deficits, borrowing a 1965 line from Milton Friedman: "Now, I am a Keynesian." Nixon was late; the Chicago Interpretation was already ascendant.

Chicago Interpretation

Founded in 1833, Chicago's location near a portage between the Great Lakes and the Mississippi river watershed made the city a transportation, trading, and industrial hub. Travelers could smell the stockyards and abattoirs before they actually reached Chicago: "It was an elemental [odor], raw and crude; it was rich, almost rancid, sensual and strong."[7] Rudyard Kipling, the British author, described Chicago as: "a gilded rabbit warren…full of people talking about money and spitting."[8]

Chicago was the ultimate trading city, the middleman to every transaction. The city became a financial hub, especially for derivative trading on the Chicago Board of Trade (CBOT) and the Chicago Mercantile Exchange (CME or the Merc). The University of Chicago exported the city's trading and market ethos to the rest of the world.

The Chicago Interpretation emphasized free markets, the primacy of individual rights, economics as a science based on empirical hypothesis testing, and the application of economic theory to all problems, even sumo wrestling. "The market always 'works'…government is always part of the problem, rather than part of the solution."[9] The rough and tumble of Chicago's markets permeated the university's teaching methods. Workshops were brutal, referred to as "bullfights" or "gunfights": "They are a bloodbath."[10] The economics was ideological, pursued with religious zeal and bigotry.

The Chicago School was the creature initially of the notoriously difficult and brilliant Frank Knight and the ferocious Jacob Viner. Knight favored laissez-faire systems but regarded capitalism as ethically indefensible. He is best remembered for his work on risk and uncertainty, and his student 1976 Nobel laureate Milton Friedman. If Knight created the first Chicago School, then Friedman created the second Chicago School.

Friedman, in the words of *The Economist*, "the most influential economist of the second half of the 20th century…possibly of all of it," made significant contributions in monetary history and theory (known as *monetarism*), consumption analysis, and stabilization policy. He had a natural affinity to free market economies and individual freedom. Leonard Silk, *The New York Times* economic writer, observed: "Adam Smith is generally hailed as the father of modern economics and Milton Friedman as his most distinguished son."[11]

Fiercely argumentative and a natural debater, Friedman reveled in the role of an influential public intellectual. In a series of popular books, including *Capitalism and Freedom* and *Free to Choose* (based on a TV series of the same name), he argued that governments could only provide a framework of enforceable contracts, secure property rights, fair competition, stable money, and limited protection for the "irresponsible." In *Capitalism and Freedom*, Friedman listed activities that the American government should not undertake, including farming subsidies, tariffs and trade quotas, minimum wages, rent control, national parks, postal services, and the regulation of various industries, especially banking. The intellectual struggle between Keynes and Friedman shaped the age of extreme money.

Economic Politics

After the Great Depression, Keynesian demand management required economists to adjust taxation and government spending to engineer desired growth levels. There was an accepted trade-off between inflation and unemployment, known as the *Phillips curve*, named after a New Zealand economist.

The Chicago School favored free markets and limited regulation. Wealth redistribution would take capital from productive sectors, transferring it to less productive activities. There was deep ambivalence about governments. Minimizing taxes would starve the beast, decreasing its ability to fund unproductive programs. The agenda reflected the social conservatism of the principals. The Cold War shaped resistance against socialism, which Keynesian economics was associated with. Chicago Business School Professor Merton Miller's distrust of behavioral economics was based on an antipathy toward "commies."[12]

Ayn Rand, the Russian-born philosopher and writer, was a major influence. Her 1943 novel *The Fountainhead* portrayed the struggle of Howard Roark, a young architect who fought against compromise in a world dominated by "second handers." *The New York Times* review was favorable: "a hymn in praise of the individual…this masterful book [raises] some of the basic concepts of our time." In her 1957 follow-up, *Atlas Shrugged*, Rand outlined her moral philosophy of "rational self interest." The book follows a group of industrialists, scientists, and artists who retreat to a mountainous hideaway to build an independent free economy. The heroes demonstrate that without their individual efforts the economy and society would collapse.

Rand's philosophy influenced conservative and liberal thinkers, including Alan Greenspan, chairman of the Federal Reserve. Greenspan was known in Rand's circles as "the undertaker" for his serious demeanor and dress habits.

Academic Warfare

The Second Chicago School set about dismantling the Keynesian mixed economy. In 1950, Frank Knight attacked Keynes as having carried "economic thinking well back to the Dark Age." Keynes' monetary theory had passed "the keys of the citadel out of the window to the Philistines hammering at the gates." Jacob Viner attacked Keynes' lack of objectivity and judiciousness, dismissing him as a prophet and a politician. Henry Simons, another protégé of Knight, saw Keynes as "the academic idol of…cranks and charlatans…and [the General Theory] as the economic bible of a fascist movement."[13]

Frederick Hayek proved a key figure in discrediting Keynes and in the resurgence of free markets. His *Road to Serfdom* attacked government intervention in the economy. His 1960 book *The Constitution of Liberty* argued that the power and role of government should be limited to maintaining individual liberty. Hayek criticized the welfare state and the role of unions. His influence on Chicago was strengthened through the Mont Pelerin Society, a collaboration of 36 like-minded scholars seeking to revive the liberal tradition.

Friedman's 1963 book *The Monetary History of the United States, 1867–1960,* written with Anna Schwartz, provided the basis for unseating Keynesian orthodoxy. According to Pierre Bayard,[14] there are four types of books: UB (books unknown to the reader); SB (books skimmed); HB (books heard about); and FB (books read but forgotten). The monumental,

900-page *Monetary History* is a book that is a SB or HB, rarely a UB or FB. Few, even hardened economists, have read the lugubrious and soporific text.

In the Friedman and Schwartz view, the Great Depression was the result of government failure rather than market failure or a failure of capitalism. Friedman and Schwartz argued that the severe contraction in output was caused by a failure of the Federal Reserve, which tightened the availability of money when it should have been loosened, creating shortages of money that triggered bank failures. The Keynesian view of the Great Depression and the need for intervention, Friedman and Schwartz argued, was wrong. Conventional causes of the Great Depression, such as the stock market crash, trade barriers, or classical boom-bust cycles, were incorrect.

The lesson learned was that central banks must not contract money supply in response to a crash. The monetarist view was that when a collapse in financial markets was avoided through a monetary solution, growth would resume after a short recession. The real difference was subtler, as monetarist doctrines owed much to Keynes. But discrediting Keynes made other parts of Keynesian economics, specifically government intervention to manage demand, vulnerable to attack.

In the late 1960s and 1970s, Western economies were gripped by *stagflation*, a combination of low growth, unemployment, and inflation that resisted Keynesian remedies. In Europe, social welfare state costs proved unsustainable. Election of conservative governments in the United States (under President Ronald Reagan) and in the UK (under Prime Minister Margaret Thatcher) hastened a return to free markets. Asked about her political philosophy, Thatcher produced a copy of Hayek's *The Constitution of Liberty*: "This is what we believe."[15] Reagan identified the nine most terrifying words in the English language: "I'm from the government and I'm here to help." Efficient markets rather than efficient government was the new battle cry.

The Gipper and the Iron Lady

In 1956, Clinton Rossiter, a political scientist, identified the skills needed by the occupant of the Oval Office: "scoutmaster, Delphic Oracle, hero of the silver screen and father of the multitudes."[16] Ronald Wilson Reagan, a Hollywood B film actor, possessed one of these qualities. A Democrat who switched to the Republican Party, Reagan was elected governor of California to send welfare bums back to work and to clean up the University of California at Berkeley, a reference to antiwar and anti-establishment student protests.

In the 1970s, growth slowed as a result of the twin oil shocks of 1974 and 1979, leading to higher oil prices. Inflation and interest rates were in double figures. Unemployment was high and there was increasing labor unrest.

America's public finances were in poor shape. The Bretton Woods system of fixed exchange rate collapsed. Since the end of the go-go years of the 1960s, the stock market had been moribund. Americans were racked with self-doubt by the effects of the Vietnam War, race problems, the Watergate scandal, as well as increasing instability and uncertainty.

The presidential race was no contest, as the *Great Communicator's* one-liners exposed the weaknesses of Jimmy Carter's presidency. "Depression is when you're out of work. A recession is when your neighbor's out of work. Recovery is when Carter's out of work." There was the *misery index*—the sum of inflation and unemployment rates. In a presidential debate, Reagan delivered the killer blow: "Next Tuesday all of you will go to the polls…and make a decision. …when you make that decision…ask yourself, are you better off than you were four years ago?" Reagan defeated President Carter easily.

In the UK, Margaret Hilda Thatcher defeated the ill-fated James Callaghan and a tired Labour government in 1979 to become the first woman prime minister of the UK. Ten years earlier Thatcher had said: "no woman in my time will be Prime Minister." Thatcher became a close ally of Reagan. An aide observed that when together a crowbar was needed to pry them apart.

Like Reagan, Thatcher was elected with a mandate to reverse the country's economic and social decline. She wrote of "a feeling of helplessness that a once great nation has somehow fallen behind." Charles Saatchi, once owner of *The Physical Impossibility of Death in the Mind of Someone Living*, created the Conservatives' successful campaign slogan "Labor isn't working" and the famous poster image of a lengthy queue of unemployed workers stretching across an empty landscape.

Reagan held firm views on government and the welfare state: "Government is like a baby. An alimentary canal with a big appetite at one end and no responsibility at the other." Reagan quipped that: "Welfare's purpose should be to eliminate, as far as possible, the need for its own existence." Thatcher believed in personal responsibility, thrift, and probity. She was christened "Milk snatcher" for stopping free milk for children at school. She earned the nickname TINA—"There is no alternative."

Economic reform focused on using monetarist tools to bring inflation under control, restoring sound money, deregulation, balanced budgets, reducing the role of government by tax cuts, and lower government spending.

Paul Volcker, chairman of the U.S. Federal Reserve, played a major part in putting the inflation genie firmly back in the bottle. The 6-foot-7, cheap-cigar-smoking model public servant was said to be able simultaneously to talk down to you and over your head.[17] Restricting the supply of money, Volcker forced interest rates up to brutal levels (above 20 percent per annum) to reduce inflationary expectations. Unemployment rose and bankruptcies increased as the economy slowed. The strategy worked and inflation eventually fell, ushering in a period of growth.

Reagan and Thatcher cut personal income and company taxes. In America the top personal marginal tax rate fell from 70 percent to 28 percent. In the UK Thatcher cut the top rate of British personal income tax rates to 40 percent from 98 percent. The UK tax base was broadened using indirect taxes.

Reagan ended the price controls on domestic oil that had aggravated the 1970s energy crisis. Banking, telecommunications, airlines, electricity, gas, water, and transport were all deregulated to increase flexibility and remove barriers to competition. Thatcher privatized British state-owned companies, reversing decades of nationalization and government ownership.

There was deregulation of the labor markets. Facing a strike by federal air traffic controllers, Reagan, once president of the Screen Actors Guild, declared an emergency and ultimately fired over 11,000 striking controllers, effectively busting the union. In the UK Thatcher and her trusted enforcer Norman Tebbit defeated the National Union of Mineworkers in a bruising, no-holds-barred battle. Reagan and Thatcher took the advice of financier Jay Gould: "hire one half of the working class to kill the other half."

Reagan cut spending, but not sufficiently to offset the reduction in tax revenue. Reagan reduced nonmilitary spending such as food stamps, federal education, and environmental programs. Politically sensitive entitlement programs, such as Social Security and Medicare, were maintained. America borrowed heavily domestically and abroad to cover large budget deficits. National debt increased from $700 billion to $3 trillion. The President was disappointed at the growing national debt, joking that: "[The deficit] is big enough to take care of itself." Thatcher balanced the books, largely through the sale of state-owned businesses.

By the late 1980s, *neo-liberalism* (as the Chicago School ideas were now called) dominated economic thinking. Even in France, home of the *dirigiste* tradition favoring state control over the economy, Socialist Prime Minister Lionel Jospin reluctantly embraced pragmatic economics: "Yes to the market economy, no to the market society."[18]

Political Economy

Growth recovered after the recession of the early 1980s. Unemployment and interest rates fell sharply, and stocks rose in a new bull market. It is unclear whether the recovery was the result of traditional Keynesian nostrums of large budget deficits, low inflation, and reduced interest rates or the new economics. Friedman grumbled that government and central banks, especially the British, were applying his ideas incorrectly. John Kenneth Galbraith's criticism was withering: "Milton's [Friedman's] misfortune is that his policies have been tried."[19]

Volcker declared himself a monetarist but rarely followed theory. Money supply proved difficult to measure or control. When the government targeted one measure of money supply, other measures changed unexpectedly. As Charles Goodhart, an English economist and central banker, identified: "observed statistical regularity will tend to collapse once pressure is placed upon it for control purposes." Christopher Fildes, an English journalist, restated Goodhart's law: "It's all very well when anthropologists observe the savages, but all bets are off when the savages start observing the anthropologists."[20]

Reaganomics flirted with *supply side theory*, advocated by little known economist Arthur Laffer. Large tax cuts would stimulate economic growth, expanding the tax base and offsetting the lost revenue from lower tax rates. Armed with a flipchart and pointer, Reagan used a presidential TV address to introduce a bemused nation to the *Laffer curve*. Half a century earlier, Cornell University Professor George Warren had convinced Franklin Delano Roosevelt to raise prices for agricultural produce by boosting gold prices to try to end the Great Depression. Warren's credentials included formulas for getting chickens to lay more eggs.[21]

Politics dictated that governments were unable to rein in spending to match the tax cuts to balance the budget. Spending was the basis of political patronage and purchased votes. In *Atlas Shrugged*, the politicians come to John Galt, the heroic businessman, for assistance to help repair the economy. Galt: "You want me to be economic dictator?" Mr. Thompson: "Yes!" "And you'll obey any order I give?" "Implicitly!" "Then start by abolishing all income taxes." "Oh no!" screams Mr. Thompson, leaping to his feet. "We couldn't do that.... How would we pay government employees?" "Fire your government employees." "Oh, no!"[22]

Governments actually became larger. Deregulating industries concentrated market power and reduced competition, necessitating renewed state intervention. Technological innovation, encouraged by free markets, rapidly reshaped industries, creating noncompetitive monopolies requiring regulation. The neo-liberal program encountered an old problem recognized by Keynes: "Capitalism is the astounding belief that the most wickedest of men will do the most wickedest of things for the greatest good of everyone."

Thatcher was not interested in pure agendas: "Economics are the method; the object is to change the soul." Conservative politician Enoch Powell ridiculed Thatcher's monetarist policies: "A pity she did not understand them!" Reagan never fully engaged with his economic program: "I have left orders to be awakened at any time in case of national emergency, even if I'm in a cabinet meeting."

Only tiny New Zealand, under Roger Douglas, finance minister in a left-of-center government, attempted the full Chicago program. *Rogeronomics* entailed large spending and tax cuts, sale of state-owned assets, cuts in subsidies and tariffs, and deregulation of industries. There were plans for a flat low rate of taxation. The program was ultimately aborted in a wave of business collapses and bank failures.

In 1973, General Augusto Pinochet, with the active support of the U.S. CIA, removed the elected left wing Allende regime in Chile in a military coup. The Pinochet regime undertook systematic and widespread human rights violations in Chile and abroad, including torture, kidnapping, illegal detention, and mass-murder of suspected opponents, as well press censorship. Pinochet was accused of enriching himself and his family. Chile imported a team from the University of Chicago—"los Cee-Ca-Go boys"—to advise on restructuring its economy. Milton Friedman visited Chile in 1975 and met with Pinochet.

Although never implicated in human rights violations, Friedman's association with Chile and Pinochet cast a shadow over his career. British Labour Prime Minister Tony Blair mocked the Conservatives as "the party of Pinochet," pointing to the Chilean dictator's close relationship with Thatcher. *The New York Times* asked: "if the pure Chicago economic theory can be carried out…only at the price of repression, should its authors feel some responsibility?"[23]

Frank Knight was suspicious of any "ism"—commun*ism*, social*ism*, capital*ism*, and liberal*ism*, even neo-liberalism. He believed that any attempt to improve public policy was doomed to failure:

> The probability of the people in power being individuals who dislike the possession and exercise of power is on a level with the probability that an extremely tender-hearted person would get the job of whipping master in a slave plantation.[24]

New Old Deal

Politicians and governments, irrespective of ideology, accepted market fundamentalism. Free markets were considered better at regulating competing forces, allocating resources, and meeting consumer demand. The role of government was to remove impediments to and ensure the proper institutional framework for free and competitive markets. Harvard economist and U.S. Treasury Secretary Lawrence Summers "tried to leave [his] students with…the view that the invisible hand is more powerful than the [un]hidden hand. Things will happen in well-organized efforts without direction, controls, plans. That's the consensus among economists."[25]

Tony Blair's New Labour government's unalloyed support for the City reflected this belief. Upon succeeding Blair as the UK prime minister, Gordon Brown even invited Thatcher to No. 10 Downing Street for tea, seemingly to lend authority to his economic credentials. Enthusiastic embrace of markets and deregulation shaped Bill Clinton's presidency. James Carville, Clinton's political adviser, summed up this attitude in an oft-quoted remark: "I want to come back as the bond market. You can intimidate everybody."[26] Politicians everywhere learned the truth of Thatcher's words: "You can't buck the markets."

Money, highly mobile capital flows, the financial sector, and financialization were the core of the new economy. Economic growth was powered by ever-larger amounts of borrowing and spending. Investors and traders moved money into and out of investments and countries with alarming rapidity, to take advantage of the latest opportunities. Lawrence Summers loudly stated his approval: "In this age of electronic money investors are no longer seduced by a financial dance of a thousand veils. Only hard accurate information…will keep capital from fleeing precipitously at the first sign of trouble."[27]

Economic historians debate the influence of the Chicago School but contradictions abound. Ronald Reagan, the beatified doyen of conservatives, ran substantial budgets deficits that had a distinct Keynesian taint. Blair and Clinton's social democrat administrations presided over the aggressive dismantling of banking regulation, which looks distinctly neo-liberal and ill-conceived. Then no pure economic model has been implemented in living memory, except perhaps in North Korea.

The Monetary Lens

The shift to a monetary focus increased the importance of money and the power of central banks. Politicians and the public were traditionally deeply suspicious of a powerful central bank. A prime mover in the creation of the American central bank was Paul Warburg, a Jewish German financier, who formed an unlikely partnership with Rhode Island Senator Nelson Aldrich. The idea of an American central bank was formulated at a secret meeting in 1910 on Jekyll Island off the Georgia coast. Participants traveled to the island pretending to be duck hunters. To ensure secrecy, they referred to each other only by their given names, giving rise to the sobriquet "The First Name Club."[28]

The Federal Reserve System (known generally as the Fed) was created in 1913 to implement banking and currency reforms to prevent periodic banking crises, such as the panic of 1907. It was a government entity with private components, consisting principally of the president-appointed board of governors of the Federal Reserve System in Washington DC, and 12 regional Federal Reserve banks located in major cities. The Fed was destined to play both Dr. Jekyll and Mr. Hyde in financialization.

In theory, central bank authority focused on ensuring that the value of money was not undermined by inflation. Hayek argued for mechanical rules to reduce the central bank's discretion.

The cult of the all-powerful central banker emerged in the 1920s. Neurotic and prone to bouts of mental collapse, Sir Montagu Norman, governor of the Bank of England, dabbled with spiritualism, apparently once informing a colleague that he could walk through walls. On central banking matters, Norman reputedly observed: "I don't have reasons. I have instincts." Hjalmar Schacht, a fierce nationalist with the stiff gait and moustache of a Prussian reserve officer, headed Germany's Reichsbank and went on to serve Hitler until a celebrated falling out. Paul Volcker's success in dealing with inflation made him immensely powerful and invested the role of chairman of the Fed with great authority. When Volcker retired in 1987, his successor Alan Greenspan expanded the role of the central bank.

The pivotal event was the stock market crash of Monday, October 19, 1987. Despite volatile stock prices during the previous week, Greenspan traveled to Dallas to speak at the American Bankers' Convention to maintain an appearance of calm and business as usual. Upon arriving in Dallas, Greenspan was told that the stock market was down "five oh eight." The Fed Chairman assumed that it meant 5.08 points, only to learn that the market had fallen 508 points, or more than 22 percent.[29]

Drawing on Friedman's criticism of the Fed's actions during the Great Depression, Greenspan announced the Fed's willingness "to serve as a source of liquidity to support the economic and financial system." The strategy worked, with the economy suffering only modest effects. The stock market stabilized and recovered quickly, establishing Greenspan's credentials.

Half a century earlier, the longest-serving chairman of the Federal Reserve William McChesney Martin stated that the job of the Fed was to take away the punch bowl just as the party gets going.[30] Alan Greenspan reversed the emphasis, believing that bubbles were difficult to identify, and the central bankers' task was not to try to prevent them. Central bankers now administered fluids to the casualties of irrational exuberance.

In 2002, at a dinner celebrating Friedman's 90th birthday, Ben Bernanke, Greenspan's successor as Fed chairman, swooned obsequiously: "I would like to say to Milton and Anna. Regarding the Great Depression. You're right, we did it. We're very sorry. But thanks to you, we won't do it again."[31] The audience sat in the manner of sinners, heads slightly bowed and the eyes moist and a bit glassy, amid the murmurs of "Amen, Brother" and "Praise the Lord."

Unstable Stability?

Friedmanites argued that Reagan and Thatcher's policies reinvigorated the economy, paving the way for the *Great Moderation*. Coined by Harvard economist James Stock, the term referred to an era of strong economic growth, increased prosperity, and the perceived end to economic cycles and volatility.

Prosperity was increasingly based on financial services and the speculation economy. The cycles were still there, papered over by the free money from central banks when necessary. Speculation and risk-taking behavior were almost risk free, as long as everybody, especially large, too-big-to-fail institutions, bet on the same color.

Manufacturing, which provided significant employment and prospects of social improvement for millions, was wound back, with production and jobs shifting to cheaper locations. Workers inhabited an insecure world of part-time or casual work or temporary contracts. Public services and public spaces were degraded. Heavily indebted consumer cultures focused on consumption. The socially unequal and atomized structures spilt over into binge drinking and casual violence in the nongentrified parts of great cities.

Hayek understood the dynamic, amoral, and unpredictable forces that underlie free markets. Like the Austrian, Knight considered free markets to be unjust because they distributed wealth based on luck and inheritance rather than capability and effort. Hayek and Knight were wary of the tendency of free markets to speculation, frenzy, and fraud. Greed, credulity, and herd instinct were likely to overwhelm economic rationality. Knight and Hayek did not consider markets an ideal tool for satisfying demand as they inevitably molded themselves to the desires of active participants and ignored other factors, like the environment and quality of life.

Knight argued that the economy is too complex and unstable to be controlled by simplistic government intervention. Intervention, he argued, is dangerous, rejecting the economic prescriptions of both the Keynesian and Friedman schools. Knight's criticism of Friedman's Second Chicago School was typically wry: "the emotional pronouncement of value judgements condemning emotion and value judgements which seems to [me] a symptom of a defective sense of humor."[32]

In his 1986 book *Stabilizing an Unstable Economy*, Hyman Minsky, an American economist, outlined a hypothesis as to why modern economies are liable to fluctuate and how obvious instability can be masked for a time. Minsky's thesis was that stability in financial markets engenders instability as a result of inherent tendencies in the financial system—stability is itself destabilizing.

Minsky viewed modern financial markets as "conditionally coherent" and characterized by "periods of tranquility." Excessive risk taking—driven in part by assumptions about the level of risk, inherent investment biases as asset prices increase, and increased leverage—led to market breakdowns. Minsky's caution about "balance sheet adventuring" presciently anticipated the crisis that was to bring the Great Moderation to its end in 2007. Ben Bernanke, a follower of Friedman and student of the Great Depression, found himself facing the type of crash that the theory said could not happen again.

8

False Gods, Fake Prophecies

Finance is what economists call money; financial economics is the economics of money. Its pioneering scholars emanated from Chicago's Graduate Business School (GBS) rather than the economics department because business schools paid better. The GBS shaped modern finance, investments, markets, asset pricing, and especially the measurement and management of risk.

In the 1950s, finance curriculums were rooted in institutional arrangements, legal issues, generalization, common sense, and judgment. Sitting through a Harvard case study on finance, Merton Miller complained: "the solution was not obvious to me…it was frustrating to have no sense of a theory…to tie all this material together."[1] Chicago changed that, using the rigorous analysis favored by the university's economic department. Today, Chicago's Booth School of Business advertises: "In 1960, we…transformed finance from a guild into a science."

Larry Summers called finance theory "ketchup economics."[2] MIT economist David Durand argued that the new finance had "lost virtually all contact with terra firma…[being] more interested in demonstrating… mathematical prowess than in solving genuine problems; often…playing mathematical games."[3] Even Friedman, sitting on Harry Markowitz's doctoral dissertation committee, grumbled: "It's not math, it's not economics, it's not even business administration."[4]

Mystery of Price

If Galileo Galilei was obsessed with the motion of celestial objects, then financial economists are obsessed with oscillations of stock prices.

In the 1950s, stocks still traded below 1929 levels and stock ownership by individuals and institutions was considered risky. In 1969, the head of the Ford Foundation, McGeorge Bundy, who as U.S. national security adviser escalated American involvement in Vietnam, increased investment in equities. Harry Markowitz and his 1952 paper *Portfolio Selection* influenced Bundy.

Markowitz's *modern portfolio theory* linked risk and return. Risk was defined and quantified as variance—how far the returns could vary from the expected average (mean) return. The *mean-variance* approach became the foundation of risk management, starting finance's fascination and reliance on the *bell-shaped* normal distribution curve.

Markowitz distinguished between the risk of an individual security and a portfolio. The risk of a portfolio was a function of the risk of an individual security but also how each security moved relative to others (the covariance or correlation between the price movements of the two securities). Diversifying a portfolio among a number of securities, whose prices do not move closely together, reduced risk.

Markowitz was restating Antonio, in William Shakespeare's *Merchant of Venice*: "My ventures are not in one bottom trusted, nor to one place; nor is my whole estate upon the fortune of this present year; therefore my merchandise makes me not sad." Despite Friedman's grumbling, Markowitz received his Ph.D.

Building on Markowitz's work, in the 1960s, Jack Treynor, William Sharpe, John Lintner, and Jan Mossin developed the *capital asset pricing model (CAPM)*. The CAPM calculated a theoretically appropriate required rate of return for assets, such as an individual security or a portfolio. Where an asset is added to a well-diversified portfolio, the additional return required is related to the risk unique to that security, which cannot be diversified away.

The CAPM is one of modern finance's iconic equations:

E[Ri] = Rf + Beta [E[Rm] – Rf]

where:

E[Ri] is the expected return on the asset.

Rf is the risk-free rate of interest on government bonds.

Beta is the sensitivity of the asset returns to market returns.

E[Rm] is the expected return of the market.

[E[Rm] – Rf] is sometimes known as the market premium or risk premium (the difference between the expected market rate of return and the risk-free rate of return).

The CAPM's insight was that the general risk of markets (*systematic risk*) could be reduced by diversification but the unique risk of a security (*unsystematic risk*) could not. A volatile or risky stock (high beta) would need to have a low price (that is, a high expected return) to attract investors. Conversely, a less volatile or lower risk stock (low beta) would have a higher price (a lower expected return). By plugging the inputs into the model, investors could determine what a security should return.

Michael Jensen, a graduate student at Chicago, used a measure developed by Sharpe called the *information ratio* to compare actual returns earned by investment managers adjusting for the risk taken. Jensen found that few funds outperformed the broad market. On average, investors buying all the stocks in the market would earn higher returns with lower risk. Fund managers with high returns simply took higher risk rather than possessing supernatural skill.

Demon of Chance

The *efficient market hypothesis (EMH)* stated that the stock prices followed a random walk, a formal mathematical statement of a trajectory consisting of successive random steps. Pioneers Jules Regnault (in the nineteenth century) and Louis Bachelier (early twentieth century) had discovered that short-term price changes were random—a coin toss could predict up or down moves. Bachelier's Sorbonne thesis established that the probability of a given change in price was consistent with the Gaussian or bell-shaped normal distribution, well-known in statistical theory.

Aware of the importance of his insights, Bachelier claimed: "the present theory resolves the majority of problems in the study of speculation."[5] His examiners disagreed. Paul Levy, the leading French probability theorist, thought Bachelier's work had too much finance. Bachelier's thesis received a *mention honorable*, below the *très honorable* needed to gain a place in the academic world.

Random movements in prices, devoid of any trend or cycle, were a depressing prospect for economists. Maurice Kendall, a British statistician, described it as the work of "the Demon of Chance," randomly drawing a number from a distribution of possible price changes, which, when added to today's price, determined the next price.

While working for a stock market newsletter, Eugene Fama noticed patterns in stock prices that would appear and disappear rapidly. In his doctoral dissertation, he laid out the argument that stock prices were random, reflecting all available information relevant to its value. Prices followed a random walk and market participants could not systematically profit from market inefficiencies. The EMH does not require market price to be always accurate. Investors force the price to fluctuate randomly around its real value. As economist Paul Samuelson put it: "if one could be sure that a price will rise, it would already have risen."[6]

The EMH was the finance version of *The Price Is Right*, the corollary of Chicago's belief in free markets. Reviewing Markowitz's work, David Durand observed that the "argument rests on the concept of the Rational Man." Durand did not think such a creature existed and thought the whole thing had "an air of fantasy."[7]

Corporate M&Ms

In the late 1950s, Franco Modigliani and Merton Miller, two professors at Carnegie Mellon University, developed two propositions influencing a company's capital structure (the mix of debt and equity) and dividend policy. In an efficient market without taxes, bankruptcy costs and differences in knowledge between participants (known as *asymmetric information*), Proposition 1 states that the value of a firm is unaffected by how that firm is financed. It does not matter if the firm finances by issuing stock or selling debt. Proposition 2 argues that the firm's dividend policy does not matter.

The *Modigliani-Miller propositions* crucially introduced the *irrelevance principle* and *arbitrage*. They argued that the earnings of a firm were independent of financing decisions with the financing mix between debt and equity only determining how earnings were split between lenders and shareholders. A company with more debt was normally considered riskier than one with less debt. Modigliani and Miller argued that, in a perfect world, investors would demand higher return for the shares and debt where a company had more borrowing. This would negate any benefits of additional borrowing, which consists mainly of the lower cost of debt when compared to the cost of equity.

The process was driven by arbitrage. Classically, arbitrage took advantage of price differentials between two markets. Assume cocaine is trading at $1,000/ounce in London and $1,100/ounce in New York, and the cost of transportation between the two centers is $25/ounce. An arbitrager could purchase an ounce in London, transport it to New York, and sell it to lock in a profit of $75 ounce without any financial risk.

In an arbitrage-free world, where the value of a firm's debt or equity differed from its intrinsic value driven by its earnings or cash flows, Modigliani and Miller showed that investors would take advantage of any discrepancy in market prices. By investing in different combinations of debt and shares, the investor could create a future income stream of the same size and risk. Dividends were irrelevant, as investors could sell shares to generate income, being indifferent to dividend policy. When the assumption of no taxes was removed, the fact that interest payments reduced tax made debt much cheaper than shares, driving increased leverage and private equity transactions.

In 1976, Michael Jensen and his co-author William H. Meckling published "Theory of the firm: managerial behaviour, agency costs and ownership structure." The paper's argument that managers' interests are different from those of shareholders was not original. What made it influential was the emphasis on using market forces, especially the stock market's collective judgment, to overcome agency conflicts and costs.

Jensen, who taught at Harvard, used academic journals and popular outlets like the *Harvard Business Review*, *The Wall Street Journal*, and *The New York Times* to propound the idea of the *market for corporate control*. He argued that: "The takeover market provides a unique, powerful and impersonal mechanism to accomplish the major restructuring and redeployment of assets continually required by changes in technology and consumer preference."[8]

Just as Friedman was the public face of its economics, Jensen and Miller were the public face of Chicago finance. Jensen combined his academic duties with a role at Monitor Group, a strategy consulting firm started by Michael Porter, another Harvard academic and consultant. Merton Miller served as a public director on the CBOT between 1983 and 1985 and the CME from 1990 until his death on June 3, 2000. They helped make the theory influential and relevant to banks and industrial corporations.

In his finance class, Miller once drew a vertical line on the blackboard, writing M & M on one side and T on the other side. Asked about the T, the combative Miller replied "them," opponents of the new finance.[9]

Risk Taming

In a 2008 BBC documentary on finance, wispy clouds over central London shape a mathematical formula:

$$P_{ce} = S \times N(d1) - K\,e^{-Rf.T} \times N(d2)$$

The clouds were the work of computer graphics; the equation is real. Just as every art movement has its defining work, the *Black-Scholes option pricing model* is the masterpiece of financial economics.

Options are insurance against rising and falling prices. Applied to stocks, a *call option* gives the buyer, in return for payment of a fee (the *premium*), any gain from increases above an agreed price (*strike price*) as at or by a certain date (*expiry*). A *put option* gives the buyer, in return for a fee, protection against falling prices. Options have skewed risks and rewards. The buyer of an option has limited loss (the premium) but potentially large gains (depending on how much the price of the underlying asset moves). Conversely, sellers of options risk large losses (the potentially large payout they must make if the price of the asset moves by a large amount) in return for a small gain (the premium received).

Insurance, with its long history, offered guidance on valuation. The insurer's profit was the difference between statistical loss experience, based on historical knowledge of claims, and the premiums paid, plus investment income on the premiums. Applying insurance theory to options proved difficult.

Louis Bachelier applied random walk models to pricing options. Paul Cootner and Paul Samuleson worked on the problem. In their 1967 book *Beat the Market*, mathematicians Sheen Kassouf and Edward Thorp outlined the relationship between the price of an option and the price of the underlying stock. Thorp, whose interest was gambling and beating the casino at roulette and baccarat, developed a model, anticipating the Black-Scholes equation.

With a background in physics and mathematics, Fischer Black worked at Arthur D. Little, a financial consulting firm. While at the University of Chicago, Black collaborated with Myron Scholes, whose Ph.D. focused on using arbitrage to ensure that securities with similar risks offered similar returns. Black and Scholes built upon Kassouf and Thorp's idea of hedging options using the underlying stock.

The value of the option must be determined by the value of the stock. As the stock price changes, so should the price of the option. If a stock price moves from $10 to $11, then the price of the call option should also increase. The relationship allows the setting up of *risk-free* portfolios where you buy a call option and at the same time short sell a share. If the stock price goes up then the value of the call option increases but you suffer a loss on the shares, as you have to buy them back at the higher price. By adjusting the ratio of options to the shares, you can construct a portfolio where the changes in the value of the options and shares exactly offset, at least, for small movements in the stock price.

Working as research assistant to Paul Samuelson, Robert Merton was also working on option pricing. Merton introduced an idea—*continuous time mathematics*. Black and Scholes assumed that the portfolio would be rebalanced to keep it free of risk by changing the number of shares held at *discrete time intervals*. Merton forced the time intervals into infinitely small fragments of time, effectively allowing *continuous and instantaneous* rebalancing. Although unrealistic and practically impossible, this allowed a mathematical solution using Ito's (pronounced "Eto") Lemma to solve the equation. Ito, an eccentric Japanese mathematician, later did not remember deriving the eponymous technique.

The Black-Scholes-Merton (BSM) option pricing model relied on the CAPM, itself reliant on the EMH, and arbitrage. While physicists searched, financial economists had arrived at their own version of the GUT (grand unifying theory).

The BSM model and its hedging logic profoundly influenced risk management. Infinite varieties of derivative instruments could be created. In awarding Scholes and Merton the 1997 Nobel prize in Economics, the Swedish Academy noted that "their valuation methodology has paved the way for…new…financial instruments and facilitated more efficient risk management."[10]

Option pricing proved pivotal because many transactions could be deconstructed into options or, more generally, derivatives. Shares, bonds, mortgage prepayment rights, and various contracts could be unbundled, evaluated, and priced. Keen to solve every financial problem, Merton led the way with his newfound Lemma gun. Derivatives were a "universal financial device,"[11] which could be used in endless ways to manage risk, create packages of risk, generate income, or simply speculate on certain outcomes.

In April 1973, shortly after publication of the Black Scholes paper, the Chicago Board of Option Exchange (CBOE), coincidentally, began trading stock options in its converted smoking lounge. The advent of handheld calculators, made by Texas Instruments and Hewlett-Packard, which could be programmed to calculate option prices using the model, appeared. Texas Instruments advertised in *The Wall Street Journal*: "you can find the Black-Scholes value using our…calculator."[12]

Black went on to a long career at Goldman Sachs. Scholes moved to Salomon Brothers and Long Term Capital Management (LTCM), where Merton joined him. As the Nobel prize in Economics is not awarded posthumously, Fischer Black's death in 1995 robbed him of a share of the award that went to Scholes and Merton for the development of option pricing models. During his life, when Black appeared infrequently on the floor of the CBOE, trading would halt momentarily and a loud cheer and clapping would break out. *The Economist* obituary described Black as "one of the most productive minds of [the] century."

In practice, it is the hedging or replication aspect of the model (the Merton perspective) that became important. Traders could hedge the risk of options by trading in the underlying asset, allowing them to make markets and trade in options and derivatives generally. Black remained equivocal about the replication approach: "Merton's derivation relies on stricter assumptions, so I don't think it's really robust."[13]

Slow and Quick Money

Initially, the ideas did not find acceptance among practitioners. The professors could point to no practical experience or track record. Baron

Rothschild once observed that only three people understood the meaning of money and none had very much of it.[14]

Diversification to reduce risk was contrary to the ethos of stock picking. While successfully managing the portfolios of an insurance company and the King's College endowment, Keynes insisted that diversification was flawed:

> To suppose that safety...consists in having a small gamble in a large number of different [stocks] where I have no information...as compared with a substantial stake in a company where one's information is adequate, strikes me as a travesty of investment policy.[15]

Mark Twain's Pudd'nhead Wilson agreed: "Put all your eggs in one basket, and watch that basket."

Academic James Lorie arrogantly advised money managers to "give up conventional security analysis. Its occasional triumphs are offset by its occasional disasters and on the average nothing valuable is produced."[16] One convert argued what fund managers were doing was "150,000 percent bullshit."[17] Burton Malkiel wryly remarked that proponents were "greeted in...Wall Street...with as much enthusiasm as Saddam Hussein addressing a meeting of the B'nai B'rith." Wells Fargo's James Vertin, whose bank was trying to commercialize the theories, understood the problem: "most practitioners feel themselves to be objects of academic ridicule, and most feel bound to resist this assault."[18]

The 1974 U.S. Employee Retirement Income Security Act required investment managers and trustees to meet the "prudent man" test in discharging fiduciary duties. As EMH and CAPM enjoyed academic acceptance, trustees and managers were forced to follow the theory to avoid failing the test by differing too radically from its prescriptions.

As money was farmed out to external specialist fund managers, investors needed to measure investment performance. Asset consultants Mercers, Frank Russell, Towers-Perrin, Watson-Wyatt, BARRA, and others, who were employed to analyze portfolios, returns, and investment practices, were well versed in the theory, helping popularize them.

Benchmarking returns and monitoring investment performance regularly became accepted wisdom. It influenced how money was allocated between different investments such as cash, bonds, and equity. Portfolio returns were compared to benchmarks such as the S&P 500. Investment return was separated into β (beta), or the return on the broad market, and α (alpha), the fund manager's outperformance.

Giving up trying to beat the market, index funds purchased all the stocks in the index to match the market return. Jack Bogle's Vanguard Group and Barclays Global Investors (BGI, now owned by Blackstone) built large businesses on the mantra of low cost indexation.

Others used a *core-satellite* approach—the bulk of funds were invested to match the index but a small portion was used to pick winners seeking outperformance (generate alpha). As fund management evolved into a professionally managed business, increasing costs, especially of attracting investors and compliance, forced economies of scale. UBS Asset Management and Blackstone now manage trillions of dollars. As size made it difficult to enter and exit markets quickly without affecting prices, indexation or core-satellite approaches grew.

Diversification encouraged new asset classes—emerging markets, currencies, commodities, infrastructure, insurance risk, and even fine arts. As long as the investment offered returns and did not move together with other asset classes held by the investor, adding them to a portfolio improved return with lower risk. The success of the unorthodox investment philosophy of David Swensen and the Yale Endowment showed the potential of hedge funds and private equity to generate alpha. Investment managers used derivatives to manage risk or create structured products. Portfolio insurance or constant proportion portfolio insurance was used to limit investor's risk of loss from a sharp fall in prices.

Acceptance was not wholehearted: "An awful lot of material is coming in…sitting on people's desk…getting talked about…But the number of people…actually using the new investment technology is still limited…Everybody is trying to look *au courant*."[19] But engagement gradually deepened.

Corporate Practice

Chicago graduate Joel Stern's Stern Stewart & Co. (a consulting firm), Marakon Consulting (which evolved out of Wells Fargo's Management Sciences Division) and Alcar (created by Professor Alfred Rappaport) spruiked shareholder value. Stern, a skilful self-promoter, wrote influential articles in *The Wall Street Journal*, a column in the *Financial Times* and, like Bill Gross, became a regular on *Wall Street Week*.

The Stern Stewart pitch was pure Modigliani and Miller, arguing that companies' share prices reflected 'expected cash flow…above and beyond the anticipated investment requirement of the business."[20] Shareholder value required maximizing cash flow and returns above the company's cost of capital.

Stern Stewart published an annual *Billboard Top 100 Chart* that analyzed corporations' EVA™—economic value added or estimate of economic profit. The idea gained traction when executive remuneration was linked to EVA and companies awarded stock or stock options to executives to align the interests of shareholders and management.

Shareholder value fueled financial innovation, new debt and equity securities, allowing companies to raise cheap equity or increase borrowing. Companies repurchased the firm's shares to boost share prices.

Traditionally, companies favored modest borrowing and high credit ratings. Now, they increased debt to reduce their cost of capital. Debt was cheaper than equity and interest was tax-deductible, allowing companies to increase shareholder return through additional leverage. By 2005 the number of companies rated AAA (the highest credit quality) declined to 6 from 32 in the early 1980s.[21]

As the volatility of currencies, interest rates and equity prices increased, banks and exchanges introduced derivative instruments. At the CME, Leo Melamed, concerned about the drop in volumes in the onion and egg futures contracts, perspicaciously steered the exchange into financial derivatives, with the support of Friedman and Miller, with immediate success. Corporations and investors increasingly needed to use available derivatives to hedge risks to be considered prudent.

The BSM model and Markowitz's work evolved into risk quantification modes, such as *value at risk* (VAR) models. VAR signifies the maximum amount that you can lose, statistically, as a result of market moves for a given probability over a fixed time.

If you own shares over a year, then most of the time the share price moves up or down a small amount. On some days you may get a large or very large price change. VAR ranks the price changes from largest fall to largest rise. Assuming that prices follow a random walk and price changes fit a normal distribution, you can calculate the probability of a particular size price change. You can answer questions like what is the likely maximum price change and loss on your holding at a specific probability level, say 99 percent, which equates to 1 day out of 100 days. A VAR figure of $50 million at 99 percent over a 10-day holding period means that the bank has a 99 percent probability that it will not suffer a loss of more than $50 million over a 10-day period.

VAR became accepted best practice, enshrined in bank regulations. Risk, the unknown unknown, was now a known unknown or even a known known. Former risk manager Barry Schacter offered an alternative definition of VAR: "a number invented by purveyors of panaceas for pecuniary peril intended to mislead senior management and regulators into false confidence that market risk is adequately understood and controlled."[22]

Everything Is Just Noise

The new theories required that everyone has rational expectations, that is, the population is correct on average even if no individual person is. Behavioral economist Amos Tversky summed it up: "When we talk about individuals, especially policy makers, they all make errors in their decisions. But in aggregate, they all get it right?"[23]

Exceptions and anomalies increasingly undermined the theory of efficient markets. There was the *turn-of-the-year effect*, where stocks seemed to rise in January each year. Small-size firms outperformed large stocks—the *small-firm effect*. In the *loser effect*, stocks that had fallen significantly outperformed stocks that performed well in previous periods. There was little relationship between beta (risk) and return.

Behavioural economists, such as Tversky, Daniel Kahneman and Richard Thaler, argued that *efficient* financial markets were rife with cognitive biases and errors in reasoning and information processing, including overconfidence, overreaction, representative bias, information bias, and the use of linear reasoning. Cliff Asness, a student of Fama and founder of hedge fund AQR Capital Management, exploited these anomalies. Hearing complaints that his strategies were not working, Asness' wife asked him incredulously: "Let me get this straight. I thought you said you make your money because people aren't completely rational. Yet now you're mad because they're *too* irrational."[24]

Risk management assumes that price changes are normally distributed. The mathematician Benoit Mandelbrot demonstrated that normal distributions do not exist in practice. In *Fooled by Randomness* and *Black Swan*, Nicholas Nassim Taleb argued against the application of statistical methods in finance, especially the normal distribution curve to measure risk.

Taleb drew on John Stuart Mill, himself rephrasing a problem posed by Scottish philosopher David Hume: "no amount of observations of white swans can allow the inference that all swans are white, but the observation of a single black swan is sufficient to refute that conclusion." Unpredictable extremes of price movement, known as *fat tails*, were more common than theory implied. Extreme price moves were perfectly intelligible in hindsight but are not predictable—just as the existence of black swans was only discovered in Australia in the eighteenth century.

In August 2007, David Viniar, Goldman Sachs' CFO, commented that: "We were seeing things that were 25-standard-deviation moves, several days in a row." In October 2008, the Dow Jones Industrial Average moved more than 10 percent on 2 days. Using a normal distribution, economists Paul De Grauwe, Leonardo Iania and Pablo Rovira Kaltwasser estimated that the moves should occur only every 73 to 603 trillion billion years. "Since our universe…exists a mere 20 billion years we, finance theorists, would have had to wait for another trillion universes before one such change could be observed…. A truly miraculous event."[25]

But nobody wanted to accept that their models were incorrect. Confronted with quantum theory, Albert Einstein refused to believe that God played dice with the universe. But as Stephen Hawking remarked: "Not only does God play dice, but…he sometimes throws them where they cannot be seen."[26]

In his 1986 presidential address to the American Finance Association, Fischer Black distinguished between *noise* and *information*. In traditional communication, noise is the disruption in the passage of information through unintended addition to the signal between transmission and reception. It makes it difficult to decode the intended signal accurately. People increasingly mistook noise for information. Traders bought and sold on rumor or misinformation. Noise occurs at every step, making observation imperfect and preventing prices from getting to real values.

Noise led to oversimplified relationships, making it impossible to determine cause and effect. Black argued:

> No matter how many variables we include...there are always...potentially important variables that we have omitted, possibly because they too are unobservable.... In the end, a theory is accepted not because it is confirmed by conventional empirical tests, but because researchers persuade one another that the theory is correct and relevant.[27]

Traders traded, fooled by noise. Even people with accurate price sensitive information could not be certain whether they were trading on information or noise, making much of the modeling meaningless.

Keynes, too, had warned about the risk in making any estimate because of incomplete knowledge:

> Professional investment may be likened to those newspaper competitions in which the competitors have to pick out the six prettiest faces from a hundred photographs...each competitor has to pick, not the faces which he himself finds the prettiest, but those which he thinks likeliest to catch the fancy of the other competitors.

He anticipated modern finance:

> We have reached the third degree when we devote our intelligences to anticipating what average opinion expects the average opinion to be. And there are some, I believe, who practice the fourth, fifth and higher degrees.[28]

Perfect Worlds

In modern economics and finance, until something is said mathematically, it isn't said at all. Soviet economists had access to the latest Western economics publications because "the Party ruled that these were mathematical works...purely technical, devoid of ideological content."[29]

Models were increasingly the product of *data mining*, trawling through historical data to find a relationship and prove or reject hypotheses. More data and improved statistical methods overwhelmed common sense. Albert

Einstein knew the problem: "*As far as the laws of mathematics refer to reality, they are not certain, and as far as they are certain, they do not refer to reality.*"

Researchers "saw" patterns in data. But strong correlation does not prove causality. In the late 1940s, before the invention of the polio vaccine, American public health experts thought they had discovered a correlation between polio cases and increased consumption of ice cream and soft drinks. In reality, polio outbreaks were simply more common in the hot summer months and not caused by eating ice cream. Eugen Slutsky cautioned that "it is always possible to detect, even in the multitude of individual peculiarities…uniformities and regularities."[30] David Weinberger, in his mathematics Ph.D. dissertation involved in arbitrage, argued that investors and traders "believe there's structure or you don't …. It's…a religious question."[31]

The models relied on over-simplified assumptions. Friedman argued that economic theory was "an engine" not "a camera"; it could analyze the world but it was not complete as it was impossible to incorporate all details. The theory would have inaccurate or unrealistic assumptions, but this was irrelevant. A theory should be judged not on its assumptions, but on the power of its conclusions. Philosopher Karl Popper argued similarly that factual evidence could never prove a theory but could only fail to disprove it.[32]

Frank Knight remained sceptical: "mathematical economists have commonly been mathematicians first and economists afterwards, disposed to simplify the data and underestimate the divergence between their premises and the facts of life."[33] Economic research increasingly resembled the view of Poo-Bah in *The Mikado*: "corroborative details intended to give artistic verisimilitude to an otherwise bald and unconvincing narrative."[34]

Theories were the work of economists who did not know any finance and a handful of financiers who learned finance from these same economists. The statisticians, mathematicians, and scientists knew neither economics nor finance. None had much actual practice, actively resisting contamination and preferring to deal with finance on a theoretical level. Much of the literature reflected the Gordon-Liebhafsky theorem that: "provided that it achieves a certain threshold of intelligibility, the greater the obscurity of a piece written by an economist, the greater is the likelihood that it will be recognized as a classic or seminal work."[35]

For financiers, theory and models were secondary to profit. Merton's dynamic hedging or replication approach allowed the creation of derivatives and their risk management, helping banks to trade a bewildering variety of instruments. In the 1950s, two economists, Kenneth Arrow and Gerard Debreu, showed that attaining the nirvana of economic equilibrium required *state securities*, contracts to buy or sell everything at any time period in every place until infinity or the end of the world, whichever was first. This theoretically perfect world now justified any and every type of derivative and financial product.

Financial Fundamentalism

In the eighteenth century, Western societies shifted from medieval systems of aristocratic and religious authority to models of reason, scientific method, rational discourse, personal liberty, and individual responsibility. A central tenet of the new faith was the ability to control the environment. In 1965, President Johnson's Council of Economic Advisers, led by Walter Heller, declared: "Tools of economic policy are becoming more refined, more effective, and increasingly freed from inhibitions imposed by traditions, misunderstanding, and doctrinaire polemics." The Council declared that economic policymakers could "foresee and shape future development."[36]

In *Against The Gods: The Remarkable History of Risk*, Peter Bernstein argued that capitalism would be impossible without quantification and hedging of risk. Investors and businesses could now undertake long-term investments with confidence, secure in the knowledge that, if necessary risk could be hedged away at a price. In 1999 *Time* featured Alan Greenspan, Robert Rubin, and Lawrence Summers as the new vaudeville act, "The Committee to Save the World." No financial risk was so great that it could not be managed.

In 130 AD, Ptolemy, a Greek mathematician, astronomer, geographer, and astrologer, developed an astronomical system. The Ptolemaic system fitted the accepted view of philosophers and the Church that the Earth was at the center of the universe and all stellar bodies moved with perfect uniform circular motion. When Galileo observed the actual movements of heavenly objects and tested Ptolemy's theories against the evidence, the system collapsed. Modern economics resembles a Ptolemaic system where deeply held philosophical and political beliefs shaped models of economies and markets.

As the Russians learned, economics is ideology. Alan Blinder, a former vice-chairman of the Fed, observed: "Some…economists are extremely ideological. If you [give] them evidence counter to their world view, they say you are wrong."[37]

The dominant theme is free and efficient markets, which have to be left alone for the common good. Thomas Frank in *One Market, One God* captured this spirit:

> Efficient markets theory holds that stock markets process economic data quickly and flawlessly…commentators…believe that stock markets perform pretty much the same operation with general will, endlessly adjusting and modifying themselves in conformity with the vast and enigmatic popular mind.[38]

American Nobel-prize-winning economist Joseph Stiglitz dissented: "[Adam Smith's] invisible hand often seems invisible [because] it is often not there."[39]

Nineteenth-century Danish philosopher Søren Kierkegaard differentiated between *objective truths* and *subjective truths*. Objective truths are filtered and altered by our subjective truths. Financial economics, in its prioritization of evidence and its models, converted objective truths into subjective truths consistent with the Chicago Interpretation. Daniel Miller, an anthropologist, argued that "economics has the authority to transform the world into its image."[40] That image was money and the speculation economy.

Fata Morgana

It was a mirage, a *fata morgana*: "poetic crap, in short."[41] The world was not structured, comprehensible or controllable. Theories were narrative fallacies where unconnected data was rearranged into a plausible story after the fact to give it an identifiable explanation.

Robert Merton's first published paper—"The 'motionless' motion of Swift's flying island"—was about Jonathan Swift's *Gulliver's Travels*. Educated people, fond of mathematics and astronomy, populated Laputa, Swift's fictional island. The Laputians were impractical, unable to construct buildings or make clothing, and insisted on taking measurements with compasses and quadrants where measuring tapes were appropriate. *La puta* means "whore" in Spanish profanity, alluding to Martin Luther's famous phrase: "that great whore, reason." Swift's allegory was a satire on rational thinking. Much of the liturgy of finance and economics was *Laputian* in nature.

In 1936 sociologist Robert K. Merton, Robert Merton's father, introduced the concept of *unintended consequences*. The world's complexity, self-deception, hubris, and biases had unintended consequences. There is *ignorance*—the impossibility of anticipating everything leading to incomplete analysis; the likelihood of *error*—the incorrect analysis of the problem or inappropriate application to a situation; *immediate interest*—which may override long-term interests; *basic values*—requiring or prohibiting certain actions; and the problem of the *self-defeating prophecy*—fear driving people to find solutions before the problem occurs. The financial theories and models had serious unintended consequenses and were deeply flawed.

Quantification of risk is difficult. The illusion that risk can be measured or managed has unintended consequences, encouraging risk taking or lulling regulators and policy makers into assuming that something is less risky than it is. Managing risk itself creates instability and increases risk. Financial markets are artificial man-made creations, not objects found in nature. As Taleb noted: "Our activities may invalidate our measurements."[42]

Keynes had modest hopes for economics: "If economists could manage to get themselves thought of as humble, competent people on a level with dentists, that would be splendid!"[43] Believing that they were able to control markets and economies, ambitious modern policy makers and economists embraced reason and scientific method, ignoring the law of unintended consequences. Ignorance, error, and immediate interest were crucial subtexts in finance.

In business to manufacture financial products and sell them to clients for profit, financiers were oblivious to the theoretical nuances and debates. Financial economics relies heavily on data collected by Chicago's Center for Research in Security Prices (CRSP), funded by Merrill Lynch. The sponsorship was not driven by altruistic interest in research and knowledge. In 1960 Louis Engle, Merrill's head of advertising and marketing, discovered that the Securities and Exchange Commission (SEC) would not allow the broker to advertise stocks as an appropriate investment without evidence. Engle funded CRSP to undertake a long-term study of returns on shares to justify Merrill selling stocks to ordinary investors. As Confucius observed: "The superior man understands what is right; the inferior man understands what will sell."

Theory and practice have always been occasional bedfellows on Wall Street. Financiers borrow and steal whatever bits and pieces of any cosmological theory and Sufi philosophy within reach.

Subtle theological debates about finance did not interest bankers. Was *The Physical Impossibility of Death in the Mind of Someone Living* really art or amateur taxidermy? Traders did not care, only being interested in whether clients would pay good money for it. They took the advice of art critic Peter Schjedahl: "Art tells you things you don't know you need to know until you know them."[44]

The new economics allowed politicians to implement their ideological agendas. The new finance provided the moral and intellectual basis for financial conquest, plunder, and pillage. The historian Bernal Díaz del Castillo, companion of Hernán Cortés de Monroy y Pizarro, the Spanish conquistador who led the Spanish colonisation of the Americas, understood this very well: "We came here (to America) to serve God and the King, and also to get rich."

The professors may have been after some elusive truth but ended up as the piano players in the whorehouse. The smart ones cut themselves a share of the action. Financiers did what they had always done—whatever it takes to make money, only now they did it with *financial alchemy*.

Part III

Alchemy

Alchemy—magical powers, traditionally associated with transmuting base metals into gold.

In medieval times, alchemists sought riches in science, by developing techniques to create gold—money. In the age of capital, financiers developed techniques based on fundamentalist money theories, which exploited society's faith in money.

Like alchemy, private equity, securitization, derivatives, and hedge funds promised unimagined riches. In reality, the techniques were merely disguised debt or new opaque risk packages that would fool customers and eventually the financiers themselves.

9

Learning to Love Debt

Financial alchemy took the form of more and more borrowing, initially in the form of private equity and junk bonds. Private equity, originally called leveraged buyouts (LBO), was about high levels of leverage—debt. Investors, *financial sponsors*, committed a small amount of the capital required to buy a company. The bulk was borrowed and repaid from the cash flow of the acquired business. The game was buying low and selling high, with other people's money.

Fixed Floor Coverings

Congoleum traced its origins back to the American Nairn Linoleum Company, established in 1887 in Kearny, New Jersey. The company manufactured linoleum, a durable floor covering made from solidified linseed oil, pine rosin, ground cork dust, wood flour, and mineral fillers on a burlap or canvas backing.

In 1978, Congoleum had $576 million of revenue and $42 million in earnings. 40 percent of revenues and 53 percent of earnings came from linoleum. The rest came from ship-building and automotive accessories. The company had negligible debt. Congoleum shares traded at a current market price of $25.375, equivalent to seven times price/earnings ratio (share price divided by current earning per share—EPS).

On July 16, 1978 First Boston (now part of Credit Suisse) and insurer Prudential Insurance Company offered $474.7 million to purchase Congoleum at $38 per share, 50 percent above the market price, financing the purchase with 87 percent debt (see Table 9.1).[1]

Table 9.1 First Boston's Offer to Purchase Congoleum

	$ million	Percentage of Total Capital
Congoleum surplus cash	95.1	
Bank loans	125.0	33
Institutional investor funds		
Senior debt	113.6	30
Subordinated debt	89.8	24
Cumulative preferred stock	26.2	7
Stock		
Common stock	16.5	4
Common stock—investment banks	4.5	1
Common stock—management	4.0	1
Total	474.7	

Note: Percentage of capital is calculated after excluding the Congoleum surplus cash.

The purchase was less risky than it appeared because the company's stable earnings and cash flows could support increased debt repayments. Following the LBO, according to First Boston's forecast, Congoleum's interest coverage (interest payable divided by earnings before interest and tax—EBIT) would be 1.7 times. Earnings would have to fall by 41 percent before it would have difficulty meeting interest payments. Although this was a low margin of safety, Congoleum's interest coverage would improve rapidly as it paid off debt. By 1984 one-third of its borrowing would be repaid and interest cover increased to around 4.6 times—an excellent margin of safety. Patents and royalty arrangements protected earnings from the floor covering business. The shipping business had a backlog of orders and contracts with its clients, including the U.S. Navy.

Following the successful acquisition of Congoleum by First Boston, the firm, in fact, reduced borrowing ahead of schedule by 1983. Congoleum then underwent a new LBO. In 1986 management liquidated Congoleum, selling off the businesses separately for $850 million, an increase in the company's value of 175 percent in 7 years. The managers turned their $4.0 million investment in Congoleum into nearly $600 million. Byron Radaker and Eddy Nicholson, who had managed Congoleum since 1975, announced: "We expect to build another company or make some interesting investments in the future. Before we're going to make any decisions we're going to take a rest."[2] For everyone, it was one huge payday, all done with leverage.

By the Bootstraps

LBOs are synonymous with KKR (Kohlberg, Kravis, and Roberts) and their $31.1 billion LBO of RJR Nabisco, chronicled in the 1990 book *Barbarians at the Gate: The Fall of RJR Nabisco*. In 2006 and 2007, larger LBOs were completed although, after adjustment for inflation, none surpassed RJR Nabisco.

While at investment bank Bear Stearns, Jerome Kohlberg, Jr. and his protégés Henry Kravis and George Roberts, a cousin of Kravis, purchased businesses for financial buyers using large amounts of debt. After strategic disagreements, the three left Bear Stearns, creating KKR in 1976.

LBOs were not new. After the Second World War there were *bootstrap acquisitions* where financial buyers bought businesses, using the acquired company's assets and cash flows to pay for the purchase. In the 1960s, James Ling and his investment conglomerate LTV purchased companies using high levels of debt, selling off the parts for profit. Ling's *modus operandi* was simple: "Jimmy looked for value.... Here's an undervalued company. [He] could leverage the whole thing and the company could buy itself."[3]

During the 1970s, with the global economy mired in low economic growth, high inflation, and high unemployment, LBO volumes grew steadily. Many were purchases of unwanted or underperforming businesses, or smaller companies whose shares were undervalued due to lack of research coverage, limited liquidity, and their unfashionable businesses. Hastily assembled conglomerates from the 1960 go-go years also needed restructuring.

LBO firms gobbled up *quiet* companies with reliable earnings and cash flow. Financial buyers and a stake for existing management and staff were attractive to a retiring generation of founders of family-owned businesses. Corporate managers who had experienced the Great Depression first hand and shunned debt were literally dying off. The new managers, many with MBAs, were more willing to borrow.

In January 1982, an investment group headed by William Simon, a former U.S. Treasury secretary, acquired Gibson Greetings, a producer of greeting cards, for $80 million. Some 16 months later the investors floated Gibson on the stock market for $290 million. Simon turned an investment of around $330,000 into approximately $70 million. The success of Gibson Greetings and the huge returns attracted attention, triggering a boom in LBOs.

Leverage for Everything

True believers argued that LBOs empowered management to improve operations and efficiency, increasing earnings, and the value of the business. The popular Boston Consultant Group (BCG) *growth-share matrix* categorized businesses as "stars," "cash cows," "question marks," and "dogs." Good management took funds generated by cash cows to invest in stars or question marks with higher growth and earnings potential. LBOs used debt to convert cash cows, question marks, and even dogs into stars—the economic equivalent of kissing the frog to turn it into a prince.

Assume you buy a company for $100 million using $10 million of equity and borrowing $90 million at 6 percent per annum. The company produces cash of $15 million each year. If you pay no dividends and do not invest in the business, diverting all the cash ($15 million) to paying back debt, then you are debt free in 8 years. If you can sell the business for the original value, then your $10 million investment is now worth $100 million, a return of 33 percent per annum. If you can extract more cash from the business, then you pay down the debt quicker, increasing returns. If cash flow increases by one-third to $20 million per annum, then debt is repaid in 6 years, increasing returns to 46 percent per annum.

Investors in Congoleum paid a premium of $154 million (50 percent over the market share price before the First Boston offer). Cost-savings from becoming a private company and large tax benefits accounted for most of the premium paid. Savings from avoiding the costs of being a public listed company were around $11 million over 5 years in 1979 dollars. Congoleum's tax deductible interest deductions were equivalent to $78 million. Congoleum's assets were written up to fair market value, increasing depreciation expenses and generating additional tax savings worth $50 million over 5 years. These savings, totalling around $139 million, made up most of the extra amount that First Boston was willing to pay.

Franco Modigliani and Merton Miller had identified that firms with larger borrowings benefited from the lower cost of debt and tax savings, because they were able to deduct the interest payable. Debt, they argued, should be increased to a point where the risk of bankruptcy was manageable to increase returns to shareholders. LBOs were a practical application of this insight. In July 1909, during a debate on introducing corporate income tax and making interest expenses tax deductible, U..S Senator Augustus O. Bacon prophetically noted: "It will be within the powers of corporations to convert their stock into bonds…in so doing, they will escape the payment of this tax."[4]

LBOs did not rejuvenate firms or improve them. John Brooks, a journalist, contrasted acquisitions of the conglomerate era of the 1960s and the LBOs of the 1980s: "the acquirers…in the sixties intended to operate them or let them operate themselves, those of the eighties…seemed…to be for the purpose of dismantling them…for a quick-cash profit."[5] One financier used rhapsodic language: "It's the leverage. What we are really doing is releasing value the way a sculptor releases a work of art from a block of stone."[6] LBOs were not art; they were about milking the cash cow.

Cutting to the Bone

Between 1979 and 1989, more than 2,000 LBOs, worth in excess of $250 billion, were completed. KKR and its competitors created investment funds to invest in their deals.

The size of the deals grew rapidly. Increasingly, the acquisitions were unfriendly—hostile and unsolicited bids. When KKR considered an unsolicited offer, Kohlberg protested: "It's not the way of the firm."[7]

Initially, transactions stuck to the script, focusing on businesses with strong, stable cash flows that were able to support debt. Over time, the margin of safety declined. Congoleum's interest coverage of 1.7 times was considered aggressive. By the late 1980s, the coverage ratios were around 0.7 times, meaning borrowers would have difficulty even paying interest.[8] Health warnings, risk factors, relating to LBO debt, stated that: "funds generated by the existing operations will be insufficient to enable the Company to meet its obligations on its borrowings." It was no longer a case of milking the cow.

Under innovative debt structures, interest was accrued but not paid in cash. It would be paid when assets were sold or from money raised by selling shares. The lenders were attracted by the higher interest rates, ignoring whether they would receive anything at all. LBOs now relied on paying down debt from selling assets, cost cutting, reducing business investment, and other corporate auto-cannibalism: "We're always cutting, cutting, cutting.... There's the risk that you may cut out something that you really need."[9]

In the 1980s, corporate raiders—T. Boone Pickens, Carl Icahn, Victor Posner, Robert M. Bass, Kirk Kerkorian, Sir James Goldsmith, Saul Steinberg—dominated LBOs.

Boone Pickens made a series of raids on major oil companies, realizing that they were literally liquidating themselves by depleting their reserves without investing in exploration and development to replenish them. Pickens was unsuccessful but earned significant profits by building up strategic stakes in companies like Cities Services, Gulf Oil, and Unocal, effectively putting them into play. It was simple *greenmail*, the use of the threat of a hostile takeover to coerce management into buying off the potential bidder. Pickens profited from selling out his stake to either white knights arranged by the board or sometimes to the company itself, which borrowed to buy back its own shares from the unwelcome intruder.

After leaving to set up his own buyout firm, Kohlberg staked out the high moral ground, speaking out against "overpowering greed" and the breakdown in Wall Street's ethical system. But Kohlberg, a "spiritual leader" questioning the evolution of the industry, continued to make millions of dollars from his investments in KKR transactions and preferential rights to invest in new transactions, including RJR Nabisco.[10]

Professor Jensen Goes to Wall Street

Professor Michael Jensen, a prominent evangelist of the Chicago School, argued that LBOs improved the efficiency of firms.[11] The discipline of debt, the obligation to make interest and principal payments, forced operational improvements. Substitution of expensive equity with cheaper debt lowered the businesses' cost of capital. Managers with meaningful equity stakes behaved like owners maximizing shareholder value, better aligning the interests of managers and shareholders. Private firms, protected from the pressures of meeting quarterly earnings targets, and the threat of takeovers, could be managed for the long term.

Critics saw LBOs as financial opportunism, exploiting tax benefits. Operational benefits of LBOs were limited and not the real motivation. They argued that lenders misunderstood risk and underpriced the debt.

In the late 1970s and early 1980s, American industry was embattled as stagflation and increased competition, especially from Japan and Germany, squeezed profitability. Product quality was often poor, costs high and sensitivity to customer requirements absent. Businesses needed radical reinvention to become competitive and viable.

Like BCG, Jensen focused on *free cash flow*—the surplus cash from operations after reinvestment to maintain or renew capacity where it was profitable. In periods of growth, firms achieved high returns but needed cash. High returns came from strong demand, high prices, in part driven by a shortage of production capacity to meet this demand, and limited competition. Cash shortfalls reflected the need to constantly invest in plant, equipment, working capital, and human resources to grow. As the market for a product matured, supply and demand aligned and competition, attracted by high returns, reduced earnings. While profits and investment returns fell, free cash flow increased, as investment needs declined.

During the growth phase, the firm needed to raise money from equity and debt investors, who provided discipline and control of the firm's activities. As it reached maturity, the firm could fund investments from its own free cash flow, reducing external scrutiny. This meant that managers paid off debt and retained surplus cash, increasing autonomy. All this increased the firm's cost of capital and frequently led to poor investments.

Management overinvested in industries already suffering from overcapacity or, worse, invested in unrelated industries to diversify. Performance anxiety caused firms to overinvest in growth businesses to disguise poor returns from their mature businesses. Alternatively, firms under-invested in growth areas because of competitive pressures in their mature markets.

Jensen saw the conflict between the owner (shareholders) and the agent (the managers) in terms of control and utilization of cash flow. LBOs increased efficiency by reducing investments in unprofitable businesses, forcing the sale of individual assets or complete business units. Buyouts encouraged businesses to concentrate on identifiable and closely related activities, giving investors direct, undiluted exposure to specific businesses, pure plays. Investors had control over their portfolios, allowing better diversification and reducing the discount attached to a bundled investment. More debt forced firms to return cash to investors through increased interest and principal repayments, increased dividends, share repurchases, and capital returns. Higher debt reduced capital cost and lowered tax paid.

The key was the discipline of debt and active shareholders, such as private equity investors. The correct management incentives, usually substantial equity ownership by managers and payments linked to performance, were the cure-all for capitalism's ills.

Drowning by Numbers

Jensen accurately identified the disease afflicting of American corporations. At RJR Nabisco the CEO's dog flew on one of ten corporate jets under the name "G. Shepherd." But Jensen identified the wrong cure. Private equity firms did not have the required operational skills to revitalize the companies they took over. Henry Kravis admitted: "We're financial people, not operating people. We don't know how to run a company. We'd only mess it up if we tried."[12]

The aim became *buy and flick*. Rather than fix deep-seated problems, expensive managers used short-term measures to boost performance—cutting costs deeply and reducing investment. Then the business was sold or its shares offered to public investors allowing the private equity firm to sell out and cash in. Henry Kravis summed up the strategy: "Don't congratulate me when we buy it. Congratulate me when I sell it."[13]

There was little direct contact between the investors and the firms themselves. Austerity measures were delivered remotely via phone, fax, and emails. The emphasis was on the numbers, meeting financial targets to pay down debt. Corporate performance was analyzed and re-analyzed on spreadsheets that were becoming part of finance: "the personal computer accomplished for Wall Street buyout boutiques what the advent of gunpowder did for Mongol warriors."[14]

Private equity firms controlled empires that were disparate in industry and geography, increasingly resembling the large companies that they dismembered. Michael Jensen found even this to be positive, comparing it to the *keiretsu* or *zaibatsu* structure in Japan where banks and financial institutions held equity stakes in companies they lent to. Unfortunately, as Edward Deming, the management expert, noted: "American management thinks that they can just copy from Japan—but they don't know what to copy!"[15]

The success of LBOs relied on management incentives and privileged access to information. Managers, either existing or especially brought in, received 10–15 percent ownership in the purchased company, more generous than the 1–3 percent in stock options they would traditionally have received. A KKR associate accurately described the strategy: "Grab a man by his W-2 [the wage and tax statement used by the U.S. Internal Revenue Service to report wages] and his heart and mind will follow."[16]

There were conflicts of interest in LBOs. Managers used privileged access to information about a company's activities to lower the price, paving the way for a LBO that might benefit them. Where they were part of the LBO, existing management claimed to know how to fix or improve the business—but only if given a large equity interest. It was legal blackmail.

Buyout firms collected a fee, typically 1 percent of each purchase. In addition, the buyout firm charged an annual management fee, around 1–2 percent, on the investors' funds, managed plus 20 percent carried interest, receiving a share of any investment gains on disposition. They charged annual monitoring and director's fees. During negotiations, Gerald Saltarelli, chairman of Houdaille, argued that KKR should not be entitled to any fee for buying the company. Kohlberg argued he was entitled to a fee: "I'm an investment banker."[17]

Lenders got high interest rates as well as substantial fees. When junk bonds started to be used for financing LBOs, Drexel Burnham Lambert (Drexel) received a fixed fee (0.50–1 percent) of the amount raised, a commitment fee, an underwriting fee, an advisory fee, warrants over the stock, and expenses. In the LBO of Triangle, Drexel earned fees of $25 million plus warrants over 16 percent of the purchased company. When banks lent to LBOs, they too were proficient at charging substantial fees. Legal fees, accounting charges, due diligence costs, and other professional fees routinely ran into tens of millions of dollars. Even the catering bill, for coffee, doughnuts and Chinese takeaways, ran into the tens of thousands.

Who was paying for this? The client. Where were the profits coming from? The massive leverage, substantial tax benefits, and "increased efficiency"—cost cutting primarily from reducing staffing levels and pay cuts for the rank and file employees. Magical debt was the stick—the sword of Damocles hanging over management forcing the right actions to be taken. There was the carrot—management would get very rich if they could meet targets.

Harvard Business School Professor Malcolm Salter referred to LBOs as "the repair shop for capitalism."[18] Finance had become the panacea for arresting America's industrial decline. There was little attempt to address problems of product, manufacturing, quality, sales, and customer service. In Phillipe Meyer's novel *American Rust*, a former employee of a U.S. steelworks who has been crippled in an industrial accident muses: "the Japs and Germans…were always investing…Penn Steel never invested a dime in its mills, guaranteed its own downfall…those welfare states, Germany and Sweden, they made plenty of steel…they were the ones supposed to go bankrupt."[19]

Censored Loans

Believing they deserved a bigger share of the rewards, the insurers, who initially supplied the money for LBOs, demanded higher fees and more equity. Buyout firms turned to bankers and ultimately the junk bond market.

Bankers found the margin of safety on LBO loans low. But self-interest and large profits led to a change of heart. Bankers Trust (BT), in the process of transforming itself into an aggressive investment bank, recognized that the risk of LBO loans was manageable, interest rates and fees were high, the volume of business was substantial, and the buyout firms paid well. Others followed, and it became possible to raise large sums quickly.

In 1986, at a lavish dinner to celebrate the successful closing of an LBO, Don Kelly, the new CEO of Beatrice, a consumer products group, told the bankers: "This is the same group of dummies who lent me too much money before…guess what? You've gone and done it again!"[20] The $6.2 billion Beatrice transaction resulted in fees to financiers and lawyers of $248 million, of which 53 banks shared $44 million.

Buyouts turned increasingly to junk bonds, the product of the mercurial Mike Milken and Drexel. Saul Fix, a KKR associate, summed it up: "Drexel's money became a key element…. If we didn't do it this way, we'd have to pay a lot more and have had to rely on a much more complex, unwieldy structure…we never would have been able to do all the things we did."[21]

Bond markets traditionally provided finance only to highly creditworthy companies. Credit quality was a function of credit rating provided by the major rating agencies—Moody's Investor Services (Moodys), Standard & Poor's (S&P), and Fitch. The rating agencies were the equivalent of film censors. Instead of rating films for sex, violence, and offensiveness, they graded the credit quality of bonds. Table 9.2 shows the rating scale.

TABLE 9.2 Rating Scales

Moodys	S&P	Fitch	Official Meaning	Unofficial Meaning
Investment grade				
AAA	AAA	AAA	Obligations are judged to be of the highest quality, with minimal credit risk.	The crème de la crème of bonds.
Aa	AA	AA	Obligations are judged to be of high quality and are subject to very low credit risk.	Doesn't have the snob value of AAA.
A	A	A	Obligations are considered upper-medium grade and are subject to low credit risk.	If you can't afford Louis Vuitton.
Baa	BBB	BBB	Obligations are subject to moderate credit risk. They are considered medium grade and as such may possess certain speculative characteristics.	Perfectly serviceable—Barneys or Wal-Mart.
Noninvestment grade (colloquially "junk" or "high yield")				
Ba	BB	BB	Obligations are judged to have speculative elements and are subject to substantial credit risk.	Seconds and rejects.
B	B	B	Obligations considered speculative and are subject to high credit risk.	You are a risk taker.
Caa	CCC	CCC	Obligations are judged to be of poor standing and are subject to very high credit risk. They may be highly speculative and have a high probability of defaulting with limited prospect for recovery of principal and interest.	Russian roulette with five bullets in the chamber.
D	D	D	In default.	Scrape your brains off the wall and place in a plastic bag.

Insurance companies, pension funds, trust and endowment funds, banks, mutual funds, and the wealthy traditionally bought only investment grade bonds (rated BBB or better). Mike Milken and Drexel created an entire new market for noninvestment grade bonds, taking the use of debt and leverage on to a different plane. Meshulam Riklis, who controlled Rapid American, a conglomerate built with leverage, referred to it as the "effective nonuse of cash"[22]—at least, your own.

High Opportunity Bonds

In August 1985, Forbes argued that Milken had "created his own universe."[23] With great tenacity, an endless appetite for work, and a monomaniac focus, Milken was "an amazing salesman" of junk bonds.[24] He disliked the term "junk," preferring *high opportunity* bonds. They would eventually become *high yield* bonds.

At the University of Pennsylvania's Wharton Business School, Milken came across the work of W. Braddock Hickman. In his 1958 *Corporate Bond Quality and Investor Experience*, which sold 934 copies, Hickman's laborious precomputer analysis showed that lower rated bond issues that paid high rates of interest to compensate for the higher risk were safer and had lower rates of default than previously thought. Even after factoring in losses when issuers defaulted, investors in low-rated bonds did better than investors in high-quality bonds. In 1984, New York University Professor Edward Altman confirmed the thesis.

Advocates now argued that junk bonds were a sound investment for investors with fiduciary responsibilities, as bond ratings overestimated the risk of noninvestment grade bonds. Numerous papers and books by independent analysts, who acted as consultants to, or were retained and paid by investment banks, extolled the case for junk bonds.

Analysis of defaulted bonds is tricky because there are few defaults, which are concentrated in specific industries (railways) or at specific times (severe recessions such as the 1920s). Markets and issuers change over time, and data is not comparable. Hickman did not conclude that ratings were incorrect but that there were errors, due to problems in forecasting the business cycle and industry developments. Lower-rated bonds outperformed at certain times of the economic cycle, mainly when markets became extremely concerned about default. It was an old investment adage—buy when everybody is selling, when there are blood and tanks on the street.

Altman's studies compared defaults in one year to the entire universe of junk bonds. The rate of default in Year x was the number of defaults divided by the volume of junk bonds on issue. The rapid increase in the size of the market (from $10 billion outstanding in 1978 to $100 billion a decade later) lowered the default rates artificially. A fairer comparison was actual defaults as a percentage of the amount issued *in the original year of issue*.

Altman's studies did not adjust for other games. Issuers routinely *overfunded*, raising excess cash, which meant borrowers would not default quickly. Financially distressed junk bonds were often exchanged for new securities, sometimes not paying interest in cash, to avoid default. No distinction was drawn between bonds issued by investment grade companies whose ratings had fallen and issuers who started as junk.[25]

In the late 1980s, as the LBO boom was ending, new research studies on junk bonds corrected the problems of previous studies. Paul Asquith, a professor at Harvard Graduate School of Business, with his colleagues David Mullins and Eric Wolf, found that junk bond default rates were higher than previously stated. Around 30 percent of all junk bonds issued in 1977–9 had defaulted or been subject to a distressed exchange. Lipper Analytical Services, an investment firm, found that over 10 years junk bonds provided lower returns than government bonds, earning the same as money market funds. Altman published new research reaching similar conclusions.[26] As Laurence J. Peter, author of *The Peter Principle*, stated: "Facts are stubborn things, but statistics are more pliable."

Fallen Angels

Milken put Hickman's theories to work at Drexel Harriman Ripley, an investment bank that had once partnered with JP Morgan. As head of fixed income research and subsequently sales and trading, Milken operated in the bond underworld, buying and selling *fallen angels* or *Chinese paper*—bonds issued by investment-grade companies that had their ratings downgraded and were trading at deep discounts.

Milken's trading made money but no friends. When Drexel traders who scorned junk bonds tried to shut down Milken, management pointed out that Milken made significant amounts of money using a modest amount of the firm's capital. Investment-grade bond traders used more capital and made large losses. "Whom should I fire?" the manager asked.[27]

Unhappy that the firm restricted his trading by limiting his ability to take risks, Milken wanted to go back to Wharton to teach. His trading limit was increased from $500,000 to $2 million (a substantial sum at that time). Milken stayed, and in 1973 made $2 million in profits (a return of 100 percent on his capital) and received 35 percent of profits as a bonus. The percentage would stay the same throughout his career at Drexel, without any cap on the amount he could receive.

Milken's success allowed him to expand, creating an autonomous unit with its own traders, sales staff, and research analysts to trade junk bonds.

The unit sealed its independence by moving to Beverly Hills on the West Coast.

Junk People

Milken's consistent mantra was that the rating of junk bonds was incorrect—the potential returns outweighed the risk. Investors in junk bonds received higher interest rates but also potential gains in the value of the bond if the company's fortunes and rating improved. Buying lower-rated bonds was less risky because higher-rated companies were more likely to be downgraded—AAA-rated companies can only be downgraded. Buying a bond for, say, 40 cents per dollar of face value was less risky than buying a bond trading at a dollar (or par), as it could only fall. Milken argued that the debt holder rather than shareholder controlled the company. If a company missed any payment of interest or principal, the lenders could move in and take over.

Investors began to take notice, especially since high-rated bonds offered low returns and some, such as securities issued by the City of New York, defaulted on payment of interest. High returns from purchasing Milken's junk bonds turned portfolio managers like David Solomon of First Investors Fund for Income into celebrities.

In 1974 Fred Carr, a former driveway repairman and manager of the Enterprise Fund in the 1960s, took over a small insurance company—First Executive Insurance. He created a product called the *single premium deferred annuity (SPDA)*. The purchasers invested a fixed amount, and the insurance company contracted to pay them an agreed amount after a fixed period. The key to the SPDA was the interest rate—the higher the rate, the higher the final payout. Purchasing junk bonds to generate high rates, First Executive became the market leader in annuities, creating a large market for junk bonds.

Thrift institutions like saving and loans associations (S&Ls) traditionally made long-term mortgage loans on fixed rates, funding them with short-term deposits where the interest rates were adjustable. When newly deregulated short-term interest rates rose sharply, as Paul Volcker tried to tame inflation, the S&L's cost of deposits exceeded the interest on loans. Congress changed regulations to help attract deposits and to improve profitability, expanding the S&L's investment powers by allowing purchases of junk bonds. In the 1980s, mutual funds specializing in junk bonds allowed individuals to invest in the market. Attracted by media campaigns promoting high returns, investors flocked to the funds.

Buyers of insurance products and policies were inadvertently purchasing junk bonds. Repackaged as *guaranteed investment contracts (GICs)*, issued by First Executive, junk bonds were being sold to pension funds. Depositors in S&Ls and the taxpayers guaranteeing the deposits were unwittingly exposed to junk bonds. Competitive pressures meant that the debate was not about buying junk bonds but why you weren't buying them.

Milken's Mobsters

But there just wasn't enough Chinese paper to match investor demand—there were far too few fallen angels. When Goldman Sachs and Lehman Brothers issued the first junk bonds in 1977, Milken and Drexel seized the opportunity, starting with a $30 million issue for Texas International. Over time, they found new issuers of junk bonds—*Milken's mobsters*.

Drexel forged relationships with the new robber barons—buyout firms, entrepreneurial outsiders like Turner Broadcasting, MCI, and McCaw Cellular, and aggressive corporate raiders like Carl Icahn and Boone Pickens. Drexel's Christian Anderson summarized the situation: "There are only two kinds of companies—the comers and the goers. We finance the comers."[28] Observers later noted: "Pumped into buyouts, Milken's junk bonds became a high-octane fuel that transformed the LBO industry from a Volkswagen Beetle into a monstrous drag race belching smoke and fire."[29]

Harvard-trained Fred Joseph, Drexel president and CEO, wanted to build the firm to rival Goldman Sachs, then, as now, the benchmark for excellence. Lacking clients within the Fortune 500, Drexel's investment banking franchise was built on the *comers* where expertise in junk bonds provided a crucial competitive edge. At a planning session, more psychotherapy than business school, Cavas Gobhai, an Indian consultant, saw the strategy as: "Merge with Mike."[30]

Drexel adopted aggressive and unconventional tactics, backing hostile acquisitions. Traditionally, companies lined up bank loans to support bids. Milken evolved the *highly confident letter*, which stated that Drexel was "highly confident" that it could obtain the necessary financing. Originally nicknamed the Air Fund, the highly confident letter lacked legal status, relying on Milken and Drexel's ability to underwrite and place bonds to raise the money. Drexel's reputation meant that the letter was as good as cash.

Modestly resourced corporate raiders, backed by a highly confident letter, were suddenly credible. Jay Higgins, head of mergers and acquisitions at rival Salomon Brothers, observed: "Big companies used to worry only about threats from other big companies. But with Drexel doing the financing, anybody long on ideas and short on capital is a threat."[31] Drexel moved from providing advice to bankrolling transactions as a principal.

The raiders, leveraged buyout funds, and investors met at the annual Drexel's High Yield Bond Conference to raise money for new deals. Held at the Beverly Hills Hotel, owned by Ivan Boesky, an investor specializing in risk arbitrage (betting on outcomes of mergers and acquisitions), the Predator's Ball was the bacchanalian centrepiece of the world of hostile takeovers and debt.

Milken always opened the conference with a simple statement: "There's $3 trillion in this room." Each year the number was higher, providing a measure of the power and influence of the players and Drexel. At the 1986 conference, Drexel screened a video (an annual tradition) showing a businessman striding into a meeting in a boardroom of The Fat and Lazy Corporation, brandishing a Drexel titanium card with a credit limit of $10 billion. After scrutinizing the card carefully, the Chairman makes an imprint of the card as the executives strap on gold-colored parachutes and jump out the windows. The businessman, played by Larry Hagman (then enjoying success as the tyrannical and ruthless J.R. Ewing in the hit TV series *Dallas*), grins and tells the audience: "Don't go hunting without it."

The Sweet Envy of Bankers

Nick Brady, CEO of the investment bank Dillon Read, saw Drexel as "junk people buying junk bonds."[32] Michel Bergerac, chairman and CEO of Revlon, subject to a hostile bid from Ronald Perelman, sneered: "Drexel has inserted itself between the pawnbrokers and the banks."[33]

Drexel's business practices failed modern tests of corporate conduct. One attendee naïvely misunderstood the presence of extremely attractive women at the firm's functions: "I've got to hand it to these guys—I've never seen so many beautiful wives." A banker observing one guest conversing at length with a woman, set him straight: "Tell Irwin he doesn't have to work so hard. She's already paid for."[34] When Perelman, a Drexel client, sought entry into the Ivy League social circle after completing the takeover of Revlon, one observer noted: "This has got to be the highest price ever paid in the history of this country to get a good table at a New York restaurant."[35]

But Drexel rapidly became the most profitable investment bank on the street, using its profits from junk bonds to diversify its clients and businesses. It was on its way to its objective: "to be as big as Salomon [Brothers] so we can be as arrogant as they are and tell them to go stuff it."[36] Drexel now pitched to corporate blue bloods with an approach straight out of *The Godfather*: You become our clients and pay us; we will protect you. Clients shopped around, moving from "the traditional concept of marriage to one-night stands."[37]

Other banks eyed Drexel's business enviously but feared that a déclassé activity like junk bonds would alienate traditional clients. By 1983/4, major investment banks caved in. Morgan Stanley, the bluest of the blue bloods, advised companies to take on debt, initiated hostile takeovers, and traded junk to protect its franchise. Eric Gleacher, Morgan Stanley's head of mergers and acquisitions, defended the strategy: "When you look at the debt of the world, the debt of the country, and the debt of the private sector, you can't with a straight face tell me that a few speculative merger deals are going to tip the balance and create disaster."[38]

Competition on fees and commissions was ferocious. Traditional syndicates formed by investment banks to market securities were redundant. Drexel frequently underwrote bond issues alone, relying on its capability to underwrite large amounts at short notice, risking its own money and trusting its placement power.

Drexel excelled in the age of trading and risk: "Sharp elbows and a working knowledge of spreadsheets suddenly counted more than a nose for sherry or membership in Skull and Bones [a secret society at Yale University]."[39] Lazard Freres' Felix Rohatyn, a veteran investment banker, did not see the changes positively: "A cancer has been spreading in our industry...Too much money is coming together with too many young people who have little or no institutional memory, or sense of tradition, and who are under enormous economic pressure to perform in the glare of Hollywood like publicity."[40]

In the 1980s, when Merrill Lynch was rumored to be merging with Drexel, the betting on the new combine's name was Burn'em & Lynch'em. The merger did not happen. A quarter of a century later, Merrill would be destroyed by a different kind of junk.

Thank You for Borrowing

Throughout the 1980s, money flowed into buyout funds floated by LBO firms. The cost of debt fell and availability increased. Purchasers paid higher prices for businesses because the availability of cheap debt made the purchase more expensive. As the margin of safety fell, buyers and the investors took on more risk.

Subordinated ("sub" or "junior") debt replaced equity. If the company went bankrupt, then the subordinated debt holders would be paid after the *senior* debt. Subordinated debt investors received higher interest rates, but the cost to the borrower was lower than equity. Zero coupon debt allowed interest to be accrued every year with payment deferred till maturity. Pay-in-kind (PIK) notes allowed the company to pay interest in new IOUs not cash. Exchangeable variable rate debentures, with low interest rates that would reset at a future date, anticipated adjusted rate subprime mortgages (ARMs). Scarce cash was stretched further to service the increasing debt.

The day of reckoning—when the debt and the interest would have to be paid—was postponed.

In November 1984, Drexel arranged a $1.3 billion bond refinancing the debt of Metromedia Broadcasting Corporation, which had been bought in a LBO by John Kluge, chairman of Metromedia, and three managers. The complex package reduced Metromedia's cash outgoings, helping Kluge to avoid selling broadcasting assets to meet loan conditions. Interest rates went up from around 14.90 percent per annum to 15.40 percent per annum, but cash interest payments fell from 14.90 percent per annum to 10.30 percent per annum for the first 5 years. Around $290 million in principal repayments were deferred for 4 years.

Critics predicted problems with the arrangements. In May 1985, Rupert Murdoch bought Metromedia's TV stations for $2 billion ($650 million in cash and $1.35 billion in assumed debt) to create the Fox Network. Kluge netted $3 billion profit from the transactions. The critics were silenced.

The ambitious 1989 RJR Nabisco deal marked the high-water mark of the boom. RJ Reynolds was a tobacco business that owned the iconic Camel brand. RJR's stable businesses, low debt levels and low investment needs made the firm an attractive LBO candidate. Ross Johnson, the CEO, put RJR into play when he joined with Shearson Lehman Hutton to take the company private. The board refused the initial offer of $75 per share, initiating an auction. KKR eventually prevailed at a price of $109 per share, valuing RJR at $31 billion. The purchasers put in around $1.5 billion in equity, leaving the remaining $29.5 billion to be financed with debt.

One Bridge Too Far

But the environment was changing. Political concerns about jobs, investment security, and the large profits from LBOs led to congressional inquiries. Fred Hartley, chairman of Unocal, which was subject to a hostile bid from Boone Pickens, told the U.S. Senate:

> Corporate raiders and bust up takeovers have not inspired one new technological innovation; they have drained off investment capital. They have not strengthened companies; they have weakened them, loading surviving firms with onerous debt.[41]

Alan Greenspan was equivocal, arguing that "the trend towards more ownership by managers and tighter control…enhanced operational efficiency" while cautioning that increased debt created "broad based risk."[42]

Susan Faludi's Pulitzer-winning 1990 *Wall Street Journal* story "The reckoning" was an exposé of KKR's LBO of Safeway Stores, purchased for $4.7 billion, of which 94 percent was borrowed. Faludi drew attention to shareholder greed and the costs borne by employees of the company and the community. It did not help that KKR completed a successful public offering of 10 percent of Safeway at 450 percent of what they had paid 4 years earlier.

Barbarians at the Gate told of mismanagement, financier greed, and ignored social costs in the buyout of RJR. Michael Jensen complained that the book ignored "clear evidence of corporate wide inefficiencies at RJR Nabisco, including massive waste of 'corporate free cash flow.'"[43]

Unmanageable debt levels, over-optimistic forecasts and falling asset values after the 1987 stock market crash led to the bankruptcy of the Federated Department Stores, Revco drug stores, Walter Industries, FEB Trucking, and Eaton Leonard LBOs. Mounting losses to lenders in LBOs reduced the availability of finance. Changes in regulation made it more difficult for S&Ls and insurance companies to hold junk bonds. As they sold, prices fell, forcing other holders to follow and causing the junk bond market to seize up.

To compete against Drexel's highly confident letter, other banks and securities firms had provided *bridge financing*, using their own money to bridge the client from the time of making the offer to actual payment. When the bank and junk bond markets closed, it proved a bridge too far. The banks that expected to refinance the bridge loans later found themselves stuck with loans.

Drexel found itself tangled in a web of allegations and investigations into insider trading. In 1986, Dennis Levine, a Drexel investment banker, was charged with insider trading. Drexel traders joked: "Anybody who had to do 54 trades to make $12 million couldn't be any good."[44] Levine implicated Ivan Boesky, the model for Gordon Gekko in the 1987 movie *Wall Street*. In 1986, Boesky had declared: "Greed is all right...greed is healthy. You can be greedy and still feel good about yourself."[45] Boesky saved himself by cooperating with the Securities and Exchange Commission (SEC) and informing on Milken.

The SEC and Rudy Giuliani, the U.S. attorney for the Southern District of New York, launched wide-ranging investigations into Drexel's operations. The SEC brought charges of insider trading, stock manipulation, defrauding its clients, and stock parking (buying stocks for the benefit of another) against Drexel and Milken. Giuliani threatened indictment under the Racketeer Influenced and Corrupt Organizations (RICO) Act, originally intended for use against organized crime. Drexel could be required to post a performance bond of as much as $1 billion or have its assets frozen. Under an agreement with the government, Drexel pleaded *nolo contendere* (no contest) to six felonies and paid a record fine of $650 million. In March 1989, Milken was indicted and left the firm. In February 1990, Drexel filed for bankruptcy.

National Treasure

The Wall Street Journal stated:

> Not since J.P. Morgan has any financier influenced Wall Street and the nation the way Michael Milken has.... Not surprisingly, Mr. Milken, 42, aroused the fear and loathing of industrialists whose companies fell to his onslaughts or seemed likely candidates for his attention.

He was "the most important financier of the century."[46] In its August 1985 article, *Forbes* considered that Milken "isn't just a step ahead of his Wall Street peers—he's a quantum leap ahead, acting as venture capitalist, investment banker, trader, investor."[47]

Milken's activities entailed inherent conflicts of interest. Clients were encouraged to overfund—raise more money than required—with the surplus funds being invested in junk bonds sold by Drexel. The firm financed insurance companies and the purchase of S&Ls that then invested in junk bonds. Drexel financed acquisitions with junk bonds placed with Milken's clients. After completion of LBOs, the company's pension fund purchased high-yielding GICs from First Executive, creating demand for junk bonds. The higher return allowed the pension fund to reduce required contributions from the sponsor or even allow any overfunding to be returned. The money flowed back to the corporate raiders and investors, fueling a new round of acquisition activity. Relentless churn, buying and selling bonds, increased earnings.

Drexel traded with and raised money for risk arbitragers, like Boesky who bet on stocks in play in mergers and acquisitions. Bank Chinese walls were meant to separate the flow of material between those that make investment and trading decisions and others privy to undisclosed material information that may influence those decisions. In April 1986, Milken, contemptuous in his disregard for such niceties, told investors that "buying high-yield securities has overpowered all regulation."[48]

In the Drexel system, each division received bonuses linked only to individual performance, creating acrimonious relationships between the immensely profitable high-yield department and other parts of the firm. In 1986, Drexel earned $545.5 million, then the largest profit ever for a Wall Street investment bank. In 1987, Milken earned $550 million. Milken organized limited partnerships that allowed him and selected employees to invest in Drexel deals. The partnerships frequently bought and sold junk bonds or ended up with options to buy shares in buyouts that made more money than Drexel on some deals.

Milken's genius was to develop a system providing financing, arranging acquisitions, and trading in bonds and shares that excluded other players. He controlled information on companies and who held specific bonds or shares, setting up purchases and sales of securities at prices that he set. Anybody who wanted to play had to involve Drexel and Milken. For a brief period of financial time, Milken was the market—a financial "god."

In April 1990, Milken pleaded guilty to six securities and reporting felonies but did not admit to insider trading. He paid $200 million in fines and a further $400 million to shareholders hurt by his actions. Accepting a lifetime ban from the securities industry, Milken served 22 months (from March 1991 until January 1993) of a 10-year prison sentence. Milken's fans argued that he was a scapegoat, brought down by the American WASP business establishment because he was Jewish.

Today Milken is worth more $2 billion and active via the Milken Foundation and Milken Institute. In November 2004, *Fortune* magazine called Milken "The man who changed medicine" for funding medical research into life-threatening diseases. On May 1, 1990 *The New York Times* provided an assessment: "Michael Milken is a convicted felon. But he is also a financial genius."

Even without Milken, the junk bond market would recover and reemerge. Debt and leverage would become part of the mainstream. The ingredients of Drexel's success, especially the emphasis on trading and using the bank's own capital, would become the rulebook for others.

10

Private Vices

In the film *Rain Man*, the institutionalized, autistic savant Raymond Babbit (Dustin Hoffman) informs his brother Charlie Babbit (played by Tom Cruise) that he won't fly on any airline except Qantas because it had never crashed. Qantas remains a profitable, full-service airline, with its safety record more or less intact. When Ralph Fiennes, the English actor, who was alleged to have been involved in an intimate encounter with a flight attendant in an aircraft toilet, some dubbed the carrier—**Q**uickies **a**vailable **n**ear **t**oilet **a**sk **s**taff.

In 2007 a consortium of private equity investors bid A$11.1 billion ($9.2 billion) for Qantas, around A$8.5 billion ($7 billion) (77 percent) borrowed from banks. LBOs were now private equity and investors were keen to join the Mile High club.

Excess Returns

After the 1987 equity crash, Milken presciently had warned of increasing risk: "The byword is equitize."[1] After Drexel's demise, the focus was on restructuring legacy deals. RJR Nabisco required $1.7 billion of additional equity from KKR in 1990. Around 1992, leveraged buyouts (LBOs) started to recover. It was back to basics, buying quiet companies and extracting value from the operational side. Margins of safety improved and leverage of 60–80 percent was down from the 85–95 percent of the boom years.

New players joined familiar players, who had never gone away. There was the Blackstone Group—originally a mergers and acquisitions boutique founded in 1985 by Pete Peterson and Stephen Schwarzman of Lehman Brothers. There was Carlyle—founded in 1987 by Stephen Norris and David Rubenstein. There was Texas Pacific Group (now TPG Capital)—created by David Bonderman and James Coulter. Citicorp Venture Capital, spun out of CitiGroup, became CVC Capital Partners. Schroder Ventures (a part of venerable English merchant bank Schroders) morphed into Permira, derived from the Latin adjective *permirus* meaning "very surprising," "very different." Guy Hands created Nomura's Principal Finance Group, which eventually became Terra Firma Capital Partners.

Disillusioned with poor returns in equities and declining interest rates in the 1990s, investors invested in *alternative assets*, including buyouts and hedge funds promising high returns. Asset consultants cited alpha, beta, and diversification benefits based on historical performance. Investors ignored industrialist Warren Buffett's advice: "If past history was all there was to the game, the richest people would be librarians."

Debt now came increasingly from banks, who formed *leveraged finance groups* covering buyout firms (rebranded *financial sponsors*) supplying acquisition debt (*leveraged loans*). In the junk bond market, investors diversified out of buyouts into borrowers from emerging markets. In 1997/8, borrowers from Asia, Latin America, and Eastern Europe defaulted, inflicting large losses. Investors retreated to traditional areas like telecommunications, only for the dot.com bubble to burst, losing from the failure of firms like WorldCom, Adelphia, and Global Crossing.

The collapse of the technology stock bubble and the events of September 11, 2001 paved the way for a new buyout boom. Corporate and accounting scandals such as Enron, Tyco, and Worldcom led to the 2002 U.S. Corporate and Auditing Accountability and Responsibility Act—the Sarbanes–Oxley Act or SOX, named after sponsors U.S. Senator Paul Sarbanes and U.S. Representative Michael G. Oxley. SOX established legislative standards of auditor independence, corporate governance, internal controls, and enhanced financial disclosure for U.S. public companies, backed by criminal penalties. Public company boards and managers became extremely cautious, retaining excess cash and setting high hurdle rates for investments, making them buyout targets. Public companies went private just to avoid SOX.

In 2002, Alan Greenspan cut interest rates sharply to prevent the U.S. economy going into recession, reducing the cost of debt and increasing the ability to borrow to finance acquisitions. Lower rates encouraged investors to invest in higher risk debt and junk bonds for higher returns.

Subordinated debt reemerged as *mezzanine* (mezz) debt. PIK (pay in kind) debt was rebranded *toggle loans*, allowing interest payments in cash or by issuing IOUs. If the PIK feature was activated, *toggled*, then the interest rate increased by 0.25 percent per annum to 0.75 percent per annum. Toggles triggered by a cash flow trigger were known as PIYW (pay if you want) and PIYC (pay if you can). *Cov-lite* (covenant light) loans dispensed with protective covenants—financial tests designed to monitor the borrower's financial condition.

Looser lending conditions were encouraged by banks that no longer held on to the loans, repackaging them using securitization and derivatives for sale to investors. Financial alchemy, in the form of securitization, allowed low-quality (noninvestment grade) buyout loans to be repackaged into investment grade, even AAA rated bonds, increasing the number of potential buyers. In a virtuous spiral, increasing availability of cheap debt drove larger transactions, which in turn increased the flow of money into buyouts driving new transactions.

Sexy Private Equity

Rebranding buyouts as *private equity* was designed to distance them from the shameful history of Milken. In the period 2003 to 2007, 13,000 deals were completed, an increase of 140 percent from the 1996–2000 period. Between 2003 and 2007, 58 deals with a size of $5 billion or more were completed, an increase of 5,700 percent from the 1996–2000 period.

Transactions included household names—Toys R Us ($6.5 billion), Hertz ($15 billion) and Metro-Goldwyn-Mayer ($4.8 billion). RJR Nabisco was finally passed in nominal dollar terms by Blackstone's acquisition of Equity Office Properties and then by KKR and TPG's acquisition of TXU (formerly Texas Utilities). Private equity deal makers mused about the first deal of $100 billion.

In 2007, commitments to new private equity funds increased by 64 percent from 2000, and 2,250 percent from 1990. Some 75 funds of $5 billion or more were raised between 2003 and 2007. The Top 20 public pension funds allocations to private equity exceeded $100 billion between 2000 and 2007. Senior loan volumes for private transactions reached $485 billion between 2005 and 2007, an increase of 386 percent from the 1999–2001 period.

In 2007, to purchase businesses, private equity firms paid on average nine to ten times the company's annual cash flow, an increase of 62 percent from 2001, when they paid around six times cash flow. The amount of debt increased by around 50 percent, as companies borrowed six times annual cash flow compared to four times in 2001. Interest coverage fell to around one to one and a half times cash flow. The margin of safety was small, with many transactions vulnerable to downturns in economic activity. Purchasers relied on squeezing more cash out to service the debt.

The emphasis was on selling businesses off quickly, piecemeal or as a whole, to private buyers or the public. Private equity firms paid themselves large cash dividends as soon as possible, sometimes from borrowings and asset sales, to improve returns. This was termed *early return of capital*; critics preferred *strip mining*. Firms worked together in *club* deals to minimize competition and spread the risk of ever-larger transactions. Sales of investments from one fund to another became commonplace to increase values.

The fees from transactions exceeded the excesses of the 1980s. In May 2006, Thomas H. Lee Partners purchased 80 percent of Hawkeye Holdings, an Iowa Falls ethanol producer, investing $312 million. Before the purchase even closed, the private equity firm registered to undertake an initial public offering expected to generate a large profit. Thomas H. Lee received a $20 million advisory fee from Hawkeye for negotiating the buyout, a $1 million management fee, and $6 million to meet its tax obligations. Private equity investors collected payments of around $27 million, while Hawkeye earned $1.5 million in the 6 months. One article described private equity as Fees R Us.

Speaking at the London Business School in July 2007, Niall Ferguson, the economic historian, asked: "Why are we here attending conferences when we should be setting up private-equity firms?"[2]

Inflight Entertainment

In December 2007, Marjorie Jackson (known as Her Madge), chairperson, and Geoff Dixon (Dicko), CEO, announced that the board endorsed a private equity proposal to purchase Qantas for A$11.1 billion. Airline Partners Australia (APA), the purchasers, included TPG and Onex Group, Allco Equity Partners, Allco Finance Group, and Macquarie Bank. Allco and Macquarie ensured that Qantas remained majority Australian-owned to maintain traffic rights.

The price—A$5.45 per share plus an interim dividend of A$0.15 per share—was 55 percent higher than the average share price over the previous 12 months, above the record high for Qantas shares of A$5.28 and almost 88 percent above its recent low of A$2.93. The chairperson urged shareholders to board flight QF 545 (as the bid came to be known).

Successful buyouts of airlines are rare. Airline earnings and cash flows are sensitive to economic conditions and unpredictable changes in oil prices. Airlines require massive investment; the industry is regulated and in some countries unionized. But QF 545 was a calculated gamble.

Qantas was forecast to generate A$2 billion in cash flow on revenue of around A$13.6 billion. It had low debt, paid a lot of tax, and also paid high dividends. The purchase would increase interest costs to A$600 million, but lower tax from higher interest would reduce the cash outflow to A$400 million. Unpaid dividends would cover the rest. Modest increases in revenue (by 5 percent) and cost cutting (around A$400 million per annum) would increase cash flow to around A$2.9 billion. Assuming Qantas was still valued at around 5.5 times cash flow (as before the buyout), the airline would be worth A$15.8 billion. After paying off A$8.5 billion of debt, the private equity investors would turn a A$2.5 billion investment into A$7.3 billion in 5 years—a return of 24 percent per annum.

The airline's loyalty scheme (with 4.6 million members) could be sold for A$2 billion. The catering unit and valuable order positions in new generation fuel-efficient aircraft from Boeing and Airbus could be sold for cash. Deal fees (A$600 million) and a planned large special dividend to investors reduced the risk to the investors and increased the prospects of large returns. Qantas wheeled out a 96-year-old former employee George Roberts, who had been with the airline since 1936 and was still a part-time volunteer at the Qantas museum, to extol the bid's virtues.

Earlier, in mid-2007, Guy Hands' Terra Firma purchased the iconic EMI Group (formerly Electric & Musical Industries). EMI was famed for its His Master's Voice record label and the legendary London Abbey Road recording studios. Its roster of artists included classical and contemporary giants such as Arturo Toscanini, Otto Klemperer, Frank Sinatra, Cliff Richard, The Beatles, The Beach Boys, Pink Floyd, David Bowie, Queen, Coldplay, Kylie Minogue, Robbie Williams, and Norah Jones.

Hands boasted that he made money out the worst businesses in difficult industries. EMI fitted the criteria perfectly, having lost £260 million in 2007. EMI's share of the British market had dropped from 16 percent to 9 percent. CD sales had fallen 50 percent since 2000, in part because of illegal music downloads. The karaoke-loving Hands, a finance rock star, purchased EMI for a stunning £4 billion.

EMI earned royalties when its artists' songs were broadcast or downloaded. Terra Firma planned to sell the future royalty cash flows of EMI Music Publishing and the EMI Music catalogue for £4 billion. Hands also planned to sell the residual businesses and cut costs (including reducing the firm's £200,000 fruit and flowers annual budget) to boost earnings.

Anticipating a large and quick profit of £1 billion, Terra Firma invested the maximum permitted 30 percent of its two funds in EMI. CitiGroup agreed to provide debt funding of £2.6 billion, hoping to earn large fees for advising EMI, providing debt and arranging the securitizations and asset sales.

In 2007, Hands presented clients and bankers with John Kenneth Galbraith's *The Great Crash*—the history of the 1929 stock market crash. In 2008, he sent Niall Ferguson's *The Ascent of Money*, highlighting the statement: "Sooner or later, every bubble bursts." In the music business, EMI stood for Every Mistake Imaginable. QF 545 and the EMI buyouts were done at the top of the market with undue haste.

Selling the Family Silver

Private equity techniques were now applied to infrastructure—roads, tunnels, bridges, ports, airports, hospitals, schools, prisons, and so on. Traditionally, infrastructure was built and financed by government. Believing that governments had a limited role, Margaret Thatcher privatized British Telecom, British Gas, and British Petroleum, using the money received to pay off government debt. Thatcher boasted of turning Britons from a race of shopkeepers into a nation of shareholders. The new shareholders unwittingly paid a second time for something that they already owned as citizens.

In an era of balanced budgets and smaller government, essential infrastructure was provided by public private partnerships (PPP), where governments would grant concessions, for example the rights to a road, for a fixed period of 30 years. A consortium raised the money, built the road and operated it, charging cars using the road a toll to pay back the investors over time. At the end of the concession period, the road reverted to public ownership. The government gained a road without having to spend money. Taxpayers paid for the road in tolls rather than taxes.

Advocates argued that the arrangement saved government money while ensuring essential infrastructure was built. Competition and private ownership would deliver infrastructure efficiently with lower prices, improved quality, greater choice, and less corruption or bureaucracy. Critics argued that infrastructure by its inherent nature was a monopoly, which was not subject to competition. This allowed private firms to charge the maximum price that the market would bear rather than focus on the delivery of affordable basic services. Governments could also raise money more cheapely than private firms to finance essential projects. But in an era of febrile neoliberalism, the case in favor of PPPs prevailed.

Infrastructure attracted investment from pension funds and individuals saving for retirement. Long-term assets providing steady *safe* income, being less affected by economic cycles and competition. As infrastructure costs are mainly incurred in construction, increasing revenues from tolls as prices rose generated higher earnings to offset the effect of inflation. As returns from infrastructure were modest, banks boosted returns by using familiar private equity techniques—large amounts of debt.

Holey Dollar

Macquarie Bank, an Australian bank, was the global leader in infrastructure.[3] The *Macquarie model* entailed buying a business or infrastructure assets using its own money. After restructuring, the assets were sold to an affiliated fund, managed by the bank. The funds, private or listed on stock exchanges, used a combination of equity, raised from individual and institutional investors, and debt from banks to finance the asset. Macquarie controlled more than $250 billion, with investments in more than 100 different projects across the world.

The usual process was that Macquarie's bankers found the projects, then advised on the transaction, charging fees around 1 percent of the value. Macquarie then sold the project to a fund at a mark-up to what it paid for the asset. Macquarie charged fees for raising money for the funds. It charged fees for managing the funds, typically 1-2 percent plus a performance fee of 20 percent. Macquarie advised the business owned by the funds and raised money for them. The bank advised the funds on sales and restructuring of the projects it owned. It was a fee factory that competitors envied.

The projects had debt. Then the funds that owned the project used additional debt. The funds individually did not own a majority stake in projects, allowing them to avoid reporting the project's borrowing. Different Macquarie managed funds owned minority stakes in the same project or stakes in each other. The structure disguised the fact the projects might be funded with high levels of borrowings, as much as 90 percent.

Australians were ambivalent about Macquarie. On one side, Australia's "can do," "underdog that punches above its weight" culture celebrated the firm as a world leader. On the other, Australians loathed the bank's arrogance, political influence, and especially the rewards for its bankers. In 2007, Chairman David Clarke, Managing Director Alan Moss, Managing-Director-in-waiting Nicholas Moore and three other senior bankers together were paid A$209 million.

Ordinary individuals also objected to private ownership of public infrastructure and perceived price gouging. Macquarie-fund-owned Sydney Airport charged A$4 for a luggage trolley, a fee for taxis waiting to pick up passengers and usurious parking fees. Purchasers at the airport's extensive duty free shopping were provided with a shorter, *special* customs queue. When Macquarie and Cintra, a Spanish operator, combined to complete a 99-year lease of the Chicago Skyway, a 7.8 mile toll road, the charges increased from $2.00 to $2.50. Taxpayers questioned the right of governments to sell public property, allowing private interests to make money.

Macquarie Bank's namesake Lachlan Macquarie, governor of New South Wales between 1810 and 1821, notoriously doubled the colony's money supply by punching out the center of Spanish silver dollars, using both the holey dollar and the punched-out piece as currency. Macquarie Bank, whose logo is the holey dollar, improved on the governor's financial engineering. Powered by its model, Macquarie's share price rose by more than 20 times since its public listing in 1996. Investors in Macquarie funds enjoyed returns of 20 percent per annum.

Money for Nothing

Unlike private equity investors that receive capital gains when the fund realizes an investment, infrastructure funds pay high levels of income, designed to attract pension funds and especially individual retirees. As these investors were happy with returns lower than the 20 percent required by private equity investors, Macquarie could pay higher prices for assets, sustain higher levels of debt, and so increase its own fees.

Unprofitable in their early phase, infrastructure projects could not pay dividends. Instead, the funds issued *stapled securities*, combinations of shares of two different companies, enabling the fund to borrow to make distributions to investors even where the funds were not making money. As the cash from the project did not cover the payments to investors, the fund's debt increased rather than decreased over time.

Macquarie used proprietary models to value its holdings and determine earnings. Projected future cash flows were discounted back to today, using an assumed discount rate to generate values. A change of 1 percent in cash flows of a 30-year project alters the value of the investment by 14 percent. For a 99-year project, the same change alters the value by 35 percent. Long lives meant that valuation mistakes would only become apparent after the bankers had moved on. Macquarie justified the valuations citing few actual sales, some of which were between the funds.

In 2006, Macquarie and Cintra paid $3.8 billion for an Indiana toll road concession, 50 times the road's annual cash flows and around $1 billion more than the next bidder. Investor returns were projected at 12.5 percent per annum. Maunsell, an engineering firm, estimated traffic for the valuation model. Maunsell had a close relationship with Macquarie, being entitled to success fees if the bank won its bid. Indiana Finance Authority's consultant came up with 50 percent lower traffic forecasts, valuing the toll road at half the $3.8 billion purchase price. A third consultant concluded that Maunsell's forecasts exceeded the highway capacity after 2020.

Macquarie used derivatives, known as *accreting interest rate swaps*, to lower early payments by increasing later payments. Complex securities, such as *TICKETs* (tradeable interest bearing convertible to equity trust securities), with low early interest rates that increased over time, were used. The arrangements were identical to those used in subprime mortgages.

Projects routinely issued debt linked to inflation, prized by pension funds and insurance companies trying to minimize risk from change in price levels. As the inflation adjustment was paid at maturity, the structure conserved cash flows, which were distributed to other investors or to the bank as fees. Issuing these securities robbed shareholders in the infrastructure projects of at least some of the inflation hedge that they purchased.

Jim Chanos, whose fund Kynikos Associates bet on Macquarie's share pricing falling, argued that the model was a giant Ponzi scheme. Edward Chancellor, a journalist, was also critical: "excessive fees, excessive leverage and excessive complexity."[4]

Public Squalor, Private Profits

Over time, *adjacency*—close enough—allowed the techniques to be applied to mobile phone antennae, casinos, car parks, parking meters, shopping centers, water utilities, and even emergency services communications networks. The common theme was debt, lots of it.

In December 2010, snowstorms closed London's Heathrow Airport, the busiest in the world, stranding thousands of passengers and revealing the dark side of private infrastructure. Heathrow Airport is owned and operated by BAA (British Airport Authority). Ferrovial, the Spanish construction company, which owns BAA, branched out into infrastructure investments financed with generous dollops of cheap debt because there was more money in running, financing, and owning infrastructure than in building it.

Although the weather was the primary cause, insufficient de-icing and snow-clearing equipment exacerbated Heathrow's problems. Critics argued that BAA had failed to invest in basic infrastructure, favoring quick profits and cash to service large borrowings. They argued that the only real investment in Heathrow was to expand the terminals' lucrative retail concessions. A Macquarie executive once described an airport as nothing more than real estate—a parking lot and shopping mall and a few runways attached. Airports are also monopolies, allowing the owner to extract large profits, with limited competition.

In the global financial crisis, the infrastructure funds and investors experienced problems due to their high level of borrowings. Many Macquarie clones went bankrupt. New infrastructure funding acronyms appeared complementing the familiar PPP—DOG (debt overburdened group), FOG (full of gearing), RTN (road to nowhere) and ROT (ruse on toll roads).

As asset values fell and debt became less abundant and more expensive, Macquarie Bank itself moved to unlisted funds reducing transparency and scrutiny of its operations even further. Infrastructure remained popular with investors. John Kenneth Galbraith once commented on America's private wealth and public squalor. Facing infrastructure needs, governments sought to alleviate public squalor by appealing to private profits, with indifferent results.

Locust Plagues

At the 2007 Super Return annual industry conference, the financier Henry Kravis argued that private equity "leads not only to value creation, but also to economic and social benefits, for example, increases in employment, innovation, and research and development."[5] The reality was short-run profit-maximizing strategies where businesses were "starved of R&D, equipment modernization and advertising funds and/or prices are set at high levels inviting competitor inroads, leaving in the end a depleted non-competitive shell."[6]

Under Terra Firma, EMI was not interested in developing new artists but exploiting its existing libraries. Investors in Qantas and EMI openly indicated their desire for an early exit. Private equity firms had never managed anything other than money. Qantas was well run and the existing management, who were adroit cost cutters, would be retained.

Many private equity deals did not live up to expectations. Blackstone paid $26 billion for Hilton Hotels, financed by Lehman Brothers, Bear Stearns, and others. Financiers spent a lot of time in hotels and somehow assumed that this qualified them to own and run them. As recession hit, the hotels fell sharply in value and the rooms stood empty. In 2008, Steve Rattner's Quadrangle, a specialist in media deals, purchased *Maxim*, a lad's magazine, for $250 million, with a view to cutting costs and expanding the *Maxim* brand into movies, restaurants, and shops selling *tchotchkes* (a term used by Jewish Americans deriving from Yiddish meaning kitsch knick-knacks or trinkets). Finding itself in financial difficulties, Quadrangle tried to give back *Maxim* to its creditors. Cerberus, a large U.S. private equity firm, invested $7.4 billion in Chrysler. In March 2009, Cerberus lost its equity stake as a condition of the U.S. Treasury's bailout of Chrysler. Chrysler Financial, in whom Cerberus maintained a controlling stake, underwent liquidation.

The private equity case relies on high investment returns. Studies found that average returns, net of fees, were roughly equal to those produced by the S&P 500 index between 1980 and 2001.[7] Adjusted for additional risks, such as the high levels of debt and the fact that investments could not be taken out for long periods, private equity investments underperformed the stock market on average, by as much as 3 percent per annum.[8] Returns were difficult to determine because of accounting practices and tricks like paying out large dividends shortly after purchases. Returns between funds and investors varied widely, some funds earning 14 percentage points above the average.

As in the 1980s, leverage, tax deductions and financial engineering drove returns. APA relied on increasing Qantas' borrowings to generate high returns. Terra Firma relied on high levels of debt and on being able to repackage and sell off future royalty streams. In 2010, a report by the Centre for the Study of Financial Innovation, a London think-tank, analyzed 542 buy-out deals in the portfolio of Yale's endowment, finding that they underperformed the stock market by 40 percent, after stripping out the impact of extra debt.[9]

The loss of tax revenues was increasingly a concern. The special status of partners and investors in private-equity firms, whose earnings were taxed at a low rate as capital gains, came under scrutiny. The lower tax rate was justified as a proper reward for risk taking. Nicholas Ferguson, chairman of SVG Capital, a listed British private equity firm, broke ranks by admitting the concessional tax rate was indefensible. The person in the boardroom was being taxed at a lower marginal rate than the person who cleaned it.

Advocates argued that management preferred to work for privately owned firms—unsurprising, given the huge rewards for managers. On QF 545, Dicko was forced to place his long-term incentives, valued at up to A$60 million, in a charitable trust to deflect criticism of the estimated A$600 million in fees and profits that would accrue to the private equity firms, financiers, and investors, including management.

As public criticism grew, trade unions picketed the launch of the Private Equity Foundation, a new charity for children. Protesters picketed the houses of leading private equity financiers. Private equity was no longer very private.

In 2008, Blackstone-owned Merlin Entertainments, a British amusement-park operator, negotiated to acquire a well-known Vienna landmark—the giant Ferris Wheel in the Wurstelprater, an amusement park in the center of Vienna, built in 1897 to commemorate the 50th anniversary of Emperor Franz Joseph I's accession to the Habsburg throne. Heinz-Christian Strache, the leader of the far-right Austrian Freedom Party, was unhappy: "Hands off our Viennese giant wheel." Strache warned darkly that it was a short step from the Ferris Wheel to a private equity acquisition of the Hofburg Imperial Palace. A German politician labeled private equity firms "locusts."

At the 2007 Davos World Economy Forum, where private equity chiefs were being feted as financial royalty, David Rubenstein of Carlyle thought that the industry did a poor job in presenting its case.[10] The Private Equity Council, formed to lobby for the industry, commissioned a research project to look at the economic impact. At Davos, financiers announced that the study would show that private equity was beneficial for the economy, generated high returns for its investors like public pension funds, created employment, and paid a lot of tax. Given that research had not commenced, the insight into its findings was impressive.

Vain Capital

Paradoxically, private equity firms now wanted to list on stock exchanges, signaling the beginning of the end of the boom. Listing of the management company contradicted private equity's oft stated competitive advantages—patience, long-term focus, avoiding the pressure of quarterly earnings, and the high cost of regulatory compliance for public companies. Stephen Schwarzman, Blackstone's CEO, previously argued that: "public markets are overrated."[11] One blogger described Schwarzman's conversion as "the most unlikely…since Saul of Tarsus fell off his horse en route to Damascus."[12]

It was Fortress envy. In February 2007, Fortress Investment Group, an alternative investment firm, sold 8.6 percent of the company for $685 million. Offered at $18.50 each, the shares rose 68 percent on listing to $31, trading at 40 times their historical earnings. It was private equity's Netscape moment, reminiscent of when the Internet neophyte floated its shares to the public and the price skyrocketed. Blackstone, KKR, and others rushed to cash in on the gold rush.

Schwarzman's $5 million 60th birthday celebration, held in February 2007, was another sign of impending doom. The venue—the Armory—was decorated to replicate Schwarzman's Park Avenue apartment, featuring a large portrait of the birthday boy. Children dressed in military regalia acted as ushers, and comedian Martin Short was master of ceremonies. Guests, including Colin Powell and New York Mayor Michael Bloomberg, dined on lobster and baked Alaska, whilst imbibing fine wines. Composer Marvin Hamlisch performed a number from *A Chorus Line*. Patti LaBelle led the Abyssinian Baptist Church choir in a song especially composed in honor of Schwarzman. Rod Stewart, the sexagenarian British rock star, performed his hits including *Maggie May* and *Do'ya Think I'm Sexy*.

In 2002, David Bonderman, co-founder of TPG, had staged a lavish $7 million party to celebrate his 60th birthday party for hundreds of his "closest" friends. Held at the Bellagio Hotel in Las Vegas, the party featured entertainment from the Rolling Stones and Robin Williams. Carlyle's David Rubinstein was unimpressed: "We have all wanted to be private—at least until now. When Steve Schwarzman's biography with all the dollar signs is posted on the web site none of us will like the furore that results—and that's even if you like Rod Stewart."[13]

In June 2007, Blackstone's share offering was priced at $31 per share listed, trading upon listing in the stock exchange at around $37. The Chinese government invested $3 billion. Schwarzman cashed out stock worth over $650 million. His remaining 24 percent stake was valued at almost $8 billion, placing him near Rupert Murdoch and Steve Jobs on the list of richest people. In 2006, Schwarzman earned $398 million, around double the combined pay of the five largest American investment bank CEOs.

Amateur Hour

A leaked internal memo written by Carlyle's William Conway dated January 31, 2007 showed that that the boom was almost over: "most investors in most assets classes are not being paid for the risks being taken...the longer it lasts the worst it will be when it ends...if the excess liquidity ended tomorrow I would want as much flexibility as possible."[14] Shortly after the Blackstone IPO, U.S. subprime problems overflowed into a general credit crunch, and the debt markets ground to a halt. As the global recession affected earnings and cash flows, companies that had been leveraged up in buyouts found it difficult to meet debt repayments. Drops in stock prices reduced values, making it difficult to offload businesses.

By July 2007, EMI was in difficulties. With CitiGroup unable to sell off the debt that it had underwritten, Terra Firma and the bank considered abandoning the deal. CitiGroup agreed to honor its commitment, becoming the sole provider of the £2.6 billion loan. The "whimpering dogs," Hands' term for bankers, had shown commendable loyalty. Hands later apologized for the term, prompting a banker to send him dog biscuits.

In the recession, EMI's revenues fell by 20 percent and losses tripled as cost savings could not offset the higher interest charges. EMI's value fell to £1.4 billion, below the level of its debt. Talent began leaving EMI. In 2009, Terra Firma wrote off half its investment in EMI—over 45 percent of its entire portfolio.

Hands, who lived on the island of Guernsey to avoid British taxes, blamed investors and banks: "We all had too much money. It was just too easy." Hands admitted that the EMI deal was a mistake. If the lenders had been slower and the deal had been a few weeks later, "We wouldn't have bought it. We'd have 90 percent of our funds still to invest and we'd look like geniuses."[15]

In late 2009, Hands offered to inject £1 billion in equity into EMI but only if CitiGroup would write off a similar amount of debt. The bank refused. Terra Firma commenced legal proceedings against CitiGroup, claiming that CitiGroup encouraged Hands to make a binding bid by the May 21, 2007 deadline even though other bidders had allegedly dropped out. Due diligence on EMI was rushed, and Terra Firma claimed reliance on a CitiGroup analyst report in making its bid. Rivals found Hands' claim puzzling: "He's [not] some half-wit amateur.... It is buyer beware...it is ludicrous to say you paid too much because of what some banker told you."[16]

In late 2010, a New York jury took only 5 hours to clear Citigroup and its bankers, but not before a jury member, Donna Gianel, a former circus performer, was removed. A Google search had revealed her part in Michael Moore's film *Capitalism: A Love Story*. Hands' hope for billions in damages to rescue his EMI investment seemed over.

In early 2011, Citigroup seized control of EMI, an event that came to be known as the "Fab Foreclosure," an allusion to The Beatles, the company's iconic stars. Citi wrote off £2.2 billion (around 65 percent) of EMI's £3.4 billion in debt, in the process taking a substantial loss on its own loans.

The intriguing question was whether the £1.75 billion loss to Terra Firma and its investors would affect Hands' ability to raise money for future deals. Investors and bankers remained loyal to him, based on past successes. The EMI deal was seen as badly timed and an unfortunate victim of unfavorable market circumstances. Given short memories, most observers thought that it would be only a year or so before everybody forgot what had happened.

Turbulence

QF 545 ran into head winds. The APA offer was subject to a minimum shareholder acceptance level of 90 percent, but two funds controlling more than 10 percent refused to sell, holding out for a higher price. The minimum shareholder acceptance level was reduced to 70 percent.

The company and private equity firms tried to convince shareholders of the "fantastic opportunity." In the hospital suffering from DVT (deep vein thrombosis), fetchingly attired in a hospital gown, Her Madge had a brain explosion. She told reporters that shareholders had "a mental problem" if they did not understand that if the bid did not proceed, then the Qantas share price would collapse.

APA failed to secure the 50 percent shareholder acceptance it needed to extend the bid to try to achieve its target 70 percent. At the close of acceptance at 7:00 p.m. May 4, 2008, APA had 46 percent, claiming that a U.S. hedge fund had agreed to sell 4.9 percent of Qantas but had not accepted in time. The financial gods apparently lacked basic numeracy and the ability to read clocks. Amid claims, counterclaims, and legal suits, the bid faded away. After peaking at around $6.00 per share in anticipation of a new higher bid, the share price fell to a low of below $1.50 as the recession and earning downgrades hit.

The failed buyout of United Airlines (UAL) marked the beginning of the end of the 1980s acquisition boom. Coincidentally, the failure of QF 545 signaled the end of the subsequent boom. The cancellation of QF 545 proved fortunate. In the recession, the debt burden would have been fatal. The *Rain Man*—Raymond Babbit—would be relieved that Qantas dodged a surface-to-air missile, narrowly avoiding crashing and burning.

Financiers privately admitted that it would take a mathematical miracle for investors in many buy-outs to recover their investments. Hands summarized the state of play:

> Neither the banks nor private equity want to come clean about mistakes...companies will live as zombies unable to grow their businesses or make long-term commitments...banks will try to suck out as much money as they can in fees and postpone recognizing the full extent of the losses. It was a case of "you're not bankrupt, until people know you're bankrupt."[17]

Blackstone's shares fell around 50 percent as earning fell almost 90 percent. Schwarzman and his partners had cashed in their chips at the top of the cycle. The Private Equity Council rebranded itself Private Equity Growth Capital Council. The new mantra was private equity created economic benefits and growth.

In the 1987 film *Wall Street*, Gordon Gecko (played by Michael Douglas) tells his star acolyte Bud Fox (Charlie Sheen) that in zero sum money games somebody wins and somebody loses but no money is ever made or lost. Private equity was always a zero sum game, with money simply being transferred between different perceptions.

In each boom cycle and period of easy money, private equity firms used large amounts of cheap debt in combination with their spreadsheets and selling skills to do deals, which enriched them extravagantly. Veteran private equity players argued that the industry would have to adapt—restructure existing deals, do smaller deals, use less leverage, and so on. It had all been said before, at the end of the last boom.

Locusts wait for favorable conditions to thrive, multiply, and devour everything in their path. The world had learned to love leverage. When market conditions were right, private equity would be back. Right on cue, in late 2010, Blackstone announced plans for a $15 billion fund, only slightly smaller than its previous November 2006 fund of $21.7 billion, the largest-ever fund. It signaled the return of private equity and leverage.

11

Dice with Debt

In 2009, London's *Daily Mirror* found the culprit responsible for the financial crisis—David Bowie, aka Ziggy Stardust and the Thin White Duke. In 1997, he issued $55 million of 7.9 percent per annum 10-year Bowie Bonds backed by future royalties from 25 albums containing 287 songs, including *Space Oddity*, *Starman*, *Jean Genie*, *Fame*, *Young American*, *Ashes to Ashes*, *Let's Dance*, *China Girl*, and *Modern Love*. Bowie gave up 10 years' worth of royalties in return for $55 million up front.

Although the Bowie Bond pioneered the securitization of intellectual property rights, the technique itself had been used since the 1970s to repackage loans, especially mortgages, into securities sold to investors. Michael Milken called it "democratization of capital."

In the Japanese TV cooking show *Ryōri no Tetsujin*, literally "Ironmen of Cooking" (the American version is called *The Iron Chef*), chefs battled against each other to create dishes around a specific theme ingredient. Over time, bankers learned to cut and dice debt in more ways than any celebrity television chef. Securitization was a bacchanalian feast of unprecedented size for bankers and their acolytes.

Securitization Recipes

Securitization is a recipe for cutting and dicing debt into more debt. Like food recipes, securitization ranges from simple dishes to haute cuisine. The only ingredient is debt—mortgage loans, credit card loans, car loans, loans to companies, loans to people, loans to people who cannot pay, any loans at all. Poor quality loans are no barrier to an acceptable and edible final securitized product.

Haute securitized debt depends on various condiments—SPVs, derivatives, bonds, tranches, over-collateralization, and excess spreads. Kitchen staff is needed—bankers and brokers to make loans; traders to structure the deal, price and hedge it; sales people; rating agencies to bless the deals as fit for investor consumption; servicers to monitor things; accountants to track the money; trustees to look after bondholders' interests; lawyers to protect everybody, especially themselves. Securitization was a bacchanalian feast of unprecedented size for bankers and their acolytes.

The structure is set out in Figure 11.1. Lenders sell loans they made to an SPV, not associated with the seller. The SPV, a trust or a company located in the tax-efficient balmy Cayman Islands, pays the lender for the purchase from the proceeds of bonds it issues to investors, *asset-backed securities* (ABSs). ABS investors, indirectly via the SPV, own the loans, relying on the cash flows from the underlying loans for the interest and principal they are entitled to receive.

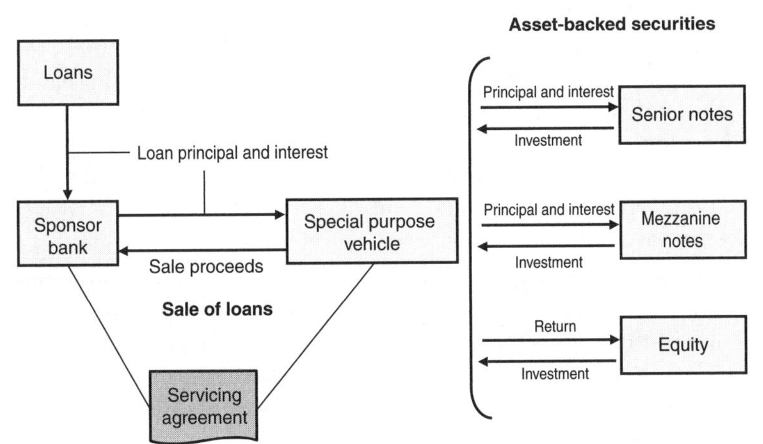

Figure 11.1 Asset-backed security structure

When sold to the SPV, the original loans and any associated borrowing disappear from the balance sheet of the original lender. As the loans are sold off, the lender can make new loans, freeing the lending institution from constraints of capital and funding resources. Lenders also raise long-term funds matching the life of loans and so reducing risk. For a poor-credit-quality lender, the cost of money is lower, as the ABS investors look through to the underlying loans as collateral. Lenders transfer the risk of loss on their loans. If the borrowers on the underlying loans do not make their contracted payments, then the ABS investors would suffer losses. In return for assuming this risk, investors earn higher rates of return than on comparable bonds. Initially, the risk of loss was low as securitization used high-quality mortgage loans to modest folk, carrying a government or near-government guarantee.

Slice and Dice

Lewis Ranieri of Salomon Brothers and Lawrence Fink (then at First Boston and subsequent founder of Blackrock, an investment manager) pioneered the structure. In 2004, *BusinessWeek* honored "Lew," immortalized in Michael Lewis' *Liar's Poker*, as one of the great innovators of the past 75 years. In March 2008, Nobel-prize-winning economist Robert Mundell included Ranieri in his list of the "Five goats who contributed to the financial crisis of 2008," together with President Bill Clinton, former AIG head Hank Greenberg, Ben Bernanke, and Henry Paulson.[1]

The key to securitization is the allocation of risks between different investors. Quantitative analysts segmented mortgage cash flow from a complex menu of choices, manufacturing investment dishes to meet investors' appetites.

U.S. mortgages are generally 30 years and fixed rate. Minimal prepayment penalties mean that if interest rates fall, then mortgagors pay back their old mortgages, refinancing at lower rates to reduce their repayments. ABS investors risk early return of their money, which must be reinvested at lower rates. CMOs (*collateralized mortgage obligation*) segmented cash *horizontally*, creating different bonds out of a pool of standard mortgages to reduce prepayment risk.

If there are four separate bonds, the first class receives prepayments before the other classes, getting repaid earlier. The first class receives a lower interest rate reflecting lower risk. The second class receives payments next and so on. The Z tranche, at the bottom, receives the highest return but does not receive any payment until all other tranches are fully paid off. CMOs allow 30-year mortgages to be converted into bonds with different, theoretically more predictable maturities to match investor needs.

Vertical segmentation, *tranching* (French for slicing) improved credit quality (see Figure 11.2). The SPV issues three different classes of securities. The most risky security is the *equity tranche*, which takes first losses on the underlying loans. The next most risky security is the *mezzanine notes*, which bear losses only if the losses exceed the amount of the equity tranche. The least risky security is the *senior tranche*, which only bears losses if the losses exceed the combined value of the equity and *mezzanine tranches*.

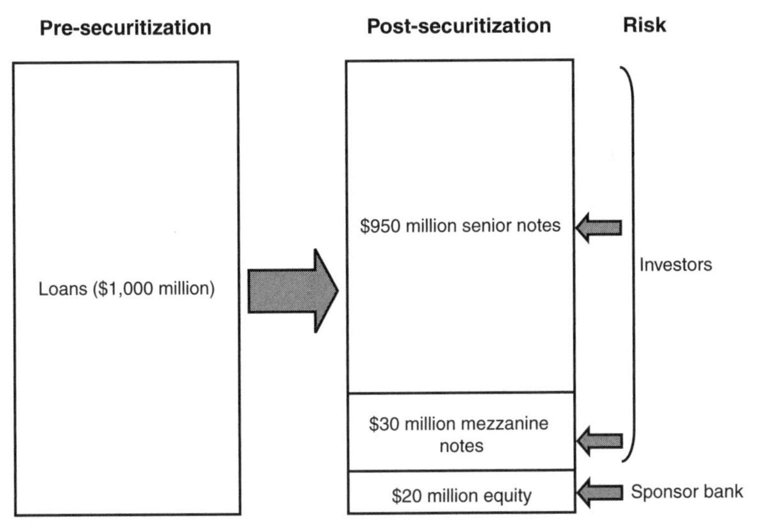

Figure 11.2 Asset-backed security tranches

Assume an underlying portfolio of $1,000 million made up of 5,000 mortgages of $200,000 each. Assume that the SPV issues $20 million in equity, $30 million in mezzanine notes, and $950 million in senior notes to finance this portfolio. If a homeowner defaults, then the lender loses 50 percent of the amount lent ($100,000 being 50 percent of $200,000). The loss is lower than the amount of the loan because the property can be sold to recover part of the amount lent, a *recovery rate* of 50 percent.

Defaults on 200 mortgages (4 percent) wipes out the equity tranche (loss of $100,000 per loan times 200) but investors in mezzanine and senior notes receive their investment back in full. If 10 percent of the mortgages default, then the loss of $50 million (loss of $100,000 times 500) wipes out the equity and mezzanine. If the entire portfolio defaults, senior note holders get back $500 million ($1,000 million minus losses of $500 million—calculated as loss of $100,000 times 5,000)—a loss of 53 percent ($500 million loss divided by $950 million face value). Only if all mortgages defaulted and all the underlying houses were worthless would the senior note holders lose their entire investment.

Betting on no or very few defaults, equity holders take the greatest risk and receive the highest return. Senior note holders take the least risk and receive low returns. Mezzanine is in the middle—less risky than equity, more risky than senior, betting on modest losses not exceeding the equity tranche (less than 4 percent of mortgages). Mezzanine note holders receive higher returns than senior note investors but less than equity.

The assumption is that the entire underlying portfolio is unlikely to default simultaneously. If the equity and mezzanine notes provide a sufficient buffer, then the risk of loss on the senior notes is reduced. The risk of individual notes can be adjusted similarly by changing the subordination level—the size of the tranches that take earlier losses.

If the average historical default rate on the mortgages is 0.5 percent, then the expected loss would be $2.5 million (0.5 percent of 5,000 mortgages times $100,000 loss per mortgage). As there would have to be 20 times the average loss ($50 million divided by $2.5 million) before they would lose, the senior notes are considered to carry very low risk, receiving the highest credit rating (AAA). The mezzanine note holders are a relatively low risk and may command an investment grade rating, as losses of eight times average loss are required for them to lose money.

Conservative investors invested in low risk AAA or AA-rated securities, preferring the return of capital to the return on their capital. Alchemy transformed portfolios of low quality and junk loans to highly rated securities, allowing investors to purchase them in the form of highly rated debt ABSs. Investors with greater risk appetite purchased mezzanine notes or the equity tranches. Investors in the equity, known as *toxic waste*, earned high returns as long as losses were zero or low. In most deals, the bank selling off the loans or arranging the securitisation took at least a part of the equity tranche to provide comfort to other investors—this was the bank's *skin in the game* or *hurt money*.

Tranching is like buying a place to live in a flood-prone area. To protect yourself from the one-in-10,000-year flood, you buy an apartment in a tower above previous known flood levels, with a large margin of safety. You pay more for your flood-safe penthouse while buyers of the lower levels trade off the lower price against the "remote" risk of the flood.

In drought years, everybody lives happily. When the flood comes, the owners of the lower levels are flooded. You congratulate yourself on your perspicacious decision, only to find that the floods damage the foundations of your tower block, weakening the structure. The utilities and services don't function. You cannot get to and from your penthouse. You cannot offload the penthouse to anybody at any price. If you miscalculated the margin of safety of the one-in-10,000-year flood, then you require full scuba gear to sit in your living room contemplating the alchemy of tranching.

Almost as Safe as Houses

Like Henry Ford, bankers are good at mass production, quickly adopting and developing a successful product. The capability to repackage all kinds of debt into highly rated securities that investors sought allowed the expansion of debt levels to reach epic proportions.

The early focus in the United States was on MBSs (*mortgage backed securities*)—repackaging and selling off mortgages guaranteed by government-sponsored entities. As securitization became accepted, bankers adapted the technique to pools of private mortgages, automobiles (CARS—*certificate for automobile receivables*) and credit card debt. In the late 1980s, Milken created CBOs (*collateralized bond obligations*) and CLOs (*collateralized loan obligations*), repackaging corporate debt. Soon, corporate loans, private equity loans, loans secured by commercial real estate, and emerging market junk bonds were all being securitized.

A bank making a loan to a company was required by regulators originally to hold capital of 8 percent ($8 for every $100 loan) against risk of loss. If the bank charged a margin of 1 percent per annum, then the return on capital was 12.5 percent per annum (1 percent divided by 8 percent), usually below the bank's cost of capital determined by the CAPM (capital asset pricing model). Loans to high-quality companies paying low margins were now pooled and sold off as CLOs. Assuming that the 2 percent equity tranche was retained by the lending bank and the CLO cost was 0.2 percent per annum (reducing the loan margin from 1 percent to 0.8 percent), this tripled the return on capital to 40 percent per annum (0.8 percent divided by 2 percent).

As banks held the equity and the likelihood of losses exceeding the equity tranche was low, the return on capital increased but the risks were unchanged. As executive compensation and stock prices were linked to return on capital, banks used securitization to boost returns.

Mirroring Anthony Trollope's 1867 novel *Last Chronicle of Barset*, whose characters invest in mortgages, investors purchased MBSs as low risk and secure investments paying regular income. The higher return available on securitized bonds relative to ordinary securities of similar quality was attractive.

Synthetic Stuff

In the 1990s, securitization underwent a makeover, being rebranded CDOs (*collateralized debt obligations*), a term subsuming various types of underlying loans and securitization formats. In 1997 JP Morgan introduced *synthetic* securitization, overcoming the unwieldy need to transfer the underlying loans to the SPV and also lowering the cost of transferring the risk. Instead of selling the loans, the lender now purchased credit insurance against the risk of loss using a *credit default swap (CDS)*.

The structure is shown in Figure 11.3. The bank purchased separate credit insurance policies from the SPV on each loan it wanted to transfer. As in a traditional ABS structure, the SPV issued securities. Instead of issuing securities equal to the face value of the loans insured, they issued a smaller amount—$80 million against an underlying portfolio of $1,000 million. The proceeds of the bonds were used to buy government bonds, such as U.S.

Treasury bonds. These bonds were then pledged to secure the SPV's payment obligations under the credit insurance policies it had sold to the bank.

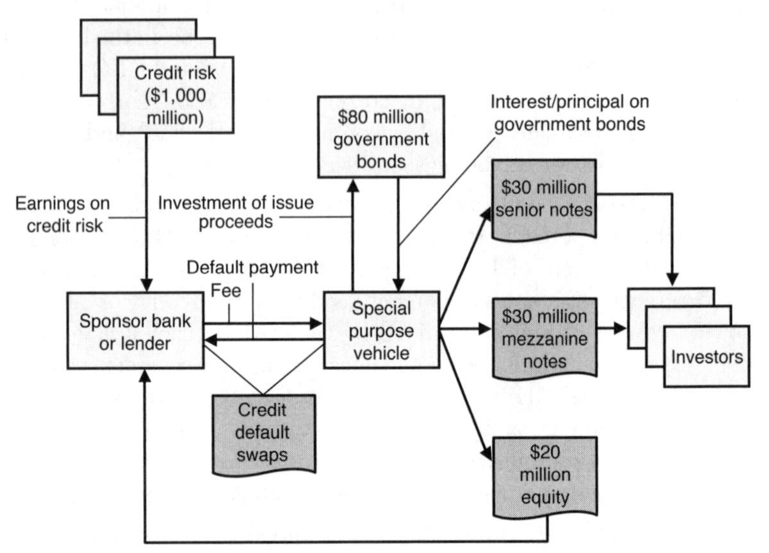

Figure 11.3 Synthetic CDO

Over the life of the deal, the bank paid insurance premiums to the SPV, which together with income from the government bonds financed the interest payments to the investors in the senior and mezzanine notes, with anything left over going to equity. If there are no defaults on the underlying loans, then at maturity of the structure the bondholders get paid from the proceeds of the maturing government bonds. If there are defaults, then the bank's claims under its insurance policies are paid out of the government bonds, reducing the amount available to equity holders, mezzanine note holders, and finally senior note holder (in that order). The structure of risk in the synthetic CDO is shown in Figure 11.4.

Assume an underlying portfolio of $1,000 million made up of 100 loans of $10 million each to companies. Assume that the SPV issues $20 million in equity, $30 million in mezzanine notes and $30 million in senior notes. The SPV issues only $80 million of securities in total, while assuming the risk of a $1,000 million portfolio of loans. This leaves $920 million unhedged, which, as described below, remains with the bank.

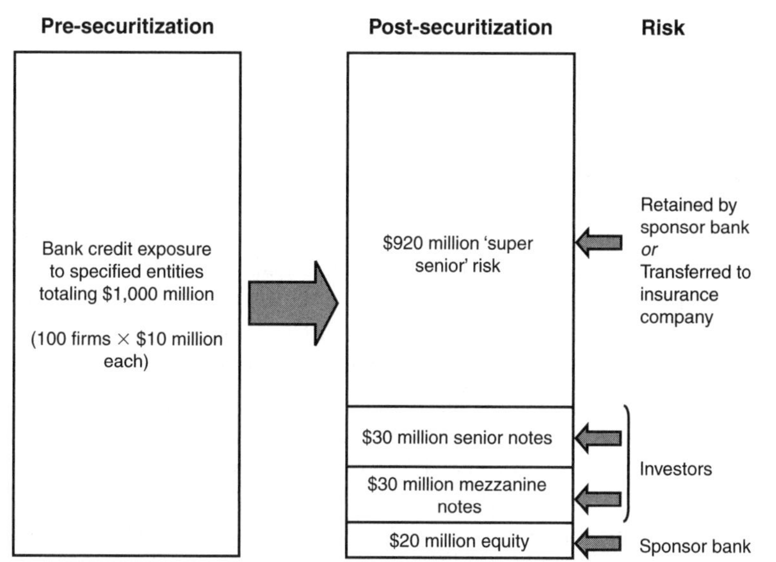

Figure 11.4 Synthetic CDO Tranches

Assume the lender will lose 60 percent of the amount loaned ($6,000,000) if any borrower defaults, a recovery rate of 40 percent.[2] Three loan defaults (3 percent of the loans) or losses of $20 million (loss of $6,000,000 per loan times 3) wipe out the equity tranche entirely. Eight defaults (8 percent of the loans) or losses of $50 million (loss of $6,000,000 times 8) wipes out the equity and the mezzanine. If losses are more than $50 million, then the senior note investors suffer losses. Thirteen defaults (13 percent of the loans) or losses of $80 million (loss of $6,000,000 times 13) wipe out the equity, mezzanine, and the senior note investors.

After 13 defaults or losses of $80 million, the SPV has no more money to cover additional defaults under the insurance policies it has entered into with the bank. The risk on the remaining $920 million (92 percent of the portfolio), known as the *super senior* tranche, reverts to the bank and is retained or must be transferred to another party. Given that losses would have to be very high relative to the risk of the loans and the AAA-rated senior tranche wiped out entirely, the super senior tranche is as close to risk free as possible. Regulators agreed, minimizing the capital that banks have to hold against the super senior risk.

Where the bank does not pay a third party to assume the super senior risk, the cost of securitization falls from around 0.2–0.3 percent per annum to around 0.05 percent per annum. Even if the super senior risk had to be transferred to a third party, the cost of around 0.1 percent per annum was lower than what bond investors required for AAA-rated bonds in a normal securitisation, so reducing the cost.

This residual risk of catastrophically large losses could be transferred using a super senior CDS (an insurance contract) to reinsurance companies (AIG, Swiss Re, Gen Re) and monolines or bond insurers (MBIA, Ambac). Large reinsurers, like AIG, were looking for insurance-type business that diversified traditional risks. Monolines' traditional business of insuring municipal bonds was declining. Local municipalities now obtained credit ratings directly or could access financing without the monoline guarantee (known as the *bond wrap*). Synthetic securitizations, where risk was packaged into insurance-like contracts, were ideal for these investors.

A synthetic securitization has high levels of leverage, as only $80 million of money supports $1,000 million of credit risk. Even where the super senior risk was hedged with a third party, the counterparty did not have to put up money initially, increasing leverage and risk. In traditional securitization, the underlying loans existed. In synthetic securitization, the bank could buy insurance without owning the underlying loan, allowing *shorting* of credit risk to profit from a decline in the credit quality or default of the named entity. There was no theoretical limit on the volume of securitizations that could be completed. Volumes became detached from the underlying loan and debt markets.

If private equity and junk bonds increased reliance on leverage and appetite for different instruments, then securitization took the availability of debt to an entirely new level.

Regulators loved the theoretical idea of breaking risk into tiny particles, distributing it widely. In practice, risk was spreading like a virulent virus through the financial system, ending up in unknown places in the hands of investors, who did not understand the complex risks that they assumed. As Iceland imploded during the financial crisis, traders speculated that the Icelandic banks' fatal dalliance with structured finance was simply confusion between the word c-o-d (an area of Icelandic expertise) and the non-piscine c-d-o (collateralized debt obligations).

Get Copula-ed

Assorted statisticians, mathematicians, scientists, and MBAs with little knowledge of banking now shaped packages of loans into complicated *objets d'art*. They built simplified models to predict patterns of cash flows from the underlying loans. In the ultra-rational world of efficient markets, prepayments were assumed to be linked to interest rates adjusted for behavioral nuances. Historical data was used to estimate the risk of nonpayment (default rates) and the loss rate (the amount lent minus the recovery rate).

Historical data was used to estimate *default correlation*, the risk that if one loan defaulted, then other loans might also default.

Statistical analysis works moderately well with mortgages, at least simple traditional residential mortgages. Performance of large numbers of loans approximates an average. Individual calamities, lost jobs, illness, fraud, do not affect the pool significantly, as most borrowers make their payments as required. The risk of all homeowners defaulting at the same time is low.

In corporate loan securitizations, the models were more problematic. There were perhaps only 100 corporate loans compared to 5,000 mortgages for the same size portfolio, making individual defaults and loss more significant. Investment grade companies also default infrequently and their recovery rates fluctuate. Correlation between defaults is complex. If a major customer defaults without paying for goods and services supplied then the firm is more likely to default. If a competitor defaults, then the firm's default risk may decrease if it picks up business, or increase if it is affected by the same problems that caused the default.

In his paper "On default correlation: a copula function approach," David Xiang Lin Li, a Chinese-born actuary, used a Gaussian copula to determine whether two companies will simultaneously default (joint default probability).[3] *Gaussian* refers to the assumption of a normal bell-shaped distribution. *Copula* in Latin means "combining."

The idea drew on changes in life expectancy when a spouse dies. In general, in the year following a loved one's death, women and men are, respectively, more than twice and six times as likely to die than normal. Actuaries used statistical techniques to model *stress cardiomyopathy* or *apical ballooning syndrome*, dying of a broken heart. Li applied this approach to the likelihood of default in a portfolio of loans.

The model's attraction was its simplicity and ease of application. Bankers and quants could get deals done. But the simple model could not capture the complex relationship between two loans. The expected default correlation could not be objectively calculated, only extrapolated from other information, like share prices or credit margins. Small changes in input changed the results significantly. Uncomfortable with his model, in 2005, Li told *The Wall Street Journal*: "Very few people understand the essence of the model." In 2006, Janet Tavakoli, a former derivative banker, reflected: "Correlation trading has spread through the psyche of the financial markets like a highly infectious thought virus."[4]

Sticky Mess

Massive investment in quantitative infrastructure to structure, trade and sell ABSs, created a relentless drive for revenue, a constant push for deals and innovation. If the returns were sufficient, any assets could be repackaged and sold to investors. Securitization of life insurance policies (death bonds), hurricane, and earthquake risk (catastrophe or cat bonds) emerged. MBS structures reached levels of complexity, requiring color-coded risk warnings originally used on ski runs.

Innovation improved tranching. *Excess spread* accounts lowered the equity and mezzanine debt required to reach a target rating, allowing sponsors with less capital to complete securitizations. *Prepayment tranching, sequential tranching*, and *parallel tranching* improved the predictability of the life of the bonds. Investors could choose between PAC (planned amortization class) bonds, TAC (target amortization class) bonds, VADM (very accurately defined maturity) bonds, and the sticky jump Z tranche. A 2008 conference agenda posed the question: "Should the taxpayers be concerned that the Fed accepts private label whole loan nonsticky jump Z-tranche CMOs as collateral when the casino doesn't?"[5]

In 1987, Howard Rubin, a Merrill Lynch trader, lost $377 million in mortgage trading. MBSs are split into IO (*interest only*) and PO (*principal only*) bonds. IOs pay out only the interest payments on the underlying pool of mortgages. Lower rates mean more prepayments, meaning less interest payments reducing the price of the IOs. Higher interest rates mean lower prepayments and more interest payments, increasing the value of the IOs. POs pay only principal, effectively like zero coupon bonds where you paid $800 for a bond that at maturity pays $1,000. POs behave exactly the opposite to IOs. If interest rates go down, then they appreciate in value, as the investor receives the face value of the bond earlier because of higher prepayments. If interest rates go up, then POs decrease in value as you get paid back later. Rubin owned a large amount of POs from Merrill Lynch's deals that the firm had not managed to sell. When interest rates went up, he made large losses and tried to make them back by buying more POs.

Merrill Lynch had no "eye deer" that Rubin had taken on so much risk. Old-fashioned stockbrokers with minimal understanding of risk and complex financial products, William Schreyer and Dan Tully, the heads of Merrill Lynch, announced that "the ship will sail closer to shore."[6] Rubin was fired but went on to a successful career at Bear Stearns. Ace Greenberg, the head of Bear Stearns, believed in "second chances" and thought Rubin "can make a real contribution."

Merrill tended to be in the thick of trouble and calamity. In 1994, Merrill was involved in the Orange County derivative losses. In 2001, when the Internet bubble burst, Merrill was there front and center. The pattern would repeat with CDO investments in 2008 under Stan O'Neal.

In 1987 a trade journal warned: "For Wall Street in general, Merrill's loss is a reminder of the dangers of financial engineering.... The pace of innovation has been breathtaking. Unfortunately, the growth in understanding has been less impressive."[7] No one understood what economic commentator James Grant stated: "Financial engineering is the science of structuring cash flows…credit analysis is the art of getting paid."[8] Risk would return over and over via new structures, each time bigger and more toxic than the last.

Several Houses of One's Own

To write fiction, according to English writer Virginia Woolf, a woman in Victorian England needed money and a room of her own. In modern America, everyone needed a large house and increasingly several houses. Money was not strictly needed, as rising house prices provided the necessary cash. The houses, the loans to finance them, and the securitized bonds based on the mortgages were classics of literary fiction.

Houses provide shelter, a dwelling place. In a hostile world, houses became self-sufficient fortresses with diversions (TV rooms and home entertainment centers), nature (gardens), recreation (home gyms) and oceans (swimming pools). You never had to leave, reflecting philosopher Søren Kierkegaard's observation: "robbers and the elite agree on just one thing—living in hiding."[9]

The average U.S. home more than doubled in size—from 1,000 square feet (93 square meters) in 1950 to 2,400 square feet (223 square meters) by the early 2000s. Microsoft co-founder Paul Allen built a 74,000-square-foot (6,882-square-meters) house, roughly the same size as the Cornell Business School where 100 people worked. Virginia Woolf would have recognized the MacMansions: "Those comfortably padded lunatic asylums which are known, euphemistically, as the stately homes of England."

As governments subsidized home ownership, believing it created a more stable society, home ownership ceased to be the preserve of the wealthy. In the UK Margaret Thatcher sold public housing to tenants at a discount. Governments provided subsidies, tax deductions on mortgage-interest payments, or lower taxes on capital gains from the sale of a residence.

The concept of home ownership was enthusiastically adopted in America. During the Great Depression, mass mortgage defaults and bank failures caused the home loan market to collapse. In 1934, the U.S. government created the Federal Housing Administration (FHA), the world's largest public mortgage insurer, to insure private banks' higher risk, nonprime home loans. In 1938, the Federal National Mortgage Association (FNMA or Fannie Mae) was created to allow low and middle-income buyers to purchase home with subsidized mortgages. In 1968, the Johnson administration privatized Fannie Mae to finance growing budget deficits, also creating the Government National Mortgage Association (GNMA or Ginnie Mae) to provide U.S. government guarantees for MBSs backed by federally insured or guaranteed loans. Two years later, the Federal Home Loan Mortgage Corporation

(FHLMC or Freddie Mac) was created, primarily to provide competition for Fannie Mae. Freddie was privatized in 1989.

These government-sponsored entities (GSEs) dominated the U.S. mortgage market. The implicit government guarantee lowered the GSEs' borrowing costs, reducing the cost of mortgages for borrowers. The GSEs enjoyed tax exemptions and lower capital requirements, allowing them to leverage more than banks. Unable to compete directly with the GSEs, banks developed riskier mortgage lending to borrowers who did not qualify for agency financing.

In the 1980s, the shift to self-funded retirement savings meant houses became a store of wealth. As homeowners paid off their mortgages, the home equity—the value of the houses less the outstanding debt—became a substantial asset, financing consumption and eventually retirement. As maintenance costs, utility bills, and property taxes mean that houses require rather than provide cash, homeowners borrowed against their home equity. Homeowners treated their properties as an automatic teller machine from which they extracted cash. Between 2000 and 2008 Americans drew more than $4 trillion of equity from their homes using home equity loans.

Investors also bought houses and apartments with borrowed money—renting them out, constantly trading up, and increasing the number of properties they owned. During the Internet gold rush, ordinary people abandoned jobs to become day traders. Now, housing day traders emerged, frequently buying off the plan and hoping to sell even before the building was completed.

Books, seminars, and TV series on property ownership outlined the infallibility of housing as an investment, assuming irreversible and continuous increases in home prices. Everyone got on the property or housing ladder. Adam Smith would have recognized the folly: "The chance of gain is by every man more or less overvalued, and the chance of loss is by most men undervalued."[10]

Rising wealth from home ownership masked declines in income levels and uncertain employment for the population. Less affected by globalization, housing sustained employment, income, and economic activity. Alan Greenspan approvingly noted one assessment of his early 2000s policy: "The housing boom saved the economy.... Americans went on a real estate orgy. [Americans] traded up, tore down, and added on."[11]

In the film *It's a Wonderful Life*, George Bailey (Jimmy Stewart) recognizes the fundamental desire of a man for his own roof, walls, and fireplace. The kind banker offers a couple entering their home (financed by a mortgage from his bank) food and wine to celebrate the happy occasion. But houses became an obsession, symbolic of over consumption and excess. In Monty Python's film *The Meaning of Life*, the obese Mr. Creosote (Terry Jones) eats an enormous amount, vomits repeatedly, and explodes after eating one last tiny mint. In the housing market, subprime mortgages were the final mint.

Cheaper Cuts of Mortgage

Prime mortgages in the United States, eligible for purchase and securitization by GSEs, conform to fixed guidelines covering the maximum loan amount (until 2008, around $417,000 for a single family home), maximum loan-to-value (LVR) ratios, debt-to-income limits, and documentation requirements. Subprime loans are given to less creditworthy borrowers, unable to qualify for conforming mortgages because of their lower income or uncertain employment histories. Most have damaged credit histories due to late payment of debts or financial problems arising from business failures, illness, or divorce. Some borrowers are subprime because of a lack of credit history—they have never borrowed.

In assessing risk, lenders rely on automated *credit scores*, a numerical measure of the creditworthiness of a person based on personal data, financial information, and credit history. The most common measure is the FICO score, named after the Fair Isaacs Corporation, which ranges between 300 and 850. In the United States, the median score is 720, with most borrowers scoring between 650 and 800. Borrowers with scores above 620 conform to GSE guidelines. Subprime borrowers typically scored between 500 and 620.

Starting in the early 1990s, governments actively promoted lending to the poor and minority groups. President George Bush sought to increase home ownership and housing affordability: "We can put light where there's darkness, and hope where there's despondency in this country…part of it is working together…to encourage folks to own their own home."[12] Construction firms, banks, lenders, and government created the National Homeownership Strategy to enhance availability of affordable housing through creative financing techniques.

The U.S. Community Reinvestment Act (CRA) encouraged financial institutions to meet credit needs of local communities, including low and moderate-income neighborhoods. Tax incentives and mandated targets encouraged GSEs to purchase mortgages and MBSs, including loans to low-income borrowers, expanding the market in securitized subprime mortgages. Legislative changes removed restrictions, allowing higher interest rates and fees for subprime loans.

As casual or part-time employment, self-employment or independent contracting increased; proof-of-income requirements were relaxed. Mortgages against second and third homes, vacation homes and nonowner-occupied investment homes to be rented out (buy-to-let) or sold later (condo flippers) were allowed. HE (home equity) and HELOC (home equity line of credit), borrowing against the equity in existing homes, became prevalent.

Empowered by high-tech models, lenders loaned to less creditworthy borrowers, believing they could price any risk. Ben Bernanke shared his predecessor Alan Greenspan's faith: "banks have become increasingly adept at predicting default risk by applying statistical models to data, such as credit scores." Bernanke concluded that banks "have made substantial strides...in their ability to measure and manage risks."[13]

Innovative affordability products included *jumbo* and *super jumbo* loans that did not conform to guidelines because of their size. More risky than prime but less risky than subprime, Alt A (Alternative A) mortgages were for borrowers who did not meet normal criteria. As lenders decreased standards, there were increases in SIVA (stated income verified assets) loans, where borrowers stated their income without proof, such as income or tax receipts, and NIVA (no income verified assets), loans where no proof of employment was required.

Traditional mortgages provide 70–80 percent of appraised value. More aggressive LVRs, including negative equity loans, where the lender lent more than the value of the house, became available. In the UK one lender offered loans for 125 percent of the value of the property. In the United States undisclosed *piggyback* loans and silent second mortgages meant that by 2005 the median down payment for first-time home buyers was only 2 percent, with more than 40 percent of buyers not making any down payment at all. The FHA website stated: "FHA-insured loans require very little cash investment to close a loan. There is more flexibility in calculating household income and payment ratios."

Balloon payment mortgages left a large balance (the balloon) due at maturity. In IO (interest only) loans, borrowers only paid the interest with repayment of principal being deferred. There were ARMs (*adjustable rate mortgages*) where the interest rate was reset periodically in line with changes in market interest rates. In an *option ARM* also known as *pick'n pay*, *pick a payment*, and *pay option*, the borrower initially paid a "teaser" rate, below the prevailing market rate. In a 2/28 ARM, the borrower paid the low rate (as low as 1 percent per annum) for 2 years, after which all the payments were adjusted based on market rates at the time for the remaining 28 years of the loan.

Under an option ARM mortgage with a 1 percent teaser rate, a borrower with a $520,000 mortgage would be paying $1,673 per month in the first year versus $3,134 monthly under a 30-year, 6.05 percent fixed rate mortgage. The lower repayments allowed borrowers to take out larger loans. As the initial repayments did not cover the interest, the loan principal increased by the unpaid interest amount (*negative amortization*). If the price of the home fell, borrowers owed more than the value of the property. After the initial "honeymoon" period, the monthly payments also increased sharply. If the loan balance increases to a set level, generally 110–125 percent of the original amount borrowed, borrowers face sharply higher payments even before the initial period expires.

Alan Greenspan championed ARMs: "many homeowners might have saved tens of thousands of dollars had they held adjustable-rate mortgages rather than fixed rate mortgages during the past decade."[14] In September 2006, Angelo Mozilo, the permanently sun-tanned CEO of Countrywide, a leading American mortgage provider, claimed shock upon discovering that 80 percent of borrowers with option ARMs were making only the very low initial payments.

Never having experienced falling house prices, borrowers bet that home values would go up very fast during the period of the teaser rate, that interest rates would stay low, and that their future income would increase to meet higher repayment. If this proved wrong, then the borrower faced payment shock—a large jump in repayments when the rate was reset. Insiders referred to these mortgages as *exploding ARMs*.

ARMs Race

Between 2004 and 2006, subprime mortgages in the United States increased to around 20–30 percent of all new mortgages. By 2007, subprime mortgage outstandings were around 10–15 percent of the total mortgage market of $10 trillion. Securitization evolved into a complex mortgage food chain (Figure 11.5).

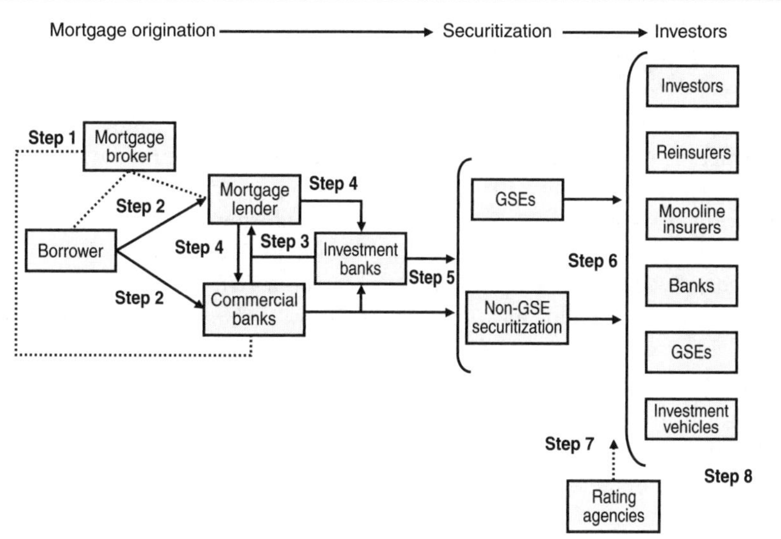

1. Borrowers seek mortgages from banks or specialist mortgage lenders, directly or through a mortgage broker.
2. Mortgage lenders and commercial banks make the loan to the borrower.
3. Mortgage lenders use lines of credit from commercial banks or investment banks (a warehouse line) to finance the mortgages, pending sale.
4. Mortgage lenders sell the loans to larger commercial banks or investment banks.
5. Commercial banks and investment banks securitize mortgages.
6. Conforming mortgages are sold to GSEs (Fannie Mae and Freddie Mac) to be sold as agency MBSs. Nonconforming mortgages (prime jumbo, Alt-A, subprime) are securitized privately without GSE support.
7. Rating agencies provide credit ratings for the MBSs.
8. MBSs are purchased by investors, which include pension funds, insurance companies, mutual funds, individual investors, specialist reinsurers, and monoline bond investors. Other MBS purchasers include banks, GSEs, SIVs and hedge funds.

Figure 11.5 Mortgage chain

Fraud by mortgage brokers, lenders, and borrowers reached epidemic proportions, ending in *liar loans*. In 2005, Mike Molden, a mortgage broker, stated: "I can get a ham sandwich a home loan if the sandwich has a job."[15] To obtain a mortgage, you only needed a pulse or to be able "to fog a mirror"—though even this was not essential, as 23 dead people were approved for new loans in Ohio.

Incentives, designed to maintain and increase volumes, encouraged declines in credit quality. Brokers received an up-front fee based on the size of mortgage—typically 1–2 percent on a conforming mortgage. Brokers received a YSP (*yield spread premium*) for higher interest rates. Where the market rate was 9 percent, the broker received a YSP of an additional commission of 1 percent for making a loan with a rate of 9.5 percent, or an additional 2 percent if the rate was 10.25 percent. This increased the proportion of subprime loans even where the borrower qualified for conventional mortgages with better terms. Valuations of properties were regularly inflated to allow larger loans.

For lenders like Countrywide, a leading nonbank mortgage lender, the only focus was growth, making more loans. One employee drove a car with the license plate FUNDEM. When a new colleague asked what it meant, he was informed that it was Countrywide's 2006 growth strategy—to fund all loans. Even if the loan applicant had no job or assets, the answer was always: "Fund 'em."[16]

No one, other than the investor who ended up with the mortgage, had any incentive to make sure that the borrower would pay back the loan. Even these investors chased higher returns, encouraging lower-quality loans to be made and repackaged.

Investors relied on the rating agencies, who relied on banks, brokers, and various third parties to ensure the quality of the loans. Banks and lenders relied on the rating agencies. The brokers relied on the banks that were buying their loans and the investors buying the securities. Everyone relied on someone else to do their job.

The automated models for approving mortgages and rating models for evaluating the quality of ABSs relied on historical data that ignored changes in the mortgage market, especially the deteriorating quality of the loans. They failed to grasp L.P. Hartley's observation in his novel *The Go-Between*: "The past is another country; they do things differently there." In a failure of common sense, smart people spent a lot of time using models and historical data to convince themselves and each other that the risks were low.

Heroes for One Day

In 2008, Adam Davidson and Alex Blumberg of America's National Public Radio (NPR) produced an award-wining episode of *This American Life* titled "The giant pool of money." In the broadcast, Mike Francis, a Morgan Stanley executive director, explained:

> We almost couldn't produce enough to keep the appetite of the investors happy. More people wanted bonds than we could actually produce...it's like, there's a guy out there with a lot of money. We gotta find a way to be his sole provider of bonds to fill his appetite. And his appetite's massive.[17]

Angelo Mozilo told his troops: "Let's look for every reason to approve applicants, not reject them."[18]

Qualifications required to be a mortgage broker were modest. A sign outside a broker's office read: "Hair Nails Mortgages."[19] The giant pool of money' profiled Mike Garner, an employee of Silver State Mortgage, the largest private mortgage bank in Nevada, who entered the mortgage business straight from his previous job as a bartender. Evangelical Christian pastors preached Earthly reward, moonlighting as mortgage brokers selling loans. Church-sponsored wealth seminars promoted home ownership, promising donations to the church in return for loans.

In the film *Boiler Room*, stockbrokers make cold calls to lists of potential monied clients using high-pressure tactics to sell them shares. In his play *Glengarry Glen Ross*, David Mamet wrote about the lives of four Chicago real estate agents prepared to lie, flatter, bribe, and threaten to sell real estate to unwilling prospective buyers. Mortgage brokers resembled the characters in *Boiler Room* and Mamet's play. They were making money by making loans to poor people with bad credit, selling high-cost mortgages to people who could not afford them. Predatory lending and fraud to close deals were de rigueur.

Some mortgage brokers were making $75,000 and $100,000 a month. In "The giant pool of money," one mortgage broker described his life style:

> We rolled up to Marquee at midnight with a line, 500-people deep out front. Walk right up to the door: Give me my table. Sitting next to Tara Reid and a couple of her friends. Christina Aguilera was doing some.... We ordered three, four bottles of Cristal at $1,000 per bottle...Whoa, who's the cool guys? We were the cool guys. They gave me the black card with my name on it. There's probably ten in existence. You know?[20]

The broker had five cars, a $1.5-million-dollar vacation house in Connecticut, and a rented penthouse in Manhattan.

Daniel Sadek of Quick Loan Funding based in California collected a fleet of cars, including a Lamborghini, a McLaren, a Ferrari Enzo, and a Porsche. Sadek also co-wrote and spent $35 million funding a feature film *Redline*, starring his girlfriend Nadia Bjorlin. The unlikely plot follows the story of a young automobile fanatic and star of a hot band, who becomes caught up in illegal drag-racing competitions. The film's message was—risk everything, fear nothing.[21]

Andy Warhol had forecast a future in which everyone would be famous for 15 minutes. Years later, during his Berlin period, David Bowie penned a song promising everyone that they could be heroes but only for one day. Mortgage brokers were both famous and heroes for a brief time, helping fulfill dreams of American home ownership.

In *Bright-Sided: How the Relentless Promotion of Positive Thinking Has Undermined America*, Barbara Ehrenreich argues that positive thinking is an ideological force that denies reality. She recounts an encounter with a popular preacher in Houston who preached that God would provide big houses and nice tables in restaurants to those who sincerely wish for them—this was "the Law of Attraction." Underlying the housing and mortgage boom was manic optimism about house prices.

Subprime lending contributed to increases in American home ownership rates to a high of 69.2 percent in 2004, up from 64 percent in 1994. Between 1997 and 2006 the higher overall demand caused average house prices to double. By late 2006, the average U.S. home cost four times the average family income, an increase from the historical two or three times. As house prices rose, Americans saved less and borrowed more. American home mortgage debt increased to 73 percent of American GDP in 2008, up from below 50 percent in the 1990s.

High house prices put home ownership beyond the means of the people that the policy was meant to assist. Borrowers were forced to enter into expensive creative mortgages to purchase houses. Eventually a surplus of unsold homes and unsustainable levels of borrowings caused housing prices to decline from mid-2006, leaving homeowners with unsustainable levels of debt. Levels of home ownership began to decline.

In 2006, Casey Serin, a 24-year old web designer from Sacramento, bought seven houses in 5 months with $2.2 million in debt. He lied about his income on *no document* loans. He had no deposit. In 2007, three of Serin's houses were repossessed. The others faced foreclosure. Serin's website—www.Iamfacingforeclosure.com—was a symbol of the excesses of the sub-prime mortgage market.

It was not lending money to poor people that was the problem. The problem was lending money poorly.

12

The Doomsday Debt Machine

Rebranded as *structured finance* or *structured credit*, securitization increasingly involved layers of complex leverage repeatedly using the same debt as collateral. The new alphabet of debt that the process created was self-dealing raised to an art form. Debt now bought more debt, as the same underlying loan was leveraged and re-leveraged in a seemingly endless spiral of borrowing. At each stage, the banks charged fees and earned margins from the money they lent.

Alpha-Debt Soup

Investor demand for securitized debt decreased the cost of loans to the borrower, in turn bringing down investor returns. Bankers were forced constantly to create highly rated bonds with attractive returns, repackaging unsellable, rancid junk in complex chains of debt (see Figure 12.1).

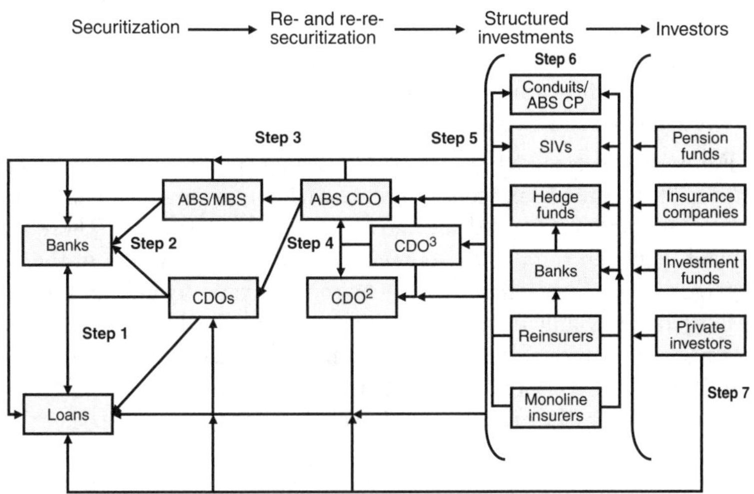

1. Banks make loans to companies and individuals, including mortgage loans.
2. Banks sell these loans to securitization vehicles that issue ABS, MBS, and CDO securities.
3. Re-securitization vehicles (structured finance CDOs, ABS CDOs, or CDO^2) purchase securitized bonds and then repackage them to sell to investors.
4. Re-securitization vehicles buy re-securitized paper issued by each other. CDO^3 vehicles buy securities issued by re-securitization vehicles to be further repackaged.
5. Structured investment vehicles purchase loans, primary securitizations (ABSs, MBSs, CDOs) and re- and re-re-securitizations.
6. Investors lend to each other or are otherwise interrelated. Banks provide lines of credit to conduits or lend to SIVs and hedge funds, secured against the securitized bonds purchased. Investment vehicles buy securities issued by each other. Reinsurers and monoline insurers guarantee the banks against losses on securities as well as investing in loans, primary securitizations, re- and re-re-securitizations and the investment vehicles.
7. Investors purchase loans, primary securitizations, re- and re-re-securitizations and invest in the structured investment vehicles and hedge funds. Some investors then borrow from banks to finance these purchases.

Figure 12.1 Securitization market

ABS CP (asset-backed securities commercial paper), conduits ("arbitrage" off-balance sheet issuers of ABS CP), SIVs (structured investment vehicles) and hedge funds purchased ABSs. SPVs issued short-dated IOUs to money market investors, indirectly taking the risk of ABSs and MBSs that they were not allowed to buy.

Figure 12.2 sets out a typical ABS CP issuing conduit structure. By early 2007, $1.2 trillion or 53 percent of the $2.2 trillion commercial paper in the U.S. market was asset-backed, around 50 percent by mortgages. There was a mismatch between the 5–30-year securitized debt and the life of the ABS CP (typically less than 6 months). If commerical paper could not be issued (considered highly unlikely), then the sponsor bank would finance the assets under a standby credit facility. SIVs bought high-quality ABS, funding it by issuing their own AAA-rated debt. One SIV even purchased highly rated debt from another SIV in an astonishing chain of risk.

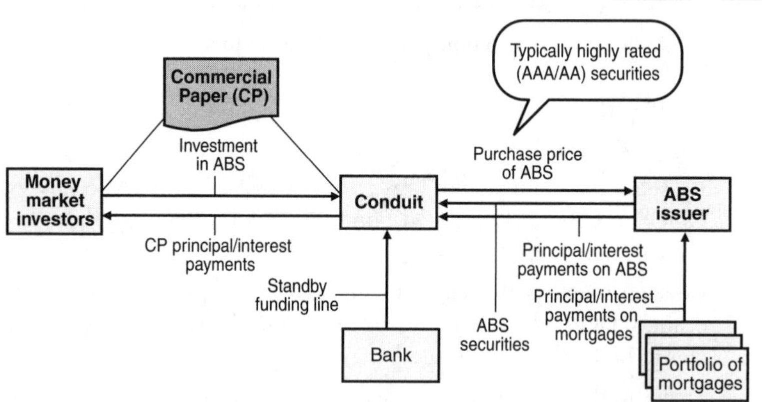

1. The conduit purchases AAA or AA securities, either ABSs, MBSs, or CDOs, with maturities of between 5 and 30 years.
2. The conduit issues commercial paper with maturities of up to 9 months (mainly 1 to 3 months) to finance the purchase of the AAA or AA-rated securities.
3. As the commercial paper has shorter maturities than the securities the conduit owns, there is a liquidity risk—commercial paper investors may not agree to keep rolling over paper when it matures. To cover this risk, the conduit takes out a standby funding line from a bank (usually the one setting up the structure). If commercial paper cannot be reissued then the conduit can draw down on this standby line to finance the securities it holds.

Figure 12.2 ABS CP structure

Hedge funds bought ABSs, funded by borrowing (up to) 98 percent of the value of AAA-rated assets. At Bear Stearns, Ralph Cioffi, a bond salesman, set up the High Grade Structured Credit Strategies Fund and High Grade Structured Credit Strategies Enhanced Leverage Fund. Promising clients steady returns with limited risk, the funds bought high-grade ABSs and MBSs, borrowing heavily against them to increase returns.

Ralphie's Funds controlled more than $15 billion of assets, funded by $14 billion of borrowings from Merrill Lynch, Goldman Sachs, Bank of America, and JP Morgan. The fees (2 percent of assets under management and 20 percent of profits) accounted for three-quarters of Bear Stearns Asset Management revenues in 2004 and 2005.

Existing securitized debt was purchased by another SPV and then repackaged into new securitized debt.

These were *re-securitizations*—structured finance CDOs, ABS CDOs, or CDO^2. There were also *re-re-securitizations*—CDO^3. Figure 12.3 sets out a typical ABS CDO or CDO^2.

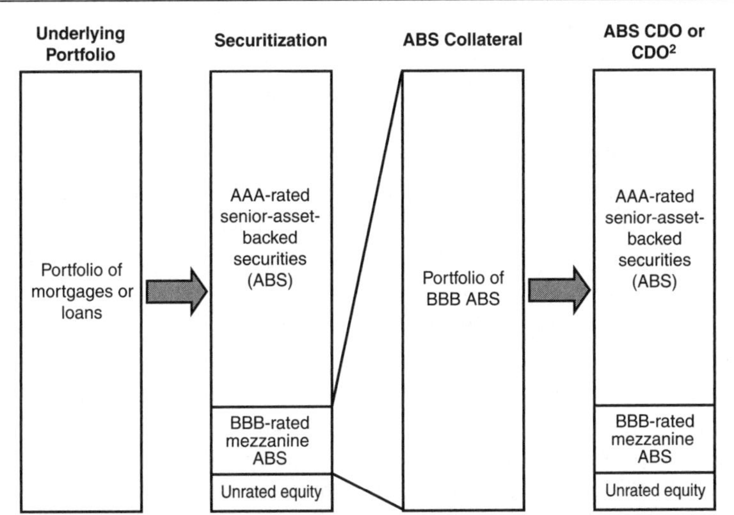

1. An underlying portfolio of mortgages and loans is assembled. This portfolio is then repackaged and securitized, being tranched into AAA-rated senior ABS, BBB-rated mezzanine, and equity.
2. The BBB-rated mezzanine from the first securitization is combined with similar securities from other deals to create a new portfolio. This portfolio is then repackaged again and resecuritized into new AAA-rated senior ABS, BBB-rated mezzanine, and equity.

Figure 12.3 ABS CDO or CDO2 structure

The complex chains of debt and leverage meant that the same loans were being churned in a merry-go-round of investors and banks chasing returns by constantly repackaging and leveraging the same debt over and over.

In the Shadow of Debt

This was the *shadow banking system*.[1] Similar to banks, the unregulated vehicles lent money raised from short-term borrowing and securitization. As the shadow banking system increased in size, risk moved from regulated banks to unregulated vehicles, where it was more difficult to identify.

Like banks, the vehicles assumed the risk that the borrower may not pay back the loan, or that the depositor financing the loan may want their money back. The vehicles held minimal capital or reserves against these risks. The vehicles depended upon the value of their assets remaining stable and also a functioning market where assets could be sold if needed.

Demand for investments from the shadow banking system, the *structured bid*, drove down borrowing costs. The vehicles constantly increased leverage and risk to maintain returns. Techniques of staggering complexity, incomprehensible to outsiders, created more debt and ever-greater levels of leverage, frequently disguised.

For example, assume a $1,000 million CDO based on a portfolio of 100 separate loans, each $10 million. If any of the loans default, then you lose $6 million (60 percent of $10 million), recovering a part of your loan (40 percent or $4 million). An investor takes the risk of the first 2 percent ($20 million, being 2 percent of $1,000 million) of losses on the entire portfolio (the equity tranche).

Investors in the CDO equity tranche take the risk of bankruptcy of the first three firms out of the 100 firms in the portfolio ($20 million of losses divided by $6 million). As they are first in line to the risk of loss of the first three firms to default, the investors are not diversified. This is because once there are three defaults causing them to lose their entire investment, they have no further interest in the performance of the remaining 97 firms in the portfolio.

Instead of purchasing the equity, the investor could invest $20 million in a diversified fashion, spreading the money equally between each of the 100 loans (that is, $200,000 in each loan—$20 million divided by the 100 loans). If three loans defaulted in the portfolio, then the investor would lose only

$0.36 million (loss of $120,000 per company (60 percent of $200,000) times 3). In contrast, where they invested in the CDO equity, for the same three losses the investor loses $20 million. For the same event (three defaults), the investor's loss is 56 times greater where they purchase the equity rather than investing in a diversified portfolio ($20 million versus $0.36 million). This is known as *embedded loss leverage*.

Linked in a dizzy spiral of debt as their modus operandi merged, banks and the inhabitants of the shadow banking sector (ABS issuers, CDO issuers, conduits, SIVs, hedge funds, reinsurers and monoline insurers) increasingly resembled each other. In a case of rinse and repeat and then repeat again, at each stage the risk was redistilled and concentrated. Figure 12.4 shows how a hedge fund uses $10 million to take the risk of the first $60 million of losses on a $850 million portfolio of mortgages.[2] Figure 12.5 shows how $1 of *real* capital now supports between $20 and $30 of loans.

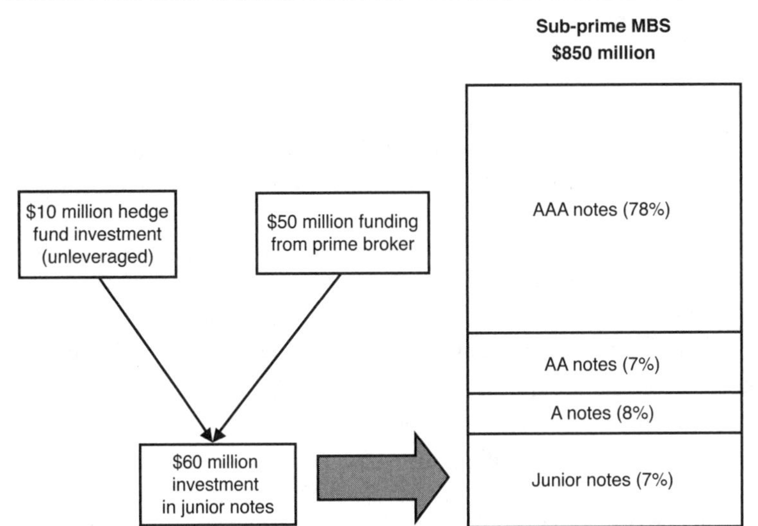

1. A hedge fund invests in $60 of the junior notes (effectively the equity tranche) of a securitization of $850 million portfolio of mortgages to create a series of different securities.
2. The hedge fund finances its $60 million with $10 million of its own money, borrowing $50 million from a bank (known as a prime broker) who will lend to it against the security of the notes.

Figure 12.4 Leveraged investment in MBS

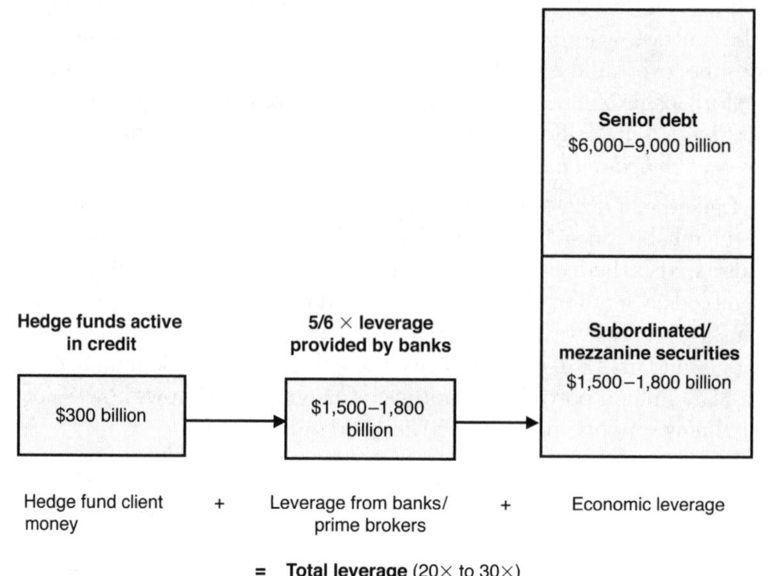

1. In 2007 there was around $300 billion of funds available from hedge funds active in credit markets that purchased debt securities and loans.
2. The available $300 million could be leveraged five or six times by borrowing $1,200–1,500 billion from banks and prime brokers, against the collateral of securities purchased by the fund. This means that the hedge funds have total buying power of $1,500–1,800 billion.
3. The hedge funds use this $1,500–1,800 billion to purchase riskier subordinated or mezzanine securities in securitizations.
4. The $1,500–1,800 billion supports additional senior debt of four to six times. This is because the subordinated and mezzanine securities absorb losses before the more highly rated senior securities. This provides investors in the senior securities comfort that they are unlikely to lose money, encouraging them to purchase the debt.
5. In total, the original $300 billion of funds now supports $6,000–$9,000 billion in assets, most of which is financed by debt.

Source: Adapted from Roger Merritt and Eileen Fahey 'Hedge funds: the new credit paradigm' (5 June 2007), Fitch Ratings, New York. Copyright © Fitch Ratings Ltd.

Figure 12.5 Systemic leverage

If the pricing models for ABSs, MBSs, and CDOs were approximate, then for more complex structures they were inadequate. If correlation between two loans in a normal portfolio was an educated guess, then the correlation input into a structured finance CDO, CDO^2, or CDO^3 was fantasy.

In the 2006 financial statements for the Bear Stearns hedge funds, auditors Deloitte & Touche noted that between 60 and 70 percent of assets were valued using estimates provided by the fund's managers, cautioning that differences in value could be significant. As Mervyn King, governor of the Bank of England, later observed: "'My word is my bond' are old words. 'My word is my CDO-squared' will never catch on."[3] King was correct.

Virtual Loans

Finally, loans became completely *virtual*—they simply did not exist. Loans were even made specifically to fail. Traditionally, lenders owned the loans that they were selling off through securitization. In a synthetic securitization, the lender purchased insurance on loans through a CDS. Increasingly, banks bought insurance on loans they did not own.

Around 2004, looking to make money from the anticipated bust of the housing bubble, a few traders short sold the shares of mortgage lenders like Countrywide, New Century, and Ameriquest, home builders and banks. But the main game was shorting the MBS referenced to the loans.

Investment banks, such as Goldman Sachs and Deutsche Bank, and hedge funds structured CDOs to benefit from the expected decline in house prices. They bought insurance against losses on loans that they simply did not own to benefit from potential defaults on mortgages. The banks and hedge funds paid modest fees (1 to 1.5 percent per annum) to bet against the U.S. housing market. Deutsche Bank's Greg Lippmann distributed T-shirts emblazoned with the words "I'm Short Your House!!!"[4]

Magnetar, a hedge fund, had a program totaling $30 billion. The name refers to a neutron star with an extremely powerful magnetic field, which as it decays emits high X-rays and gamma rays. The hedge fund bought mainly BBB-rated mezzanine ABSs that were re-securitized. As the mezzanine part of the capital structure was small (say between 3 and 7 percent), the total size of the deals had to be large. Assuming demand for $30 billion of mezzanine debt, this translated into up to $128 billion of underlying mortgages, compared to total subprime loans of around $450 billion in 2006, 28 percent of the total market.[5] As other hedge funds and banks started doing the same thing, volumes exceeded the underlying stock of mortgage loans.

The normal CDS was designed for companies where payment was triggered by bankruptcy or failure to make interest and principal repayments on loans. In June 2005, ABS PAYG CDS (asset-backed securities pay-as-you-go credit default swaps) were introduced. Under this form of credit insurance, buyers of insurance received payments where there was simply a permanent write down in the underlying loans, a downgrade to CCC credit rating or extension of maturity. Traders benefited from any deterioration in the quality of the underlying loans, making it easier to short the housing market.

In 2006, the ABX.HE (asset-backed securities home equity), an index of MBSs similar to a stock index, was created. The ABX allowed trading in portfolios of virtual mortgages—bets on the price of mortgages going up (less defaults and lower loss) or down (more defaults and more losses). Like the CDS on mortgages, the ABX was virtual, unconstrained by the size of the underlying pool of mortgages. All this had nothing to do with providing loans for homes.

In 2006/7, the shorts made a killing as the values of mortgages collapsed when house prices fell and buyers could not make repayments. Many of the securitizations structured by banks performed poorly, resulting in substantial losses for investors. Critics complained that the securitizations were structured specifically with high-risk mortgages to increase the likelihood of loss to the investors and gain to the bank. The banks argued that they had merely structured deals to meet demand from sophisticated investors.

The investors were rarely equal parties in negotiating the deals. The term "sophisticated investor" was an oxymoron, as most barely understood the structures. There was a potential conflict of interest between the banks (shorting the market) and the investors (buying the market). Sylvain R. Raynes, a structured finance specialist, told *The New York Times*: "When you buy protection against an event that you have a hand in causing, you are buying fire insurance on someone else's house and then committing arson."[6]

Amherst, a small investor, made a killing, by avoiding defaults and preventing foreclosures. Amherst insured $130 million of a pool of $29 million of highly toxic mortgages, more than 4.4 times the actual mortgages in existence. The investment banks that bought protection paid around $100 million to Amherst for the insurance. Amherst then paid off the $29 million of mortgages that it insured, avoiding having to pay out up to $130 million under the insurance policies they sold. The transaction netted Amherst around $71 million (the premium received of $100 million less the amount spent paying off the mortgages—$29 million).

Counting on the Abacus

In April 2010, the U.S. Securities and Exchange Commission (SEC) filed a lawsuit against Goldman Sachs, dismissed by Kenneth Griffin, the founder of hedge fund Citadel, as "childish."[7] The lawsuit concerned an

April 2007 CDO—Abacus 2007 AC1 (see Figure 12.6). Widely used by Asian merchants, an abacus is a calculating tool consisting of a bamboo frame with beads sliding on wires.

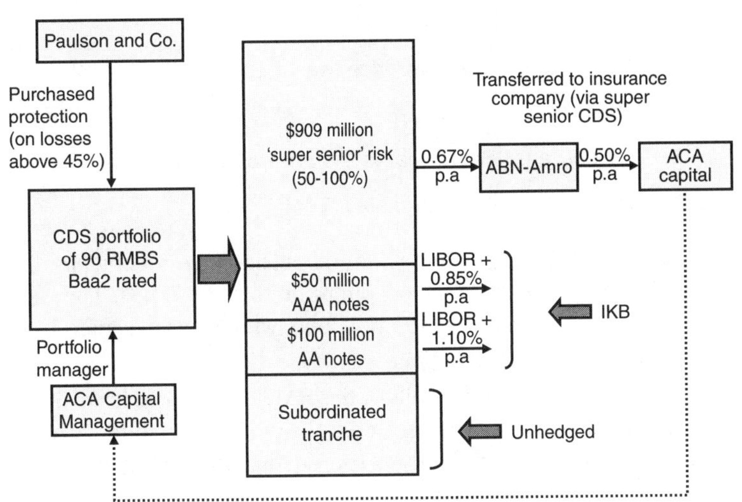

Figure 12.6 Abacus transaction

Arranged by Goldman, Abacus was a synthetic securitization, referencing a portfolio of 90 residential MBSs rated Baa2 by Moody's. The portfolio contained a high percentage of adjustable rate mortgages, relatively low borrower FICO scores, and was concentrated in U.S. states where there had been very high house price rises, like Arizona, California, Florida, and Nevada. ACA Capital Management was the portfolio selection agent. Paulson & Co. purchased protection on losses above 45 percent of the principal on the mortgages. Paulson did not own the mortgages or MBSs, betting that the securities would suffer large losses from the housing collapse.

Goldman placed $50 million AAA notes, paying LIBOR plus 0.85 percent per annum, and $100 million of AA notes, paying LIBOR plus 1.10 percent per annum, with IKB, a German bank. Goldman paid 0.67 percent per annum to hedge its super senior risk with ACA Capital, a reinsurance company (parent of the portfolio selection agent). Dutch bank ABN-Amro was interposed between Goldman and ACA Capital to guarantee ACA's performance, for a fee of 0.17 percent per annum.

In October 2007, 6 months after completion, 83 percent of underlying Baa2 RMBSs was downgraded. By January 2007, 8 months after completion, 99 percent of underlying securities had been downgraded. Paulson made $1 billion on its CDS position as the mortgages lost all value. IKB lost its entire

$150 million investment. With ACA in financial difficulties, RBS, who purchased ABN-Amro, lost $841 million on the super senior CDS.

There were parallels to 1929 and the Goldman Sachs Trading Corporation, a listed investment trust. After the crash, at a 1932 U.S. Senate hearing, there were questions about the transaction:[8]

Senator Couzens	At what price [was it sold to the public]?
Mr. Sachs	$104
Senator Couzens	And what is the price of the stock now?
Mr.Sachs	Approximately $1\frac{3}{4}$?

In 2010, the SEC alleged that Goldman misled investors by not disclosing material information on Paulson's intention to short MBSs. They alleged that Paulson, not ACA, selected the portfolio, which was designed to maximize losses from a housing collapse.

Goldman argued that full details of the RMBSs were disclosed and ACA was a reputable manager and had selected the portfolio as stated. There had been no representation that Paulson owned the underlying RMBSs. Any short position taken by Goldman was hedging its own RMBS positions. Goldman, who made $15 million for arranging the transaction, claimed to have actually lost $90 million. Goldman's claim, that IKB was a sophisticated investor, elicited humorous comments. In Michael Lewis' *The Big Short*, a trader shorting the mortgage market asks: "Who's on the other side, who's the idiot?" The answer is: "Düsseldorf. Stupid Germans. They take rating agencies seriously. They play by the rules."[9]

Intellectual Masturbation

Examination of several terabytes (billions of pages) of emails revealed Tom Montag, a senior Goldman executive, describing one CDO, Timberwolf, as: "one shi**y deal." Matthew Bieber, the trader responsible, considered the day that Timberwolf was issued as "a day that will live in infamy." Like Abacus, within 5 months of issuance, Timberwolf, whose investors included Bear Stearns' hedge funds, lost 80 percent of its value.[10]

During a Senate hearing, Goldman's CFO David Viniar was asked: "when you heard that your employees, in these e-mails, when looking at these deals, said God, what a shi**y deal...do you feel anything?" Viniar responded: "I think that's very unfortunate to have on e-mail."[11] Goldman instituted policies against using swear words in emails, cleaning up language rather than sales practices.

The SEC indictment cited Fabrice Tourre, a French employee of Goldman, who sold the Abacus deals to unwitting "widows and orphans." Among tender emails to his girlfriend Serres, the "super-smart French girl in London," the self-styled "Fabulous Fab" observed in January 2007:

> More and more leverage in the system. The whole building is about to collapse anytime now?.?.?.? Only potential survivor, the fabulous Fab[rice Tourre] standing in the middle of all these complex, highly leveraged, exotic trades he created without necessarily understanding all of the implications of those monstrosities!!!

Abacus was "pure intellectual masturbation," "a "thing," which has no purpose, which is absolutely conceptual and highly theoretical and which nobody knows how to price."

Tourre had no self-doubt:

> Anyway, not feeling too guilty about this, the real purpose of my job is to make capital markets more efficient and ultimately provide the U.S. consumer with more efficient ways to leverage and finance himself, so there is a humble, noble, and ethical reason for my job :) amazing how good I am in convincing myself !!![12]

Tourre insisted that he reasonably relied on material prepared by other Goldman staff. His insouciant Gallic defense stated that "he cannot be liable for any omissions that he did not make."

In July 2010, Goldman settled, paying a $550 million fine, around 4 percent of its annual earnings of $13 billion. Charles Geisst, author of *A History of Wall Street*, was unimpressed: "a fine is not going to bother these people.... [It] is like passing around the church collection plate and collecting a few extra bucks for sins."[13] Goldman admitted that statements in the Abacus marketing material that the reference portfolio was "selected by" ACA without disclosure of Paulson's role and economic interests, which were adverse to CDO investors, were incomplete.

The settlement avoided the real issue—the conflicts of interest within investment banks. Goldman Sachs feared that the separation of client business and trading with its own capital limited its ability to compete. Under CEO Lloyd Blankfein, the son of a postal worker born in the Bronx, Goldman embraced the conflict, emphasizing intelligence from trading with clients and other banks to place bets with its own money. As a former counsel to the Federal Reserve Board observed:

> It's all about the score. Just make the score, do the deal. Move on to the next one. That's the trader culture. Their business model has completely blurred the difference between executing trades on behalf of customers versus executing trades for themselves. It's a huge problem.[14]

Used to Be Smart

Smart banks now drank their Kool-Aid, investing their own money aggressively in ABSs. Bankers had not grasped painter Robert Motherwell's observation that "the deep necessity of art is the examination of self-deception."

Originally a self-help movement for artisans based in Newcastle, Northern Rock for much of its 150 years in existence took deposits from savers and lent to people to buy homes. Originally owned by its members, in 1997 the company demutualized and offered its shares on the London Stock Exchange. Between 1997 and 2007, under CEO Adam Applegarth, Northern Rock's loan portfolio increased from £16 billion to £101 billion, a rate of more than 20 percent per annum. Northern Rock's share of the UK's residential mortgage market more than tripled from 6 percent to 20 percent in ten years. One mortgage product allowed homebuyers to borrow 125 percent of the value of the home, or up to six times their income.

As growth outstripped the ability to finance loans from deposits from its customers, Northern Rock relied on securitization, arguing that issuing MBSs provided access to large pools of money from investors, cheaper borrowing costs and shifted the risk away from Northern Rock. Northern Rock issued £17 billion of MBSs in 2006 alone. In early 2007, bankers reaping large fees from Northern Rock securitizations voted them the best financial borrower in capital markets. In late 2007, Northern Rock's dependence on securitization would destroy it when the market failed.

CitiGroup, Merrill Lynch, and UBS committed *seppuku*, ritualized suicide. New regulations, low interest rates, and stable markets led banks to borrow more to invest in securitized bonds. At Merrill Lynch the strategy was known as a "million for a billion"—a million dollars in bonus money for every billion the bank invested in mortgage securities.

Under changed banking regulations (known as *Basel 2*), credit ratings and the bank's own models were used to calculate risk and set the amount of capital required. Under the new system, AAA and AA assets attracted minimal capital: 0.5–0.6 percent of the asset.

Following its merger and struggling to meet market expectations, Citi increased risk taking, armed with analysis from a consulting firm that Citi's risk taking lagged competitors. Chairman of the executive committee, Robert Rubin, former head of Goldman Sachs and secretary of the Treasury under President Clinton, was at the center of this push, arguing that "the only undervalued asset is risk."[15] Citi's "riverboat gamblers" created a production line to buy mortgages and repackage them into MBSs.[16] The high credit quality securities were sold to ABS CP conduits and SIVs, managed by Citi or increasingly, retained on the bank's books. Citi's trading desk's motto was "Live for today."[17]

Having worked his way to CEO of Merrill Lynch, America's largest brokerage firm, Stanley O'Neal, the grandson of a slave, struggled to change the firm, known to its employees as "Mother Merrill." Merrill Lynch's bovine image was related to a 1970 TV commercial featuring a thundering herd of cattle stampeding straight at the camera and the tagline "Merrill Lynch: bullish on America." Like Citi, "Stan Bin Laden" or "Osama O'Neal" was bullish on risk, especially mortgages.

In 2006, Merrill Lynch purchased mortgage broker First Franklin for $1.3 billion to provide raw material for its securitization machine. Merrill's portfolio of securitized mortgages peaked at $50 billion. Lacking Citi's vast balance sheet and capital, Merrill hedged some risk with reinsurers and monoline insurance companies, many of whom would turn out to be undercapitalized.

A large respected Swiss bank, UBS had a logo of three keys, signifying confidence, security, and discretion. Originally focused on private banking, UBS increased exposure to investment banking through its acquisition of S.G. Warburg, Dillion Read, and PaineWebber. UBS also invested heavily in securitization.

An internal report, prepared after UBS suffered large losses, revealed rampant risk taking.[18] Every UBS desk (internal hedge fund, bond trading, currency trading, funding) and every trading strategy (ABS relative value strategy, ABS CDO trading, and overall relative value trading) involved purchases of high-quality MBSs or CDOs. If you only had to hold 0.6 percent capital against the security, then a margin on 0.15 percent per annum translated into a return of 25 percent per annum (0.15 percent divided by 0.6 percent), well above the bank's target. Irrespective of the relationship between loan defaults, the correlation between traders and trading strategies was high.

At UBS, investments were financed with cheap money from the bank's depositors. Glass-Steagall was originally enacted to prevent depositors money being risked in this way. The banks did not heed the advice of economist Walter Bagehot in his 1873 book *Lombard Street*: "The only securities which a banker, using money that he may be asked at short notice to repay, ought to touch are those which are easily saleable and easily intelligible."[19]

Citi and Merrill would lose more than $50 billion each, whereas UBS would lose more than $30 billion. Chuck Prince, Citi's CEO, a lawyer appointed to deal with regulatory problems, lacked the requisite risk skills. Robert Rubin abnegated responsibility, citing his lack of operational responsibilities. Prince's nickname was "One Buck Chuck," a reference to the fact that Citi's stock price barely moved $1 under his leadership. Losses on mortgages drove Citi's stock price perilously close to the one-buck figure as the bank struggled to survive. Merrill was taken over by BA, after a short and troubled period with John Thain at the helm. UBS survived with the assistance of the Swiss government. UBS, observers noted acidly, meant **u**gly **b**alance **s**heet, **u**sed to **b**e **s**mart, or **u** **be** **s**tupid.

Warren Buffet and Charlie Mauger at Berkshire Hathaway believed that investors should eat their own cooking, that is, have their money at stake. In 2010, John Mack, CEO of Morgan Stanley, ruefully observed that the banks "did eat our own cooking and we choked on it."[20]

Chain Reaction

In an atomic chain reaction, a sequence creates additional reactions as positive feedback leads to a self-amplifying chain of events. In late 2007, a similar chain reaction started in securitization markets. In 2004, U.S. interest rates rose from their abnormally low levels after 2001. U.S. housing prices stalled, then fell, and mortgage defaults increased, especially on subprime loans. In a 2007 report, the Center for Responsible Lending predicted that 15 percent of loans would end in foreclosure. In the third quarter of 2009 alone, 15 percent of subprime loans were foreclosed, while another 27 percent were delinquent.

Homeowners, who qualified for mortgages based on gambling income and eBay earnings, defaulted within months of drawing down the loan. In securitizations, originators were obligated to repurchase loans if they went delinquent within an agreed time. As mortgages defaulted, the brokers did not have the money to buy them back.

In a February 2007 conference call, New Century Financial, a California-based major subprime mortgage lender, warned that loan volumes would decrease by 20 percent because of early defaults. New Century had $8.2 billion in repurchase obligations and was in default on its lines of credit. New business had ground to a halt, reducing cash flow and earnings.

In 2002 HSBC, the once staid conservative Hong Kong and Shanghai Bank, purchased Household Finance, a subprime pioneer. In February 2007, HSBC wrote off $10.56 billion in loan losses. HSBC management once spoke in glowing terms of Household's staff—of Ph.D.s skilled at cutting and dicing mortgages. In hindsight, HSBC should have stuck to old-fashioned bankers able to establish the borrower's ability to repay by means developed during the Spanish inquisition. As bankers say: "The best loans are made during the worst times, the worst loans are made during the best times."

By September 2009, one in ten U.S. householders were at least one mortgage payment behind. If foreclosures were included, then one in seven American homeowners were in housing distress. In subprime, delinquencies in some kinds of loans were 40–50 percent. The dream of home ownership had become a national nightmare.

Speaking before the Joint Economic Committee of the U.S. Congress on March 28, 2007, Ben Bernanke appeared unconcerned: "The impact on the broader economy and financial markets of the problems in the subprime markets seems likely to be contained." The Fed chairman had probably never heard of James Howard Kunstler or read his prophetic warning of October 17, 2005:

> The mortgage industry, a mutant monster organism of lapsed lending standards and arrant grift on the grand scale, is going to implode like a death star under the weight of these nonperforming loans and drag every tradable instrument known to man into the quantum vacuum of finance that it creates.[21]

Subprime losses radiated out, infecting the entire global financial system (see Figure 12.7). Loan losses meant that the riskier equity and mezzanine tranches of securitized mortgages were worthless. Paradoxically, the major problem related to high-quality-rated securities unlikely to suffer cash loss. In a typical securitization, losses would need to reach 15–30 percent before the better-rated securities lost money. As losses mounted and the lower layers on which the high rating of senior securities was based disappeared, AAA tranches were downgraded. Simultaneously, credit margins increased. Investors had *paper* or *mark-to-market* losses if the securities were sold today. If the investor could ignore the current value, then the investor was unlikely actually to lose money.

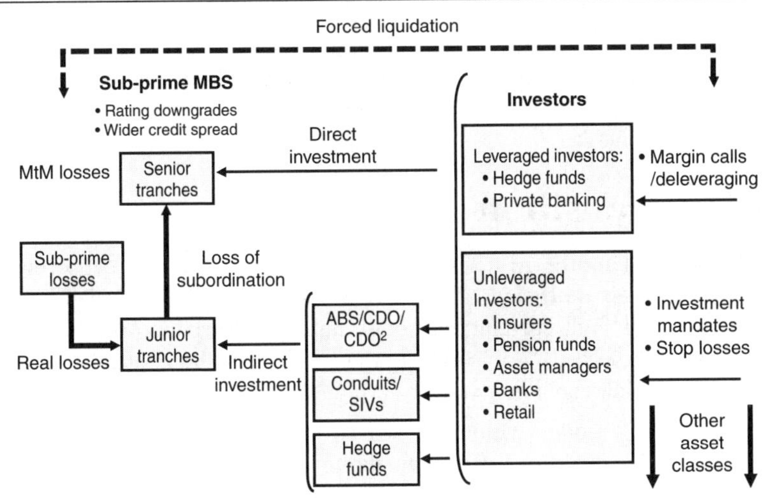

Figure 12.7 Transmission of subprime losses

Traditional investors who had not themselves borrowed to buy the securities found themselves having to sell as paper losses reached certain levels, triggering *real* losses. They were also indirectly caught up in the death throes of leveraged funds. Unable to borrow directly, they had invested in hedge funds, SIVs and CDOs to access the hidden fruit of leverage.

As the value of the securities used as collateral fell, investors who had borrowed found lenders asking for more collateral. Hedge funds, conduits, and SIVs did not have the money to meet the margin calls. Forced selling set off of a new round of price falls, restarting the entire cycle.

At Bear Stearns, Ralphie's Funds owned AAA and AA-rated MBSs funded by $600 million in equity and $10 billion in short-term borrowings. In good times, the leverage ensured good returns but now it worked in reverse. A 1 percent fall in the value of the fund assets was roughly equivalent to a loss of $100 million (about 16 percent of the equity). A 6 percent move wiped out all equity investors. A 24 percent fall in the value of the underlying bonds translated into a $1.8 billion loss for the lending banks.

Bear Stearns agreed, under pressure, to provide a $1.6 billion loan (over 10 percent of the firm's equity) to the less leveraged High Grade Structured Credit Fund, letting its more leveraged sibling fail. Jimmy Cayne, cigar-smoking, bridge-playing, and (allegedly) pot-smoking Bear Stearns' CEO, sought a one-year moratorium on margin calls. In 1998, when Wall Street bailed out Long Term Capital Management (LTCM), Bear famously rejected a similar proposal. Merrill, a big lender, now seized and tried to auction off $800 million of collateral. There were few buyers in sight and the prices were in free fall.

Shortly after the Bear funds collapsed, the UK hedge fund Peleton Partners (the name refers to the leading group in a bicycle road race) failed. Following a similar strategy to the Bear Stearns funds, Peleton had recently won an industry award for best new fixed-income hedge fund.

Phase Transition

Banks with mortgage assets suffered large losses because borrowers failed to pay their mortgages. The models used to value securitized bonds, especially the default correlation model, failed, exacerbating the loss. Will Rogers was vindicated: "You can't say that civilization don't advance; for in every war they kill you a new way."

In the Ising model, within a lattice of interacting magnetic moments, heat causes the direction of the magnetic moments to be uncorrelated, behaving randomly. Where the temperature drops below a critical temperature, the magnetic moments become spontaneously correlated. This is a *phase transition* in thermal mechanics and *spontaneous symmetry breaking* in statistical quantum field theory. As long as the economy's temperature was high, loan defaults were uncorrelated and risk was low. When the economy's temperature dropped, the correlation between defaults as well as the level of defaults increased. As the economy experienced a phase transition, losses and risk increased to catastrophic levels.

Increases in default correlation caused the value of highly rated tranches to fall as the probability of defaults and higher losses increased. Reinsurance companies and monoline insurers that had hedged mortgage exposures now experienced spontaneous symmetry breaking, failing in sympathy with the defaulting mortgages leaving the banks that they had insured exposed. As the markets seized up, banks were left with low-quality loans that they were unable to repackage and sell off, as planned.

Despite minimal exposure to subprime mortgages, Northern Rock was unable to raise money as the securitization market seized up. In mid-September 2007, queues of panicked customers outside Northern Rock branches waited to withdraw deposits. In the Internet banking age, the signs of an old-fashioned bank run sealed Northern Rock's fate. Adam Applegarth confessed to a UK parliamentary hearing that he understood: "the logic of somebody who has their life savings invested in an institution and who sees pictures of people queuing outside the door and they go join that queue."[22]

Unable to issue commercial paper as holdings of toxic assets fell in value, conduits triggered parent bank credit lines, returning the assets to the mother ship. SIVs unable to issue debt faced the choice of trying to sell their assets or file for bankruptcy and liquidate their investments. Although there was no legal obligation to do so, sponsoring banks were forced to support their off balance sheet vehicles to preserve their reputation.

In an interview, Robert Rubin admitted that he had no knowledge of the *liquidity put* mechanisms under which assets held by Citi's shadow banks could come back to the firm.[23] The risks, including the liquidity put, were disclosed in the financial statements. One trader who briefed Boards observed: "These guys wouldn't know a CDO from a PowerBar and they didn't want to learn."[24]

Terra incognita

In the years preceding the financial crisis, the United States absorbed around 85 percent of total global capital flows ($500 billion each year). Asia and Europe were the largest suppliers of capital, followed by Russia and the Middle East. This money funded U.S. government debt, the housing market and high levels of home equity lending.[25] Global money funded the U.S. debt binge and global investors suffered losses. In 2007 Jochen Sanio, a German regulator, asked: "Does anyone know who holds the risk [in modern financial deals]?...Market participants are operating in terra incognita."[26]

In Australia, one of the last terra incognitas, the local arm of Lehman Brothers sold $2 billion of CDOs (grandly named Federation, Tasman, Parkes, Flinders, Kokoda, Kiama, and Torquay) to Tumbarumba Council, Wingecarribee Council, St. Vincent De Paul Society, the Starlight Children's Cancer Foundation, the Boystown Charity for underprivileged children, and the Anglican, Baptist, Uniting, and Catholic churches. Tax money to fund civic works and charitable donations were invested in these securities.

Like their counterparts elsewhere, Australian investors did not understand the risks and did not receive sufficient return to compensate for the additional risk. Investors relied on credit ratings, assuming that the securities were just like conventional bonds. ABS, MBS, CDO, and others were *terra nullius*—there was nothing there.

Banks, especially senior managers and directors, did not understand the products that they were creating and selling. Risk was broken up into exotic fragments that were difficult to understand and value. David Skeel and Frank Partnoy in a study of CDOs concluded that the costs were high, the benefits questionable and that the structures were used to transform existing debt instruments that are accurately priced into new ones that are overvalued.[27] Warren Buffett told the *Financial Times* on October 26, 2007:

> One of the lessons that investors seem to have to learn over and over again, and will again in the future, is that not only can you not turn a toad into a prince by kissing it, but you cannot turn a toad into a prince by repackaging it. But very imaginative people in the securities market try to do that. If you have bad mortgages they do not become better by repackaging them.

Investors learned the rules of financial gravity.[28] If the value of the whole is less than the price of its parts, then some parts are overpriced. Separating out and selling risk through securitization was not necessarily a source of value. If you segment value, then you also segment liquidity. You have many securities with a smaller market for each part. When you want to sell, there are no buyers. Risk transfer encourages people to take more risk and to shift risks to those least able to understand and bear them. There is a strong correlation between the complexity of an instrument, its remoteness from the real economy and its likelihood to spread contagion.

In a Tom Satherwaite short story *Masquerade*, the American hero eats *andouillettes*. Finding them initially delicious, he is later horrified to discover that they are pigs entrails stuffed with tripe and chitterlings, offcuts, and rejects of his own culture. Securitized bonds were the *andouillettes* of high finance.

By 2007 CDOs came to mean *Chernobyl death obligations*.[29] In an atomic explosion, deadly radiation causes a slow, painful death for those not killed by the blast. Half-life measures the rate of radioactive decay, which can range from seconds to 760 million years for Uranium 238. Toxic assets from collapsed securitization markets emitted toxic radiation that lingered, poisoning financial markets.

Securitization was alchemy, creating, multiplying, and refracting borrowing for a debt-addicted world. Designed to allow transfer and reduction of risk, it ended up burning everything and everybody it touched.

13

Risk Supermarkets

On August 4, 1930, Michael Cullen opened King Kullen, the first supermarket in Jamaica Queens in New York City, aiming to sell large volumes at discounted prices. King Kullen's marketing slogan was: "Pile it high. Sell it low." Increasingly resembling financial supermarkets, banks packaged risk into discrete, tradable bundles, known as derivatives.

Derivatives have no intrinsic worth, deriving their value from an underlying financial asset—share, bond, commodity, or currency. They allow hedging the risk of changes in the price of assets. Peter Bernstein argued that: "The revolutionary idea that defines the boundary between modern times and the past is the mastery of risk: the notion that the future is more than a whim of the gods and that men and women are not passive before nature."[1] Mastery of derivative instruments, the tool for managing risk, defined the new finance. Derivatives were the ultimate in financial alchemy—the powerful, magic "ring" that allows the holder to rule and control money.

Mind Your Derivatives

Derivatives are a system of price guarantees and price insurance. *Forwards* (known as *futures* when traded on an organized exchange) guarantee the price at which you can buy or sell something at a future date. If the copper price goes up, then a copper mining company earns more from its sales.

If the price goes down, then it earns less. If the mining company wants to guarantee the future price of copper, then it sells its copper forward to an agreed date at a known price to guarantee revenues.

Options offer price insurance. By selling forward, the mining company gives up potential gains from higher than expected copper prices. Instead, the mining company could purchase a *put option* that protects against declines in the copper price. If copper prices fall then the put option pays the difference between actual market price at the future date and the agreed price (the *strike price*), compensating the mining company for losses. If prices are above the agreed strike price then the option lapses, allowing the mining company to benefit from higher copper prices. To purchase the put option, the mining company (the *option buyer*) pays a fee (the *premium*) to the provider of the insurance (the *option seller*). A *call option* protects a copper purchaser, for a fee, from higher prices by paying out the difference between the actual market price of copper at the future date and the agreed price if prices go up.

Derivatives have a number of special features, which make them attractive. The copper mining company does not actually deliver the copper to the providers of price guarantees or insurance but settles in cash, based on price changes from the time the contract was struck. If copper prices go down, then the mining company receives a payment from the price guarantor to compensate for lost revenue. If copper prices go up, the copper mining company makes a payment to the price guarantor from its higher earnings. If the copper mining company bought price insurance, then it receives only a payment if the copper price falls. Cash settlement allows traders with no position in copper to buy or sell to take advantage of expected price changes.

Using derivatives, traders can also bet on future price changes without commitment of money to actually buy the asset. Instead of buying $10 million of shares with cash, the trader can enter a derivative, a *total return swap* (TRS) over the shares (see Figure 13.1). The trader receives the return on the share (dividends and increases in price) in return for paying the cost of holding the shares (decreases in price and the funding cost of the dealer). The TRS requires no funding other than any collateral required by the dealer, substantially less than the $10 million required to buy the shares. The trader acquires the same exposure as buying the shares but increases the return and risk through leverage.

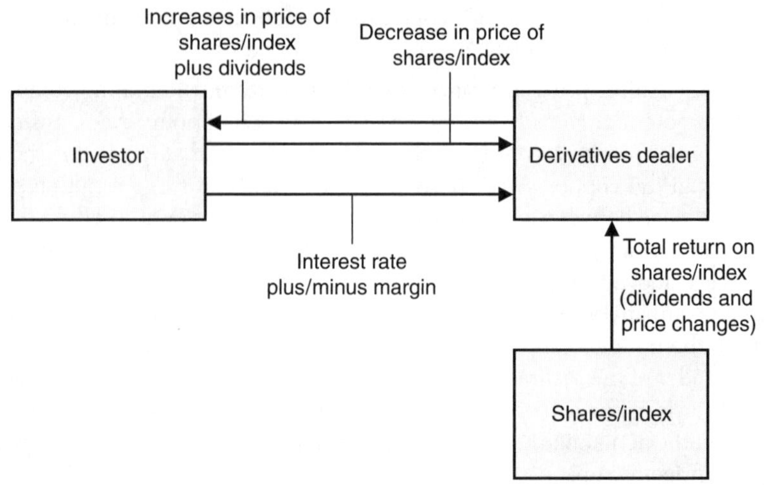

Figure 13.1 Total return swap over shares

Derivative contracts are also difficult to account for under accounting systems that date back to the Renaissance. They are off-balance sheet because all payments take place in the future. The special characteristics of derivatives allow their use to circumvent accounting regulations, investment rules, securities and tax legislation.

Particle Finance

Derivatives trading in a world where people merely hedge risk requires a party with an equal but opposite exposure to price movements. For example, the copper mining company could trade with an electronics manufacturer exposed to higher copper prices. As someone with an equal but opposite position or view on future price movements is not always available, banks increasingly supplied the derivatives. They managed the risk by trading in the underlying assets, using the Black-Scholes option pricing model. Banks now used the models to create and trade endless varieties of derivative products.

In his story *The Lottery of Babylon*, the Argentinian author Jorge Luis Borges describes a world of infinite combinations emerging from infinite subdivision where "no decision is final; all branch into others."[2] Derivatives increasingly resembled the Babylonian lottery. Like matter, financial instruments were now fractured into risk particles to be reconstituted at will using derivatives. In physics, electrons, neutrons, and protons gave way to quarks, leptons, and the probabilistic world of quantum theory. Derivative finance also became more complicated as complex derivatives divided and multiplied risk exponentially.

Quants, highly qualified POWS (physicists on Wall Street),[3] created derivative products that sometimes defied comprehension. There were swaps (price guarantees) as well as caps, floors, and collars (different types and combinations of options). There were exotic options—knock-in, knock-outs, digitals, one-touch, rainbows, worst-off, quantos. Most derivatives were on interest rates, bonds, currencies, shares or commodities. There were also derivatives on inflation, economic statistics, property prices, freight rates, catastrophe risk (hurricanes and earthquakes) and the weather. Emission derivatives were promoted as a way of combating climate change.

Just as the laws of classical physics alter at the quantum level, the rules of finance operate differently at the derivative level. Particle physics could generate electricity or create weapons of unimaginable power. Like nuclear weapons, derivatives were the culmination of centuries of intellectual endeavor. In 2002 Warren Buffett described derivatives "as time bombs both for the parties that deal in them and the economic system.... In our view...derivatives are financial weapons of mass destruction, carrying dangers that, while now latent, are potentially lethal."[4]

Derivatives now allowed trading of risks, increasingly for speculation. Even where used to manage risk or investments, derivatives frequently introduced new risks with unintended consequences.

Hedging Your Bets

In *Liar's Poker* (by Michael Lewis), the potent threat to the Salomon Brothers recruits is that if they do poorly in the training program, they might end up in municipal finance, *munis*. Municipal finance, where local governments raise funds to build schools, roads, and sewers was a backwater, safe, stable, and boring job, at least until they started dabbling in derivatives.

Jefferson County, Alabama, is centered on the iron, coal, and limestone belt in the Appalachian Mountains. The County seat, Birmingham, was the center of the civil rights struggle in the 1950s and 1960s. By 2008, Jefferson County was near bankruptcy, as a result of derivative transactions—supposedly hedges reducing risk.[5]

In 1993, three taxpayers, later joined by the U.S. Environmental Protection Agency, filed a lawsuit against the County alleging discharge of untreated sewage into the Cahaba river watershed. As part of a settlement, the County agreed to build a sewer system collecting overflows and cleaning the water. The original $3.2 billion cost ultimately doubled. Between 1997 and 2002, Jefferson County issued $2.9 billion in sewer bonds.

In 2002, bankers advised refinancing the debt using adjustable rate bonds and interest rate swaps, saving millions of dollars in interest cost. In an adjustable rate bond, the interest rate is reset periodically by reference to market rates. Between 2002 and 2004, Jefferson County issued more than $3 billion of adjustable rate bonds, predominantly auction rate securities (ARSs), bonds with a long maturity where the rate is regularly reset through a Dutch auction[6] typically held every 7, 28, or 35 days.

ARSs provided borrowers with low cost, adjustable rate debt. Institutional investors and high-net-worth individuals received a higher interest for short-term investments because of the assurance of liquidity through the auction process. The investor's risk was low, as highly rated bond or monoline insurers guaranteed repayment.

Jefferson County entered into interest rate swaps, with JP Morgan, Bank of America, and Lehman Brothers, to hedge its exposure to fluctuating interest rates. Under the swaps, the County paid a pre-agreed fixed rate in return for receiving floating rate payments. Where the payments received matched the payments under the adjustable rate bonds, the swaps converted the County's debt into fixed rates, guaranteeing a fixed cost of approximately 4.2 percent for 40 years. Figure 13.2 sets out Jefferson County's financing transactions. The County saved money, in the process building the largest portfolio of swaps ($5.8 billion) among US counties.

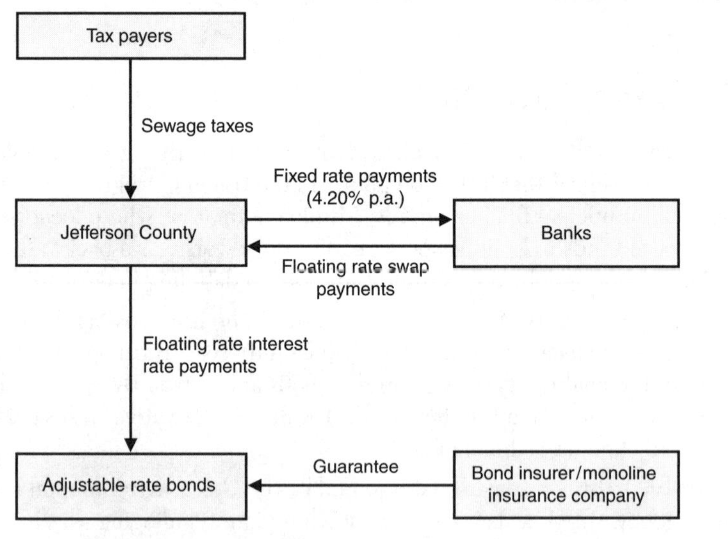

Figure 13.2 Jefferson County swaps

Sewer Bonds

Proud of its success, Jefferson County held seminars, educating other counties in sophisticated financing techniques. Wall Street bankers extolled the advantages of derivatives with sessions like "Derivatives: getting the right deal done right." Bankers quoted Fed Chairman Alan Greenspan's enthusiastic advocacy of derivatives: "New financial products have enabled risk to be dispersed more effectively to those willing, and presumably able, to bear it."[7]

The transactions assumed that the floating rate received under the swap matched the floating rate paid on the adjustable rate bonds. ARS rates are based on money market rates, like 1-month London Inter-bank Offered Rate (LIBOR) or the Securities Industry and Financial Markets Association (Sifma) municipal swap index. Jefferson County paid fixed rate and received a floating rate of, say, 67 percent of one-month LIBOR. Historical studies going back to 1986 showed that the notes typically trade at 67 percent of 1-month LIBOR. If the relationship did not change (known as *basis risk*), Jefferson County saved between 0.75 and 1.25 percent per annum.

In January 2008, when monoline insurers were downgraded by rating agencies because of exposure to subprime mortgage debt, the ARSs guaranteed by them also got downgraded. Investors exited the ARS market and auctions failed. Where there is an auction failure, the rate increases to a pre-agreed maximum level, as high as 20 percent, to compensate investors unable to sell their investments. In February 2008, Jefferson County's interest rate rose to 10 percent from 3 percent. The interest costs of Jefferson County's sewer debt reached more than $250 million, against the $138 million in revenue the system produces.

As the ARS interest rate went up, receipts under the swaps fell as central banks cut interest rates. The receipts supposed to track the County's adjustable bonds now added to its costs. Long-term interest rates fell sharply, causing losses on the swaps. The downgrade in Jefferson County's rating required lodgement of cash to cover the loss under the swap. If the County did not meet this margin call, the banks had the right to cancel the swaps, at a cost of $277 million. In March 2008, Jefferson County failed to post collateral and defaulted under the swaps.

As Jefferson County's sewer bonds were downgraded to junk status, the banks left holding unwanted ARSs became entitled to cancel arrangements to act as buyers of last resort in auctions and force the County to buy back its bonds. Downgrading the sewer bonds, Moody's noted "the unique, risky structure of Jefferson County's highly leveraged debt portfolio, which is hedged by swaps and comprised almost entirely of insured variable-rate demand bonds and auction-rate securities, and hedged by interest rate swaps."[8] Earlier, the agency had concluded that the County's use of derivatives to manage its debt portfolio did *not* present undue risks for bondholders.

The County increased taxes and cut back services. Residents faced the choice of paying heating bills or paying the water and sewer bill, which had increased fourfold in the past decade. School children were asked to bring toilet paper, soap, and paper towels to school, as the County could no longer afford them. Residents sold replica sewer bonds as toilet paper and distributed bumper stickers saying "Wipe out sewer debt." Having survived the U.S. Civil War and racial strife, Jefferson County scrambled unsuccessfully to avert the biggest municipal bankruptcy in U.S. history.

Harvard Case Studies

Located in Cambridge, Massachusetts, Harvard University is a long way from Alabama. In 2005, Lawrence (Larry) Summers, the 27th president of Harvard, announced a major campus expansion. A Harvard Ph.D. in economics and a tenured professor since 1982, Summers served as chief economist of the World Bank and secretary of the Treasury in the Clinton Administration. He told Faculty of Arts and Sciences professors in May 2004 that: "The only real limitation faced by the Faculty was the limit of its imagination."[9]

Harvard's financial position was strong, with its $22.6 billion endowment fund returning 16 percent per annum during the previous decade. To finance the expansion, Harvard issued bonds, planning to borrow $1.8 billion in 2008 and a further $500 million through to 2020. In December 2004, Harvard entered into $2.3 billion interest rate swaps to lock in financing costs at historically low rates.[10] The university gained budgetary certainty—a hedge.

In 2008, as credit markets seized up and central banks slashed rates, the swaps went into loss because Harvard was contracted to pay higher rates than current market rates. As the value of the contracts plunged, Harvard, like Jefferson County, was forced to lodge cash with its bankers, coinciding with a fall in the value of Harvard's endowment fund of 30 percent (from $36 billion at its peak to $26 billion). Its cash account used to fund ongoing expenditure lost $1.8 billion.

To limit losses, Harvard borrowed money to terminate the swaps, paying $498 million to banks during 2009 to cancel $1.1 billion of interest rate swaps. It agreed to pay $425 million over 30–40 years to offset an additional $764 million in swaps. Harvard implemented austerity measures—freezing salaries, reducing staff, and cutting capital spending, including the planned expansion. Harvard's swaps had created a liquidity crisis of their own, which no one, least of all Summers, had imagined.

Along with Robert Rubin and Alan Greenspan, Summers was instrumental in defeating the U.S. Commodity Futures Trading Commission's attempt in 1998 to regulate over-the-counter derivatives, including interest rate swaps. In 2009 Summers, now director of President Obama's National Economic Council, sought to regulate the derivatives market "to protect the American people."

The Italian Job

Europeans once had the art but only Americans had the money to buy it. Now, Americans had the financial engineering and Europeans adopted the ideas. As Summers boasted: "what Harvard does and says has an enormous resonance that goes beyond ZIP code 02138."[11]

In 2009, Alfredo Robeldo, an Italian prosecutor, began an investigation of financing arrangements for the City of Milan. In 2005, Milan restructured existing debt and cash into a €1.68 billion bond. Four banks arranged Europe's biggest-ever municipal bond sale at a fee of just 0.01 percent of the face value of the bonds, well below the normal fees of 0.3–0.45 percent. The City of Milan and the banks simultaneously entered into two derivatives—a complex *amortizing swap* converting the fixed rate bond into floating rate and a contract that allowed Milan's interest cost to fluctuate within certain ranges.

Milan used the new borrowing to pay off old loans and cancel related swaps. Milan owed the banks €96 million upon termination of the old swaps. Milan paid the banks €20 million. €48 million was paid by the group of four banks, it is alleged, covered by hidden payments, fees, and earnings received from Milan in the derivative contracts. Milan paid the remaining €28 million via another derivative contract that cost Milan around €2 million. The public prosecutor alleged that the dealers misrepresented the transactions, unfairly enriching the banks by around €100 million.

According to city officials, the bankers had presented the transactions as being favorable to Milan, saving interest costs of €60 million. Officials did not grasp that interest costs would be higher if rates fell. Italian law only allows councils to restructure funding arrangements if it leaves them in a better position than before. The banks claimed that Milan was a financially sophisticated party and understood the transactions.

In 2009, around 600 Italian town councils disclosed losses from derivative transactions entered into in the belief that they were hedges. Around 700 German local authorities were also found to have similar problems. In

Austria the state-owned railway made a loss of €420 million on derivatives, suing a bank alleging that risks had not been disclosed.

It is unclear whether Jefferson County, Harvard, and Milan had been fooled by bankers or were foolish in entering into transactions without understanding the risks. Michael Lewis' warning that munis were a financial backwater was wrong. It was a place where bankers could make large profits.

Betting Your Hedge

Facing relentless pressure to meet earnings targets, companies relied increasingly on speculative trading to boost profits. Globalization reduced trade barriers, increased competition, and reduced profit margins. These narrow profit margins could be wiped out by fluctuations in volatile currency, interest rates, and commodity markets, sometimes overnight. Companies entered into complex derivatives, believing that they could get something for nothing. When things went wrong, the banks restructured the transaction, hiding the loss. All sides kept up the pretense that the transaction was a hedge until things went awry.

Sons of Gwalia (SoG) was the third largest gold mining company in Australia, producing 500,000 ounces each year. The company hedged, selling forward its gold production. Well-versed in digging holes in the ground to extract the precious metal, SoG dug itself a bigger hole by its hedging.[12]

When gold miners sell gold forward, guaranteeing a fixed price, they gain if the gold price falls but lose if the price goes up. If the gold price goes down, then there is a temptation to *take profits*, closing out the hedge which shows gains to boost current earnings. If the gold price goes up, then the company loses on the hedge, causing it to underperform unhedged competitors, who benefit from higher earnings from selling gold at higher prices. The mining company also owes the bank cash as collateral for losses on the hedge from the higher prices. The cash is required today, while the gold must be dug up and sold over time.

Mining companies can buy insurance against the gold price falling (put options) but the cost of insurance is expensive. To minimize cost, SoG bought insurance against lower gold prices (put options) but paid for them by *selling* insurance against higher gold prices (call options). If prices fell, then SoG was protected. If prices rose, SoG benefited until the gold price reached a certain level (the strike price of the call option). As prices rose above this level, SoG had to pay out under the insurance contracts that it had sold. It gained from selling the physical gold that it had produced at higher prices, but the payments under the sold insurance contracts would reduce its earnings.

Over time, SoG migrated to indexed gold put options (IGPOs), complex combinations of bought and sold insurance. The IGPOs entailed SoG selling between five and six times the insurance against the price going up (the call options) than it bought against the price going down (the put options). As the insured amount sold was larger than that bought, the IGPOs provided SoG with cash upfront, which was used to achieve higher prices for selling its gold or to hide losses on existing hedges.

SoG was committing to selling more and more gold if the price rose. By 2004, SoG had commitments to sell between 6 and 8 million ounces of gold against 3.1 million ounces of reserves. SoG did not have any gold but it did have a magnificent hedge. It was forced to file for bankruptcy with massive hedging losses.

TARDIS Trades

In 2008, exporters in many countries suffered large currency losses. The companies exported to Europe and North America, who paid in dollars that had to be converted into the exporter's home currency—Japanese yen, South Korean won, Taiwanese dollar, Chinese renminbi, or the Indian rupee—to meet costs. If the dollar fell, then the exporters lost money as revenues fell in local currency terms.

In 2007, the dollar started to fall, causing panic amongst exporters with unhedged dollar revenues. Exporters sought help from financial engineers, who helped clients travel back in time on Dr Who's TARDIS (Time And Relative Dimension(s) In Space) to when the dollar was stronger.

Assume that the Japanese exporter, with yen as its currency of operation, has $1 million of export revenue. It has budgeted on an exchange rate of $1 equal to ¥100, giving it ¥100 million of revenue. If the dollar falls to ¥90 (dollar depreciation or yen appreciation), then the exporter's revenue falls to ¥90 million, a loss of ¥10 million (10 percent). The bank enters into a hedge where the exporter sells dollars at ¥95 (¥9.5 million in revenue), better than the current market rate of ¥90; a level at which the exports are still profitable to the company. It has the right to convert at ¥95 only if the yen does not strengthen above ¥85. At that level, the contract disappears, *knocks out*. If the yen weakens below ¥100 then the exporter must sell double the amount of dollars ($2 million) at ¥100 to the bank, the *knock-in* provision. This was known as the *currency accumulator*. Its relative, the *target redemption forward*, was similar but knocked out after the exporter made an agreed profit on the contract.

The exporter sold its dollars at better than market rates but risked large losses. It was selling double the amount of insurance on a stronger dollar than it was getting against a weaker dollar. If the yen strengthened significantly, the exporter was *not* hedged, precisely when it most needed to be hedged.

In early 2008, as U.S. investors repatriated overseas funds to cover losses, the dollar strengthened sharply, triggering the knock-in provision, which forced the exporter to sell double the dollars. If the exporters had dollars then they sold them at unfavorable rates. Some did not have sufficient dollars because exports had fallen, due to the global financial crisis, or had sold more dollars than they actually were contracted to receive.

As many as 50,000 companies in at least 12 countries, including Korea, Taiwan, China, Philippines, India, Eastern Europe, and Latin America, lost as much as $530 billion.[13] Mexican cement producer Cemex revealed a loss of $500 million on derivatives. Controladora Comercial Mexicana SAB, Mexico's third-largest supermarket operator, filed for bankruptcy after losing $1.1 billion from currency derivative deals.

In Hong Kong, Citic Pacific announced a $1.9 billion loss on derivative transactions involving Australian dollars, forcing its major shareholder—China's biggest state-owned investment company Citic Group—to provide additional capital to ensure its survival. Citic claimed it was hedging its currency risks. Henry Fan, Citic Pacific's managing director, told the *Financial Times* that he was "shocked" by the events: "I asked Leslie [Leslie Chang, Citic Pacific's group finance director] how could this happen...he said he omitted to assess the downside risk."[14] It was a lack of "horse sense," which as humorist Raymond Nash knew is: "what keeps horses from betting on what people will do."

I Will Kill You Later

Dressed in school uniform and fishnet stockings, Christina Amphlett, vocalist with the Australian rock band The Divinyls, sang about the fine line separating pleasure and pain. For investors, the line between investment and speculation was finer still.

Concerned about stagnant incomes and inadequate retirement savings, individual investors chased higher returns. To meet forecast retirement benefits or insurance payouts, pension funds and institutional investors resorted to derivatives to enhance returns through leverage and taking on complex cocktails of risk.

The toxic currency structures of 2008 were copies of an earlier product—*equity accumulators*, known to traders as "I will kill you later" contracts. In a typical accumulator contract, the investor commits to purchase, or accumulate, a fixed number of shares per day at a pre-agreed price (the accumulator price) for a fixed period, typically 3–12 months. The accumulator price is set typically 10–20 percent below the market price of the shares at the time you enter the contract.

If the market price of the shares rises above a prespecified level (the knock-out price), the investor's right to buy the shares knocks out, limiting upside gains. The knock-out price typically is set 5 percent above the market price of the shares at the time you enter the contract. If the market price remains below the knock-out price, the investor continues to accumulate the shares. If the market price falls below the accumulator price (typically a decline of more than 10–20 percent from the commencement of the contract), the investor must keep purchasing the shares, meaning unlimited downside risk. In most contracts, the number of shares the investor must purchase increases if the market price falls below the accumulator price. This step-up feature would occur typically two times, meaning that if the price fell below the accumulator price, the number of shares the investor purchased doubled.

In accumulator contracts, investors buy and sell a series of options that mature daily. The packaging of the product does not generally mention options, especially the fact that investors are selling options, a risky activity. Any disclosure is buried in the "risk section" of the Product Disclosure Statement. The print size and impenetrable legal prose mean that Sherlock Holmes would struggle to find the risks and a linguist would struggle to understand them.

Accumulators allow investors to buy shares at a price lower than the current price of the underlying shares. This is the byproduct of the option transactions. The options sold by investors are more expensive than the options the investor bought because the gain to the share buyer is limited while the potential losses are much larger. The difference in premiums creates the benefit. Dealers routinely benefit even more from selling accumulators, generally 4–5 percent of the total value of the contract upfront.

The investor gains where the share prices remain stable—between the knock-out price and the accumulator price. If the price goes up sharply then the accumulator knocks out, limiting the gain to the investor. If the price goes down sharply then the investor must purchase more shares, suffering losses because the purchase price is above market prices.

When the market fell in 2008, investors had to purchase larger number of shares under the step-up provision. Even where the share price had fallen but not below the accumulator price, the investor often lost because the current value of the contract had deteriorated as a result of changes in the volatility of underlying shares. Typically, investors put up around 10–25 percent of the value, agreeing to make margin calls where the value of the contract moved adversely. When the accumulator contracts showed money owing to the bank, the investor had to pledge more cash to cover the losses. If they could not come up with the cash then the contract was closed out, triggering losses for the investor. One dealer opined that: "a lot of investors have underestimated the cash flow commitment."

First to Lose

In Asia, investors, often with limited education, purchased complex investments that offered slightly higher returns than bank deposits. Issued by a Cayman Islands' SPV, Lehman Brothers' Minibonds were marketed as simple bonds paying a high interest rate. In fact, they were complex, highly financially engineered derivatives, where the higher return required taking the risk that none of seven or eight companies would default or file for bankruptcy.

The SPV invested the money subscribed by investors in high-quality AAA-rated securities, initially investments in money market funds. The investments secured a credit derivative known as a *first-to-default* (FtD) swap. The investors received an annual fee that together with the interest on the money invested gave the investors the higher return. The investors agreed to make a contingent payment if any one of the identified firms defaulted. Under the FtD swap, the investors were exposed to all seven or eight entities, although the loss was limited to the first entity to default and the face value of the Minibonds.

Documents emphasized the *remote* risk of loss. The companies to which the investor was exposed were solid, well-known global institutions. While the sales literature highlighted the good credit rating (generally AA or A) of the individual companies, the investors were taking two risks—the likelihood of any of the firms in the FtD basket defaulting and the likelihood of one reference entity defaulting if another reference entity defaulted (*default correlation*).

Perfect default correlation (1) assumes that if any entity defaults then all other reference entities within the basket will default simultaneously. A zero default correlation (0) assumes that the risk of default of the reference entities is independent. If the default correlation within the basket is 1, then the FtD is equivalent to selling insurance on the most risky firm in the basket. If the default correlation is 0, then the FtD is equivalent to selling insurance on all the entities within the basket with a limit on the maximum loss. Assuming low or zero default correlation, the risk of any one entity within a basket of eight well-rated firms defaulting is significantly higher than for any single entity defaulting. A FtD basket based on investment grade companies may be equivalent to noninvestment grade credit risk.

Over time, instead of placing the investor's money in money market funds, the cash was invested in CDOs and CDO^2s, arranged and sold by Lehman, adding to the risk of the arrangements.

In Hong Kong, in accordance with local superstitions, no series of Minibonds were issued with the number 4, considered unlucky in Chinese culture. Advertisements and flyers prominently featured symbols of potency, luck or profit—tigers, rhinoceroses, and whales. Investors were enticed with prizes, including video cameras and flat-screen televisions.

Billions of Lehman Minibonds were sold to tens of thousands of investors in Asia, Australia, New Zealand, and Europe, especially in Switzerland, Germany, and Eastern Europe. Other banks emulated Lehman. As Pablo Picasso, the Spanish artist, observed: "Good artists copy, great artists steal."

In October 2008, when Lehman filed for legal protection from its creditors under bankruptcy laws, investors suffered large unexpected losses. In most cases, none of the entities in the baskets had defaulted. Where Lehman was the purchaser of credit insurance from investors, the bankruptcy filing terminated the contract. Because of changes in market conditions, investors suffered mark-to-market or paper losses that had to be settled, requiring sale of the underlying investments. Where the money was invested in CDOs, the losses were large.

The documentation included a *flip clause*, providing that the underlying collateral should be applied firstly to amounts owed to Lehman and then to the amounts owed to investors. If Lehman defaulted, then there was a change in priority. Lehman would rank behind investors in the distribution of underlying proceeds.

When Lehman applied for bankruptcy protection, it triggered the change in priority of payment. However, on November 25, 2008 Lehman's legal counsel notified investors that the flip clause breached the U.S. Bankruptcy Code and was unenforceable. The alteration of priority on default was found to be enforceable as a matter of English insolvency law, but unenforceable as a matter of U.S. Bankruptcy Law. If the U.S. position is upheld by appellate courts, the investor's loss will be exaggerated.

In the Minibonds, initially bankers and, after the problems, lawyers, and insolvency practitioners cleaned up. Always first to lose, the investors were just completely cleaned out.

Toxic Municipal Siblings

Located around 125 miles (200 kilometers) south of the Arctic Circle in Norway, Narvik's ice-free harbor and proximity to the iron ore mines in Sweden make the town strategically important. In the Second World War the Germans tried to gain control of the town to access the ore, triggering a naval battle. The wrecks of German, Norwegian, and British ships in the Fjords and the town's history are a tourist attraction.

In November 2007 Narvik, together with other Norwegian investors, lost money in investments involving American municipalities manufactured by CitiGroup and sold by Terra Securities, a Norwegian securities firm.

In 2004, using a loophole in their regulations, Narvik and other Norwegian municipalities—all large producers of hydroelectricity—borrowed using future energy revenue as collateral. The money raised was invested in complex securities offering high returns, such as highly leveraged securities linked to American municipal TOBs (tender option bonds), a form of ARS. The Norwegians received between 0.5 and 3 percent per annum more than they would receive on bank deposits but risked losing their entire investment.

In 2007 and 2008, as the problems in the U.S. municipal debt markets emerged, the investments linked to the underlying muni bonds lost value, causing large losses. Narvik was at the other end of the fuse lit by Jefferson County across the Atlantic. The investments were a quarter of the Narvik annual budget. To cover the losses, the town took out a long-term loan to be paid back by cutting back on civic services, such as childcare, health services, and cultural institutions. In late 2007, Narvik missed making the payroll for municipal workers. Narvik's museum, chronicling its war history, was a victim of the crisis.

Playing Swaps and Robbers

Derivatives were frequently part of elaborate arrangements to avoid regulations. Fiat S.p.A. (Fabbrica Italiana Automobili Torino or Italian Automobile Factory of Turin) is an Italian carmaker, created in 1899 by a group of investors led by Giovanni Agnelli. In the early 2000s, Fiat faced financial and operating difficulties, losing over €8 billion. Following restructuring, Fiat, now led by CEO Sergio Marchionne, recovered, making a profit of €1 billion in 2005.

To survive, Fiat borrowed €3 billion through a convertible bond, where the banks could exchange the loan into Fiat shares. On April 26, 2005 Fiat announced that the loan would be converted into Fiat shares on 20 September 2005, giving the banks 24 percent of Fiat and diluting the Agnelli family's interest, held through IFIL Investments (IFIL), from 30 percent to 23 percent.

To maintain control of Fiat, IFIL needed to buy shares in Fiat. If it purchased shares in Fiat before 20 September 2005, pushing its ownership interest over 30 percent, then under Italian law IFIL would be forced to launch a takeover bid for the entire company at a premium to the market price. Instead, IFIL used derivatives—total return swaps on shares or equity swaps—to preserve control of Fiat.

On April 26, 2005 Exor, a private company 70-percent-owned by the Agnelli family, entered into a swap with Merrill Lynch. Under the terms of the swap, Merrill would pay Exor the total return on 90 million Fiat shares (around 7 percent of the share capital), worth €495 million at €5.50 per Fiat share, the price at which Merrill purchased Fiat shares in the market.

Under the swap, Exor assumed the full economic risk of the shares, receiving any increase in the value of Fiat shares above €5.50 and paying Merrill any decrease below €5.50. Exor covered Merrill's funding cost on the shares. The swap was to be settled at maturity in cash, with no delivery of Fiat shares, avoiding disclosure to Italian regulators.

On September 15, 2005 Exor and Merrill amended the original swap, allowing settlement by physical delivery of the shares. At maturity, Exor would receive 90 million Fiat shares in return for paying €495 million to Merrill (equivalent to the agreed price of €5.50 per share). The conversion was disclosed as required under Italian security laws. In late September, after the bank loan was converted, IFIL purchased the shares acquired by Exor under the swap from Merrill at €6.50 per share, giving Exor a profit on the sale of the shares.

The swap allowed IFIL to maintain its shareholding in Fiat at 30 percent. The Agnelli family through Exor acquired the required shares without triggering a full takeover of Fiat, as IFIL never exceeded the 30 percent threshold. The Agnelli family acquired the required 7 percent of Fiat at favorable prices, €5.50 per share against €7 per share in late September 2005. By early 2007, Fiat shares were trading above €17 per share.

In February 2007, in a civil case, the Italian regulators (Consob) fined IFIL, a related company and directors €16 million. The chairman of IFIL and two senior officers of the company were suspended from holding posts in public companies for between 2 and 6 months. IFIL appealed against the decision. Italian regulators also fined two Merrill Lynch bankers €250,000 for failing to disclose that the firm had equity swaps that entitled it to more than 5 percent of Fiat.

In 2010, luxury goods firm LVMH made a bid for control of Hermès, surprising the descendants of Thierry Hermès, a saddle maker who founded the company in 1837. Just like of Fiat, LVMH built the stake through cash-settled equity swaps with three banks in 2008, when the luxury industry was in crisis. The derivative contracts allowed LVMH to avoid disclosure requirements, producing a nice profit for LVMH when Hermès shares rose.

The Greek Job

In the 1990s, Japanese companies and investors pioneered the use of derivatives to hide losses, a practice called *tobashi* (from the Japanese verb *tobasu* meaning "to make fly away"). Subsequently, a number of European countries used derivatives to disguise their borrowings.

Derivatives, such as interest rate and currency swaps, are normally used to alter the nature and currency of cash flows on assets or borrowings. Transactions involve exchanging one stream of payments for another. At commencement, if the contract is priced at current market rates, then the value of the two sets of cash flows should be roughly equal.

Using artificial or "off-market" interest or currency rates, it is possible to create differences in value between payments and receipts. If the value of future payments is higher than future receipts, then the party making the future payments receives an up-front amount reflecting the positive value of the contract. In effect, the participant receives a payment today that is repaid by the higher than market payments in the future—identical to a loan. Figure 13.3 sets out the strategy using a simple currency swap.

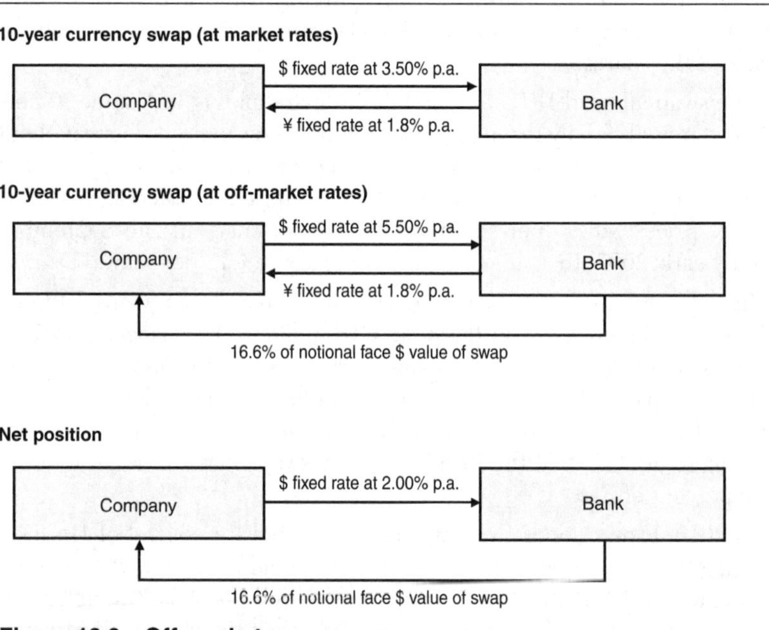

Figure 13.3 Off-market currency swap

In 2008, Greece was found to have entered into a series of transactions with Goldman Sachs to disguise its debt. Earlier, academic Gustavo Piga identified an unnamed European country, generally assumed to be Italy, using derivatives to provide similar window dressing.

In December 1996, Italy allegedly used a currency swap against an existing ¥200 billion bond ($1.6 billion) to lock in profits from the depreciation of the yen. Done at nonmarket rates, the swap was really a loan where Italy accepted an unfavorable exchange rate and received cash in return. The payments were used to reduce Italy's deficit, helping meet the European Union target of less than 3 percent of GDP under the EU Maastricht Treaty.

The Greek transactions were similar off-market cross-currency swaps linked to the country's foreign currency debt. The swaps were for a notional principal of approximately $10 billion, with maturities between 15 and 20 years. The cash received may have reduced the country's debt/GDP ratio from 107 percent in 2001 to 104.9 percent in 2002 and lowered interest payments from 7.4 percent in 2001 to 6.4 percent in 2002. The future payment obligations under the swaps were not reported as a future liability for Greece.

Dealers made money by helping clients hedge or take on more risk using derivatives. Clients also paid dealers handsomely for structures that took advantage of regulatory loopholes. Goldman Sachs allegedly made around $300 million from the Greek job.

Madman's Games

Much of the financial innovation was designed to conceal risk or leverage, obfuscate investors, and reduce transparency. Complexity was used to make products difficult to understand and analyze, allowing them to be priced inefficiently to produce excessive profits for traders. After the Narvik problems surfaced, the CEO of Terra Securities admitted that he did not know how the product worked. When the original CitiGroup prospectus for the product was translated from English to Norwegian, the original risk disclosures appeared to have been omitted. As Warren Buffett once remarked, derivative contracts are "limited only by the imagination of man—or, sometimes, it seems, madmen."[15]

Harvard Professor Elizabeth Warren noted that in the pharmaceutical industry innovators once earned large profits by skillfully marketing quack cures and ineffective products, exploiting the customers' poor understanding of products. The U.S. Food and Drug Administration developed disclosure rules, helping foster safer, effective drugs and treatments. Complex derivative products, incomprehensible structures, and sharp sales practices are relatively unregulated. Complexity, she argued, is the handmaiden of deception.[16]

14

Financial Arms Race

Over time, seduced by their allure, dealers began trading derivatives, risking their own money. Like narcotic dealers, they discovered the pleasure of their illicit, highly addictive products. They had not heard the warning of the seventeenth-century French author François de La Rochefoucauld: "We are so accustomed to disguise ourselves to others that in the end we become disguised to ourselves."

Derivative professionals, especially quants, were taken in by an elegant vision of a scientific and mathematically precise vision of risk. As the English author G.K. Chesterton wrote: "The real trouble with this world [is that].... It looks just a little more mathematical and regular than it is; its exactitude is obvious but its inexactitude is hidden; its wildness lies in wait."[1]

Shock-Gen

Société Générale (SG or Soc-Gen) was the crème de la crème of French banking, synonymous with complex, state-of-the-art derivatives. On January 24, 2008 the French bank announced losses of €5.9 billion from trading equity derivatives. The *Financial Times* Lex Column rechristened the bank ShockGen.

Jerome Kerviel, a junior SG trader, used derivative contracts to take positions on stocks, trading in equity indexes like Dow Jones Eurostoxx 50,

Germany's DAX, and London's FTSE 100 indexes. Kerviel's job was to buy from and sell to clients, offsetting positions with other banks to minimize risk. It turned out that Kerviel had not matched the positions, creating fictitious trades to hide purchases of €50 billion of shares.

La Défense, the nouveau, très moderne Paris business district bordering a graveyard, where SG is based, is named after an 1884 statue commemorating the soldiers who defended Paris during the Franco-Prussian War. In damage control mode, SG's public relations defended the bank with the same determination. Kerviel was a "super villain" with an "extraordinary talent for dissimulation." Using his knowledge of SG's operations, he carefully hid the positions using derivatives and falsified documents. The bank's version lost credibility as the facts emerged.

SG had not detected the huge positions because the bank focused on the *net* position, the difference between bought and sold positions. Kerviel's positions escaped detection because the fictitious portfolio of trades balanced the real transactions, giving the impression there was no net position and therefore no risk. The positions required SG to lodge cash to support transactions. SG had not noticed the size of the margin calls. Eurex, the European derivative exchange, actually sent detailed data that allowed the bank to tie specific positions and cash movements to individual traders. SG had not reconciled the information.

Between June 2006 and January 2008, on more than 90 occasions, there were internal queries about Kerviel's trading. The trader's explanation of anomalies was accepted without further investigations, despite oddities like products scheduled to mature on days when the market was closed. Eurex queried Kerviel's trading in late 2007. SG responded, but considered the queries "technical." Daniel Bouton, SG's chief executive, admitted that the bank's derivatives business designed to run at 80 mph was actually doing 130.

Evil Kerviel

Whenever a bank loses a large sum trading, it is always blamed on a *rogue trader*. In 1995, Nick Leeson of Barings lost £860 million ($1.4 billion) in equity trading. In 1996 Yasuo Hamanaka of Japan's Sumitomo lost $1.8 billion in copper trading. In 2006, Brian Hunter and hedge fund Amaranth lost $6 billion in natural gas trading. Recycled French homilies could not explain the largest derivative trading loss in history.

Banks do not want to admit that risk taking and profits from speculation are part and parcel of modern finance. In 2007, around 35 percent of the profits of SG's corporate and investment bank came from trading, both with clients and on the bank's own account. Like competitors, SG encouraged and allowed aggressive risk taking and competition between traders.

In 2004, the National Australia Bank (NAB) lost hundreds of millions in currency trading. Sentencing two former traders, Judge Geoff Chettle identified a culture in which traders were seemingly "invincible." The NAB team described themselves in Olympian terms—BOAT or Best of All Time. The judge identified "a culture of profit-driven morality...you [had] to take risks in order to achieve the projections and targets set for your desk. To further your career, you had to succeed."[2]

Like Leeson, Kerviel was an unlikely rogue. Unlike the bulk of SG traders who were graduates of France's prestigious *grande écoles* in quantitative disciplines, Kerviel studied at second-tier universities in Nantes and Lyon. Like Leeson, Kerviel joined SG in a support role, making the rare transition from back office to a junior trader in 2005.

Despite his job entailing low risk, Kerviel started taking positions to bet on the movements in shares. Kerviel claimed that unauthorized trading was widespread and tolerated when it made money. In late December 2007, his positions showed profits of $2 billion, before the markets turned and the gains became losses.

Kerviel was not greedy, hoping only for a modest €300,000 bonus. But he wanted recognition as an exceptional trader: "This will show the power of Kerviel."[3] Kerviel admitted: "You lose a sense of the sums involved in this type of work. You get desensitized."[4]

Soldier Monks

ShockGen damaged French banking's image of cutting-edge quantitative finance. In May 2007, Christian Noyer, the governor of the Banque de France, praised French banks' derivative skills: "French expertise in this field is founded on a solid teaching in math and finance, the key to excellency in financial fields, and on an important hive of university-level talents."[5]

At SG Antoine Paille built the derivative business in the 1980s, drawing on the skills of highly trained engineers and mathematicians from the *grande écoles*. SG's reputation was for complex derivatives, especially in stocks and currencies. There was no insurance or guarantee structure that they would not price or trade. Like the devout and disciplined monks who fought in the Crusades, Paille's traders—*les moines-soldats*—personified innovation, skill, confidence, and arrogance.

The French *grande écoles* propound a system based on the work of René Descartes, the seventeenth-century French mathematician and philosopher. SG's traders believed in the Cartesian system—an ordered world where models can be built to understand and predict outcomes. Kerviel circumvented sophisticated systems with crude, simple strategies.

SG's vaunted risk management systems and risk managers did not detect the unhedged €50 billion exposure to European markets. Foreigners joked that, as a result of ShockGen, France finally achieved a world record in finance.

Kerviel emerged as a heroic figure—the Che Guevara of finance or the James Bond of SocGen. Some called for Kerviel to be awarded the Nobel Prize for economics. There were Kerviel T-shirts. The social-networking site Facebook hosted groups dedicated to the support of Kerviel. Kerviel went on to publish his own book, *L'engrenage, Mémoires d'un trader*.

Mystère Kerviel

In 2010, Kerviel appeared in a French court charged with breach of trust, computer abuse, and forgery. The judge's first question was: "Tell me who you are—who is Mr. Kerviel?"[6]

The trial featured France's two best-known lawyers—Olivier Metzner defending Kerviel and Jean Veil for SG. Metzner noted: "When it is a case of a man against the system, I defend the man and not the system."[7]

Daniel Bouton, who resigned as SG's CEO, testified that the trading scandal was a "catastrophe" and a "hurricane" that nearly destroyed the bank. Bouton spoke of his "formidable anger" at learning of the "monstrous" bets and losses: "It is not the business of a bank to risk its very existence." Bouton rejected claims that SG knew of the positions taken by the "evil genius": "I cannot believe for one second any of Jérôme Kerviel's supervisors were aware. I'm sorry, my dear fellow."[8] Jean-Pierre Mustier, the former head of SG's investment bank, told the court that traders were encouraged not to take risks but to "know how" to take risks.[9] SG's failure was in creating an environment of "too much trust."[10]

Summing up, Olivier Metzner told the Paris courtroom that Kerviel was a young man "formed—deformed—by Société Générale." He was a 33-year-old country boy from Brittany who entered a "virtual" world where "numbers had no meaning." Turning the judge's first question around, Metzner asked: "Who are you, Société Générale? Who are you? How do you create men like this?" It echoed the testimony of another SG employee Nicolas Huc-Morel: "There is no 'Kerviel mystery.' The mystery is rather Société Générale. How could the bank allow [such] massive positions to be taken? How could Mr. Kerviel's superiors not have known?"[11]

Kerviel maintained that his superiors were aware of his risk taking. Metzner claimed: "It is not a man at fault here but a system." Kerviel revealed the ambiguity in the relationship between traders and banks that employ them: "I've said it, and I repeat it: It's in my mandate when I'm making money, it's no longer there when I'm losing it."[12]

On Tuesday, October 5, 2010 Jérôme Kerviel was convicted of breach of trust and other crimes and sentenced to 5 years in prison and ordered to pay SG €4.9 billion. The impossible level of damages made the French court the "laughing stock" of the world.[13] SG indicated that the damage award was symbolic. Based on his salary as a computer security consultant, it would take Kerviel 177,000 years to pay.

The damages left Kerviel bankrupt and crippled for life, unable to make trouble for the French establishment: "a token ball and chain attached to him for the rest of his life. The €4.9 billion fine is a little illusory as it makes little difference whether one drowns in 10 feet of water or two miles."[14] The French court's decision also made it difficult for related American class action lawsuits to be pursued against SG, its directors and management.

When ShockGen's losses were revealed, Christian Noyer told reporters he was "totally serene." About 8 months later, Noyer's American peers were anything but calm as AIG, the world's largest company, found itself in serious financial difficulty from a toxic combination of derivatives, model failure, and an old-fashioned need for cash.

Risk Is Our Business

Cornelius Van der Starr founded AIG in 1919 in Shanghai, China. Under Maurice R. "Hank" Greenberg, Starr's successor and CEO for 37 years, AIG became one of the largest underwriters of commercial and industrial insurance in the world, with $110 billion in revenues and $1 trillion in assets.

AIG's marketing boasted that "the biggest risk is not taking one." In September 2008, AIG's poor risk management required a government rescue, with an initial $85 billion line of credit.

AIG's problems related to AIG Financial Products (FP), a specialist derivative trading operation, the brainchild of former Drexel Burnham Lambert trader Howard Sosin. Restricted by Drexel's low credit ratings, he saw the opportunity to create a derivatives business using AIG's AAA credit rating and large balance sheet.

Fortuitously, Greenberg was looking to expand outside insurance at the time. Aware of the risk of the complex joint venture, Sosin negotiated the arrangements carefully. As his legal advisor put it: "let us plan your divorce while we're planning your marriage."[15] Sosin got autonomy and a generous financial share of the business. AIG got 65 percent of earnings, while Sosin's team received 35 percent.

Initially, FP focused on traditional derivatives, interest rate, and currency swaps. FP focused on long-dated transactions, up to 30 years, taking advantage of AIG's AAA status. In July 1987, FP completed a $1 billion swap with the Republic of Italy, ten times a typical trade at the time, earning $3 million. In its first 6 months of operation, FP made around $60 million, establishing itself as the go-to shop for complex, long-dated derivatives.

FP became a beautiful money-making engine, contributing more than $5 billion to AIG's pretax income. Sosin was well rewarded. Even a company lawyer received a $25 million bonus at the end of 1 year.

The autocratic Greenberg mistrusted the equally autocratic Sosin's independence. Sosin resented Greenberg's interference in operations that AIG did not understand. The central issue was the calculation of FP's *profits*.

Derivative transactions are accounted for on a *mark-to-market (MtM)* basis—the current market price of the instrument. MtM accounting allows earnings to be recognized up front, even if the deal has a life of 30 years. As derivatives trade privately, market prices for specific transactions are not directly available. Derivative profits are *mark-to-model* or *mark-to-myself* rather than mark-to-market. Model variations and small differences in input can result in large changes in values for some products. Investment blogger Nicholas Vardy compared mathematical models to bikinis: "What they reveal is suggestive; but what they conceal is vital."[16]

As there is no real market for long-term, complex deals, Sosin and FP were the market. Trading was illiquid. In the words of the trader: "I would take your time and have your cup of coffee."[17] FP's deals created the quotes against which their transactions were valued. FP and Sosin received *theoretical* profits up front based on models while AIG remained at risk over the life of the transaction. FP had access to AIG's credit ratings and capital, largely rent-free. Sosin and FP had powerful incentives to chase short-term profits, leaving AIG with potential future losses.

Warren Buffett inherited Gen Re Securities, a smaller operation modeled on FP, when Berkshire Hathaway bought General Reinsurance. Buffett told shareholders that derivatives were like hell: "easy to enter and almost impossible to exit."[18] One contract was for 100 years.

Buffett discovered valuation problems:

> Marking errors in the derivatives business have not been symmetrical. Almost invariably they...favored the trader who was eyeing a multimillion dollar bonus.... Only much later did shareholders learn that the reported earnings were a sham.[19]

Buffet's feelings on Gen Re's derivatives were like a Country and Western song: "I liked you better before I got to know you so well."[20]

In 1993, Greenberg terminated the agreement, forcing Sosin out. Many of the FP team stayed on, ensuring the continuation of the unit. Under the new agreement, AIG received 70 percent and the employees 30 percent of profits, but were forced to reinvest 50 percent of what they received in FP.

At the time of its demise, employees had more than $500 million invested in FP.

In 2005, Sosin's payout from AIG emerged in the course of his real divorce. His wife received a $40 million settlement—a $24 million payment, $3.6 million Manhattan apartment, $2 million Utah ski house, $800,000 home in Wallkill, NY, $6 million in brokerage accounts, eight cars and $2.9 million in jewelry. The settlement revealed that Howard Sosin had received $182 million from AIG upon termination.

Free Money

Around 1997, banks began using synthetic securitization to get risk off their books to reduce capital needs. The structure created the low-risk super senior tranche that banks wanted to sell off. After JP Morgan introduced the idea, FP began selling credit insurance, in the form of credit default swaps (CDS). Under the contract, AIG received a fee from the bank. In return, FP agreed to insure the bank against the small risk of loss on the super senior tranche. By 2008, FP had insured around $450 billion of this risk. AIG's AAA rating and ability to take these risks more cheaply than a regulated bank made FP the go-to house now for super senior risk.

When FP entered into any contract on interest rates, currencies, equities, or commodities, it simultaneously entered into offsetting contracts to minimize its own risk. The focus was protecting AIG's AAA credit rating. Greenberg warned Tom Savage, Sosin's successor, that he would come after him "with a pitchfork" if FP endangered the AAA rating.[21]

Under the quantitatively trained Sosin and Savage, FP did not enter trades that "we can't correctly model, value, provide hedges for, and account for."[22] Savage was skeptical about the credit business, especially valuing the risk. Joseph Cassano, Savage's successor, was versed in accounting and credit but had limited quantitative skills.

Under CDS contracts, FP retained the risk unhedged. FP viewed the super senior risk like the catastrophe risk that AIG routinely insured—remote events unlikely to ever happen. In an investor presentation in May 2008, AIG pointed out the similarities between excess casualty insurance (catastrophe insurance) and FP's super senior CDS portfolio.

FP relied on a model built by Yale Professor Gary Gorton, "guided by a few, very basic principles, which are designed to make them very robust and to introduce as little model risk as possible."[23] The model used historical data to estimate the likelihood of losses on the insured portfolios of corporate debt and mortgages. Based on the models, the chance of losses on the super senior tranches that FP insured was remote: a one-in-a-million-year event. As Warrant Buffet quipped: "All I can say is, beware of geeks…bearing formulas."[24]

FP's models convinced Cassano and AIG that they would never have to cover any losses, making hedging unnecessary. The payments to take on this risk amounted to *free money*. In a 2007 conference call with investors, Cassano argued: "It is hard for us, without being flippant, to even see a scenario within any kind of realm of reason that would see us losing $1 in any of those transactions." AIG CEO Martin Sullivan added: "That's why I am sleeping a little bit easier at night."[25] AIG ignored German writer Ernst Jünger's warning: "a half witted mathematician could cause more damage in a second than Frederick the Great in three Silesian campaigns."

Credit's Fatal Attraction

FP's model focused on the risk of loss if the insured securities defaulted, not changes in the value of the contracts over its life, especially unrealized MtM losses. Initially, FP insured corporate debt but subsequently began insuring complex securitized loans and mortgages. In 2005, FP was surprised to find that it had insured bundles of loans that were 95 percent U.S. subprime mortgages, rather than an assumed 10–20 percent. As the nineteenth century American humorist Josh Billings observed: "It is better to know nothing than to know what ain't so."

In 2007/8, the fall in values of subprime mortgages triggered large MtM losses on FP's CDS portfolio. Credit risk spreads or margins rose, reflecting increased risk. Increased systemic risk pushed up default correlation (implying more defaults and losses if any borrower failed). In many cases, there were no actual losses. Where there were losses, losses did not threaten the super senior pieces that FP had insured. But the contracts showed substantial MtM losses. Responding to the altered market environment, the rating agencies downgraded the super senior tranches, triggering further losses.

To reassure banks, FP had agreed to post-cash collateral if the super senior tranches were downgraded, the current loss reached a threshold level, or AIG got downgraded below AA–. Now, as the insured super senior tranches showed losses, AIG was downgraded because of losses on the FP CDS portfolio and its investment portfolio, which was separately exposed to mortgage markets. One FP employee warned another: "the problem that we're going to face is that we're going to have just enormous downgrades on the stuff we got...we're...f***ed basically."[26]

In November 2007, the CDS portfolio showed mark-to-market losses of $352 million. By December 2007, the losses increased to $1.1 billion. In May 2008, AIG announced a record quarterly loss of $7.8 billion, driven by write-downs of the value of the swaps. By August 2008, AIG estimated CDS losses at $8.5 billion. FP's risk models still showed that there was a 99.85 percent chance that there would be no actual losses.

As MtM losses climbed, collateral calls flowed in. Goldman Sachs, who insured more than $20 billion of risk with AIG, demanded $1.5 billion in August 2007, and a further $3 billion in October. FP paid $450 million in August and a further $1.5 billion in October. By September 2008, AIG had posted in excess of $10 billion in collateral. FP suspected that trading partners were manipulating prices to increase losses and the collateral demanded. Commenting on the battles over collateral, Gary Gorton later seemed surprised: "It is difficult to convey the ferocity of the fights over collateral."[27]

Investigating differences between the FP's prices and the collateral demanded by dealers, PwC, AIG auditors, identified serious problems in risk management. Former New York Federal Reserve president Gerald Corrigan, now a managing director at Goldman Sachs, had warned in 2007: "Anyone who thinks they understand this stuff is living in lala land."[28]

Lehman Brothers, whose operating principle was demonstrating smart risk management, filed for bankruptcy protection on 15 September 2008. Rating agencies reduced AIG's credit ratings below AA on the same day. AIG now had to post $18 billion in further collateral to trading partners. In 2007 Gary Gorton wrote that "while financial intermediaries have changed in many ways, at root their problems remain the same. Indeed, the old problem of banking panics can reappear in new guises."[29] Now, AIG simply did not have the cash.

FP dealt with a "global swath" of sovereigns, supranationals (like the World Bank), municipalities, banks, investment banks, insurance companies, pension funds, endowments, hedge funds, fund managers, and high-net-worth individuals. All major market participants were linked to each other by a complex network of contracts that few fully understood. In October 2008, Gorton wrote:

> You have this very, very complicated chain of...risk, which made it very opaque about where the risk finally resided...the whole infrastructure of the financial market became kind of infected, because nobody knew exactly where the risk was.[30]

If AIG failed, then the institutions that relied on it to insure its risk would have a problem, and then the institutions that relied on those institutions, and so on. The entire intricate structure would unravel if AIG failed to meet the collateral calls and filed for bankruptcy. The U.S. Government was forced to intervene to prevent the collapse of the global financial system, at an ultimate cost of around $180 billion.

The weekend after the AIG bailout, fans of UK soccer club Manchester United, sponsored by AIG, put a line through the company's logo displayed on the front of the club's shirt. In its place were the words "U.S. Treasury."

Post-Modern Contradictions

In June 2009, the global derivative market totaled $605 trillion in notional amount, up from less than $10 trillion 20 years earlier. The volume compares to global GDP of $55–60 billion. As author Richard Duncan pointed out, the global derivatives market at its peak in June 2008 ($760 trillion) was equal to "everything produced on Earth during the previous 20 years."[31]

Proponents argue that derivatives are used principally for hedging and arbitrage. They are essential to risk transfer, savings, investment, and lowering the cost of capital. But volumes of derivative products traded are inconsistent with hedging. In the credit derivatives market, at the peak, volumes were in excess of four times outstanding underlying bonds and loans. While they can be used for hedging, derivatives are now used extensively for speculation, manufacturing risk, and creating leverage.

Relatively simple derivative products, forwards or options, provide ample scope for hedging. Dealers argue that the proliferation of complex, opaque products was customer demand for "financial solutions." In reality, derivatives are used to provide leverage to investors and corporations, increasing gains and losses for a particular event, such as a change in market prices of an asset, in accordance with customer requirements.

In 1999, Alan Greenspan remarked: "the profitability of derivative products has been a major factor in the dramatic rise in large banks' noninterest earning...the value added of derivatives themselves derives from their ability to enhance the process of wealth creation."[32] The Fed chairman missed the true source of derivative profitability. Opaque and inefficiently priced financial products produced high profit margins.

Derivatives allow risk to be altered and reconstituted in infinite combinations and transferred between participants. In aggregate, the risk remains constant. Sometimes a risk is converted into a different, more dangerous exposure. The law of risk conservation means that risk in financial markets rarely decreases. Derivatives are powerful instruments but: "It's like a hammer. You could use it to hammer in a nail with perfect precision. But you could also use it to pound someone's brains out."[33]

Derivative Deconstruction

Academics, who created models to price derivatives, failed to make money trading when they tried to identify and buy undervalued options on stocks. The market knew things that the model did not. Wall Street's PSDs, "**p**oor, **s**mart, and a **d**eep desire to get rich," turned derivatives into an extraordinary business. Rather than using derivatives to manage risks, dealers structured transactions to create risks, disguise true values, delay competition, and prevent clients from unbundling products. They reduced transparency and skewed the risk-reward relationship against the client.

In a January 2009 speech, Lord Adair Turner, chairman of UK's Financial Services Authority, agreed:

> Much of the structuring and trading activity involved in the complex version of securitized credit was not required to deliver credit intermediation efficiently, but achieved an economic rent extraction made possible by the opacity of margins and the asymmetry of information and knowledge between...users of financial services and producers...financial innovation which delivers no fundamental economic benefit, can for a time flourish and earn for the individuals and institutions which innovated very large returns.[34]

Economist John Kay added: "There was never an economic rationale for structured products on the scale on which the financial services industry created them. They were the result of a frenetic search for commissions and bonuses."[35]

In the global financial crisis, Buffett's label of "weapons of mass financial destruction" was literal. After it filed for bankruptcy protection, Lehman was found to own enough uranium cake to make a nuclear bomb. The investment bank acquired the uranium under a matured derivative contract.

Derivatives also created a false sense of security, encouraging greater risk taking. When the problems began, not only did derivatives fail to transfer risk, they increased the losses through leverage.

Jacques Derrida, the French philosopher, developed deconstruction, the pursuit of meaning, usually of a text, to expose its complex and sometimes unstable foundations. Deconstructing derivatives was "not a dismantling of the structure of a text, but a demonstration that it has already dismantled itself. Its apparently solid ground is no rock, but thin air."[36]

Piñata Parties

In 2010, concern shifted to sovereign debt, reflecting massive government spending to prevent the global economy from slipping into depression. Markets traded CDSs on sovereign nations. The specter of banks, some needing capital injections and liquidity support from governments to ensure survival, offering to insure other market participants against the risk of default by sovereign government (sometimes their own), was surreal.

Traders and derivatives need volatility to make their games profitable. Greece provided the first example of this new version of a piñata party, a tradition that originated among the Aztecs and Mayans in Mexico. A piñata is a brightly colored container, usually made from clay, cardboard, or papier-mâché. The container is beaten forcefully with poles and sticks, so that it breaks and the contents spill out to signify abundance or favors from the gods. In the financial version of a piñata party, a company or country was singled out. Traders grabbed their sticks and beat it until it broke apart.

Greece was running unsustainable budget deficits and was overly indebted. Greek public debt statistics were fudged with derivatives. Initially, banks and investors with exposure to Greek debt purchased credit insurance on Greece in the form of CDSs. They paid premiums to investors willing to earn a return for accepting the risk that the country might default. As the supply of CDS contracts was not restricted by the amount of Greek debt, hedge funds and other rubber-necked financial accident voyeurs joined the party, looking to make profits. Dealers in CDSs made large spreads from standing in between the buyers and sellers.

As with all insurance, higher risks mean higher premiums. The CDS markets became a visible benchmark of Greece's problems. The price of insurance was not anchored to the real underlying risk or the public finances of Greece. Traders were not interested in whether Greece was likely to default or in protecting themselves from this risk. They just kept beating the Greek piñata. Traders pushed around the thinly traded insurance contracts, making money from the volatility. Price movements triggered collateral requirements, causing further problems. Eventually, the EU agreed to bail out Greece, with help from the International Monetary Fund.

The financial piñata was stuffed with money rather than divine favors. Pension funds earned premiums from selling insurance, hedge funds made trading profits or losses, and banks earned fees. Everybody had fun except the inhabitants of the country, whose economy was decimated.[37]

The contagion effect provided further opportunity for traders. Volatile markets are like natural catastrophes—highly destructive and entirely indiscriminate in inflicting damage on anything in their path. The process was repeated in rapid succession with Ireland, Portugal, and Spain.

In the CDS market, traders holding insurance policies without owning the underlying bonds had a perverse incentive to ensure the default or, at least, a deterioration in the financial condition of the underlying companies and countries. This was nothing "much more than a floating craps game in an alley off Wall Street."[38]

Derivatives were now central to this world of speculation. Derivatives possessed the "violence of abstraction":

> Derivatives [must] be capable of computing all concrete risks...on a single metric. They must...translate concrete risks into quantities of abstract risk...the crisis of value measurement is expressed in the first instance in markets for financial instruments, like derivatives...it is at root a classic case of a crisis of value measurement, caused by collapses in value brought on by over-accumulation, falling profits, and unsustainable build-ups in fictitious capitals.[39]

Economist Jagdish Bhagwati contrasted the "destructive creation" of financial innovation and the "creative destruction" of industrial innovation in the real economy.

The promise of derivatives was the measurement and management of risk. In 2009, Alan Greenspan, once an ardent advocate of all things derivative, elliptically noted: "A Nobel Prize was awarded for the discovery of the pricing model that underpins much of the advance in derivatives markets. This modern risk management paradigm held sway for decades. The whole intellectual edifice, however, collapsed in the summer of last year."[40]

If the *Mirrored Room* by Lucas Samaras is the ultimate symbol for extreme money, then derivatives are the ultimate, universal financial instrument for manipulating that world, creating, and chasing endless reflections of real things. In a thoroughly post-modern contradiction, far from reducing risk, derivatives increase risk, often with catastrophic consequences.

15

Woodstock for Hedge Funds

In and around New York's Helmsley building, Stanford Connecticut, or London's St James and Mayfair (known as "Hedge Fund Alley"), brass plates acknowledge congregations of hedge funds. The funds are frequently named after birds of prey—"falcon," "peregrine," or "osprey." Other names conjure images of solidity, Wesley R. Edens' Fortress or Kenneth C. Griffin's Citadel. The word "capital" is ubiquitous. If private equity, securitization, and derivatives were alchemy, then hedge fund managers had to be the alchemists of the age of capital.

Journalist Martin Baker described the formula for hedge funds:

> Take a speculative cocktail shaker. Add four parts public ignorance and 33 parts greed. Toss in a little perceived genius. If you don't have any freshly ground perceived genius to hand, a little dried genius status will do. Season generously with mystique. Add apparent publicity shyness to taste. Serve in opaque tumbler of awed, ill informed media coverage.[1]

Hedge fund managers: "considered [themselves] part of the new era and the new breed, a Wall Street egalitarian, a Master of the Universe, who was only a respecter of performance."[2] The original Masters of the Universe were HeMan and his Friends in the 1980s popular children's cartoon. Tom Wolfe used the term to satirize his bond trader protagonist in *Bonfire of the Vanities*. In 2009, Lloyd Blankfein, CEO of Goldman Sachs, unconsciously borrowed from Wolfe to justify bumper profits: "performance is the ultimate narrative."[3] By the new millennium, Wolfe admitted that hedge fund managers had superseded bankers as the *new* Masters of the Universe.

Keeping Up with the Joneses

Hedge funds came to prominence when Soros *broke* the Bank of England and the pound sterling on Black Wednesday, September 16, 1992. Founded in 1970, Soros' Quantum Fund sold short the pound sterling to profit from a fall in the UK's currency. After vain attempts to defend the currency, the UK devalued the pound, handing Soros a $1.1 billion gain. George Soros later stated:

> Our total position by Black Wednesday had to be worth almost $10 billion. We planned to sell more than that. In fact, when Norman Lamont [the UK chancellor] said just before the devaluation that he would borrow nearly $15 billion to defend sterling, we were amused because that was about how much we wanted to sell.[4]

Black Wednesday cost the UK taxpayer an estimated £3.4 billion.

The idea of a hedge fund is attributed to Alfred Winslow Jones, an academic, diplomat, steamboat purser, and journalist. Jones sought profits while minimizing risk of losses from unpredictable market movements. In the 1950s he began buying undervalued stocks and selling overvalued stocks—an *equity long-short strategy*. The shorts hedged the longs, reducing exposure to general market movements, hence the moniker—*hedge fund*. Jones outperformed other mutual funds handsomely over a long period.

As the short positions were around 50 percent of the value of the longs, risk was reduced but not eliminated entirely. Jones bet that the market would go up. Jones also used leverage. If he was long $1.5 million and short $1 million, then the total exposure to stock price movements was around $2.5 million on $0.5 million of *net* risk. Jones received 20 percent of performance. He invested his own money in the fund. Later, anticipating future developments, Jones acted as an *incubator* for two employees who left to set up their own funds, and transformed his fund into a *fund-of-funds*, investing in other hedge funds with different expertise and investment styles.

In the late 1960s, Carol Loomis, a *Fortune* journalist, published an influential article about Jones' fund. Others copied Jones' hitherto secret investment strategies. By 2008, there were more than 8,000 hedge funds with more than $1,500 billion in assets under management (AUM) around the world.

In Search of Moby Dick

Today, 30–40 percent of hedge fund money comes from the usual suspects—the simply wealthy, Mafia barons, drug lords, arms merchants, and despotic dictators of tin-pot countries. The rest comes from pension funds, insurance companies, mutual funds, foundations, endowment funds, and banks.

Investors were initially attracted by stellar returns. Investments were segmented into *beta* (market returns) and *alpha* (outperformance). Alpha was Captain Ahab's Moby Dick, the "white whale of the investment community—coveted, precious, sought with a maniacal fury."[5] A *core* portfolio targeted beta using index-tracking funds, like exchange-traded funds with low costs, to closely match market moves. A *satellite* portfolio, consisting of actively managed funds or alternative investments, chased alpha. Investors lashed themselves to hedge funds, seeking outperformance.

Few traditional investment managers outperform the market, after trading costs and fees, over long periods. If you outperform, then people give you more money to invest, which reduces flexibility—the *winner's curse*. Large funds also create diseconomies of scale: every time a large investor tries to trade, the market moves against them. Investment managers tried to beat benchmarks, usually a diversified index like a stock market index. If the portfolio was down 50 percent but the benchmark fell 53 percent, then the fund manager outperformed by +3 percent. In contrast, hedge funds focused on absolute returns, trying to make money under all market conditions.

In the early 1990s and again in the early 2000s, equity markets were moribund and interest rates were at record lows. Forced to look elsewhere, investors increased investment in hedge funds.

Suspicious of new products, traditional institutions reluctantly entered new markets to boost declining returns. Not allowed to buy structured securities, short sell, leverage or use derivatives, conservative funds gave money to hedge funds that could. The new mantra was "hedge funds for everybody."

Style Gurus

Hedge fund managers argued that only they knew what they do, reminiscent of a prospectus from the 1920s: "the credit and status of the company are so well known that it is scarcely necessary to make any public statement."[6] At a 2009 Congressional Inquiry, Citadel's Ken Griffin argued against disclosure by comparing it to "asking Coca-Cola to disclose their secret formula to the world."[7]

One manager explained his investment strategy as throwing light on "fragmented information" and "opaque" track records. George Soros was honest:

> I don't have a particular style of investing or, more exactly, I try to change my style to fit the conditions...I assume that markets are always wrong.... Most of the time we are punished if we go against the trend. Only at an inflection point are we rewarded.[8]

Hedge funds pursue high absolute returns, whilst trying to reduce risk, by combining long and short positions that move in opposite directions as markets move. Leverage is used to increase earnings.

Equity long-short funds follow Jones's model. Some funds match exactly, while others take views on the likely trend, known as the portion *outside the hedge*. Stock selection uses fundamental analysis or quantitative models to identify over and undervalued stocks.

Market neutral or *relative value funds* arbitrage market inefficiencies. There's fixed income arbitrage, convertible bond arbitrage, derivative arbitrage, MBS arbitrage, capital structure arbitrage, and arbitrage arbitrage. All use quantitative analysis to identify small, low-risk pricing discrepancies, amplified by leverage to generate high returns.

Event-driven funds take advantage of mergers and takeovers (*risk arb*) or bankruptcy (*vulture funds* or *distressed debt trading*). Event-driven trading uses knowledge of regulations, legal documentation, and (sometimes critics suspect) inside information to make profits. Investment periods can be long and, as the name implies, there is "event risk" (a merger not proceeding).

Quantitative funds use computer-driven trading strategies. Trend-following models identify the market's *mo* (momentum) and ride the bucking bronco bareback. Sophisticated models identify undervalued and overvalued securities. *Algorithmic trading*, known as algo, black-box, or robo trading, uses computer programs to decide timing, price or quantity of trading orders. It divides large trades into smaller trades or vice versa to manage market impact and risk. It generates small but frequent returns by providing liquidity to other buyers and sellers.

Macro funds make large, speculative, leveraged bets on currencies, stocks, interest rates, and commodities. Strategies are based on fundamental analysis, computer-generated trading signals, market price action, and a certain vibration in the intestinal tract. According to Dion Friedland, chairman of Magnum Funds, macro hedge funds are: "mammoth and quick, keen and powerful, sudden and aggressive; they go for the kill, they want it all, not content with only a mere morsel of their prey."[9]

As opportunities within their expertise dry up, single strategy hedge funds undertake other strategies—known as *style drift*. Over time, hedge funds became *multistrategy*. In his 1940 book *Where Are The Customer's Yachts?* Fred Schwed, Jr. anticipated hedge fund investing: "At the close of day's business they take all the money and throw it up into the air. Everything that sticks to the ceiling belongs to the clients."[10]

In 2010, Paul the Octopus established a prefect record, predicting winners in the Football World Cup. Bloomberg reported that Paul raised $2 billion in seed funding for a new hedge fund. The backer was reported as saying that:

> He is an octopus but his track record is great. It may be just pure luck to you, but we call that alpha in our business and it is no more stupid an idea than correlation trading or structured credit arbitrage. Besides, as a spineless bottom feeder we think he will be a natural with investors.[11]

Magic Wand

While some do show high returns, hedge fund returns on average appear only slightly higher than that available on the broader stock markets.[12]

Percentage returns can be misleading. In its first 18 years, Julian Robertson's Tiger Fund generated returns of 30 percent per annum. In its last two years, the fund made losses of 50 percent. Taking the losses into account, Tiger returned 25 percent per annum over its life. Starting life in 1980 with $10 million, it had $22 billion under management by 1998. The fund's highest percentage returns were on a small dollar base. The losses came from a larger base (a 50 percent loss on $22 billion is a loss of $11 billion). Tiger may have lost more dollars than it made over its life.[13]

Historical returns exclude funds that fail or no longer accept new investment—*survivorship bias*. Only funds with a successful track record report performance—*backfill bias*. The difference between the best and worst performing funds is large. For investors seeking alpha, high average returns are meaningless, like a comfortable average ambient temperature where your feet are in the oven and your head is in the refrigerator.

A confluence of events boosted hedge fund returns. Macro funds benefited from the growth of emerging economies, the end of communism in Eastern Europe, world trade and deregulation of financial markets. Soros' currency profits came from the collapse of a flawed system for European currencies. In 1997/8, hedge funds made substantial returns when pegged Asian currencies collapsed. In recent years, many macro funds, like the fabled Quantum and Tiger Funds, restructured or disappeared.

Some hedge fund managers are exceptionally skilful. Soros, Tudor Jones, and James Simons, an ex-mathematics professor and former code breaker, have outstanding records. For others, investment Viagra boosted performance.

Some, like the Bear Stearns hedge funds, used leverage to increase returns. In 2009, in a Freudian slip, George Soros referred to Long Term Capital Management (LTCM) as "leveraged capital."[14] Others increased returns by investing in illiquid or complex securities.

Some managers seek an information edge. The credo of SAC, a hedge fund operated by billionaire art collector Steve Cohen, is: "Get information before anyone else."[15] Hedge funds test the boundary of insider trading and market abuse.

In 2010, U.S. Federal Investigators began investigating a spider-web of insider trading, involving billionaire investor Raj Rajaratnam, founder of the Galleon hedge fund. For hedge funds, insider-trading profits offered large returns as they receive a share of trading profits, and artificially enhanced returns attract more investments generating higher management fees. The alleged inside information came from lawyers at Ropes & Gray, a prestigious corporate law firm, a senior executive at IBM, a partner at Ernst & Young and a director at the big management consulting firm McKinsey. Although not identified by name, two traders at SAC were also accused of involvement.

The biggest name caught up in the investigation was Rajat Gupta who it was alleged had passed on information to Rajarantnam. Gupta had been McKinsey's global managing director for almost a decade until 2003 and remained on its partnership board until 2007. Gupta faced civil insider trading charges for allegedly sharing secret information acquired as a board member of Goldman Sachs and Procter & Gamble. Robert Khuzami, director of enforcement at the Securities and Exchange Commission, described Rajaratnam as "a master of the Rolodex" rather than "a master of the universe."

The investigation focused on expert network firms, which provided "independent investment research." Redefining the concept of expertise, these firms seemed to specialize in matching insiders with traders hungry for privileged information, routinely allowing access to non-public sensitive inside information on sales forecasts and earnings. The investigations recalled the investigations and convictions of Ivan Boesky and Michael Milken for corruption on Wall Street in the late 1980s. Regulators suggested that the practice was so widespread as to verge on a "corrupt business model."[16]

Some fund managers dispense with pretence and fabricate returns. In 2008, Bernard Madoff confessed to an investment fraud totaling more than $60 billion, involving nearly 5,000 clients. Madoff's hedge funds, operating from three floors of the Lipstick Building, generated solid returns, trading stocks, and options. In reality, since the mid-1990s, Madoff had operated a Ponzi scheme.

Lucky Man

Jones charged 20 percent of performance, but no management fee, and paid expenses from his performance fee. Traditional hedge funds charged 1 percent management fee and a performance fee of 20 percent of returns above a benchmark, the *watermark*. There was also a high watermark. If it makes losses, then the fund must recoup these before performance fees resume.

Funds now routinely charge 2 percent and 20 percent with *no* watermark. *Hot hedge funds* charge even more: 5 percent of assets and 35 percent of profits, 4 percent of assets and 44 percent of profits. One manager candidly admitted: "A hedge fund is just an excuse to charge two and twenty; they do not do anything else very different." A cartoon shows a road sign for Connecticut, home to a large number of hedge funds: "Entering Greenwich, speed limit 2 percent and 20 percent."[17]

Performance fees and the manager's investment in the fund supposedly align the interests of investor and the manager. In fact, the fee structure favors the manager. Assume a $100 million fund where the manager's fees are 1 percent and 20 percent of performance. The manager has a $5 million (5 percent) interest in the fund. If the hedge fund loses $20 million (20 percent), then the manager loses $1 million (20 percent of $5 million) offset by the management fee received (1 percent of $100 million equaling $1 million). If the hedge fund makes $20 million (20 percent), then the manager earns $4 million (20 percent of $20 million) plus the management fee ($1 million)—a 100 percent return. *The Economist* described it as "catch two-and-twenty."

Many investors use FoFs (fund-of-funds) to screen and select portfolios of hedge funds. Where investing in hedge funds, diversification makes no sense, earning average or worse returns. The investor pays a fee to the FoF manager (1 percent of AUM and 10 percent of performance) as well as the hedge fund manager's fee (2 percent and 20 percent). FoF might stand for "fee-of-fees."

Skewed payoffs for the manager encourage aggressive risk taking.[18] The economist Thorstein Veblen identified this: "It is always sound business to take any obtainable net gain, at any cost and at any risk to the rest of the community."

In 2007, three hedge fund managers took home more than $1 billion. At the congressional inquiry into the industry, Maryland Democratic representative Elijah Cummings reported that his neighbor asked him: "How does it feel to be going before five folks that have gotten more money than God?"[19]

It is unclear whether well-performed managers are lucky or skilful. Bill Miller's Legg Mason Value Trust Fund, one of the world's biggest funds, beat the S&P 500 Index for 15 consecutive years from 1991 to 2005. Paeans to his legend, investing style, and success were duly penned. Miller's performance faltered during the financial crisis. Echoing the author Nassim Taleb, Michael Mauboussin, one of Miller's colleagues observed: "We have difficulty in sorting skill and luck in…business and investing."[20]

Investors look for the idiot savants of money management. Unfortunately, they frequently trusted idiots without the savant. In selecting fund managers, investors should have followed Napoleon's approach to selecting generals: "Are you lucky?"

Sharpe Practice

Investors use Sharpe or information ratios to measure investment performance. Assume risk-free government securities yield 5 percent and hedge fund A has returns of 20 percent with a volatility of 10 percent while hedge fund B has returns of 15 percent and a volatility of 5 percent. The Sharpe ratios are respectively:

Hedge Fund A = [20%—5%] / 10% = 1.5

Hedge Fund B = [15%—5%] / 5% = 2.0

Despite lower absolute performance, B provides investors with greater returns relative to risk.

Sharpe ratios are *ex post* (based on actual risk) rather than *ex ante* (expected risk). Actual returns should be compared to expected risk at the time the position was taken. Insufficient attention is paid to the asymmetry of hedge fund returns, which do not follow the familiar bell-shaped normal distribution. Risk models grossly underestimate *tail risk*, exposure to large price moves. Traders arb internal risk metrics to inflate risk-adjusted returns to increase bonuses. Real hedge fund risks—correlation, liquidity, complexity, and model risk—are not measured properly.

If the portfolio of long and short positions is perfectly balanced and prices move identically, then the gains and losses should cancel out, reducing risk but earning zero return. To make money, the correlation, the relationship between the long and short securities, must change. Correlation may move unfavorably—the asset you are long falls in value; the asset you are short rises in value, triggering losses. Models based on historical price movements do not properly capture this correlation risk.

Risk models assume that investors can buy, sell, hedge, or borrow whatever is required. This liquidity risk is compounded by leverage. Hedge funds trade on margin, putting up a small fraction of the value of the asset as collateral. If prices fall, then the hedge fund must post more collateral. If losses exceed the hedge fund's ability to meet margin calls, then the position must be liquidated, realizing losses.

To value and hedge positions, funds use quantitative models that are sensitive to minor changes in parameters and inputs. While prices scroll across computer screens every second of every day, few instruments actually trade with sufficient liquidity to allow positions to be valued against actual prices. Hedge funds do not measure the possibility of model failures when quantifying risk. They follow actress Tallulah Bankhead's advice: "If I had to live my life again, I'd make the same mistakes, only sooner."

Hedge funds buy or sell mispriced securities, reducing risk through an offsetting trade. If market prices converge, then the trader unwinds their trades at a profit. If the market prices do not correct, then the trader may have to hold the position to maturity, up to 30 years. Given risk horizons of 6–12 months, changes in market values, margin calls, and investor redemptions make it difficult to manage this risk.

Adjusted properly for leverage, liquidity risk, model errors, and complexity, most hedge funds return, at best, the same as or frequently less than traditional investments. Sharpe practice not only underestimates risk but also overstates returns.

Embedded

Hedge funds are courtesans, high-class prostitutes whose clients come from the wealthy. Banks are the pimps and bordello keepers. As *Forbes* magazine noted: "It's easy to guess who is likely to make most money in the long term."[21]

Banks have prime brokerage units that settle and clear hedge fund trades as well as financing hedge funds. Banks make *capital introductions*, raising capital for hedge funds (for a fee of 2–4 percent). They set up incubators to help budding traders create hedge funds, including training in etiquette at formal lunches and investor communications. Banks invest in and trade with hedge funds. They trade derivatives on hedge funds.

Lending money to hedge funds provides the major part of the profits. Lending is through *repos* (repurchase agreements), where the bank lends money against the value of securities. Alternatively, derivatives are used. The hedge fund lodges cash or securities equal to a small percentage of the face value as surety.

To reduce risk, banks use a *haircut* or over collateralization. Banks estimate the worst-case daily change in the value of positions to cover the risk. Event risk, where the value of the position changes a lot quickly, is difficult to measure. Competition reduces the haircuts. LTCM was special, not requiring any haircut. As one observer asked: "Would hedge funds even exist without a fatty dollop of moral hazard somewhere along the great protein chain of lending?"[22]

At their peak, hedge funds accounted for 30–40 percent of total investment bank earnings. Citadel paid $5.5 billion in trading costs to investment banks,[23] the largest portion being interest on borrowings. Citadel's total and net assets were $166 billion and $13 billion respectively. Trading costs totaled one-third of net assets.

Bank dealings with hedge funds frequently entail conflicts of interest. Senior bank executives, who were personal investors in LTCM, negotiated its bailout. It was all part of the "special" relationship.[24]

Banks copied from the best and brightest, creating internal hedge funds to replicate successful trading strategies borrowed from smart hedge funds. Once their own risk limits were full, they marketed the strategies to other banks and hedge funds. Even if the hedge fund failed, banks made money buying the positions at distressed prices. Banks provided a true cradle-to-grave service for hedge funds.

In the Long Run, We Are All Dead

LTCM was known as Salomon North, reflecting its Greenwich, Connecticut base. After leaving Salomon Brothers in 1991 following a trading scandal, John Meriwether established LTCM in 1994 with capital of $4 billion. Investors paid a 2 percent management fee and 25 percent incentive fee on earnings after a threshold level of return.

The operation sought to replicate Salomon Brothers' successful fixed income arbitrage unit. Joining Meriwether were key Salomon traders Eric Rosenfield, Lawrence Hilibrand, Victor Haghani, and Greg Hawkins. Nobel Prize winners Robert Merton and Myron Scholes, as well as former Fed vice-chairman David Mullins, also joined. The principals invested, in some cases their entire wealth, in LTCM. They bristled with indignation at suggestions that LTCM was a hedge fund.

LTCM's strategies were vague, emphasizing research, sophisticated analysis, proprietary modeling, relative value, and convergence trading. It identified small pricing discrepancies between securities, taking advantage of opportunities when prices deviated from long-run equilibrium values, due to short-term market disturbances. LTCM purchased cheap, underpriced securities, hedging with short sales of expensive securities with similar characteristics. Profits were made when pricing differences corrected. The fund did not take directional risks and outright positions, reducing risk and allowing the use of leverage, up to 25 times, to accentuate returns.

When an investor questioned how the fund would earn high returns with low risk, the abrasive Scholes snapped: "because of fools like you."[25] Scholes told his old mentor at the University of Chicago, Merton Miller:

"think of us [LTCM] as a gigantic vacuum cleaner sucking up nickels from all over the world."[26] LTCM was trying to pick up nickels in front of a bullet train.

In 1995 and 1996, the fund generated returns of more than 40 percent per annum, using trading strategies perfected during the Salomon years. In 1997, U.S. stocks returned 33 percent, LTCM's returns fell to 17 percent. To improve performance, LTCM increased leverage, returning $2.7 billion of its accumulated capital of $7 billion to investors. LTCM broadened into credit spread trading, volatility trading, and equity risk arbitrage.

In 1998, LTCM lost 92 percent of its capital. The Asian monetary crisis created uncertainty, a general aversion to risk and a flight to quality. Sensing an opportunity, LTCM placed bets on credit spreads (the margin between corporate bonds and government bonds) and stock volatility. The market dubbed LTCM the "Central Bank of Liquidity and Volatility," a risk re-insurer.

In May/June 1998, LTCM took a big loss in mortgage-backed securities. In August 1998, when Russia defaulted on its debt, LTCM took more losses. On August 21, LTCM lost $550 million, mainly on its credit spread and equity volatility positions. LTCM needed cash to cover losses. The unflappable Meriwether advised that: "we've had a serious markdown but everything's fine with us."[27] LTCM discovered what John Maynard Keynes knew: "the market can remain irrational longer than you can remain solvent."[28]

On September 2, 1998 John Meriwether advised investors that LTCM had lost 52 percent of its value:

> As you are all too aware events surrounding the collapse of Russia caused large losses and dramatically increased volatility in global markets.... Many of the fund's investment strategies involve providing liquidity to the market. Hence, our losses across strategies were correlated after-the-fact from the sharp increase in the liquidity premium: the use of leverage has accentuated the losses.

LTCM sought new investment from investors: "Since it is prudent to raise capital the fund is offering you the opportunity to invest on special terms related to LTCM's fees."[29] There were no takers.

On September 18, 1998 Bear Stearns was rumored to have frozen the fund's cash account, following a large margin call. On September 23, 1998 AIG, Goldman Sachs, and Warren Buffet made an unsuccessful offer to buy out LTCM's partners and inject $4 billion into the fund. Facing the specter of a massive default affecting the entire financial system, the New York Federal Reserve brokered a recapitalization of LTCM. Fourteen banks invested $3.6 billion in return for 90 percent of LTCM. Keynes was correct: "There is nothing so disastrous as a rational investment policy in an irrational world."[30]

The Game

At the beginning of 1998, LTCM's risk models showed that there was a 1 percent chance of losses exceeding $45 million. After May/June 1998, LTCM reduced risk limits to $35 million. Yet in August 1998, LTCM's daily profits and losses were up to $135 million. By September 1998, LTCM's profit and loss was moving $100 million to $200 million daily, three to six times the limit.

Risk models underestimated volatility and used incorrect correlation. The principals were blind to the dangers of a firm reliant on borrowed money holding large positions. LTCM held 10 percent of the entire global dollar interest rate swap market. To reduce positions rapidly, LTCM sold liquid positions first, leaving only illiquid positions. Closing out large or illiquid positions increased losses.

While trading at Salomon Brothers, the purpose of specific trades—client or proprietary—was not apparent to the market. At LTCM, all trades were proprietary. Dealers had worked out LTCM's trading strategies, replicating them using their bank's money, or selling the ideas to other hedge funds and banks. Everybody tried to exit the *crowded trade* at the same time.

Rumors of LTCM's problems triggered more selling, anticipating LTCM's need to sell its massive portfolio. Traders tried to force LTCM into default and purchase its portfolio at distressed prices. LTCM's Victor Haghani commented later: "It was as if there was someone out there with our exact portfolio only it was three times as large as ours and they were liquidating all at once."[31]

As losses mounted, LTCM had to meet margin calls on its positions. Louis Bacon, the principal of Moore Capital, once remarked that: "There are those who know that they are in the game; there are those who don't know they are in the game; and there are those who don't know they are in the game and have become the game."[32] By late 1998, LTCM were the game. In the end, LTCM simply ran out of cash.

The More Things Change

Amaranth was a $9.2 billion multistrategy hedge fund named after the Greek *amarantos*—"one that does not wither" or "the never-fading flower." In August/September 2006, Amaranth lost $6 billion, almost twice the loss when LTCM collapsed.[33]

Starting life as a low-risk convertible arbitrage fund, Amaranth was a recent entrant into volatile energy trading. In 2005, Brian Hunter, a 32-year old Canadian in charge of Amaranth's energy trading, used derivatives to bet successfully that natural gas prices would rise following Hurricane Katrina. Hunter placed a similar but larger bet in 2006. Another trader sent Hunter the following message: "Brian, what the hell is going on out there, rumor is you are getting even more rich!!! According to the market you are brilliant!!!!!! Can do no wrong ever!"[34]

Amaranth bought natural gas for delivery in March 2007, while selling it for delivery in April 2007. Historically, natural gas prices increase during winter, and fall after March as demand for heating decreases. In early September 2006, natural gas prices fell as supply exceeded demand. Hunter bet that a hurricane or a cold winter would push natural gas prices upward. An uneventful hurricane season meant that the difference in natural gas prices for delivery in March and April 2007 (the *spread*) fell. Amaranth's position, which profited from widening spreads, showed losses as the March/April spread narrowed from 2.05 points on September 1 to 0.75 points on September 18.

Like LTCM, Amaranth believed that it was involved in low risk trading. But it was exposed to correlation, changes in the relationship between the two components. Correlation changes rapidly, like a piece of elastic snapping. On September 22, 2006 Nick Maounis, chief executive of the fund, announced: "A series of unusual and unpredictable market events caused the funds' natural gas positions, including spreads, to incur dramatic losses."[35] Maounis noted: "Although the size of our natural gas exposure was large, we believed, based on input from both our trading desk and the stress testing performed by our energy risk team, that the risk capital ascribed to the natural gas portfolio was sufficient."[36]

Amaranth had a large, concentrated position in natural gas, representing 10 percent of the global market in natural gas futures. Bruno Stanziale, a former colleague, commended Hunter's contribution in helping the market and gas producers to finance new exploration: "He's opened a market up and provided a new level of liquidity to all players."[37] Stanziale had confused Hunter with Mother Teresa.

When losses occurred, Nick Maounis reprised the aria made famous by the principals of LTCM in 1998: "The markets provided no economically viable means of exiting those positions. Despite all our efforts, we were unable to close out the exposures in the public markets."[38]

As news got around of Amaranth's problems, traders took advantage:

> When people get a sense that someone is on the ropes, they're going to exacerbate the problems that he has. Those with risk capital are going to short whatever he has, believing the guy will have to capitulate and that they will be there to take his capitulation selling.[39]

In the end, Amaranth was forced to transfer its energy positions to JP Morgan and Citadel at a $1.4 billion discount to their mark-to-market value. Amaranth provided the following analysis: "We did not expect that the market would move so aggressively against our positions."[40]

Sophisticated fund-of-funds and investors such as Goldman Sachs, Morgan Stanley, Credit Suisse, Bank of New York, Deutsche Bank and Man Group, failed to pick up any problems at Amaranth. In a speculative environment, critical ability greatly diminishes. Most people fail to look beyond the profits. In better times, Amaranth had given out gift chess sets inscribed with the words of grandmaster Alexander Kotov: "It often happens that a player carries out a deep and complicated calculation, but fails to spot something elementary right at the first move."[41]

Hedgestock

In 2006, hedge funds staged *Hedgestock*, 2 days of "networking and finance." The title paid homage to Woodstock, the historic three days of peace, love, promiscuity, rock 'n' roll, drugs, and shockingly bad dancing on Max Yasgur's farm in Bethel, New York in 1969. Adam Smith understood "networking": "People of the same trade seldom meet together, even for merriment and diversion, but the conversation ends in conspiracy against the public, or in some contrivance to raise prices."[42]

Hippies celebrated the counterculture movement at Woodstock. Hedge fund managers advertised their movement—*alternative investments*. It was "the age of money" not "the age of Aquarius." Hedgestock's "free market" message was far removed from Woodstock's message of "free love."

16

Minsky Machines

Gradually problems emerged. Hedge funds did not consistently deliver alpha, and returns were disappointing—in some periods lower than the broader equity market.[1] Average returns dropped from 18.3 percent per annum in the 1990s to 7.5 percent in the 2000s.[2]

Investment genius was always little more than a short memory and a rising market. Edwardian novelist Max Beerbohm was vindicated: "The dullard's envy of brilliant men is always assuaged by the suspicion that they will come to a bad end."

But investors still chased yesterday's returns. The focus now shifted to diversification, using hedge funds to balance the risk of traditional investments. Hedge funds were "a perfectly hedged financial institution [that] loses money in every conceivable interest rate environment."[3]

Affinities and Curses

Clever people can make money if there are few clever people and lots of opportunities. Steve Cohen, owner of *The Physical Impossibility of Death in the Mind of Someone Living*, sounded a cautionary note: "It's hard to find ideas that aren't picked over and harder to get real returns and differentiate yourself. We're entering a new environment. The days of big returns are gone."[4]

There is also the problem of *scalability*—what works on a small scale may not work on a larger scale. Some strategies need liquid markets. If you exploit inefficiency, then other investors must supply it. To be *alternative*, there must be a majority; the alternative cannot be the majority.

Inflow of money into successful hedge funds eroded returns. Louis Bacon (of Moore Capital) observed: "Size matters. It is the bane of the successful money manager."[5] Size forces style drift. LTCM drifted from its métier, relative value trading in fixed income, into volatility trading, credit spread trading, and merger arbitrage. In 2006, when market neutral hedge funds losses mirrored the fall in the market, hedge fund managers explained: "Everything in the market was a compelling buy. We could find nothing to short."

The market changed. Banks *cloned* hedge funds, replicating returns by using simple instruments, with lower fees and less risk of an Amaranth or LTCM.[6] Investors were looking for grand masters at knock-off prices.

Smart money focused on incubators, identifying traders and seeding start-ups. After established with a track record, the hedge fund raised third-party funding. The original investors exited, retaining the real investment crown jewel, the interest in the fund manager.

In 2006, hedge funds, led by trailblazer Pirate Capital, started selling shares to investors.[7] Used to timing for purchases or sales, the Masters of the Universe were astutely selling out at the top. Banks convinced themselves that they needed to own hedge fund managers. Holding trading positions in hedge funds was capital efficient. Hedge funds could leverage more than the banks. Hedge funds alleviated problems of attracting and remunerating star traders.

Wall Street and the City are bad judges of value. Having enjoyed the milk, in a moment of confusion they tend to over pay for the cow. An orgy of billion-dollar buying ensued.

Crowded Hours

Investment in just two types of funds—quantitative equity market neutral and long short equity—increased from $10 billion to $160 billion between 1995 and 2007. As returns fell, from 1.3 percent to 0.13 percent, managers increased leverage, from two times to ten times. Because of the limited opportunities, funds ended up holding similar positions.

In August and September 2008, increased volatility and changes in correlation between stocks led to losses. Forced selling caused the cheap or value stocks (which the funds bought) to fall in value, and expensive stocks (which they short sold) to rise. MIT Professor Andrew Lo used a nautical analogy:

> We have so many boats in the harbor, you can't whiz by at 50 knots without rocking a few boats.... In the middle of the ocean, your wake has no impact, but in a crowded harbor, a fast exit can cause quite a disruption.

Clifford Asness, founder of AQR, a $37 billion hedge fund, discovered: "There is a new risk factor in our world and it is us."[8]

Everybody had borrowed money in low interest currencies to purchase illiquid investments paying high returns. Traders had taken on the same event risk—likelihood of low losses in mortgages, the emergence of the BRIC economies, higher commodity prices, and corporate actions (mergers, LBOs, and bankruptcy). Hedge funds leveraged up bets on the big stories using *volatility swaps* (bets on the level of volatility), *correlation swaps* (bets on correlation) and *gamma* or *dispersion swaps* (bets on both volatility and correlation). The concentration of risk meant that any event spread through the highly leveraged financial system, creating volatility that fed on itself.

Lack of liquidity affected market prices. Banks valued position conservatively, exacerbating already large losses and necessitating margin calls that the funds could not meet. Mark Twain's observation held true: "A banker is a fellow who lends you his umbrella when the sun is shining, but wants it back the minute it begins to rain."

Bankers moved to reduce their risk by either requiring additional collateral which hedge funds did not have or forcing the sales of investments at distressed prices to pay their loans back. The experience of hedge funds now paralleled the organizers of Woodstock. Joel Roseman wrote in the *Woodstock Experience* that: "We had a pretty conservative banker.... Next to his desk was a fish tank containing a piranha and another tank containing goldfish, and as he put a goldfish into the piranha's tank, he'd say, "Everybody repays their loans here at the National Bank of North America."[9]

As investors began to withdraw money in response to investment losses, many hedge funds suspended redemption rights, known as *gating*. Managers hid in their fortresses and citadels behind high gates, as the perils of leverage and investment in complex illiquid securities were exposed.

Crime Without Punishment

In 2008, hedge fund returns averaged *negative* 20 percent. Even marque funds took large losses. Hedge fund investments fell by around $600 billion. Over 3,300 hedge funds out of 8,000 ceased operations. John Devaney, a hedge fund manager and *bon vivant* with a taste for high living, lost $100 million and was forced to sell prized personal assets—properties in Aspen, Colorado, and Miami, Florida, his helicopter, a Gulfstream jet, and his cherished 142-foot yacht *Positive Carry*.

Hedge funds tried to calm investors' anxiety and anger with literary gems. Griffin's Citadel Funds, which lost $8 billion and was down 55 percent, said: "We did not foresee the financial disaster that was to unfold in September." Tosca moaned: "It is emotionally and financially draining that after eight solid years the fund should be so damaged by the failed global monetary system." Oaktree took a different tone: "We're grabbing at falling knives.... We consider it our job to catch falling knives—in a careful, skillful manner."[10] Another fund blamed regulators: "The next time anyone tells you, as the geniuses who run our financial system have done, that the ever-rising prices of homes should be counted in savings, you should lean close to his/her ear and scream: "IDIOT!"[11]

David Harding, a London-based fund manager, defended failed models: "People aren't going to give up their computers and go back to insider information and tips."[12] An anonymous blogger provided useful advice: "You may want to re-calibrate your abacus, most all the ones I've used always have seven poles and ten beads on each pole, are you sure you have the right 'model'?"[13]

Trader Paul Tudor Jones wrote that he would earn back losses, quoting polar explorer Admiral Richard Evelyn Byrd: "The mantle of leadership rests easily when the compass needle does not move."[14] After suffering a loss of 16 percent in the third quarter of 2008, David Einhorn, a famed short seller, admitted that: "In hindsight, our suggestion from last quarter's letter to go to cash and go to the beach would have been the better option."[15]

Large losses that would not be recouped quickly reduced the opportunity for hedge fund managers to earn performance fees where there was a watermark. To get around the problem, some managers simply closed the existing funds, starting new funds. An article on hedge funds asked: "Gaming the system: are hedge fund managers talented, or just good at fooling investors?"[16]

Not everybody lost money. Paulson & Co., run by John Paulson, made $3 billion from shorting subprime securities. For the first 10 months of 2007, Paulson's Credit Opportunities fund made a gross return of 690 percent and a net return (after fees) of 551 percent. His Credit Opportunities II fund made a gross return of 410 percent and a net 328 percent. Paulson's fund assets increased from $6 billion to $27.5 billion, entering the top ten global funds. Philip Falcone's Harbinger Capital, Mike Burry's Scion Funds and Lahde Capital, a Santa-Monica-based fund set up by Andrew Lahde, all recorded substantial returns.

Burry wrote to his investors: "The opportunity in 2005 and 2006 to short subprime mortgages was an historic one." Lahde, a small fund, returned money to investors, recognizing that: "The risk/return characteristics are far less attractive than in the past."[17]

The funds that profited from the collapse were generally smaller funds, outside the mainstream. Before the crisis, when asked about John Paulson, a banker at Goldman Sachs told a potential investor that he was "a third rate hedge fund guy who didn't know what he was talking about."[18]

One person noted: "In the hedge-fund industry the only bad thing you can do is lose people's money."[19] Even that wasn't strictly speaking true.

In 1999, after the collapse of LTCM, John Meriwether had no difficulties raising new funds for JWM Partners LLC (JWM), a lower risk version of LTCM. In 2008 the $2.3 billion JWM fund found itself in trouble. In a familiar message, Meriwether told investors: "We have sharply reduced the risk and balance sheet of the portfolio." JWM closed its main fund after losing 44 percent between September 2007 and February 2009.[20] Subsequently, in 2010, Meriwether opened his third hedge fund venture—JM Advisors Management. As Mark Twain pointed out: "All you need in this life is ignorance and confidence; then success is sure."

At the time of the creation of JWM, a member of the banking consortium that bailed out LTCM stated that Meriwether's re-emergence highlighted "the ongoing vitality of the Wall Street system." F. Scott Fitzgerald was wrong when he said there are no second acts in American lives. For hedge fund managers, there are second acts, third acts, fourth acts, and fifth acts. Potential investors seem to take comfort in physicist Niels Bohr's observation: "An expert is a man who has made all the mistakes which can be made in a very narrow field."

Fast Cars, Slow Hedge Funds

The Masters of the Universe were even beaten at their own game by a German carmaker Porsche Automobil Holding SE (Porsche). Porsches are synonymous with prestige, luxury, and performance, making them the conveyance of choice for hedge fund managers.

Porsche is majority owned by the Piëch and Porsche families. Ferdinand Piëch, the grandson of the founder, dreamed of uniting Porsche and Volkswagen (VW). In 2005 Porsche, led by Wendelin Wiedeking, CEO, and Holger Härter, the chief financial officer, announced it would become the largest shareholder in VW by purchasing a 20 percent stake. In April 2007, Porsche crossed the 30 percent threshold, requiring it to submit a takeover offer for VW. Porsche's supervisory board announced it would raise its voting stake in VW from 31 percent to more than 50 percent. Porsche was trying to gain control of a company more than 80 times its size as measured by sales.

Call options, the right to purchase VW shares, were central to the acquisition strategy. The options protected against higher VW share prices, while enabling Porsche to mask its exact shareholding in VW.

In a weakening economic environment, hedge funds believed that VW shares were overvalued and bet that the share price would fall. As Porsche's share purchases and option activity pushed up VW's share price, hedge funds sold VW shares short, looking to buy them back when the price fell. Some funds sold VW shares and bought the shares of other car companies to capture the correction in relative prices. Merger arbitrage funds sold VW shares and bought Porsche shares, betting that the prices would converge. Others shorted VW ordinary shares and bought the preference shares trading at a 50 percent discount to ordinary shares, betting that the spread would decrease.

Around September 2009, Porsche announced it intended to lift its shareholding to 75 percent, allowing it to enter into a domination agreement, giving it effective control of VW. Earlier, on March 10, 2008, Porsche had dismissed suggestions that it was going to increase its shareholding to 75 percent as "speculation." On September 16, 2008 Porsche stated that its shareholding in VW was 35.14 percent, ignoring the options.

At 3:00 p.m. on Sunday, October 26, 2008, concerned about the level of short positions in VW, Porsche disclosed that it held 42.6 percent of VW's ordinary shares and also 31.5 percent of outstanding VW shares via call options. Designed to hedge its risk to higher prices, the options did not entail Porsche physically buying the shares. They would be cash-settled when the contract expired. But if Porsche acquired the shares underlying the options, then its total stake in VW was 74.1 percent.

Traders did some basic arithmetic. Lower Saxony, the German state, owned 20.1 percent of VW. Porsche owned or controlled 74.1 percent. Investment funds tracking the German market index, the DAX (Deutscher Aktien IndeX), owned an estimated 5 percent. All this added up to a simple fact—the less than 1 percent of VW shares available to trade, the free float, was substantially below short positions in VW of over 12 percent of outstanding shares. As one hedge fund manager described it: "I was on a wet walk and checked my BlackBerry—I ran like a madman back to my house. I assumed the numbers were wrong, but when a broker told me he'd had a dozen panicked calls already, I knew it was true."[21] There were insufficient shares available to buy back the hedge fund's short positions.

Panicked hedge funds rushed to close the short positions at any price. On October 28, 2008 VW shares briefly touched €1,005.01, up four-fold from €210.52 on 24 October, making VW the world's most valuable company—its market value greater than Apple, Philip Morris, and Intel combined. The shares fell back to €512 on October 29 and by November 26 were at €300.05. Porsche's shares went up to €62.60 on 23 October before falling to €52.95 on November 26, well above its low of €37.61 on 27 October.

Porsche made €6.83 billion gains on the options, a large part of overall profits of €8.6 billion for the year. Lower Saxony was another winner, its

20.1 percent of VW was worth €47 billion. Hedge funds betting on VW's share price falling lost €10–15 billion. Unable to hedge their exposure under the options and exposed to hedge funds that they financed or traded with, banks also took losses.

Like their precise handling cars, Porsche had cornered the market perfectly. The hedge funds had been caught in a classic short squeeze. Analysts questioned whether Porsche made cars or was a hedge fund with a few car plants. The company explained the difference: "We make money from hedging and building cars. The difference is that hedge funds don't make cars the last time I checked."[22]

Fast Cornering

Hedge funds complained that Porsche manipulated the market in VW shares, taking advantage of inside information to profit at the hedge fund's expense. Porsche denied the allegations, blaming the hedge funds that chose to take positions. Porsche argued that it had used derivatives to hedge the price of the planned purchase of VW shares, in compliance with German laws.

The surprise of the hedge funds was surprising. Porsche repeatedly stated its intentions regarding VW publicly. Porsche's financial statements disclosed its option trading. On October 8, 2008, a Morgan Stanley analyst, Adam Jonas, warned against playing "billionaire's poker," drawing attention to the size of the short position on VW relative to the free float. Earlier, on February 27, 2008, JP Morgan identified the risk of a short squeeze, predicting that Porsche would continue to increase its stake in VW.[23] Porsche made disclosures, giving investors who short sold VW the opportunity to manage their positions and risks.

When their arguments did not gain traction, hedge funds argued that the trades, while legal, were not within the spirit of the law. They argued about the "lack of transparency" and "reputational damage" to the German financial markets. A trader complained that: "This sort of behavior by a public company wouldn't be allowed in the UK or U.S. But we can't expect help from the German authorities—this is pay back."[24]

One analyst reported: "I have hedge fund managers literally in tears on the phone."[25] Putting a brave face on the loss, Larry Robbins, the chief executive of Glenview Capital, wrote to investors that the fund was "committed to maintaining the short exposure for the eventual recoupling between the stock and its intrinsic value." David Einhorn told investors that it expected to profit as "on a fundamental basis, we believe that Volkswagen is highly overvalued."[26]

Bundesanstalt für Finanzdienstleistungsaufsicht (BaFin), the German financial regulator, launched a market manipulation probe, investigating the circumstances around Porsche building its stake in VW. Hedge funds and investors commenced legal proceedings, alleging that Porsche, Wiedeking, and Holger misled investors and lied about the positions and intentions with respect to VW. In December 2010, a U.S. federal court dismissed the lawsuit against Porsche and two of its former managers.

Contemptuous of hedge funds and private equity investors, Germans were secretly pleased. Wiedeking and Härter were folk heroes who beat the London and New York hedge funds at their own game. The headline from *Neues Deutschland*, the former East German newspaper, read: "Porsche eats the locusts."

Porsche's victory was pyrrhic. When the options expired, Porsche's option gains were the difference between the guaranteed price and actual market price for VW shares. Porsche still needed money to actually purchase the VW shares. As the financial crisis hit and banks became reluctant to lend, Porsche was unable to raise the cash to complete the takeover. In May 2009, Porsche dropped its takeover plans, announcing plans to merge with VW. In June 2009, Porsche announced the Gulf State of Qatar would take a 25 percent stake in the combined company to reduce its level of debt.

In November 2009, Porsche revealed losses of €4.4 billion before tax and announced that it expected a further multibillion euro loss the following year. The company would eventually become just another marque brand in the VW range. Wiedeking, who turned the near-bankrupt Porsche in the early 1990s into one of the world most profitable carmakers, left the company.

The whisky-drinking, cigar-smoking Wiedeking was one of the highest paid managers in the world, taking home a reputed €60–80 million. Accepting an award in 2003, he joked that at Porsche: "We produce nothing but superfluous things. That is very rewarding because superfluous things cannot be replaced by even more superfluous things."[27] Superfluous things had come to be dominated by the ultimate superfluity, extreme money.

One investor thought that Porsche would: "struggle to sell 911s to hedge-fund managers for years and years to come."[28] Wiedeking showed no Schadenfreude at the losses of the hedge funds: "We all have to get used to the fact that quick money is not a healthy business. Values played no role in what happened."[29]

Children of Privilege

The economist Hyman Minsky theorized that in the early stages of a business cycle money is only available to creditworthy borrowers, known ironically as *hedge finance*. As the cycle develops, financial conditions look rosy and competing lenders extend money to marginal borrowers, a phase known as *speculative finance* and ultimately *Ponzi finance*. The cycle ends in a *Minsky moment* when the supply of money slows or shuts off. Borrowers unable to meet financial obligations try to sell assets, leading to a collapse in prices that triggers a spiral of economic decline.

Hedge funds are *Minsky machines*. They borrow to purchase assets, a strategy that works in moderation. Increased borrowing to buy assets artificially boosts asset values, generating profits that allow further leverage until the supply of money ceases. When the asset price bubble eventually bursts, the pressure to liquidate assets triggers losses, triggering a run on the funds, leading to larger losses and failure. Minsky machines are creatures of stable, benign environments that through their actions create the conditions for instability and their own demise. Ian Macfarlane, the former governor of the Australian Central Bank, observed: "Hedge funds have become the privileged children of the international financial scene, being entitled to the benefits of free markets without any of the responsibilities."[30]

Hedge fund managers themselves take few risks. As Alan Howard, co-founder of Brevan Howard, a large London-based hedge fund, put it: "I have no interest in getting excited or upset." After an accident, Howard, known in London's trading community as "Mr. Bond," gave up skiing. He does not even drive, to avoid the dangers of London traffic: "I see all these nutty drivers."[31] In a "heads I win tails you lose world," only investors and lenders are at risk.

In 2008 Warren Buffett, the CEO of Berkshire Hathaway, bet $1 million with Protégé Partners, a New York fund of hedge funds, that even a rigorously selected portfolio of hedge funds would not beat the return on the market over 10 years. Buffett argued that large fees mean that hedge funds have to earn substantially greater returns than the S&P 500 index to match let alone beat its performance.[32] The Buffet bet paralleled a $20,000 wager between Lotus founder Mitchell Kapor and futurist Ray Kurzweil that by 2029 no computer or machine intelligence will pass the Turing Test, where a computer successfully impersonates a human being.

In 2010, Stanley Druckenmiller, who had been one of the traders at Soros' Quantum Fund that broke the pound, announced that he was closing his fund Duquesne Capital Management. Druckenmiller confessed that increased volatility following the global financial crisis made it difficult to make money. It suggested a difficult outlook for Minsky machines.[33]

Make Money Not War

Known as "Woodstock for capitalists," Berkshire Hathaway's annual shareholder meeting in the Qwest Center in Omaha, Nebraska, is characterized by folksy, comic wisdom. Hedgestock, the "Woodstock for hedge funds," was short on such self-deprecating humor.

Investment banks sponsored Hedgestock, their way of "putting something back." Proceeds went to the Teenage Cancer Trust. The image of hedge funds needed to be softened, brought into line with societal norms.

Knebworth House was chosen as the location because of its history of legendary concerts featuring Led Zeppelin, Queen, and Oasis, and its proximity to London, the hedge fund capital of Europe. Entry to Hedgestock was £500 plus VAT (value added tax) and limited to 4,000 guests. The original Woodstock was attended by around half a million, most of whom simply turned up and did not pay anything.

There was talk of vintage Woodstock-era VW camper vans, costumes, and dress codes of the psychedelic 1960s. On the day, hedge fund managers turned up in Porsches, BMWs, Mercs, Ferraris, and the odd Bentley. The preppy cool dress code was out of *The Graduate*. Only the organizers wore tie-dyed shirts and jeans. BlackBerries and mobile phones were conspicuous.

Hedgestock's house rules were *new age*. There was a 10:30 p.m. curfew. Drugs were *verboten* but the Pimm's and champagne bar traded actively. There were raincoats to counter risk, the UK's fickle weather. As for promiscuity, there were debates on "Esoterica—new risk and new returns for consenting adults" or "Insourcing or outsourcing—how saucy are you?" or "Multi strat versus fund of funds: strange bedfellows."

The original Woodstock is mostly associated with rain, mud, and bad acid (LSD) by the few people who were there and can actually remember it. Hedgestock promised alternative entertainment—poker tournaments and other forms of betting—to allow the hedge fund managers to exercise their natural animal instincts, testosterone, and considerable egos.

The entertainment draw card or *kick asset* concert was The Who—at least, its surviving members: Pete Townshend and Roger Daltrey. The occasion did not however rival the memory of the band's legendary performance at the original Woodstock. One reporter observed of the audience: "I've seen more passion at Waitrose [a UK retail grocery chain] on a Friday night."[34]

Woodstock's anthem was "make love not war." Hedgestock's less catchy mantra was "make money not war." As John Kenneth Galbraith, the American economist, noted: "Wealth, in even the most improbable cases, manages to convey the aspect of intelligence."

The 30-year history of financial alchemy is the rise of private equity, securitization, derivatives, and ultimately the Masters of the Universe and their Minsky machines. The growth of these instruments owed everything to financial fundamentalism.

Woodstock marked an end, not a beginning. It was a celebration and high watermark of the counterculture. Within a few years, its iconic stars, Jimi Hendrix and Janis Joplin, would be dead. Hedgestock, too, may have marked an end—the high watermark of financial alchemy.

Part IV

Oligarchy

Oligarchy—government by a powerful, dominant class with deep-vested interests.

Extreme money created a powerful coalition of financiers, business interests, regulators, and politicians that increasingly dominated the economy. This oligarchy set the agenda and set policies, which benefited them and their constituencies. Similar backgrounds, education, and interests, especially a common cognitive view of the world, shaped the oligarchy.

17

War Games

The age of capital was the conscious creation of policymakers and regulators. Central banks even played *war games* to test their ability to deal with a financial crisis.

In 2002 the U.S. military staged the Millennium Challenge, the largest war game, costing over $250 million and featuring an attack on an unknown oil-rich Middle East country. The good guys, the Blue Force, defeated the bad guys, the Red Force, vindicating Donald Rumsfeld's new high-tech warfare.

But the Red Force, under iconoclastic retired Marine General Paul Van Riper, actually won the battle, using unconventional strategies. Riper used small boats and planes to sink the Blue Fleet, which if it had really occurred would have been the worst naval defeat since Pearl Harbor. Riper's Red Force communicated via motorbikes and the muezzin's calls to prayer, avoiding the Blue Force's electronic surveillance and destruction of Van Riper's command and communication infrastructure. The Red Force changed its position and tactics repeatedly, combating the superior strength of the Blue Force.

When it became clear that the Blue Force would not prevail, the script was rewritten for the right result. For Riper, the games were a "mistruth": "There's very little intellectual activity.... What happens is a number of people are put into a room, given some sort of a slogan and told to write to the slogan. That's not the way to generate new ideas."[1] Like the Millennium Challenge, modern economies were built upon incorrect theories and flawed belief systems in a triumph of expediency over inconvenient truths.

In their war games, central bankers looked at bank failures and even the effects of a flu pandemic, but failed to grasp the flimsy foundations of the entire financial system. As Jeremy Grantham, chairman of investment manager GMO, remarked: "I want to emphasize how little I understand all of the intricate workings of the global financial system. I hope that someone else gets it, because I don't."[2]

Borrowed Times

The brave new economy was built on debt. Individuals borrowed to buy houses, cars, gadgets, or take holidays. They borrowed to get an education, to get healthcare. They even borrowed to save, using debt-financed investments. Companies borrowed to invest and to buy each other. They borrowed to pay dividends or repurchase their own stock.

Governments in Australia and the UK swore off debt. But at the first sign of trouble, they fell off the wagon, borrowing furiously. America borrowed in good times because it could and borrowed in bad times because it needed to. Vice-President Dick Cheney stated: "Reagan proved deficits don't matter."[3]

Borrowing levels, especially household, and government, increased rapidly. Figure 17.1 sets out the rapid build-up in debt in the United States. Others—British, Canadians, Australian and New Zealanders—also started to live on borrowed time. Even in the traditionally abstemious eurozone countries, household debt rose from 49 percent of GDP at the end of 1999 to 63 percent by mid-2009. The growth in European debt was driven mainly by the "Club Med" countries (Spain, Portugal, Italy, Greece) as well as Ireland. But other economies also ran up debt, mainly government debt, to finance social spending and entitlements. Savings of thrifty Germans and Asians were recycled to the borrowers and back again as payments for goods they sold.

In *Hamlet*, Polonius counseled: "Neither a borrower nor a lender be; for loan oft loses both itself and friend, and borrowing dulls the edge of husbandry." It was advice for a different time.

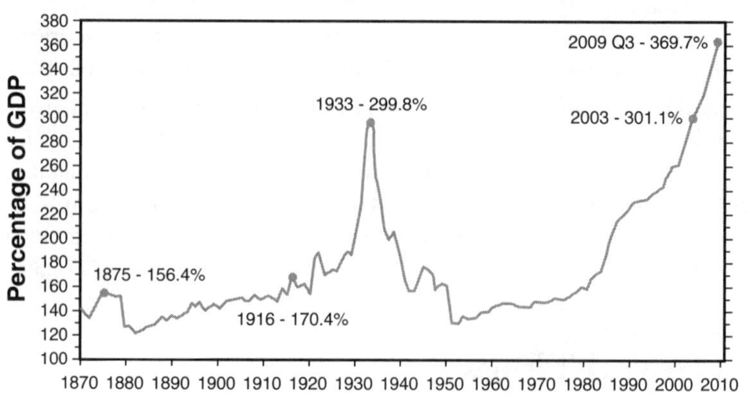

Source: U.S. Bureau of Economic Analysis, Federal Reserve, Census Bureau.

Figure 17.1 U.S. debt levels as a percentage of GDP

Saving is consumption deferred. Borrowing accelerates consumption, providing instant gratification. All debt borrows from tomorrow to pay for today. To be sustainable, future income must be sufficient to pay the interest and repay the loan. But much of the borrowing in the new economy was now unproductive, financing consumption or larger houses that did not produce income. Earnings from investments were frequently insufficient to meet interest and principal payments.

Debt was inextricably linked to the value of assets, especially houses purchased with borrowed money. Figure 17.2 shows the relationship between the supply of debt and the price of assets.

Assume an investor uses $20 of its own money—equity—and borrows $80 (80 percent of the value) to purchase an asset for $100. If the asset increases in value by 10 percent to $110, then the investor's equity increases on paper to $30 ($110 minus the fixed amount of debt of $80). If the investor maintains its leverage at 5 times then it can buy $150 of assets (funded by $30 of equity and $120 of debt). If the investor can now leverage 6 times then it can buy $180 of assets (funded by $30 of equity and $150 of debt). The investor still only has its original $20 investment in cash, unless it sells the asset to realize its paper gains, which can vanish. But now, this $20 supports even more debt, as much as $160 (the $180 of assets that the investor can buy if it leverages 6 times less its original investment). The real leverage is around 9 times, which means an 11 percent fall in the value of the asset purchased can wipe out the investor's wealth entirely.

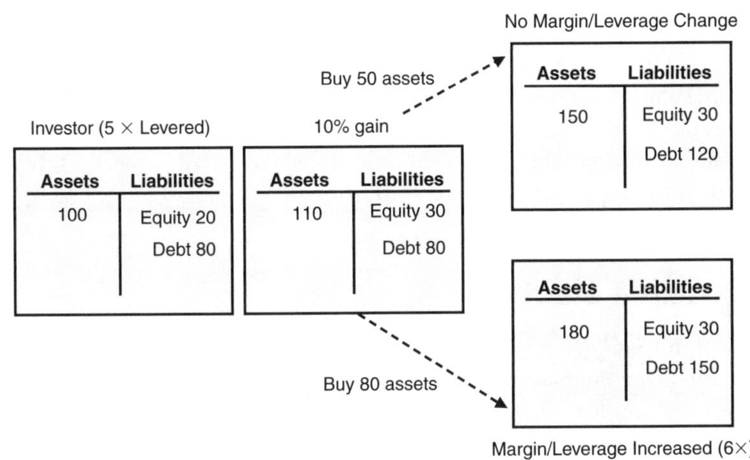

Figure 17.2 Asset purchases using borrowings

Where the supply of assets does not increase as quickly as the supply of debt, the price increases allow the process to continue. Many borrowers could not pay the interest on their debt, needing prices to rise to allow them to borrow more to repay the original loan. The gains are fictitious until converted to cash by selling the asset and paying off the debt. Where prices are rising, no one wants to give up future gains, leaving everyone vulnerable to prices falling.

In America and the UK, increasing paper wealth encouraged reduced savings. The future relied on a spiral of guaranteed rising prices.

Alan Greenspan theorized that "a rising, debt-to-income ratio for households or of total non-financial debt to GDP" did not signify stress but was "a reflection of dispersion of a growing financial imbalance of economic entities that in turn reflects the irreversible up-drift in division of labor and specialization."[4] In 2005, Ben Bernanke, Greenspan's successor as chairman of the US Federal Reserve, provided an apology for high levels of debt: "Concerns about debt should be allayed by the fact that household assets (particularly housing wealth) have risen even more quickly than household liabilities."[5] In the *Great Moderation*, debt-driven speculation drove prosperity.

For Bernanke, it was not even a debt problem but a savings problem. He blamed the Germans, Japanese and Chinese for saving too much.[6] America was being "neighborly," helping out. After the global crisis, in a case of severe cognitive dissonance, Bernanke continued to blame the foreign savers for the problems.[7]

In 1933, the economist Irving Fisher identified the danger: "over-investment and over-speculation are often important; but they would have far less serious results were they not conducted with borrowed money."[8] In 2005, William White, chief economist at the Bank of International Settlement, broke ranks by warning that easy money was creating a boom that would end painfully, reflecting "the size of the real imbalances that, preceded it." He warned "mistakes...take a long time to work off."[9]

Liquidity Factory

Cotton Candy (candyfloss or fairy floss) is spun sugar, consisting mostly of air. Financial engineering spun real money, expanding it into ever-larger servings—*candyfloss money*.[10] Figure 17.3 sets out the modern money pyramid.

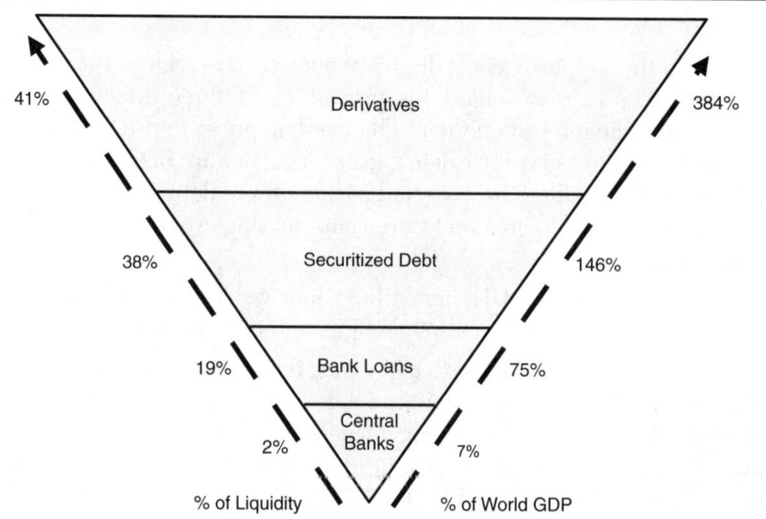

Source: David Roche, Independent Strategy (www.instrategy.com). Reproduced with permission.

Figure 17.3 The new liquidity factory

Until the mid-1980s the money that existed in the world consisted primarily of funds created by central banks (notes, reserves and money held by financial institutions with the central bank) and bank loans. By 2006, this traditional money made up only 21 percent of the total liquidity available. Central banks and bank loans consisted of 2 percent and 19 percent of available money respectively. In dollar terms, central bank money was equivalent to around $4 trillion (7 percent of global GDP of around $56 trillion). Bank loans were around $42 trillion (75 percent of global GDP).

The new liquidity factory or market-based credit[11] was based on financial alchemy. Securitization and derivatives now provided most of the money, around 79 percent of total liquidity. Around 38 percent of global money was in the form of securitization, around $82 trillion (146 percent of global GDP). Around 41 percent was in the form of derivative contracts, around $215 trillion (384 percent of global GDP).[12] The astonishing growth in global liquidity was driven by financialization.

Banks moved assets off-balance sheet into the opaque, unregulated shadow banking system. The shadow banks depended on short-term debt from professional money markets to fund long-term, illiquid assets. Borrowing against the value of the assets, they were vulnerable to falls in their price. Banks increased the volume of lending and risk, confident in their ability to transfer them to the shadow banks.

Fund manager Pimco's Paul McCulley identified the trend:

> The bottom line is simple; shadow banks use funding instruments that are not just as good as old-fashioned [government]-protected deposits. But it was a great gig so long as the public bought the notion that such funding instruments were "just as good" as bank deposits—more leverage, less regulation and more asset freedom were a path to (much) higher returns on equity in shadow banks than conventional banks.[13]

The liquidity factory increased debt to levels without historical parallel. The tsunami of debt fuelled price increases in equity, property, infrastructure, and commodities.

Cotton candy eventually collapses into a sticky mess that is a fraction of its original size. In the financial crisis, the entire money pile would collapse in a similar way, entangling the global economy.

Six Degrees of Separation

John Guare's *Six Degrees of Separation* popularized the idea that everyone is no more than six steps away from any other person on Earth. Guare's play borrows from Hungarian Frigyes Karinthy's story *Chains or Chain Link*: "using no more than five individuals, one of whom is a personal acquaintance, [you] could contact the selected individual using nothing except the network of personal acquaintances."[14] Financial institutions were now similarly linked through complex networks.

Securitization and derivatives were supposed to deliver a safer financial system. Donald Kohn, vice-chairman of the Federal Reserve, argued that *originate and distribute* would "enable risk and return to be divided and priced to better meet the needs of borrowers and lenders...permit previously illiquid obligations to be securitized and traded." Derivatives would convert risk into another commodity to be traded, making "obsolete previous divisions among types of financial intermediaries and across geographical regions in which they operate." The new business model made "banks and other financial institutions 'more robust' and [make] the financial system 'more resilient and flexible' and better able to absorb shocks without increasing the effects of such shocks on the real economy."[15]

Originate and hide was a more accurate description. Complex chains of transactions allowed risk and debt to move from a place where it was observable to places where it was hidden and unregulated. Trading linked market participants in networks of relationships and interdependence. Bear Stearns was linked to 5,000 parties via 750,000 contracts. Lehman Brothers had more than a 1 million contracts with a notional value of $40 trillion, including more than $5 trillion in credit default swaps alone.

Having insured banks against risk, if AIG was unable to perform under the contracts then the banks lost twice—on the risk hedged and on its hedge for which it had paid. If one bank had financial problems then banks that dealt with it were exposed to losses. If required to post collateral, AIG needed to raise money or sell assets. If AIG sold assets, then as prices fell other holders suffered losses, forcing them to sell their holdings or post additional collateral. It was the epidemiology of sexually transmitted diseases—it wasn't who you had sex with, but whom those people had slept with, and so on.

At each stage in the chains of risk, information was lost. Figure 17.4 sets out the information lost in the process of securitizing mortgages. Everybody now relied on someone else to do their risk analysis. William Heyman, former head of market regulation at the US SEC, observed: "In manufacturing, the market price is set by the smartest guy with the best, cheapest production process. In securities markets, the price is set by the dumbest guy with the most money to lose."[16]

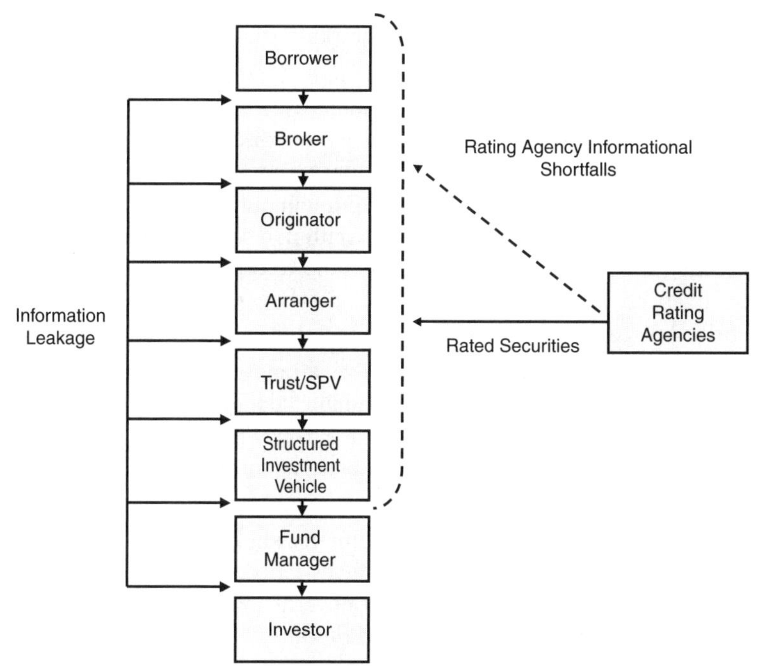

Source: Adapted from BIS Committee on the Global Financial System.

Figure 17.4 Information asymmetries in securitization

Paper Chains

These risk chains relied on voluminous documents, which only lawyers read but without necessarily understanding what was going on. As became apparent later, the legal basis for some transactions was also flawed. The key to mortgages is the *note*, the actual IOU where the borrower agrees to pay back the loan. Only the note holder has legal standing to ask a court to foreclose and evict delinquent borrowers from their homes.

When loans are repackaged into securities, the title to the loan must be transferred to one or more SPVs, where the loan is sliced and diced. Once securitized, the loan is entirely virtual as the different MBS tranche holders do not own the loan but have complex claims against payments made by the borrower.

The MERS (*Mortgage Electronic Registration System*) was created to hold the digitized notes from the actual mortgage loans. Somewhere, the chain of title was broken; the transfer of ownership and the note was not done correctly. The holder of the loan or MBS could not prove ownership.

The person who took out the mortgage no longer knew whom to pay. The lender could not foreclose and sell the property to recover the money lent.

As more and more mortgages became delinquent and foreclosures increased, lawyers acting on behalf of home-owners and courts looked into the chain of title, finding the botched paperwork. *Foreclosure mills*, law firms specializing in foreclosures, allegedly faked and falsified documentation to repair the chain of title on delinquent mortgages. In one firm, a woman deceased in 1995 miraculously continued to sign foreclosure documents until 2008—a phenomenon that came to be known as *robo signing*. On her website (www.nakedcapitalism.com), blogger Yves Smith even put up a price list from companies specializing in these types of services.

The U.S. government launched investigations and banks were forced to stop foreclosures. Unless remedied, the faulty documentation would mean that delinquent mortgagors would not have to pay back their loans, increasing the losses to lenders and holders of repackaged mortgage loans.

CDO^2 transactions re-securitizing MBSs could involve 93,750,000 mortgages and 1,125,000,300 pages of documentation. The Bank of England's Andrew Haldane recommended that investors deal with the complexity "with a Ph.D. in mathematics under one arm and a Diploma in speed-reading under the other." He concluded that the task would "have tried the patience of even the most diligent investor." This meant that "with no time to read the small-print, the instruments were instead devoured whole" and "food poisoning and a lengthy loss of appetite have been the predictable consequences."[17]

Toxic Pathologies

Financial systems now comprised a small number of financial hubs with multiple linkages. Between 1985 and 2005 a Bank of England's analysis of financial networks showed that the linkages had become markedly more dense, complex and concentrated between countries and institutions within countries.[18] The system was very vulnerable to disturbances. Problems were transmitted rapidly through the tightly linked system.

The linkages were exacerbated because major players had near-identical business models and risk management practices. Everybody wanted to be Goldman Sachs, JP Morgan or Deutsche Bank, concentrating on the latest fashionable products, equity derivatives, structured credit or prime brokerage. In 1994 Charles Bowsher, comptroller general of the USA, identified the risk: "The sudden failure or abrupt withdrawal from trading of any of these large US dealers could cause liquidity problems in the markets and could also pose risks to others and the financial system as a whole." Anticipating the events of 2008, he warned that this could require "a financial bailout paid for or guaranteed by taxpayers."[19]

In a 2005 paper, economist Hyun Song Shin argued that financial markets are relatively calm and orderly most of the time. In the case of a crisis, all participants rush to decrease their risk, leading to heightened instability and potentially complete breakdown. Markets exhibited *synchronous lateral excitation* when "individuals react to what's happening around them, and where individuals' actions affect the outcomes."[20] It was a sophisticated version of yelling "fire" in a crowded theatre.

In 2006, central banks, responsible for financial stability, assessed the financial system as being healthy. They did not see any emerging threats. In August 2008, central bankers, regulators and bankers were reluctantly forced to admit that:

> As late as the summer of 2007, virtually none of us...imagined that, as of July of 2008, financial sector write-offs and loss provisions would approach $500 billion...the underlying complexity and risk characteristics of certain financial instruments were so opaque that even some of the most sophisticated financial institutions in the world and their supervisors were simply caught off guard.[21]

The entire system was an accident waiting to happen. Charles Calomiris, an economic historian, wrote in 2008 that: "The most severe financial [crises] typically arise when rapid growth in untested financial innovations...[coincides] with...an abundance of the supply of credit."[22]

Relying on the Zohar

Financial crises were increasingly the result of the toxic pathologies inherent in the financial system, rather than economic downturns, geopolitical events or natural disasters.[23] Economic cycles became less pronounced as a result of government actions, improvements in information, monetary and fiscal policies. At the same time, risk increased, driven by the structure of markets, flawed regulatory regimes and volatile capital flows.

Trading shifted risk within the system in complex ways. While hedge funds and banks provided liquidity and dispersed risk, they placed large bets on the same event using different instruments increasing risk. The relationship between hedge funds and banks that financed and traded with them created risk concentrations. Pricing, risk management and valuation of instruments relied on very similar models that did not capture the behavior of the underlying market, asset price dynamics and limitations in trading liquidity and funding.

Risk managers with a "brain the size of a caraway seed and the imagination of a parsnip"[24] slavishly used inadequate techniques. Like the philosopher of science Thomas Kuhn, financial markets persisted with flawed models, arguing that they worked in normal conditions and were superior to alternatives. David Einhorn compared risk systems to: "an airbag which works all the time except when you get into a crash."[25]

Financiers were reluctant to use qualitative approaches that were inconsistent with their scientific self-image. As Benoit Mandelbrot, the creator of *chaos theory*, observed: "Human Nature yearns to see order and hierarchy in the world. It will invent it if it cannot find it."[26]

Psychologist B.F. Skinner created "superstitious pigeons." Unlike in normal experiments, he fed the pigeons with no reference to the bird's behavior. Even though the food was given out on a fixed schedule, each bird developed its own superstitious behavior, trying to uncover a pattern associated with food. One pigeon turned counter-clockwise about the cage, another repeatedly thrust its head into an upper corner of the cage, while others developed a pendulum motion of the head and body. Financial models were like the behavior of the superstitious pigeons.

Mathematical finance lent credibility and false precision to the dismal reality of risk management. A South Vietnamese officer questioned about U.S. Defense Secretary Robert MacNamara's application of quantitative methodology to the Vietnam War replied: "Ah 'Les Statistiques.' Your secretary of defense loves statistics. We Vietnamese can give him all he wants. If you want them to go up, they will go up. If you want them to go down, they will go down."[27]

Mastery of risk had not enabled human beings to overcome the notion that the future was divine whim or chance. Financial economists and risk management just replaced oracles and soothsayers. Banks and regulators relied on the power of the Zohar, a 23-volume, $415 work essential to the study of the Kabbalah: "By simply possessing the books, power, protection, and fulfillment came into their lives."[28]

Blind Capital

A wall of liquidity drove the global economy: "[There are] capital flows around the market from what feels like limitless sources—from CDOs, CLOs, hedge funds, private equity and recycled foreign trade surpluses."[29] Steven Rattner, founder of hedge fund Quadrangle, told *The Wall Street Journal* on June 18, 2007: "No exaggeration is required to pronounce unequivocally that money is available today in quantities, at prices and on terms never before seen in the 100-plus years since U.S. financial markets reached full flower."[30]

But the new economy was a toxic mix of increasing debt, risk, speculation, and "unrealistic aspirations and the expectations that they can be fulfilled."[31] British clinical psychologist Oliver James noted that great swathes of the population "believe that they can become rich and famous."[32] Dinner parties reverberated with: "Did you hear how much they got for the house down the road?"[33]

Reinventing its traditional economy of fishing and geothermal energy, Iceland, a country of 330,000, became a global banking player—"Wall Street on the tundra."[34] Icelandic bank Kaupthing (meaning "marketplace") aspired to be the Goldman Sachs of the Arctic. Icelandic firms owned Eastern Europe's telecommunication firms, well-known UK high street retailers such as House of Fraser, Arcadia and Hamleys and much of the Nordic banking system. When Bakkavor, an Icelandic food company, purchased Geest, creating UK's largest ready-made food company, Ólafur Ragnar Grímsson, the CEO, explained where the money was coming from: "It comes from Barclays Bank."[35]

With local interest rates at an asphyxiating 15.5 percent, ordinary Icelanders borrowed Japanese yen, Swiss francs or euros at low rates to buy houses. Fishermen did the same, until financial profits overwhelmed piscatorial earnings. The risk of devaluation of the krona, Iceland's currency, against the borrowing currencies was ignored. Writing about the Mississippi Company speculation of 1719/20, Matthieu Marais, an advocate in the Parisian Parliament, noted: "It is trade where you do not understand anything, where all precautions are useless, where the most enlightened spirit doesn't see a flicker and which turns according to the designs of the Movement of the Machines. Yet all the fate of the Kingdom depends on it."[36]

Prime Minister David Oddsson, a key architect of Iceland's transformation, was heavily influenced by Friedman, Hayek, Thatcher and Reagan. He lowered taxes, privatized government-owned assets, reduced trade restrictions and deregulated the banking system. In 2005, Iceland even hosted a meeting of the Mont Pelerin Society, the free-market think tank associated with Hayek and Friedman.

Iceland was quintessentially American in its "can do attitude." Anticipating Barrack Obama's "Yes, we can!" call to arms, Sigurdur Einarsson, the CEO of Kaupthing, told employees of his then small brokerage firm: "If you think you can, you can."[37] Tony Shearer, CEO of Singer & Friedlander, an English bank, acquired by Kaupthing, observed: "They were very different. They ran their business in a very strange way. Everyone there was incredibly young. They were all from the same community in Reykjavík. And they had no idea what they were doing."[38]

Iceland had absorbed the key lesson of the new economy: buy as many assets as possible with borrowed money because asset prices only rise. Between 2002 and 2007 Icelanders increased their ownership of foreign assets by 50 times. When the financial crisis hit, Americans could point to Iceland and say: "Well, at least we didn't do that."[39]

Rent Collectors

Warren Buffet tells a story about a soapbox orator speaking to a Wall Street audience about the evils of drugs. At the end, he asked if there were any questions. One investment banker asked: "Yeah, who makes the needles?" Now bankers made the needles and the most of the opportunity. In the virtual age, anonymous bankers set about shaping the modern world—or, at least, its economy. Banks grew in size, increasing their lending and growing their balance sheets.

Between 1980 and 2008, the total debt of U.S. financial firms grew from around 20 percent of GDP to slightly greater than 100 percent. In the United Kingdom, the total size of the banks reached more than 4 times the country's GDP, well above the United States but also larger than other countries reliant on the financial services sector such as Switzerland and the Netherlands. In the 4 years to October 2008, RBS (formerly the Royal Bank of Scotland) tripled the size of its balance sheet to more than £1.9 trillion (over $3 trillion), 15 times the size of the Scottish economy and larger than the UK's GDP of £1.5 trillion ($2.7 trillion). In Iceland, between 2003 and 2007, the assets of the three largest banks grew from a few billion dollars to more than $140 billion, "the most rapid expansion of a banking system in the history of mankind."[40]

America made less but bought more from Germany, Japan, and China, paying with newly printed IOUs. As its financial sector grew, UK manufacturing fell from more than 30 percent in 1970 to 11 percent of the economy in 2009. The people employed in the sector fell to 2.6 million workers or 10 percent of the workforce from 6.9 million or around 28 percent in 1978. According to the World Intellectual Property Organization, UK ranked below North Korea in terms of number of patents granted.

In 2007, the U.S. financial sector's share of domestic corporate profits reached a peak of 41 percent, up from 21 percent to 30 percent in the 1990s. Between 1973 and 1985 the financial sector's share was below 16 percent. Between the early 1980s and 2007, the combined value of these firms grew from 6 percent to 23 percent of the stock market. Between 1996 and 2007 alone, the profits of finance companies in the S&P500 increased from $65 billion to $232 billion, or from 19.5 percent to 27 percent of the total. In tiny Australia, bank profits rose from 1 percent of GDP to 6 percent between 1960 and 2010, tripling in the last 10 years.

Compensation levels rose sharply, to 181 percent of the average for U.S. private industry. Between 1948 and 1982 they had been between 99 percent and 108 percent. In 2006 and 2007, Wall Street bonuses totaled $34.3 billion and $33 billion respectively, an increase from $9.8 billion in 2002.

Financiers earned large *economic rents*—excess earnings above the amount required to ensure adequate supply of the goods or services. Free markets and competition should reduce economic rents. But the structure of financial markets, especially the lack of transparency, ensured high profitability. Specialized products, combined with information and skill asymmetries between banks and customers, created profit opportunities. Investors hired advisers, who hired consultants, who hired fund managers, who hired other fund managers, who bought products from banks, who laid off the risk with other banks or investors. Everybody along the chain earned a share of the action.

There is no "try before you buy" with financial products. Marketed on the basis of past returns, complex and long-term in nature, financial products lend themselves to economic rent seeking. When fund management fees were reduced by migration to low-cost index tracking funds, investment managers tempted investors into new higher margin products, structured investments, private equity and hedge funds, with the promise of high returns. Simple derivatives were repackaged into complicated and opaque exotic structures to increase profit margins.

High rewards encouraged the best and brightest to sign up, helping create newer more complex products. Ragnar Arnason, a professor of fishing economics at the University of Iceland, found that: "Everyone was learning Black-Scholes.... The schools of engineering and math were offering courses on financial engineering."[41]

Best in Best Possible World

All financial bubbles start with a convincing and plausible theory of "this time it's different." It may be new technology (railways, cars, computers, or the Internet) or new markets (China). People start to extrapolate boldly into regions where common sense has never gone before, leading to over-investment helped by easy money and excess credit. Rising debt drives up asset prices leading to even more debt that cannot be supported by values or income produced.

The system is underpinned by faith in the competence of legislators, regulators and the chattering classes—commentators, gurus and financial journalists. Faux theories, such as Alan Greenspan and Ben Bernanke's *Great Moderation*, reassure investors that old problems have been overcome. Moral hazard increases as excessive risk taking and speculation become commonplace. There are increases in *beezle*[42]—fraud or embezzlement—as sharp people take advantage of the favorable conditions and abundance of money.

As Dr. Pangloss, professor of "metaphysico-theologo-cosmolo-nigology" in Voltaire's *Candide*, knew: "All is for the best in the best of all possible worlds." Bankers were the best of the best. Nick Sibley, former managing director of Jardine Fleming, predicted the result: "Giving liquidity to bankers is like giving a barrel of beer to a drunk. You know exactly what is going to happen. You just don't know which wall he is going to choose."[43]

Until 2007 prices went up, and everybody made money. In 1856 Walter Bagehot wrote:

> At particular times a great deal of stupid people have a great deal of stupid money.... At intervals...the money of these people—the blind capital, as we call it—of the country is particularly large and craving; it seeks for someone to devour it, and there is a "plethora"; it finds someone, and there is "speculation"; it is devoured, and there is "panic."[44]

Visiting the London School of Economics in November 2008, Queen Elizabeth asked why nobody saw the global financial crisis coming. The real reason why economists were unprepared was simple. In a wonderfully titled blog, "The unfortunate uselessness of most 'state of the art' academic monetary economics," economist Willem Buiter pointed out that for decades economic research had become "haiku like,"[45] preoccupied by its internal logic and aesthetic puzzles. It was largely uninterested in how the economy really worked. It completely ignored how the economy would work in times of stress and financial instability because such conditions were deemed impossible in the new age.[46]

In June 2009, Professors Tim Besley and Peter Hennessy drafted a letter to Her Majesty summarizing the views of the economic establishment. Many economists had apparently foreseen the crisis, merely failing to specifically identify the timing of its onset, specific dynamics and extent. The economists hoped to "develop a new shared, horizon-scanning capability so that you never need to ask that question again."[47]

Nobody really understood how risky the economy had become or how it functioned. The economy grew and people prospered, as their houses and retirement savings increased in value. Company earnings rose every quarter. People talked about quick four-bagger and five bagger returns (a four-bagger is four times or 400 percent return). As Walter Bagehot knew: "People are most credulous when they are happy...when money has been made."[48]

In the film *Transformers*, a meditation on the dangers of advanced technology, a mobile phone turns into a homicidal robot. Advanced finance posed the same danger to the global economy.

In David Hare's play *The Power of Yes*, a central banker identifies the moment the crisis hit the UK. At a celebratory opening night dinner for a conference celebrating the era of stability and confidence, everyone was complacent. At least, they were until one staff member reported to the Governor of the Bank of England that the imminent demise of Northern Rock was being reported in the news.[49]

18

Shell Games

In the new economy, central banks and bank regulators were all-powerful. In 2005, David Oddsson, the former prime minister of Iceland, became governor of Iceland's Central Bank. Economist Brad DeLong mused: "It is either our curse or our blessing that we live in the Republic of the Central Banker."[1]

In 1933, President Roosevelt argued for financial regulation:

> The money changers have fled from their high seats in the temple of our civilization. We may now restore that temple to the ancient truths.... There must be strict supervision of all banking and credits and investments; there must be an end to speculation with other people's money.[2]

Over time, the regulations were relaxed. Enacted to regulate the financial sector, the UK Financial Services Act 2001 specifically required the regulator "not to discourage the launch of new financial products" and avoid "erecting regulatory barriers."[3] Deregulation of financial markets now maintained the flow of money.

Central Bank Republics

Central bankers, led by Alan Greenspan, believed that lightly regulated markets promoted prosperity: "government regulation cannot substitute for individual integrity…the first and most effective line of defense against fraud and insolvency is counterparties' surveillance…. JP Morgan thoroughly scrutinizes the balance sheet of Merrill Lynch before it lends."[4] In 2008, defending deregulated markets, Greenspan stated: "You can have huge amounts of regulation and I will guarantee nothing will go wrong, but nothing will go right either."[5]

In his review of the global banking crisis, Lord Adair Turner noted that:

> An underlying assumption of financial regulation in the U.S., the UK and across the world has been that financial innovation is by definition beneficial, since market discipline will winnow out any unnecessary or value destructive innovations. As a result, regulators have not considered it their role to judge the value of different financial products, and they have in general avoided direct products regulation, certainly in wholesale markets with sophisticated investors.[6]

It was a matter of faith:

> Our soundness standards should be no more or no less stringent than those the market place would impose. If banks were unregulated, they would take on any amount of risk they wished, and the market would price their capital and debt accordingly.[7]

Capital held by banks and brokers against loss decreased, increasing their leverage. The definition of capital was expanded to include hybrid capital, debt ranking below deposits and senior borrowings. Cheaper than normal equity, hybrids avoided dilution of existing shareholders. Increases in debt and leverage reflected "improved financial flexibility…the results of massive improvements in technology and infrastructure."[8] Banks' liquidity reserves, designed to cover withdrawal of deposits, were reduced, freeing up money for lending. The risk was ignored: "The lack of a spare tire is of no concern if you do not get a flat."[9]

In 1999, commenting on the Asian crisis, Greenspan argued that the lack of well-developed financial markets in Asia had contributed to the problems. Economist Robert Wade disagreed:

> [Greenspan] and other U.S. officials see it as imperative to make sure that the troubles in Asia are blamed on the Asians and that free capital markets are seen as key to world economic recovery and advance; the idea that international capital markets are themselves the source of speculative disequilibria and retrogression must not be allowed to take root.[10]

The *Greenspan put* ensured that at the first sign of trouble central bankers—"pawnbrokers of last resort"[11]—flooded the system with money, lowering interest rates to protect risk takers. The strategy ensured successive, larger blow-ups in financial markets in 1987, 1991, 1994, 1998, 2001, and 2007. Martin Wolf, the chief economics writer for the *Financial Times*, argued: "What we have [in banking] is a risk-loving industry guaranteed as a public utility."[12]

Greenspan did not see any contradictions in the bailout of LTCM: "some moral hazard, however slight, may have been created by the Federal Reserve's involvement. Such negatives were outweighed by the risk of serious distortions to market prices had [LTCM] been pushed suddenly into bankruptcy."[13] As English philosopher Herbert Spencer knew: "the ultimate result of shielding men from the effects of folly is to fill the world with fools."

Games of Old Maid

Central bankers' assumption about securitization and derivatives reducing risk were wrong. Figure 18.1 shows how transferred credit risk finds its way back to the bank.

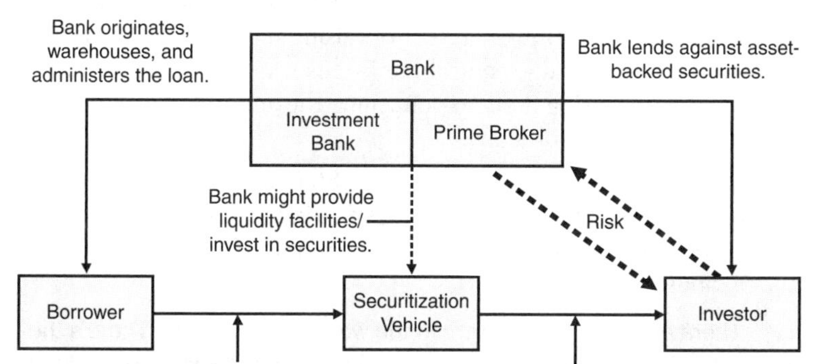

Figure 18.1 Risk transfer games

Where it sells risky loans, the bank may invest in the securities created, sometimes to reassure other investors. Banks also hold the loans until sold, exposing them to market disruptions. Banks provide *liquidity*, standby lines of credit, to SPVs to cover funding shortfalls. If the vehicle cannot fund, then the bank may be forced to lend against the assets that have supposedly been sold.

Risk also returns to the bank via the back door. Where a bank finances investors, such as hedge funds that use borrowing to increase returns, it is exposed to the securities lodged as surety. If the value of the securities used as collateral falls and the investor does not have the cash to meet the call for additional margin to cover the amount now owing, then the bank must sell the securities to recover the loan. Where illiquid structured assets created by the bank are used as collateral, they end up back on the bank's books. As

Charles Caleb Cotton observed in 1825: "There are some frauds so well conducted that it would be stupidity not to be deceived by them."

One commentator accurately pointed to the regulators' abject lack of understanding:

> Alan Greenspan was mistaken in believing that the largely unregulated hedge fund industry can be effectively controlled by regulating creditors... Creditors can be just as prone to greed as the latest wizard of Wall Street, but they are often the last to understand the risks that would ordinarily help fear counterbalance greed.[14]

Protection Rackets

Markets increasingly relied on bond ratings, opinions of the likelihood of payment of interest and principal based on mathematical models using historical default experience. Ratings determined whether investors could purchase particular securities, the cost of raising money and the parties you could deal with. Eventually, central banks enshrined the role of ratings in banking regulations, using them to determine the amount of capital required to be held against bonds or loans.

Moody's Investor Services (Moody's), Standard & Poor's (S&P), and Fitch controlled 95 percent of the ratings market. Moody's and S&P's combined market share was 80 percent. The columnist Tom Friedman pointed out the obvious:

> There are two super powers in the world in my opinion. There's the United States and there's Moody's Bond rating service. The United States can destroy you by dropping bombs, and Moody's can destroy you by downgrading your bonds. And believe me, it's not clear sometimes who's more powerful.[15]

Forbes rated the CEO of one of the rating agencies as the 35th most powerful man, just below Saddam Hussein.

Credit ratings involve conflicts of interest—do agencies work for investors who use their ratings, the companies they rate or banks that pay them to rate issues? Originally investors paid subscription fees for ratings information. Today, 90 percent of revenues are from issuers wanting to be rated.

For rating straightforward corporate bonds, the agencies receive 0.03 or 0.04 percent of the size of the issue, with a minimum fee of $30,000 and a maximum fee of $300,000. For rating complex structured bonds, the agencies get paid more, 0.10 percent capped at $2–3 million. Securitization drove rapid increases in the revenues of rating agencies. In 2007, Moody's revenues from rating structured securities were $900 million, an increase of over 5 times from $172 million in 1999, far in excess of fees from rating government, municipal and corporate bonds.

The rating business paid well, with Moody's (17 percent owned by Warren Buffett's investment company) showing a profit margin of over 50 percent. Glenn Reynolds, head of CreditSights, a research firm, called it: "As close to Shangri-La as you can get, at Microsoft-plus margins."[16] A cumbersome, slow approval process restricted new entrants, creating a lack of competition. Toronto-based Dominion Bond Rating Service took 13 years to obtain approval.

In 2000, when Moody's became a public company, senior management received stock options and performance incentives. Senior rating agency staff, traditionally graduates who missed out on prestigious Wall Street jobs, now earned seven-digit salaries, up from the high-five or low-six levels. Protecting investors gave way to maximizing revenues. In a Freudian slip, one journalist referred to Fitch as Filch.

Stockholm Syndrome

In 1994 the agencies failed to anticipate the collapse of Orange County from derivative trading losses. *Insufficient disclosure* was the reason offered. In 1997, they failed to predict the financial collapse of Asian countries, blaming insufficient disclosure and lack of *informational transparency*. After Enron and WorldCom went bankrupt, they argued insufficient disclosure and *fraud*.

In 2007, Moody's upgraded three major Icelandic banks to the highest AAA rating, citing new methodology that took into account the likelihood of government support. Although Moody's reversed the upgrades, all three banks collapsed in 2008. Unimpeded by insufficient disclosure, lack of information transparency, fraud, and improper accounting, traders anticipated these defaults, marking down bond prices well before rating downgrades.

Rating-structured securities required statistical models, mapping complex securities to historical patterns of default on normal bonds. With mortgage markets changing rapidly, this was like "using weather in Antarctica to forecast conditions in Hawaii."[17] Antarctica from 100 years ago!

The agencies did not look at the underlying mortgages or loans in detail, relying instead on information from others. Moody's Yuri Yoshizawa stated: "We're structure experts. We're not underlying-asset experts."[18] Jamie Dimon, the CEO of JP Morgan, later observed: "There was a large failure of common sense.... Very complex securities shouldn't have been rated as if they were easy-to-value bonds."[19]

As high rating levels were crucial for success and profitability, bankers frequently pressured the agencies. Taking advantage of different models used by individual agencies, bankers shopped around for higher ratings. One S&P employee compared the people rating mortgage-backed securities to hostages who have embraced the ideology of their kidnappers—the *Stockholm Syndrome*. At the 2005 annual off-site meeting, three members of Moody's structured finance department, dressed as the Blues Brothers, performed an original song called "The Compliance Blues," mocking the agency's quality control team.

Lawyer David Grais identified the changed role of the agencies:

> An analogy...is with the restaurant critic. If the restaurant critic dons his disguise and goes to the restaurant and eats dinner and writes a review, he's clearly a journalist. But if he steps into the kitchen and samples the sauce and makes suggestions to the chef about how to correct the seasoning, and then comes back out and writes a review of the meal that he helped to create, he's acting as something more than a journalist...journalists do not participate in the events that they cover...in structured finance the rating agencies were back in the kitchen.[20]

In October 2007, Raymond McDaniel, CEO, admitted that at times: "We drink the Kool-Aid."[21] American politicians described it as a "bone-chilling definition of corruption."[22]

Free Speech

Rating anomalies emerged.[23] Table 18.1 shows the percentage of CDOs that defaulted in the period till 2003. While no AAA-rated CDO defaulted, the 22 percent default rate for BBB CDO securities (investment grade) was not materially different from the 24 percent for BB CDOs (junk). Many investors can only purchase investment grade securities, but in a CDO the risks appear the same. Defaults on BBB CDOs were around ten times that for equivalent conventional securities.

In 2010, Donald MacKenzie of the University of Edinburgh compared the actual defaults on mortgage backed securities against predictions based on typical models used by rating agencies. For AAA rated securities, the actual defaults were more than 12 times the model predictions. For securities with ratings AA, A, and BBB, the actual defaults were anywhere from 75 to over 300 times higher than the model estimates.[24] Between November 2007 and May 2010, 93 per cent of all AAA securities in synthetic securitisations had their rating downgraded.

Facing criticism, chairman and chief executive Harold "Terry" McGraw, III defended S&P: "A couple of assumptions we made didn't work out and we just totally missed on the U.S. housing recession."[25] Moody's Brian Clarkson explained: "We were preparing for a rainstorm and it was a tsunami."[26]

When criticized, the agencies claimed their ratings were opinions, protected under the U.S. constitution as free speech.

Table 18.1 Actual CDO Default Rates

Rating	CDO Default Rate (%)
AAA/Aaa	0.00
AA/Aa	1.10
A	5.44
BBB/Baa	21.59
BB/Ba	24.25
B	55.56

Source: Jian Hu, Richard Cantor, and Gus Harris "Default and Loss Rates of US CDOs: 1993–2003" (March 2005) *Moody's Investor Services*: Figure 10. © Moody's Investors Services, Inc. and/or its affiliates. Reprinted with permission. All Rights Reserved.

"Ratergate," a 2008 SEC investigation, turned up embarrassing internal emails. "It could be structured by cows and we would rate it." The analyst confessed to being able to measure "half" of a deal's risk prior to providing a rating. Another wrote: "Let's hope we are all wealthy and retired by the time this house of cards falters." One analyst admitted: "We do not have the resources to support what we are doing now."[27] Pimco's Bill Gross colorfully observed that the CDO ratings were a "tramp stamp" and the agencies were seduced by "hookers in six-inch stilettos."[28]

Investors ascribed magical properties to the alphabet soup of letters, remaining willfully ignorant about how ratings are determined or their meaning. In 2010, Robert Rubin stated that "AAA securities had always been considered money good," that is, no loss was likely.[29]

Stan Correy, an Australian journalist, was confused: "They have become both critic and chef in the big financial kitchens, but they say they're really journalists and take no responsibility for their advice. [Credit rating agencies] are probably beyond the law, yet governments have said their advice is mandatory. Weird."[30]

No Accounting for Values

Harvard professor Eddie Riedl told his MBA class that "Accounting = Economic truth + Measurement error + Bias."[31] Accounting was now mainly "measurement error" and "bias."

Developed in the late fifteenth century by Venetian monk Luca Pacioli, double-entry accounting was not designed for modern finance. Robert Merton, the Nobel Prize-winning economist, thought that it was asking "a plough horse to gallop on a race track."[32] Accountants frequently resorted to

Pacioli's *De viribus quantitatis*, a treatise on mathematics and magic, describing card tricks, juggling, eating fire, and making coins dance. American comedian David Letterman noted: "There's no business like show business, but there are several businesses like accounting."

Modern accounting struggles to provide tolerably accurate, reasonably objective, and meaningful information about financial positions. Accounting standard setters admit that users of accounting statements untrained in the nuances find them difficult to follow. Users need experts to help them understand the information. Alan Greenspan noted that:

> It has been my experience that competency in mathematics, both in numerical manipulations and in understanding its conceptual foundations, enhances a person's ability to handle the more ambiguous and qualitative relationships that dominate our day-to-day financial decision making.[33]

He may be the only one who understands modern financial statements.

Mark to Make Believe

Financial statements relied on mark-to-market (MtM) accounting, using market values for assets and liabilities rather than original cost adjusted for impairment. Academics assumed: "Financial assets, even complex pools of assets, trade continuously in markets." They advocated the use of models for valuation:

> To provide estimates of the fair values of their assets.... Banks can similarly use models to update the prices that would be paid for various assets. Trading desks in financial institutions have models that allow them to predict prices to within 5 percent of what would be offered for even their complex asset pools.[34]

In practice, as few things had true markets, market value became *fair value* accounting.

Financial Accounting Standard Board (FASB) Standard 157 (FAS157), provided a three-level hierarchy of valuation (three levels of enlightenment). Level 1 required observable prices for identical assets or liabilities in active markets (true *mark-to-market*). Level 2 used observable inputs put through a model as actual prices for the instruments were unavailable (*mark-to-model*). Level 3 required subjective assumptions as observable inputs or prices were unavailable (*mark-to-make-believe* or *mark-to-myself*).

Fair value accounting gave financial institutions and auditors considerable latitude in valuing assets. During the boom, this helped create an illusion of high earnings and financial strength. In a letter to *The Times* dated July 27, 2010, a group of UK academics and accountancy experts wrote that: "the 'fair weather' model significantly overstated bank profits, resulting in excessive dividends. It also obscured true gearing and capital destructive business models. In 'storm' mode it accelerated and exaggerated losses, resulting in taxpayer-funded recapitalizations."[35]

During the financial crisis, only government bonds, large well-known stocks and listed derivatives remained liquid. Valuation for anything else required a higher degree in a quantitative discipline, a super computer and a vivid imagination. David Goldman, a credit strategist, described quotes for credit default swap contracts:

> The business looks like the window of a Brezhnev-era Soviet butcher shop. Mouldy scraps hanging in the window. Old women lining up at 4 a.m. to try and buy credit protection on General Motors. What are reported as trades are really ways to establish prices to satisfy the auditors.[36]

Dubious market prices drove real investment and credit decisions, through asset values, profits and losses, risk calculations, and the value of collateral supporting loans. A current market price of 85 percent for an AAA security does not mean that you will lose 15 percent. It is an estimate of likely losses *if you sell today*. In volatile markets, values deviate significantly from actual values if the security is held to maturity.

Prices are prone to manipulation. Banks may mark positions at high prices to prevent complex, illiquid securities being sold at a discount, and pushing down values. If the securities actually traded, then the lower market price would be used to value positions, increasing losses and margin calls for more collateral on already cash-strapped investors. Alternatively, a lower price is used to force margin calls and selling, allowing dealers to buy the assets cheaply.

The entity's own credit risk was now required to be used to establish the value of its liabilities, resulting in gains for credit downgrades and losses for credit upgrades. If a bank has issued $100 bonds and the market price drops to $80 (80 percent), then it records a *gain*. During the financial crisis, banks recorded substantial profits from revaluing their own liabilities—bizarrely increasing profits as their financial condition deteriorated.

In volatile markets, instead of providing an accurate picture of the financial position, market value accounting increased volatility as behavior became linked by accounting disclosures. Coordinated actions of participants led to sharp movements in asset prices, distorting financial position and value, exacerbating uncertainty and destroying market confidence.

Market value accounting eliminated one market imperfection (poor information) magnifying another imperfection (illiquid markets). In 2008, with the capital markets frozen, a Congressional Oversight Panel noted that:

> The risks troubled assets continue to pose...depend on how many troubled assets there are. But no one appears to know for certain.... It is impossible to ever arrive at an exact dollar amount of

troubled assets, but even the challenges of making a reliable estimate are formidable.[37]

The ability to recognize earnings immediately really drove market value accounting. Tony Shearer, CEO of Singer and Friedlander, told the UK House of Commons that virtually all Icelandic bank Kaupthing's stated profits were from inflated prices of assets: "The actual amount of profits that were coming from…banking was less than 10 percent."[38]

Bankers paid themselves substantial bonuses on profits that were expected to show up in cash some time in the future—that is, if they showed up at all. In Lucy Prebble's play *Enron*, Jeffrey Skilling explained that profits needed to be recognized when the deal was concluded: "Life is short. If you have a moment of genius [you] will be rewarded now."[39]

Out of Sight

Banks and companies used special structures to park assets and associated funding off-balance sheet, reducing the firm's size. Financial institutions moved assets to QSPEs (qualified special purpose entities), recording a sale and the amount received as revenue. Securitization and derivatives shifted assets off-balance sheet, but liquidity puts and standby funding arrangements meant that the risk remained with the bank.

Following the collapse of Lehman Brothers, a court-appointed examiner found that the investment bank used *repos* (repurchase agreements) to shift assets off-balance sheet.[40] In a repo, the borrower sells an asset, simultaneously agreeing to repurchase it at an agreed price plus interest for funds advanced at a future date. Normally, a repo is treated as a secured loan. But where the securities are worth significantly more than the loan, the repo is treated as a sale.

Lehman did $50 billion of *repo 105* (the assets were 105 percent of the loan) at the end of each quarter, reversing it a few days later. The repos reduced assets and debt, lowering Lehman's leverage and risk. In March 2008, Erin Callan, briefly the CFO of Lehman Brothers, affirmed the firm's commitment to "trying to give the group a great amount of transparency on the balance sheet."[41] At about the same time, Herbert McDade, a Lehman executive known as the firm's balance sheet czar, referred to repo 105 as "another drug we're on."[42] Banks reduced their balance sheets by as much as 40 percent over quarter ends, effectively hiding their leverage and risk from the world.

Off-balance sheet treatment relied on the fiction that the banks did not control the assets and the vehicles. In the financial crisis, the fiction evaporated as assets held by SIVs and securitization vehicles returned to the balance sheet from whence they came.

Creeping Crumble

Sir David Tweedie, head of the International Accounting Standards Board, criticized accountants as having "all the backbone of a chocolate éclair," when facing pressure to massage client's financial statements. He complained of "creeping crumble" when:

> Auditors [were picked off] by investment bankers, selling a scheme that perhaps was just within the law to a client, persuading two major auditing firms to accept it whereupon it became accepted practice and QCs would tell a third auditor that he could not qualify [the company's financial report] as the scheme was now part of "true and fair."[43]

Market values were acceptable when there were gains, but everybody wanted historical or adjusted model prices when there were losses. The International Institute of Finance (IIF) proposed a return to using historical prices to facilitate stable valuations in order to increase market confidence. Goldman Sachs dismissed it as "Alice in Wonderland accounting."

Resisting calls for changes in accounting standards, one accountant argued that: "It's the market that needs to change, not the accounting." French accountants concluded that "market prices [had been] squeezed by a crisis discount" and proposed adjusting the valuation using an "upgraded fair value" model for serious crises. The accounting regulator would arbitrate when the crisis discount was abnormally high, allowing a switch from market value to fair value based on a mark-to-model approach.[44] The proposal highlighted French strengths first identified by Napoleon III: "We do not make reforms in France; we make revolution."

Radical proposals retreated to the position before market value accounting. Instruments held to maturity would be valued at book value, adjusted for impairments and trading instruments at market. Accountants decided that it was better to manipulate the values and pretend that there were no losses in preference to inconvenient truths.

Standard setters unveiled a more pressing project, plain English accounting. To simplify the language of accounting, they proposed *people who owe us money* instead of *debtors*. *Current assets* would become *assets we have at the present time*. *Liabilities* would become *where the money came from*.

Sir David Tweedie outlined the heroic role of the accountant:

> The accountant is an artist, but he has to portray his subject faithfully.... If the reporting accountant lacks integrity; if raw economic facts are unpalatable and smoothing devices are sought; if he fails to support fellow professionals who have carefully documented their view of the principle, researched the literature and sought advice and made an honest judgment; if regulators

> demand one answer and one alone, not those within a range; or if the profession constantly seeks answers for all questions—the reporting accountant will paint by numbers and deserve the rule-based standards he has requested. This will be the profession of the search engine, not one of reasoned judgment.[45]

Management by Neglect

Empty words like *governance* and *oversight* masked a lack of adult supervision of business and markets. A culture of benign neglect presided over increasing debt, greater leverage, higher risk, lower capital, and accounting fudges.

Financial statements were filled with page after page of disclosure about meetings of audit and risk committees—how often they met, who attended. It was form over substance, a case of ticking boxes. A character in David Hare's play *The Power of Yes* describes it like a fast-moving vessel that everyone thinks is running fine, but no one seems to care that it's like the *Titanic* heading toward an iceberg.[46]

Senior management rarely understood the spells and potions cast by the financial alchemists in their employ. Elite senior securitization and exotic derivative wizards were reluctant to let others in on the lucrative magic and voodoo they practiced. Managers needed Roosevelt's March 12, 1933 fire-side chat on banking, which, according to Will Rogers: "made everyone understand it, even the bankers."[47]

Few senior bankers understood transactions outside their expertise. Even then, their knowledge was frequently dated. Today, a 55-year-old rarely understands a 25-year-old. In banking, the rapid rate of innovation and change meant that a 35-year-old did not understand a 30-year-old, and the 30-year-old did not understand a 25-year-old. John Gutfreund, former CEO of Salomon Brothers, told Michael Lewis that CEOs could not oversee large financial institutions: "I didn't understand all the product lines and they don't either."[48]

Vikram Pandit, CEO of CitiGroup (replacing Prince), had multiple degrees from Columbia University and had run his own hedge fund. When MBIA, a bond insurer, was in trouble, Pandit was stunned to discover that CDS contracts insuring Citi's portfolio of MBSs only paid out if there were *actual* losses, not *unrealized* mark-to-market losses.[49] Richard Fuld, CEO of Lehman, had traded simple instruments that did not prepare him for the firm's complex transactions. The Lehman CEO had no knowledge of repo 105 as he did not use a computer and did not have the ability to open attach-ments on his BlackBerry.[50] Jamie Dimon, CEO of JP Morgan, noted that:

"It's very dangerous to fly at 40,000 feet if you don't have the ability to drill down and have deep knowledge of the company and its various businesses."[51]

CitiGroup's senior managers blamed their disastrous foray into mortgage securitization on advice from external consultants. They created small inner cabals to mask their insecurity and inability to control the underlying business.

It was *management by deal*—buying and selling businesses, creating fiefdoms run by trusted associates. When Bank of America (BA) suffered large losses, CEO Ken Lewis confessed that: "I've had all the fun I can stand in investment banking right now."[52] Lewis said that he would not use BA's petty cash to buy an investment bank. Shortly afterward BA purchased Merrill Lynch, Lewis deciding: "I like it again."[53] Lewis predicted that the acquisition would be a thing of beauty.

The only strategy was follow the leader. Richard Posner, U.S. federal judge, argued that competition and fear of falling behind meant that managers had no choice.[54] Former CitiGroup chairman Sandy Weill candidly admitted that: "If you look at the results of what happened on Wall Street, it became, 'well, this one's doing it, so how can I not do it, if I don't do it, then people are going to leave my place and go some place else.' "[55] In *The Power of Yes*, the character David Freud summarizes it. When people tell you that they can get higher returns and more money, it is difficult to refuse. People begin to think that there is something wrong with you.[56]

Senior management frequently did not seem to have a good grasp of what was going on in their own firm. John Thain, a former Goldman Sachs executive and head of the New York Stock Exchange, replaced Stan O'Neal at Merrill Lynch. Asked about Merrill's need for capital, on January 15, 2008, Thain stated that "[recent capital raisings] make certain that Merrill is well-capitalized." On March 8, 2008 Thain reiterated: "Today I can say that we will not need additional funds.... We will not return to the market." On March 16, Thain went further: "We have more capital than we need, so we can say to the market that we don't need more injections." In April 2008, Merrill Lynch issued $9.55 billion of preferred shares to raise capital. On July 17, 2008 Thain returned to the same theme: "Right now we believe that we are in a very comfortable spot in terms of our capital." Later, in July 2008, Merrill would sell its stake in Bloomberg for US $4.5 billion and issue $8.5 billion in shares to raise capital.

After hearing testimony from senior CitiGroup executives, Phil Angelides, chairman of the Financial Crisis Inquiry Commission, remarked: "One thing that is striking is the extent to which senior management either didn't know or didn't care to know about risks that ultimately helped bring the institution to its knees."[57]

Directing Traffic

Compliant nonexecutive boards of directors, hand-picked by CEOs, were even further removed from the action. Taking their independence seriously, they chose to function without any knowledge of the industry, firm, or what was actually going on.

Former U.S. President Gerald Ford, a member of the Lehman Brothers board, asked about the difference between equity and revenue.[58] Robert Rubin, vice-chairman of Citi, argued that: "A board cannot know what is in the position books of a financial services firm. You cannot know the granularity of the positions." [59] Upon joining the Salomon Brothers Board, Henry Kaufman found that most nonexecutive directors had little experience or understanding of banking. The board reports were "neither comprehensive...nor detailed enough...about the diversity and complexity of our operations." Nonexecutive directors relied "heavily on the veracity and competency of senior managers, who in turn ...re beholden to the veracity of middle managers, who are themselves motivated to take risks through a variety of profit compensation formulas."[60]

Kaufman later joined the board of Lehman Brothers. Nine out of ten members of the Lehman board were retired, four were 75 years or more in age, only two had banking experience, but in a different era. The octogenarian Kaufman sat on the Lehman Risk Committee with a Broadway producer, a former Navy admiral, a former CEO of a Spanish-language TV station, and the former chairman of IBM. The Committee only had two meetings in 2006 and 2007. AIG's board included several heavyweight diplomats and admirals; even though Richard Breeden, former head of the SEC told a reporter: "AIG, as far as I know, didn't own any aircraft carriers and didn't have a seat in the United Nations."[61]

Under-resourced, under-skilled, and under-paid, regulators struggled to enforce legislation. Emasculated by lack of power and will, regulators resembled the unarmed policeman in a Robin Williams' sketch trying to apprehend a fleeing suspect with the exhalation: "Stop! Or...I'll shout stop again!"

Shown the exemplary returns of the Madoff fund, Harry Markopolos, an analyst at a small Boston firm, detected a telltale funny smell. Unraveling the secrets of Madoff's money machine, he found the world's largest Ponzi scheme. Motivated partly by the possibility of a bounty for whistleblowers, Markopolos tried on no less than five occasions to have the SEC investigate Madoff.

The SEC's failure to follow up and take any enforcement action, in Markapolos' view, was driven by ignorance, incompetence, arrogance, and unwillingness to take on a non-executive former chairman of NASDAQ and industry grandee. Markapolos observed that the SEC was "overlawyered… poisoned by lawyers…. If you can't do math and if you can't take apart the investment products of the 21st century backward and forward and put them together in your sleep, you'll never find the frauds on Wall Street."[62]

When things were going well, regulators favored self-regulation, which bears the same relationship to regulation that self-importance does to importance. In *Holidays in Hell*, P.J. O'Rourke provides an example of self-regulation. At a Syrian hillside roadblock, the soldier wants to search the trunk of a car. Told that the hand brake is faulty, the soldier volunteers to sit in the car holding the brake pedal while the driver opens the trunk. "Is there any contraband in there?" he inquires of the driver.[63]

When problems arose, regulators switched to a different plan. At a different roadblock, P.J. O'Rourke observed a soldier searching a rear-engined VW Beetle for stolen goods. Opening the luggage compartment in front and failing to find anything, he searches the trunk. Finding the engine, the soldier triumphantly exclaims: "You have stolen a motor…you have just done it because it's still running."[64]

A *shell game* is a confidence trick used to perpetrate fraud. It requires three shells and a small, soft round ball, about the size of a pea. The pea is placed under one of the shells; then the shells are shuffled around quickly while the audience bets on the location of the pea. Through sleight of hand, the operator easily hides the pea, undetected by the victims. Risk transfer, ratings, and accounting standards were the shell games of financial markets. Central bankers, regulators, rating agencies, accountants, managers, and directors played the game, over the years.

19

Cult of Risk

As money and debt became key drivers of economies, bankers gained "juice"—influence. Related industries, like housing, also lobbied relentlessly for initiatives that increased the supply of money for a home of one's own.

In *The Logic of Collective Action* and *The Rise and Decline of Nations*, American economist Mancur Olson argued that in democratic societies and market economies small coalitions form over time. They use intensive, well-funded lobbying to influence policies that benefit members, leaving large costs to be borne by the rest of the population. Coalitions accumulate, ultimately paralyzing the economic system and causing inevitable and irretrievable economic decline.

In the article "The quiet coup"[1] and book *13 Bankers*, Simon Johnson, a former IMF chief economist and James Kwak, a former McKinsey consultant, argued that *banksters* had captured regulators. The idea echoed President Dwight Eisenhower's 1961 warning about the military industrial complex, an influential and powerful combination of the military establishment and arms industry with the "potential for the disastrous rise of misplaced power."[2]

If it were a conspiracy, then it was one of convenience among pickpockets. If it was a coup, then it was by engraved invitation, like the sadomasochistic sexual encounter between Howard Roark and Dominique Francon in Ayn Rand's *The Fountainhead*.[3] While increasing debt and risk was dangerous, it had become the accepted way to generate economic growth and improve living standards.

Growth for All Seasons

As in ancient Rome, where the perpetuation of Empire and Caesar's reign required ample supplies of bread and games for the population, all politics and economics is now informed by the necessity of maintaining strong economic growth:

> We have entered a period of sustained growth that could double the world's economy every dozen years and bring increasing prosperity for...billions of people on the planet. We are riding the early waves of a 25-year run of a greatly expanding economy that will do much to solve seemingly intractable problems like poverty and to ease tensions throughout the world. And we'll do it without blowing the lid off the environment.[4]

The belief that governments and central banks could control the economy was widespread:

> Faster economic growth is the panacea for all...economic (and for that matter political) problems and that faster growth can be easily achieved by a combination of inflationary demand-management policies and politically appealing fiscal gimmickry.[5]

Economic growth was a perennial and persistent preoccupation. In 1929, the New York *Daily Mirror* wrote: "The prevailing bull market is just America's bet that she won't stop expanding."[6] In 1936, Wilhelm Röpke looked back at the roaring 1920s: "with production and trade increasing month by month throughout the world, the moment actually seemed in sight when social problems would be solved by prosperity for all."[7] At the time, the 1920s were also regarded as a period of remarkable social progress.

Historically, increasing population, new markets, productivity increases, and industrial innovation drove growth. As the world grew older, growth slowed but "when the monster stops growing, it dies. It can't stay one size."[8] After the Berlin Wall fell, the reintegration of Eastern Europe, China, and India into global trade provided low-cost labor supplying cheap goods and services and creating new markets for products. But demand for improved living standards needed even greater growth. Chinese novelist Ma Jian saw this in his native country: "As society changes, new words and terms keep popping up such as sauna, private car ownership, property developer, mortgage, and personal installment loan...no one talks about the Tiananmen protests...or...official corruption."[9]

Financial engineering replaced real engineering as the engine for growth. Debt-fueled consumption drove growth, particularly in the developed world. Investors, such as central banks with large reserves, pension funds, and asset managers, eagerly purchased the debt. Borrowing fueled higher asset prices, allowing greater levels of borrowing against the value of the asset. Spending that normally would have taken place over a period of years was squeezed into a short period because of the availability of cheap borrowing. Business over-invested in production capacity, assuming exaggerated growth would continue indefinitely.

Over half the recorded growth in the United States over recent years was the result of debt. Spiraling levels of debt were needed to maintain growth. By 2008 $4–5 of debt was required to create $1 of growth, up from $1–2 needed 20 years earlier. In the frenzy of low interest rates and rising asset prices, collateral cover and ability to service the loans deteriorated, increasing debt levels to unsustainable levels.

A perpetual motion machine indefinitely produces more energy than it consumes. The new economy was a perpetual growth machine, producing high rates of growth using debt. Perpetual motion is a *Gedanken*—thought experiment—designed to test a hypothesis. The new economy ultimately proved impossible to sustain. Sigmund Freud remarked that:

> Illusions commend themselves to us because they save us pain and allow us to enjoy pleasure instead. We must therefore accept it without complaint when they sometimes collide with a bit of reality against which they are dashed to pieces.[10]

The financial crisis was the reality on which the fake pleasure of the *Great Moderation* and the *Goldilocks Economy* was smashed.

Financial Groupthink

Asked about why regulators did not see the problems and excesses, Richard Breeden, a former chairman of the SEC, remarked: "It's probably a better question for a psychologist. There's a group dynamic…nobody likes to be the person who sends everybody home from the party when they're having a good time."[11]

Groupthink, suggested by William Whyte, author of *The Organisation Man*, and developed by psychologist Irving Janis, describes a process where a group with similar backgrounds and largely insulated from outside opinions makes decisions without critically testing, analyzing and evaluating ideas.[12] It involves collective rationalizations, conviction about the inherent morality of its views, and illusions about unanimity and invulnerability. The group holds stereotyped views of outsiders and no toleration of dissent.

The financial system was a case of financial groupthink, the *madness of crowds*. Alan Greenspan, the former Fed chairman, was the chief mind-guard of financial groupthink. In the early 1950s, Greenspan wrote for Ayn Rand's newsletter and contributed essays to her book *Capitalism: The*

Unknown Ideal. In 1974, after a successful career as an economic consultant, Greenspan joined President Gerald Ford's Council of Economic Advisers. Rand attended the swearing-in ceremony. In 1982, Greenspan attended Rand's funeral.

Born Alisa Rosenbaum, Rand, a Russian Jew, was a trenchant critic of popular collectivism movements of the twentieth century. Based on her experience of the Russian revolution, Rand was fervently anticommunist, devoted to the rights and liberty of the individual. She shaped the libertarian self-image—the gifted individual restricted, brought down and in permanent conflict with power-hungry bureaucrats, officials, and the untalented second-handers who populate life.

Rand argued that thriving societies are not possible without freedom, entrepreneurs, and innovation. China's embrace of market economics was validation of Rand's point of view. Refracted through economic and finance theory, this was the core belief of extreme money.

The academic establishment found Rand's polemic novels and views shallow and limited. But Rand's absolute values and intolerance were attractive to an adolescent sensibility and a Manichean worldview, a simple cosmology divided between good and evil. Encouraging mystique, she anticipated the cult of celebrity thought leadership before the term existed. Her glare "could wilt a cactus." She wore a brooch in the shape of a dollar sign. With a talent for self-promotion, Ayn Rand was her greatest creation.

Within her inner circle—known ironically as *the collective*—the promoter of individual liberty did not tolerate dissent. Her stifling worldview encompassed politics, interior design, and dancing. Despite a failure to create a lasting legacy or political movement, Rand remains an influence on conservative thinking. *The New York Times* dubbed Rand the "novelist Laureate" of the Reagan administration, citing her influence on Greenspan.[13] Paul Samuelson, the economist, recalled that:

> The trouble is that [Greenspan] had been an Ayn Rander. You can take the boy out of the cult but you can't take the cult out of the boy. He actually had instructions, probably pinned on the wall: "Nothing from this office should go forth which discredits the capitalist system. Greed is good."[14]

Like his mentor, Greenspan was his own splendid creation.

Celebrity Central Banking

Greenspan reveled in the age of celebrity central bankers: "The only central bankers ever to achieve…rock star status…. No one has yet credited Alan Greenspan with the fall of the Soviet Union or the rise of the Boston Red Sox, although both may come in time as the legend grows."[15] In 2000,

U.S. Senator John McCain suggested that if Greenspan died, it would be necessary to adopt a *Weekend at Bernie's* strategy—put dark glasses on him and prop him up in his office.

Lacking the talent to be a successful musician, Greenspan became the bandleader of the new economy. Critics muttered that his Ph.D. thesis in economics from New York University was a collection of articles that he wrote in the 1950s. Like Elvis, who claimed in his line of work that knowledge of music was not strictly necessary, Greenspan did not need to know much about economics.[16]

In oracular pronouncements, Greenspan excelled at "lacquering a slate of ignorance with a thin coating of knowledge."[17] At a July 1996 meeting, discussing the target rate of inflation, Governor Janet Yellen argued for 2 percent. Greenspan waffled about price stability. Asked to define the term, Greenspan said that it was "the state in which expected changes in price level do not effectively alter business or household decisions." Pressed further, Greenspan expressed preference for zero inflation, correctly measured. The consensus was for 2 percent incorrectly measured. Greenspan cautioned the other governors not to reveal the target.[18]

In 1998, Greenspan told the U.S. Securities Industry Association that: "The financial instruments of a bygone era, common stocks and debt obligations, have been augmented by a vast array of complex hybrid financial products...which, in many cases, seemingly challenge human understanding."[19] In *The Power of Yes*, Adair Turner, head of the English FSA, is asked whether the fact that nobody understood what was going on was an issue. Turner responds that no, it wasn't a problem as, for people like Alan Greenspan, it was just a matter of faith.[20]

There was no evidence that Greenspan was accurate at forecasting economic events. At the Fed, Greenspan had at his disposal: "an entire department of economists who can provide a brilliant ex post facto explanation of what happened."[21] He grasped that sound economics and ideas were irrelevant as long as the stock market kept rising and people felt that they were getting wealthier. Obscure, pseudo-scientific language masked the paucity of substance. Han de Jong, chief economist of ABN Amro Bank, confessed to the *Financial Times* on February 21, 2008: "The role of serious economists in financial institutions is very limited today. We are little more than clowns, whose purpose is to entertain." It was parlor economics by parlor intellectuals.

But Greenspan did have an acute understanding of power and political savvy. During the Reagan years, White House staff members marveled at his omnipresence, and the way he worked government officials. His limbo-dancer like flexibility on policy issues was legendary. Greenspan supported President Bush's 2001 tax cuts but was highly critical of his 2003 tax cut plans, urging a return to fiscal rectitude. Shortly after, he switched tack, praising Bush's plan to eliminate taxes on dividends, and arguing that the cuts would have limited effects on the budget. Democratic Senator Harry

Reid called Greenspan "one of the biggest political hacks we have here in Washington."[22]

Greenspan's true constituency was the markets. He exemplified deregulation and the extraordinary gains they provided to bankers. The *Greenspan put* guaranteed that the central bank would save them from their folly.

Greenspan's policies were grounded in "asymmetric ignorance."[23] As Fed chairman, he repeatedly stated that central bankers could not anticipate price bubbles or do anything about them because it was impossible to know when asset prices were too high. Nevertheless, he always knew when falling asset prices would create a crisis and the central bank should pump money into the system to support prices. Underlying the policies was his deep-seated, fundamental belief that irrational bubbles were simply impossible in an efficient, modern market. After retirement, Greenspan gained powers of clairvoyance, warning about developing bubbles and urging action to prevent them.

Traditional central bankers shunned publicity, being reluctant to disclose anything. Asked about the level of its gold reserves by a Royal Commission, one governor of the Bank of England would only say that they were "very, very considerable." In 1929, in an inquiry before a select parliamentary committee, the deputy governor responded that "it was [the Bank of England's] practice to leave our actions to explain our policy." The Bank thought it "dangerous to start to give reasons" and unwise to defend itself against criticism, finding it "akin to a lady starting to defend her virtue."[24]

In contrast, Greenspan courted the press—literally. He dated journalists Barbara Walters and Susan Mills before marrying Andrea Mitchell, a television personality. He manipulated the press cleverly, pumping up his profile. When he became Fed chairman, fewer than 10 percent of Americans could identify the holder of the office. By the time he retired in 2006, more than 90 percent knew him.

Like Rand, Greenspan cultivated a contrived popular image. Journalists granted interviews would inevitably find him poring over reams of data or obscure economic statistics, building the aura of deep technical knowledge. His mannered speech gave the impression of superior elevated wisdom. Greenspan himself provided guidance to interpreting his pronouncements: "I know you believe you understand what you think I said, but I am not sure you realize that what you heard is not what I meant."[25] He once further clarified his position: "If I have made myself clear then you have misunderstood me."[26]

In Turkmenistan, President Berdymukhamedov, a former dentist, settled for the title of *hero*. Based on a hagiographic, uncritical biography, Greenspan was the *maestro*. Like Greenspan, President Berdymukhamedov was often shown on state TV performing heroic tasks. The day after one such operation, the security services confiscated newspapers carrying a photo that showed the President holding an X-ray upside down. Greenspan's Delphic obscurity and airbrushed history belied the fact that he wasn't actually saying or doing much and had a term in office littered with mistakes.

Greenspan's genius was to grasp the need for an oracle to satisfy deep-seated longings for certainty and infallibility. As Friederich Nietzsche observed:

> To trace something unknown back to something known is alleviating, soothing, gratifying and gives moreover a feeling of power. Danger, disquiet, anxiety attend the unknown—the first instinct is to eliminate these distressing states. First principle: any explanation is better than none.... The cause-creating drive is thus conditioned and excited by the feeling of fear.[27]

Dealing with Dissent

Like Rand, Greenspan purged dissenters with Stalinist efficiency: "You challenge Greenspan and he tolerates it—at first. If you keep going...it's like a cartoon: a sixteen-ton weight drops on you from the ceiling, and it's clear the conversation is over."[28] Time and again, Greenspan ensured that proposals for regulation of the financial system were stillborn.

Brooksley Born, the head of the Commodity Futures Trading Commission (CFTC), tried to engender debate on the regulation of the growing volume of privately negotiated derivative contracts and the risk to the financial system. She testified repeatedly before Congress to that effect. In 1998, the CFTC issued a draft release proposing regulation, greater disclosure, and more reserves against losses.

A furious Greenspan, together with Treasury secretary Robert Rubin, deputy Treasury secretary Larry Summers, and SEC chairman Arthur Levitt, launched an extraordinary attack against regulation of derivatives and personally on Born. Michael Greenberger, a director at the CFTC, noted: "Brooksley was this woman...not playing tennis with these guys...not having lunch with these guys...this woman was not of Wall Street."[29]

Greenspan told Born that she did not understand what she was doing: "regulation of derivatives transactions that are privately negotiated by professionals is unnecessary."[30] Regulation would reduce market efficiency, create uncertainty, and reduce standards of living. The market place was automatically self-regulating. Market regulation was superior to even minimal intervention. Acknowledging that derivatives create linkages that transmit risks, Greenspan dismissed the possibility of problems in the financial system as extremely remote. Regulation would cause a flight of capital from America, reducing its financial influence.

Arguing that the CFTC had no authority over derivatives, Rubin offered Born an education in the applicable laws on the powers of the regulator.

Larry Summers, later an advocate of reregulation of the financial system, chastised Born: "There are thirteen bankers in my office. They say if this is published we'll have the worst financial crisis since World War II."[31]

When Born stubbornly continued, Greenspan, Rubin, and Levitt used their influence in Congress to stall the proposals. Born's case gained support when later that year LTCM collapsed, necessitating a hasty Fed-orchestrated rescue. Greenspan's views on derivatives remained unaffected. After Born departed in 1999, Greenspan, Summers (now Treasury secretary), and Levitt pushed through the Commodity Futures Modernization Act, stripping the agency of much of its powers over derivatives. Later Rubin and Summers argued that they had actually favored regulating derivatives but the system and public opinion militated against it.

After leaving the CFTC, Born received the John F. Kennedy Profiles in Courage Award in recognition of the "political courage she demonstrated in sounding early warnings about conditions that contributed to the current global financial crisis."

In 2005, in his paper *Has Financial Development Made the World Riskier?* at the Fed's annual conference held at Jackson Hole, Raghuram Rajan, a former IMF chief economist and professor at the University of Chicago, presciently highlighted the increased risks and the interdependence of markets that made them vulnerable. Donald Kohn, Greenspan's Fed flunky, and Summers rushed to defend their master, launching a virulent attack. Rajan had not followed John Kenneth Galbraith's advice: "The conventional having been made more or less identical with sound scholarship, its position is virtually impregnable. The skeptic is disqualified by his very tendency to go brashly from the old to the new. Were he a sound scholar…he would remain with the conventional wisdom."[32]

Greenspan's personal authority was influential in convincing both legislators and regulators. None of them had the knowledge to understand the issues or challenge the maestro, who modestly claimed credit for the rising stock market and growing economy. Within banks, managers concerned with risk were weeded out. During a meeting in 2007 between academics and banks, a risk manager told Rajan (who was surprised at the lack of concern): "You must understand, anyone who was worried was fired long ago."[33]

The world slavishly followed the American example. As William White, chief economist of the BIS, remarked: "In the field of economics, American academics have such a high reputation that they sweep all before them. If you add to that the personal reputation of the 'Maestro,' it was very difficult for anybody else to come in and say the problems building."[34]

Free markets and deregulation were conventional wisdom—everyone was paid to agree with the broad consensus. As Hyman Minsky wrote: "As a previous crisis recedes in time, it's quite natural…to believe that a new era has arrived. Cassandra-like warnings that nothing has changed, that there is a financial breaking point that will lead to a deep depression, are naturally ignored in these circumstances."[35]

Noneofuscouldanode

On October 22, 2008, as the global economy and financial system dissolved into crisis, Alan Greenspan appeared before the U.S. House Oversight Committee.

Well-meaning and ineffectual hearings, irrespective of topic, typically conclude that any failure was systemic, not attributable to any individual. The inadvertent, unconscious clan and class sympathies of men and women dressed in similar attire on both sides of the bar are a factor in the outcome. In January 2011, the Financial Crisis Inquiry Commission (FCIC) would issue a weighty report, which was dubbed the financial equivalent of *Murder on the Orient Express*—everybody did it but no one would be held responsible.

Since leaving the Fed, Greenspan had carved out a lucrative career as a speaker and adviser to a bank (Deutsche Bank), fund manager (Pimco) and hedge fund (Paulson & Co.). He had a best-selling book *The Age of Turbulence*, promoted relentlessly through interviews and public appearances on popular TV shows. Aware of the importance of the event, Greenspan hired a PR consultant to help him prepare.

This time, the interrogation, led by Congressman Henry Waxman, the chairman, was less adulatory: "Were you wrong?" Looking frail and uncomfortable, Greenspan responded: "I made a mistake in presuming that the self-interest of organizations [was] such that they were best capable of protecting their own shareholders and their equity in the firms…. I've found a flaw…in the model that I perceived as the critical functioning structure that defines how the world works, so to speak."[36] He was even, he allowed, "partially" wrong for opposing tougher regulation of derivatives: "30 percent wrong."[37]

Greenspan's confession of shocked disbelief echoed the admission of Robert Stadler, the physicist in *Atlas Shrugged*, who betrays his faith in exchange for political favors. Greenspan seemed nothing more than an icon of an economy that was disintegrating.

In October 2008, speaking before business leaders in Edinburgh, Hector Sants, CEO of the UK FSA, apologized that bank "business models [were] ill-equipped to survive the stress…a fact we regret…. We are sorry that our supervision did not achieve all it should have done."[38] As journalist Simon Jenkins commented: "It was like a pilot protesting that his plane was flying fine except for the engines."[39]

As markets recovered, disbelief turned to defiance. In October 2009, at the Yalta European Conference, Greenspan clashed with George Soros and

Dominique Strauss-Kahn, head of the IMF, on the need for regulation: "I think you have to allow the market to make those judgments…[markets would ensure] that many practices would naturally find themselves "off the table."[40]

Keynes argued that models were weak expressions of conventional wisdom: "Like other orthodoxies it stands for what is jejeune and intellectually sterile; and since it has prejudice on its side, it can use claptrap with impunity."[41] The EMH—*efficient market-hypothesis*—was really a case of the *extreme money hypocrisy*, which in times of stress transformed into the *emotional market hypothesis*.[42]

Je Ne Regrette Rien!

In 2010, the now *Dr.* Greenspan defended his record before the USFCIC[43] and at the Brooking Institute. Greenspan was careful to look prescient, drawing on past praise of achievements, especially from the late Milton Friedman. Contrition was in short supply, Greenspan telling an interviewer: "I have no regrets on any of the Federal Reserve's policies that we initiated back then."[44]

An unrepentant Greenspan refused to acknowledge any failure to take action to rein in excessive lending, aggressive risk-taking by banks. and subprime mortgages. The banking system had had inadequate capital for at least 40 to 50 years. Asked to defend his deregulatory policies, Greenspan told the FCIC that it was not his fault: "The notion that somehow my views on regulation were predominant and effective at influencing the Congress is something you may have perceived. But it didn't look that way from my point of view."[45] He had warned about subprime lending and low-down-payment mortgages in 1999 and 2001. He was powerless, as legislators would have prevented him from taking action. It was an odd admission of helplessness from the second most important man on the planet.

Greenspan's analysis of the crisis was conventional; central banks were innocent voyeurs to events. He recited Ben Bernanke's global saving glut thesis—an excess of global saving created the problems. He steadfastly denied that loose money or deregulation of the financial system were key elements of the crisis.

Keynes argued that "the difficulty lies not so much in developing new ideas as in escaping from old ones."[46] But as John Kenneth Galbraith realized, "faced with the choice between changing one's mind and proving there is no need to do so, almost everyone gets busy on the proof."[47]

Patrick Artus, economic adviser to the French government and author of *Les incendiaires: Les banques centrales dépassées par la globalisation* (The Arsonists: Central Banks Overtaken by Globalisation), called

Greenspan a "very bad Fed chairman" who created four major crises—savings and loans, LTCM, new-technology shares and subprime mortgages. When asked about Greenspan's contribution in rescuing markets with his actions, Artus replied: "Yes, but after the fact. He's congratulated for his role as fireman, but he's the one who started the fire."[48]

In 2009. the economics profession voted Alan Greenspan the economist most responsible for causing the global financial crisis—the Dynamite Prize in Economics. Milton Friedman and Larry Summers finished in second and third place. Greenspan could take solace in John Kenneth Galbraith's advice: "If all else fails, immortality can always be assured by spectacular error."

Last Supper

In November 2008, hedge fund manager John Paulson celebrated unparalleled gains from betting on the collapse of the U.S. subprime mortgage market. Investors in Paulson's funds gathered for an exclusive dinner at New York's Metropolitan Club facing Central Park. The human misery that this celebration was built on did not trouble the invited.

The evening started with a cocktail reception where Krug Grande Cuvée champagne and 2006 Chassagne-Montrachet from Domaine Marc Morey were served. The dinner menu featured jumbo crabmeat and avocado, Colorado rack of lamb with tarragon jus and Parmesan, polenta cake, and a warm chocolate cake. Oenophiles enjoyed the evening's libations—1999 Château Haut-Brion, 1999 Château Margaux, and 1999 Château Lafite-Rothschild (at more than $500 a bottle).

The man instrumental for the investor's good fortune provided the evening's entertainment. Greenspan, an adviser to Paulson, was the after-dinner speaker. Greenspan believed that: "There is a lot of amnesia that's emerging, apparently."[49] The 83-year-old Dr. Greenspan was not immune from this affliction, especially where preserving his legacy. He took the advice of author Gabriel Garcia Márquez: "What matters in life is not what happens to you but what you remember and how you remember it."[50]

Greenspan's FCIC testimony was followed by executives from CitiGroup, propped up by more than $45 billion of US taxpayer funds. They acknowledged deterioration of lending standards and investment in mortgage backed securities. A former CitiGroup lending officer told the Commission how lending decisions were altered from "turned down" to "approved" and of futile attempts to draw violations of credit risk policies to the attention of senior management, including Robert Rubin.

When it was their turn, senior CitiGroup personnel parroted that the super senior CDO tranches held were "super safe." Thomas Maheras, the executive in charge of Citi's mortgage activities, told the FCIC that no one could have conceived that house prices would fall by 30–40 percent. David Bushell, CitiGroup's head of risk, pointed out that everybody, including the regulators, assumed the same things.

Citi's behavior was merely a rational of poor business judgment. As John Kenneth Galbraith pointed out: "The conventional view serves to protect us from the painful job of thinking.... In any great organization it is far, far safer to be wrong with the majority than to be right alone." The large profits, as Upton Sinclair observed, made it "difficult...for a man to understand something if he's paid a small fortune to not understand it."[51]

In October 2008 Dean Jay Light told Harvard Business Schools students and alumni:

> We failed to understand how much the system had changed...and how fragile it might be because of increased leverage, decreased transparency and decreased liquidity...we have witnessed...a stunning and sobering failure of financial safeguards, of financial markets, of financial institutions and mostly of leadership at many levels. We will leave the talk of fixing the blame to others, that is not very interesting. But we must be involved...in fixing the problems.[52]

Having failed to see looming problems, the same people, Light argued, should be in charge of solving the problem. As Benjamin Franklin remarked: "The definition of insanity is doing the same thing over and over and expecting different results."

Boom and bust cycles had not been consigned to the dustbin of history. High levels of debt and leverage were not the elixir of endless growth. Housing prices did go down as well as up. Wealth did not flow endlessly from buying and selling claims on future properties off the plan in exotic investment hot spots. The finest financial minds proved incapable of understanding the risk of modern financial markets, though they had greater success in convincing central bankers and bankers of their models. As the Renaissance scholar Michel de Montaigne asked: "How many things we regarded yesterday as articles of faith that seem to us only fables today?"

The financial economy proved unable, ultimately, to overcome deficiencies in the real economy. Modern markets proved dangerously circular and self-referential. The crisis highlighted what John Stuart Mill knew in 1867: "Panics do not destroy capital; they merely reveal the extent to which it has been previously destroyed by its betrayal into hopelessly unproductive works."

At a meeting of the collective, Greenspan once expressed concern that he might not exist, causing Rand to remark caustically: "By the way, who is making that statement?"[53] During Greenspan's FCIC testimony, the lights went out mysteriously in the hearing room as Phil Angelides, the commission's chairman, asked Greenspan: "Do you feel there was a failure of regulation?" The financial system that Greenspan fostered had grown large and risky, eventually creating the conditions for the crisis that brought the global economy to the brink of a new depression. But it had not been forced on the world. As Alsatian humanist and satirist Sebastian Brant observed in 1494: "The world wants to be deceived."

The ability of governments and policy mandarins to control the economic engines had been overrated. The crisis exposed politicians, bureaucrats, and central bankers as the *Wizards of Oz*, behind the curtain, running from one lever to another in a desperate attempt to maintain illusions. The incompleteness of knowledge would not have surprised Keynes. In an essay titled *The Great Slump of 1930* published in December of that year, he wrote: "We have involved ourselves in a colossal muddle, having blundered in the control of a delicate machine, the workings of which we do not understand."[54]

20

Masters of the Universe

During the Great Depression, finance was unfashionable: "Don't tell my mother I'm a banker, she thinks I play piano in a brothel." Now, the best and brightest business school, mathematics, science, and computing graduates take jobs on Wall Street: "When it's profit you're after, why go after it the hard way? I intend to be a stockbroker...One attempts to make the most money with the least work."[1]

In Lucy Prebble's play *Enron*, the character Jeffrey Skilling, Harvard MBA, CEO of Enron and soon to be convicted felon, outlines the basis of the new economy: "the only difference between me and the people judging me is they weren't smart enough to do what we did."[2] Money and brilliance became synonymous: "One of our culture's deepest beliefs is expressed in the question, 'If you are so smart, why ain't you rich?'...people in finance are rich—so it logically follows that everything they chose to do must be smart."[3] John Kenneth Galbraith's caution would prove well founded: "Nothing so gives the illusion of intelligence as personal association with large sums of money. It is also alas an illusion."[4]

Money Illusions

Between 1980 and 2005 in the United States, jobs trading financial assets increased from 2.8 to 9 percent of all finance jobs. During the same period, jobs entailing risk modeling increased from 1.2 to 5 percent. The value contributed by finance to the economy increased from 2.3 percent after the Second World War to 4.4 percent in 1997 and 8.1 percent by 2006. In 1980, finance professionals earned the same as engineers. By 2005, financial engineers, on average, earned around 30–40 percent more than real engineers.[5] In the UK the financial sector made up 10 percent of the economy, contributing 27 percent of tax revenue.

Banking embodies a clear class structure. The vast majority of bankers remained ordinary men and women involved in mundane activities, helping their customers and keeping the wheels of the financial system turning. But now a new super class of bankers and elite financiers emerged, reflecting the changes in banking and the financial system.

In 1989, Michael Lewis, in *Liar's Poker*, set out his experiences at Salomon Brothers, as a highly paid 24-year-old with minimal training providing investment advice and making large bets with other people's money. Intended to highlight the absurdity, the book instead became the manual for how to succeed in banking.

In the 1970s, Pierre Bourdieu, a French anthropologist, introduced the idea of *habitus*—how each society and culture orders its world subconsciously according to a cognitive framework based on its experiences. He argued that: "The most successful ideological effects are those which have no need of words, but ask no more than a complicitous silence."[6] Class, affinities, education, and the work itself shaped the financial elite.

In the sixteenth century the Conquistadors brought the ambitions, prejudices, attitudes, and values of Spain to the New World. Achievements were validated with riches, rank, and power. Failures brought disease and death, mollified by the consolations of faith and the afterlife. The financial elite undertook similar conquest and plunder, marshaling vast sums of money and creating intricate financial structures. In the new age, Masters of the Universe strutted through the City of London, Wall Street, Finanzplatz Deutschland, Zurich's Bahnofstrasse, Singapore's Raffles Place, Hong Kong's Exchange Square, and Tokyo's Marunouchi, parodying a banker in the movie *The Bank* who believes he is just like God, but with a better suit.

Factories for Unhappy People[7]

In the 1967 film *The Graduate*, Dustin Hoffman's character Ben Braddock received career advice. Then it was "PLASTICS," now it was "MONEY." Finance now was the "hot" professional ticket, attracting between 20 and 40 percent of graduates from the best universities.

MBAs (**me**diocre **b**ut **a**rrogant or **mo**stly **b**loody **a**wful) became conveyor belts for the finance mill. In cocooned campuses resembling Baghdad's Green Zone,[8] students focused on courses like Biggie (business, government, and international economics). Laboring long hours, one student thought he was gaining a "Swiss army knife…toolkit of skills' and becoming a real ninja at using [them]." He sought solace in the aura: "the great thing about studying economics at the University of Chicago is that most of what you learn…was invented, or…affected significantly, by research done within one square mile of where you are."[9] Business Schools boasted that you were never more than two degrees of separation from powerful figures—the president of a nation, the head of a central bank or CEO of an investment bank.

MBAs gave graduates a narcissistic self-confidence—the belief that they were 100 percent right, 100 percent of the time. Asked about the benefits of a MBA in 1986, Russell Ackoff, a professor at the Wharton Business School, replied:

> The first was to equip students with a vocabulary that enabled them to talk with authority about subjects they did not understand. The second was to give students principles that would demonstrate their ability to withstand any amount of disconfirming evidence. The third was to give students a ticket of admission to a job where they could learn something about management.[10]

An MBA was nothing more than a union card for the financial elite.

War Versus Money

Scientists traded in real union cards to trade on Wall Street as available academic and defence jobs decreased. They flocked to make money not war.

Each year 150,000 people in the United States alone sit examinations to earn the letters CFA—*certified financial analyst*. The CFA and financial engineering program such as CQF (*certificate in quantitative finance*) were an entrance ticket to lucrative careers on Wall Street. Sylvain Raines, an experienced quant, joked that quantitative finance was an oxymoron as "finance is quantitative by definition…this is like saying aerial flight or wet swimming."[11]

Newly graduated financial experts applied simple "phenomenological toys" to markets. Most financial models are wrong, only the degree of error is in question. Differential equations, positive definite matrices or the desirable statistical properties of an estimator rarely determine the price of traded financial instruments.

Goldman Sachs' Emanuel Derman, a trained physicist, identified the difference: "In physics, a model is correct if it predicts the future trajectories of planets or the existence and properties of new planets.… In finance, you cannot easily prove a model right by such observations." Derman ruefully concluded: "Trained economists have never seen a really first-class model."[12]

Commenting on the required level of quantitative knowledge of people involved in financial markets, Derman once observed that Tour de France bicyclists did not need to know the laws of physics. But it helped to know that at certain speeds and angles you come off the bike.

Quants and bankers barely understood each other: "The members of each discipline are proud of the fact they know nothing about other disciplines."[13] MBAs believed the models. Quants worshipped the models they built. But turning models into money-making machines required the skills of the traders: "Reeling and Writhing, of course, to begin with, and the different branches of Arithmetic—Ambition, Distraction, Uglification, and Derision."[14]

Traders understood that prices are based on ever-changing, frequently irrational opinions. They understood that the players "don't know when they've lost, so they keep trying."[15] In *Wall Street*, Gordon Gecko (Mike Douglas) derisively dismisses Harvard MBA types as not adding up to dog shit. He wants guys who are poor, smart, hungry, without feelings and who keep on fighting.

During the global financial crisis, the *Financial Times* published a spoof ad for the Central Intelligence Agency (CIA) targeting financiers: "You didn't see the financial crisis coming. We missed 9/11 and the end of the cold war. Sounds like a match made in heaven—particularly now that you're unemployed."[16]

Shop Floors

The ritual theater of campus recruitment, the *hunting season*, is dominated by words like "smart," "intelligent," and "challenging." It is the idealized vision of bankers: 'They are the elite of Wall Street. Their offices are as furnished with expensive antiques and original works of art. They…are as quick to place a telephone call to Rome or Zurich or Frankfurt as most Americans are to call their next door neighbor…. His art is arcane."[17]

New recruits rapidly discover a different reality. Banks don't even trust the skills of recruits, putting them through extensive training programs: "You are perfect, now could you please change?" Then, there's the work.

Investment banking is *coverage* or *product*. Coverage is constant client meetings and spending 24/7 preparing thick, glossy, spurious *pitch books*, glanced at cursorily and thrown into waste bins. Reams of analysis are only to persuade clients to do something, anything, which results in fees for the bank.

Product means mergers and acquisitions or fund raising. Mergers involve endless research, positing what a company *should* do. Dense, stupefying valuations are prepared, showing how every proposed transaction will boost share prices. Fund raising is proposals to raise more money, more cheaply, via the latest opportunities and market windows.

Trading is *selling* or *speculation*. Selling is endless cold calling, puffery or inane chatter, masquerading as market *color* (commentary) or trading ideas. No one can provide what everybody is really interested in—the sure, sure thing. Traders chafe under the relentless pressure of making money or not losing money.

In risk management, you learn that you are irrelevant, despite everybody saying you are vital. In the back office, you are chained to the oars of the banking trireme, processing an avalanche of paper. If you are not a producer then you are a cost center, expected to perform magic tricks daily to keep the machine going.

Misinformed

Banks take smart people and plug "them into [their] dull, trivial culture" where they "waste their lives on the hamster wheel of corporate life."[18] There is a mismatch between expectations and the reality of banking, echoing a scene in the film *Casablanca*. Asked by Captain Renault what brought him to Casablanca, Rick (played by Humphrey Bogart) replies that he came because of his health, to take the waters. A surprised Captain Renault informs Rick that they are in the desert. Rick ironically rejoinders that he was misinformed.

The assumed sophistication of finance and financiers is greatly overrated:[19]

Banker	Financial markets are, to use the common phrase, driven by sentiment.
Interviewer	What does that mean?
Banker	Suddenly, one day, out of the blue, one of these very sharp and sophisticated people says, my god something awful's going to happen. We've lost everything. Oh my god, what are we going to do? What are we going to do?
Interviewer	Shall I, ah, jump out of the window?
Banker	Shall I jump out of the window? Exactly. Let's all jump out of the window.

Gaining an edge is crucial, sometimes involving unusual initiatives. A trader at Steve Cohen's SAC Capital was allegedly forced by his boss to take female hormones and wear articles of women's clothing at work, leading to a sexual relationship between the men, one of whom was married. The bizarre behavior was to eliminate the trader's aggressive male attitude, making him a more obedient and detail-oriented trader.[20]

Amar Bhide, a professor of business at Harvard, coined the phrase *hustle as strategy*. Banks have no strategy, only hustle. One bank decided its strategy was to have no strategy. Instead it hired smart people and backed them. Imitation is the only real strategy.

The culture does not create leaders, instead producing tyrants and dictators. Richard Fuld, CEO of Lehman Brothers for almost two decades, was "neither a leader nor a dazzling intellect."[21] In the culture of the deal, banks endlessly copy each other's strategies or products, chasing the same customers, competing on price and the ability to take risk. Complex systems of fealty exist within firms. Fiercely secretive, bankers are reluctant to share information, seeking an edge over their internal and external competitors. People eat what they kill.

Despite affirmative action programs and considerable lip service to modern employment practices, the firms are backward in their treatment of women, minorities, and cultural differences. A proudly misogynist culture dominates at every level. Joseph Akermann, head of Germany's Deutsche Bank, thought that adding women to the firm's men-only management board would make the forum "more colorful and prettier."[22] In 2007 Morgan Stanley agreed to pay $62 million to settle a number of gender discrimination claims bought by female employees.

Writing about her experiences at the 2011 World Economic Forum in Davos, journalist Anya Schiffrin, the wife of economist Joseph Stiglitz, recorded the humiliation of the women who make up a small portion of attendees. In a world where titles on conference badges are everything, the plain white name badges defined a wife's low status. The only position that is worse is that of a Davos mistress, who usually does not get a badge at all.[23]

Smiling and Killing

French philosopher Michel Foucault identified a *carceral continuum*, the system of cruelty, power, supervision, surveillance, and enforcement of acceptable behavior affecting working and domestic lives. Banking has its equivalent. It is the world of the film *Crimson Tide*, where Captain Ramsay tells sailors that rules are not open to personal interpretation, intuition, gut feeling, the behavior of the hairs on the back of the neck, or the whispers of little devils and angels sitting on your shoulder. Recruits must adapt to the unforgiving culture or die.

Sociologist Zygmunt Bauman's metaphor of *liquid* and *solid* modernity captures the shift from a society of producers to a society of consumers. Security gives way to increased freedom to purchase, to consume and to enjoy life. In liquid modernity, individuals have to be flexible and adaptable, pursuing available opportunities, calculating likely gains and losses from actions under endemic uncertainty. It was a metaphor for the rise of financiers and the financialization of everyday life in a volatile world where risk taking and speculation was an essential survival strategy.

In *Liquidated*, anthropologist Karen Ho documented the culture of modern banking.[24] Instead of the expected royal treatment, the best and brightest must work like indentured slaves for up to 140 hours a week. Lacking job security and facing constant performance pressure, bankers survive by trading things or cutting deals. Ho's title evokes Bauman's idea of liquid modernity. Bankers made assets liquid or tradable. As highly liquid assets themselves that could be easily liquidated, they lived in constant fear. They learned the truth of an old Wall Street saying: "Never tell anyone on Wall Street your problems. Some don't care. Most are glad you have them."

The environment creates a culture where narrow, short-term self-interest dominates. It drives creation and sales of products of no intrinsic value. Fear of liquidation eliminates misgivings about profitable transactions that might result in enormous pain for others.

Bernard Madoff perfected *affinity fraud*, preying upon unwitting members of his religious and ethnic communities, enlisting leading figures to promote fraudulent investments through the country clubs of Long Island and Palm Beach. Former Salomon Brothers economist and Lehman Brothers board member Henry Kaufman, along with stars such as Steven Spielberg, Jeffrey Katzenberg, Kevin Bacon, John Malkovich, Zsa Zsa Gabor, and Larry King lost money. The Elie Wiesel Foundation for Humanity, founded by holocaust survivor Elie Wiesel, lost $15.2 million. Investors should have heeded Groucho Marx's observation about not belonging to any club that would have him as a member.

In Bret Easton Ellis' novel *American Psycho*, Patrick Bateman is a successful, intelligent, and charming Wall Street banker who outside working hours is a vicious psychopathic killer. But elite bankers don't only behave this way at night. At the start of the book, Bateman stares at blood-red graffiti that alludes to Dante's hell: "Abandon all hope ye who enter here." At the end of the book, Bateman sits in a bar staring at a sign: "This is not an exit."[25] Any Faustian bargain comes with a price.

Pay Grades

The pay was the only thing that made it all tolerable. As Jeffrey Skilling, the former president of Enron, knew: "all that matters is money.... You buy loyalty with money...touchy feely stuff isn't as important as cash."[26] The character Jeffrey Skilling in the drama *Enron* says: "Money and sex motivate people...money...gets their hand off their d**k and into work."[27]

In 2006, investment banking accounted for just 0.1 percent of all U.S. private sector jobs (173,340 out of 132.5 million jobs), yet accounted for 1.3 percent of all wages. The average weekly wage of investment bankers was

$8,367, compared to $841 for all private sector jobs. In Fairfield County, Connecticut, where many hedge funds were based, the average pay was $23,846 a week.[28] In 2007, the combined remuneration at the five major Wall Street investment banks alone exceeded the world's total foreign aid budget of $850 billion.

The leading 20 hedge fund and private equity managers earned $657.5 million in 2007—$12.6 million a week or $210,737 an hour (assuming a 60-hour week). They earned the $29,500 average annual income in the U.S. in just over 8 minutes. They earned the President's salary (around $400,000 per year) in less than 2 hours.[29]

At a conference on the Australian economy, CEO of Macquarie Bank Allan Moss, who annually earned A$33.5 million, was shocked to discover that the best paid teachers earned A$65,000 per year (less than 0.2 percent of his remuneration). Moss was not entirely out of touch with domestic economics, being spotted presenting a voucher entitling him to a 4-cent-per-litre discount on fuel purchases.[30]

Bankers get paid a base salary, $35,000 to $500,000, but performance based bonuses can total up to 100 times that. The structure makes compensation costs variable, matching the volatile nature of investment banking.

Although senior bankers everywhere were well paid, the über bonus is a recent phenomenon. Until the mid 1990s, multimillion dollar bonuses were unusual. Traditionally, investment banks were partnerships where gentlemen worked together, sharing profits. For employees, the *golden ring* of partnership was the prize. At "Goldmine" or "Golden Sachs," becoming a partner was winning the lottery, *every year*. As investment banks became publicly owned or part of commercial banks, the promise of the partnership was lost and bonuses became important in compensating and retaining staff.

Large bonuses and increasing profits went hand in hand. Traditional partnerships had limited capital, confining themselves to primarily arranging deals. Access to more capital from shareholders (where publicly held) or commercial banks (who owned them) allowed investment banks to trade on their own account and take greater risks.

Much More Than This

Learning about former CEO of Goldman Sachs and U.S. Treasury secretary Hank Paulson's bucolic lifestyle, playwright David Hare mused: "Why does anyone need $500 million, or whatever he got from Goldman, to live in Idaho?"[31] Bankers argued that it was reward for talent and expertise. Society benefited from the banker's work: "Tell the masses...you are inferior and all the improvements in your conditions which you simply take for granted you owe to the effort of men who are better than you."[32]

Larry Summers believed that the market allowed skilled talent to capture their fair share of returns, consistent with productivity and contribution to economic outcomes. Between government jobs, Summers earned $5 million at hedge fund D.E. Shaw & Co., playing down his role as a mere part-time job.

Bankers blamed the high cost of living in major financial centers like London and New York. There was the need to maintain an expected life style—private schools, private trainers, private chefs, etc. It was pure Woody Allen: "Money is better than poverty, if only for financial reasons."

Large bonuses were based on high profits, the product of excessive risk and leverage. Some of the earnings were imaginary, based on mark-to-market accounting not true cash profit. Bankers mastered the art of "seeing where the arrow of performance lands and then painting the bull's eye around it."[33] Banks paid out non-existent earnings to employees because everybody was doing it.

In 2008, Stan O'Neal, CEO of Merrill Lynch, said that: "As a result of the extraordinary growth at Merrill during my tenure as CEO the board saw fit to increase my compensation each year." In 2006, when Merrill had record earnings of $7.5 billion, the firm handed out over $5 billion in bonuses. Dow Kim, head of the Merrill's fixed income business including mortgages, received a bonus of $35 million on top of his salary of $350,000. A 20-something year old analyst collected a bonus of $250,000 on top of a base salary of $130,000. A 30-something year old trader collected a bonus of $5 million on top of a base salary of $180,000. Merrill ultimately lost vast sums when the basis of the profits, mortgage investments, fell sharply in value.[34]

Joining CitiGroup after his term as Treasury secretary, Robert Rubin was paid $20 million a year, as a non-executive board member with poorly defined duties. During the tenure of Rubin and CEO Chuck Prince, Citi lost over $50 billion and its market value fell by more than $60 billion, ultimately requiring a government bailout.

Even failure was well rewarded. Upon leaving, Merrill's Stan O'Neal received $30 million in retirement benefits as well as $129 million in stock and option holdings, in addition to the $160 million he earned during nearly five years as CEO. Chuck Prince was paid an exit bonus of $12.5 million, additional to $68 million already received in stock and options, a $1.7 million annual pension, as well an office, car, and driver for up to 5 years. Prince signed a 5-year noncompete agreement. Citi may have benefited more by allowing their former CEO to manage a competitor, given the results of his tenure at the bank.

Tight circles of directors, senior managers, and consultants determine salaries. Benchmarking exercises merely reinforce the norm, with packages justified as "needing to buy the best talent" or "meeting the demands of a competitive market." John Kenneth Galbraith identified this pattern: "The salary of the chief executive of the large corporation is not a market award for achievement. It is frequently in the nature of a warm personal gesture by the individual to himself."[35]

The conventional view was that the global financial crisis wiped out the wealth of senior executives, because they were significant shareholders of their banks. While executives suffered losses, top executives of Bear Stearns and Lehman Brothers had cashed out. The top five executives at Bear Stearns and Lehman pocketed cash bonuses exceeding $300 million and $150 million respectively (in 2009 U.S. dollars). Although the earnings on which the remuneration was based were reversed in 2008, the executives did not return the payments received.[36]

Salli Krawcheck, a former CFO at Citi, observed: "it's better to be an investment bank employee than shareholder."[37] Andy Kessler, a former Wall Street research analyst, noted: "Wall Street is just a compensation scheme.... They literally exist to pay out half their revenue as compensation. And that's what gets them into trouble every so often—it's just a game of generating revenue, because the players know they will get half of it back."[38]

There were crumbs from the bankers' feast for all. Regulators were seduced with invitations to all-expense-paid lavish conferences and speaking engagements. Modest current salaries were compensated for by post-retirement sinecures in banks. In Japan, each summer senior government officials retired and underwent amakudari (descent from heaven), taking up lucrative jobs in private firms in the industries they had previously regulated.

Charles Ferguson's film *Inside Job* exposed prestigious academics and former regulators who were paid large consulting fees by financial institutions and even countries to espouse a particular point of view. Former Federal Reserve vice-chairman Frederic Mishkin, the film revealed, was paid $124,0000 for touting Iceland as a well-run banking center shortly before it imploded. A study originally titled "Financial stability in Iceland" was included mysteriously in Mishkin's CV as "Financial instability in Iceland." Confronted on camera about conflicts of interest, the film captured Harvard's Martin Feldstein glowering, squirming, and smiling, in the words of one reviewer "like Yoda with a hemorrhoid."[39]

Warren Buffet recognized that the system produced "wildly capricious" results. "I've worked in an economy that rewards someone who saves the lives of others on a battlefield with a medal, rewards a great teacher with thank-you notes from parents, but rewards those who can detect the mispricing of securities with sums reaching into the billions."[40]

Attached

Attachment theory in psychology focuses on a child's need to develop a relationship with someone for normal social and emotional development.

The banking elite attached themselves to money: "in the real world...[if] people aren't making that much money, then they don't really matter. They don't count, so you can treat the guy who gives you coffee as a lesser citizen."[41] Converted into commodities, in fear of being liquidated, bankers sought the safety of liquidity: "As long as I get the bonus that I want, I'll stay. Otherwise...I will just leave...everyone is looking out for himself."[42]

Originally the primary means of acquiring wealth was robbery, privateering, and force rather than capital accumulation. Bankers reverted to these traditional activities to generate rewards, vacuuming up every last entitlement. They worked just past the hour entitling them to free meals and a car-service ride home. Travel expenses were routinely misstated. Goldman Sachs offered a generous health benefits package, including coverage of sex reassignment surgery.[43]

If you liked to go hunting or shooting then you just invited your clients along for the day. In Japan, salary men bankers routinely entertained Western clients on the bank's account. They lost the client quickly to get on with the night's revelry unhindered. Everywhere, sporting events, and expensive restaurants co-existed with adult entertainment. Some bankers regularly paid prostitutes to entertain clients. One broker described a fishing trip as an extended orgy, a customer drinking, and drug party.

For the jaded palate, there was London's *ginger pig butcher*. Clad in white coats, bankers, investors, hedge fund managers, and lawyers paid more than £120 each to learn how to carve up carcasses. As banks routinely butcher and carve up clients, the parallel was appropriate.

The system of entitlement was visceral. Gaining entry to MBA courses, students deliberately ran down bank accounts to qualify for larger student support by buying expensive new cars—"financial aid" BMWs. As cars were not listed as assets, the students qualified for more financial assistance. When Lehman Brothers filed for bankruptcy, bankers filed out grasping plaintively at small cardboard boxes, full of sandwiches, drinks, chocolate bars, and other food items. As the firm's canteen worked on a still-functioning internal staff credit system, the bankers were in fact looting its contents.

Bonus Season

Each year, from around September, the bonus season is in full swing. Donors huddle in meetings, while supplicants lobby, submitting *puff* sheets of exaggerated contributions to earnings. Timely opinion pieces in trade magazines, speeches at conferences or increased press profile lend support to their case for larger bonuses. Some solicit form letters of commendation from clients extolling their talents. Some resort to veiled threats of opportunities elsewhere.

Managers use the *number* to manage their charges, while keeping the lion's share of the plunder themselves. If a manager has ten people in their department, then reducing each person's bonus by $100,000 increases the manager's own share by $1 million. Happy employees mean that you have paid them too much. Disgusted employees mean that you have paid them so little that they will leave. The optimal point is between satisfied and dissatisfied—enough to keep you but not enough to make you complacent or diminish the manager's own bonus.[44]

On the day of announcement, the earlier you are called in the better. The later you attend, the more difficult the conversation is likely to be. "The firm and markets are facing challenging times." "You are being promoted to head of EMEA Trading in Local Currency." "We have stretched to pay you one of the highest bonuses within your comparable group." "There is a mismatch between your talents and the job." All these mean that your bonus is low. The really out-of-favor have already been removed from the bonus pool by transfers to other departments late in the year or outright dismissal. The better conversations home in quickly on the money, there being so little else to say.

In 2009, one junior trader protested that he could not possibly maintain his lifestyle or his investments on the number. The recipients of larger bonuses register a muted protest, to establish the ground for a higher number next year and demonstrate the hunger that firms value. The real angst comes when you discover that you got $1 million but someone else got a dollar more.

Plenty

Successful bankers, like Lehman's Richard Fuld and Bear Stearns' James Cayne, took nearly 2 decades to become multimillionaires and finally billionaires. A less patient, new generation aspired to become hedge fund and private equity managers where the 2/20 percent formula gave them a share of the action. Brian Hunter, responsible for energy trading at hedge fund Amaranth before it imploded, earned between $75 million and $100 million in 2005, ranking him a middling 29th highest paid in his profession. Several hedge fund managers routinely earn $1 billion each year.

When hedge fund Fortress went public in 2007, at the end of the first day of trading Wes Edens, one of the founders, was worth $2.3 billion on paper and Fortress's total market value was $12.5 billion. By 2007, nearly half of the 40 richest people in the United States had made their fortunes in private equity or hedge funds—David Bonderman and James Coulter of TPG, William Conway, Daniel D'Aniello, and David Rubenstein of The Carlyle Group, Peter Peterson and Stephen Schwarzman of The Blackstone Group, Daniel Och of Och-Ziff Capital Management, and Steven Cohen of

SAC Capital. The youngest was 33-year-old John Arnold, a former Enron trader, who set up hedge fund Centaurus Energy and was worth an estimated $1.5 billion.

Chuck Prince's successor as CEO of Citi, Vikram Pandit, started the hedge fund Old Lane Partners after leaving Morgan Stanley. After Citi purchased the fund for $800 million, Pandit joined Citi as head of its Investment Management Unit—the "$800 million man." After poor performance, Citi shut down the fund and wrote down its investment.

The monetary measure of true success was "never having to fly commercial." In *Wall Street*, Gordon Gecko thought that having your own jet was what qualified a true player in the game—someone who was rich enough not to have to waste time. Everything else amounted to nothing.

Tipping Points

Bankers were getting a disproportionate share of the profits with no liability for losses, under a bonus system that encouraged excessive risk taking. Firms tinkered with the bonus system. In 1994 Warren Buffett tried to stop bonus payments until Salomon Brothers' profitability returned to satisfactory levels. Buffett was forced to abandon the proposal when many senior staff left, joining competitors. A financial firm's assets well and truly go down in the elevator at the end of every day.

The mobility of and competition for staff made it difficult to change the system. Payouts were deferred over a number of years and a portion was in deferred stock or stock options. Competitors poached successful bankers or traders, matching deferred compensation in new stock or cash, adding large signing on bonuses and multi-year guarantees.

During negotiations with the U.S. government to invest $10 billion of tax payers' money directly in Merrill Lynch to avoid risk of failure, John Thain, Stan O'Neal's successor, was concerned about how this would affect executive compensation.[45] Even the U.S. Bankruptcy Court approved a bonus pool of $50 million for the remaining derivative traders at bankrupt Lehman Brothers, who had been kept on to wind down its transactions.

Dissatisfied with his number, a young banker protested that it "was not a bonus! It's a tip!" A tip or gratuity is a noncontractual payment for special service, sometimes related to the relative status of the parties. No doctor or surgeon expects to or receives a tip for doing their job properly.

The bonus culture encouraged *moral hazard*—a focus on narrowly quantifiable outcomes while ignoring wider risks and costs. Elite bankers and traders took risks with other people's money, aware that if they won the bet they would get a significant share of profits, while suffering no permanent damage if they lost.

In a comedy sketch featuring British comedians John Bird and John Fortune, the interviewer asks: "Can we talk about moral hazard?" The banker responds: "About what?" The interviewer reiterates the question: "Moral hazard?" The banker says: "I know what 'hazard' means, but what's the other word?"[46] As Adam Smith bemoaned: "All for ourselves, and nothing for anyone else seems, in every age, to have been the vile maxim of the masters of mankind."[47]

21

Financial Nihilism

When bankers say that it's not about the money, it may even be true. Ron Beller, a Goldman Sachs partner, was one of a group of bankers who had more than £4 million stolen from them by Joyti De-Laurey, their secretary. The bankers made so much money that they did not notice the theft of large amounts for many years.

Ceasing to be ordinary—anyone with a net worth less than $100 million—elite bankers discovered that they actually had always been art experts, public intellectuals, men or women of letters, or all of these. Their ambition rivaled that of Salvador Dali: "At the age of six I wanted to be a cook. At seven I wanted to be Napoleon. And my ambition has been growing steadily ever since."[1] As poet T.S. Eliot knew: "Most of the trouble in the world is caused by people wanting to be important."

The financial elite is narrow and limited, too smart, too fast, wanting too much, lacking any sense of history, and reinforcing each other's opinion. In agriculture, monocultures are inherently dangerous—increasing production but with a lack of diversity that makes crops less resilient to parasites and disease. In the 1840s, potato crops in Ireland became blighted, causing famine. Collapses in the French wine industry and U.S. corn production highlighted the risk of focusing on a single strain. The monocultural financial elites ignored this lesson of history.

Cosmetic Consumption

Rich bankers sought to convert their earnings into something approximating satisfaction, happiness, or social respectability. Keen to promote his wife Lori's writing ambitions, the ordinarily frugal Michael Milken offered to buy her a publishing company. A keen bird watcher and naturalist, Hank Paulson bought up swathes of endangered wetlands. Michael Steinhardt, a hedge fund manager, wanted to collect every duck and swan variety in the world to populate his estate. Some traded up partners to fit corporate exigencies, ambitions, and evolving tastes. Attractive women found bankers irresistible, as research showed that a "woman's orgasm frequency increases with the income of their partner."[2]

In 2008, hedge fund manager Steve Cohen applied to add 1,145 square feet (106 square meters) to an existing 35,085-square-foot (3,263-square-meter) residence on 14 acres (5.5 hectares) in Greenwich, Connecticut. The $14 million *Xanadu on Crown Lane* featured a basketball court, an indoor pool, and a Zamboni machine to smooth out a 6,734-square-foot (626-square-meter) ice rink. Cohen also owned a 6,000-square-foot (559-square-meter) pied-à-terre in Manhattan and a 19,000-square-foot (1,767-square-meter) bungalow in Delray Beach, Florida. A neighbor, Valery Kogan, another hedge fund manager, proposed a new 54,000-square-foot (5,022-square-meter) house with a 12-car garage, a Finnish spa, a dog-grooming salon, and no less than 26 toilets.

Transport was private jets, helicopters, European marque cars, or SUVs. Based on the Ferrari 599 GTB, a flying car, the Autovolanter, was on the drawing board. Costing £500,000, the Autovolantor was designed to travel at 100 mph on the ground and 150 mph in the air at altitudes of up to 5,000 feet (465 meters). The vehicle targeted businessmen and financiers, allowing occupants to avoid traffic.

Holiday homes in exotic locations, vacations in seven-star resorts, boats, clothes, and every possible electronic gadget supported by an array of private staff were also part of the appearance. As American media personality Tyra Banks put it: "I love the confidence that make-up gives me."

A minority succumbed to drugs and depravity. In 2007, the death of Seth Tobias, a hedge manager, became a steamy soap opera of cocaine abuse and sex with gay prostitutes, especially a male go-go dancer known as Tiger and a one-time California psychic claiming to be the deceased's former assistant.

Warren Buffett, worth about $60 billion, famously continued to live in his home in Omaha, Nebraska, purchased in 1958 for $31,500. He drove a modest 2006 Cadillac DTS, having traded in his 6-year-old Lincoln Town Car (with the personalized registration THRIFTY). He favored hamburgers and soft drinks. Buffet bought his second wife's wedding ring from Borsheim's Fine Jewelry in Omaha, owned by Buffett's Berkshire Hathaway, asking for and receiving a staff discount. Rupert Murdoch's third wife,

Wendy Deng, told a woman's magazine that her husband, worth more than $8 billion, wore $9 shirts bought at U.S. discount store Wal-Mart. But Buffett and Murdoch also owned top-of-the-line business jets to ease the rigors of frequent business travel.

The Physical Impossibility of Spending the Amount Earned by Someone Living

Life imitated fiction as wealthy bankers mirrored *Wall Street*'s fictitious, art collecting villain—Gordon Gekko.

Art was an alibi for networking, providing natural opportunities to meet members of the financial elite and identify deals.

Hedge fund manager Steve Cohen was typical of new buyers who increasingly drove the market for high-end art. His $700 million art collection included Damien Hirst's *The Physical Impossibility of Death in the Mind of Someone Living*. Given a net worth of $8 billion and an annual income of $500 million, the work cost a few days' income: "after you have a fourth home and a [Gulfstream] G5 jet, what else is there?"[3]

Finance and art share an abstract nature as well as constant debates about value and significance. Art was an expensive meta-object unrelated to anything else. It was self-referential, using itself as the point of departure and benchmark—it was the fact that it was an *artist*'s work that made it *art*. Modern money, too, was a meta-concept, capable of infinite expansion, circular and entirely trapped in its own ambiguous reality. Damien Hirst recognized the parallel: "art is a more powerful currency than money.... But you start to have this sneaking feeling that money is more powerful."[4]

Art was an investment with "liquidity" that "diversified your portfolio." Like emerging markets, collectors spoke of "emergent art." Art prices paralleled finance: "in the long run, economic and cultural values correlate...[but] in the short term, you get fictional markets." There was the language of derivatives: "collectors are effectively buying futures option on a work's cultural significance...people coming into my private mausoleum/ museum are going to be thrilled by the painting."[5]

Sotheby's and Christie's were the centerpiece of modern art:

> Auctions are a bizarre combination of slave market, trading floor, theater and brothel...rarefied entertainments where speculation, spin, and trophy hunting merge as an insular caste enacts a highly structured ritual in which the codes of consumption and peerage are manipulated in plain sight.[6]

For the alpha males of banking, buying and selling art approximates trading: "They study the form, they read the magazine, they listen to the word on the street, they have hunches." Art dealers talk of "making markets in art works" and "pulling the trigger on a trade."[7]

Like financial assets, critic Robert Hughes thought that prices for artworks "are determined by the meeting of real or induced scarcity with pure irrational desire, and nothing is more manipulable than desire…a fair price is the highest one a collector can be induced to pay."[8] Mimicking the behavior of financial markets, herds chase works by a handful of fashionable painters.

Previous generations of bankers collected Old Masters, like the Impressionists. Newer generations favored modern art, which expressed the artist's angst at the discovery of their inability to draw or paint at all. Distillation of suffering exorcising the guilt of wealth did well. Charles Saatchi famously profited from Marc Quinn's *Self*—a cast of the artist's head made from his frozen blood.

Art confirming the self-image of financiers attracted especially high prices. Inspired by Hokusai's famous nineteenth-century woodblock print *The Great Wave of Kanagawa*, the Japanese artist Takashi Murakami's 727 paintings showed Mr. DOB, a post nuclear Mickey Mouse character, as a god riding on a cloud or a shark surfing on a wave. The first 727 is owned by New York's Museum of Modern Art, the second by Steve Cohen. With its jaws gaping, poised to swallow its prey, *The Physical Impossibility of Death in the Mind of Someone Living* mirrored the killer instincts of hedge funds—feared predators in financial markets. Cohen "liked the whole fear factor."[9]

Celebrity Finance

Financiers, especially celebrity financiers, increasingly wielded significant political power, shaping economic and sometimes social agendas.

Since the late nineteenth century, idolization of speculators and financiers alternated with occasional calls for their scalps. J.P. Morgan, known as "Financial Titan," "Finance's Napoleon", or simply "Zeus" or "Jupiter," exemplified the banker's influence. *Life* magazine clarified his powers: "God made the world in 4004 BC and it was reorganized…by J.P. Morgan."[10] When Morgan said, "America is good enough for me," the politician William Jennings Bryan retorted: "Whenever he doesn't like it, he can give it back."[11] In the July 2010 issue of *Vanity Fair*, hedge-fund billionaire Steve Cohen told correspondent Bryan Burrough that even he might be ready to walk away from trading. Burrough, awestruck, wrote that it's "a little like saying that God is ready to walk away from Earth."[12]

Popular media portrayed glamorous, corporate predators, junk bond kings, securitization virtuosos, and derivative wizards. The idea of energetic, inventive, and cunning financiers operating at the edge of morality and legality, taking on governments, was heroic. The media celebrated George Soros' 1992 attack on the pound sterling as victory over an inept and poor government.

Bankers joined industrialists and celebrities as *Davos men and women*.[13] At the Davos World Economic Forum, the Boao Forum in Asia and the

IMF/World Bank annual meetings, the financial elite meets to exchange views, coordinate strategies, and shape policy, captured by the paparazzi.

The events are open to people whose adoring and uncritical media profiles promote their purported business genius and ability to walk on water. Believing that they are *special*, they associate only with *special* others who understand them. At Davos the diverse mix is confusing—celebrities wanting to be intellectuals, intellectuals wanting to be celebrities, and bankers wanting to be both celebrities and intellectuals. Perspectives are self-serving, promoting views beneficial to their business and financial interests.

In 2006, using his network, Stephen Schwarzman arranged to meet with Chancellor Angela Merkel to counter German hostility toward private equity locusts. Eight weeks later, Blackstone (Schwarzman's firm) purchased a stake in Deutsche Telekom.[14] In 2010, facing proposals to tax private equity executives at higher income tax rates, Schwarzman compared President Obama's administration's *war* against business to Hitler's invasion of Poland in 1939.[15]

The avuncular Warren Buffett freely dispenses finely crafted financial homilies. Criticism of derivative weapons of mass destruction contrasts with Berkshire Hathaway's extensive use of derivatives and investments in Salomon Brothers and General Reinsurance, both participants in derivative markets.

During the crisis, Buffett, a significant investor in Moody's, was silent about the problems surrounding rating agencies. Having uncharacteristically declined an invitation to appear, in June 2010 Buffett testified before the Financial Crisis Inquiry Commission under subpoena. Buffett emphasized that he knew little about the rating process other than its profit margins. He had never visited Moody's offices, not even knowing where they were located.

Buffett defended Moody's:

> They made a mistake that virtually everybody in the country made. There was the greatest bubble I've ever seen in my life.... Very, very few people could appreciate the bubble.... Rising prices are a narcotic that affect the reasoning power up and down the line.[16]

He did not acknowledge any failure or complicity of the agencies in creating the bubble.

When Goldman Sachs was indicted for alleged violations in structuring and selling CDOs, Buffett, a major investor in Goldman, defended the firm, its actions and its CEO.

In 2011, David Sokol, the CEO of Netjets, a company in which Buffett had a significant shareholding, resigned. Sokol had been a candidate for succeeding Buffett at Berkshire Hathaway. Sokol's resignation came after disclosure of his purchase of Lubrizol shares before Berkshire bought the chemicals company, netting him a $3 million personal profit. Buffett initially defended Sokol's actions arguing that the purchases were not unlawful.

Buffett also initially did not comment on the ethical issues or conflicts of interst. Similar personal trading in the shares would be unambiguously barred at banks, themeselves hardly paragons of virtue.

Whatever his record as an investor, the Sokol episode drew attention to the differences between Buffett's pronouncements about the standard of conduct he required of others and that followed at Berkshire Hathaway. Critics pointed out anomalies in the firm's corporate practices. Berkshire Hathaway's dual class share arrangement gives Buffett voting control, whilst owning 34 percent of the equity. Until a decade ago, Berkshire Hathaway's seven person board of directors consisted of mainly insiders such as Buffett's son. The new "independent" directors include Bill Gates, a close friend of Buffett and his regular bridge partner as well as co-investor in the Gates Foundation. Critics also pointed to the fact that Buffett's partner Charlie Munger's family owned a 3 percent stake in BYD, the Chinese electric battery maker, before Bershire bought a stake in 2008.

Nothing anaesthetizes, it seems, better than financial self-interest. Ambrose Bierce, the American writer, described hypocrisy as "prejudice with a halo."

Elite bankers also sought to influence social policy, through generous donations to charities. Their model was Richard Gere: "Hi, I'm Richard Gere and I'm speaking for the entire world."[17] Bear Stearn's Ace Greenburg donated $1 million to a hospital so that homeless men had access to free Viagra.[18] George Soros supported free markets and democratic initiatives in Eastern Europe. Of course, hedge funds were beneficiaries from the opening up of these economies.

Veteran campaigner Ralph Nader's book, *Only the Super Rich Can Save Us*, urged billionaires to use their wealth to clean up America in a form of practical utopianism. Warren Buffett has indicated that he will leave 85 percent of his multibillion-dollar fortune to charity to be managed by his friend Bill Gates. One blogger urged everybody to go and get rich, so they could help more people. Others saw the contradiction: "The uber-rich try to do good once they have done their damage.... I admire Gates and Buffett for their generosity...but...loathe the system that put them at the top of the food chain."[19]

Arthur Hugh Clough in *Spectator ab Extra* captured the dichotomy:[20]

> I sit at my table en grand signeur
> And when I have done, throw a crust to the poor;
> Not only the pleasure of good living,
> But also the pleasure of now and then giving:
> So pleasant it is to have money, heigh ho!

The philanthropy of the financial elite was really an exercise in damage control against any backlash from increasing inequality.

Manqué Not Monkey

Some financier's creative tendencies manifested themselves in *billionaire drivel*.[21] Ray Dalio, founder of fund manager Bridgewater, sent out an 83-page management "manifesto" setting out 296 principles.[22] Highlights included banning gossip, "personalizing mistakes" to humiliate staff, and managing employees as baseball cards. Meetings were recorded and distributed, and there were firm-wide emails of recordings of individuals being mercilessly shredded.[23] Bridgewater's pursuit of *truth* and *honesty* was Orwellian.

In a memo to his "gang" while on "yacht time" after "an agonizingly tough couple of weeks," Tom Barrack, CEO of Colony Capital, wrote of discovering his daughter's copy of *Twilight*, a series of adolescent vampire-romance novels: "I don't get it…but I feel it. Taking the agenda-less time to absorb a point of view that I had ignored while loved ones around me relished it was an oasis for my soul." Barrack experienced an epiphany: "It is hard for us to dream…it is time for all of us…to spend more time outside the strict arithmetic cadence of our business…we must really find the 'moment.'"[24]

George Soros craves acceptance as a thought leader. Appearing before the U.S. Congress, Soros brought along a copy of his latest book to promote it. For Soros, a man of letters and a hedge fund manager were identical career choices:

> The main difference between me and other people who have amassed this kind of money is that I am primarily interested in ideas, and I don't have much personal use for money. But I hate to think what would have happened if I hadn't made money: My ideas would not have gotten much play. I wish I could write a book that will be read for as long as our civilization lasts.... I would value it much more highly than any business success.[25]

The centerpiece of Soros' philosophy is the idea of *reflexivity*. Markets do not tend toward equilibrium but feed on their own misconceptions to produce exaggerated price changes until they reach an inflection point when it changes. Soros suggests following the trend, selling as it reaches the peak.

Soros thinks of himself as a financial philosopher, even a philosopher *manqué*—past participle of the French verb *manquer*, "to miss," and means unfulfilled or potential, generally with reference to a profession. It is the philosophy of Gene Simmons, bass player of the rock band KISS: "Life is too short to have anything but delusional notions about yourself."

In December 1998, *The Economist* reviewed Soros' *The Crisis of Global Capitalism*:

> Because of who he is there will always be buyers for his books, publishers for his books, and cash-strapped academics to say flattering things about his books. None of this alters the fact that his

> books are no good.... A remarkable thing happens to money when it passes through Mr. Soros; it emerges multiplied, but otherwise unchanged. With other inputs the results are more disappointing—to be blunt, more in line with biology. Mr. Soros gorged on chopped philosophy, mashed economics, and facts and figures swimming in grease. It was too much. Before he knew what was happening out rushed this book.[26]

During the Asian financial crisis of 1997/8, Mahathir Mohammed, prime minister of Malaysia, also a less benign view of Soros: "All these countries [in East Asia] have spent 40 years trying to build up their economies and a moron like Soros comes along with a lot of money to speculate and ruin things."[27] The Prime Minister made no mention of his own Pharaonic projects funded by borrowings from foreigners. Slovenian philosopher Slavoj Žižek captured the essence of Soros: "Half the day he engages in the most ruthless financial exploitations, ruining the lives of hundreds of thousands, even millions. The other half [of the day] he just gives part of it back."[28]

Wizard and Muggles

In J.K. Rowling's *Harry Potter* fantasies, *muggle*, derived from "mug" or someone gullible, refers to people lacking magical ability. Foolish, befuddled muggles are contrasted to wizards born into the magical world. If muggles happen to observe the working of the wizard's magic, then *Obliviators*, sent by the Ministry of Magic, cast memory charms, causing them to forget the event. Wizards, the financial elite, used sorcery to rule over the muggles of the world, exploiting what John Kenneth Galbraith called the "inordinate desire to get rich quickly with a minimum of physical effort."

Bankers and extreme money brought about sociologist Georg Simmel's *vapidity of life*, a loosening of beneficial and human connections between the worlds of real industry and money, allowing each to develop independently of the other. Following the Great Depression, Wall Street became irrelevant to the wider economy. Now the wider economy was irrelevant to Wall Street.

Only elite bankers knew how to get things done: "We've made everyone smarter. We know much more...we're the grease that makes things turn more efficiently."[29] Jeffery Skilling, the character in *Enron*, sees the banker's role in driving growth as heroic:

> There's your mirror. Every dip, every crash, every bubble that's burst, that's you. Your brilliant stupidity. This one gave us railroads. This one the Internet. This one the slave trade. And if you wanna do anything about saving the environment or reaching other worlds, you'll need a bubble for that, too.[30]

None was more delusional than Angelo R. Mozilo, former CEO of Countrywide Financial, a mortgage lender that profited from the subprime lending debacle. He told the U.S. Financial Crisis Inquiry Commission that

Countrywide had "prevented social unrest" by providing loans to 25 million borrowers, many from minority groups: "Countrywide was one of the greatest companies in the history of this country and probably made more difference to society, to the integrity of our society, than any company in the history of America."[31]

In a 2010 essay, Malcolm Gladwell, the author, saw John Paulson, the hedge fund manager who profited from the collapse in subprime mortgages, as an archetypal entrepreneur.[32] Paulson was an opportunistic speculator who enriched himself and his investors, taking advantage of the housing disasters and resultant problems of the global financial system. Rather than heroic, their actions were parasitical, taking advantage of human misery. They did not create jobs, wealth nor produce or leave behind anything except money.[33] As the journalist H.L. Mencken knew: "The most common of all follies is to believe passionately in the palpably not true. It is the chief occupation of mankind."

In the Midnight Hour

While the money flowed, everything was fine. Chuck Prince told the *Financial Times* on July 10,2007: "When the music stops, in terms of liquidity, things will be complicated. But as long as the music is playing, you've got to get up and dance. We're still dancing." Warren Buffett foresaw the end:

> Nothing sedates rationality like large doses of effortless money...normally sensible people drift into behavior akin to that of Cinderella at the ball...they...hate to miss a single minute of what is one helluva party...the giddy participants all plan to leave just seconds before midnight. There's a problem, though: They are dancing in a room in which the clocks have no hands.[34]

In 2007, the clock turned to midnight and the music stopped. The subprime collapse set off a chain reaction that decimated financial markets and economies. Psychiatrist Elizabeth Kübler-Ross identified five stages of grieving—denial, anger, bargaining, depression, and acceptance.[35] As losses mounted and they were fired, bankers found it difficult to move beyond denial and anger.

When an investment manager's quantitative stock selection model underperformed, they had been undone by the "dash for cash" as markets fell. When markets recovered, they lost because of the "dash for trash." The market sentiment model found no sympathy, the quality-based model proved to be of low quality and the valuation model's ability was overvalued. It wasn't the manager's fault or a faulty model, but the fact that the risk trade was back on.

Lehman Brothers' CFO (thought by some now to stand for "conspicuous female officer") Erin Callan was pictured in *Condé Nast Portfolio* in a coquettish pose, dressed in a short dress and heels, stepping out of a limousine. As the firm battled to survive, she told *The Wall Street Journal* of her personal shopper at Bergdorf Goodman, an up-market fashion store.

The successor to Stan O'Neal at Merrill Lynch, John Thain optimistically spent $1.2 million redecorating his office while Merrill slipped closer to insolvency. After the U.S. Treasury arranged a shotgun marriage with Bank of America (BA) to save the firm, John Boy, now president of the Merrill Lynch Division, allegedly sought a $30–40 million bonus for "his good work." Rebuffed, he enquired whether a smaller bonus was available.[36] On *The Daily Show*, Jon Stewart showed a clip of Thain defending bonuses as a way to keep "your best people." An angry Stewart was unimpressed: "You don't have 'best people'! You lost $27 billion! Do you live in Bizarro World?"

The sense of entitlement remained to the end. A group of traders at a bar learned that one had had his employment terminated. Upon his return to the office, he was asked to return his corporate credit card. He was unable to comply. The card was behind the bar paying the tab for his colleagues carousing.

In 2008, Andrew Lahde, a hedge fund manager who made the highest percentage profits (870 percent) in a single year from the subprime collapse, filed a memorable resignation letter in the *Financial Times*. Lahde was generous in his praise for those who helped in his success:

> The low hanging fruit, i.e. idiots whose parents paid for prep school, Yale, and then the Harvard MBA, was there for the taking. These people who were (often) truly not worthy of the education they received (or supposedly received) rose to the top of companies...all levels of our government. All of this behavior supporting the Aristocracy only ended up making it easier for me to find people stupid enough to take the other side of my trades. God bless America.

He was refreshingly honest about his motivations: "I was in this game for the money." Lahde was satisfied to leave with his winnings:

> Some people, who think they have arrived at a reasonable estimate of my net worth, might be surprised that I would call it quits with such a small war chest. That is fine; I am content with my rewards. Moreover, I will let others try to amass nine, ten or eleven figure net worths. Meanwhile, their lives suck. Appointments back to back, booked solid for the next three months, they look forward to their two week vacation in January during which they will likely be glued to their BlackBerries.

He was retiring to:

> ...repair my health, which was destroyed by the stress I layered onto myself over the past two years, as well as my entire life—where I had to compete for spaces in universities and graduate schools, jobs and assets under management—with those who had all the advantages (rich parents) that I did not.[37]

But Lahde too benefited from the economic catastrophe that the Masters of the Universe unleashed. He was like author Kurt Vonnegut, Jr., who had profited from the fire bombing of Dresden and loss of 25,000 lives, the subject of his book *Slaughterhouse-Five*.[38]

In 2010 an email pinging around financial institutions summarized bankers' reaction to being considered "overpaid a***holes" by average Joes:[39]

> We are Wall Street. It's our job to make money. Whether it's a commodity, stock, bond, or some hypothetical piece of fake paper, it doesn't matter. We would trade baseball cards if it were profitable. I didn't hear America complaining when the market was roaring to 14,000 and everyone's 401k doubled every 3 years. Just like gambling, it's not a problem until you lose. I've never heard of anyone going to Gamblers Anonymous because they won too much in Vegas.
>
> Well now the market crapped out, & even though it has come back somewhat, the government and the average Joes are still looking for a scapegoat. God knows there has to be one for everything. Well, here we are.
>
> Go ahead and continue to take us down, but you're only going to hurt yourselves. What's going to happen when we can't find jobs on the Street anymore? Guess what: We're going to take yours. We get up at 5 a.m. & work till 10 p.m. or later. We're used to not getting up to pee when we have a position. We don't take an hour or more for a lunch break. We don't demand a union. We don't retire at 50 with a pension. We eat what we kill, and when the only thing left to eat is on your dinner plates, we'll eat that.
>
> For years teachers and other unionized labor have had us fooled. We were too busy working to notice. Do you really think that we are incapable of teaching 3rd graders and doing landscaping? We're going to take your cushy jobs with tenure and 4 months off a year and whine just like you that we are so-o-o-o underpaid for building the youth of America. Say goodbye to your overtime and double time and a half. I'll be hitting grounders to the high school baseball team for $5k extra a summer, thank you very much.
>
> So now that we're going to be making $85k a year without upside, Joe Mainstreet is going to have his revenge, right? Wrong! Guess what: we're going to stop buying the new 80k car, we aren't going to leave the 35 percent tip at our business dinners anymore. No more free rides on our backs. We're going to landscape our own back yards, wash our cars with a garden hose in our driveways. Our money was your money. You spent it. When our money dries up, so does yours.
>
> The difference is, you lived off of it, we rejoiced in it....We aren't dinosaurs. We are smarter and more vicious than that, and we are going to survive.

In *The Power of Yes*, a female journalist, resembling the *Financial Times'* Gillian Tett, tells playwright David Hare that the bankers don't believe that they are guilty of anything. This is because they make so much more money than anybody else. They equate their pay with being smarter than anyone else. They actually believe that they are Masters of the Universe.[40]

Last Rites

The world that the financiers helped create was one where exploitation was deeply ingrained, justified by financial fundamentalism. It would end badly for the financiers, but much worse for ordinary citizens who had placed such faith in the financiers' powers of alchemy.

As the crisis intensified, early one morning in Canary Wharf a young man was wandering around in distress, sobbing hysterically: "I have lost everything I had. Every last f***ing cent." In 1929, after the Great Crash, ruined stockbrokers committed suicide, often jumping to their death from high-rise offices. Will Rogers joked that in New York hotels the desk clerks asked bankers: "You wanna room for sleeping or jumping?"

As financial institutions suffered near-fatal losses, they cut staff and pay. Employees awash with debt could not bring themselves to tell their partners. Check-book marriages held together by the glue of wealth floundered.

Bankers commenced divorce proceedings using the downturn to reduce the settlements, or returned to court to renegotiate terms, pleading difficult financial circumstances.

Some bankers downsized to smaller houses, expressing relief at not having to live in an art gallery. Gilded lifestyles were pared back. Some flew "commercial" rather than take a private jet to vacation destinations. The line "we are starting a family" fell flat. Bloomberg's marketplace had dozens of Land Rovers, Porsche Cayennes, and even a Bentley for sale at a fraction of its retail price. Those with jobs spoke of not being in it for money, but assisting clients with interesting and challenging problems.

Safe As

In Hong Kong, tens of billions of dollars of structured products based on exotic derivatives on stocks and credit risk had been sold to ordinary investors. Investors in Germany bought €130 billion of more than 300,000 different products, reassuringly called *Zertifikate*, certificate. The structures were rated investment grade by the rating agencies, or 100 percent capital guaranteed by major institutions, like Lehman Brothers.

Bankers aggressively enticed customers to switch from bank deposits to these products in return for higher rates. Where the return was dependent upon events, like a stock's price changes, the salesperson sold the products as "a sure thing." Bankers received large up-front commissions, up to 5 percent. To encourage investment, one Hong Kong bank gave away supermarket coupons worth $20. Bankers even used pyramid-selling techniques, recruiting members of families to sell to other relatives and rewarding them with a cash bonus.

Banks claimed that the risks were set out in thick prospectuses, but these were barely comprehensible even to experts. Questioned by regulators, bankers readily confessed that they did not understand how the products worked. Investors with limited education and limited financial literacy never understood the structures. Misled by bankers or tempted by their own greed, ordinary men and women lost all or a substantial part of their life savings when Lehman Brothers filed for bankruptcy protection in September 2008.

Some investors committed suicide from despair. In Hong Kong other investors kept a vigil outside the I.M. Pei-designed Bank of China building that dominates the skyline. They banged drums, keeping up a loud cacophony to draw attention to their cause. Megaphones connected to an iPod chanted: "Rotten deal—money back." One protestor wore a sign in Chinese characters: "The Bank of China is a hooker. Give me back my money earned with blood and sweat."

Poor subprime bank lending resulted in over 30,000 foreclosures in the U.S. city of Baltimore alone, reversing efforts to arrest decades of urban decline and regenerate the city. David Simons, creator of the HBO series *The Wire*, set in Baltimore, noted:

> [The show] is a meditation on the death of work and the betrayal of the American working class...it is a deliberate argument that unencumbered capitalism is not a substitute for social policy; that on its own, without a social compact, raw capitalism is destined to serve the few at the expense of the many.[41]

The city sued Wells Fargo, the fourth largest bank in the United States, for lost property taxes, the cost of boarding up vacant properties and policing attendant crime.

In the recession, as millions were thrown out of work, individuals experienced severe hardship. In her blog (www.theboxcarkids.com), Jayne Reid, a pseudonym, wrote poignantly of her family's experience living in a trailer. Her tale was of an older single mother with four adopted children, including one with a serious illness, and sundry pets. It was of lives destroyed by the crisis, day-to-day survival without wealthy friends, retirement accounts, or silver linings. It was about losing a grip on a precarious middle-class existence and becoming marginalized. It was about life on unemployment benefits for five human beings in 207 square feet (19 square meters), including a bed, sofa, kitchen diner, and bathroom. For the victims of the Masters of the Universe, it was all about uncertainty, loss, and constant struggle.

Snuff Movies

In 2006, food and oil prices rose sharply: Wheat rose by 80 percent, maize by 90 percent, rice by 320 percent, and oil prices doubled. The rise in prices meant that the poor could not afford basic foodstuffs or fuel for cooking, triggering riots in countries like Bangladesh and Haiti. The UN's Jean Ziegler called it "silent mass murder."[42]

Explanations focused on increased demand from emerging countries like China and India, lower supply, including growing demand for bio-fuels, trade protectionism, subsidies, and low productivity. But according to the International Grain Council, global wheat production increased and demand for grain fell during the period.[43] The rises were due, in part, to the financialization of the commodity market and speculation.

In the late 1980s, as commodities became a class of investment, traders bet on volatile commodity prices. Banks produced research reports, developed trading strategies and set up specialist funds to invest in food, energy, agriculture, and water. Rather than real investment in commodities, derivatives were used to bet on commodity prices. Banks and traditional commodity traders gained unprecedented ability to control markets or manipulate prices through operations spanning the entire supply chain—land ownership, production, trading physical commodities, storing, transportation, refining, sales, and trading derivatives.

In 2008, Michael Masters, a hedge fund manager, testified before the U.S. Congress that the price of oil (then $130 a barrel) was double what it would be in the absence of speculation.[44] On regulated U.S. exchanges speculators held 64 percent of all open wheat contracts. In July 2010, Armajaro, a London-based hedge fund, purchased 7 percent of the world's annual cocoa-bean production (240,100 tonnes) for $1 billion, promoting complaints of market manipulation. Anthony Ward, the head of Armanjo, was dubbed "Chocfinger."[45]

As the U.S. real estate bubble burst, investors, and traders moved into agricultural commodities and energy, betting that people would still need to eat and get around. The price rises triggered greater buying as investors who tracked specific indices had to purchase more. Higher prices encouraged producers and traders of the actual commodity to hoard, betting on further price rises, creating supply shortages with potentially catastrophic human consequences.

In 2008, the CFTC dismissed the role of speculators in price rises, relying on a narrow definition of speculation.[46] But prices of commodities not traded on derivatives markets, including millet, cassava, and potatoes, had not risen as much as commodities traded in derivative markets.[47] Financial investment and speculative activity rather than traditional forces of supply and demand increasingly determined food prices.

After falling from their high levels, food prices surged again in late 2010. The reasons for the rise were similar to those during the earlier episode of higher prices. An added influence now was the policies of the U.S. government and the U.S. Federal Reserve. By flooding the financial system with money, in an attempt to restore growth, they reduced the value of the U.S. dollar. As most commodities are priced and traded in dollars, the lower value drove sellers to increase prices to maintain the purchasing power of their commodities. The weaker U.S. dollar and the actions of central banks in the USA, UK, Europe, and Japan also reduced the faith of investors in paper money, driving increased investment in hard commodities with real value and ready use.

Snuff movies are motion pictures that depict the real death or killing of a person for entertainment. Investors and traders routinely pursue actions to make money, which could cause hardship and suffering to fellow human beings. Speculators trading necessities effectively bet on human life and suffering in the market casinos. In a reversal of the dictum of TV personal finance adviser Suze Orman, money and profits were placed before people, especially poor people.

Silent Mass Murder

In a famous series of experiments delivering electric shocks to people, Stanley Milgram found that:

> Ordinary people can become agents in a terrible destructive process.... Even when the destructive effects of their work becomes patently clear, and they are asked to carry out actions incompatible with fundamental standards of morality, relatively few people have the resources needed to resist authority.[48]

Bankers became willing agents in a highly destructive process, even when they were aware of the consequences of their actions. It was as Marcel Proust wrote in *À la recherche du temps perdu*: "indifference to the sufferings one causes, an indifference which whatever other names one may give to it is the permanent form of cruelty."[49]

Money was the game but also the prize. In the end, financial nihilism was not moral, it did not create anything lasting. Exploiting the trust they enjoyed and relying on the fake legitimacy of dubious science, financiers, governments, and societies fooled each other with the promise of universal prosperity built on a system of speculation and debt. In the end, everyone fooled themselves.

Part 5

Cracks

Crack—a fissure without a complete separation of the parts, also failure or a break with a loud sudden sound.

The global financial crisis that began in 2006/7, commencing with problems in the U.S. subprime mortgage market, exposed the deep-seated problems in the "extreme money economy."

Economic growth and prosperity were based on excessive debt and speculation. Individual wealth had been based on borrowing against future gains from investments. Savings were inadequate to provide for old age. Company profits had been exaggerated by demand from artificial consumption based on borrowing and financial tricks. Entire countries had tried, unsuccessfully, to financialize their way to higher living standards.

The economic and financial models were deeply flawed and had failed. The available tools and knowledge were insufficient to manage the crisis and restore the health of the global economy.

22

Financial Gravity

In 2007, everyone discovered what Joseph Conrad knew: "[a civilized life is] a dangerous walk on a thin crust of barely cooled lava which at any moment might break and let the unwary sink into fiery depths."[1] The end arrived unexpectedly, reflecting author Alexander Pope's description of the collapse of the 1720 South Sea Bubble: "Most people thought it wou'd come but no man prepar'd for it; no man consider'd it would come like a thief in the night, exactly as it happens in the case of death."[2]

Air Pockets

As interest rates increased from 1 percent to 5.25 percent per annum, reflecting higher oil and food prices, U.S. house prices stalled and then fell. Subprime mortgages predicated on low rates, rising house prices and the ability to refinance on favorable terms defaulted. Losses were significant but not huge. But mortgage defaults also triggered paper losses on highly rated securities used as collateral for borrowing. Borrowers sold everything to meet the need for cash to margin calls, forcing down prices setting off new margin calls, causing losses to radiate through the financial system.

In 1929, JP Morgan's Thomas Lamont had tried to calm markets: "There has been a little distress selling.... Air holes caused by a technical condition...the situation was 'susceptible of betterment.'"[3] As the stock market fell, John D. Rockefeller issued a statement: "Believing that the fundamental conditions of the country are sound...my son and I have for some time been purchasing sound common stocks." Actor Eddie Cantor, who lost a substantial sum in the collapse of Goldman Sachs Trading Corporation, replied: "Sure, who else had any money left?" Cantor created a skit where a stooge walks out on stage violently squeezing a lemon. Cantor asks: "Who are you?" The stooge replies: "I'm the margin clerk for Goldman Sachs."[4]

Heading for the exit at the same time, traders learned that everybody owned the same securities, all financed with borrowed money. Liquidity evaporated. Nobody had any idea what anything was worth, marking them down aggressively and fearing the worst. Markets were awash with rumors. As the Roman poet Virgil wrote in the *Aeneid*: "Of all the ills there are, rumour is the swiftest. She thrives on movement and gathers strength as she goes." Everybody feared that everyone except them was insolvent.

On August 3, 2007, on CNBC, a more out-of-control than usual Jim Cramer made the panic palpable: "Bernanke is being an academic. He has no idea how bad it is out there. [He's] nuts! They're nuts! They know nothing." Earlier on April 20, 2007, speaking on CBS Marketwatch, Treasury Secretary Henry Paulson had been upbeat, the U.S. economy was "robust" and "very healthy," and "the housing market is at or near the bottom." Here was a man who had jumped off a 50-story building without a parachute saying that it was all plain sailing so far, as he passed the 40th floor.

Mass Extinction

In June 2007, Damien Hirst tried to sell a life-size platinum cast of a human skull, encrusted with £15-million-worth of 8,601 pave-set industrial diamonds, weighing 1,100 carats, including a 52.4-carat pink diamond in the centre of the forehead valued at £4 million. Entitled *For the Love of God*, it was a *memento mori*, in Latin "remember you must die." Betting on demand from wealthy financiers, the work was offered for sale at £50 million as part of Hirst's *Beyond Belief* show. In September 2007 *For the Love of God* was "sold" to Hirst and some investors for full price, for later "resale."

The sale of *The Physical Impossibility of Death in the Mind of Someone Living* marked the last phase of the irresistible rise of markets. The failure of *For the Love of God* to sell marked its zenith as clearly as any economic marker.

In July 2007, Bear Stearns injected $1.6 billion into one of its hedge funds. On 7, August 2007, on the brink of collapse due to investments in mortgage-backed securities including the ill-fated Goldman Sachs CDO

Abacus, German lender IKB Deutsche Industriebank was rescued. On August 9, 2007 BNP Paribas, a French bank, suspended redemptions on some of its investment funds. On Thursday, September 13, 2007 the run on Northern Rock forced the UK government to guarantee all existing bank deposits to stop the run. In March 2008, JP Morgan purchased Bear Stearns for a price lower than that paid by the LA Galaxy for the footballer David Beckham.

In September 2008, Fannie Mae and Freddie Mac were nationalized. In desperate shotgun marriages, Merrill Lynch merged with Bank of America, and Wachovia merged with California-based Wells Fargo. Washington Mutual failed. On September 15, 2008 Lehman Brothers filed for bankruptcy protection in the world's largest corporate failure, with debts of $768 billion and assets worth $639 billion. A few days later the U.S. government took a majority stake in AIG to stave off failure.

In *Cat's Cradle*, Kurt Vonnegut wrote about *ice-nine*, a hypothetical substance which, if brought into contact with liquid water, freezes. Ice-nine had been dropped into the world's money markets, freezing up the global financial system. Investors pulled money out of banks and money market funds. They were following Tennessee Williams' advice for survival: "We have to distrust each other. It is our only defense against betrayal."

Some 65 million years ago, the impact of an asteroid in Mexico, equivalent to an explosion of 100 million tons of TNT, created the Chicxulub crater, 120 miles (180 kilometers) in diameter. 300,000 years later (an eye blink in geological time), a second much larger celestial object, named Shiva, the Indian God of destruction, hit India with a force estimated at 100 times that of the Chicxulub asteroid, creating a 310-mile (500-kilometre) crater. Debris ejected into the atmosphere shut out the sun, creating a *nuclear winter* that prevented photosynthesis by plants, slowly starving most life and leading to the extinction of millions of species, including dinosaurs.

Something similar had happened to the global economy. A lack of money slowly caused normal economic activity to stop. Money was the oil lubricating the economy. Now the oil was leaking out via a large crack, and the moving parts were seizing up.

In Indian mythology, Brahma is the creator of the world. In his next incarnation or *avatar* as Vishnu, the preserver, he sustains the world. In his final transformation, Vishnu becomes Shiva. At the Trinity test site, watching the power released by the explosion of the world's first atomic bomb, Robert Oppenheimer resorted to the sacred text of the *Bhagavad Gita*: "I am become Death, Shiva, destroyer of worlds."[5] Money had created and preserved modern economies. Now, it unleashed its destructive power, ironically by its absence.

ER

Panicked market participants searched for nonexistent exits, confirming Lloyd George's observation: "Financiers in a fright do not make a heroic picture."

The Fed resorted to a tried and tested solution, cutting interest rates from 5.25 percent to 0.00 percent. An alphabet soup of facilities was hastily assembled, desperately pumping money into the economy—PCF (primary credit facility); TAF (term auction facility); TSLP (term securities lending facility); and PDCF (primary dealer credit facility). Ultimately, the Fed resorted to printing money, known as *quantitative easing*. Wanting to hug the Fed chairman, Jim Cramer thought that Bernanke "got it."

Bernanke once boasted that dropping money from a helicopter would stop such a crisis. Central banks assumed that price falls reflected a temporary shortage of cash and confidence. Elizabeth Warren, chair of the Troubled Asset Relief Program (TARP), Oversight Panel Report, questioned the approach:

> One key assumption...is [US Treasury's] belief that...the decline in asset values...is in large part the product of temporary liquidity constraints...it is possible that Treasury's approach fails to acknowledge the depth of the current downturn and the degree to which the low valuation of troubled assets accurately reflects their worth.[6]

Figure 22.1 shows how falling prices affect values of assets financed with debt. Assume an investor with $20 of their own money—equity—is allowed to leverage five times, allowing the purchase of $100 of assets (funded with $20 of equity and $80 of debt). If the asset falls 10 percent in price to $90, then the investor's leverage increases to 9 times ($10 of capital (the original amount less the loss) and $80 of debt supporting $90 of assets). If the permitted leverage stays constant at 5 times then the investor must sell $50 of assets (50 percent) to reduce borrowing—$10 of capital and $40 of debt funding $50 of assets. If lenders reduce leverage to 3 times, then the investor must then sell $70 of assets (70 percent) with $10 of capital and $20 of debt funding $30 of assets.

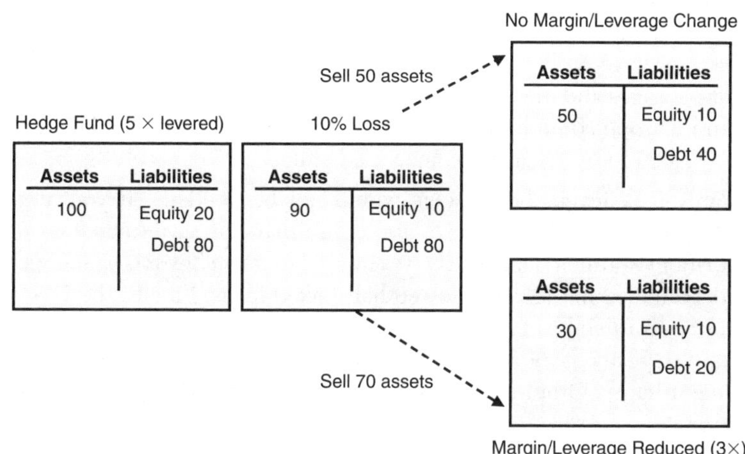

Figure 22.1 Effect of falling prices on assets purchased with debt

Reduction of debt requires liquid markets and buyers with money to purchase the assets. In the absence of buyers, prices fell as the system reduced debt. In January 2008, George Soros observed:

> Boom-bust processes usually revolve around credit and always involve a bias or misconception. This is usually a failure to recognize a reflexive, circular connection between the willingness to lend and the value of the collateral. Ease of credit generates demand that pushes up the value of property, which in turn increases the amount of credit available.[7]

The process was now working in reverse.

This Is Not a Seminar!

By September 2008, images of people unable to draw money out of ATMs and banks closing down destroying people's life savings did not seem farfetched. Kent and Edgar's apocalyptic vision in Shakespeare's *King Lear* now haunted the world: "Is this the promised end? Or image of that horror?"

The FOMC (the Federal Open Market Committee) was openly derided as the "Open Mouth Committee." Realizing the need for more radical action, U.S. Treasury Secretary Henry Paulson briefed President George Bush, describing the conditions as "cardiac arrest." The President grasped the problem: "This sucker could go down."[8] The satirical magazine *Onion* parsed it as "Bush calls for panic."

On September 18, 2008 Paulson and Bernanke proposed a $700 billion emergency bailout. Bernanke told skeptical legislators: "If we don't do this, we may not have an economy on Monday."[9] Other countries followed with bailout packages and measures to stimulate the economy. The United States, UK, and Europe committed $14 trillion, 25 percent of global GDP, equivalent to $7,000 for every man, woman, and child.

Paulson believed the package would not be needed: "If you've got a bazooka, and people know you've got it, you may not have to take it out."[10] The former Goldman Sachs CEO was unable to move beyond banking's deal culture. Bungled initiatives followed half-baked ideas. Finally, the U.S. government was forced to take significant stakes in major banks, guaranteeing debt and deposits of the banks. The UK government also partially nationalized major banks. Other countries throughout the world implemented similar measures.

The concern was that another big financial institution would fail, affecting firms that they had dealings with and triggering a collapse of the global financial system. In 1902, Paul Warburg warned James Stillman, president of National City Bank: "Your bank is so big and powerful, Mr. Stillman, that when the next panic comes, you may wish your responsibilities were smaller."[11] Asked about government assistance to firms considered too big to fail, George Schultz, secretary of the Treasury under President Nixon, snapped: "If they are too big to fail, make them smaller."[12] But now big financial institutions were all TBTF—"too big to fail." Governments everywhere rushed to prop them up.

Dubbed WIT (whatever it takes) by British Prime Minister Gordon Brown, or WIN (whatever is necessary) by U.S. President Obama, the actions were designed to stabilize the financial system and maintain economic growth. Bank of England Governor Mervyn King summed up the strategy: "The package of measures announced yesterday by the Chancellor are not designed to protect the banks as such. They are designed to protect the economy from the banks."[13] Upon announcement of the $700 billion TARP bailout package, Republican Senator Jim Bunning quipped: "When I picked up my newspaper yesterday…I thought I woke up in France. But no, it turned out it was socialism here in the United States."[14] The Chinese joked that the United States was adopting Chinese socialism with American characteristics.

In good times, bankers are capitalists. During crises, bankers are socialists. In every crisis, policy makers argue that people's life savings and pension entitlements are at risk if the system is not bailed out. No one asks who put them at risk in the first place. Bankers' excuses are of someone having murdered their parents seeking clemency on the grounds that he is an orphan.

The social activist Naomi Klein termed it *disaster capitalism*.[15] Having unknowingly underwritten a system allowing banks to generate vast private profits, ordinary men and women were forced to bear the cost of bailing out banks. As his friend Dink tells author Joe Bageant: "Sounds like a piss-poor solution to me, cause they're just throwing money we ain't got at the big dogs who already got plenty. But hell what do I know?"[16]

On CBS's *60 Minutes*, Bernanke defended the policy: "I come from Main Street. That's my background. I've never been on Wall Street. And I care about Wall Street for one reason and one reason only: because what happens on Wall Street matters to Main Street." As Nick, in F. Scott Fitzgerald's *The Great Gatsby*, observes about Tom and Daisy, scions of the monied classes: "It was all very careless and confused...they smashed up things and creatures and then retreated back into their money or their vast carelessness, or whatever it was that kept them together, and let other people clean up the mess."[17]

ICU

Banks choked on bad loans. In a phenomenon dubbed IAG, *involuntary asset growth*, loans hidden in the shadow banking system came back on to the bank's own books. No one knew how to do any of this. One SIV manager joked: "I need to read the instruction manual."

Jim Cramer called banks' financial statements "works of fiction." To survive, banks needed capital and money. No one thinks that they are going to need extra capital or money. If they need it, then they think they can get it at a price. If you wait until you need it, you can't get it at any price. Financial institutions rummaged in the backs of sofas looking for spare change to stay afloat.

The sense of *Schadenfreude*, Masters of the Universe receiving their comeuppance, evaporated. The financial crisis spread quickly to the real economy. In the United States, more than 8 million jobs were lost, with unemployment rising to 10 percent (over 15 million workers), the highest level since the early 1980s. The State of Ohio received 80,000 calls per day for unemployment claims (versus a normal 7,500 per day). Ohio hired temporary staff to handle the volumes of unemployment claims. Including people not seeking work because none was available or forced to work part-time, real unemployment in the United States hovered around 16–18 percent of the workforce. In Europe, unemployment rose above 10 percent.

Global trade volumes decreased 12 percent, the first fall in 25 years. In the third quarter of 2007, Sweden's Volvo AB, the second largest global truck maker, received 41,970 European orders. In the same quarter of 2008 the firm received orders for 155 vehicles, a decline of 99.63 percent. As exports fell, 20 million Chinese workers in the southern province of Guangzhou were thrown out of work. As Karl Mayer von Rothschild noted in 1875 in relation to a different crisis: "The whole world has become a city."[18]

By December 2008, the Baltic Dry Index, a measure of shipping costs, had fallen more than 90 percent from its May 2008 peak of 11,793. The cost of sending a 40-foot (12-metre) steel container from China to the UK fell from $1,400 to $150 before rebounding to $300. By late 2008, a tenth of the vessels that transport the world's trade were idle. In the Strait of Malacca near Singapore, a vast ghost fleet of cargo vessels sat idle at anchor.

Bellwether GE missed earning forecasts, then lowered earnings guidance. As its stock price fell, former CEO Jack Welch threatened to get a gun and shoot his successor Jeff Immelt. Warren Buffett bought $3 billion in GE preferred stock, paying an annual dividend of 10 percent with options to purchase $3 billion of common stock at $22.25. The 10 percent rate was what junk bond companies, not a AAA company like GE, would expect to pay. GE also sold another $12 billion of additional shares at $22.25 to the public.

Focused on beating short-term earnings goals, over the previous three years GE had spent $30 billion on share buybacks. Now needing capital, GE sold shares at low prices, having bought them back at higher prices.

Chrysler was bought out by Fiat. Bailed out by the government, GM (nicknamed "Government Motors") filed for a prepackaged bankruptcy to try to salvage a viable business. Larry Flynt (founder of *Hustler*) and Joe Francis (creator of *Girls Gone Wild*) sought $5 billion to bailout the adult entertainment industry where revenues were falling: "Americans can do without cars...but they cannot do without sex."[19]

Country for Sale

As the boom in Ireland got "boomier," household debt increased to 160 percent of GDP, up from 60 percent. Irish banks lent aggressively to property developers in an unprecedented real estate boom. Having doubled in price in a few years, a modest family home in Dublin cost the same as one in Beverly Hills. A three-bedroom penthouse in the Elysian, the tallest building in Ireland, complete with Porsche SE taps and views over Cork, cost €1.8 million ($2.6 million).

Intoxicated at the success of the "Celtic tiger" and the country's double-digit growth, the Irish splashed out, behaving like "a poor person who had won the lottery." As novelist Anne Enright expressed it: "We're very narcissistic...[believing] our boom was better than anyone else's."[20]

Now, house prices fell by 50 percent and the cranes that dotted Dublin's skyline stood idle. The Irish banking system collapsed under the weight of bad loans, unable to raise money. In September 2008, Ireland was the first major nation forced to guarantee the debts of its banks totaling €400 billion, nearly three times Ireland's annual GDP.

The economy contracted by 20 percent with unemployment expected to reach 15–20 percent. Ireland spent more than 30 percent of its GDP to bailout its banks. Government debt rose sharply from the low 25 percent of GDP it reached during the good times to more than 100 percent of GDP. Businesses, like Waterford Wedgwood, owner of the luxury crystal and china brands, downsized or closed down. The downturn exposed the problems of corruption and close associations between business people, bankers and politicians.

Lack of prospects revived a historical trend of Irish emigration to the United States, Canada, or Australia. This reversed a trend during the boom years when many émigrés returned to Ireland and immigrants sought employment in the country's construction boom. The tired joke was that the difference between Iceland and Ireland was a "c."

When their country collapsed earlier, Icelanders overseas could not draw money out of ATMs. Individuals, local government and charities, who had deposited their savings at high-interest rates with Icelandic banks in the UK, like Icesave, could not access their money. Iceland's government took over the largest banks as they collapsed with debts equal to about 12 times the total economy. In an attempt to protect British depositors, the UK used 2001 antiterrorism laws to freeze the British assets of a failing Icelandic bank. Iceland was listed alongside Al Qaeda, Sudan, and North Korea.

Overnight, the Icelandic economy and the Icelandic currency, krona or kronur, collapsed. Reopening after a three-day suspension of trading, Iceland's stock market fell 77 percent. Depositors lost their savings or found them much reduced in value. The repayments on borrowings in low-interest foreign currencies, like euro and Swiss franc, increased to unsustainable levels. As much of Iceland's requirements must be imported, costs skyrocketed.

Foreigners left Iceland. More than one-third of Icelanders contemplated emigrating. A proud, independent country had been brought to its knees by the crisis. The new government approached the IMF, seeking a €4 billion loan (over €13,000 for each Icelander) to shore up the economy.

Iceland was for sale on eBay: "Located in the mid-Atlantic ridge of the North Atlantic Ocean, Iceland will provide the winning bidder with a habitable environment, Icelandic horses, and admittedly a somewhat sketchy financial situation." You had to pick it up yourself. Bjork, Iceland's famous pop star, and Sigur Ros, a rock band, were not included. Buyers inquired whether COD (cash on delivery) was acceptable, joking that their payments might be frozen.

Iceland's Kaupthing Bank, Landsbanki, Glitnir and the Central Bank were awarded the Ig Nobel Economics Prize, recognizing their work on how small banks could be transformed rapidly into big banks and vice versa. The Ig Nobel Mathematics Prize went to Gideon Gono, governor of Zimbabwe's Reserve Bank, for printing bank notes with denominations ranging from 1 cent to 1 hundred trillion dollars to help Zimbabweans cope with hyperinflation.

In 2008, a banker was transferred from New York to London. To finance a Range Rover, he sold his modest shareholding in his employer, a bank. The banker was subsequently transferred to Dubai. When selling his Range Rover, he suffered a loss of 50 percent of the price he paid 6 months ago. The proceeds from the sale of the car (despite the 50 percent loss) would have allowed the banker to purchase five times the number of bank shares he originally sold to finance the car. In Iceland, there was an oversupply of Range Rovers, now known as "Game Overs."

Crying Games

Nicolas Sarkozy, president of France, pronounced laissez faire capitalism dead: "C'est fini!" Wang Qishan, vice-premier of China, tartly observed: "The teachers now have some problems."[21] Luiz Inácio "Lula" da Silva, president of Brazil, blamed the global financial crisis on "the irrational behavior of white people with blue eyes, who before the crisis appeared to know everything, but are now showing that they know nothing."[22] He termed it "an eminently American crisis" caused by people trying to make a lot of "third-class money."

Archbishop of Canterbury Rowan Williams called traders who cashed in on falling prices "bank robbers and asset strippers." Archbishop of York John Sentamu thundered: "We have all gone to this temple called money. We have all worshipped at it. No one is guiltless." The Church had lent stock to short sellers, sold a mortgage portfolio and bought shares in the biggest listed hedge fund.[23]

Politicians blamed bankers. Bankers blamed the borrowers who borrowed excessively. Borrowers blamed bankers for forcing them to borrow, stagnant income levels, job insecurity, the high cost of living and poverty. Reborn Keynesians blamed free-market economists, who argued that the problem was not too little regulation but too much interference in markets. Familiar with the demon drink, George Bush blamed alcohol, claiming that bankers got drunk.

Vikram Pandit singled out short sellers as the cause of Citi's problems. Bad loans, excessive investments in structured securities, inadequate capital relative to risk and a host of other failures were irrelevant. Blaming the messenger of bad news, short selling was banned or restricted in many countries. The debate was informed by Mark Twain's observation that: "I am not one of those who in expressing opinions confine themselves to facts."

In South Korea an online blogger, using the pseudonym Minerva, the Roman goddess of wisdom, predicted the imminent collapse of Lehman Brothers and made dire forecasts about the South Korean currency (the won), his site registering 40 million hits. When the won fell 26 percent, an unimpressed Korean government arrested the celebrity blogger, known to netizens as "the Internet Economic President."

Newtonian Economics

In 2003, Robert Lucas, a Nobel-Prize-winning economist, declared: "macroeconomics...has succeeded. Its central problem of depression-prevention has been solved, for all practical purposes, and has been solved for many decades."[24] Gordon Brown boasted that under New Labour's stewardship the boom-bust cycles of the UK economy had been banished. As the global economy slid into crisis, economists and analysts contemplated the D-word that dare not say its name—*depression*. Terrified of losing money on their vast holdings of U.S. dollars, the Chinese resuscitated Keynes' proposal for a global reserve currency—the *bancor*.

Dead economists were resurrected in support of political positions. Upsurge in government intervention and massive spending to stimulate demand marked the return of Keynesian economics. In 1996 Lucas told a journalist: "One cannot find good under-forty economists who identify themselves as Keynesian...people don't take Keynesian theorizing seriously anymore: the audience start to whisper and giggle to one another."[25] After a period when free markets, the Chicago School and Friedman's ideas dominated, Keynes was back in vogue. Minsky, too, had a good crisis.

Keynes is always the economist for a crisis, providing desperate governments with the intellectual basis for massive and dramatic fiscal stimulus. Benn Steil, of the Council on Foreign Relations, succinctly explained the resurrection: "when the facts are on our side, we pound the facts; when theory is on our side, we pound theory; and when neither the facts nor theory are on our side, we pound Keynes."[26] Just as there are no atheists under bombardment, Robert Lucas joked that "everyone is a Keynesian in a fox-hole."[27]

As Keynes himself observed:

> The ideas of economists and political philosophers, both when they are right and when they are wrong, are more powerful than is commonly understood. Indeed the world is ruled by little else. Practical men, who believe themselves to be exempt from any intellectual influences, are usually the slaves of some defunct economist. Madmen in authority, who hear voices in the air, are distilling their frenzy from some academic scribbler of a few years back.[28]

In 1929, investment analyst Roger Babson anticipated the stock market crash. In his pamphlet *Gravity—Our Enemy Number One*, Babson argued that gravity was an evil force.[29] In the credit boom, prices rose, defying gravity. Financial gravity had reasserted its malevolent power.

23

Unusually Uncertain

In Carl Sagan's novel *Contact*, an unknown alien, encountered by Dr. Ellie Arroway, talks of Earth's "astonishingly backward economic systems." Abandoning the *Great Moderation* and *Goldilocks economy*, the world embraced *Botox economics*. Botox is a toxin, commonly used to improve a person's appearance by removing signs of ageing. However, the effect is only temporary, with significant side effects.

As the global financial crisis rolled on, *Financial Botox*, a flood of money from central banks and governments, covered up unresolved and deep-seated problems. The prevailing thinking was from Will Rogers: "If stupidity got us into this mess, then why can't it get us out?"

Botox Economics

Government spending, industry support schemes such as "cash for clunkers," tax cuts, investment incentives, and subsidies all boosted activity. Low or zero interest rate policies (ZIRP) engineered a recovery in stocks and financial markets. Historically low interest rates, especially in dollars, made anything offering reasonable income look attractive. One analyst told investors: "We like the junkiest of the junk."[1]

Capital injections into banks, central bank purchases of toxic assets and explicit government support for bank borrowings helped stabilize the financial system. Changes in accounting rules deferred write-downs of potentially bad loans and suspect securities, allowing banks to create their own reality. For investors "a bubble is a rising market that one is not invested in; if one is invested, then it is a bull market." Naysayers were dismissed.

Coordinated government action across the globe on an unprecedented scale stopped the crisis turning into depression. Policy makers everywhere gambled on growth and inflation, as a painless means to adjust the deeply indebted global economy. In the words of François Duc de La Rochefoucauld in the seventeenth century: "Hope, deceitful as it is, serves at least to lead us to the end of our lives by an agreeable route."

Behind the glossy and smooth surface, the interior remained decayed and rotten. In the U.S. mortgage market one in ten householders was at least one payment behind. If foreclosures were included, then one in seven mortgagors was in distress. Commercial real estate, office, and retail properties experienced high vacancy rates, falling rentals and declining values. In 2009 Japanese investment bank Nomura secured a 20-year lease of the 12-story Watermark Place on London's River Thames for £40 per square foot, 40 percent lower than the rents of nearly £70 per square foot prior to the global financial crisis. Nomura did not have to pay any rent *until 2015*.

Unemployment remained high, even though enforced reduction in working hours, and taking paid or unpaid leave reduced the rise in unemployment levels significantly. Working hours and personal income fell.

Global trade stabilized after precipitous earlier falls. By late 2009, world trade was 8 percent above the low of May 2009 but 14 percent below the peak of April 2008. Trade protectionism threatened recovery in global trade as countries followed beggar-thy-neighbor policies. While paying lip service to free trade, governments encouraged the purchase of locally produced goods, happily subsidizing local industries. Each country sought to lower the value of its currency to gain a vital edge over competitors to capture a larger share of the market in an effort to maintain growth. It had all been seen before, especially during the 1930s.

Société Générale bank analyst Dylan Grice wrote: "Apparently heroin addicts can become so drug dependent that their bodies cannot withstand the shock of withdrawal, and failure to continue taking the drug triggers multiple organ failures. I just wonder how apt that analogy is to our government debt dependency today."[2] The global economy had exchanged a heroin addiction (debt) for a methadone addiction (government support).

Joseph Tainter in *The Collapse of Complex Societies* identified the approach:

> Where under the [Roman] Principate the strategy had been to tax the future to pay for the present, the Dominate paid for the present by undermining the future's ability to pay taxes. The Empire emerged from the third century crisis, but at a cost that weakened its ability to meet future crises.[3]

No one knew how long governments could keep the economic life support system switched on.

China Syndrome

First suggested in 2007, the *decoupling hypothesis* argued that emerging markets would be immune to the problems of developed countries, with China driving the global economy, fueling the next global investment boom. Instead, recession in the United States and Europe triggered a collapse in exports and a slowdown in China's economic activity.

Facing the specter of unemployed workers plotting revolution, comrade leaders directed massive spending and bank lending, embracing Botox economics. Ghost cities, unoccupied and empty, rose in China, driven by cheap money. No one knew who would buy the new condominiums that sprang up everywhere or travel on the new super highways and super fast trains. The revival drove *decoupling hypothesis 2.0*, a theory in which a billion Chinese would overnight urbanize and consumerize, driving 10 percent growth forever. China would replace America as global consumers of last resort, rescuing the world.

Analysts relied on Chinese statistics, which were unreliable and frequently manipulated by officials to meet political and personal objectives. Commenting on the time taken to compile growth data, Derek Scissors, from the Washington-based Heritage Foundation, wryly observed: "Despite starkly limited resources and a dynamic, complex economy, the state statistical bureau again needed only 15 days to survey the economic progress of 1.3 billion people."[4] Another commentator expressed surprise that revenue and cost gymnastics were not an official event at the 2008 Beijing Olympics. Investors just took playwright Lillian Hellman's advice: "It is best to act with confidence, no matter how little right you have to it."

Within China, a new class of wealthy individuals, usually affiliated with the Chinese Communist Party, aped their overseas peers—at least in their consumption of luxury goods.

Despite taxes on imported goods, sales of luxury goods grew at 25 percent annually in 2010, more than twice the rate of increase of overall consumption. For handbag maker Louis Vuitton, the "Middle Blingdom" was its largest single market, accounting for 15 percent of its global sales. China's share of the global luxury market was forecast to rise to 44 percent by 2020, despite average wages of about 25 percent of that in developed countries. Wealthy Chinese, analysts noted, now had everything they needed and were progressing to buy a whole lot of things they didn't need as well.[5]

With rising inflation eating away savings earning low interest rates in banks, the Chinese who could afford to bought up property, betting that the government would ensure that real estate prices would keep rising. This was the *Wen Jiabao put*, named after the Chinese premier, consciously referring to the famed Greenspan put. The assumption was that the Chinese government would ensure high growth. In many cases, the properties stood empty, awaiting future sale at a large profit.

A viral 2010 email captured the anger about China's growing differences in living standards. To purchase a 1,076-square-foot (100-square-meter) apartment in central Beijing costing 3 million renminbi ($450,000), a peasant farmer would have had to work since the Tang dynasty that ended in A.D. 907. A Chinese blue-collar worker on the average monthly salary of 1,500 renminbi ($225) would have had to work since the opium wars of the mid-nineteenth century. Prostitutes would have to entertain 10,000 customers; a thief would need 2,500 robberies. *Snail House*, a popular Chinese TV soap opera, combined house prices, sex, corruption, and political intrigue. A woman becomes the mistress of a party official to obtain his help to buy a flat, while a young couple struggles unsuccessfully to raise the deposit for an apartment.

Another email described the fate of ordinary Chinese with sardonic humor:

> Can't afford to be born because a Caesarean costs 50,000 renminbi [$7,500]; can't afford to study because schools cost at least 30,000 renminbi [$4,500]; can't afford to live anywhere because each square meter is at least 20,000 renminbi [$3,000]; can't afford to get sick because pharmaceutical profits are at least 10-fold; can't afford to die because cremation costs at least 30,000 renminbi [$4,500].[6]

These were the consumers whom Western economists had tasked with driving global growth.

In China, ordinary people felt increasingly abandoned by the state, which now favored the wealthy and well-connected. Economic growth of 10 percent each year papered over a lot of sins—over-investment in ambitious infrastructure projects, frequently with poor economic rationale, environmental degradation, confiscation of land, growing social inequality, and institutionalized corruption. Insiders worried that China's economic success was unsustainable. They feared that a slowdown in growth would expose the problems.

Wolfgang Münchau, columnist for the *Financial Times*, observed:

> Instead of solving the problems to generate a recovery, the political strategies have consisted of waiting for a recovery to solve the problem. The Europeans are relying on the Americans to generate growth. The Americans are relying on the Chinese, who in turn are waiting for the rest of the world.[7]

In London's Science Museum, there is a contraption consisting of yellow tubes connecting a number of tanks and cisterns where colored water is pumped through sluices and valves governing its flow. Built in 1949 by William Phillips, an engineer who converted to economics, the model demonstrates the flow of money within an economy. By pouring a lot of water into a bucket with a large hole, the world now sustained the impression that the receptacle was almost full.

Regulatory Dialectic

Regulators and economists, who contributed to the crisis, offered *solutions*, confirming Goethe's observation: "There is nothing more frightening than ignorance in action." Regulatory initiatives relied on self-confidence, which Samuel Johnson observed is "the first requisite to great undertakings."

Former Fed Chairman Paul Volcker put his name to restrictions on banks trading on their own account or investing in hedge or private equity funds. Proprietary trading is hard to define. Testifying to Congress, Volcker indicated elliptically that bankers knew whether they were trading on proprietary account, recalling U.S. Supreme Court Justice Potter Stewart's statement that while it was hard to define, he knew pornography when he saw it.

Hitherto little-known Arkansas Democratic Senator Blanche Lincoln and her Committee on Agriculture, Nutrition, and Forestry controversially proposed that banks spin off their derivative activities and be prevented from hedging their own genuine risks. Faced with a close re-election race, Senator Lincoln only wanted to be identified in voters' minds for her anti-Wall Street stance: "My legislation brings a $600 trillion market into the light of day and ends the days of Wall Street's backroom deals…that nearly destroyed our economy, hurting Arkansas small businesses and costing millions of Americans their jobs."[8]

Regulators and legislators held *educational* sessions with banks and economists, ignoring author Thomas Pynchon's warning: "If they can get you to ask the wrong questions then the answers don't matter."[9]

In January 2011, a new business-friendly study opposed steps to bring transparency to derivative markets, claiming that proposed regulations would result in 130,000 lost jobs and a $6.7 billion reduction in corporate spending. The study's release was timed for maximum impact, coinciding with regulatory debate about proposed derivatives rules.

The study was undertaken by an "independent" economics and public policy consulting firm and included contributions by all-star academics. Except many of the firm's advisers, including Nobel-prize-winner Joseph Stiglitz, were not advisers at all. When confronted, the consulting firm confirmed that Stiglitz had not contributed to the report, but had worked on other reports.

The firm stated that it had undertaken the report at a client's request: "It was a hypothetical study." The firm suggested that the reason a number of academics advisers wanted to distance themselves from the report had nothing to do with the report's conclusions. It was because of the movie *Inside*

Job, which raised questions about economists and their consulting arrangements with big business.[10]

Banks and their lobbyists believed, like English poet William Davenant: "Had laws not been, we never had been blam'd; / For not to know we sinn'd is innocence." Wolfgang Schäuble, the German finance minister, had the right idea: "If you want to drain a swamp, you don't ask the frogs for an objective assessment of the situation."[11]

Familiar arguments were trotted out—loss of competitive advantage, diminished financial innovation, slower capital formation, and higher cost of capital. If arguments for self-regulation failed, then banks tried to minimize scrutiny, masterfully narrowing proposed rules limiting impediments to profitable activities via exclusions and exemptions. As American radio and television commentator Charles Osgood observed: "There are no exceptions to the rule that everybody likes to be an exception to the rule."

Bankers threatened relocation to *friendly* locales, with the loss of jobs and taxes. When London introduced higher taxes and intrusive regulations, banks considered moving to Geneva, Monaco, Bulgaria, or Macedonia—any place with lower taxes, the required infrastructure, minimal regulations, good-looking women or men, recreational facilities, and favorable divorce laws.

The U.S. Financial Reform Act that emerged was 2,300 pages long. The Congress website warned: "This bill is very large, and loading it may cause your web browser to perform sluggishly, or even freeze." As one commentator put it: "it's no longer an act, it's word processors gone mad."[12] In 2010, 500 central bankers and regulators from 27 nations produced Basel III, 440 pages of new rules. The frenetic activity recalled Italian author Giuseppe di Lampedusa: "everything must change so that everything can stay the same."

As before, the revised rules were susceptible to being manipulated, through regulatory arbitrage. Many of the rules had little to do with improving regulation, instead focusing on familiar regulatory turf wars or battles for power, staff and budgets, as well as settling of old scores. Regulatory initiatives did little to address the quality of regulators and the acuity of oversight or enforcement of breaches of the law.

The case for greater oversight of the financial system was not helped by the fact that the U.S. Government Accountability Office (GAO) had found faults with the SEC's financial statements, since it began producing audited statements in 2004. In November 2010, the GAO found that the SEC's books were in disarray, failing in fundamental tasks such as accurately accounting for income from fines, filing fees and the return of illegal profits. Ironically, if any company's auditor had identified similar long-standing weaknesses in its accounting, the SEC would have investigated it immediately.

The much-touted *Volcker rule*, limiting the ability of banks to trade with client money, emerged riddled with loopholes, most notably allowing banks to take positions where they are trading securities and instruments with or for clients. Reviewing the legislation, a leading derivative lawyer told banks: "Given so much of proprietary trading has a client nexus to it, I'll be embarrassed if I don't manage to exempt all your activities from the rule." Large banks promptly shut down their proprietary trading desks, transferring traders to client-focused market-making operations where they continue to trade as before.

Legislators and regulators discovered that Groucho Marx was right: "[government] is the art of looking for trouble, finding it, misdiagnosing it and then misapplying the wrong remedies." The complexity of the issues means that ultimately no laws may be effective. As one famous law maker, Adlai Stevenson, observed "Laws are never as effective as habits."

Recurrent financial crises may not be preventable, being embedded in the DNA of markets. As John Kenneth Galbraith warned: "Euphoria leading on to extreme mental aberration is a recurring phenomenon…there are no very obvious regulations that act as a safeguard and preventive; only acute personal and public awareness can do so."[13]

Patient Zero

Greece, the cradle of Western civilization, was *Patient Zero* of the next phase of the crisis. As historian Arnold Toynbee observed: "An autopsy of history would show that all great nations commit suicide."

Greece's significance was not size (0.5 percent of global GDP) but its sizeable debts—€270 billion (113 percent of GDP) projected to rise by 2014 to around €340 billion (150 percent of GDP). Greece's budget deficit was around 12 percent. Profligate public spending, generous welfare systems, low productivity, an inadequate tax base, rampant corruption and poor government were responsible for the parlous state of public finances.

In 2010, Greece found itself unable to borrow around €50 billion to pay back maturing debt and fund its budget deficit.

Greece was the canary in the coalmine, highlighting similar problems in the *PIGS* (Portugal, Ireland, Greece, and Spain), countries, which had €2 trillion of debt. Larger countries, the *FIBS* (France, Italy, Britain, and the States), had similar problems—high public debt, unsustainable budget deficits, and (in most cases) unfavorable trade deficits. There were long-term problems of ageing populations and unfunded social welfare schemes (pensions and health systems). Greece highlighted that government debt levels may be unsustainable and investors may not continue to finance them.

After prevaricating, the EU proposed a highly conditional €110-billion rescue package for Greece, including a contribution from the IMF, which would supervise implementation of the economic cure. Continued market skepticism forced the EU to *go nuclear*—a €750-billion stabilization fund to support eurozone countries.

Journalists spoke of financial 'shock and awe'. 'Panic' better summed up the actions. Initially, stock markets rose sharply, especially shares of banks exposed to Greece who would benefit from the rescue. The interest rates on Greek, Irish, Italian, Portuguese, and Spanish bonds fell sharply. President Nicolas Sarkozy turned the eurozone's sovereign-debt crisis into a personal triumph, letting it be known that the rescue was 95 percent French. *Le Figaro* reported Sarkozy's comment that 'in Greece they call me 'the savior'."

Karl Dunninger, a trader, captured the madness:

> The most amusing part of this is that nations seriously in debt and without a pot to piss in will be 'contributing' some of the money to fund the debt. Spain, for instance, has pledged to do so. Where is Spain going to get the money from? Will they sell bonds at 8 percent to fund a loan at 5 percent? That's a very nice idea...let's see, we lose 3 percent on those deals. That ought to help Spain's fiscal situation, don't you think?[14]

It was reminiscent of the U.S. subprime debt crisis. Deeply troubled members of the eurozone could not bail out each other. On any reasonable analysis, the PIGS would still need to restructure debt—a polite term for default. Shock and awe quickly proved more shocking and less awe-inspiring than hoped. Only covering immediate financing needs, repaying maturing debt, and financing deficits, the plan did not address the problem of unsustainable levels of borrowing. The cost of borrowing for European countries rose to levels above those before the Greek bailout.

The IMF outlined the challenges facing the bankrupt countries: "a dysfunctional labor market, the deflating property bubble, a large fiscal deficit, heavy private sector, and external indebtedness, anemic productivity growth, weak competitiveness, and a banking sector with pockets of weakness."[15]

Based on per capita income of $30,000 (roughly 75 percent of Germany), Greece gives the appearance of a developed economy. In fact, Greece's economy and its institutional infrastructure are weak with low productivity, low quality, and endemic corruption. Around 30 percent of the Greek economy is unreported and informal, resulting in tax revenue losses of $30 billion per annum.

While entry into the euro assisted Greece's ascension into major league status, it decreased competitiveness as the country priced itself out of many markets. The euro provided access to low-cost funds, financing a construction boom and generous social benefits. Greece's borrowing fueled consumption or was channeled into unproductive uses. One commentator mused:

> It's a moot point whether Greece is a poor country masquerading as a wealthy country or vice versa.... If the old illusion was that Greece was a wealthy country, the new illusion is that Greece will, in short order, become wealthy enough to pay back ever-growing sums of debt.[16]

The same was true of many countries.

Russian writer Leo Tolstoy wrote that: "All happy families resemble one another, every unhappy family is unhappy in its own way." The same could be said for the beleaguered European countries.

If Greece had a bloated public sector and an uncompetitive economy, then Ireland's problems arose from exessive dependence on the financial sector, poor lending, and a property bubble. Portugal had slow growth, anemic productivity, large budget deficits, and poor domestic savings. Spain had low productivity, high unemployment, an inflexible labor market, and a banking system with large exposures to property and European sovereigns. Italy suffered from low growth, poor productivity, and a close association with the other peripheral European countries.

Ireland voluntarily implemented a draconian austerity program, trying to shrink its way to solvency. The Irish economy promptly fell into a deep recession. In late 2010 Ireland, too, needed an EU rescue package, prompting public anger at the humiliation. *The Irish Times* editorial referred to the Easter Rising against British rule, asking whether this: "was what the men of 1916 died for: a bail-out from the German chancellor with a few shillings of sympathy from the British chancellor on the side."[17] An Irish radio show played the new Irish national anthem to the tune of the German anthem. In Greece, the severe cutbacks in government spending saw strikes and violent protests on the streets of Athens.

Portugal, Spain, Italy, and Belgium now came under siege. In dealing with the threat, European politicians and central bankers preferred geography to economics. Prior to succumbing to the inevitable, Ireland told everyone that it was not Greece. Portugal now told everyone that it was not Greece or Ireland. Spain insisted that it was not Greece, Ireland, or Portugal. Italy said it was not in the PIGS in the first place. Belgium, a deeply divided country where the two main ethnic groups shared little more than a king and a large amount of public debt, insisted there was no "B" in PIGS or even PIIGS (if Italy was included with the other troubled economies).

Meetings of the EU in late 2010 and early 2011 broke up without clear agreement about how to deal with the European debt crisis. In April 2011, Portugal too sought a bailout. The predators of the financial markets now stalked the remaining over indebted countries, looking to pick them off one by one.

Amid talk of an even larger permanent safety net, Europe resembled a group of mountaineers roped together. As the members fell one by one, the survival of the stronger ones was increasingly threatened. With uncharacteristic common sense and clarity, Jyrki Katainen, the Finnish finance minister, identified the unpopular but obvious solution: "There's no miracle which we should wait for. If you have more expenditures than income, then you have to adjust it."[18]

Nowhere to Run, Nowhere to Hide

Policymakers had gambled that government support and public debt could keep the game going. David Bowers of Absolute Strategy Research set out the strategy: "It's the last game of pass the parcel. When the tech bubble burst, balance sheet problems were passed to the household sector [through mortgages]. This time they are being passed to the public sector [through governments' assumption of banks' debts]. There's nobody left to pass it to in the future."[19] It was the grifter's *long con*, great if it works but difficult to pull off.

The European sovereign debt crisis showed that governments were now the problem, calling time on the wishful thinking of financial markets. Governments throughout the world were forced to embrace the *new austerity* to reverse the deterioration in public finances, with new taxes and cutting expenditures. In a CNBC interview in June 2010, New York Governor Patterson described it as "an unavailability of spending crisis."

Withdrawal of government support would reduce global demand, threatening to create a prolonged period of stagnation, like Japan's two lost decades. But the alternative—problems of public sector solvency and a clutch of sovereign debt rescheduling—risked a sharper deterioration in financial and economic conditions.

The problems in Europe masked the bigger problem—US government debt, growing at $1 trillion a year. Commentator David Rosenberg observed in 2011:

> In the past three years...the U.S. public debt [exploded] by $5 trillion—the country is 244 years old and over one-third of the national debt has been created in just the past three years.... The U.S .government now spends $1.60 in goods and services for every dollar it is taking in with respect to revenues which is unheard of—this ratio never got much above $1.20, not even during the previous severe economic setbacks in the early 1980s and early 1990s.[20]

US national debt approached 100 percent of GDP. U.S. states and municipalities toiled under large debt burdens. In 2009, the U.S. Treasury received $3.1 million in gifts from citizens trying to pay down the country's massive debt. Given that the United States owed its creditors $13.4 trillion, it would take 4,322,581 years of similar gifts to pay back the debt.

Government debt problems were almost universal. Japan's public debt approached 200 percent of GDP, and the government each year borrowed more than it raised in taxes. The Ministry of Finance ran ads promoting ownership of government bonds: "Men who hold JGBs [Japanese Government Bonds] are popular with women!"

There was no shortage of ideas of trying to finance government debts. Bankers suggested the US issue perpetual debt, that is, the government would not be obligated to pay back the amount borrowed at all. Peter Orzag, former director of the U.S. Office of Management and Budget under President Obama and now a vice-chairman at Citigroup, suggested another creative way to correct the problem—lotteries. To encourage savings, banks should offer lottery-linked accounts offering a lower rate of interest, but also a one-in-a-million chance of winning $1million for each $100 deposited.[21]

As governments printed money to service their debts, the U.S. Postal Service issued 44-cent first class "forever stamps" that had no face value but were guaranteed to cover the cost of mailing a first class letter, regardless of how high that cost might be in the future. Between 2007 and 2010 the public bought 28 billion forever stamps. The scheme summed up government approaches to public finance—USPS was cleverly hiding its financial problems, receiving cash upfront against the uncertain promise to pay back the money somewhere in the never, never future.

Concerns about banks reemerged, as games of *extend and pretend* failed. Banks had lent over $2.2 trillion to the PIGS, with French and German banks alone lending over $1 trillion. In Spain the government was forced to rescue the regional savings banks, the *cajas*, who had made bad property loans. Once a pawn shop run by Christian charities, CajaSur opened board meetings with the blessing: "In the name of Jesus Christ, amen." One incredulous European regulator asked: "How was a priest in Córdoba able to weaken the Euro? The world has gone mad."[22]

It was unclear how increasingly facile money games were going to fix the problems of excessive levels of debt. Like a man told that he is going to die in a particular place and who tries to avoid going there, governments refused to face the inevitability of reducing debt and with it economic growth.

Borrowing is repaid by selling assets or by redirecting income towards repayments. For private borrowers, the current value of their assets, such as their house, did not cover the outstanding debt. The income and cash flow generated was insufficient to cover interest costs or repay the borrowing. Governments had few assets to show for the money they spent. Unable to continue to borrow or raise sufficient taxes to pay down their borrowings, their only choice was to print money, destroying the value of the currency.

In Germany, the paymaster and strength behind the EU, ordinary citizens resented footing the bill for rescuing profligate European neighbors. Germany's biggest tabloid *Bild* asked "First the Greeks, then the Irish, then…will we end up having to pay for everyone in Europe?"

Germans wanted the return of their Deutschemark, replaced by the euro, pining for a time when "Mark gleich Mark—paper or gold, a Mark is a Mark."[23] The nightmare of Weimar, the erosion of the value of money, hovered in the background. As governments borrowed ever-larger sums, ordinary citizens feared that even gilt-edged government securities would become worthless. As a banker asks an old woman in 1918: "where is the State which guaranteed these securities to you? It is dead."[24]

In Germany, gold was available from vending machines in airports and railway stations—*gold to go*. Shoppers could buy a 1-gram wafer of gold for €30 or a larger 10-gram bar priced in early 2011 at €245. Refiners were unable to keep up with demand for gold bars and coins. As poet John Milton wrote: "Time will run back and fetch the age of gold."

In the 1930s, Herbert Hoover prematurely predicted recovery: "Gentleman, you have come sixty days too late. The Depression is over."[25] In early 2011, as policy makers announced "economic mission accomplished," self-reinforcing events drove a pernicious reversal. The logo on a black T-shirt worn by Lisbeth Salander, the heroine of Stieg Larsson's *Girl with the Dragon Tattoo*, represented the outlook: "Armageddon was yesterday—today we have a serious problem."

Built to Fail

Paul Volcker identified the deeper problem:

> We have another economic problem which is mixed up in this of too much consumption, too much spending relative to our capacity to invest and to export. It's involved with the financial crisis but in a way it's more difficult than the financial crisis because it reflects the basic structure of the economy.[26]

Modern economies worshipped quantifiable economic growth following Lord Kelvin, the scientist: "When you cannot measure it, when you cannot express it in numbers, your knowledge is of a meager and unsatisfactory kind." As Senator Robert Kennedy argued: "It measures everything, in short, except that which makes life worthwhile."[27]

Economic growth meant consumption, mostly optional. Philosopher Henry David Thoreau identified the tendency: "Most of the luxuries, and many of the so-called comforts of life, are not only not indispensable, but positive hindrances to the elevation of mankind." Václav Havel, the Czech playwright, led the 1989 Velvet Revolution overthrowing communism. Twenty years on, he criticized the "palaces of consumerism" and an emerging society dominated by mobsters and bankers.[28] In Poland this new economy was known as the *Glitzkrieg*.

In the age of capital, financial assets and real wealth were confused. Money was a claim on real things, to be used or enjoyed. Increasing financial wealth, dividing real things into a larger number of pieces, did not create wealth. Trading things and boosting prices does not change a loaf of bread or its nourishment value. The world maximized something without understanding what it represented.

A strong stock market and high prices for houses and other financial investments were now barometers of growth, wealth and economic health.

Investors in China used the Shanghai Stock Market to measure China's economic progress. Unrepresentative of China's economy, the stocks traded were characterized by inadequate information, poor economic data and questionable accounting disclosure. Regulation and corporate governance was poor, with frequent government intervention. Trading was speculative, anticipating investment fashions, changes in liquidity and government intervention.[29] Bill Miller, a famed fund manager, even saw the stock market as a substitute for the real economy: "Using the outlook for the economy to predict the direction of the stock market...is to look at things the wrong way round."[30]

Over 50 percent of stock trading was now between super-fast super computers using mathematical algorithms. The average holding period was a few seconds. In *The Girl with the Dragon Tattoo*, journalist Mikael Blomkvist sums up the stock market's role:

> You have to distinguish between two things—the...economy and the...stock market. The ...economy is the sum of all the goods and services that are produced every day.... The Stock Exchange is something very different. There is no economy and no production of goods and services. There are only fantasies in which people from one hour to the next decide that this or that company is worth so many billions more or less. It doesn't have a thing to do with reality or with the...economy.[31]

Asked what the stock market would do, J.P. Morgan a century ago had given the correct response: "Fluctuate."

By the late twentieth century, houses, providing shelter and refuge, were a financial investment, even though rising prices did not actually make anyone richer. Tapping into this seemingly increased wealth required borrowing money, which, as it had to be paid back together with interest, did not increase wealth.

Monetary values also shaped attitudes and behavior, at a deeper level. The anonymity of money and distance from the effects of their decisions allowed bankers to justify their decisions. Bankers structuring, selling or trading shares or bonds did not relate it to the factory or business that the instruments helped finance. Traders did not see that short selling shares or bankrupting a business resulted in workers losing their livelihoods and the hardship that families and communities suffered. As they did not make or create anything, the only measure was the money they made or lost.

In *The Grapes of Wrath*, John Steinbeck captured the confusion:

> No man touched the seed, or lusted for the growth. Men ate what they had not raised, had no connection with the bread.... Owners no longer worked on the farms. They farmed on paper; and they forgot the land, the smell, the feel of it and remembered only that they owned it, remembered only what they gained and lost by it.[32]

End of Ponzi Prosperity?

Economic growth and wealth was also based on borrowed money and speculation. It relied on allowing unsustainable degradation of the environment and the uneconomic, profligate use of non-renewable natural resources, like oil.

Aggressive increases in debt globally increased economic growth, allowing society to borrow from the future. It accelerated consumption, with spending that would have taken place normally over a period of many years squeezed into a short period because of the availability of cheap borrowings.

When few people were rich and most were poor, gambling was necessary to survive. Over time, society developed a risk-averse predictability, built around high levels of employment, job security, improving living standards, and welfare systems, including pensions and healthcare. As post-war certainties eroded, speculation, once associated with horse racing or glamorous casinos, became an essential means of assuring survival and financial security.

When the housing bubble collapsed, the American satirical magazine *The Onion* demanded that the American people be given another bubble to invest in. As Adam Smith recognized: "The chance of gain is by every man more or less overvalued, and the chance of loss is by most men undervalued."[33]

There are similarities between the financial system, irreversible climate change, and shortages of vital resources like oil, food, and water. In each case, society borrowed from the future, shifting problems to generations to come. In the end, you literally devour the future until eventually the future de-vours you.

Once, religious belief preached forgoing the pleasure of the present for the promise of reward in the afterlife. Now, society literally sacrificed the future for the ephemeral pleasures of the present. As Ireland's boom collapsed, Abbot Mark Patrick Hederman encapsulated the triumph of material ambition over faith: "People lost interest in the other world while they were so successful in this one."[34]

Short-term profits were pursued at the expense of risks that were not evident and would only emerge later. Financiers entered into increasingly destructive transactions, extracting large fees and leaving taxpayers to cover the cost of economic damage. In a March 2010 paper, the Bank of England's Andrew Haldane compared the banking industry to the auto industry. Both produced pollutants—for cars, exhaust fumes; for banks, systemic risk. Extreme money polluted the economy.

In 2010, the failure of a deep-water undersea oil well in the Gulf of Mexico caused an environmental disaster. BP believed any spill unlikely, not anticipating any risk to walruses, sea otters and sea lions. This was unsurprising as none of these species were found in the area. BP's disaster-recovery plans for the Gulf of Mexico had been cut-and-pasted from a similar document *for the Arctic*.[35] Four days before the disaster, a BP employee defended a short cut: "Who cares, it's done, end of story, will probably be fine."[36] The failure cost 11 lives, and 4,900,000 barrels of oil leaking into the ocean. People of the Gulf Coast lost their livelihoods. Uncounted millions of animals, birds and other living organisms died.

The UK government and press defended BP, arguing that UK pensioners depended on its dividends. They pointed out that strictly speaking BP was not entirely a British company, as 30 percent of its shares were held by U.S. investors. When President Obama sought a temporary suspension of deep-water drilling in the Gulf of Mexico, oil companies argued the destruction of the eco-system of business. Financial considerations exculpated one of the biggest environmental disasters in history.

Bankers proposed creating tradable carbon credits to combat climate change. The credits would give businesses the right to pollute up to a specified level. The real driver was that banks could trade the credits, earning profits. John Maynard Keynes anticipated the environmental debate: "We are capable of shutting off the sun and the stars because they do not pay a dividend." James Lovelock, who warned of climate change before it was fashionable, dismissed subsidised renewable energy and financial initiatives to control climate change as a money-making scam that "doesn't do a damn thing as far as reducing climate change."[37]

The world tried, unsuccessfully, to defy financial gravity, with a variety of tricks. Their wealth and prospects greatly diminished, men and women everywhere found that, like Alexander Pope: "They have dreamed out their dream and awaking have found nothing in their hands." As always, the reality was more complex. A few had gotten out before the problems started, through prescience or luck. Some lost the lot. Most people gave back the gains of the good years and more, finding themselves with a lot less than they thought. Their houses were worth less. The value of their savings and retirement funds had decreased substantially. But expectations had been built upon their recent "wealth" and belief in the inevitability of continued future gains from rising house and share prices. As writer Anne Enright reflected after the collapse of the Irish boom: "Ireland is a series of stories it tells itself. None of them are true." [38] The same was true everywhere.

As Malthus and the Club of Rome warned, there are limits to growth. Computer engineer Jay Forrester observed:

> Growth is a temporary process. Physical growth of a person ceases with maturity. Growth of an explosion ends with destruction. Past civilizations have grown into overshoot and decline. In every growth situation, growth runs its course, be it in seconds or centuries.[39]

Environmental advocate Edward Abbey put it more bluntly: "growth for the sake of growth is the ideology of a cancer cell."[40] At the launch of the

"Redefining prosperity" project exploring limits on economic growth, Tony Jackson, professor of sustainable development at the University of Surrey, wrote in the *New Scientist* that a UK Treasury official accused the authors of wanting to "go back and live in caves."

In *Rabbit Is Rich*, John Updike's Harry Angstrom ruminates: "Seems funny to say it, but I'm glad I lived when I did. These kids coming up, they'll be living on table scraps. We had the meal."[41]

Losing the Commanding Heights

The crisis called into question the capability of government and policy makers to maintain control of the economy—Lenin's "commanding heights." All competing economic philosophies were underpinned by the same reliance on growth and built-to-fail economic models. An elite class of *mandarins*, economists, and bankers, uninterested in and unresponsive to the concerns of the wider public, believed that the economy could be managed by deliberate actions.

But governments and central banks may not be able to address deep-rooted problems in the current economic order. In 2008, Andrew Gelman, professor of statistics and political science at Columbia University, wrote:

> The law of unintended consequences is what happens when a simple system tries to regulate a complex system. The political system is simple. It operates with limited information (rational ignorance), short time horizons, low feedback, and poor and misaligned incentives. Society in contrast is a complex, evolving, high-feedback, incentive-driven system. When a simple system tries to regulate a complex system you often get unintended consequences.[42]

The economic model itself is the source of the problem. Zhou Xiaochuan, governor of the Chinese central bank, commented:

> Over-consumption and a high reliance on credit is the cause of the U.S. financial crisis. As the largest and most important economy in the world, the U.S. should take the initiative to adjust its policies, raise its savings ratio appropriately, and reduce its trade and fiscal deficits.[43]

More ominously Chinese President Hu Jintao noted: "From a long-term perspective, it is necessary to change those models of economic growth that are not sustainable and to address the underlying problems in member economies."[44]

Governments and central banks have intervened in the economy to protect and boost the prices of financial assets repeatedly over the last 30 years. The policies had little to do with real things—the goods and services that the economy produces in the long run. It is not clear how, if at all, printing money or other financial alchemy can really create wealth. In the financial crisis, their actions propped up prices at exaggerated levels, not reflecting their true value. In the eighteenth century John Law used similar strategies to prop up the price of shares in his Mississippi trading company until everybody realized that the delta was nothing more than a swamp.

Policy makers and bankers are united in denial. As John F. Kennedy knew: "The greatest enemy of the truth is very often not the lie—deliberate, contrived, and dishonest—but the myth, persistent, persuasive, and unrealistic. Belief in myth allows the comfort of opinion without the discomfort of thought."[45]

In 2009, Lloyd Blankfein, chairman of Goldman Sachs, described by Matt Taibbi of *Rolling Stone* as a "great vampire squid wrapped around the face of humanity,"[46] told the UK's *Sunday Times* that he was "doing God's work." Facing public anger, Blankfein, who earned $54 million for a year's work just before the crisis, remained unapologetic about the firm's behavior. In a piece of historical revisionism that Joseph Stalin would have admired, Goldman Sachs claimed that it never needed government assistance and would have survived the crisis without it.[47] As old communists knew, it is difficult to know what will happen yesterday.

As Keynes wrote in 1933:

> We have reached a critical point. We can...see clearly the gulf to which our present path is leading.... [If governments did not take action] we must expect the progressive breakdown of the existing structure of contract and instruments of indebtedness, accompanied by the utter discredit of orthodox leadership in finance and government, with what ultimate outcome we cannot predict.[48]

Zen Finance

Prospects of a less wealthy world with lower growth prompted erudite papers, books, and seminars, including *The Future of Capitalism* and *The Economics of Happiness*. There were *downshifting* and *slowness* movements, advocating a higher quality of life, and more leisure rather than material wealth. French President Nicolas Sarkozy commissioned a report by two Nobel prize-winning economists to develop a new measure—GNH or *gross national happiness*. One commentator termed it "gross domestic fudging if feminine attractiveness, length of vacations, and quantity of garlic in the food can be included, France will rank much higher than in more old-fashioned measures."[49]

An economic system built on a Zen Buddhist renunciation of wealth and materialism is unlikely. In 1979, U.S. President Jimmy Carter argued that consumption did not provide humans with meaning. He was defeated by Ronald Reagan, who asked voters if they felt better off after 4 years of Carter's presidency, dogged by high unemployment, high inflation, high oil prices, and low growth. GNH acknowledged the end of high growth. The new measure allowed politicians to manipulate statistics, maintaining the fiction of improving living standards.

The global financial crisis prompted public demonstrations across the world, against bankers, finance, and government bailouts. In 2010, workers went out on strike, protesting against cuts in jobs, salaries, benefits, pensions, and working conditions as governments embraced austerity to restore public finances.

In the short run, ordinary people, paying for the costs of the crisis, were angry with financiers. During the 1789 French Revolution, financiers blamed for the social conditions were called the "rich egoists." In the longer run, the effects of reductions in living standards, reduced wealth, and social hardship for the worst-affected members of society are unpredictable. In 1944, President Roosevelt called for a "second bill of rights" recognizing that "true individual freedom cannot exist without economic security and independence." Roosevelt's words resonate today: "People who are hungry and out of a job are the stuff of which dictatorships are made."[50]

But the complicity of ordinary people is difficult to ignore. Many were investors, directly or indirectly through retirement schemes, who turned a blind eye to excess. Investors ignored generous pay packets for bankers while the bankers made investors richer and facilitated economic growth. Home owners did not complain when their properties rose in value. Socially progressive people accepted the position of graffiti artist Banksy: "We can't do anything in the world until capitalism crumbles. In the meantime we should all go shopping to console ourselves."[51]

After the Bear Stearns hedge fund managers were found not guilty of all charges, a member of the jury said that not only was Ralph Cioffi innocent but that she would be happy to have him manage her money. 1980s' New York Downtown performance artist Sue Anne Harkey captured this acquiescence: "It's not about them, it's about us. We are them and they are us. I have no pride, I have no shame. I have no guilt, hiding behind blame."[52]

Indian activist Arundhati Roy, who has waged countless battles against India's drive for development while ignoring the human cost, wrote optimistically: "Another world is not only possible, she is on her way. On a quiet day I can hear her breathing."[53] She echoed Pa in *The Grapes of Wrath*: "They's a change a-comin'. I don't know what. Maybe we won't live to see her. But she's a-comin'."[54]

But unable or unwilling to change, policy makers modeled themselves on the English ruling classes during the twilight of the British Empire as captured by George Orwell:

> Clearly there was only one escape for them—into stupidity. They could keep society in its existing shape only by being unable to grasp that any improvement was possible. Difficult though this

> was, they achieved it, largely by fixing their eyes on the past and refusing to notice the changes that were going on round them.[55]

Like F. Scott Fitzgerald's tragic hero Gatsby, they looked back: "Can't repeat the past? Why of course you can!"[56]

Unknown Unknowns

Money was the mirror of the times. Extreme money was money made endless, capable of infinite multiplication, completely unreal. It changed everything—individual life, business, even countries. Voodoo banking made financiers the heart of the economy, increasing their profits. False gods and fake prophets, "los Cee-Ca-Go boys," provided the text for debt and speculation. As Shakespeare wrote in *The Merchant of Venice*: "Even the devil can cite Scripture for his purpose."

Everybody came to love leverage. To meet the need for debt, bankers built doomsday debt machines, slicing and dicing debt. Thinking risk had been tamed, traders engaged in financial arms races, stocking supermarkets with cocktails of risk for eager speculators. Hedge funds, the Minsky machines, emerged to play extreme money games.

The Masters of the Universe and their cult of risk had come to dominate economies and lives. Marshall McLuhan argued that "any technology gradually creates a totally new environment." The human race created money and the finance economy. Somewhere thereafter, money and the finance economy recreated the human race, not always for the better.

Governments and policy makers now play financial games and pump money into the economy to try to restore growth and stability. There is increasing risk of a further more severe crisis, with a loss of confidence in government, *risk-free* sovereign debt and, of course, money itself. The risk of unavoidable financial, economic and social dislocation is ever present.

Ben Bernanke told the US Congress that the future now was "unusually uncertain."[57] John Maynard Keynes understood "uncertainty":

> By "uncertain" knowledge...I do not mean merely to distinguish what is known for certain from what is only probable...the prospect of a European war is uncertain, or the price of copper and the rate of interest twenty years hence...about these matters there is no scientific basis on which to form any calculable probability whatever. We simply do not know.[58]

The future had always been uncertain. Human ability to predict and control the economic future had been an illusion. It was *hubris*—arrogant, excessive pride in achievements. In the end, *Nemesis*, the goddess of retribution and downfall, ends all dreams.

Epilogue

Nemesis

Nemesis—in classical Greek mythology, the goddess of retribution and downfall.

Marginal

"What the f**k do you think you are doing!" Uncertain whether the question was rhetorical, I replied: "Good to hear from you, Mailer." "Are you acting for JR against us?" As it happens, I am acting for the administrator appointed by the fund's investors. Earlier, I accompanied the administrators, the insolvency firm of Check & Charge Partners, to a meeting at Mailer's employer. JR's Leveraged Structured Credit Fund (LSCF) owns several billion AAA and AA-rated MBSs, CDOs, and CDO^2s, funded 95 percent by money borrowed from Mailer's bank.

The market value of the securities had fallen 50 percent, well below the level of debt. The bank wanted LSCF to lodge $1,100 million additional collateral to secure the loan. LSCF didn't have the money. Alarmed, the fund's major investor called in Check & Charge, who called me. Ralph Smitz, one of the principals of JR Capital who manage the hedge fund, surprisingly recommended me. I had always thought he disliked me. Just in case, I secured an upfront payment, making sure, at least, I would get paid.

Dick Gormless, the senior insolvency partner, instructs me to do the "heavy hitting." Asked what he wants, he takes off his glasses, rubs his eyes several times, and mutters: "Live to fight another day." The meeting begins badly and gets worse. We front the money or the bank seizes the securities and sells them, wiping out the LSCF's investors. The agreement enables them to do what they please—determine the value of the securities, or change the level of collateral at any time.

"I think you're right! Those securities are worth at most, say, 10 cents, 20 cents in the dollar." My agreement with our torturers catches the bank and Gormless by surprise. "You agree?" O'Connor, vice-president in charge of risk management, asks cautiously. "Absolutely!" There is no turning back.

"First, we understand that your bank is holding around $20 to $30 billion of the same paper. We also understand that you are valuing your holdings at 90 percent of face value or even higher. You obviously think that there will be minimal losses if you hold them till they mature. Unfortunately, as administrators, we must advise the court and also bank regulators of the discrepancy between where you are valuing us and where you are valuing what you are holding. Second, if you seize the collateral, it will go on to your balance sheet. You will have to mark them down further. Third...."

"How do you know our holdings and marks?" Rogers, the managing director in charge of prime brokerage, interrupts. "Third," I continue, ignoring him, "we will file for bankruptcy. Any collateral we place with you gives you unfair preference over other creditors. The administrators are duty bound to challenge this in court. Fourth, we believe that your bank misrepresented the details of the securities to us. The collateral risk was not properly explained...."

"Blackmail." O'Connor sounds shocked. I smile: "You know these issues are fascinating ones. They would be interesting to test in court. There is the issue of valuations, your models. The regulators, I'm sure, would be very interested. So would all your other clients, I imagine." I pause. "Can you give us a few minutes alone," Rogers finally speaks. The bank team leaves the room. Gormless is about to say something but doesn't.

Returning after 20 minutes, Rogers reopens hostilities: "What do you want, really?" "Time. 30 days. We can arrange for a new capital injection into the fund. We need you to extend the maturity of your financing. Renegotiate the terms." Rogers thinks about it. "I can't do that on my own. Can I give you our answer this afternoon?" Straight after lunch, Gormless rings me to confirm that the bank has given us 10 days.

I spend the rest of the day at another bank, advising them to increase the level of collateral on positions with hedge funds and other banks to ensure sufficient cover in case things continue to get worse. I help tweak their valuation models, ensuring low prices that increase the margin calls and the cash the other side must pay up. In finance, flexibility and split personalities are important.

Widows and Orphans

Morrison Lucre and I are reunited for the first time since the Asian crisis of 1997/8. Crises are kind to scavengers like me.

Lucre & Lucre have merged with a large global legal practice—the establishment American firm of *Tink Notting*. "Sad. Family started the firm in the eighteenth century," Morrison mused. "You won't believe this. They sent in a management consultant!" Morrison is indignant. "What would they know about the law?" He rails. Morrison has romantic notions about justice.

I provide expert evidence in disputes between banks and their clients. *I will kill you later* products have killed several European and Asian investors sooner than expected. Lehman Brothers Principal Guaranteed equity notes guaranteed only large losses. The Lehman Minibonds generated minuscule returns and maximum losses. Fund managers purchased products because other funds managers were buying them. Individuals bought them for higher interest, believing the investments were safe. Companies bought them thinking they could make money easily because their real business was unprofitable.

I study prospectuses and voluminous documentation. The "pulp fiction" claims and counterclaims are depressing. Clients bleat about being egregiously misled about risks and unsuitable products. Sophisticated dealers have taken advantage of them. Dealers claim that the clients are sophisticated, understood the risks, and entered the transactions while fully clothed and conscious. Banks rely on documents—PDS (*product disclosure statement*) explaining the risks; RDS (*risk disclosure statement*) signed by clients stating that they understood the risks; NRA (*non-reliance agreement*) stating that the client was not relying on the bank to explain the risks.

Innocents who have lost their life savings cannot afford legal help. Morrison and I help the deserving ones that can afford us. An Oriental dowager, worth several hundred million dollars, claims to have invested under the influence of her prescription drugs and a charming banker. Having completed several hundred transactions, she is hardly the proverbial widow and orphan, with no experience of such dealings. When we point this out, the old woman frostily advises us that she is a widow and her parents are dead.

Bank claims that the risks explained are disingenuous. The salesperson did not understand the products sold and could not explain them. Local language PDSs struggle to find translations for English words like *risk* and *loss* but have no difficulty finding local words for *profit* or *gain*.

In court proceedings, lawyers with scant understanding of what they are arguing present cases before judges who understand less. Experts resemble ventriloquist dummies through which parochial arguments favoring their clients emerge. Neither the lawyers nor the judges understand the experts.

Like a scene from the film *The Reader,* I spend an entire day in court reading my expert report of more than 200 pages into the court record, as it seems that no one has or can be bothered reading it.

Summary proceedings become epics. First-instance hearings go to a second and third. Omnibus hearings require trucks to transport the paperwork. Arbitration proves arbitrary. Alternative dispute resolution processes resolve nothing. There are appeals to higher powers, which prove indifferent and uninterested. Clients learn the reality of the words of Dennis Wholey, an American TV host: "Expecting the world to treat you fairly because you are a good person is a little like expecting a bull not to attack you because you are a vegetarian."

By October 2010, the fees paid to lawyers, advisers, and managers involved in the bankruptcy of Lehman Brothers reaches more than $1,000 million. Partners command $1,000 an hour; junior associates out of law schools are charged out at $500 an hour. One law firm charges $150,000 to compile bills and time records. Expenses include $263,000 for a few weeks' photocopying, thousands for business class air travel, five-star hotels, and charges for limos waiting for meetings to finish. One bill includes a charge for $2.54 for gum at the airport. The fees include a payment of $1.5 million to a firm to monitor the fees paid.

Unsecured Lehman creditors expect less than 15 cents on the dollar for their claims, sometime in the future. A Basil Boothroyd poem about movies applies to finance: "Isn't it funny / How they never make any money / When everyone in the racket / Cleans up such a packet."

Nausea

The ambitious investments of Euro Swiss Bank (ESB) in AAA-rated MBSs, ABSs, and CDOs as well as private equity and hedge funds result in huge losses. In bridging the gap, the bank seems to be disappearing into it. At the annual shareholders' meeting, hearing that Eduard Keller, ESB's *wunderkind* CEO, will forgo his bonus, one elderly shareholder speaks of buying a larger handkerchief for his tears. Worried that Keller cannot dine at the Michelin-rated restaurant Stucki in Zurich, favored by bankers, a shareholder presents the CEO with a packet of sausages, a tin of Sauerkraut, and a tube of mustard. Keller resigns shortly afterward.

LSCF's investors refuse to put in more money, forcing the fund to file for bankruptcy. Smitz asks me to continue advising on restructuring of several SIVs, CDOs, and hedge funds as JR fights for survival.

Mailer's employer has survived, bloodied but unbowed. Over a drink, I outline my thesis on banking—back to the future, return to basics. Commercial banks take deposits, make loans. Investment banks provide advice and arrange equity and debt issues. Trading is curtailed. Finance becomes highly regulated, a smaller part of the economy. Mailer is unconvinced. "Dull. It'll be dull."

He rails about his bank's "stupid" cost-cutting—crackdowns on first-class travel, five-star hotels, and gourmet restaurants. Employees fly economy, take buses, and trains. Taxis are permitted only during transport strikes. Limos are off the menu. Employee meals are $15 per person, matching the cost in the bank's cafeteria. Client entertainment is limited to $150 for two. Mailer bemoans the "good old days" when salacious outings at an adult entertainment venue or brothel could be passed off as a restaurant where the name wasn't obvious. The days of excess—bankers spending £44,000 just on wine during a meal at Gordon Ramsay's Pétrus or spraying bars with vintage champagne, imitating Grand Prix drivers—are gone.

Mailer complains about banking salaries. "You can't live in New York decently for less than a couple of million a year! And that's just the basics." The mortgage is $150,000 a year. The co-op maintenance and property taxes another $150,000, private school fees are $50,000 a child, the nanny is $60,000, and then there are private tutors. That's before living expenses ($50,000). "They don't have any idea of what a decent suits costs?" Mailer vents. There are cars, drivers, and summer vacations in the Hamptons or on Martha's Vineyard.

Holly Peterson, daughter of Blackstone Group founder Pete Peterson and author of *The Manny*, an Upper East Side novel of manners, tells a reporter: "As hard as it is to believe, bankers who are living on the Upper East Side making $2 or $3 million a year have set up a life for themselves in which they are also at zero at the end of the year with credit cards and mortgage bills that are inescapable." Candace Bushnell, the author of *Sex and the City*, observes that:

> People inherently understand that if they are going to get ahead in whatever corporate culture they are involved in, they need to take on the appurtenances of what defines that culture. So if you are in a culture where spending a lot of money is a sign of success, it's like the same thing that goes back to high school peer pressure. It's about fitting in.[1]

In the Unites States, unemployment remains high with few new jobs being created. People downsize from houses to trailers, from trailers to streets. Wall Street wives shop for cheaper cuts of meat as the less fortunate go hungry. Speaking about the bankers, Ken Auletta, author of *Greed and Glory on Wall Street: The Fall of the House of Lehman* remarked: "Honestly, I was relieved that I'd never have to see many of them ever again. They were, with some exceptions, a greedy, selfish, deeply unpleasant bunch of people."[2]

Crunch Porn, Crash Lit

Sales of Ayn Rand's *The Fountainhead* and *Atlas Shrugged* rise, coinciding with massive state intervention in the economy following market failures. One new group on the social networking site Facebook writes: "Read the news today? It's like *Atlas Shrugged* is happening in real life."

Alongside the *Twilight* series of vampire tales and Stieg Larsson's *Millennium* trilogy, bookshops create *crunch porn* or *crash lit* sections. All authors saw the writing on the wall, predicted the crisis, and now offer solutions to the crisis to end all crises. Nouriel Roubini's best-seller *Crash Economics* leaves no doubt that he predicted a crisis: "Roubini's prescience was as singular as it was remarkable: no other economist in the world foresaw the recent crisis with nearly the same level of clarity and specificity."[3] But no one matches the prescience of Pope Benedict XVI. According to the Italian finance minister Giulio Tremonti, the Pope, then Cardinal Joseph Ratzinger, in 1985 predicted that "an undisciplined economy would collapse by its own rules."[4]

Books on economics by economists criticize other economists. As John Kenneth Galbraith pointed out, economics only provides employment for economists. It provides fruitful employment to authors explaining the theories (in good times) and debunking them (in bad times).

Journalists rush out blow-by-blow accounts of the collapse of Lehman Brothers and the subsequent financial market meltdown. Hastily written histories of firms and banking figures as well as personal perspectives and memoirs proliferate. Many find links between cocaine snorting, binge drinking, lap dancing, and the crisis.

Journalists go for the racy rippin' yarn, achieving an immediacy of style that comes when the book was produced over a weekend or two. Economists aim for a desiccated drone (reminiscent of John Cage's experimental work in the 1960s) to achieve the correct type of unreadability. Memoirs owe more to Gestalt sessions or accounting than Shakespeare. Some works read like nineteenth-century pamphlets, with equal measures of vitriol, self-righteousness, and broad prescriptions.

Reviewing *Lecturing Birds on Flying*, a polemic against the Black-Scholes-Merton option pricing model, *The Economist* questions a style exemplified by the final sentence: "Deliciously paradoxically, the Nobel could end up diminishing, not fortifying, the qualifications-blindness and self-enslavement to equations-led dictums that, fifth-columnist style, pave the path for our sacrifice at the altar of misplaced concreteness."[5] One reviewer on www.amazon.co.uk queries the book's use of terms like "tumultuous tumultuousness," "unconventional conventionalism," and "dogmatic dogmatism." He seeks clarification that a reference to an argument as "non-incoherent" means "coherent."

Readers wander around like the Russian harlequin in Joseph Conrad's *Heart of Darkness*, a cross between a star-struck cult member and a Shakespearean fool: "I tell you this man has enlarged my mind."[6]

Economic Rock Stars

The financial media analyses every confused development in absurd detail. Crisis documentaries and films multiply at the same rate as losses.

Fêted as a rock star at Davos, the *black swan* thesis of Nassim Taleb attracts attention. The crisis may be a black swan (an unknown unknown), white swan (a known unknown) or gray (all of the above) swan. Taleb combatively attacks the *charlatans*—anyone who does not agree with him.

Economists and statisticians do not react well to being labeled *pseudo-scientists* of financial risk who disguised their incompetence behind maths. In August 2007, the *imbeciles*, *knaves*, and *fools* (Taleb's descriptions) devoted an entire issue of *The American Statistician* to the black swan hypothesis. On the *Charlie Rose Show*, Taleb dismisses all criticism as *ad hominen*, a logical fallacy that the validity of a premise is linked to the advocating person. Statisticians do not like the grandiose prose or tangential literary flights that Taleb defends, arguing that his book is a work of literature and philosophy.

Taleb suggests that Myron Scholes, the co-author of the famed option pricing model, return his Nobel Prize as he is responsible for the crisis. He points to the failures of LTCM (where Scholes was a partner) and a subsequent hedge fund he started. Taleb suggests Scholes should be playing Sudoku in a retirement home, not lecturing anyone on risk. Stating he does not play Sudoku, Scholes accuses Taleb of being 'popular', trying to make money selling his book. It is unclear why Taleb wants to be taken seriously in the academic circles he despises.

Nouriel Roubini is everywhere—CNBC, Bloomberg TV, CBS, ABC, WSJ, NYT, NPR, HBO, FT, and *Der Spiegel*. If you want to know where the man is going to appear next, then you just check Roubini's Tweet. His ubiquity suggests that there are several clones of the man. His exotic background, accented English, and the moody look of the Ancient Mariner who has seen catastrophe makes Roubini the iconic crisis brand. To monetize his celebrity status, Roubini rebrands his consulting service as roubini.com, rather than RGE Monitor. Detractors argue that Roubini predicted a different kind of crisis for a long time, switching in late 2006 to warnings about U.S. housing and a global recession, adroitly fitting his narrative to events.[7]

Financial people believe strongly in their superior intelligence. On July 22, 2001, in an open letter to the economist Joseph Stiglitz, Kenneth Rogoff wrote: "One of my favourite stories…is a lunch with you…you started discussing whether Paul Volcker merited your vote for a tenured appointment at Princeton. At one point, you turned to me and said, 'Ken, you used to work for Volcker at the Fed. Tell me, is he really smart?' I responded something to the effect of 'Well, he was arguably the greatest Federal Reserve Chairman of the twentieth century.' To which you replied, 'But is he smart like us?'"

Reviewing Stiglitz's book *Globalisation and its Discontents*, Rogoff wrote that:

> I failed to detect a single instance where you, Joe Stiglitz, admit to having been even slightly wrong about a major real world problem. When the US economy booms in the 1990s, you take some credit. But when anything goes wrong, it is because lesser mortals like Federal Reserve Chairman Greenspan or then-Treasury Secretary Rubin did not listen to your advice.

Rogoff concluded that Stiglitz was "a towering genius…you have a 'beautiful mind.' As a policymaker, however, you were just a bit less impressive."[8]

Writing in his preface to Benjamin Graham's *Intelligent Investor*, Warren Buffet observed that: "not only does a sky-high IQ not guarantee success but it could also pose a danger…nobody would be allowed to work in the financial markets in any capacity with a [IQ] score of 115 or higher. Finance is too important to be left to smart people."

Showtime

A 2006 book *Traders, Guns & Money*, pointing out the dangers and risks of derivatives, attracts occasional media interest. My naturally pessimistic view of the world proves useful, coinciding with the times. People are forgiving if things turn out better than predictions.

In 2009, an Asian stockbroking firm invites me to speak at investment conferences in Tokyo and Hong Kong. I am part of the chorus, support for the mega-stars. In Japan, celebrity anti-exuberance advocate[9] Robert Shiller in the course of a short speech, manages to mention his forthcoming book at least a dozen times.

In Hong Kong, the world's first and only celebrity economic historian[10] Niall Ferguson gives a keynote address on *Chimerica*, the relationship between China and America. Well-known for his books and Channel 4 series, Ferguson was named by *Time* magazine in 2004 as one of the 100 most influential people in the world. Jealous colleagues acknowledge his brilliance but criticize his love of celebrity, adulation, and money. The Harvard heartthrob reportedly charges around $100,000 per speech, earning $5 million a year, comparable to a high-ranking banker.

The speech takes its inspiration from the film *The Painted Veil*, based on Somerset Maugham's story of infidelity. China and America have a marriage, Ferguson argues, that is on the metaphorical rocks. A few months after the speech, the London *Daily Mail* carries a story of Ferguson's own marital problems. The article chronicles a £30,000 40th-birthday party for his mistress, Somali-born former Dutch politician Ayaan Hirsi Ali, to which Ferguson also invited his wife.[11]

In Lewis Carroll's tale, Alice confesses that: "One can't believe impossible things." The Queen disagrees: "Why, sometimes I've believed as many as six impossible things before breakfast."[12] In the *Alice in Wonderland* world of financial media, it is essential to say and believe six impossible things every minute. In a March 2009 interview with *Today Show*'s Jon Stewart, Jim Cramer admits that *Mad Money* was "an entertainment show about business." Stewart eviscerates Cramer: "It's not a f***ing game."

Meta Money

At a *Festival of Ideas*, I meet a French semiotician, a branch of linguistics that studies signs and symbols. The global financial crisis is, he assures me, a test of post-modernism. Money and financial markets manifest a modern anxiety about the nature of reality. As in all modernism, the problem is the meta level. Modern finance creates instruments enabling the creation of new forms of money, abstracted from real things. Derivatives and securitization are meta-money, making traditional concepts of money otiose.

For him, the crisis is obvious. In post-modernity, the meta level eventually dominates the primary level it emanates from. The cotton-candy money of financial alchemy dominates ordinary money. This leads to circularity and self-reference—value becomes driven by itself, prices become a function of what you can borrow against the collateral, driving up value feeding on itself. Instruments designed to manage risk create new risks. Hedging of risks by individual participants creates risks for the system.

New instruments emerge, being traded in huge volumes among institutions essentially trading with themselves. They undertake transactions, and price them and book fictitious earnings, neglecting to establish whether any of it is real or makes economic sense. The function of money markets to raise and invest money is systematically undermined. The true function of money as a mechanism for exchange, a store of buying power, and a measure of value is corrupted.

He explains: "All this is absolutely obvious, of course, except to economists and bankers." This may explain why Siegmund Warburg, the founder of the eponymous UK merchant bank, favored hiring graduates with a background in the classics, believing that all other knowledge was ephemeral.

In November 2009, the auction of Andy Warhol's 1962 silk-screen painting *200 One Dollar Bills* confirms the French semiotician's view. The painting's title is literal, as the work is simply an accurate rendition of 200 $1 bills. The catalogue describes the piece as Warhol's response "to the post-war world's media and consumerist saturation" via "a form of art that would remove the hand of the artist, creating the same sense of distance and disconnect that was emerging in the world around him."[13] At a time when real money was rapidly losing value, the price paid for the painting meant that each painted dollar bill depicted in the work was worth $219,000.

Economic Trivialities

Asked to explain what has happened, I draw on the back of a napkin (Figure E.1). There is a box—the original real economy. In the age of capital, a larger economy appeared, really two boxes stacked on top of each other—the real economy and the extreme money economy, with its excessive debt and speculation. In the global financial crisis, the extreme money box disappeared, leaving only the smaller real economy once more.

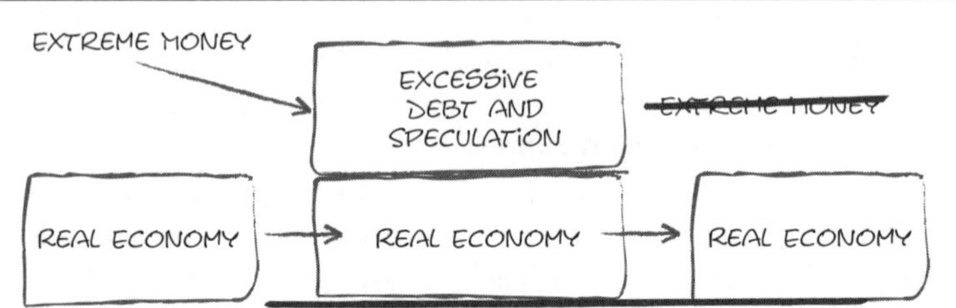

Figure E.1 The extreme money economy

The world now has less wealth and more debt and may grow at a lower rate. Improvements in living standards, once accepted as routine, are likely to slow. For some countries or parts of society, which have lived beyond their means, living standards will need to fall, perhaps sharply.

In a world of increasing inequality, a small group will get even richer, parlaying scarce skills into a greater share of the economic pie. Many people will be marginalized, leading an increasingly precarious and uncertain existence in a netherworld of job insecurity and stagnant incomes. As journalist Peter Gosselin forecast: "comparatively few enjoy great wealth at almost no risk, while the majority must accept the possibility that any reversal—whether of their own or someone else's making—can destroy a lifetime of endeavor."[14]

In an economically fragile world, ordinary people everywhere view the future for themselves and their children with trepidation. Facing uncertain career prospects, even well-educated young people can feel hopeless and increasingly disenfranchised: "I have every possible certificate. I have everything except a death certificate."[15]

Companies torture themselves financially to survive and maintain profitability. In the short run, businesses make money, squeezing costs, cutting back staff, and reducing benefits. They create jobs only in countries where labor is cheap and growth prospects are better. But eventually low economic growth will bite, eroding profits.

The heroic bet on growth and inflation to rescue the world from the problem of excessive debt levels may not succeed. Public borrowing cannot substitute fully or indefinitely for private demand and eventually governments will be forced to reduce debt. In 1939 Henry Morgenthau, secretary of the U.S. Treasury, admitted as much: "We have tried spending money. We are spending more than we have ever spent before and it does not work."[16]

Anticipating increased scrutiny from investors in the aftermath of the continuing European debt crisis, governments everywhere try to improve the state of public finances. They cut back welfare payments. Increases in the retirement age force most workers to work literally until the grave, as their private retirement savings are generally inadequate. Governments put up taxes, creating employment for a vast industry of accountants, lawyers, and private bankers, who will ensure that those who can afford to pay their fees will not pay any more than the bare minimum of tax.

World leaders flit between summits, performing John Holbo's "two step of terrific triviality" for the media: "say something that is ambiguous between something so strong it is absurd and so weak that it would be absurd even to mention it. When attacked, hop from foot to foot as necessary, keeping a serious expression on your face."[17] The level of the policy debate barely rises above the level of undergraduate economics. Despite mathematical pretensions, the discussion is "conducted in terms that would be quite familiar to economists in the 1920s and 1930s" highlighting "the lack of advance in our knowledge in 80 years."[18]

There is no simple, painless solution. The world has to reduce debt, shrink the financial part of the economy, and change the destructive incentive structures in finance. Individuals in developed countries have to save more and spend less. Companies have to go back to real engineering. Governments have to balance their books better. Banking must become a mechanism for matching savers and borrowers, financing real things. Banks cannot be larger than nations, countries in themselves. Countries cannot rely on debt and speculation for prosperity. The world must live within its means.

Reforming the economy, reining in extreme money, is not difficult but comes with short-term painful costs and longer-term slower growth and lower living standards. Unpopular and politically untenable trade-offs mean that policymakers take a path of least resistance, committing more money to restoring the *status quo ante* using public debt to prop up the system, absorbing private losses and slowing the reduction in debt. German finance minister Peer Steinbruck questioned the approach: "When I ask about the origins of the crisis, economists I respect tell me it is the credit financed growth of recent years and decades. Isn't this the same mistake everyone is suddenly making again?"[19]

The world desperately wills itself to believe that the crisis is over, the good times are returning. Gatsby, too, built himself an illusion to live by. Briefly his dream seemed so close that it was almost within reach. But "he did not know that it was already behind him."[20]

This Time, It Is No Different!

Failure is generally not fatal but failure to change can be. But no real progress is possible until everybody faces up to the fundamental problems. Yet no one seems to have learned anything at all.

At the 2011 World Economic Forum at Davos, a Report—*More Credit with Fewer Crises: Responsibly Meeting the World's Growing Demand for Credit*—forecasts that global borrowings will double between 2009 and 2020 to $213 trillion, a growth rate of 6.3 percent per annum. This follows a doubling of global credit between 2000 and 2009 from $57 trillion to $109 trillion, a 7.5 percent compound annual growth rate. There is little acknowledgment of the need to curtail the growth of debt or the problems of debt-fueled economic growth.

Policy makers and academics continue to mistake the beauty of their models for reality. New bank regulations rely on discredited models and ratings for assessing creditworthiness. Regulators argue that there is nothing better or that the new models are improved.

The intellectual commitment to defend the old ways is formidable. In a 2010 paper, economists Olivier Coibion and Yuri Gorodnichenko provide an elegant and inventive reinterpretation of recent history, arguing that the Great Moderation was the product of "good public policy." The crisis that had thrown millions out of work, created untold hardship, and required massive government support to avoid a total collapse of the global financial system is dismissed as a "transitory volatility blip of 2009."[21] Economist Richard Posner identified the barriers to progress: "Professors have tenure…They have techniques that they know and are comfortable with. It takes a great deal to drive them out of their accustomed way of doing business."[22]

At the 2011 Davos Forum, the world's major banks tell politicians to stop bashing bankers, as it is a barrier to economic growth. Earlier, Robert

Diamond, CEO of Barclays Bank, told a UK parliamentary committee investigating bankers' bonuses that: "the period of remorse and apology…needs to be over."[23] Banks and financiers argue that what is good for them is good for everybody. The lobbying power of financial institutions means that real change will not or cannot be made: "The banks are still the most powerful lobby on Capital Hill: they frankly own the place."[24]

Remuneration in the financial sector returns to pre-crisis levels. In 2010, hedge fund manager John Paulson earned $5 billion, higher than the $4 billion payday from his successful 2007 bets against subprime mortgages. The amount was almost equal to the $6.4 billion total net worth of Steven Cohen, the head of hedge fund SAC Capital. Appaloosa Management's David Tepper made $2 billion; Bridgewater Associates' Ray Dalio made $3 billion. Steve Cohen was rumored to have earned $1 billion in 2010.

The huge payments do not always reflect exceptional returns. Appaloosa and Bridgewater earned high returns of around 30 percent from successful bets, anticipating the government's actions, flooding the world with money. But the average hedge fund gained a little more than 10 percent in 2010, below the 15 percent gain of the Standard & Poor's 500 stock index and 19 percent return of average stock mutual funds. Paulson's $36 billion Advantage Plus fund earned 17 percent, whereas another fund returned 11 percent. Despite this, Paulson earned a 20 percent performance fee.

Bankers' earnings also recover, largely underwritten by government support of the financial system. Apologists argue that bankers are doing vital work to support the economy, justifying their pay as merely sharing in the profits that they generate. They complain that they are poor cousins to the hedge fund managers. The 36,000 employees at Goldman Sachs, the most lucrative of investment banks, took home just more than $8 billion in 2010, less than twice John Paulson's earnings. Goldman Sach's CEO Lloyd Blankfein, who earns a few tens of millions, must feel like a mere pretender at gatherings of the business elite.

Hedge fund managers receive all earnings in cash. Some of the profits are classified as long-term capital gains, taxed at lower rates than normal income tax rates. Bankers complain that they receive only part of their bonuses in cash now. Regulators want them to receive most of their bonuses in shares or other instruments, which are deferred in time and linked to the performance of their institutions. The protests are disingenuous. Derivative traders devised strategies long ago to hedge shares received by bankers and executives as part of compensation packages, breaking the link between compensation and the firm's ongoing performance, dooming regulators' efforts.

The problem is that a large part of the profits are not actually cash, but unrealized paper gains based on sometimes dubious market values for illiquid instruments and even more dubious models. The deadly pathology of finance—the gaming of bonus systems, manipulation of valuations, and accounting tricks—continues. As one observer notes: "It is simply amazing to me how much money you can make by shuffling papers. We have come a long way from our industrial giants."[25]

In New York, credit-crunch tours take in the original Lehman Brothers building and New York's Federal Reserve. In Bowling Green Park, downtown Manhattan, visitors still pose to have their photos taken near Arturo di Modica's statue of a charging bull. Guides show tourists a real toxic asset—a thick prospectus for a 2006 $1.5-billion subprime CDO that was rated AAA where investors lost almost all their investment. The guide explains that the $185 billion of the taxpayer bailout would fill an entire alley near the AIG building to a height of nearly 7 feet (2 metres).

In their offices, financiers are little changed. Traders bet the house's money in the same old "double up." You bet $100 on a coin toss—tails! If you win then you have a $100 profit. But if you lose, you simply bet double the amount—$200—on tails the next coin toss. If the coin comes up tails, then you win $100—the $200 you bet less the $100 loss on the first toss. If the coin comes up heads, you simply double up again, betting $400. The assumption is that the coin must come down tails eventually, allowing you to win your $100 back. The only problem is that you could run out of money and be bankrupt before the coin comes up tails. You are risking higher and higher losses betting that the coin must come up tails at some stage.[26] But traders don't play the game with their own money, they play with other people's money.

Trading culture remains largely untouched. A drinking game, *icing*, sweeps banks. You surprise a bro with a bottle of Smirnoff Ice any time, any place. If caught, the bro gets down on one knee, chugs the bottle. If he happens to whip out his own bottle, the icer gets owned, having to drink both. Andy Serwer, managing editor of *Fortune*, captured the period:

> The party is over until it comes back again...I've been around long enough to see that we have these cycles. These guys get their cigars and champagne. They have a great time. The whole thing blows up. But then they re-emerge years later. This one is a really bad one. But I don't think Wall Street is dead.[27]

As Scottish philosopher David Hume knew: "All plans of government, which suppose great reformation in the manners of mankind, are plainly imaginary."

Suicide Is Painless

Financial problems, environmental issues, management of finite energy, food and water resources, and lower wealth increasingly converge in a toxic brew. The choices are pure Woody Allen: "More than any other time in history, mankind faces a crossroads. One path leads to despair and utter hopelessness. The other, to total extinction. Let us pray we have the wisdom to choose correctly."

Ordinary people everywhere bear the cost. I think back to the people at the Money Show, wondering how Mary and Greg and the others are doing in their efforts to secure prosperity.

After the Investment Conference in Hong Kong, I leave the hotel and make my way to the airport train, through the Central Business District. Tens of thousands of Filipino women, who work as maids to monied business people, crowd every inch of the public space and sidewalks outside stylish skyscrapers, luxury hotels, and fashionable shops. Hotels and shopping arcade guards keep the women from using their restrooms.

On their only day off, the women meet to picnic on pieces of cardboard, read books, and write letters to the families they left behind. Poorly paid, often abused, they work long hours to support extended families back in the Philippines. In the hustle and bustle of Hong Kong's financial center, they are the only people who smile and laugh. Among them, there is a rare sense of community.

Talking about the human effects of the crisis, a friend tells me a story about Indonesia during the Asian financial crisis more than a decade ago. Fluent in Bahasa Indonesia, he overheard a conversation one night outside the hotel where he was staying. A mother and her two daughters were discussing who would sell herself that night to feed the family.

The crisis has led to cutbacks in the number of Filipino maids in Hong Kong. They face competition from women from mainland China. On the street, an older woman comforts her younger companion. She lightly touches the other woman's head in a sympathetic gesture, recalling playwright Harold Pinter's last words in *No Man's Land*: "Tender the dead as you would yourself be tendered, now, in what you would describe as your life."

Arriving early for a meeting in London's Canary Wharf, I notice a small street stand erected near the Underground station by the English Teachers Union to recruit teachers. Two affable women explain that they heard that there is "a bit of financial crisis." Well-educated and highly motivated bankers who were losing their jobs might consider a new career teaching. Questioned about the 90 percent reduction in salary, one recruiter responds: "If you haven't got a job then it's not relevant is it? It was never real money and it wasn't going to ever last was it?"

One turns to attend to her small baby. The child's eyes catch mine for a brief moment. I think about the future of all children, everywhere. I think of the words of Viktor Chernomyrdin, the malapropism-inclined former Russian prime minister, describing government policies designed to ensure: "We are going to live so that our children and grandchildren will envy us!" [28]

Former soccer star Eric Cantona calls for a new French revolution, urging citizens to withdraw money from banks. *Le Monde* jokes that Cantona would need a van to withdraw his savings, which he has built up through celebrity endorsements. Baudouin Prot, CEO of France's largest bank BNP Paribas, considers: "This recommendation to withdraw deposits is criminal." French Finance Minister Christine Lagarde considers Cantona "a great footballer" but recommends against following his financial reform proposals.[29] Cantona does not carry out the threat. Ordinary people everywhere lack "the power to translate their hatred into active opposition…cherishing it within their bosoms, warming themselves with its rancorous fire."[30]

The Turning World

Poet Lord Tennyson wrote in *Locksley Hall*: "Forward, forward let us range, / Let the great world spin for ever down the ringing grooves of change." Past my use-by-date, I wind up my business affairs.

On a trip to London finishing off some business, I travel to the De La Warr Pavilion at Bexhill-on-Sea to view an exhibition of the d'Offay collection of Joseph Beuys's work. In an upstairs room in the gallery, there is a sculpture, *Scala Napoletana*, a piece the artist finished a few months before his death. The work consists of an old ladder, which Beuys found on the Island of Capri. It is suspended from two lead spheres by wire. Worn, fragile, its paint peeling, the ladder hangs in the middle of the display space, elegiac and solemnly eloquent. Beuys was deeply influenced by shaman beliefs of ascending the upper regions of existence. Steeped in the artist's awareness of his own death, the ladder seems to symbolize the final ascent that we all make, conveying its danger, desperate hope, uncertainty, and inevitability.

In the train back to London, I turn my attention to a book by German philosopher Walter Benjamin. His unfinished *Arcades Project* was to have been a study of capitalist modernity, based on Paris's neglected covered passages, symbolic of a golden age of production, consumption, and consumer society. For Benjamin, the alcoves were the repository of discredited dreams. The ninth thesis from the essay "Theses on the philosophy of history" catches my attention:

> A Klee painting named "Angelus Novus" shows an angel looking as though he is about to move away from something he is fixedly contemplating. His eyes are staring, his mouth is open, his wings are spread. This is how one pictures the angel of history. His face is turned toward the past. Where we perceive a chain of events, he sees one single catastrophe [that] keeps piling wreckage and hurls it in front of his feet. The angel would like to stay, awaken the dead, and make whole what has been smashed. But a storm is blowing in from Paradise; it has got caught in his wings with such a violence that the angel can no longer close them. The storm irresistibly propels him into the future to which his back is turned, while the pile of debris before him grows skyward. This storm is what we call progress.[31]

Was the global financial crisis bringing to a close a grand arc of human history? Over the last 40 years, financial fundamentalism and financial oligarchs changed the world. *Extreme money*, the idea of universal wealth and prosperity engineered by financial alchemy, was immensely powerful, impossible to resist. Was it possible to turn back? As Dom Cobb (played by Leonardo DiCaprio) understands in the film *Inception*, the hardest virus to kill is an idea.

Notes

The original reference source for most quotes in the text is provided where they are uncommon. In recent years, the availability of the Internet, online quotation databases, and websites and search engines (such as www.google.com) mean that many quotes are readily available online. In the interest of minimizing notes, where the quote is well known, specific sources have not been included. Quotes from films can be found at www.imdb.com

Prologue—Hubris

1. George W. Bush, Remarks on Signing the American Dream Downpayment Act (16 December 2003) (www.presidency.ucsb.edu/ws/index.php?pid=64935).
2. Quoted in Ron Chernow (1990) *The House of Morgan: An American Banking Dynasty and the Rise of Modern Finance*, Touchstone Books, New York: 154.
3. Quoted in Don Thompson (2008) *The $12 Million Stuffed Shark: The Curious Economics of Contemporary Art*, Palgrave Macmillan, New York: 219.
4. Quoted in John Kay "A stakeholding society—what does it mean for business?" (1997) *Scottish Journal of Political Economy* 44/4: 425–36.
5. John Kenneth Galbraith (1975) *The Great Crash 1929*, Penguin Books, London: 187.
6. Quoted in "The pop star and the private equity firms" (26 June 2009) *New York Times*.
7. Edwin Lefèvre (2005) *Reminiscences of a Stock Operator*, John Wiley, New Jersey: 12.
8. F. Scott Fitzgerald (1973) *The Great Gatsby*, Penguin Books, London: 188.
9. Alain de Botton (2002) *The Art of Travel*, Penguin Books, London: 40.
10. Ibid: 57.
11. Quoted in Andrew Ross Sorkin "A 'bonfire' returns as heartburn" (24 June 2008) *New York Times*.

Chapter 1—Mirror of the Times

1. Michael Jackson "Money" from History—Past, Present And Future Book 1 (2009).
2. Adam Smith (1776) An Inquiry into the Nature and Causes of the Wealth of Nations: Book 1 Chapter 2 (http://geolib.com/smith.adam/won1-02.html).
3. Glyn Davies (2002) *A History of Money: From Ancient Times to the Present Day*, University of Wales Press, Cardiff: 13, 14.
4. Ibid: 18, 20.
5. Christian Oliver and Jan Cienski "North Korea offers ginseng to pay Czech debt" (10 August 2010) *Financial Times*.
6. Jack Wetherford (1997) *The History of Money*, Three Rivers Press, New York: Chapter 1.
7. Ibid: 20.
8. Quoted in Justyn Walsh (2009) *Keynes and the Market*, John Wiley & Sons, Chichester: 148.
9. William Jennings Bryan, Speech concluding debate on the Chicago Platform (9 July 1896), Democratic National Convention, Chicago, Illinois (http://en.wikisource.org/wiki/Cross_of_Gold_Speech).
10. Wetherford, *The History of Money*: 175–7.
11. Quoted in Brook Larmer "The price of gold" (January 2009) National Geographic: 42.
12. Ian Fleming (2009) *Goldfinger*, Penguin Books, London: 73.
13. John Updike (1982) *Rabbit is Rich*, Penguin Books, London: 201.
14. Adam Smith (2007) *The Wealth of Nations*, Cosmino, New York: 241.
15. John Kenneth Galbraith (1975) *Money: Whence It Came, Whence It Went*, Houghton Mifflin, Boston: 45.
16. Dylan Grice "Popular delusions: a Minskian roadmap to the next gold mania" (18 November 2009), Société Générale Cross Asset Research.
17. Walsh, *Keynes and the Market*: 167.
18. George Bernard Shaw (2005) *The Intelligent Woman's Guide to Socialism and Capitalism*, Transaction Publishers, New Jersey: 263.
19. Quoted in Francis J. Gavin (2004) *Gold, Dollars, and Power: The Politics of International Monetary Relations 1958–1971*, University of North Carolina Press: 3.
20. Lewis Carroll (1871) *Through the Looking Glass*: Chapter 6 (www.sabian.org/Alice/lgchap06.html).
21. John Maynard Keynes (2010) *The Economic Consequences of the Peace*, Indo European Publishing, Los Angeles: 108.
22. Quoted in William Grieder (1987) *Secret of the Temple: How the Federal Reserve Runs The Country*, Simon & Schuster, New York: 231.
23. Alan Greenspan "Gold and economic freedom" (1966) *The Objectivist*; reprinted in Ayn Rand (1986) *Capitalism: The Unknown Ideal*, Signet, New York (www.321gold.com/fed/greenspan/1966.html).
24. Galbraith, *Money: Whence it Came, Where it Went*: 15.
25. University of Virginia Library Electronic Text Center, Thomas Jefferson Digital Archive (http://etext.lib.virginia.edu/jefferson/quotations/jeff1325.html).

26. John Maynard Keynes (2006) *The General Theory of Employment, Interest and Money*, Atlantic Books, New Delhi: 268.
27. Quoted in Niall Ferguson (2008) *The Ascent of Money*, Allen Lane, London: 85.
28. Paul Seabright (2004) *The Company of Strangers: A Natural History of Economic Life*, Princeton University Press, New Jersey.
29. Quoted in Grieder, *Secret of the Temple*: 234, 236.
30. Quoted in Wetherford, *The History of Money*: 137–9.
31. William Shakespeare (1599), *Julius Caesar*: Act I Scene ii (www.readprint.com/chapter-7839/Julius-Caesar-William-Shakespeare).
32. Robert Hughes (1980) *The Shock of the New—Art and the Century of Change*, British Broadcasting Corporation, London: 398; Leonard Shilan (1991) *Art and Physics: Parallel Visions in Space, Time and Light*, Quill William Morrow, New York: 270.

Chapter 2—Money Changes Everything

1. Quoted in Niall Ferguson (2008) *The Ascent of Money*, Allen Lane, London: 85.
2. F. Scott Fitzgerald (1926) *The Rich Boy* (http://en.wikiquote.org/wiki/Talk:F._Scott_Fitzgerald).
3. Robert Frank (2007) *Richistan: A Journey through the 21st Century Wealth Boom and the Lives of the New Rich*, Crown, New York.
4. Robert J. Gordon and Ian Dew-Becker "Where did the productivity growth go? Inflation dynamics and the distribution of income" (December 2005), National Bureau of Economic Research Working Paper 11842.
5. Quoted in Louis Uchitelle "The wage that meant middle class" (20 April 2008) *New York Times*.
6. John Kenneth Galbraith (1981) *A Life In Our Times*, André Deutsch, London: 122.
7. John Kenneth Galbraith (2001) "Economics and the quality of life" in *The Essential Galbraith*, Houghton Mifflin, New York: 103, 104.
8. Alan Greenspan (2007) *The Age of Turbulence—Adventures in a New World*, Allen Lane, London: 270, 271.
9. Quoted in Zygmunt Bauman (2007) *Liquid Times: Living in an Age of Uncertainty*, Polity Press, Cambridge: 105.
10. Suketu Mehta "What they hate about Mumbai" (28 November 2008) *New York Times*.
11. Quoted in Doug Wakefield "Fear and perception—the speed at which investor sentiment can change" (1 November 2007) (www.marketoracle.co.uk/Article2634.html).
12. James Quinn "The shallowest generation" (3 November 2008) (www.financialsense.com/editorials/quinn/2008/1103.html); based on data from the U.S. Census Bureau.
13. John Updike (1996) *Rabbit: Rest*, Penguin Books, London: 7.
14. Peter Watson (2001) *A Terrible Beauty: The People and Ideas that Shaped the Modern Mind—A History*, Phoenix Press, London: 594.
15. Robert Frank "A risky profile" (4 March 2007) *Wall Street Journal*.

16. Quoted in Norman Berlin (1998) "The late plays," in Michael Mannheim (ed.) *The Cambridge Companion to Eugene O'Neill*, Cambridge University Press, Cambridge: 82.
17. Quoted in John Hills, John Ditch, and Howard Glennerster (1994) *Beveridge and Social Security: An International Retrospective*, Oxford University Press, Oxford: 10.
18. Quoted in Robin Blackburn (2002) *Banking on Death*, Verso, London: 31.
19. Quoted in Robert Winnett and Myra Butterworth "Savers told to stop moaning and start spending" (27 September 2010) *Daily Telegraph*.
20. Thomas Friedman (1999) *The Lexus and the Olive Tree*, Random House, New York: 58.

Chapter 3—Business of Business

1. Lawrence E. Mitchell (2007) *The Speculation Economy: How Finance Triumphed Over Industry*, Berrett-Koehler Publishing Inc., San Francisco: 13–15, 95.
2. Sir W. S. (William Schwenck) Gilbert "Songs of a Savoyard" (http://infomotions.com/etexts/gutenberg/dirs/etext97/svyrd10.htm).
3. Tom Hadden (1972) *Company Law and Capitalism*, Weidenfeld & Nicolson, London: 14.
4. Oscar Wilde (1965) *The Works of Oscar Wilde*, Spring Books, London: 93.
5. Betsy Morris "Tearing up the Jack Welch playbook" (7 November 2006) *Fortune* (www.CNNmoney.com).
6. The term was coined by Tony Golding, see (2001) *The City: Inside the Great Expectations Machine*, FT Prentice Hall, London.
7. Francesco Guerrera "Welch condemns share price focus" (12 March 2009) *Financial Times*.
8. Frank Partnoy (2003) *Infectious Greed: How Deceit and Risk Corrupted the Financial Markets*, Henry Holt, New York: 298–9.
9. "The Hondoyota GT89th" (12 September 1987) *International Financing Review*: 690.
10. "Mystery after China copper trader vanishes following heavy losses" (15 November 2005) *Fortune*.
11. Larry McDonald (2009) *A Colossal Failure of Common Sense*, Ebury Press, London: 165.
12. Bethany McLean and Peter Elkind (2003) *The Smartest Guys in the Room: The Amazing Rise and Scandalous Fall of Enron*, Penguin Books, New York: 39.
13. Alan Greenspan (2008) *The Age of Turbulence*, Allen Lane, London: 360.
14. Ibid: 472.
15. Andrew Smithers and Stephen Wright (2000) *Valuing Wall Street—Protecting Wealth in Turbulent Markets*, McGraw-Hill, Illinois.
16. *Institutional Investor* (4 February 1987). Reproduced with permission from BP.
17. Satyajit Das "Key trends in Treasury management" (May 1992) *Corporate Finance*: 39.
18. Ron Chernow (1993) *The Warburgs*, Vintage Books, New York: 647–54.
19. Ibid: 653.

20. John Cassidy (2002) *dot.con*, Perennial, New York: 261–4.
21. This discussion of GE draws on Julie Froud, Sukhdev Johal, Adam Leaver, and Karel Williams (2006) *Financialization and Strategy: Narrative and Numbers*, Routledge, London: Part II, Chapter 3, 299–368.
22. *The Economist* (2 May 2002).
23. Robert Slater (2003) *29 Leadership Secrets from Jack Welch*, McGraw–Hill, New York: 66.
24. Ibid: 171.
25. Quoted in John Plender "When clever insiders are pitted against naive outsiders" (20 April 2010) *Financial Times*.
26. Quoted in Berkshire Hathaway Letter to Shareholders (1995).
27. Maryann Keller (1989) *Rude Awakening: The Rise, Fall, and Struggle for Recovery of General Motors* (www.generalwatch.com/quotes.cfm).
28. Quoted in Niall Ferguson (2008) *The Ascent of Money*, Allen Lane, London: 89.

Chapter 4—Money for Sale

1. Quoted in John Lanchester (2010) *Whoops! Why Everyone Owes Everyone and No One Can Pay*, Allen Lane, London: 161.
2. Walter Bagehot (2006) *Lombard Street: A Description of the Money Market*, Cosimo, New York: 270.
3. Ron Chernow (1990) *The House of Morgan: An American Banking Dynasty and the Rise of Modern Finance*, Touchstone Books, New York: 20.
4. David Gaffney (2008) *Never Never*, Tindal Street Press, Birmingham: 35.
5. Chernow, *The House of Morgan*: 612.
6. James Grant (1993) "Why not platinum?" in *Minding Mr. Market: Ten Years on Wall Street with Grant's Interest Rate Observer*, Times Books, New York: 152–4.
7. Adapted from a saying by columnist Earl Wilson.
8. Jonathan A. Knee (2007) *The Accidental Investment Banker*, John Wiley, Chichester: 49.
9. John Cassidy (2002) *dot.com*, Perennial, New York: 340.
10. John Maynard Keynes (2006) *The General Theory of Employment, Interest and Money*, Atlantic Books, New Delhi: 176.
11. John Kenneth Galbraith (1993) *A Short History of Financial Euphoria*, Viking Books, New York: 19.
12. "A special report on the future of finance" (24 January 2009) *The Economist*: 17.

Chapter 5—Yellow Brick Road

1. Alfred Marshall (1920) *Principles of Economics*, Macmillan, London: 271.
2. Patrick Hosking and Suzy Jagger "'Wake up, gentlemen', world's top bankers warned by former Fed chairman Volcker" (9 December 2009) *The Times*.
3. Michael Lewis (1989) *Liar's Poker: Two Cities, True Greed*, Hodder & Stoughton, London: 182–3.

4. Philip Augar (2000) *The Death of Gentlemanly Capitalism*, Penguin Books, London: 76.
5. Ibid: 3.
6. Philip Augar (2009) *Chasing Alpha: How Reckless Growth and Unchecked Ambition Ruined The City's Golden Decade*, Bodley Head, London: 4.
7. Margaret Pagano "A matchless talent pool" (14 June 1999) *Financial News*; Tony Golding (2003) *The City: Inside the Great Expectations Machine*, FT Prentice Hall, London: 2.
8. William J. Bernstein (2009) *A Splendid Exchange: How Trade Shaped the World*, Grove Press, New York: 105, 106.
9. *New York Times* (20 December 2007); Kevin Phillip (2009) *Bad Money: Reckless Finance, Failed Politics, and the Global Crisis of American Capitalism*, Scribe Publications, Melbourne: 191.
10. http://thinkexist.com/quotes/federico_garcia_lorca/2.html
11. William H. McNeill (1998) *Plagues and People*, Anchor Books, New York: 130.
12. Bernstein, *A Splendid Exchange*: 287.
13. David Roche and Bob McKee (2008) *New Monetarism*, Independent Strategy Publications, London.
14. Martin Hutchinson "The return of Thomas Mun" (27 July 2009) (www.prudentbear.com/index.php/thebearslairview?art_id=10254).
15. Andy Warhol (2007) *The Philosophy of Andy Warhol*, Penguin Books, London: 229.
16. Niall Ferguson (2008) *The Ascent of Money*, Allen Lane, London: 335–9.
17. Piers Brendon (2000) *The Dark Valley: A Panorama of the 1930s*, Pimlico, London: 222.
18. "Impact of US financial crisis will be felt around world: Chinese PM" (28 September 2008), AFP.
19. Robert A. Mundell and Paul J. Zak (2003) *Monetary Stability and Economic Policy: A Dialog Between Leading Economists*, Edward Elgar Publishing, Cheltenham: 136.
20. Jeffrey Thompson Schnapp and Matthew Tiews (2006) *Crowds*, Stanford University Press, California: 273.
21. John Maynard Keynes (2006) *The General Theory of Employment, Interest and Money*, Atlantic Books, New Delhi: 142.

Chapter 6—Money Honey

1. Thomas A. Bass "The future of money" (October 1996) *Wired* 4.10.
2. Robert Sobel (1993) *Dangerous Dreamers: The Financial Innovators from Charles Merrill to Michael Milken*, John Wiley, New York: 221.
3. Donald Rumsfeld (22 September 2002) quoted in Hart Seely (2005) *Pieces of Intelligence: The Existential Poetry of Donald H. Rumsfeld*, Free Press, New York: 60.
4. www.youtube.com/results?search_query=two+johns+subprime&aq=1
5. Julian Lee "TV news is not factual program, says regulator" (12 February 2010) *Sydney Morning Herald*.
6. John Pilger "The invisible government" (16 June 2007) (www.inminds.co.uk/article.php?id=10196).

7. http://en.wikipedia.org/wiki/Louis_Rukeyser
8. Chrystia Freeland "Lunch with the FT: Jim Cramer" (22 February 2008) *Financial Times.*
9. Sean Collins, a senior producer with NPR News, quoted in Dan Gardner (2008) *Risk—The Science and Politics of Fear*, Virgin Books, London: 200.
10. Donald Rumsfeld (28 February 2003) quoted in Hart Seely (2005) *Pieces of Intelligence: The Existential Poetry of Donald H. Rumsfeld*, Free Press, New York: 57.
11. Ibid: 23.
12. Richard Feynman in a letter to Armando Garcia Jr (11 December 1985).
13. Attributed to Albert Einstein.
14. Attributed to Winston Churchill.
15. On CBS in October 2008, responding to a question to name another Supreme Court decision, she disagreed with other than Roe v. Wade, which legalized abortion in the USA.
16. "Network effects" (17 December 2009) *The Economist.*
17. Paul J. Bolster and Emery A. Trahan "Investing in mad money: price and style effects" (Spring 2009) *Financial Services Review.*
18. Robert Pari (1987) "Wall Street Week recommendations: yes or no?" *Journal of Portfolio Management* 14: 74–6; Jess Beltz and Robert Jennings (1997) "Recommendations: trading activity and performance: 'Wall Street Week with Louis Rukeyser,'" *Review of Financial Economics* 6: 15–27.
19. William J. Bernstein (1996) "The basics of investing and portfolio theory" (www.efficientfrontier.com).
20. Devin Leonard "Treasury's got Bill Gross on speed dial" (20 June 2009) *New York Times.*
21. Ibid.
22. Louis Rukeyser (26 July 2002) *Wall Street Week*, CNBC.
23. Peter Applebome "Contemplating the boobs we were" (27 December 2008) *New York Times.*
24. Kevin Kelly "Prophets of boom" (September 1999) *Wired.*
25. Ibid: 151.
26. John Cassidy (2002) *dot.con*, Perennial, New York: 254–5.

Chapter 7—Los Cee-Ca-Go Boys

1. Milton Friedman "Schools: Chicago" (Autumn 1974) *University of Chicago Magazine* 11–16: 11.
2. P.J. O'Rourke (1998) *Eat The Rich*, Atlantic Monthly Press, New York: 123.
3. Adam Smith (1776) *An Inquiry into the Nature and Causes of the Wealth of Nations*: Book 1 Chapter 2 (http://geolib.com/smith.adam/won1-02.html).
4. John Maynard Keynes (1973) *The General Theory of Employment, Interest and Money* in *The Collected Writings of John Maynard Keynes*, Macmillan, London: 321, 322.
5. Daniel Yergin and Joseph Stanislaw (2002) *The Commanding Heights: The Battle for the World Economy*, Touchstone Books, New York: 125.

6. Quoted in Kai Bord and Martin J. Sherwin (2006) *American Prometheus: The Triumph and Tragedy of J. Robert Oppenheimer*, Vintage Books, New York: 62.
7. Upton Sinclair (1965) *The Jungle*, Dover Publications: 32.
8. Quoted in Peter Watson (2000) *A Terrible Beauty: The People and Ideas that Shaped the Modern Minds—A History*, Phoenix Press, London: 81.
9. Philip Mirowski (2002) *Machine Dreams: Economics Becomes a Cyborg Science*, Cambridge University Press, Cambridge: 203, 204.
10. Johan van Overtveldt (2007) The Chicago School: How the University of Chicago Assembled the Thinkers Who Revolutionised Economics and Business, Agate Books, Chicago: 9.
11. Ibid: 91.
12. Justin Fox (2009) *The Myth of the Rational Market: A History of Risk, Reward and Delusion on Wall Street*, Harper Business, New York: 252.
13. van Overtveldt, The Chicago School: 85–7.
14. Pierre Bayard (2007) *How to Talk About Books You Haven't Read*, Bloomsbury, London.
15. Yergin and Stanislaw, *The Commanding Heights*: 89. The quote is derived from John Ranelagh's book, (1991) *Thatcher's People: an insider's account of the politics, the power, and the personalities*, Harper Collins, London. It is not verifiable but is likely to be true.
16. Quoted in "Lexington: the Obama cult" (25 July 2009) The Economist.
17. Yergin and Stanislaw, *The Commanding Heights*: 346.
18. Ibid: 333.
19. Quoted in Wolfgang Munchau "Recession is not the worst possible outcome" (6 July 2008) *Financial Times.*
20. James Grant (2008) *Mr. Market Miscalculates: The Bubble Years and Beyond*, Axios Press, Mount Jackson: 298, 299.
21. Ron Chernow (1993) *The Warburgs*, Vintage Books, New York: 393.
22. Quoted in Stephen Moore "*Atlas Shrugged*: from fiction to fact in 52 years" (9 January 2009) *Wall Street Journal.*
23. Niall Ferguson (2008) *The Ascent of Money: A Financial History of the World*, Allen Lane, London: 214.
24. van Overtveldt, *The Chicago School*: 60.
25. Yergin and Stanislaw, *The Commanding Heights*: 132, 133.
26. Quoted in Ferguson, *The Ascent of Money*: 65.
27. Quoted in Emmanuel Tumusiime-Mutebile (Governor of the Bank of Uganda) "Partnering with the media for effective communication and quality reporting", Speech at the Bank of Uganda/Media Top executives' dialogue (6 November 2009), Kampala (www.bis.org/review/r100120e.pdf).
28. Chernow, *The Warburgs*: 132–40.
29. Alan Greenspan (2007) *The Age of Turbulence: Adventures in a New World*, Allen Lane, London: 104–10.
30. The actual statement is: "The Federal Reserve…is in the position of the chaperone who has ordered the punch bowl removed just as the party was really warming up." William McChesney Martin Jr, Address to New York Group of the Investment Bankers Association of America (19 October 1955), Waldorf-Astoria Hotel, New York.

31. Ben S. Bernanke, Remarks at the Conference to Honor Milton Friedman (8 November 2002), University of Chicago, Chicago, Illinois.
32. Frank Knight "What is truth in economics?" (1940) *Journal of Political Economy*.

Chapter 8—False Gods, Fake Prophecies

1. Quoted in Justin Fox (2009) *The Myth of the Rational Market: A History of Risk, Reward and Delusion on Wall Street*, Harper Business, New York: 79.
2. Donald MacKenzie (2008) *An Engine, Not a Camera: How Financial Models Shape Markets*, MIT Press, Cambridge, Massachusetts: 5.
3. Ibid: 71.
4. Peter Bernstein (2005) *Capital Ideas: The Improbable Origins of Modern Wall Street*, John Wiley, New Jersey: 60.
5. Ibid: 22.
6. MacKenzie, An Engine, Not a Camera: 62.
7. Quoted in ibid: 50.
8. Quoted in Leonard Silk "The peril behind the takeover boom" (29 December 1985) *New York Times*.
9. Fox, *The Myth of the Rational Market*: 98, 99.
10. Johan van Overtveldt (2007) The Chicago School: How the University of Chicago Assembled the Thinkers Who Revolutionised Economics and Business, Agate Books, Chicago: 271.
11. Bernstein, *Capital Ideas*: Chapter 11.
12. Ibid: 227.
13. MacKenzie, An Engine, Not a Camera: 136.
14. Bernstein, *Capital Ideas*: 143.
15. Quoted in ibid: 48.
16. MacKenzie, *An Engine, Not a Camera*: 79.
17. Ibid: 79, 80.
18. Ibid: 80.
19. Ibid: 83, 84.
20. Joel Stern "Let's abandon earnings per share" (18 December 1972) *Wall Street Journal*.
21. MacKenzie, An Engine, Not a Camera: 254.
22. Barry Schachter "An irreverent guide to value at risk" (August 1997) *Financial Engineering News* 1/1 (www.debtonnet.com/newdon/files/marketinformation/varguide.asp).
23. Quoted in Fox, *The Myth of the Rational Market*: 191.
24. Quoted in ibid: 260.
25. Paul De Grauwe, Leonardo Iania and Pablo Rovira Kaltwasser "How abnormal was the stock market in October 2008?" (11 November 2008) (www.eurointelligence.com/article.581+M5f21b8d26a3.0.html).

26. Stephen Hawking, during a 1994 debate with Roger Penrose at the Isaac Newton Institute for Mathematical Sciences, University of Cambridge; in Stephen Hawking and Roger Penrose (1996) *The Nature of Space and Time*, Princeton University Press, New Jersey: 26.
27. Fischer Black "Noise" (1986) *Journal of Finance* 41: 529–43.
28. John Maynard Keynes (2006) *The General Theory of Employment, Interest and Money*, Atlantic Books, New Delhi: 140.
29. Alan Greenspan (2007) *The Age of Turbulence: Adventures in a New World*, Allen Lane, London: 124.
30. Fox, The Myth of the Rational Market: 41.
31. MacKenzie, An Engine, Not a Camera: 95.
32. Ibid: 8–12.
33. van Overtveldt, *The Chicago School*: 67.
34. Dan Gardner (2008) *Risk—The Science and Politics of Fear*, Virgin Books, London: 53.
35. van Overtveldt, *The Chicago School*: 291.
36. Quoted in Greenspan, *The Age of Turbulence*: 55.
37. Quoted in van Overtveldt, *The Chicago School*: 172.
38. Quoted in Fox, The Myth of the Rational Market: 269.
39. Daniel Altman "Managing Globalization: Q & A with Joseph Stiglitz" (11 October 2006) *The International Herald Tribune*.
40. MacKenzie, An Engine, Not a Camera: 24.
41. Kurt Vonnegut Jr (1963) *Cat's Cradle*, Holt, Rhinehart & Winston, New York: 75.
42. "Roundtable: the limits of VAR" (April 1998) *Derivatives Strategy*.
43. John Maynard Keynes (1991) *Essays in Persuasion*, W.W. Norton, New York: Chapter 5.
44. Quoted in Don Thompson (2008) The $12 Million Stuffed Shark: The Curious Economics of Contemporary Art, Palgrave Macmillan, New York: 53.

Chapter 9—Learning to Love Debt

1. "Congoleum Corporation (abridged)" (2008), Harvard Business School Case Study 9-287-029, Harvard Business School Publishing, Boston, MA.
2. *Boston Globe* (20 August 1986) quoted in "Congoleum Corporation (abridged)" Teaching Notes (1997), Harvard Business School Case Study 9-292-081, Harvard Business School Publishing, Boston, MA: 5.
3. Robert Sobel (1993) *Dangerous Dreamers: The Financial Innovators from Charles Merrill to Michael Milken*, John Wiley, New York: 40.
4. Quoted in George Anders (1992) *Merchants of Debt: KKR and the Mortgaging of American Business*, Basic Books, New York: 21.
5. John Brooks (1987) *The Takeover Game*, Truman Talley Books, New York: 29.
6. Anders, *Merchants of Debt*: 112.
7. Ibid: 148.
8. Ibid: 105.

9. Ibid: 191.
10. Ibid: 148, 152–5.
11. Michael C. Jensen "The modern Industrial Revolution, exit, and the failure of internal control systems" (1993) *Continental Bank Journal of Applied Corporate Finance*: 4–23.
12. Anders, *Merchants of Debt*: xix.
13. Quoted in George B. Baker and George David Smith (1998) *The New Financial Capitalists: Kohlberg Kravis Roberts and the Creation of Corporate Value*, Cambridge University Press, New York: 90.
14. Anders, *Merchants of Debt*: 41.
15. *If Japan can ... Why can't we?* (1980), TV show introducing the methods of W. Edwards Deming to American managers, produced by Clare Crawford-Mason, NBC (http://en.wikipedia.org/wiki/If_Japan_Can..._Why_Can't_We%3F).
16. Quoted in Anders, Merchants of Debt: 162.
17. Quoted in ibid: 35.
18. Quoted in Baker and Smith, *The New Financial Capitalists*: 204.
19. Philipp Meyer (2009) *American Rust*, Simon & Schuster, London: 348.
20. Quoted in Anders, *Merchants of Debt*: 74.
21. Quoted in Baker and Smith, *The New Financial Capitalists*: 82.
22. Connie Bruck (1988) *The Predators' Ball: How Michael Milken and his Junk Bond Machine Staked the Corporate Raiders*, Simon & Schuster, New York: 37.
23. Benjamin J. Stein (1992) *A License to Steal: The Untold Story of Michael Milken and the Conspiracy to Bilk the Nation*, Simon & Schuster, New York: 24, 25.
24. Sobel, *Dangerous Dreamers*, John Wiley, New York: 99.
25. Stein, *A License to Steal*: Chapter 9.
26. Sobel, *Dangerous Dreamers*: 187–91.
27. Bruck, *The Predators' Ball*: 29.
28. Quoted in Sobel *Dangerous Dreamers*: 79.
29. Bryan Burroughs and John Helyar (1990) *Barbarians at the Gate: The Fall of RJR Nabisco*, Harper & Row, New York.
30. Bruck, The Predators' Ball: 66.
31. Quoted in Sobel, *Dangerous Dreamers*: 146.
32. Ibid: 90.
33. Bruck, *The Predators' Ball*: 197.
34. Ibid: 15.
35. Ibid: 66.
36. Ibid: 295.
37. Sobel, *Dangerous Dreamers*: 124.
38. Quoted in Ron Chernow (1990) *The House of Morgan*, Simon & Schuster, New York: 693.
39. Sobel, Dangerous Dreamers: 105.
40. Quoted in ibid: 120.
41. Quoted in ibid: 168.

42. Alan Greenspan, Statement before the Senate Finance Committee (26 January 1989).
43. Michael Jensen "Corporate control and the politics of finance" (Summer 1991) *Journal of Applied Corporate Finance* 4/2.
44. Bruck, *The Predators' Ball*: 254.
45. James B. Stewart (1992) *Den of Thieves*, Simon & Schuster, New York: 261.
46. Sobel, *Dangerous Dreamers*: 2.
47. Stein, *A License to Steal*: 24, 25.
48. Bruck, *The Predators' Ball*: 266.

Chapter 10—Private Vices

1. Robert Sobel (1993) *Dangerous Dreamers: The Financial Innovators from Charles Merrill to Michael Milken*, John Wiley, New York: 191.
2. http://resident-alien.blogspot.com/2007/07/public-v-private-equity.html
3. Edward Chancellor with Lauren Silva "The Wizards of Oz: not making sense of Macquarie's business model" (1 June 1007) *Breaking Views*; Gideon Haigh "Who's afraid of Macquarie Banks? The story of the millionaire's factory" (July 2007) *The Monthly*; Bethany McLean "Would you buy a bridge from this man?" (18 September 2007) *Fortune*.
4. Chancellor with Silva, "The Wizards of Oz."
5. "The uneasy crown: the buy-out business is booming, but capitalism's new kings are attracting growing criticism" (8 February 2007) *The Economist*.
6. Connie Bruck (1988) *The Predators' Ball: How Michael Milken and his Junk Bond Machine Staked the Corporate Raiders*, Simon & Schuster, New York: 261–2.
7. Steven Kaplan and Antoinette Schoar "Private equity performance: returns, persistence and capital flows" (August 2005) *Journal of Finance*.
8. Ludovic Phalippou, Oliver Gottschalg and Maurizio Zollo (2007) "Performance of private equity funds: another puzzle," Society for Financial Studies Working Paper.
9. Martin Arnold "Buy-out study queries performance" (25 July 2010) *Financial Times*.
10. "The uneasy crown" (8 February 2007) *The Economist*.
11. Andrew Capon "Endgame for private equity" (May 2009) *Euromoney*: 72.
12. "Blackstone's IPO: bigger than Rod" (22 March 2007) *The Economist*.
13. Quoted in Henny Sender and Monica Langley "Buyout mogul: How Blackstone's chief became $7 billion man—Schwarzman says he's worth every penny," (13 June 2007) *Wall Street Journal*.
14. http://media.washingtonpost.com/wp-srv/business/documents/conwaymemo.pdf
15. Andrew Ross Sorkin "A financier peels back the curtain" (21 September 2009) *New York Times*.
16. "Citicorp defiant over EMI lawsuit" (13 December 2009) *Financial Times*.
17. Quoted in Sorkin "A financier peels back the curtain."

Chapter 11—Dice with Debt

1. Robert Mundell, Presentation at Conference on Globalization and Problems of Development (2–6 March 2008), Havana, Cuba.
2. Please note that all numbers here are rounded to whole numbers, as a company either defaults or it does not.
3. "Felix Salmon recipe for disaster: the formula that killed Wall Street" (23 February 2009)" *Wired*; Sam Jones "Of couples and copulas" (24 April 2009) *Financial Times*.
4. "Felix Salmon recipe for disaster."
5. www.wib.org/conferences__education/past_programs/2008_bond_university/08_index.html
6. Charles Gasparino (2009) *The Sellout: How Three Decades of Wall Street Greed and Government Mismanagement Destroyed the Global Financial System*, Harper Business, New York: 64.
7. Kevin Commins "The haunted world of mortgage-backeds" (July 1987) *Intermarket*: 22.
8. James Grant (2008) *Mr. Market Miscalculates: The Bubble Years and Beyond*, Axios Press, Mount Jackson: 326.
9. Quoted in Rebecca Solnit (2000) *Wanderlust: A History of Walking*, Penguin Books, New York: 256.
10. Adam Smith (2007) *Wealth of Nations*, Cosimo, New York: 113.
11. Alan Greenspan (2007) *The Age of Turbulence: Adventures in a New World*, Allen Lane, London: 230.
12. Jo Becker, Sheryl Gay Stolberg and Stephen Labaton "The reckoning—White House philosophy stoked mortgage bonfire" (20 December 2008) *New York Times*.
13. Ben Bernanke "Modern risk management and banking supervision" (12 June 2006), Remarks at the Stonier Graduate School of Banking, Washington.
14. Alan Greenspan "Understanding household debt obligations" (23 February 2004), Address to Credit Union National Association 2004 Governmental Affairs Conference, Washington DC.
15. Joe Bageant (2009) *Deer Hunting with Jesus: Dispatches from America's Class War*, Scribe Publications, Melbourne: 99.
16. Gretchen Morgenson "How a whistle-blower conquered Countrywide" (19 February 2011) *New York Times*.
17. www.thisamericanlife.org/radio-archives/episode/355/the-giant-pool-of-money
18. Gasparino, *The Sellout*: 162.
19. Richard Bitner (2008) *Confessions of a Sub-prime Lender: An Insider's Tale of Greed, Fraud and Ignorance*, Icon Books, London: 41.
20. www.thisamericanlife.org/radio-archives/episode/355/the-giant-pool-of-money
21. Bob Ivry "Deal with devil funded Carrera crash before sub-prime shakeout" (18 December 2007) *New York Times*.

Chapter 12—The Doomsday Debt Machine

1. The term "shadow banking system" is attributed to Paul McCulley of PIMCO, who coined it at the 2007 Jackson Hole conference; see Paul McCulley "Teton reflections" (July/August 2007), Pimco Global Central Banking Focus.
2. Roger Merrit, Ian Linnell, Robert Grossman and John Shiavetta "Hedge funds: an emerging force in global credit markets" (18 July 2005), Fitch Ratings, New York.
3. Speech at the Lord Mayor's Banquet for Bankers and Merchants of the City of London (17 June 2009), Mansion House, London.
4. Gretchen Morgenson and Louise Story "Bundled bad debt, bet against it and won" (23 December 2009) *New York Times*.
5. Based on Yves Smith (2010) *ECONned: How Unenlightened Self Interest Undermined Democracy and Corrupted Capitalism*, Palgrave Macmillan, New York: 257–6 1. It is assumed that 80 percent of the underlying loans were subprime, 80 percent of the Magnetar transactions were synthetic, and 20 percent of subprime component of these CDOs were 2006 vintage BBB subprime tranches. This leads to the following estimate: (\$30 billion × 80% × 80% × 20%) / 3% = \$128 billion. See also Jesse Eisinger and Jake Bernstein "The Magnetar trade: how one hedge fund helped keep the bubble going" (9 April 2010) *ProPublica*.
6. Morgenson and Story "Bundled bad debt."
7. Andrew Ross Sorkin "A crowd with pity for Goldman" (26 April 2010) *New York Times*.
8. John Kenneth Galbraith (1975) *The Great Crash 1929*, Penguin Books, London: 90.
9. Michael Lewis (2010) *The Big Short: Inside the Doomsday Machine*, Allen Lane, London: 67.
10. Henny Sender and Francesco Guerrera "Goldman criticised \$1bn loan product" (27 April 2010) *Financial Times*.
11. Nicole Bullock and Telis Demos "It pays to think before you click" (21 July 2010) *Financial Times*.
12. Steve Eder and Karey Wutkowski "Goldman's 'fabulous' fab's conflicted love letters" (26 April 2010), Reuters; Patrick Jenkins and Francesco Guerrera "Goldman versus the regulators" (18 April 2010) *Financial Times*.
13. Quoted in Louise Story "The generals who ended Goldman's war" (16 July 2010) *New York Times*.
14. Quoted in Gretchen Morgenson and Louise Story "Clients worried about Goldman's dueling goals" (18 May 2010) *New York Times*.
15. Eric Dash and Julie Cresswell "The reckoning: CitiGroup pays for a rush to risk" (23 November 2008) *New York Times*.
16. The phrase "riverboat gambler' is used to describe Tommy Maheras, a senior Citi executive in charge of this activity, in Charles Gasparino (2009) *The Sellout: How Three Decades of Wall Street Greed and Government Mismanagement Destroyed the Global Financial System*, Harper Business, New York.
17. Gasparino, *The Sellout*: 195.
18. Shareholder Report on UBS Writedowns (18 April 2008).

19. Walter Bagehot (2004) *Lombard Street: A Description of the Money Market*, Kessenger Publishing, Montana: 111.
20. "Quotes from US financial crisis commission hearing" (13 January 2010), Reuters.
21. http://jameshowardkunstler.typepad.com/clusterfuck_nation/2005/10/no_direction_ho.html
22. "The run on the Rock" (24 January 2008) House of Commons Treasury Select Committee 1: 67.
23. Gasparino, *The Sellout*: 318.
24. Ibid: 318, 319.
25. McKinsey Global Institute "Mapping the global capital markets—third annual report" (January 2007).
26. Gillian Tett "Should Atlas still shrug? The threat that lurks behind the growth of complex debt deals" (15 January 2007) *Financial Times*.
27. David A. Skeel Jr and Frank Partnoy "The promise and perils of credit derivatives" (2007) *University of Cincinnati Law Review* 75: 1019.
28. www.derivativesstrategy.com/magazine/archive/1999/0899qa.asp
29. Ian Kerr referred to them as Chernobyl decay obligations (www.efinancialnews.com/homepage/content/2448260317).

Chapter 13—Risk Supermarkets

1. Peter L. Bernstein (1996) *Against The Gods: The Remarkable Story of Risk*, John Wiley, New York: 1.
2. Jorge Luis Borges (1999) *Collected Fiction*, Penguin Books, New York: 105.
3. Emanuel Derman (2004) *My Life As A Quant: Reflection on Physics and Finance*, John Wiley, New Jersey.
4. Berkshire Hathaway Letter to Shareholders (2002).
5. Martin Z. Braun, Darrell Preston and Liz Willen "The banks that fleeced Alabama" (September 2005) *Bloomberg Markets*; William Selway and Martin Z. Braun "The fleecing of Alabama: the bills come due" (July 2008) *Bloomberg Markets*.
6. In a Dutch auction, the auctioneer begins with a high asking price that is lowered until some bidder accepts the auctioneer's price, or a predetermined reserve price (the seller's minimum acceptable price) is reached. The winning bidder pays the last announced price. The name derives from its use during the Dutch tulip bubble.
7. Alan Greenspan "Finance: United States and global" (22 April 2002), Institute of International Finance, New York, New York (via videoconference).
8. Joe Mysak "Moody's, S&P help push Alabama county to insolvency" (4 March 2008), Bloomberg.
9. Michael McDonald, John Lauerman, and Gillian Wee "Harvard swaps are so toxic even Summers won't explain" (18 December 2009), Bloomberg.
10. Ibid; John Lauerman and Michael McDonald "Harvard's bet on interest rate rise cost $500 million to exit share business" (17 October 2009), Bloomberg.
11. Quoted in Philip Kennicott "The man in the ivory tower—Harvard's Lawrence Summers is a study in controversy" (15 April 2005) *The Washington Post*.

12. Stephen Bartholomeusz "Sons of Gwalia's gold hedging had big holes" (4 September 2004) *Sydney Morning Herald*; "A cautionary tale: how sons of Gwalia fell" (June 2006) *Asia Risk*.
13. Randall Dodd "Exotic derivatives losses in emerging markets: questions of suitability, concerns for stability" (July 2009), IMF Working Paper.
14. Tom Mitchell and Justine Lau "Citic Pacific badly scarred by its currency speculation" (22 October 2008) *Financial Times*.
15. Berkshire Hathaway Letter to Shareholders (2002).
16. Make Markets be Markets Conference (3 March 2010), New York City.

Chapter 14—Financial Arms Race

1. G.K. Chesterton (2009) *Orthodoxy*, BiblioLife: 131.
2. "Former NAB traders jailed" (4 July 2006) *Sydney Morning Herald*.
3. Adam Sage "SocGen trader's fear of being caught and jailed in Paris" (11 February 2008) *The Times*.
4. Ben Hall "Former trader: SocGen says he got 'a bit carried away'" (6 February 2008) *Financial Times*.
5. Nelson D. Schwartz and Jad Mouawad "A French style of capitalism is now stained" (28 January 2008) *New York Times*.
6. "Crowds and cameras greet Kerviel's day in court" (8 June 2010) *Financial Times*.
7. Scheherazade Daneshkhu "Top guns to trade legal blows in SocGen clash" (6 June 2010) *Financial Times*.
8. Nicola Clark "Former SocGen chairman has sharp words for trader" (22 June 2010) *New York Times*.
9. Scheherazade Daneshkhu "SocGen must have seen Kerviel risky trades—witness" (11 June 2010) *Financial Times*.
10. Nicola Clark and Katrin Bennhold "A Société Générale trader remains a mystery as his criminal trial ends" (25 June 2010) *New York Times*.
11. Scheherazade Daneshkhu "Kerviel was a 'creation' of SocGen" (25 June 2010) *Financial Times*.
12. Karen Maley "The making of a rogue trader" (17 June 2010). http://www.businessspector.com.au/bs.nsf/Article/The-making-of-a-rogue-trader-pd20100617-6H767.
13. "SocGen, La Banque clown" (5 October 2010) *Financial Times*.
14. Scheherazade Daneshkhu "Kerviel faces jail and fine in SocGen trial" (5 October 2010) *Financial Times*.
15. Robert O'Harrow Jr and Brady Dennis "The beautiful machine" (29, 30, 31 December 2008) *Washington Post*.
16. Marc Lackritz "Beware the biggest moral hazard of them all" (10 June 2010) *Financial Times*.
17. "The world according to Lee Wakeman" (www.derivativesstrategy.com/ magazine/ archive/1997/0797qa.asp).
18. Berkshire Hathaway Letter to Shareholders (2004).
19. Berkshire Hathaway Letter to Shareholders (2002).

20. Berkshire Hathaway Letter to Shareholders (2008).
21. O'Harrow and Dennis "The beautiful machine."
22. Ibid.
23. Carrick Mollenkamp, Serena Ng, Liam Pleven and Randall Smith "Behind AIG's fall, risk models failed to pass real-world test" (3 November 2008) *Wall Street Journal*.
24. Quoted in Dennis Overbye "They tried to outsmart Wall Street" (9 March 2009) *New York Times*.
25. O'Harrow and Dennis "The beautiful machine."
26. Norges Bank v. CitiGroup Inc. and other Case 1:10-cv-07202-UA Document 1 (17 September 2010), United States District Court, Southern District of New York.
27. Gary Gorton (2010) *Slapped by the Invisible Hand: The Panic of 2007*, Oxford University Press, Oxford: 133.
28. Alister Bull "Fed focus-credit derivatives—a tool with a sharp edge" (16 May 2007), Reuters.
29. Gary Gorton "Banks, banking, and crises" (2007) *NBER Reporter: Research Summary* 4.
30. "A root of the financial crisis" (18 September 2008) (http://mba.yale.edu/news_events/CMS/Articles/6603.shtml).
31. Richard Duncan (2009) *The Corruption of Capitalism*, CLSA Books, Hong Kong: 140.
32. Alan Greenspan "Financial derivatives" (19 March 1999), Futures Industry Association, Boca Raton, Florida.
33. Martin Z. Braun and William Selway "Hidden swap fees by JP Morgan, Morgan Stanley hit school boards" (1 February 2008), Bloomberg.
34. Adair Turner "The financial crisis and the future of financial regulation" (21 January 2009) *The Economist*'s Inaugural City Lecture.
35. John Kay "Wind down the market in five-legged dogs" (21 January 2009) *Financial Times*.
36. J. Hillis Miller "Stevens' rock and criticism as cure" (1976) *Georgia Review* 30: 34.
37. James Rickards "How markets attacked the Greek piñata" (11 February 2010) *Financial Times*.
38. Ibid.
39. David McNally "From financial crisis to world slump: accumulation, financialization, and the global slowdown" (15 December 2008), expanded version of a paper presented to the plenary session ("The global financial crisis: causes and consequences"), 2008 Historical Materialism Conference, University of London (http://marxandthefinancialcrisisof2008.blogspot.com/2008/12/david-mcnally-from-financial-crisis-to.html).
40. Alan Greenspan, Testimony to the House Committee on Oversight and Government Reform (23 October 2008).

Chapter 15—Woodstock for Hedge Funds

1. Martin Baker (1995) *A Fool and His Money*, Orion Books, London: 157, 158.
2. Tom Wolfe (1988) *The Bonfire of the Vanities*, Picador, London: 64.
3. Tony Tassell "The Goldman Sachs narrative" (8 February 2010) *Financial Times*.

4. Quoted in Robert Slater (2009) *Soros: The World's Most Influential Investor*, McGraw Hill, New Jersey: 178.
5. Philip Delves Broughton (2009) *Ahead of the Curve: Two Years at Harvard Business School*, Penguin Books, New York: 99.
6. Ron Chernow (1990) *The House of Morgan: An American Banking Dynasty and the Rise of Modern Finance*, Touchstone Books, New York: 43.
7. "Live-blogging the hedge fund hearing" (13 November 2008) New York Times.
8. George Soros (1995) *Soros on Soros: Staying Ahead of the Curve*, John Wiley, New Jersey.
9. Quoted in Peter Temple (2001) *Hedge Funds: The Courtesans of Capitalism*, John Wiley & Sons, Chichester: 61.
10. Fred Schwed Jr (2006) *Where Are The Customers' Yachts? Or A Good Hard Look: Wall Street*, John Wiley, New Jersey: 140.
11. Bloomberg (12 July 2010).
12. John Griffin and Jun Xu "How smart are the smart guys? A unique view from hedge fund stock holdings" (2009) *Review of Financial Studies*: 2531–70; Burton G. Malkiel and Atanu Saha "Hedge funds: risk and return" (2005) *Financial Analysts Journal* 61/6.
13. Richard Bookstaber (2007) *A Demon of our Own Design*, John Wiley, New Jersey: 179–80.
14. "Live-blogging the hedge fund hearing."
15. Marcia Vickers "The most powerful trader on Wall Street you've never heard of" (21 July 2003) *Bloomberg Businessweek*.
16. David S. Hilzenrath and Jia Lynn Yang "Federal investigators expose vast web of insider trading" (12 February 2011) *Washington Post*.
17. James Grant (2008) *Mr. Market Miscalculates: The Bubble Years and Beyond*, Axios Press, Mount Jackson: 86.
18. Dean P. Foster and H. Peyton Young "The hedge fund game: incentives, excess returns, and piggy backing" (November 2007, revised 2 March 2008), Economic Series Working Papers, University of Oxford.
19. "Live-blogging the hedge fund hearing."
20. Vivek Kaul "What's luck got to do with investing?" (28 December 2009), DNA India.
21. Temple, Hedge Funds: 5.
22. Holman W. Jenkins "How a cat becomes a dog" (5 April 2000) *Wall Street Journal*.
23. David Wighton, Ben White and Deborah Brewster "Citadel trading costs hit $5.5 bn" (2–3 December 2006) *Financial Times*: 1.
24. Merrill Lynch, Bear Stearns and Paine Webber senior executives are understood to have had invested in LTCM; see Roger Lowenstein (2002) *When Genius Failed: The Rise and Fall of Long-Term Capital Management*, Fourth Estate, London.
25. Scholes denies having used the word "fool" in Lowenstein, *When Genius Failed*: 33, 34.
26. "Trillion dollar bet" (8 February 2000), PBS; Sam Jones "Meriwether setting up new hedge fund" (22 October 2009) *Financial Times*.
27. Lowenstein, *When Genius Failed*: 147.

28. As quoted in Lowenstein, *When Genius Failed*: 123; actually "Markets can remain irrational a lot longer than you and I can remain solvent" from A. Gary Shilling (1993) *Forbes* 151/4: 236.

29. Quoted in Nicolas Dunbar (2000) *Investing Money*, John Wiley, Chichester: 208, 209.

30. Adam Smith (2006) *Super Money*, John Wiley, New Jersey: 180.

31. Michael Lewis "How the eggheads cracked" (24 January 1999) *New York Times Magazine*: 24–42.

32. Peter Temple (2001) *Hedge Funds: The Courtesans of Capitalism*, John Wiley & Sons, Chichester: 41, 42.

33. Hilary Till "Comments on the Amaranth Case: Early Lessons from the Debacle" (2006), EDHEC Working Paper; Chris C. Finger "The lights are on?" (October 2006) *RiskMetrics Group—Research Monthly*.

34. Jeremy Grant "Did Amaranth cause harm?" (25 June 2007) *Financial Times*.

35. "Amaranth hit by $6bn loss" (October 2006) *Risk*.

36. Ibid.

37. Katherine Burton and Jenny Strasburg "Amaranth's slide began with offer to keep star trader" (6 December 2006), Bloomberg.

38. "Amaranth hit by $6bn loss" (October 2006) *Risk*.

39. Ibid.

40. Burton and Strasburg "Amaranth's slide."

41. www.wilmott.com/messageview.cfm?catid=11&threadid=76822&FTVAR_MSGDBTABLE=

42. Adam Smith (1776) *An Inquiry into the Nature and Causes of the Wealth of Nations*: Book 1, Chapter 27 (http://geolib.com/smith.adam/won1-02.html).

Chapter 16—Minsky Machines

1. William Fung, David Hsieh, Narayan Naik, and Tarun Ramadorai "Hedge funds: performance, risk and capital formation" (19 July 2006) (www.ssrn.com/abstract=778124).

2. "Rolling in it" (16 November 2006) *The Economist*.

3. Michael Lewis (2010) *The Big Short: Inside the Doomsday Machine*, Allen Lane, London: 3.

4. "The hedge fund king is getting nervous" (16 September 2006) *Wall Street Journal*: A.1.

5. Peter Temple (2001) *Hedge Funds: The Courtesans of Capitalism*, John Wiley & Sons, Chichester: 42.

6. H. Kat and H. Palaro "Who needs hedge funds? A copula-based approach to hedge fund return replication" (2005), Alternative Investment Research Centre Working Paper 27, Cass Business School, City University London; H. Kat and H. Palaro "Replication and evaluation of fund of hedge fund returns" (2006), Alternative Investment Research Centre Working Paper 28, Cass Business School, City University London; H. Kat and H. Palaro "Superstars or average Joes? A replication-based performance evaluation of 1917 individual hedge funds" (2006), Alternative Investment Research Centre Working Paper 30, Cass Business School, City University,

London; H. Kat and H. Palaro "Tell me what you want, what you really, really want! An exercise in tailor-made synthetic fund creation" (2006), Alternative Investment Research Centre Working Paper 36, Cass Business School, City University London; Jasmina Hasanhodzic and Andrew W. Lo "Can hedge-fund returns be replicated? The linear case" (16 August 2006) (www.ssrn.com/abstract=924565).

7. Thorold Barker "Does it do what it says on the tin?" (2–3 December 2006) *Financial Times*: 11.
8. Jenny Anderson "Papers study August crisis, from first wave to last ripple" (28 September 2007) *New York Times.*
9. Quoted in Peter Aspden "From free love to free market" (31 July 2009) *Financial Times.*
10. "Hedge funds: what they told clients" (2 November 2008) *The Sunday Times.*
11. Ibid.
12. "Hedge funds: behind the veil" (16 August 2007) *The Economist.*
13. See blog associated with Geoffrey Rogow "Hedge funds: defensive in tone, aggressive in strategy" (21 October 2008) *Wall Street Journal.*
14. Louise Story "Paul Tudor Jones's rules of investing" (1 December 2008) *New York Times.*
15. Rogow "Hedge funds."
16. http://knowledge.wharton.upenn.edu/article.cfm?articleid=1931
17. William Hutchings "Hedge fund makes $3bn from sub-prime bet" (12 November 2007) (www.efinancialnews.com/story/2007-11-12/hedge-fund-makes-from-sub-prime-bet).
18. Michael Lewis (2010) *The Big Short: Inside the Doomsday Machine*, Allen Lane, London: 106.
19. "Back in business: A trader's trespasses are forgiven" (12 October 2006) *The Economist*.
20. Jenny Strasburg "A decade later, John Meriwether must scramble again" (27 March 2008) *New York Times*; Katherine Burton and Saijel Kishan "Meriwether said to shut JWM hedge fund after losses" (8 July 2008), Bloomberg; Henny Sender "The storms that hit Meriwether's fund" (9 July 2009) *Financial Times.*
21. Louise Armitstead and Richard Fletcher "How Porsche took the wind out of the hedge funds' sails" (29 October 2008) *New York Times.*
22. Richard Milne and Kate Burgess "Hedge funds left reeling as VW races on" (28 October 2008) *Financial Times.*
23. "Equity derivatives: the Volkswagen squeeze" (December 2008) *Risk* 21/12.
24. Armitstead and Fletcher "How Porsche took the wind out of the hedge funds' sails."
25. Milne and Burgess "Hedge funds left reeling."
26. Louise Story, Michael J. De La Merced and Carter Dougherty "Panicked traders take VW shares on a wild ride" (28 October 2008) *New York Times.*
27. Richard Milne "Man in the news: Wendelin Wiederking" (31 October 2008) *Financial Times.*
28. "Porsche and VW: squeezy money" (30 October 2008) *The Economist.*
29. Milne "Man in the news."
30. Quoted in Temple, *Hedge Funds*: 133.

31. Richard Teitelbaum and Tom Cahill "Brevan Howard shows paranoid survive in hedge fund of time outs" (1 April 2009), Bloomberg.
32. Carol J. Loomis "Buffett's big bet" (9 June 2008) *Fortune.*
33. Henny Sender "Druckenmiller exit marks end of era" (18 August 2010) *Financial Times.*
34. Penny Wary "Selling themselves short" (9 June 2006) *The Times.*

Chapter 17—War Games

1. Sean D. Naylor "War games rigged?" (16 August 2002) (www.armytimes.com/legacy/new/0-292925-1060102.php).
2. Lawrence C. Strauss "Jeremy Grantham: still holding back" (13 October 2008) *Barron's.*
3. Ron Suskind (2004) *The Price of Loyalty*, Simon & Schuster, New York: 291.
4. Alan Greenspan (2007) *The Age of Turbulence: Adventures in a New World*, Allen Lane, London: 360, 361.
5. Ben Bernanke "The economic outlook" (5 May 2005), Testimony to the Joint Economic Committee, US Congress.
6. "Savings versus liquidity" (11 August 2005) *The Economist.*
7. Robin Harding "Bernanke says foreign investors fuelled crisis" (18 February 2011) *Financial Times.*
8. Fisher, Irving "The debt-deflation theory of great depressions" (1933) *Econometrica*: 337–57.
9. William White "Is price stability enough?" (April 2006) *Bank of International Settlements.*
10. Gillian Tett of the *Financial Times* coined the phrase; see Gillian Tett "Should Atlas still shrug?" (15 January 2007) *Financial Times.*
11. The phrase "new liquidity factory" was coined by Mohamed El-Erian.
12. Total outstanding volumes of derivative contracts are greater, around $600 trillion (see Chapter 14). The figure here is adjusted for double counting of derivative volumes and the estimated portion that is used for hedging.
13. Paul McCulley "The paradox of deleveraging will be broken" (November 2008), Pimco.
14. Mark E. J. Newman, Albert-László Barabási and Duncan J. Watts (2006) *The Structure and Dynamics of Networks*, Princeton University Press, New Jersey: L-22.
15. Donald L. Kohn "Commentary: has financial development made the world riskier?" (August 2005), Federal Reserve Bank of Kansas City Economic Symposium, Jackson Hole, Wyoming.
16. Quoted in Yves Smith (2010) ECONned: How Unenlightened Self Interest Undermined Democracy and Corrupted Capitalism, Palgrave Macmillan, New York: 126.
17. Andrew Haldane "Rethinking the financial network" (April 2009), Speech delivered at the Financial Student Association, Amsterdam.
18. Haldane "Rethinking the financial network."
19. Testimony before Senate Committee on Banking, Housing and Urban Affairs (18 May 1994).

20. Hyun Song Shin "Commentary: has financial development made the world riskier?" (August 2005), Federal Reserve Bank of Kansas City Economic Symposium, Jackson Hole, Wyoming.
21. "Containing systemic risk: the road to reform" (6 August 2008), Report of the Credit Risk Management Policy Group.
22. Charles W. Calomiris "The subprime turmoil: what's old, what's new and what's next" (2 October 2008), Federal Reserve Bank of Kansas City Economic Symposium, Jackson Hole, Wyoming.
23. Richard Bookstaber (2007) *A Demon of Our Own Design*, John Wiley, Hoboken, New Jersey: 2–6.
24. Larry McDonald (2009) *A Colossal Failure of Common Sense*, Ebury Press, London: 175.
25. John Lanchester (2010) *Whoops! Why Everyone Owes Everyone and No One Can Pay*, Allen Lane, London: 142.
26. Benoit Mandlebrot (2004) *The (Mis)behavior of Markets*, Basic Books, New York: 237.
27. Quoted in Philip Delves Broughton (2009) *Ahead of the Curve: Two Years at Harvard Business School*, Penguin Books, New York: 283.
28. Marina Hyde (2009) *Celebrity: How Entertainers Took Over the World and Why We Need an Exit Strategy*, Harvill Secker, London: 67.
29. Victor Consoli (11 May 2006) *Financial Times.*
30. Steven Rattner "The coming credit meltdown" (18 June 2007) *Wall Street Journal.*
31. Zygmunt Bauman (2010) *Living on Borrowed Time*, Polity Press, Cambridge: 43.
32. Ibid: 43.
33. Lanchester, *Whoops!*: 71.
34. Michael Lewis "Wall Street on the tundra" (April 2009) *Vanity Fair.*
35. Kate Burgess, Tom Braithwaite and Sarah O'Connor "A cruel wind" (10 October 2008) Financial Times.
36. Quoted in Alex Preda (2009) *Framing Finance*, University of Chicago Press, Chicago and London: 63.
37. Asger Jonsson (2009) Why Iceland? McGraw Hill, New York: 36.
38. Lewis "Wall Street on the tundra."
39. Ibid.
40. Ibid.
41. Ibid.
42. The term is associated with John Kenneth Galbraith (1975) *The Great Crash 1929*, Penguin Books, London.
43. Quoted in Smith, ECONned: 109.
44. Walter Bagehot "Edward Gibbon" (January 1856) in (1978) *The Collected Works: Literary Essays*, The Economist, London: 352.
45. The phrase is used in Olivier Blanchard "The state of macro" (2008), NBER Working Paper 14259: 27.
46. Willem Buiter (2009) "The unfortunate uselessness of most "state of the art" academic monetary economics" (http://blogs.ft.com/maverecon/2009/03/the-unfortunate-uselessness-of-most-state-of-the-art-academic-monetary-economics).

47. Samuel Brittan "Economists shuffle the deckchairs" (6 August 2009) *Financial Times.*
48. Walter Bagehot (1877) *Lombard Street: A Description of the Money Market*, Henry S. King & Sons, London: Chapter 6 (www.econlib.org/library/Bagehot/bagLom6.html).
49. David Hare (2009) *The Power of Yes*, Faber & Faber, London: 45.

Chapter 18—Shell Games

1. Brad DeLong "Republic of the central banker" (27 October 2008) *The American Prospect.*
2. Paul Mason (2009) *Meltdown: The End of the Age of Greed*, Verso, London: 61.
3. Philip Augar (2009) *Chasing Alpha: How Reckless Growth and Unchecked Ambition Ruined the City's Golden Decade*, Bodley Head, London: 47.
4. Alan Greenspan (2008) *The Age of Turbulence: Adventures in a New World*, Penguin Books, London: 256, 257.
5. Peter S. Goodman "Taking a hard new look: a Greenspan legacy" (8 October 2008) *New York Times.*
6. "The Turner Review: A regulatory response to the global banking crisis" (March 2009), Financial Services Authority: 49.
7. Alan Greenspan "Banking in the global marketplace" (18 November 1996), Speech to Federation of Bankers Association of Japan, Tokyo.
8. Greenspan, *The Age of Turbulence*: 360.
9. Alan Greenspan "Do efficient financial markets mitigate financial crises?" (19 October 1999), Financial Markets Conference of the Federal Reserve Bank of Atlanta.
10. Robert Wade "The Asian financial crisis and the global economy" (November 1998) (www.wright.edu); Peter Temple (2001) *Hedge Funds: The Courtesans of Capitalism*, John Wiley & Sons, Chichester: 141.
11. Yves Smith "Covert nationalization of the banking system" (3 August 2008) (www.nakedcapitalism.com).
12. Martin Wolf "Why banking is an accident waiting to happen" (27 November 2007) *Financial Times.*
13. Roger Lowenstein (2000) *When Genius Failed: The Rise and Fall of Long Term Capital Management*, Fourth Estate, London: 230.
14. Quoted in Temple, *Hedge Funds*: 110.
15. NewsHour with Jim Lehrer (13 February 1996), PBS.
16. "Measuring the measurers" (31 May 2007) *The Economist.*
17. Roger Lowenstein "Triple-A failure" (27 April 2008) *New York Times Magazine.*
18. Ibid.
19. Ibid.
20. Stanley Correy "Background briefing: credit rating agencies" (27 July 2009), Australian Broadcasting Corporation.
21. Gretchen Morgenson "Credit rating agency heads grilled by lawmakers" (22 October 2008) *New York Times.*
22. Jamil Anderlini "S&P owner rejects Chinese criticism" (3 August 2010) *Financial Times.*

23. Arturo Cifuentes and Georgios Katsaros "CDO ratings: chronicle of a disaster foretold" (4 June 2007) *Total Securitisation* 11–12; Charles Calomiris and Joseph Mason "We need a better way to judge risk" (24 August 2007) *Financial Times.*
24. Based on Donald MacKenzie, University of Edinburgh, in "A special report on financial risk–The gods strike back" (11 February 2010). *The Economist*; to be published as Donald MacKenzie, "The credit crisis as a problem in the sociology of knowledge" (forthcoming) *The American Journal of Sociology*.
25. Anderlini "S&P owner rejects Chinese criticism."
26. Sam Jones "When junk was gold" (17 October 2008) *Financial Times.*
27. Committee on Oversight and Government Reform (22 October 2008) (http://oversight.house.gov/documents/20081022112325.pdf).
28. Bill Gross "Looking for contagion in all the wrong places" (July 2007) *Investment Outlook*, Pimco.
29. Robert Rubin, Testimony before the Financial Crisis Inquiry Commission (8 April 2010).
30. Correy "Background briefing."
31. Philip Delves Broughton (2009) *Ahead of the Curve: Two Years at Harvard Business School*, Penguin Books, New York: 58.
32. "True and Fair: fair is not hard and fast: the future of accounts" (26 April 2003) *The Economist.*
33. www.alangreenspan.org/more.html
34. Robert Kaplan, Robert Merton and Scott Richard "Disclose the fair value of complex securities" (17 August 2009) *Financial Times.*
35. www.nakedcapitalism.com/2011/01/ian-fraser-is-the-house-of-lords-crisis-inquiry-putting-the-fcic-to-shame.html
36. Quoted in John Dizard "Put the credit default swaps market out of its misery" (9 December 2008) *Financial Times.*
37. Congressional Oversight Panel "Oversight report—the continued risk of troubled assets (11 August 2009).
38. Michael Lewis "Wall Street on the tundra" (April 2009) *Vanity Fair.*
39. ©Lucy Prebble, *Enron*, and Methuen Drama, an imprint of Bloomsbury Publishing Plc., London: 8, 9.
40. Report of Anton R. Valukas, Examiner (11 March 2010), United States Bankruptcy Court Southern District of New York in re Lehman Brothers Holdings Inc., et al.
41. "Accounting: fooled again" (19 March 2010) *Financial Times.*
42. Michael J. De La Merced and Andrew Ross Sorkin "Report details how Lehman hid its woes" (11 March 2010) *New York Times.*
43. Sir David Tweedie, Speech to the Institute of Chartered Accountants of Scotland (September 2008) (www.iasb.org).
44. Jean-Francois Lepetit, Etienne Boris and Didier Marceau "How to arrive: fair value during a crisis" (28 July 2008) *Financial Times.*
45. Sir David Tweedie, Speech to the Institute of Chartered Accountants of Scotland.
46. David Hare (2009) *The Power of Yes*, Faber & Faber, London: 36.
47. "Will Rogers claps hands for the President's speech" (14 March 1933) *New York Times.*
48. Michael Lewis (2010) *The Big Short: Inside the Doomsday Machine*, Allen Lane, London: 255

49. Roger Lowenstein (2010) *The End of Wall Street*, Scribe Publications, Melbourne: 120, 121.
50. Francesco Guerrera "Fuld 'knew about accounting trick'"(12 March 2010) *Financial Times*.
51. Francesco Guerrera "Man in the news: Jamie Dimon" (16 April 2010) *Financial Times.*
52. 18 October 2007 in a conference call.
53. 15 September 2008 in a conference call.
54. Richard Posner (2009) A Failure of Capitalism: The Crisis of '08 and the Descent into Depression, Harvard University Press, Cambridge.
55. See The Financial Crisis Inquiry Report: Final Report Of The National Commission On The Causes Of The Financial And Economic Crisis In The United States - Official Government Edition; The Financial Crisis Inquiry Commission Submitted By Pursuant To Public Law 111-21 (January 2011) At 83
56. Hare, The Power of Yes: 29, 30.
57. Bradley Keoun, Jesse Westbrook and Ian Katz "Citigroup "liquidity puts" draw scrutiny from crisis inquiry" (13 April 2010), Bloomberg.
58. Vicky Ward (2010) *The Devil's Casino: Friendship, Betrayal and the High Stakes Games Played Inside Lehman Brothers*, John Wiley, New Jersey: 69
59. Robert Rubin, Testimony before the Financial Crisis Inquiry Commission (8 April 2010).
60. Henry Kaufman "The fallout from Enron: lessons and consequences" (April 2002), Address to Boston Economic Club.
61. "Financial crisis stemmed from a lack of will" (15 July 2009), ABC Radio.
62. Deborah Solomon "Math is hard" (25 February 2010) New York Times.
63. P.J. O'Rourke (1988) *Holidays in Hell*, Grove Press, New York: 37.
64. Ibid: 36.

Chapter 19—Cult of Risk

1. Simon Johnson "The quiet coup" (May 2009) *The Atlantic.*
2. President Dwight Eisenhower, Farewell Address to the Nation (17 January 1961).
3. Jennifer Burns (2009) *How Markets Fail: The Logic of Economic Calamities*, Oxford University Press, Oxford: 84.
4. Peter Schwartz and Peter Leyden "The long boom: a history of the future, 1880–1920" (July 1997) *Wired.*
5. Harry Johnson and Elizabeth Johnson (1978) *The Shadow of Keynes*, Basil Blackwell, Oxford: 222–5.
6. Liaquat Ahamed (2009) *Lords of Finance: The Bankers Who Broke The World*, Penguin Books, London: 313.
7. Wilhelm Röpke (1936) *Crises and Cycles*, William Hodge & Co., London: 64 (http://mises.org/books/crisis.pdf).
8. John Steinbeck (1992) *The Grapes of Wrath*, Penguin Books, New York: 44.
9. Ma Jian (2009) *Beijing Coma*, Vintage Books, London: 557.

10. Quoted in James H. Austin (1999) *Zen and the Brain: Toward an Understanding of Meditation and Consciousness*, MIT Press, Massachusetts:129.
11. "Financial crisis stemmed from a lack of will" (15 July 2009), ABC Radio.
12. Irving Janis (1982) *Groupthink: Psychological Studies of Policy Decisions and Fiascoes*, Houghton Mifflin, New York.
13. Maureen Dowd "Where Atlas Shrugged is still read—forthrightly" (13 September 1987) *New York Times.*
14. "An interview with Paul Samuelson, part one" (17 June 2009) *The Atlantic.*
15. Alan Blinder and Ricardo Reis "Understanding the Greenspan standard" (August 2005), Federal Reserve Bank of Kansas City, Jackson Hole Conference.
16. Fred Sheehan "Clowning around" (19 May 2008) (www.prudentbear.com).
17. James Grant (2008) *Mr. Market Miscalculates: The Bubble Years and Beyond*, Axios Press, Mount Jackson: 264.
18. Ibid: 296.
19. Alan Greenspan, Remarks on the structure of the international financial system (5 November 1998), Annual Meeting of the Securities Industry Association, Boca Raton, Florida.
20. David Hare (2009) *The Power of Yes*, Faber & Faber, London: 33.
21. John Lanchester (2010) *Whoops! Why Everyone Owes Everyone and No One Can Pay*, Allen Lane, London: 167.
22. "Pimco hires Greenspan as consultant" (16 May 2007) *Reuters.*
23. The phrase was used by Charles Dumas of Lombard Street Research; see "Losing confidence—looking at the dollar in the old-fashioned way" (22 July 2010) *The Economist.*
24. Ahamed, *Lords of Finance*: 80, 81, 372.
25. Daniel Kadlec "Summing up Greenspan" (17 December 2000) *Time.*
26. David James "Wot's all this then, Alan?" (10–16 July 2003), BRW.
27. Friedrich Wilhelm Nietzsche, R. J. Hollingdale and Michael Tanner (2003) *Twilight of the Idols and Anti-Christ*, Penguin Books, London: 62.
28. David Wessel (2010) *In Fed We Trust: Ben Bernanke's War on the Great Panic*, Scribe Publications, Melbourne: 125.
29. Peter S. Goodman "Taking a hard new look: a Greenspan legacy" (8 October 2008) *New York Times.*
30. Alan Greenspan "The regulation of OTC derivatives" (24 July 1998), Testimony to the Committee on Banking and Financial Services, US House of Representatives.
31. Roger Lowenstein (2010) *The End of Wall Street*, Scribe Publications, Melbourne: 59.
32. John Kenneth Galbraith (1998) *The Affluent Society*, Mariner Books, Boston: 9.
33. Raghuram Rajan (2010) *Fault Lines: How Hidden Fractures Still Threaten the World Economy*, Princeton University Press, Princeton and Oxford: 141.
34. John Cassidy (2009) *How Markets Fail: The Logic of Economic Calamities*, Allen Lane: 226.
35. Hyman Minsky (2008) *Stabilizing an Unstable Economy*, McGraw-Hill, New York: 233.
36. Testimony to the House Oversight and Government Reform Committee (22 October 2008).

37. Alan Beattie "Lunch with the FT: Alan Greenspan" (30 July 2010) *Financial Times.*
38. Christopher Andrews "Watching your stocks?" (1 November 2008) *Continuity, Insurance and Risk Magazine.*
39. Simon Jenkins "It's a bull market for humility, and shares in kindness are soaring" (17 October 2008) *Guardian.*
40. Alan Rappeport "Greenspan and Strauss-Kahn clash on regulation" (1 October 2009) *Financial Times.*
41. Quoted in Ahamed, *Lords of Finance*: 237–8
42. Gillian Tett "The emotional markets hypothesis and Greek bonds" (9 April 2010) *Financial Times.*
43. Alan Greenspan, Testimony to the Financial Crisis Inquiry Commission (7 April 2010).
44. "Greenspan, on CNBC: US in recession" (8 April 2008), Reuters.
45. Sewel Chan and Eric Dash "Greenspan rejects criticism of policies at hearing" (7 April 2010) *New York Times.*
46. John Maynard Keynes (2006) *The General Theory of Employment, Interest and Money*, Atlantic Books, New Delhi: Preface.
47. John Kenneth Galbraith (2001) *The Essential Galbraith*, Mariner, Boston: 241.
48. "Interview by Farah Nayeri: Greenspan was "very bad" Fed chairman, says Artus of Natixis" (30 November 2007), Bloomberg.
49. Denny Gulino "Greenspan: Congress has "amnesia" re its part in crisis" (7 April 2010) (http://imarketnews.com/node/11417).
50. Vanessa Thorpe "Magical realism…and fakery: the ailing Nobel Laureate is writing the definitive account of his life" (21 January 2001) *The Observer.*
51. John C. Bogle (2007) *The Little Book of Common Sense Investing: The Only Way to Guarantee Your Fair Share of Stock Market Returns*, John Wiley, New Jersey: 39.
52. Philip Delves Broughton (2009) *Ahead of the Curve: Two Years at Harvard Business School*, Penguin Books, New York: 285.
53. Jennifer Burns (2009) *How Markets Fail: The Logic of Economic Calamities*, Oxford University Press, Oxford: 149.
54. John Maynard Keynes (1930) *The Great Slump of 1930* (www.gutenberg.ca/ebooks/keynes-slump/keynes-slump-00-h.html).

Chapter 20—Masters of the Universe

1. Louis Aunchincloss in his 1954 novel *A World of Profit*, quoted in Robert Sobel (1993) *Dangerous Dreamers: The Financial Innovators from Charles Merrill to Michael Milken*, John Wiley, New York: 29.
2. ©Lucy Prebble, *Enron*, and Methuen Drama, an imprint of Bloomsbury Publishing Plc., London: 106.
3. John Lanchester (2010) *Whoops! Why Everyone Owes Everyone and No One Can Pay*, Allen Lane, London.
4. John Kenneth Galbraith "The 1929 parallel" (January 1987) Atlantic Monthly: 62.
5. Thomas Philippon and Ariell Reshef "Wages and human capital in the financial industry: 1909–2006" (December 2008), Working Paper, New York University and University of Virginia.

6. Quoted in Gillian Tett "Silos and silences: why so few people spotted the problems in complex credit and what that implies for the future" (July 2010) Financial System Review—Derivatives: Financial Innovation and Stability, Banque de France: 122.
7. The term was coined by Philip Delves Broughton (2009) *Ahead of the Curve: Two Years at Harvard Business School*, Penguin Books, New York.
8. Ibid: 50.
9. Rahul Bajaj "The privilege of living in extraordinary times" (26 January 2009) *Financial Times.*
10. Stephen Crittenden "Background briefing, mostly bloody awful" (29 March 2009), ABC Radio, Australia.
11. Sylvain Raynes "The state of financial engineering" (3 December 2008) (www.quantnet.com/forum/showthread.php?t=3978).
12. Emanuel Derman (2004) *My Life as a Quant: Reflections on Physics and Finance*, John Wiley, New Jersey: 266, 267.
13. "Prophet of climate doom a scientific black sheep" (17 September 2009), AFP (www.terradaily.com/reports/Prophet_of_climate_doom_a_scientific_black_sheep_999.html).
14. Lewis Carroll (1960) *The Annotated Alice: Alice's Adventures in Wonderland*, Penguin Books, London: 129.
15. Derman, *My Life as a Quant*: 266, 267.
16. "The CIA on Wall Street" (19 June 2009) *Financial Times.*
17. Michael Jensen (1976) The Financiers: The World of the Great Wall Street Investment Banking House, Weyright & Talley, New York: 1, 2.
18. Broughton, Ahead of the Curve: 212.
19. YouTube sketch by English comedians John Bird and John Fortune (www.youtube.com/watch?v=kEL0g3As2vE).
20. Paul Tharp and Jana Winter "Two in the sac: Feds probing hedge fund hormone charges" (12 October 2007) New York Post.
21. Vicky Ward (2010) *The Devil's Casino: Friendship, Betrayal and the High Stakes Games Played Inside Lehman Brothers*, John Wiley, New Jersey: 4.
22. Tom Bawden and Julia Kollewe "Pretty and colourful: what women bring to the DB boardroom, says Ackermann" (7 February 2011) The Guardian.
23. Gillian Tett "The trouble with men" (4 February 2011) *Financial Times.*
24. Karen Ho (2009) *Liquidated: An Ethnography of Wall Street*, Duke University Press, Durham and London.
25. Bret Easton Ellis (1991) *American Psycho*, Picador, Melbourne: 4, 399.
26. Bethany McLean and Peter Elking (2003) *The Smartest Guys in the Room: The Amazing and Scandalous Fall of Enron*, Penguin Books, London: 55.
27. Prebble, *Enron*: 29.
28. www.nytimes.com/interactive/2008/10/07/business/20080929-payout-graphic.html
29. "Executive excess" (2007), Institute for Policy Studies and United for a Fair Economy.
30. Jessica Irvine "Shock of real world for business chiefs" (21 April 2008) *Sydney Morning Herald.*
31. Gillian Tett "Lunch with the FT: David Hare" (25 September 2009) *Financial Times.*

32. Jennifer Burns (2009) *How Markets Fail: The Logic of Economic Calamities*, Oxford University Press, Oxford: 177.
33. Warren Buffett, Berkshire Hathaway Letter to Shareholders (2009).
34. Louise Story "On Wall Street, bonuses, not profits, were real" (17 December 2008) *New York Times.*
35. Quoted in Robert A.G. Monks and Nell Minow (2008) *Corporate Governance*, John Wiley, Chichester: 311.
36. Lucian Bebchuk, Alma Cohen and Holger Spamann "Bankers had cashed in before the music stopped" (6 December 2009) *Financial Times.*
37. Quoted in Yves Smith (2010) *ECONned: How Unenlightened Self Interest Undermined Democracy and Corrupted Capitalism*, Palgrave Macmillan, New York: 169.
38. Quoted in Duff McDonald "Please, Sir, I want some more: how Goldman Sachs is carving up its $11 billion money pie" (5 December 2005) New York Magazine.
39. Owen Gleiberman "Cannes: in the dark documentaries "Inside Job" and "Countdown to Zero" it's the end of the world as we know it" (16 May 2010) Entertainment Weekly.
40. Hugh Son "Buffett says "wildly capricious" economy inspires his charity" (16 June 2010) Bloomberg News.
41. Ho, *Liquidated*: 260.
42. Ibid: 270.
43. Althea Chang "Unusual perks: Goldman Sachs covers sex changes" (8 February 2008) (http://money.cnn.com/2008/02/08/news/companies/gender.fortune/index.htm).
44. Michael Lewis (2010) The Big Short: Inside the Doomsday Machine, Allen Lane, London: 63.
45. David Wessel (2010) *In Fed We Trust: Ben Bernanke's War on the Great Panic*, Scribe Publications, Melbourne: 239.
46. www.youtube.com/watch?v=hXBcmqwTV9s
47. Adam Smith (1776) *An Inquiry into the Nature and Causes of the Wealth of Nations*: Book 3, Chapter 4 (www.marxists.org/reference/archive/smith-adam/works/wealth-of-nations/book03/ch04.htm).

Chapter 21—Financial Nihilism

1. Salvador Dali (1962) *The World of Salvador Dali*, Macmillan, London.
2. "Little gold-diggers" (27 January–9 February 2009) *The Big Issue* 321: 9.
3. Sarah Thornton (2009) *Seven Days in the Art World*, Granta, London: xvi.
4. Don Thompson (2008) *The $12 Million Stuffed Shark: The Curious Economics of Contemporary Art*, Palgrave Macmillan, New York: 177.
5. Thornton, *Seven Days in the Art World*: xvi; 17, 37, 83, 91.
6. Jerry Saltz, an art critic, quoted in Thompson, *The $12 Million Stuffed Shark*: 116.
7. Thornton, *Seven Days in the Art World*: 17, 37, 83, 91.
8. Thompson, *The $12 Million Stuffed Shark*: 189.
9. Carol Vogel "Swimming with famous dead sharks" (1 October 2006) *New York Times.*

10. John Steele Gordon (2004) An Empire of Wealth: The Epic History of American Economic Power, HarperCollins, New York: 262.
11. Ron Chernow (1990) *The House of Morgan: An American Banking Dynasty and the Rise of Modern Finance*, Touchstone Books, New York: 78.
12. "Steve Cohen Steps Out" (2 June 2010) Vanity Fair.
13. The term "Davos man" was suggested by Samuel Huntington "Dead souls: the denationalization of the American elite" (Spring 2004) National Interest: 5–18.
14. David Rothkof (2008) *Superclass: The Global Power Elite and the World They are Making*, Farrar, Straus & Giroux, New York: 129.
15. "Survival of the richest" (19 August 2010) The Economist.
16. Quoted in Tom Braithwaite and Aline van Duyn "Buffett bats off criticism of Moody's" (2 June 2010) Financial Times.
17. Quoted in Marina Hyde (2009) *Celebrity: How Entertainers Took Over the World and Why We Need an Exit Strategy*, Harvill Secker, London: 1.
18. Charles Gasparino (2009) *The Sellout: How Three Decades of Wall Street Greed and Government Mismanagement Destroyed the Global Financial System*, Harper Business, New York: 365.
19. Alex Preda (2009) *Framing Finance*, University of Chicago Press, Chicago and London: 250.
20. Felipe Fernández-Armesto (2002) *Food: A History*, Pan Books, London: 117.
21. The phrase is from Lucy Kellaway "Why financiers are leaders in drivel" (1 August 2010) Financial Times.
22. Ray Dalio (2010) *Principles*, Bridgewater Associates, Westport.
23. James Thomson "Trouble over: Bridgewater" (10 July 2010) (www.businessspectator.com.au).
24. Quoted in Kellaway "Why financiers are leaders in drivel."
25. Quoted in Mark Tier (2006) *The Winning Investment Habits of Warren Buffett and George Soros*, St Martin's Griffin, New York: 219.
26. "A tract for the times" (3 December 1998) The Economist.
27. N.N. Baily, D. Farrell and S. Lund "The color of hot money" (2000) Foreign Affairs 79/2: 99–109.
28. www.izlese.org/slavoj-a-34-ia-34-ek-the-reality-of-the-virtual-1-7.html
29. Karen Ho (2009) *Liquidated: An Ethnography of Wall Street*, Duke University Press, Durham and London: 104.
30. ©Lucy Prebble, *Enron*, and Methuen Drama, an imprint of Bloomsbury Publishing Plc., London: 106.
31. "The financial crisis inquiry report: final report of the National Commission on the Causes of the Financial and Economic Crisis in the United States—official government edition" (January 2011), submitted by the Financial Crisis Inquiry Commission pursuant to Public Law 111–21: 105.
32. Malcolm Gladwell "The sure thing: how entrepreneurs really succeed" (January 2010) *The New Yorker.*
33. Luke Johnson "Malcolm Gladwell's business blindspot" (2 February 2010) *Financial Times.*
34. Quoted in David L. Western (2004) *Booms, Bubbles, and Busts in US Stock Markets*, Routledge, London: 84.

35. Elizabeth Kubler-Ross (1975) *Death: The Final Stage of Growth*, Prentice Hall, New Jersey.
36. Greg Farrell and Henny Sender "The shaming of John Thain" (13 March 2009) *Financial Times*.
37. Andrew Lahde "Letter: Andrew Lahde, Lahde Capital Management" (17 October 2008) *Financial Times.*
38. John Gapper "Yours truly, angry mob" (24 October 2008) *Financial Times.*
39. Stacy-Marie Ishmael "We are Wall Street …" (30 April 2010) *Financial Times,* Copyright © The Financial Times Ltd.
40. David Hare (2009) *The Power of Yes*, Faber & Faber, London: 61.
41. Richard Vine "Totally wired" (2005) *The Guardian Unlimited* (http://blogs.guardian.co.uk/theguide/archives/tv_and_radio/2005/01/totally_wired.html).
42. Johann Hari "How Goldman Sachs gambled on starving the poor—and won" (2 July 2010) *The Independent.*
43. Jayati Ghosh "The unnatural coupling: food and global finance" (2009), The Ideas Working Paper Series, Paper 8.
44. Michael W. Masters, Testimony before the Permanent Subcommittee on Investigations Committee on Homeland Security and Governmental Affairs United States Senate (20 May 2008).
45. "Sweet dreams: a hedge fund bets big on chocolate" (5 August 2010) *The Economist*.
46. Interagency Task Force on Commodity Markets, "Interim report on crude oil" (July 2008), CFTC.
47. Ghosh "The unnatural coupling."
48. Stanley Milgram (1983) *Obedience to Authority*, Harper, New York: 6.
49. Kai Bord and Martin J. Sherwin (2006) *American Prometheus: The Triumph and Tragedy of J. Robert Oppenheimer*, Vintage Books, New York: 51.

Chapter 22—Financial Gravity

1. Quoted in Bertrand Russell (1956) *Portraits from Memory and Other Essays*, Simon & Schuster, London: 152.
2. Quoted in Edward Chancellor (2000) *Devil Take The Hindmost: A History of Financial Speculation*, Plume Books, New York: 84.
3. Quoted in Liaquat Ahamed (2009) *Lords of Finance: The Bankers Who Broke the World*, Penguin Books, London: 355.
4. Ron Chernow (1990) *The House of Morgan*, Grove Press, New York: 319, 320.
5. Attributed to physicist Robert Oppenheimer, Supervising Scientist Manhattan Project (05.29 hours, 16 July 1945) in the Jornada del Muerto desert near the Trinity site in the White Sands Missile Range, witnessing the first atomic detonation by mankind. The exact quote from the *Bhagavad-Gita* is: "If the radiance of a thousand suns were to burst at once into the sky, that would be like the splendor of the Mighty one…I am become Death, the shatterer of Worlds."
6. Congressional Oversight Panel "Oversight report—assessing Treasury's strategy: six months of TARP" (7 April 2009).
7. George Soros "The worst market crisis in 60 years" (23 January 2008) *Financial Times.*

8. "The financial crisis: an inside view of a stormy White House summit" (27 September 2008) *Wall Street Journal.*
9. Joe Nocera "As credit crisis spiraled, alarm led to action" (1 October 2008) *New York Times.*
10. Ibid.
11. Quoted in Ron Chernow (1993) *The Warburgs: The Twentieth-Century Odyssey of a Remarkable Jewish Family*, Vintage Books, New York: 89.
12. PBS Newshour "How big is too big to fail?" (15 December 2009) (www.pbs.org/newshour/bb/business/july-dec09/schultz_12-15.html).
13. Mervyn King, Governor of the Bank of England, Speech to the CBI Dinner (20 January 2009), East Midlands Conference Centre, Nottingham.
14. Senator Jim Bunning, Statement to the Senate Banking Committee on the Federal Reserve Monetary Policy Report (15 July 2008), Senate Banking Committee.
15. Naomi Klein (2008) *The Shock Doctrine: The Rise of Disaster Capitalism*, Picador, New York.
16. Joe Bageant (2007) *Deer Hunting with Jesus: Despatches from America's Class War*, Scribe Publications, Melbourne: viii.
17. F. Scott Fitzgerald (1973) *The Great Gatsby*, Penguin Books, London: 186.
18. Quoted in Charles P. Kindelberger (1978) *Manias, Panics and Crashes: A History of Financial Crisis*, Basic Books, New York: 130.
19. "Americans "too depressed" for sex, porn barons seek US bailout" (8 January 2009) (www.abc.net.au/news/stories/2009/01/08/2461638.htm).
20. "After the race" (19 February 2011) *The Economist.*
21. Matthias Nass "A year of awkward anniversaries" (January 2009) *The Atlantic Times.*
22. Peter Hartcher "Double standard brings down rich white club" (4 April 2009) *Sydney Morning Herald.*
23. John Willman "Fear and loathing in the aftermath of the credit crisis" (3 October 2008) *Financial Times.*
24. Robert Lucas "Macroeconomic priorities" (2003) *American Economic Review* 93/1: 1703.
25. John Cassidy "The decline of economics" (2 December 1996) *New Yorker*: 54.
26. Benn Steil "Keynes and the triumph of hope over economics" (5 February 2009) *Financial Times.*
27. Justin Fox "The comeback Keynes" (27 January 2009) *Time.*
28. John Maynard Keynes (1931) *Essays in Persuasion*, Macmillan, London: 383.
29. Ahamed, *Lords of Finance*: 349.

Chapter 23—Unusually Uncertain

1. Henny Sender "On Wall Street: A tonic that works too well" (23 December 2009) *Financial Times.*
2. Dylan Grice "Popular delusions: government hedonism and the next policy mistake" (11 February 2010), Société Générale Cross Asset Research.

3. Joseph Tainter (1988) *The Collapse of Complex Societies*, New Studies in Archaeology, Cambridge University Press, Cambridge, quoted in John Dizard "Irish bail-out"s unintended consequences" (18 December 2010) *Financial Times*.
4. Quoted in John Chan "China's dubious statistics cover up economic crisis" (10 August 2009) (www.wsws.org/articles/2009/aug2009/chin-a10.shtml).
5. "China's luxury boom: the middle blingdom" (17 February 2011) *The Economist*.
6. Jamil Anderlini "Beijing's housing price fury goes viral" (23 December 2010) *Financial Times*.
7. Wolfgang Münchau "Optimism is not enough for a global recovery" (14 June 2009) *Financial Times*.
8. Press release, "Lincoln hails Senate passage of tough Wall Street reforms" (20 May 2010) (http://lincoln.senate.gov/newsroom/2010-05-20-6.cfm).
9. http://en.wikipedia.org/wiki/Thomas_Pynchon
10. Andrew Ross Sorkin "Vanishing act: "advisers" distance themselves from a report" (14 February 2011) *New York Times*.
11. Brooke Masters and David Oakley "Markets take fright: political disorder" (20 May 2010) *Financial Times*.
12. Sam Jones "Hedge funds hope 'Volcker rule' will clip banks' wings" (30 June 2010) *Financial Times*.
13. Quoted in Masayuki Oku "A cure that could do more harm than good" (13 July 2010) *Financial Times*.
14. www.seekingalpha.com
15. Patrick Hosking and Grainne Gilmore "Spain's challenges are severe: IMF" (25 May 2010) *The Times*.
16. Tyler Cohen "How will Greece get off the dole?" (21 May 2010) *New York Times*.
17. David Gardner, Tony Barber and Peter Spiegel "Ireland: A punt too far" (19 November 2010) *Financial Times*.
18. Peter Spiegel "EU leaders back new bail-out system" (16 December 2010) *Financial Times*.
19. John Authers "A risky revival" (25 September 2009) *Financial Times*.
20. www.zerohedge.com/article/rosenberg-probability-another-qe-round
21. Peter Orszag "Taking a chance can be a better way to save" (16 February 2011) *Financial Times*.
22. Sarah Gordon and Megan Murphy "European banks: leaning lenders" (3 June 2010) *Financial Times*.
23. Adam Ferguson (2010) *When Money Dies: The Nightmare of the Weimar Hyper-Inflation*, Old Street Publishing, London: 5.
24. Ibid: 24.
25. Liaquat Ahamed (2009) *Lords of Finance: The Bankers Who Broke The World*, Penguin Books, London: 363.
26. Nick Baker and Mary Childs "US Stocks gain on signs economic recovery is strengthening" (12 December 2009), Bloomberg.
27. Robert F. Kennedy, Address (18 March 1968), University of Kansas, Lawrence, Kansas.
28. Interview (18 June 2008), Bloomberg.

29. Michael Pettis "Don't rely on the performance of China's markets" (16 June 2010) *Financial Times*.
30. Bill Miller "US large-cap stocks are bargains of a lifetime" (31 August 2010) *Financial Times*.
31. Stieg Larsson (2008) *The Girl With The Dragon Tattoo*, Quercus, London: 519, 520.
32. John Steinbeck (1992) *The Grapes of Wrath*, Penguin Books, New York: 49, 317.
33. Adam Smith (2007) *The Wealth of Nations*, Cosmino Books, New York: 113.
34. "After the race" (19 February 2011) *The Economist*.
35. Matt Taibi "The spill, the scandal and the President" (8 June 2010) *Rolling Stone*.
36. "The oil well and the damage done: BP counts the political and financial cost of Deepwater Horizon" (17 June 2010) *The Economist*.
37. "Prophet of climate doom a scientific black sheep" (17 September 2009), AFP (www.terradaily.com/reports/Prophet_of_climate_doom_a_scientific_black_sheep_999.html).
38. "After the race" (19 February 2011) *The Economist*.
39. Quoted in Yves Smith (2010) *ECONned: How Unenlightened Self Interest Undermined Democracy and Corrupted Capitalism*, Palgrave Macmillan, New York: 55.
40. Edward Abbey (1990) *Desert Solitaire: A Season in the Wilderness*, Touchstone, New York: 113.
41. John Updike (1981) *Rabbit is Rich*, Penguin Books, London: 13.
42. Andrew Gelman "What kind of law is the Law of Unintended Consequences?" (22 January 2008) (www.stat.columbia.edu/~cook/movabletype/archives/2008/01/what_kind_of_la.html).
43. Geoff Dyer "China lectures US on economy" (4 December 2008) *Financial Times*.
44. Hu Jintao President of the People's Republic of China, Remarks at the 16th APEC Economic Leaders' Meeting (22 November 2008), Lima, Peru.
45. Smith, *ECONned*: 1.
46. Matt Taibbi "The Great American bubble machine" (5 April 2010) *Rolling Stone*.
47. John Gapper "Master of risk who did God's work for Goldman Sachs but won it little love" (23 December 2009) Financial Times.
48. John Maynard Keynes (1933) The Means to Prosperity, Macmillan, London: 37 (www.gutenberg.ca/ebooks/keynes-means/keynes-means-00-h.html).
49. Martin Hutchinson "Gross domestic fudging" (21 September 2009) (www.prudentbear.com).
50. President Franklin D. Roosevelt, State of the Union Address (11 January 1944).
51. Banksy (2006) Wall and Piece, Century, London: 204.
52. www.nakedcapitalism.com/2009/10/guest-post-still-the-masters-of-the-universe.html
53. Arundhati Roy "Confronting empire" (27 January 2003), Porto Alegre, Brazil (www.ratical.org/ratville/CAH/AR012703.html).
54. Steinbeck, The Grapes of Wrath: 471.
55. George Orwell "England My England" in (2001) *Orwell's England*, Penguin Books, London: 266.
56. F. Scott Fitzgerald (1973) *The Great Gatsby*, Penguin Books, London: 117.

57. Ben Bernanke used the phrase to describe the economic outlook; see Richard Leong "Treasuries-Bonds slip as equities rise renews risk appetite" (23 July 2010), Reuters.
58. John Maynard Keynes "The general theory of employment" (1937) *Quarterly Journal of Economics* 51/2: 213–14.

Epilogue—Nemesis

1. Quoted in Allen Salkin "You try to live on 500K in this town" (6 February 2009) *New York Times.*
2. Quoted in Vicky Ward (2010) *The Devil's Casino: Friendship, Betrayal and the High Stakes Games Played Inside Lehman Brothers*, John Wiley, New Jersey: 1.
3. Nouriel Roubini and Stephen Mihm (2010) *Crisis Economics: A Crash Course in the Future of Finance*, Allen Lane, London: 3.
4. Bloomberg News (20 November 2008).
5. "First draft of history" (25 June 2009) *The Economist.*
6. Joseph Conrad (1995) *Heart of Darkness*, Wordsworth Editions, Ware: 82.
7. Justin Fox "What exactly is Nouriel Roubini good for?" (26 May 2010) HBR (http://blogs.hbr.org/fox/2010/05/what-exactly-is-nouriel-roubini.html).
8. www.imf.org/external/np/vc/2002/070202.htm
9. Aaron Brown "The economist's new clothes" (May/ June 2010) *Wilmott Magazine*: 20.
10. Ibid: 20.
11. Richard Kay and Geoffrey Levy "Naughty Niall Ferguson: the dashing TV historian and the string of affairs that could cost him millions" (20 February 2010) *Daily Mail.*
12. Lewis Carroll (1976) *The Annotated Alice: Through The Looking Glass*, Penguin Books, London: 251.
13. Sotheby's Catalogue (11 November 2009), Contemporary Art Evening Auction (www.sothebys.com/app/live/lot/LotDetail.jsp?lot_id=159564574).
14. Peter Gosselin (2009) *High Wire: The Precarious Financial Lives of American Families*, Basic Books, New York: 234.
15. Rachel Donadio "Europe's young grow agitated over future prospects" (1 January 2011) *New York Times.*
16. http://en.wikipedia.org/wiki/New_Deal
17. http://crookedtimber.org/2007/04/11/when-i-hear-the-word-culture-aw-hell-with-it
18. Gregory Clark "Dismal scientists: how the crash is reshaping economics" (16 February 2009) *Atlantic Monthly.*
19. *Newsweek* (15 December 2008).
20. F. Scott Fitzgerald (1973) *The Great Gatsby*, Penguin Books, London: 188.
21. Olivier Coibion and Yuriy Gorodnichenko "Does the great recession really mean the end of the great moderation?" (www.voxeu.org).
22. Quoted in John Cassidy "After the blowup (letter from Chicago)" (11 January 2010) *New Yorker*: 28.
23. "Round three: the annual ding-dong over bank bonuses is under way" (13 January 2011) *The Economist.*

24. US Senator Dick Durbin, quoted in Adam Doster "Durbin on Congress: the banks "own the place"" (29 April 2009) (www.huffingtonpost.com/2009/04/29/dick-durbin-banks-frankly_n_193010.html).
25. Gregory Zuckerman "Trader racks up a second epic gain: $5 billion profit for John Paulson" (28 January 2011) *Wall Street Journal*.
26. Jordan Ellenberg "We're down $700 billion. Let's go double or nothing" (2 August 2008), Slate Magazine.
27. Abbie Bordeau, David Fitzpatrick and Scott Zamost "Wall Street: fall of the fat cats" (17 October 2008), CNN.com.
28. I am indebted to Simon Mihailovich from Eidesis for pointing this quote out to me.
29. Ben Hall "Banks cry foul: "King Eric" revolution" (6 December 2010) Financial Times.
30. Sir John Wheeler-Bennet's description of the German people in 1919; see Adam Ferguson (2010) When Money Dies: The Nightmare of the Weimar Hyper-Inflation, Old Street Publishing, London: 14.
31. Walter Benjamin (1973) *Illumination*, Fontana/Collins, London: 259, 260.

Select Bibliography

Viral Acharya and Matthew Richardson (eds) (2009) *Restoring Financial Stability: How to Repair a Failed System*, John Wiley, New Jersey.

Liaquat Ahamed (2009) *Lords of Finance: The Bankers Who Broke the World*, Penguin Books, London.

Al Alletzhauser (1990) *The House of Nomura*, Bloomsbury, London.

Daniel Altman (2007) *Connected: 24 Hours in the Global Economy*, Macmillan, London.

George Anders (1992) *Merchants of Debt: KKR and the Mortgaging of American Business*, Basic Books, New York.

Philip Augar (2000) *The Death of Gentlemanly Capitalism*, Penguin Books, London.

Philip Augar (2006) *The Greed Merchants: How the Investment Banks Played the Free Market Game*, Penguin Books, London.

Philip Augar (2009) *Chasing Alpha: How Reckless Growth and Unchecked Ambition Ruined the City's Golden Decade*, Bodley Head, London.

John Authers (2010) *The Fearful Rise of Markets: A Short View of Global Bubbles and Synchronised Meltdowns*, FT Prentice Hall, London.

Joel Bakan (2004) *The Corporation*, Constable & Robinson, London.

George B. Baker and George David Smith (1998) *The New Financial Capitalists: Kohlberg Kravis Roberts and the Creation of Corporate Value*, Cambridge University Press, New York.

Martin Baker (1995) *A Fool and His Money*, Orion Books, London.

Erik Banks (1999) *The Rise and Fall of the Merchant Banks*, Kogan Page, London.

Maria Bartiromo with Catherine Whitney (2010) *The Weekend that Changed Wall Street: An Eyewitness Account*, Portfolio/Penguin Books, New York.

Zygmunt Bauman (2008) *Does Ethics Have a Chance in a World of Consumers?* Harvard University Press, Boston.

Zygmunt Bauman (2007) *Liquid Times: Living in an Age of Uncertainty*, Polity Press, Cambridge.

Zygmunt Bauman (2010) *Living on Borrowed Time*, Polity Press, Cambridge

Alan Beattie (2009) *False Economy: A Surprising Economic History of the World*, Viking, London.

Gary Belsky and Thomas Gilovich (1999) *Why Smart People Make Big Money Mistakes— and How to Correct Them*, Simon & Schuster, New York.

Peter L. Bernstein (1996) *Against The Gods: The Remarkable Story of Risk*, John Wiley, New York.

Peter L. Bernstein (2000) *The Power of Gold: The History of An Obsession*, John Wiley, New York.

Peter L. Bernstein (2005) *Capital Ideas: The Improbable Origins of Modern Wall Street*, John Wiley, New Jersey.

Peter L. Bernstein (2007) *Capital Ideas Evolving*, John Wiley, New Jersey.

William J. Bernstein (2009) *A Splendid Exchange: How Trade Shaped The World*, Grove Press, New York.

Barton Biggs (2006) *Hedge Hogging*, John Wiley, New Jersey.

Richard Bitner (2008) *Confessions of a Sub-prime Lender: An Insider's Tale of Greed, Fraud and Ignorance*, Icon Books, London.

Robin Blackburn (2002) *Banking on Death*, Verso, London.

John Bogle (2009) *Enough: True Measures of Money, Business and Life*, John Wiley, New Jersey.

Bill Bonner and Addison Wiggin (2006) *Empire of Debt: The Rise of an Epic Financial Crisis*, John Wiley, New Jersey.

Richard Bookstaber (2007) *A Demon of Our Own Design*, John Wiley, New Jersey.

Piers Brendon (2000) *The Dark Valley: A Panorama of the 1930s*, Pimlico, London.

Dan Briody (2003) *The Iron Triangle: Inside the Secret World of the Carlyle Group*, John Wiley, New Jersey.

Samuel Brittan (2005) *Against the Flow: Reflections of an Individualist*, Atlantic Books, London.

Po Bronson (1995) *Bombardiers*, Secker & Warburg, London.

John Brooks (1998) *The Go-Go Years: The Drama and Crashing Finale of Wall Street's Bullish 60s*, John Wiley, New Jersey.

Philip Delves Broughton (2009) *Ahead of the Curve: Two Years at Harvard Business School*, Penguin Books, New York.

J.C. Bruce (2010) *The 'Rogue' Myth: Demon Traders or Convenient Scapegoats?*, CreateSpace, Seattle.

Connie Bruck (1988) *The Predators' Ball: How Michael Milken and his Junk Bond Machine Staked the Corporate Raiders*, Simon & Schuster, New York.

Robert F. Bruner and Sean D. Carr (2007) *The Panic of 1907: Lessons Learned from the Market's Perfect Storm*, John Wiley, New Jersey.

Jennifer Burns (2009) *How Markets Fail: The Logic of Economic Calamities*, Oxford University Press, Oxford.

Bryan Burroughs and John Helyar (1990) *Barbarians at the Gate: The Fall of RJR Nabisco*, Harper & Row, New York.

Christopher Byron (2004) *Testosterone: Tales of CEOs Gone Wild*, John Wiley, New Jersey.

John Cassidy (2002) *dot.con*, Perennial, New York.

John Cassidy (2009) *How Markets Fail: The Logic of Economic Calamities*, Allen Lane, London.

Edward Chancellor (2000) *Devil Take The Hindmost*, Plume Books, New York.

Ron Chernow (1990) *The House of Morgan: An American Banking Dynasty and the Rise of Modern Finance*, Touchstone Books, New York.

Ron Chernow (1993) *The Warburgs*, Vintage Books, New York.

Ron Chernow (1997) *The Death of the Banker: The Decline and Fall of the Great Dynasties and the Triumph of the Small Investor*, Vintage Books, New York.

William D. Cohan (2007) *The Last Tycoons: The Secret History of Lazard Fréres & Co.*, Broadway Books, New York.

William D. Cohan (2009) *House of Cards: How Wall Street's Gamblers Broke Capitalism*, Allen Lane, London.

Lawrence A. Cunningham (2009) *The Essays of Warren Buffett: Lessons for Investors and Managers*, John Wiley, Singapore.

Satyajit Das (2010) *Traders Guns and Money: Knowns and Unknowns in the Dazzling World of Financial Derivatives*, FT Prentice Hall, London.

Glyn Davies (2002) *A History of Money: From Ancient Times to the Present Day*, University of Wales Press, Cardiff.

Emanuel Derman (2004) *My Life as a Quant: Reflections on Physics and Finance*, John Wiley, New Jersey.

Kevin Dowd and Martin Hutchinson (2010) *Alchemists of Loss: How Modern Finance and Government Intervention Crashed the Financial System*, John Wiley, New Jersey.

Steven Drobny (2006) *Inside the House of Money*, John Wiley, New Jersey.

Nicolas Dunbar (2000) *Investing Money*, John Wiley, Chichester.

Richard Duncan (2009) *The Corruption of Capitalism*, CLSA Books, Hong Kong.

David Einhorn (2008) *Fooling Some of the People All of the Time, A Long Short Story*, John Wiley, New Jersey.

Larry Elliot and Dan Atkinson (2008) *The Gods That Failed: How Blind Faith in Markets Has Cost U.S. Our Future*, The Bodley Head, London.

Charles D. Ellis (2009) *The Partnership: The Making of Goldman Sachs*, Penguin Books, London.

Adam Ferguson (2010) *When Money Dies: The Nightmare of the Weimar Hyper-Inflation*, Old Street Publishing, London.

Niall Ferguson (1998) *The House of Rothschild: Money's Prophets 1798–1848*, Penguin Books, London.

Niall Ferguson (2000) *The House of Rothschild: The World's Banker 1849–1999*, Penguin Books, London.

Niall Ferguson (2001) *The Cash Nexus: Money and Power in the Modern World 1700–2000*, Penguin Books, London.

Niall Ferguson (2008) *The Ascent of Money*, Allen Lane, London.

Niall Ferguson (2010) *High Financier: The Life and Times of Siegmund Warburg*, Allen Lane, London.

Joel L. Fleishman (2007) *The Foundation: A Great American Secret—How Private Wealth is Changing the World*, Public Affairs, New York.

Justin Fox (2009) *The Myth of the Rational Market: A History of Risk, Reward and Delusion on Wall Street*, Harper Business, New York.

Loren Fox (2003) *Enron: The Rise and Fall*, John Wiley, New Jersey.

Robert Frank (2007) Richistan: *A Journey through the 21st Century Wealth Boom and the Lives of the New Rich*, Crown, New York.

Guy Fraser-Sampson (2007) *Private Equity as an Asset Class*, John Wiley, Chichester

Julie Froud, Sukhdev Johal, Adam Leaver and Karel Williams (2006) *Financialization and Strategy: Narrative and Numbers*, Routledge, London.

Peter C. Fusaro and Ross M. Miller (2002) *What Went Wrong at Enron*, John Wiley, New Jersey.

John Kenneth Galbraith (1975) *The Great Crash 1929*, Penguin Books, London.

John Kenneth Galbraith (1994) *A Short History of Financial Euphoria*, Penguin Books, London.

John Kenneth Galbraith (1998) *The Affluent Society*, Mariner Books, Boston.

John Kenneth Galbraith (2001) *The Essential Galbraith*, Houghton Mifflin, New York.

John Kenneth Galbraith (2004) *The Economics of Innocent Fraud*, Penguin Books, London.

Andrew Gamble (2009) *The Spectre at the Feast: Capitalist Crisis and the Politics of Recession*, Palgrave Macmillan, London.

Dan Gardner (2008) *Risk: The Science and Politics of Fear*, Virgin Books, London.

Charles Gasparino (2009) *The Sellout: How Three Decades of Wall Street Greed and Government Mismanagement Destroyed the Global Financial System*, Harper Business, New York.

Francis J. Gavin (2004) *Gold, Dollars, and Power: The Politics of International Monetary Relations 1958–1971*, University of North Carolina Press, Chapel Hill.

Charles R. Geisst (1997) *Wall Street: A History from its Beginning to the Fall of Enron*, Oxford University Press, Oxford.

Charles R. Geisst (2002) *Wheels of Fortune: The History of Speculation from Scandal to Respectability*, John Wiley, New Jersey.

Charles R. Geisst (2009) *Collateral Damaged: The Marketing of Consumer Debt to America*, Bloomberg, New York.

Tony Golding (2001) *The City: Inside the Great Expectations Machine*, FT Prentice Hall, London.

Gary Gorton (2010) *Slapped by the Invisible Hand: The Panic of 2007*, Oxford University Press, Oxford.

James Grant (1992) *Money of the Mind: Borrowing and Lending in America from the Civil War to Michael Milken*, Farrar Strauss Giroux, New York.

James Grant (1993) *Minding Mr. Market: Ten Years on Wall Street with Grant's Interest Rate Observer*, Times Books, New York.

James Grant (2008) *Mr. Market Miscalculates: The Bubble Years and Beyond*, Axios Press, Mount Jackson.

Alan Greenspan (2007) *The Age of Turbulence: Adventures in a New World*, Allen Lane, London.

William Grieder (1987) *Secret of the Temple: How the Federal Reserve Runs the Country*, Simon & Schuster, New York.

David Harvey (2010) *The Enigma of Capital and the Crisis of Capitalism*, Oxford University Press, Oxford.

Michael Hirsh (2010) *Capital Offense: How Washington's Wise Men Turned America's Future Over to Wall Street*, John Wiley, New Jersey.

Karen Ho (2009) *Liquidated: An Ethnography of Wall Street*, Duke University Press, Durham and London.

Marina Hyde (2009) *Celebrity: How Entertainers Took Over the World and Why We Need an Exit Strategy*, Harvill Secker, London.

William Isaac (2010) *Senseless Panic: How Washington Failed America*, John Wiley, New Jersey.

Tetsuya Ishikawa (2009) *How I Caused the Credit Crunch: An Insider's Story of the Financial Meltdown*, Icon Books, London.

Michael Jensen (1976) *The Financiers: The World of the Great Wall Street Investment Banking House*, Weyright and Talley, New York.

Simon Johnson and James Kwak (2010) *13 Bankers: The Wall Street Takeover and the Next Financial Meltdown*, Pantheon Books, New York.

Asgeir Jonsson (2009) *Why Iceland: How One of The World's Smallest Countries Became The Meltdown's Biggest Casualty*, McGraw Hill, New York.

Anatole Kaletsky (2010) *Capitalism 4.0: The Birth of a New Economy in the Aftermath of Crisis*, Public Affairs, New York.

Craig Karmin (2009) *Biography of the Dollar: How the Mighty Buck Conquered the World and Why It's Under Siege*, Three Rovers Press, New York.

Henry Kaufman (2009) *The Road to Financial Reformation: Warnings, Consequences, Reforms*, John Wiley, New Jersey.

John Kay (2004) *The Truth About Markets: Why Some Nations Are Rich But Most Remain Poor*, Penguin Books, London.

John Kay (2009) *The Long and the Short of It: Finance and Investment for Normally Intelligent People Who Are Not in the Industry*, Erasmus, London.

Charles P. Kindelberger (1978) *Manias, Panics and Crashes: A History of Financial Crisis*, Basic Books, New York.

Naomi Klein (2008) *The Shock Doctrine: The Rise of Disaster Capitalism*, Picador, New York.

Jonathan A. Knee (2007) *The Accidental Investment Banker*, John Wiley, Chichester.

Richard C. Koo (2008) *The Holy Grail of Macro Economics: Lessons from Japan's Great Recession*, John Wiley, Singapore.

Jesse Kornbluth (1992) *Highly Confident: The Crime and Punishment of Michael Milken*, William Morrow & Co. Inc, New York.

Paul Krugman (2005) *The Great Unraveling: Losing Our Way in the New Century*, W.W. Norton & Company, New York.

Paul Krugman (2009) *The Conscience of a Liberal*, W.W. Norton & Company, New York.

Howard Kurtz (2000) *The Fortune Tellers: Inside Wall Street's Game of Money, Media and Manipulation*, Free Press, New York.

Amielle Lake, Andrew Kakabadse and Nada Kakabadse (2008) *The Elephant Hunters: Chronicles of the Moneymen*, Palgrave Macmillan, London.

John Lanchester (2010) *Whoops! Why Everyone Owes Everyone and No One Can Pay*, Allen Lane, London.

Randall Lane (2010) *The Zeroes: My Misadventures in the Decade Wall Street Went Insane*, Scribe Publications, Melbourne.

Edwin Lefèvre (2005) *Reminiscences of a Stock Operator*, John Wiley, New Jersey.

Michael Lewis (1989) *Liar's Poker: Two Cities, True Greed*, Hodder & Stoughton, London.

Michael Lewis (1991) *The Money Culture*, Penguin Books, New York.

Michael Lewis (1999) *The New New Thing: A Silicon Valley Story*, Coronet, London.

Michael Lewis (ed.) (2008) *Panic: The Story of Modern Financial Insanity*, Penguin Books, London.

Michael Lewis (2010) *The Big Short: Inside the Doomsday Machine*, Allen Lane, London.

Michael E. Lewitt (2010) *The Death of Capital: How Creative Policy Can Restore Policy*, John Wiley, New Jersey.

Roger Lowenstein (1995) *Buffett: The Making of an American Capitalist*, Broadway Books, New York.

Roger Lowenstein (2000) *When Genius Fails: The Rise and Fall of Long-Term Capital Management*, Fourth Estate, London.

Roger Lowenstein (2004) *Origins of the Crash: The Great Bubble and Its Undoing*, Penguin Books, New York.

Roger Lowenstein (2008) *While America Aged: How Pension Debts Ruined General Motors, Stopped the NYC Subways, Bankrupted San Diego and Loom as the Next Financial Crisis*, Penguin Books, New York.

Roger Lowenstein (2010) *The End of Wall Street*, Scribe Publications, Melbourne.

Peter Maass (2009) *Crude World: The Violent Twilight of Oil*, Allen Lane, London.

Charles MacKay and Joseph de la Vega (1996) *Extraordinary Popular Delusions and the Madness of Crowds*; Confusion de Confusiónes, John Wiley, New Jersey.

Donald MacKenzie (2008) *An Engine, Not a Camera: How Financial Models Shape Markets*, MIT Press, Cambridge, Massachusetts.

George Magnus (2009) *The Age of Aging: How Demographics Are Changing the Global Economy and Our World*, John Wiley, New Jersey.

Sebastian Mallaby (2010) *More Money Than God: Hedge Funds and the Making of the New Elite*, Bloombsbury, London.

Benoit Mandlebrot (2004) *The (Mis)behavior of Markets*, Basic Books, New York.

Harry Markapolos (2010) *No One Would Listen: A True Financial Thriller*, John Wiley, New Jersey.

Paul Mason (2009) *Meltdown: The End of the Age of Greed*, Verso, London.

Mark McCormack (1984) *What They Don't Teach You At Harvard Business School: Notes From A Street-Smart Executive*, Bantam, New York.

Larry McDonald (2009) *A Colossal Failure of Common Sense*, Ebury Press, London.

Bethany Mclean and Peter Elkind (2003) *The Smartest Guys in the Room: The Amazing Rise and Scandalous Fall of Enron*, Penguin Books, New York.

John Micklethwaite and Adrian Wooldridge (1996) *The Witch Doctors: What the Management Gurus Are Saying, Why It Matters and How to Make Sense of It*, Heinemann, London.

Stephen Mihm (2007) *A Nation of Counterfeiters: Capitalists, Con Men, and the Making of the United States*, Harvard University Press, Boston.

Hyman P. Minsky (2008) *Stabilizing An Unstable Economy*, McGraw-Hill, New York.

Lawrence E. Mitchell (2007) *The Speculation Economy: How Finance Triumphed Over Industry*, Berrett-Koehler, San Francisco.

Perry Mehrling (2005) *Fischer Black and the Revolutionary Idea of Finance*, John Wiley, New Jersey.

Charles Morris (2005) *The Tycoons: How Andrew Carnegie, John D. Rockefeller, Jay Gould and J.P.Morgan Invented the American Supereconomy*, Henry Holt, New York.

Charles Morris (2008) *The Two Trillion Dollar Meltdown: Easy Money, High Rollers and the Great Credit Crash*, Public Affairs, New York.

Charles Morris (2009) *The Sages: Warren Buffett, George Soros, Paul Volcker and the Maelstrom of Markets*, Public Affairs, New York.

Paul Muolo and Matthew Padilla (2008) *Chain of Blame: How Wall Street Caused The Mortgage and Credit Crisis*, John Wiley, New Jersey.

Victor Niederhoffer (1997) *Education of a Speculator*, John Wiley, New Jersey.

Anastaia Nesvetailova (2007) *Fragile Finance: Debt Speculation and Crisis in the Age of Global Credit*, Palgrave Macmillan, London.

Joe Nocera and Bethany McLean (2010) *All the Devils Are Here: The Hidden History of the Financial Crisis*, Portfolio, New York

James O'Shea and Charles Madigan (1997) *Dangerous Company, Management Consultants and the Businesses They Save and Ruin*, Penguin Books, New York.

Johan van Overtveldt (2007) *The Chicago School: How the University of Chicago Assembled the Thinkers Who Revolutionised Economics and Business*, Agate Books, Chicago.

Jim Paul and Brendan Moynihan (1994) *What I Learned Losing A Million Dollars*, Infrared Press, Nashville.

Frank Partnoy (1999) *Fiasco: The Inside Story of a Wall Street Trader*, Penguin Books, New York.

Frank Partnoy (2003) *Infectious Greed: How Deceit and Risk Corrupted the Financial Markets*, Henry Holt, New York.

Frank Partnoy (2009) *The Match King: The Financial Genius Behind A Century of Wall Street Scandals*, Henry Holt, New York.

Scott Patterson (2010) *The Quants: How a New Breed of Math Whizzes Conquered Wall Street and Nearly Destroyed It*, Crown Business, New York.

Michael Pettis (2001) *The Volatility Machine: Emerging Economies and the Threat of Financial Collapse*, Oxford University Press, Oxford.

Kevin Phillips (2009) *Bad Money: Reckless Finance, Failed Politics and the Global Crisis of American Capitalism*, Scribe, Melbourne.

John Plender (2003) *Going Off The Rails*, John Wiley, Chichester.

Robert Pozen (2010) *Too Big To Save: How to Fix the U.S. Financial System*, John Wiley, New Jersey.

Alex Preda (2009) *Framing Finance*, University of Chicago Press, Chicago and London.

Nomi Prins (2004) *Other People's Money: The Corporate Mugging of America*, The New Press, New York.

John Quiggin (2010) *Zombie Economics: How Dead Ideas Still Walk Among Us*, Princeton University Press, Princeton and Oxford.

Raghuram G. Rajan (2010) *Fault Lines: How Hidden Fractures Still Threaten the World Economy*, Princeton University Press, Princeton and Oxford.

Carmen Reinhart and Kenneth Rogoff (2010) *This Time Is Different: Eight Centuries of Financial Folly*, Princeton University Press, Princeton and Oxford.

Barry Ritholtz (2009) *Bailout Nation: How Greed and Easy Money Corrupted Wall Street and Shook The World Economy*, John Wiley, New Jersey.

David Roche and Bob McKee (2008) *New Monetarism*, Independent Strategy Publications, London.

John Rolfe and Peter Troob (2000) *Monkey Business: Swinging Through the Wall Street Jungle*, Warner Business Books, New York.

David Rothkof (2008) *Superclass: The Global Power Elite and the World They Are Making*, Farrar, Straus & Giroux, New York.

Nouriel Roubini and Stephen Mihm (2010) *Crisis Economics: A Crash Course in the Future of Finance*, Allen Lane, London.

Gary R. Saxonhouse and Robert M.Stern (eds) (2004) *Japan's Lost Decade: Origins, Consequences and Prospects for Recovery*, Blackwell Publishing, Oxford.

Michael Schuman (2009) *The Miracle: The Epic Story of Asia's Quest for Wealth*, Harper Business, New York.

Jack D. Schwager (1992) *The New Market Wizards: Conversations with America's Top Traders*, John Wiley, New Jersey.

Fred Schwed Jr (2006) *Where Are The Customers' Yachts? Or A Good Hard Look at Wall Street*, John Wiley, New Jersey.

Robert Shiller (2005) *Irrational Exuberance*, Currency Doubleday, New York.

Georg Simmel (1990) *The Philosophy of Money*, Routledge, London.

Robert Skidelsky (2003) *John Maynard Keynes 1883–1946: Economist, Philosopher, Statesman*, Penguin Books, London.

Robert Skidelsky (2009) *Keynes: The Return of the Master*, Public Affairs, New York.

Robert Slater (2009) *Soros: The World's Most Influential Investor*, McGraw Hill, New Jersey.

Adam Smith (1976) *The Money Game*, Vintage Books, New York.

Yves Smith (2010) *ECONned: How Unenlightened Self Interest Undermined Democracy and Corrupted Capitalism*, Palgrave Macmillan, New York.

Andrew Smithers and Stephen Wright (2000) *Valuing Wall Street: Protecting Wealth in Turbulent Markets*, McGraw-Hill, Illinois.

Robert Sobel (1993) *Dangerous Dreamers: The Financial Innovators from Charles Merrill to Michael Milken*, John Wiley, New York.

Andrew Ross Sorkin (2009) *Too Big To Fail: Inside the Battle to Save Wall Street*, Allen Lane, London.

Benjamin J. Stein (1992) *A License to Steal: The Untold Story of Michael Milken and the Conspiracy to Bilk the Nation*, Simon & Schuster, New York.

James B. Stewart (1992) *Den of Thieves*, Simon & Schuster, New York.

Joseph Stiglitz (2002) *Globalisation and its Discontents*, Penguin Books, London.

Joseph Stiglitz (2003) *The Roaring Nineties: Why We're Paying The Price for the Greediest Decade in History*, Penguin Books, London.

Joseph Stiglitz (2010) *Freefall: Free Markets and the Sinking of the Global Economy*, Allen Lane, London.

Andy Stone and Mike Brewster (2002) *King of Capital: Sandy Weill and the Making of Citigroup*, John Wiley, New Jersey.

Matt Taibbi (2010) *Griftopia: Bubble Machines, Vampire and the Long Con That Is Breaking America*, Random House, New York.

Nicolas Nassim Taleb (2004) *Fooled by Randomness: The Hidden Role of Chance in Life and in the Markets*, Thompson Texere, New York.

Nicolas Nassim Taleb (2007) *The Black Swan: The Impact of the Highly Improbable*, Allen Lane, London.

John R. Talbott (2009) *The 86 Biggest Lies on Wall Street*, Scribe, Melbourne.

Janet Tavakoli (2009) *Dear Mr. Buffett: What An Investor Learns 1,269 Miles from Wall Street*, John Wiley, New Jersey.

Joseph Teaster (2004) *Paul Volcker: The Making of a Financial Legend*, John Wiley, New Jersey.

Peter Temple (2001) *Hedge Funds: The Courtesans of Capitalism*, John Wiley & Sons, Chichester.

Gillian Tett (2004) *Saving the Sun: Shinsei and the Battle for Japan's Future*, Random House, London.

Gillian Tett (2009) *Fool's Gold: How Unrestrained Greed Corrupted A Dream, Shattered Global Markets and Unleashed a Catastrophe*, Little Brown, London.

Don Thompson (2008) The *$12 Million Stuffed Shark: The Curious Economics of Contemporary Art*, Palgrave Macmillan, New York.

Pablo Triana (2010) *Lecturing Birds on Flying: Can Mathematical Theories Destroy the Financial Markets?*, John Wiley, New Jersey.

Jerome Tuccille (2002) *Alan Shrugged: The Life and Times of Alan Greenspan*, the World's Most Powerful Banker, John Wiley, New Jersey.

The Turner Review: *A Regulatory Response to the Global Banking Crisis (2009) Financial Services Authority*, London.

Justyn Walsh (2009) *Keynes and the Market*, John Wiley & Sons, Chichester.

Vicky Ward (2010) *The Devil's Casino: Friendship, Betrayal and the High Stakes Games Played Inside Lehman Brothers*, John Wiley, New Jersey.

Peter Watson (2001) *A Terrible Beauty: The People and Ideas that Shaped the Modern Mind: A History*, Phoenix Press, London.

David Wessel (2010) *In Fed We Trust: Ben Bernanke's War on the Great Panic*, Scribe Publications, Melbourne.

Jack Wetherford (1997) *The History of Money*, Three Rivers Press, New York.

R. Christopher Whalen (2011) *Inflated: How Money and Debt Built the American Dream*, John Wiley, New Jersey.

Mark T. Williams (2010) *Uncontrolled Risk: The Lessons of Lehman Brothers and How Systemic Risk Can Still Bring Down the World Financial System*, McGraw-Hill, New York.

Martin Wolf (2010) *Fixing Global Finance*, Yale University Press, London.

Christopher Wood (2006) *The Bubble Economy: Japan's Extraordinary Speculative Boom of the 80s and the Dramatic Bust of the 90s*, Solstice Publishing, Jakarta.

Bob Woodward (2000) *Maestro: Greenspan's Fed and the American Boom*, Simon & Schuster, New York.

Daniel Yergin and Joseph Stanislaw (2002) *The Commanding Heights: The Battle for the World Economy*, Touchstone Books, New York.

Mark Zandi (2009) *Financial Shock: A 360° Look at the Subprime Mortgage Implosion, and How to Avoid the Next Financial Crisis*, Pearson Education, New Jersey.

INDEX

D

E

F

G

I

J

K

L

M

N

O

P

Q

R

S

U

X–Y–Z

In an increasingly competitive world, it is quality of thinking that gives an edge—an idea that opens new doors, a technique that solves a problem, or an insight that simply helps make sense of it all.

We work with leading authors in the various arenas of business and finance to bring cutting-edge thinking and best-learning practices to a global market.

It is our goal to create world-class print publications and electronic products that give readers knowledge and understanding that can then be applied, whether studying or at work.

To find out more about our business products, you can visit us at www.ftpress.com.

EAST BATON ROUGE PARISH LIBRARY
3 1 6 5 9 0 3 7 0 7 2 3 4 1